P9-DMP-554

Life Science

interactive SCIENCE

Go to MyScienceOnline.com to experience science in a whole new way.

Interactive tools such as My Planet Diary connect you to the latest science happenings.

MY PLANET DiaRY

- **Search Earth's Journal** for important science news from around the world.

- **Use Earth's Calendar** to find out when cool scientific events occur.

- **Explore science Links** to find even more exciting information about our planet.

- **Visit Jack's Blog** to be the first to know about what is going on in science!

PEARSON

Glenview, Illinois • Boston, Massachusetts • Chandler, Arizona • Upper Saddle River, New Jersey

Program Authors

You're an author!

As you write in this science book, your answers and personal discoveries will be recorded for you to keep, making this book unique to you. That is why you are one of the primary authors of this book.

✎ In the space below, print your name, school, town, and state. Then write a short autobiography that includes your interests and accomplishments.

YOUR NAME _____

SCHOOL _____

TOWN, STATE _____

AUTOBIOGRAPHY _____

_____

_____

_____

_____

_____

_____

Your Photo

Acknowledgments appear on pages 712-717, which constitute an extension of this copyright page.

Copyright © 2013 Pearson Education, Inc., or its affiliates. All Rights Reserved. Printed in the United States of America. This publication is protected by copyright, and permission should be obtained from the publisher prior to any prohibited reproduction, storage in a retrieval system, or transmission in any form or by any means, electronic, mechanical, photocopying, recording, or likewise. For information regarding permissions, write to Rights Management & Contracts, Pearson Education, Inc., One Lake Street, Upper Saddle River, New Jersey 07458.

Pearson, Prentice Hall, Pearson Prentice Hall, Lab zone, and Planet Diary are trademarks, in the U.S. and/or other countries, of Pearson Education, Inc., or its affiliates.

Certain materials herein are adapted from *Understanding by Design, 2nd Edition*, by Grant Wiggins & Jay McTighe © 2005 ASCD. Used with permission.

UNDERSTANDING BY DESIGN® and UbD™ are trademarks of ASCD, and are used under license.

ISBN-13:   978-0-13-320922-8
ISBN-10:   0-13-320922-9
            18   20

ON THE COVER
Ghost Crabs
Although many crab species do use gills for gas exchange on land, gills are better suited for underwater respiration and generally pose challenges for terrestrial organisms. In crab species that spend part of their lives on land, other organs may supplement the gas-exchange function of the gills to varying degrees.

Program Authors

KATHRYN THORNTON, Ph.D.
Professor and Associate Dean, School of Engineering and Applied Science, University of Virginia, Charlottesville, Virginia
Selected by NASA in May 1984, Dr. Kathryn Thornton is a veteran of four space flights. She has logged more than 975 hours in space, including more than 21 hours of extravehicular activity. As an author on the *Scott Foresman Science* series, Dr. Thornton's enthusiasm for science has inspired teachers around the globe.

DON BUCKLEY, M.Sc.
Information and Communications Technology Director, The School at Columbia University, New York, New York
A founder of New York City Independent School Technologists (NYCIST) and long-time chair of New York Association of Independent Schools' annual IT conference, Mr. Buckley has taught students on two continents and created multimedia and Internet-based instructional systems for schools worldwide.

ZIPPORAH MILLER, M.A.Ed.
Associate Executive Director for Professional Programs and Conferences, National Science Teachers Association, Arlington, Virginia
Ms. Zipporah Miller is a former K–12 science supervisor and STEM coordinator for the Prince George's County Public School District in Maryland. She is a science education consultant who has overseen curriculum development and staff training for more than 150 district science coordinators.

MICHAEL J. PADILLA, Ph.D.
Associate Dean and Director, Eugene P. Moore School of Education, Clemson University, Clemson, South Carolina
A former middle school teacher and a leader in middle school science education, Dr. Michael Padilla has served as president of the National Science Teachers Association and as a writer of the National Science Education Standards. He is professor of science education at Clemson University.

MICHAEL E. WYSESSION, Ph.D.
Associate Professor of Earth and Planetary Science, Washington University, St. Louis, Missouri
An author on more than 50 scientific publications, Dr. Wysession was awarded the prestigious Packard Foundation Fellowship and Presidential Faculty Fellowship for his research in geophysics. Dr. Wysession is an expert on Earth's inner structure and has mapped various regions of Earth using seismic tomography. He is known internationally for his work in geoscience education and outreach.

Instructional Design Author

GRANT WIGGINS, Ed.D.
President, Authentic Education, Hopewell, New Jersey
Dr. Wiggins is a co-author with Jay McTighe of *Understanding by Design, 2nd Edition* (ASCD 2005). His approach to instructional design provides teachers with a disciplined way of thinking about curriculum design, assessment, and instruction that moves teaching from covering content to ensuring understanding.
UNDERSTANDING BY DESIGN® and UbD™ are trademarks of ASCD, and are used under license.

Planet Diary Author

JACK HANKIN
Science/Mathematics Teacher, The Hilldale School, Daly City, California, Founder, Planet Diary Web site
Mr. Hankin is the creator and writer of Planet Diary, a science current events Web site. He is passionate about bringing science news and environmental awareness into classrooms and offers numerous Planet Diary workshops at NSTA and other events to train middle and high school teachers.

ELL Consultant

JIM CUMMINS, Ph.D.
Professor and Canada Research Chair, Curriculum, Teaching and Learning department at the University of Toronto
Dr. Cummins focuses on literacy development in multilingual schools and the role of technology in promoting student learning across the curriculum. *Interactive Science* incorporates essential research-based principles for integrating language with the teaching of academic content based on his instructional framework.

Reading Consultant

HARVEY DANIELS, Ph.D.
Professor of Secondary Education, University of New Mexico, Albuquerque, New Mexico
Dr. Daniels is an international consultant to schools, districts, and educational agencies. He has authored or coauthored 13 books on language, literacy, and education. His most recent works are *Comprehension and Collaboration: Inquiry Circles in Action* and *Subjects Matter: Every Teacher's Guide to Content-Area Reading*.

Reviewers

Contributing Writers

Edward Aguado, Ph.D.
Professor, Department of
Geography
San Diego State University
San Diego, California

Elizabeth Coolidge-Stolz, M.D.
Medical Writer
North Reading, Massachusetts

Donald L. Cronkite, Ph.D.
Professor of Biology
Hope College
Holland, Michigan

Jan Jenner, Ph.D.
Science Writer
Talladega, Alabama

Linda Cronin Jones, Ph.D.
Associate Professor of Science and
Environmental Education
University of Florida
Gainesville, Florida

T. Griffith Jones, Ph.D.
Clinical Associate Professor
of Science Education
College of Education
University of Florida
Gainesville, Florida

Andrew C. Kemp, Ph.D.
Teacher
Jefferson County Public Schools
Louisville, Kentucky

Matthew Stoneking, Ph.D.
Associate Professor of Physics
Lawrence University
Appleton, Wisconsin

R. Bruce Ward, Ed.D.
Senior Research Associate
Science Education Department
Harvard-Smithsonian Center for
Astrophysics
Cambridge, Massachusetts

Content Reviewers

Paul D. Beale, Ph.D.
Department of Physics
University of Colorado at Boulder
Boulder, Colorado

Jeff R. Bodart, Ph.D.
Professor of Physical Sciences
Chipola College
Marianna, Florida

Joy Branlund, Ph.D.
Department of Earth Science
Southwestern Illinois College
Granite City, Illinois

Marguerite Brickman, Ph.D.
Division of Biological Sciences
University of Georgia
Athens, Georgia

Bonnie J. Brunkhorst, Ph.D.
Science Education and Geological
Sciences
California State University
San Bernardino, California

Michael Castellani, Ph.D.
Department of Chemistry
Marshall University
Huntington, West Virginia

Charles C. Curtis, Ph.D.
Research Associate Professor
of Physics
University of Arizona
Tucson, Arizona

Diane I. Doser, Ph.D.
Department of Geological
Sciences
University of Texas
El Paso, Texas

Rick Duhrkopf, Ph.D.
Department of Biology
Baylor University
Waco, Texas

Alice K. Hankla, Ph.D.
The Galloway School
Atlanta, Georgia

Mark Henriksen, Ph.D.
Physics Department
University of Maryland
Baltimore, Maryland

Chad Hershock, Ph.D.
Center for Research on Learning
and Teaching
University of Michigan
Ann Arbor, Michigan

Jeremiah N. Jarrett, Ph.D.
Department of Biology
Central Connecticut State
University
New Britain, Connecticut

Scott L. Kight, Ph.D.
Department of Biology
Montclair State University
Montclair, New Jersey

Jennifer O. Liang, Ph.D.
Department of Biology
University of Minnesota–Duluth
Duluth, Minnesota

Candace Lutzow-Felling, Ph.D.
State Arboretum of Virginia &
Blanding Experimental Farm
Boyce, Virginia

Joseph F. McCullough, Ph.D.
Physics Program Chair
Cabrillo College
Aptos, California

Heather Mernitz, Ph.D.
Department of Physical Science
Alverno College
Milwaukee, Wisconsin

Sadredin C. Moosavi, Ph.D.
Department of Earth and
Environmental Sciences
Tulane University
New Orleans, Louisiana

David L. Reid, Ph.D.
Department of Biology
Blackburn College
Carlinville, Illinois

Scott M. Rochette, Ph.D.
Department of the Earth Sciences
SUNY College at Brockport
Brockport, New York

Karyn L. Rogers, Ph.D.
Department of Geological
Sciences
University of Missouri
Columbia, Missouri

Laurence Rosenhein, Ph.D.
Department of Chemistry
Indiana State University
Terre Haute, Indiana

Sara Seager, Ph.D.
Department of Planetary Sciences
and Physics
Massachusetts Institute of
Technology
Cambridge, Massachusetts

Tom Shoberg, Ph.D.
Missouri University of Science
and Technology
Rolla, Missouri

Patricia Simmons, Ph.D.
North Carolina State University
Raleigh, North Carolina

William H. Steinecker, Ph.D.
Research Scholar
Miami University
Oxford, Ohio

Paul R. Stoddard, Ph.D.
Department of Geology and
Environmental Geosciences
Northern Illinois University
DeKalb, Illinois

John R. Villarreal, Ph.D.
Department of Chemistry
The University of Texas–Pan
American
Edinburg, Texas

John R. Wagner, Ph.D.
Department of Geology
Clemson University
Clemson, South Carolina

Jerry Waldvogel, Ph.D.
Department of Biological Sciences
Clemson University
Clemson, South Carolina

Donna L. Witter, Ph.D.
Department of Geology
Kent State University
Kent, Ohio

Edward J. Zalisko, Ph.D.
Department of Biology
Blackburn College
Carlinville, Illinois

Museum of Science.

Special thanks to the Museum of
Science, Boston, Massachusetts,
and Ioannis Miaoulis, the
Museum's president and director,
for serving as content advisors for
the technology and design strand
in this program.

Teacher Reviewers

Herb Bergamini
The Northwest School
Seattle, Washington

David R. Blakely
Arlington High School
Arlington, Massachusetts

Jane E. Callery
Capital Region Education Council
Hartford, Connecticut

Jeffrey C. Callister
Former Earth Science Instructor
Newburgh Free Academy
Newburgh, New York

Colleen Campos
Cherry Creek Schools
Aurora, Colorado

Scott Cordell
Amarillo Independent School
    District
Amarillo, Texas

Dan Gabel
Consulting Teacher, Science
Montgomery County Public
    Schools
Montgomery County, Maryland

Wayne Goates
Kansas Polymer Ambassador
Intersociety Polymer Education
    Council (IPEC)
Wichita, Kansas

Katherine Bobay Graser
Mint Hill Middle School
Charlotte, North Carolina

Darcy Hampton
Science Department Chair
Deal Middle School
Washington, D.C.

Sean S. Houseknecht
Elizabethtown Area Middle School
Elizabethtown, Pennsylvania

Tanisha L. Johnson
Prince George's County Public
    Schools
Lanham, Maryland

Karen E. Kelly
Pierce Middle School
Waterford, Michigan

Dave J. Kelso
Manchester Central High School
Manchester, New Hampshire

Beverly Crouch Lyons
Career Center High School
Winston-Salem, North Carolina

Angie L. Matamoros, Ed.D.
ALM Consulting
Weston, Florida

Corey Mayle
Durham Public Schools
Durham, North Carolina

Keith W. McCarthy
George Washington Middle
    School
Wayne, New Jersey

Timothy McCollum
Charleston Middle School
Charleston, Illinois

Bruce A. Mellin
Cambridge College
Cambridge, Massachusetts

John Thomas Miller
Thornapple Kellogg High School
Middleville, Michigan

Randy Mousley
Dean Ray Stucky Middle School
Wichita, Kansas

Yolanda O. Peña
John F. Kennedy Junior High
    School
West Valley, Utah

Kathleen M. Poe
Fletcher Middle School
Jacksonville Beach, Florida

Judy Pouncey
Thomasville Middle School
Thomasville, North Carolina

Vickki Lynne Reese
Mad River Middle School
Dayton, Ohio

Bronwyn W. Robinson
Director of Curriculum
Algiers Charter Schools
    Association
New Orleans, Louisiana

Shirley Rose
Lewis and Clark Middle School
Tulsa, Oklahoma

Linda Sandersen
Sally Ride Academy
Whitefish Bay, Wisconsin

Roxanne Scala
Schuyler-Colfax Middle School
Wayne, New Jersey

Patricia M. Shane, Ph.D.
Associate Director
Center for Mathematics & Science
    Education
University of North Carolina
    at Chapel Hill
Chapel Hill, North Carolina

Bradd A. Smithson
Science Curriculum Coordinator
John Glenn Middle School
Bedford, Massachusetts

Sharon Stroud
Consultant
Colorado Springs, Colorado

Master Teacher Board

Emily Compton
Park Forest Middle School
Baton Rouge, Louisiana

Georgi Delgadillo
East Valley School District
Spokane Valley, Washington

Treva Jeffries
Toledo Public Schools
Toledo, Ohio

James W. Kuhl
Central Square Middle School
Central Square, New York

Bonnie Mizell
Howard Middle School
Orlando, Florida

Joel Palmer, Ed.D.
Mesquite Independent School
    District
Mesquite, Texas

Leslie Pohley
Largo Middle School
Largo, Florida

Susan M. Pritchard, Ph.D.
Washington Middle School
La Habra, California

Anne Rice
Woodland Middle School
Gurnee, Illinois

Richard Towle
Noblesville Middle School
Noblesville, Indiana

Table of Contents

 Lab zone® Enter the Lab zone for hands-on inquiry.

Chapter Lab Investigation:
  • Directed Inquiry: Please Pass the Bread
  • Open Inquiry: Please Pass the Bread

Inquiry Warm-Ups: Is It Living or Nonliving? • Can You Organize a Junk Drawer? • What Organism Goes Where? • Observing Similarities

Quick Labs: React! • Compare Broth Samples • Classifying Seeds • Make a Classification Chart • Living Mysteries • Staining Leaves • Common Ancestors

my SCIENCE online.com

Go to MyScienceOnline.com to interact with this chapter's content. Keyword: Introduction to Living Things

> UNTAMED SCIENCE
• What Can You Explore in a Swamp?

> PLANET DIARY
• Introduction to Living Things

> INTERACTIVE ART
• Redi's and Pasteur's Experiments
• Taxonomic Key

> ART IN MOTION
• Finding a Common Ancestor

> VIRTUAL LAB
• Classifying Life

 Enter the Lab zone for hands-on inquiry.

Chapter Lab Investigation:
• Directed Inquiry: Design and Build a Microscope
• Open Inquiry: Design and Build a Microscope

Inquiry Warm-Ups: • What Can You See?
• How Large Are Cells? • Detecting Starch
• Diffusion in Action

Quick Labs: • Comparing Cells • Observing Cells • Gelatin Cell Model • Design a Cell
• What Is a Compound? • What's That Taste?
• Effect of Concentration on Diffusion

my science online

Go to MyScienceOnline.com to interact with this chapter's content.
Keyword: Introduction to Cells

> UNTAMED SCIENCE
• Touring Hooke's Crib!

> PLANET DIARY
• Introduction to Cells

> INTERACTIVE ART
• Plant and Animal Cells • Specialized Cells

> ART IN MOTION
• Passive and Active Transport

> VIRTUAL LAB
• How Can You Observe Cells?

CHAPTER 3

Cell Processes and Energy

Enter the Lab zone for hands-on inquiry.

Chapter Lab Investigation:
• Directed Inquiry: Exhaling Carbon Dioxide
• Open Inquiry: Exhaling Carbon Dioxide

Inquiry Warm-Ups: • Where Does the Energy Come From? • Cellular Respiration • What Are the Yeast Cells Doing?

Quick Labs: • Energy From the Sun • Looking at Pigments • Observing Fermentation • Observing Mitosis • Modeling Mitosis

my science online.com

Go to MyScienceOnline.com to interact with this chapter's content.
Keyword: Cell Processes and Energy

> **UNTAMED SCIENCE**
• Yum...Eating Solar Energy

> **PLANET DIARY**
• Cell Processes and Energy

> **INTERACTIVE ART**
• Photosynthesis • Cellular Respiration • Cell Growth and Division

> **ART IN MOTION**
• Opposite Processes

> **VIRTUAL LAB** • The Inner Workings of Photosynthesis

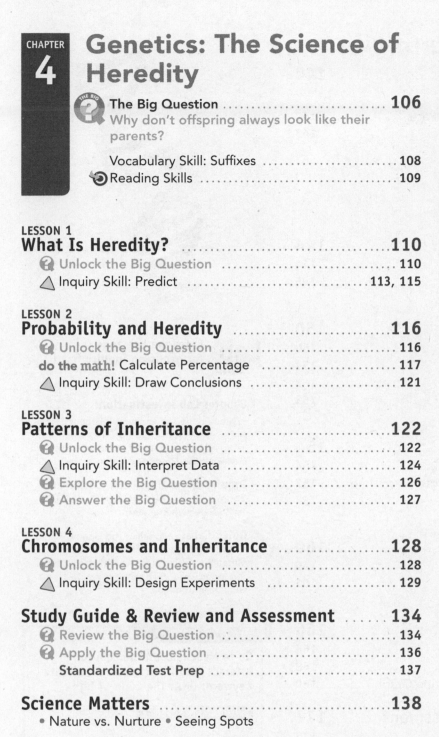

Lab zone® Enter the Lab zone for hands-on inquiry.

Chapter Lab Investigation:
• Directed Inquiry: Make the Right Call!
• Open Inquiry: Make the Right Call!

Inquiry Warm-Ups: • What Does the Father Look Like? • What's the Chance? • Observing Traits • Which Chromosome Is Which?

Quick Labs: • Observing Pistils and Stamens • Inferring the Parent Generation • Coin Crosses • Patterns of Inheritance • Is It All in the Genes? • Chromosomes and Inheritance • Modeling Meiosis

MY SCIENCE ONLINE.COM

Go to MyScienceOnline.com to interact with this chapter's content.
Keyword: Genetics: The Science of Heredity

> UNTAMED SCIENCE
• Where'd You Get Those Genes?

> PLANET DIARY
• Genetics: The Science of Heredity

> INTERACTIVE ART
• Punnett Squares • Effects of Environment on Genetic Traits • Meiosis

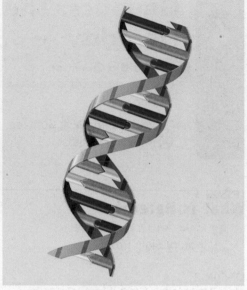

Enter the Lab zone for hands-on inquiry.

Chapter Lab Investigation:
• Directed Inquiry: Guilty or Innocent?, How Are Genes on Sex Chromosomes Inherited?
• Open Inquiry: Guilty or Innocent?, How Are Genes on Sex Chromosomes Inherited?

Inquiry Warm-Ups: • Can You Crack the Code? • What Is RNA? • Oops! • How Tall Is Tall? • Selective Breeding

Quick Labs: • Modeling the Genetic Code • Modeling Protein Synthesis • Effects of Mutations • What Happens When There Are Too Many Cells? • The Eyes Have It • Using Genetic Information

my science online.com

Go to MyScienceOnline.com to interact with this chapter's content.
Keyword: DNA: The Code of Life

> UNTAMED SCIENCE
• Why Is This Lobster Blue?

> PLANET DIARY
• DNA: The Code of Life

> INTERACTIVE ART
• Copying DNA • Making Proteins

> ART IN MOTION
• Understanding DNA • Understanding Genetic Engineering

> VIRTUAL LAB
• Track Down the Genetic Mutation • Why Does My Brother Have It and I Don't?

 Enter the Lab zone for hands-on inquiry.

Chapter Lab Investigation:
• Directed Inquiry: Nature at Work
• Open Inquiry: Nature at Work

Inquiry Warm-Ups: • How Do Living Things Vary? • How Can You Classify a Species?
• Making a Timeline

Quick Labs: Bird Beak Adaptations
• Finding Proof • Large-Scale Isolation
• Slow or Fast?

my science online.com

Go to MyScienceOnline.com to interact with this chapter's content.
Keyword: Change Over Time

> **UNTAMED SCIENCE**
• Why Would a Fish Have Red Lips?

> **PLANET DIARY**
• Change Over Time

> **INTERACTIVE ART**
• What Is It Adapted To?
• Homologous Structures

> **ART IN MOTION**
• Rate of Evolution

> **REAL-WORLD INQUIRY**
• What Affects Natural Selection?

 Enter the Lab zone for hands-on inquiry.

Chapter Lab Investigation:
• Directed Inquiry: Comparing Disinfectants
• Open Inquiry: Comparing Disinfectants

Inquiry Warm-Ups: • Which Lock Does the Key Fit? • How Quickly Can Bacteria Multiply? • What Lives in a Drop of Pond Water? • There's a Fungus Among Us

Quick Labs: • How Many Viruses Fit on a Pin? • How Viruses Spread • Classifying Bacteria • Drawing Conclusions • Observing Pseudopod Movement • Predicting • Observing Slime Mold • Do All Molds Look Alike? • Considering Fungi as Decomposers

my science online.com

Go to MyScienceOnline.com to interact with this chapter's content. Keyword: Viruses, Bacteria, Protists, and Fungi

> UNTAMED SCIENCE
• What Good Are Mushrooms?

> PLANET DIARY
• Viruses, Bacteria, Protists, and Fungi

> INTERACTIVE ART
• Virus Reproduction • Exploring Protozoans

> ART IN MOTION
• The Benefits of Bacteria

> REAL-WORLD INQUIRY
• Using Organisms in the Environment

CHAPTER

8

Plants

Lab® zone Enter the Lab zone for hands-on inquiry.

Chapter Lab Investigation:
• Directed Inquiry: Investigating Stomata
• Open Inquiry: Investigating Stomata

Inquiry Warm-Ups: • What Do Leaves Reveal About Plants? • Will Mosses Absorb Water? • Which Plant Part Is It? • Make the Pollen Stick • Can a Plant Respond To Touch? • Feeding the World

Quick Labs: • Algae and Other Plants • Local Plant Diversity • Masses of Mosses • Examining a Fern • Common Characteristics • The In-Seed Story • Modeling Flowers • Plant Life Cycles • Where Are the Seeds? • Watching Roots Grow • Seasonal Changes • Everyday Plants

my science online.com

Go to MyScienceOnline.com to interact with this chapter's content. Keyword: **Plants**

> UNTAMED SCIENCE
• Amazing Plant Defenses

> PLANET DIARY
• Plants

> INTERACTIVE ART
• Plant Cell Structures • The Structure of a Flower • Seed Dispersal

> ART IN MOTION
• Plant Tropisms

> VIRTUAL LAB
• Classifying Plants

Lab zone® Enter the Lab zone for hands-on inquiry.

Chapter Lab Investigation:
• Directed Inquiry: Earthworm Responses
• Open Inquiry: Earthworm Responses

Inquiry Warm-Ups: Is It an Animal? • How Many Ways Can You Fold It? • How Do Natural and Synthetic Sponges Compare? • How Is an Umbrella Like a Skeleton? • Exploring Vertebrates

Quick Labs: Get Moving • Classifying Animals • Organizing Animal Bodies • Front-End Advantages • Characteristics of Vertebrates • Keeping Warm • It's Plane to See

MY SCIENCE ONLINE.com

Go to MyScienceOnline.com to interact with this chapter's content.
Keyword: **Introduction to Animals**

> UNTAMED SCIENCE
• Eating Like an Animal

> PLANET DIARY
• Introduction to Animals

> INTERACTIVE ART
• Structure of a Sponge • Where Could They Live?

> ART IN MOTION
• Invertebrate Diversity

> VIRTUAL LAB
• Classifying Animals

 Enter the Lab zone for hands-on inquiry.

Chapter Lab Investigation:
• Directed Inquiry: A Snail's Pace
• Open Inquiry: A Snail's Pace

Inquiry Warm-Ups: • Will It Bend and Move? • Sending Signals • Hydra Doing? • How Do Snakes Feed? • Making More • "Eggs-amination"

Quick Labs: • Comparing Bone and Cartilage • What Do Muscles Do? • Design a Nervous System • Compare Nervous Systems • Webbing Along • Planarian Feeding Behavior • Comparing Respiratory Systems • Comparing Circulatory Systems • Types of Reproduction • Types of Fertilization "Eggs-tra" Production • Cycles of Life • To Care or Not to Care

MY SCIENCE ONLINE.com

Go to MyScienceOnline.com to interact with this chapter's content.
Keyword: Animal Life Processes

> UNTAMED SCIENCE
• Science in a Bat Cave

> PLANET DIARY
• Getting Around

> INTERACTIVE ART
• Types of Skeletons • Water Vascular System • Adaptations for Movement • Alien Mouth Match-Up • Build a Life Cycle

> ART IN MOTION
• Nervous Systems at Work • Respiratory Structures at Work

> REAL-WORLD INQUIRY
• Responding to the Environment

CHAPTER 11

Introduction to the Human Body

Lab zone® Enter the Lab zone
for hands-on inquiry.

Chapter Lab Investigation:
• Directed Inquiry: A Look Beneath the Skin
• Open Inquiry: A Look Beneath the Skin

Inquiry Warm-Ups: How Is Your Body
Organized? • How Does Your Body Respond?
• Out of Balance • Hard as a Rock? • How
Do Muscles Work? • What Can You Observe
About Skin?

Quick Labs: • Observing Cells and Tissues
• Working Together, Act I • Working Together,
Act II • Working to Maintain Balance • The
Skeleton • Observing Joints • Soft Bones?
• Observing Muscle Tissue • Modeling How
Skeletal Muscles Work • Sweaty Skin

my science online.com

Go to MyScienceOnline.com to
interact with this chapter's content.
Keyword: Introduction to the
Human Body

> **UNTAMED SCIENCE**
• Keeping Cool and Staying Warm

> **PLANET DIARY**
• The Human Body

> **INTERACTIVE ART**
• Body Systems • Build a Skeleton
• The Skeletal and Muscular Systems

> **ART IN MOTION**
• Body Systems in Action • Muscle Motion

 Enter the Lab zone for hands-on inquiry.

Chapter Lab Investigation:
• Directed Inquiry: As the Stomach Churns, A breath of Fresh Air

Inquiry Warm-Ups: • Food Claims
• Observing a Heart • How Big Can You Blow Up a Balloon? • How Does Filtering a Liquid Change the Liquid?

Quick Labs: • Predicting Starch Content
• Direction of Blood Flow • Do You Know Your A-B-Os? • Modeling Respiration • Kidney Function • Perspiration

my science online.com

Go to MyScienceOnline.com to interact with this chapter's content.
Keyword: Managing Materials in the Body

> **UNTAMED SCIENCE**
• Blood Lines

> **PLANET DIARY**
• Managing Materials in the Body

> **ART IN MOTION**
• Gas Exchange

> **INTERACTIVE ART**
• Nutrients at Work • The Heart
• The Respiratory System

> **VIRTUAL LAB**
• Up Close: Components of Blood

> **REAL-WORLD INQUIRY**
• A Digestive Journey

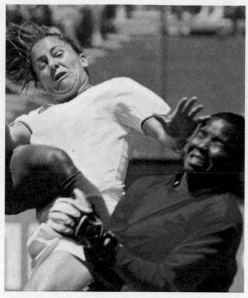

Lab zone® Enter the Lab zone for hands-on inquiry.

Chapter Lab Investigation:
• Directed Inquiry: Ready or Not!
• Open Inquiry: Ready or Not!

Inquiry Warm-Ups: • How Simple Is a Simple Task? • What's the Signal? • What's the Big Difference? • Prenatal Growth

Quick Labs: • How Does Your Knee React? • Working Together • Making Models • Modeling Negative Feedback • Reproductive Systems • Looking at Hormone Levels • Way to Grow! • Egg-cellent Protection • Labor and Delivery

my science online.com

Go to MyScienceOnline.com to interact with this chapter's content.
Keyword: Controlling Body Processes.

> UNTAMED SCIENCE
• Think Fast!

> PLANET DIARY
• Controlling Body Processes

> ART IN MOTION
• How a Nerve Impulse Travels • Stages of Prenatal Development

> INTERACTIVE ART
• The Nervous System • Negative Feedback in the Endocrine System • Reproductive Anatomy

> REAL-WORLD INQUIRY
• Sensing the World

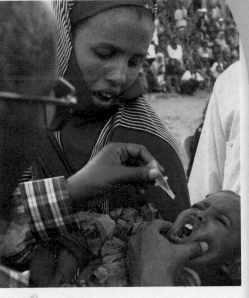

Enter the Lab zone for hands-on inquiry.

Chapter Lab Investigation:
• Directed Inquiry: The Skin as a Barrier
• Open Inquiry: The Skin as a Barrier

Inquiry Warm-Ups: • The Agents of Disease • Which Pieces Fit Together? • How Does HIV Spread? • Types of Immunity • Causes of Death, Then and Now

Quick Labs: • How Do Pathogens Cause Disease? • How Does a Disease Spread? • Stuck Together • How Does HIV Attack? • What Will Spread HIV? • Modeling Active and Passive Immunity • What Substances Can Kill Pathogens? • What Happens When Air Flow Is Restricted? • What Does Sunlight Do to the Beads?

my science online.com

Go to MyScienceOnline.com to interact with this chapter's content.
Keyword: Fighting Disease

> UNTAMED SCIENCE
• Flu Detectives

> PLANET DIARY
• Fighting Disease

> INTERACTIVE ART
• Immune Response

> ART IN MOTION
• How Do Vaccines Work?

> REAL-WORLD INQUIRY
• Diagnosis Please, Doctor

> VIRTUAL LAB
• Up Close: Pathogens

Lab zone® Enter the Lab zone for hands-on inquiry.

Chapter Lab Investigation:
• Directed Inquiry: World in a Bottle
• Open Inquiry: World in a Bottle

Inquiry Warm-Ups: • What's in the Scene?
• Populations • Can You Hide a Butterfly?
• How Communities Change

Quick Labs: • Organisms and Their Habitats
• Organizing an Ecosystem • Growing and
Shrinking • Elbow Room • Adaptations for
Survival • Competition and Predation • Type
of Symbiosis • Primary or Secondary

my science online.com

Go to MyScienceOnline.com to
interact with this chapter's content.
Keyword: Populations and
Communities

> **UNTAMED SCIENCE**
• Clown(fish)ing Around

> **PLANET DIARY**
• Populations and Communities

> **INTERACTIVE ART**
• Changes in Population • Animal Defense
Strategies

> **ART IN MOTION**
• Primary and Secondary Succession

> **REAL-WORLD INQUIRY**
• An Ecological Mystery

 Lab zone Enter the Lab zone for hands-on inquiry.

Chapter Lab Investigation:
• Directed Inquiry: Ecosystem Food Chains
• Open Inquiry: Ecosystem Food Chains

Inquiry Warm-Ups: • Where Did Your Dinner Come From? • Are You Part of a Cycle? • How Much Rain Is That? • Where Does It Live? • How Much Variety Is There?

Quick Labs: • Observing Decomposition • Following Water • Carbon and Oxygen Blues • Playing Nitrogen Cycle Roles • Inferring Forest Climates • Dissolved Oxygen • Modeling Keystone Species • Grocery Gene Pool • Humans and Biodiversity

my science online.com

Go to MyScienceOnline.com to interact with this chapter's content.
Keyword: **Ecosystems and Biomes**

UNTAMED SCIENCE
• Give Me That Carbon!

PLANET DIARY
• Ecosystems and Biomes

INTERACTIVE ART
• Ocean Food Web • Water Cycle • Cycles of Matter • Earth's Biomes

VIRTUAL LAB
• Where's All the Food? • Life in a Coral Reef

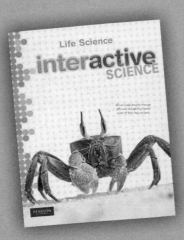

Interactive Science

Interactive Science is a program that features 3 pathways to match the way you learn.

- The write-in student edition enables you to become an active participant as you read about science.

- A variety of hands-on activities will not only engage you but also provide you with a deep understanding of science concepts.

- Go to MyScienceOnline.com to access a wide array of digital resources built especially for students like you!

 Interact with your textbook.

 Interact with inquiry.

 Interact online.

interactive SCIENCE

WHAT MAKES THESE SNOWBOARDERS "FLY" DOWNHILL?

? THE BIG How is energy conserved in a transformation?

These women are competing in the sport of snowboard cross. They "fly" down a narrow course, filled with jumps, steep sections, and ramps. Disaster looms at every turn. If they don't crash into each other or fall, then the first one across the finish line wins.

Develop Hypotheses What do you think makes these snowboarders go so fast?

_____

_____

_____

_____

▶ UNTAMED SCIENCE Watch the **Untamed Science** video to learn more about energy.

342 Energy

mY SCI

 Get Engaged!

At the start of each chapter, you will see two questions: an Engaging Question and the Big Question. Each chapter's Big Question will help you start thinking about the Big Ideas of Science. Look for the Big Q symbol throughout the chapter!

Start with the Big Question

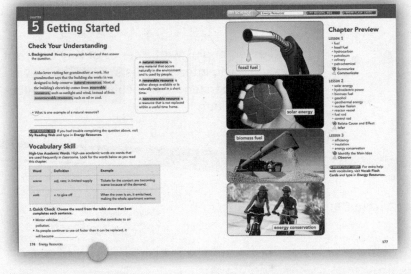

Build Reading, Inquiry, and Vocabulary Skills

- In every lesson you will learn new Reading 🔄 and Inquiry skills △ to help you read and think like a scientist.

- Go online to MyScienceOnline.com and click on My Reading Web to get additional reading at your level.

Go Online!

At MyScienceOnline.com, you will find a variety of engaging digital resources such as the Untamed Science videos. Follow the Untamed Science video crew as they travel the globe exploring the Big Ideas of Science.

Unlock the Big Question

my science online.com
Go to MyScienceOnline.com to access a wide array of digital resources such as Virtual Labs, additional My Planet Diary activities, and Got It? assessments with instant feedback.

Explore the Key Concepts

Each lesson begins with a series of Key Concept questions. The interactivities in each lesson will help you understand these concepts and Unlock the Big Question.

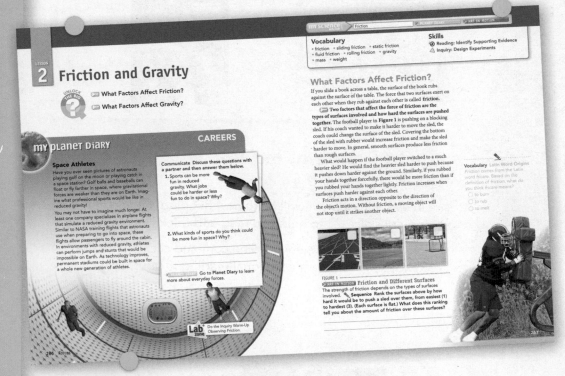

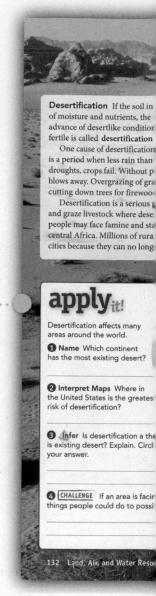

Desertification
If the soil in ... of moisture and nutrients, the ... advance of desertlike conditions ... fertile is called **desertification** ...

One cause of desertification ... is a period when less rain than ... droughts, crops fail. Without p... blows away. Overgrazing of gra... cutting down trees for firewoo...

Desertification is a serious p... and graze livestock where dese... people may face famine and sta... central Africa. Millions of rura... cities because they can no long...

apply it!

Desertification affects many areas around the world.

1 Name Which continent has the most existing desert?

2 Interpret Maps Where in the United States is the greates... risk of desertification?

3 Infer Is desertification a th... is existing desert? Explain. Circl... your answer.

4 CHALLENGE If an area is facin... things people could do to possi...

132 Land, Air, and Water Reso...

my planet diary

At the start of each lesson, My Planet Diary will introduce you to amazing events, significant people, and important discoveries in science or help you to overcome common misconceptions about science concepts.

apply it!

Elaborate further with the Apply It activities. This is your opportunity to take what you've learned and apply those skills to new situations.

Lab zone

Look for the Lab zone triangle. This means that it's time to do a hands-on inquiry lab. In every lesson, you'll have the opportunity to do a hands-on inquiry activity that will help reinforce your understanding of the lesson topic.

ertile area becomes depleted
become a desert. The
reas that previously were
t uh fih KAY shun).
te. For example, a **drought**
falls in an area. During
er, the exposed soil easily
by cattle and sheep and
use desertification, too.
People cannot grow crops
n has occurred. As a result,
Desertification is severe in
there are moving to the
rt themselves on the land.

Key
- Existing desert
- High-risk area
- Moderate-risk area

y in areas where there
a on the map to support

rtification, what are some
its effects?

Land Reclamation Fortunately, it is possible to replace land damaged by erosion or mining. The process of restoring an area of land to a more productive state is called **land reclamation**. In addition to restoring land for agriculture, land reclamation can restore habitats for wildlife. Many different types of land reclamation projects are currently underway all over the world. But it is generally more difficult and expensive to restore damaged land and soil than it is to protect those resources in the first place. In some cases, the land may not return to its original state.

FIGURE 4
Land Reclamation
These pictures show land before and after it was mined.

✏ **Communicate** Below the pictures, write a story about what happened to the land.

🔒 Assess Your Understanding

1a. Review Subsoil has (less/more) plant and animal matter than topsoil.

b. Explain What can happen to soil if plants are removed?

c. Apply Concepts Wha
that could prevent
land reclamation?

got it?

○ I get it! Now I know that soil management is important because

○ I need extra help with
Go to MY SCIENCE ⓢ COACH online for help with this subject.

 Do the Quick Lab
Modeling Soil Conservation.

got it?

Evaluate Your Progress

After answering the Got It question, think about how you're doing. Did you get it or do you need a little help? Remember, **MY SCIENCE ⓢ COACH** is there for you if you need extra help.

Assess the Big Question

Explore the Big Question

At one point in the chapter, you'll have the opportunity to take all that you've learned to further explore the Big Question.

Pollution and Solutions

What can people do to use resources wisely?

FIGURE 4

▶ **REAL-WORLD INQUIRY** All living things depend on land, air, and water. Conserving these resources for the future is important. Part of resource conservation is identifying and limiting sources of pollution.

✎ **Interpret Photos** On the photograph, write the letter from the key into the circle that best identifies the source of pollution.

Land
Describe at least one thing your community could do to reduce pollution on land.

_____

_____

_____

_____

_____

Air
Describe at least one thing your community could do to reduce air pollution.

_____

_____

_____

_____

_____

Water
Describe at least one thing your community could do to reduce water pollution.

_____

_____

_____

_____

_____

Pollution Sources

A. Sediments

B. Municipal solid waste

C. Runoff from development

Lab zone   Do the Q
Getting C

▭ **Assess Your Understa**

1a. Define What are sediments?

_____

_____

b. Explain How can bacteria help cle
spill in the ocean?

_____

_____

c. ANSWER What can people do to use
resources wisely?

_____

_____

d. [CHALLENGE] Why might a compa
to recycle the waste they produc
would reduce water pollution?

_____

_____

_____

_____

got it?

○ I get it! Now I know that water
can be reduced by _____

_____

○ I need extra help with _____

Go to MY SCIENCE COACH on
with this subject.

Answer the Big Question

Now it's time to show what you know and answer the Big Question.

Review What You've Learned

Use the Chapter Study Guide to review the
Big Question and prepare for the test.

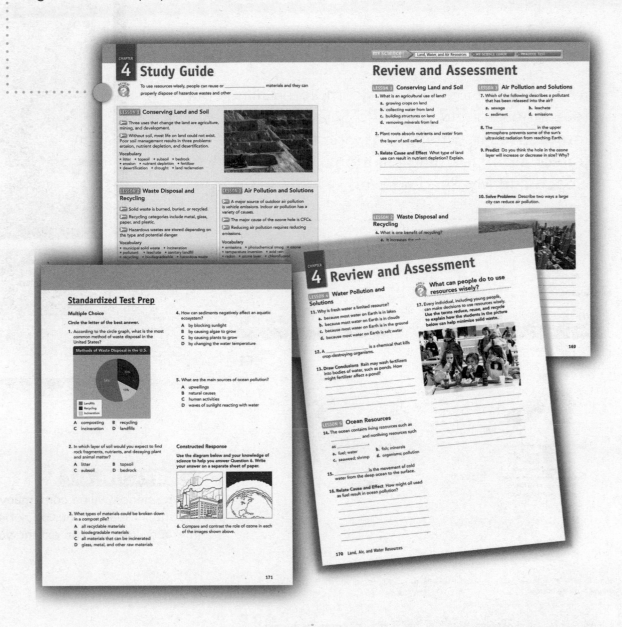

Practice Taking Tests

Apply the Big Question and take a practice test in
standardized test format.

Explore Your Complete Online Course

MyScienceOnline.com is a complete online course featuring exciting Untamed Science Videos, Interactive Art Simulations, and innovative personalized learning solutions like My Science Coach and My Reading Web.

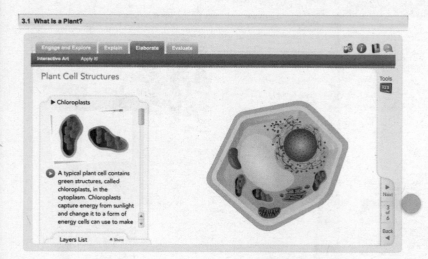

> INTERACTIVE ART

At MyScienceOnline.com, many of the beautiful visuals in your book become interactive so you can extend your learning.

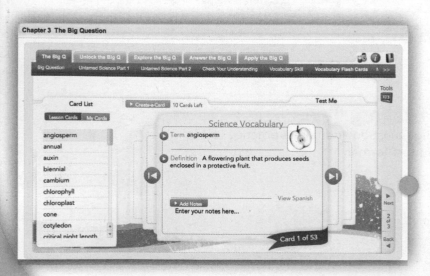

> VOCAB FLASH CARDS

Practice chapter vocabulary with interactive flash cards. Each card has an image, definitions in English and Spanish, and space for your own notes.

▷ VIRTUAL LAB

Get more practice with realistic virtual labs. Interact with on-line labs without costly equipment or clean-up.

Your Online Student Edition

Create an online notebook! Highlight important information and create sticky notes. Notes and highlights are saved in your own personal Online Student Edition.

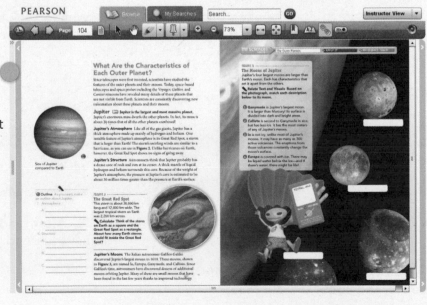

? BIG IDEAS OF SCIENCE

Have you ever worked on a jigsaw puzzle? Usually a puzzle has a theme that leads you to group the pieces by what they have in common. But until you put all the pieces together you can't solve the puzzle. Studying science is similar to solving a puzzle. The big ideas of science are like puzzle themes. To understand big ideas, scientists ask questions. The answers to those questions are like pieces of a puzzle. Each chapter in this book asks a big question to help you think about a big idea of science. By answering the big questions, you will get closer to understanding the big idea.

✎ **Before you read each chapter, write about what you know and what more you'd like to know.**

BIGIDEA

Living things are alike yet different.

Grasses and wildflowers look different, but they all grow in soil and need sunlight and water.

What do you already know about how all living things are alike yet different? ✎ **What more would you like to know?**

_____

_____

_____

Big Questions:

❓ How are living things alike yet different? Chapter 1

❓ How are living things other than plants and animals important to Earth? Chapter 7

❓ How do you know a plant when you see it? Chapter 8

❓ How do you know an animal when you see it? Chapter 9

✎ **After reading the chapters, write what you have learned about the Big Idea.**

_____

BIGIDEA

Living things are made of cells.

Nerve cells like this one transmit messages in your body. Other kinds of cells do different jobs.

What do you already know about what a cell does? What more would you like to know?

_____

_____

_____

Big Questions:

❓ What are cells made of? Chapter 2

❓ How do living things get energy? Chapter 3

✎ **After reading the chapters, write what you have learned about the Big Idea.**

_____

_____

BIGIDEA
Genetic information passes from parents to offspring.

Once in a while, a koala joey is born with white fur instead of the usual gray fur. Even with such a striking difference, you can tell the joey is related to its mother.

What do you already know about how offspring resemble their parents? What more would you like to know?

_____
_____
_____
_____

Big Questions:

❓ Why don't offspring always look like their parents? Chapter 4

❓ What does DNA do? Chapter 5

✏️ After reading the chapters, write what you have learned about the Big Idea.

_____
_____

BIGIDEA
Living things change over time.

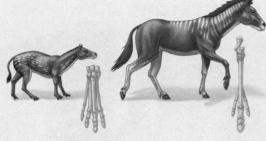

Modern horses are descended from much smaller animals with toes instead of hooves.

What do you already know about how life forms change? What more would you like to know?

_____
_____
_____

Big Question:

❓ How do life forms change over time? Chapter 6

✏️ After reading the chapter, write what you have learned about the Big Idea.

_____
_____

Structures in living things are related to their functions.

Using its wings, a hawk flies through the air and coasts to a landing.

What do you already know about how animals move in water, on land, or in air? ✎ **What more would you like to know?**

_____
_____
_____
_____
_____

Big Question:

❓ How do animals move? Chapter 10

✎ **After reading the chapter, write what you have learned about the Big Idea.**

_____
_____
_____
_____
_____
_____
_____
_____
_____
_____
_____

Living things maintain constant conditions inside their bodies.

Like a rock climber who carefully adjusts to changing conditions on the mountain, your body adjusts to changes in your surroundings.

What do you already know about your body temperature regardless of how warm or cold it is outside? ✎ **What more would you like to know?**

_____
_____
_____

Big Questions:

❓ How does your body work? Chapter 11

❓ How do systems of the body move and manage materials? Chapter 12

❓ What systems regulate and control body processes? Chapter 13

❓ Why do you sometimes get sick? Chapter 14

✎ **After reading the chapters, write what you have learned about the Big Idea.**

_____
_____
_____
_____

BIGIDEA

Living things interact with their environment.

What do you already know about how the animals and plants in your neighborhood live together? ✏️ **What more would you like to know?**

_____

_____

_____

_____

Big Questions:

❓ How do living things affect one another? Chapter 15

❓ How do energy and matter move through ecosystems? Chapter 16

✏️ **After reading the chapters, write what you have learned about the Big Idea.**

_____

_____

_____

_____

_____

_____

These prairie dogs live in grasslands and make their homes underground. To stay alive, prairie dogs search for food and water and hide from animals that eat them.

HOW ARE THIS MANATEE AND HYRAX ALIKE?

How are living things alike yet different?

Living in Florida waters, a manatee can grow to be longer than 3 meters and weigh over 350 kilograms. A rock hyrax is a small, tailless, rodentlike animal that lives in rocky areas of Africa. While these animals appear to be very different, they are actually related.

△**Develop Hypotheses** What could these two animals have in common?

_____

_____

_____

_____

_____

_____

> UNTAMED SCIENCE Watch the **Untamed Science** video to learn more about living things.

Introduction to Living Things

1 Getting Started

Check Your Understanding

1. **Background** Read the paragraph below and then answer the question.

You eat **microscopic** organisms all the time without realizing it! Some microscopic organisms are necessary to prepare common foods. **Yeast,** for example, is a tiny organism that is used to make bread. **Bacteria** are used to make yogurt, sauerkraut, and many other foods.

> Something **microscopic** is so small that it cannot be seen without a magnifying lens or a microscope.
>
> **Yeast** is a single-celled organism that has a nucleus.
>
> **Bacteria** are single-celled organisms that do not have nuclei.

• What is one kind of food that bacteria are used to make?

_____

> MY READING WEB If you had trouble completing the question above, visit **My Reading Web** and type in *Introduction to Living Things.*

Vocabulary Skill

Greek Word Origins Many science words come from ancient Greek words. Learning the word parts that have Greek origins can help you understand some of the vocabulary in this chapter.

Greek Word Part	Meaning	Example
autos	self	autotroph, *n.* an organism that makes its own food
taxis	order, arrangement	taxonomy, *n.* the scientific study of how living things are classified
homos	similar, same	homeostasis, *n.* the maintenance of stable internal conditions

2. **Quick Check** Circle the part of the word *taxonomy* that lets you know that the word's meaning has something to do with ordering or classifying things.

organism

species

eukaryote

branching tree diagram

Chapter Preview

LESSON 1

- organism
- cell
- unicellular
- multicellular
- metabolism
- stimulus
- response
- development
- asexual reproduction
- sexual reproduction
- spontaneous generation
- controlled experiment
- autotroph
- heterotroph
- homeostasis

↻ **Compare and Contrast**
△ **Control Variables**

LESSON 2

- classification
- taxonomy
- binomial nomenclature
- genus
- species

↻ **Ask Questions**
△ **Observe**

LESSON 3

- prokaryote
- nucleus
- eukaryote

↻ **Identify the Main Idea**
△ **Classify**

LESSON 4

- evolution
- branching tree diagram
- shared derived characteristic
- convergent evolution

↻ **Summarize**
△ **Infer**

> **VOCAB FLASH CARDS** For extra help with vocabulary, visit **Vocab Flash Cards** and type in *Introduction to Living Things.*

What Is Life?

🔑 **What Are the Characteristics of All Living Things?**

🔑 **Where Do Living Things Come From?**

🔑 **What Do Living Things Need to Survive?**

MY PLANET DIARY

TECHNOLOGY

It's Kismet!

If you hear a loud noise, do you turn toward the sound to see what caused it? When someone smiles at you, do you smile back? If somebody shook something in front of your face, would you back away? Most people react in these ways, and so does Kismet, a humanlike robot! Scientists developed Kismet to interact with, cooperate with, and learn from humans. Kismet can understand information that it sees and hears as if it were a young child. When responding to information, Kismet's face changes so that it seems interested, happy, or frightened. Kismet's expressions are so convincing that it is sometimes hard to remember that Kismet isn't really alive!

Answer the questions below.

1. What does Kismet do that makes it seem human?

Reacts like humans and responds like humans

2. What are some things you think Kismet might not be able to do that humans can?

Go without sleep or food.

▷ **PLANET DIARY** Go to **Planet Diary** to learn more about living things.

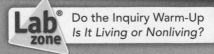 Do the Inquiry Warm-Up
Is It Living or Nonliving?

Vocabulary

- organism • cell • unicellular • multicellular • metabolism
- stimulus • response • development • asexual reproduction
- sexual reproduction • spontaneous generation
- controlled experiment • autotroph • heterotroph • homeostasis

Skills

↻ Reading: Compare and Contrast
△ Inquiry: Control Variables

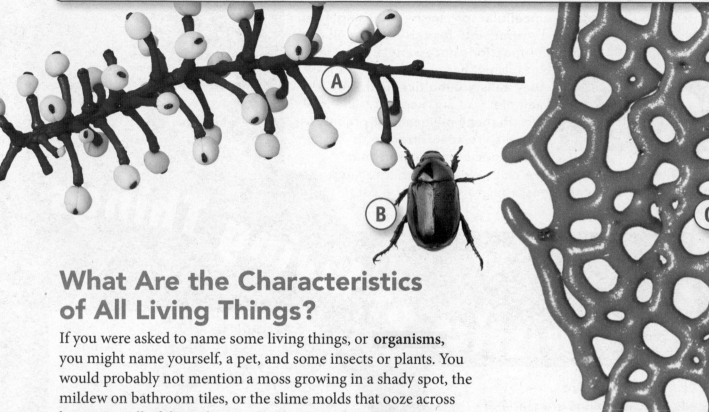

What Are the Characteristics of All Living Things?

If you were asked to name some living things, or **organisms**, you might name yourself, a pet, and some insects or plants. You would probably not mention a moss growing in a shady spot, the mildew on bathroom tiles, or the slime molds that ooze across lawns. But all of these things are organisms that share several important characteristics with all other living things. 🔑 **All living things have a cellular organization, contain similar chemicals, use energy, respond to their surroundings, grow and develop, and reproduce.**

FIGURE 1 ....

It's Alive . . . or Is It?

✎ **Look at the photos. Then answer the questions.**

1. **Identify** List the letter of the photo(s) that you think show living thing(s). ___4___

2. **Describe** What characteristics helped you decide whether or not the things shown were living or nonliving?

the looks

_____

_____

5

Cellular Organization

All organisms are made of small building blocks called cells. A **cell,** like the one shown here, is the basic unit of structure and function in an organism. Organisms may be composed of only one cell or of many cells.

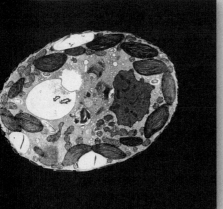

Single-celled organisms, like bacteria (bak TIHR ee uh), are **unicellular** organisms. The single cell is responsible for carrying out all of the functions necessary to stay alive. Organisms that are composed of many cells are **multicellular.** For example, you are made of trillions of cells. In many multicellular organisms, the cells are specialized to do certain tasks. Specialized cells in your body, such as muscle and nerve cells, work together to keep you alive. Nerve cells carry messages to your muscle cells, making your body move.

Characteristics of Living Things

The Chemicals of Life

The cells of living things are made of chemicals. The most abundant chemical in cells is water. Other chemicals, called carbohydrates (kahr boh HY drayts) are a cell's main energy source. Two other chemicals, proteins and lipids, are the building materials of cells, much as wood and bricks are the building materials of houses. Finally, nucleic (noo KLEE ik) acids are the genetic material of cells—the chemical instructions that cells need to carry out the functions of life.

Energy Use

Organisms get energy from taking in and breaking down materials. The combination of chemical reactions through which an organism builds up or breaks down materials is called **metabolism.** The cells of organisms use energy to do what living things must do, such as grow and repair injured parts. An organism's cells are always hard at work. For example, as you read these words, not only are your eye and brain cells busy, but most of your other cells are working, too. Young sooty terns, like the one shown above, need lots of energy to fly. These birds can fly four to five years without ever setting foot on land! An organism's metabolism can vary through it's life span. Diet, exercise, hormones, and aging all affect metabolism.

FIGURE 2 ·······················

Living Things

All living things share the same characteristics.

✎ **Make Judgments** Which characteristic on these two pages do you think best identifies an object as a living thing? Explain your choice.

the plant moving to the an light because its cells move for self gain

Response to Surroundings

If you've ever seen a plant in a sunny window, you may have observed that the plant's stems have bent so that the leaves face the sun. Like a plant bending toward the light, all organisms react to changes in their environment. A change in an organism's surroundings that causes the organism to react is called a **stimulus** (plural *stimuli*). Stimuli include changes in light, sound, and other factors.

An organism reacts to a stimulus with a **response**—an action or a change in behavior. For example, has someone ever knocked over a glass of water by accident during dinner, causing you to jump? The sudden spilling of water was the stimulus that caused your startled response.

Lab® **zone** Do the Quick Lab
React!

Growth and Development

All living things grow and develop. Growth is the process of becoming larger. **Development** is the process of change that occurs during an organism's life, producing a more complex organism. As they develop and grow, organisms use energy and make new cells.

Reproduction

Another characteristic of organisms is the ability to reproduce, or produce offspring that are similar to the parents. Organisms reproduce in different ways. **Asexual reproduction** involves only one parent and produces offspring that are identical to the parent. **Sexual reproduction** involves two parents and combines their genetic material to produce a new organism that differs from both parents. Mammals, birds, and most plants sexually reproduce. Penguins lay eggs that develop into young penguins that closely resemble their parents.

🔑 Assess Your Understanding

1a. Review A change in an organism's surroundings is a (stimulus/response).

b. Infer A bird sitting in a tree flies away as you walk by. Which of the life characteristics explains the bird's behavior?

_____

c. [CHALLENGE] Trees do not move like birds do, but they are living things. Why?

because they both produce carbon dioxide

_____
_____
_____

got it?..

○ **I get it!** Now I know that all living things

yes

_____
_____
_____
_____

○ **I need extra help with** *nothing*

_____

Go to **MY SCIENCE** Ⓢ **COACH** *online for help with this subject.*

Where Do Living Things Come From?

Today, when people see weeds poking out of cracks in sidewalks or find mice in their cabinet, as shown in **Figure 3,** they know that these organisms are the result of reproduction. 🔑 **Living things arise from other living things through reproduction.**

Four hundred years ago, however, people believed that life could appear from nonliving material. For example, when people saw flies swarming around decaying meat, they concluded that flies were produced by rotting meat. The mistaken idea that living things can arise from nonliving sources is called **spontaneous generation.** It took hundreds of years of experiments to convince people that spontaneous generation does not occur.

FIGURE 3 ·····························

Spontaneous Generation
Sometimes unexpected visitors, like this mouse, can be found in kitchen cabinets.

✎ **Answer the questions.**

1. **Develop Hypotheses** If you lived 400 years ago, where might you think the mouse in the cabinet came from?

   Cheese

2. **CHALLENGE** Describe a way in which you could test your hypothesis.

   Mice like to eat cheese.

Redi's Experiment

In the 1600s, an Italian doctor named Francesco Redi helped to disprove spontaneous generation. Redi designed a controlled experiment to show that maggots, which develop into new flies, do not arise from decaying meat. In a **controlled experiment,** a scientist carries out a series of tests that are identical in every respect except for one factor. The one factor that a scientist changes in an experiment is called the manipulated variable. The factor that changes as a result of changes to the manipulated variable is called the responding variable. Redi's experiment is shown in **Figure 4.**

FIGURE 4 ··

Redi's Experiment

Francesco Redi designed one of the first controlled experiments. Redi showed that flies do not spontaneously arise from decaying meat. Here's how he did it:

STEP 1 Redi placed meat in two identical jars. He left one jar uncovered. He covered the other jar with a cloth that let in air.

STEP 2 After a few days, Redi saw maggots (young flies) on the decaying meat in the open jar. There were no maggots on the meat in the covered jar.

STEP 3 Redi reasoned that flies had laid eggs on the meat in the open jar. The eggs hatched into maggots. Because flies could not lay eggs on the meat in the covered jar, there were no maggots there. Redi concluded that decaying meat did not produce maggots.

Uncovered jar   Covered jar

apply it!

Use **Figure 4** to answer the following questions about Redi's experiment.

1 Control Variables What is the manipulated variable in this experiment?

covering one jar

2 Control Variables What is the responding variable?

no flies get to it

3 Analyze Sources of Error Name two factors that would need to be kept constant in this experiment to avoid causing error. Why?

Allow flies to come into the area where the jars are and keep the one jar covered

Pasteur's Experiment Even after Redi's experiment, many people continued to believe in spontaneous generation. In the mid-1800s, Louis Pasteur, a French chemist, designed another experiment to test spontaneous generation. That experiment, shown in **Figure 5,** along with Redi's work, finally disproved spontaneous generation.

FIGURE 5 ·······························

> **INTERACTIVE ART** **Pasteur's Experiment**
Louis Pasteur's carefully controlled experiment demonstrated that bacteria arise only from existing bacteria. ✎ **Design Experiments** Read each step of the experiment below. Why do you think flasks with curved necks were important?

So nothing could get bacteria
in

Step ❶ Experiment Begins

Pasteur put clear broth into flasks with curved necks. The necks let in air but kept out bacteria. He boiled the broth in the flasks to kill all bacteria present.

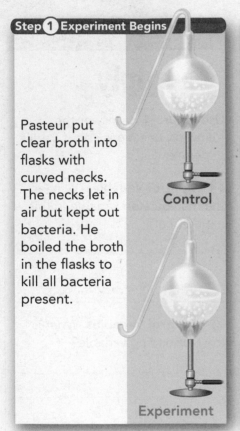

Control

Experiment

Step ❷ A Year Passes

The boiled broth remained clear. Pasteur then left some of the flasks as is.

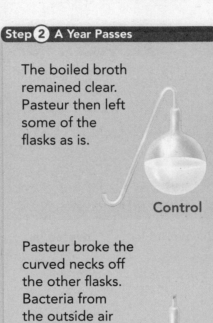

Control

Pasteur broke the curved necks off the other flasks. Bacteria from the outside air now entered these flasks.

Experiment

Step ❸ A Few Days Later

The broth in the unbroken flasks remained clear. Pasteur concluded that bacteria could not arise from the broth.

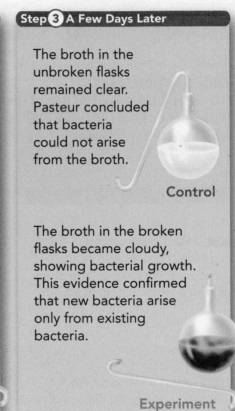

Control

The broth in the broken flasks became cloudy, showing bacterial growth. This evidence confirmed that new bacteria arise only from existing bacteria.

Experiment

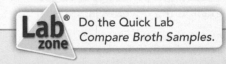

Lab zone® Do the Quick Lab
Compare Broth Samples.

🔑 **Assess Your Understanding**

2a. Identify A ___cover___ is the one factor that changes in a controlled experiment.

b. Explain Why is the idea of spontaneous generation incorrect?

because things prote
from living things

got it?

○ I get it! Now I know that living things come from _____

_____

○ I need extra help with _nothing_

Go to **MY SCIENCE** 💬 **COACH** *online for help with this subject.*

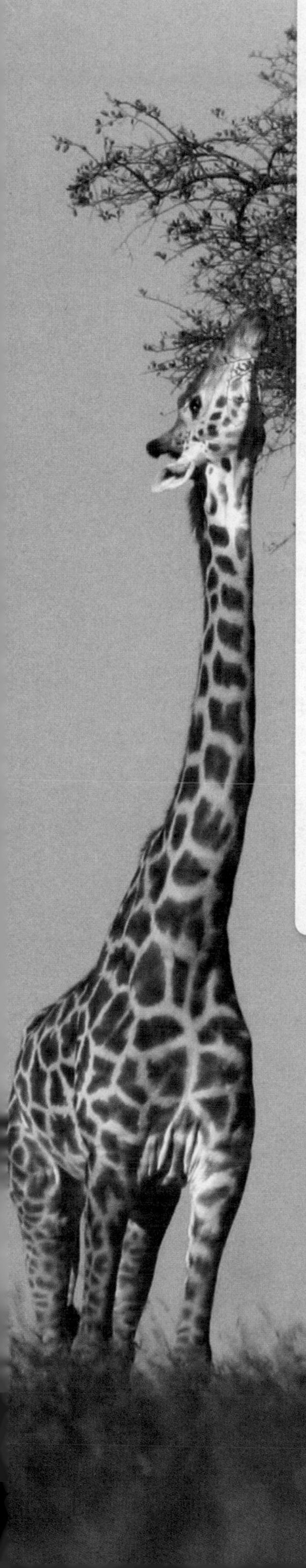

What Do Living Things Need to Survive?

Though it may seem surprising, flies, bacteria, and all other organisms have the same basic needs as you. 🔑 **All living things must satisfy their basic needs for food, water, living space, and stable internal conditions.**

Food Recall that organisms need a source of energy to live. They use food as their energy source. Organisms differ in the ways they obtain energy. Some organisms, such as plants, capture the sun's energy and use it to make food. Organisms that make their own food are called **autotrophs** (AW toh trohfs). *Auto-* means "self" and *-troph* means "feeder." Autotrophs use the food they make to carry out their own life functions.

Organisms that cannot make their own food are called **heterotrophs** (HET uh roh trohfs). Heterotrophs obtain energy by feeding on other organisms. Some heterotrophs eat autotrophs for food. Other heterotrophs consume heterotrophs that eat autotrophs. They use the energy in the autotrophs' bodies. Therefore, a heterotroph's energy source is also the sun—but in an indirect way. Animals, mushrooms, and slime molds are examples of heterotrophs.

✏️ ⊙ **Compare and Contrast** As you read, circle how autotrophs and heterotrophs are similar and underline how they are different.

✏️ **Vocabulary** Greek Word Origins The Greek word part *hetero-* means "other." How does this word help you to understand how heterotrophs get their food?

They need to feed off of others

FIGURE 6

Food

This giraffe, a heterotroph, obtains its energy by feeding on trees and shrubs.

✏️ **Identify** From your own habitat, name two examples of autotrophs and two examples of heterotrophs.

Humans and dogs are hetero trophs and algae and corn

11

did you
know?

During the summer, when desert temperatures can exceed 47°C, a camel only needs to drink water every five days. At that time, a camel can drink up to 189 liters of water in just a few hours!

Water

All living things need water to survive. In fact, most organisms can live for only a few days without water. Organisms need water to obtain chemicals from their surroundings, break down food, grow, move substances within their bodies, and reproduce.

One property of water that is vital to living things is its ability to dissolve more chemicals than any other substance on Earth. In fact, water makes up about 90 percent of the liquid part of your blood. The food that your cells need dissolves in blood and is transported to all parts of your body. Waste from cells dissolves in blood and is carried away. Your body's cells also provide a watery environment for chemicals to dissolve.

Living Space

All organisms need a place to live—a place to get food and water and find shelter. Whether an organism lives in the freezing Arctic or the scorching desert, its surroundings must provide what it needs to survive.

Because there is a limited amount of space on Earth, some organisms must compete for space. Trees in a forest, for example, compete with other trees for sunlight above ground. Below ground, their roots compete for water and minerals.

FIGURE 7

Desert Oasis

You might be surprised to see so much green in the middle of a desert. In a desert oasis, there is water beneath the surface. The groundwater can bubble to the surface and create springs.

✎ **Draw Conclusions** How can a small area in the middle of a desert provide an organism what it needs to survive?

a well could bring water

FIGURE 8 ....

Homeostasis

During the winter months, birds rely on their feathers to maintain homeostasis. By fluffing its feathers, this bluebird is able to trap body heat to keep warm. ✎ **Make Generalizations** How do people maintain homeostasis when exposed to cold temperatures?

by body heat clothes or a blanket

Lab zone® Do the Lab Investigation *Please Pass the Bread.*

🔑 Assess Your Understanding

3a. Describe Which basic need is a fox meeting by feeding on berries?

food

b. Apply Concepts The arctic fox has thick, dense fur in the winter and much shorter fur in the summer. How does this help the fox maintain homeostasis?

It stays warm in the winter and a normal tempeature inzno summer

got it? ....

○ I get it! Now I know that to survive, living things need *food water and shelter.*

○ I need extra help with *nothing*

Go to **MY SCIENCE ⓢ COACH** *online for help with this subject.*

Stable Internal Conditions

Organisms must be able to keep the conditions inside their bodies stable, even when conditions in their surroundings change significantly. For example, your body temperature stays steady despite changes in the air temperature. The maintenance of stable internal conditions is called **homeostasis** (hoh mee oh STAY sis).

Homeostasis keeps internal conditions just right for cells to function. Think about your need for water after a hard workout. When water levels in your body decrease, chemicals in your body send signals to your brain, which cause you to feel thirsty.

Other organisms have different mechanisms for maintaining homeostasis. Consider barnacles, which as adults are attached to rocks at the edge of the ocean. At high tide, they are covered by water. But at low tide, the watery surroundings disappear, and barnacles are exposed to hours of sun and wind. Without a way to keep water in their cells, they would die. Fortunately, a barnacle can close up its hard outer plates, trapping some water inside. In this way, a barnacle can keep its body moist until the next high tide. Refer to **Figure 8** to see another example of how an organism maintains homeostasis.

Classifying Life

UNLOCK THE BIG ?

🔑 **Why Do Biologists Classify Organisms?**

🔑 **What Are the Levels of Classification?**

🔑 **How Are Taxonomic Keys Useful?**

MY PLANET DiARY

CAREER

Birds of a Feather

When people first began to travel in airplanes, birds often caused crashes. In 1960, 62 people were killed when birds flew into an airplane's engine. Something had to be done, but no one knew what kinds of birds were causing the crashes. Usually only a tiny, burnt piece of feather remained. Engineers didn't know how big or heavy the birds were, so they couldn't design planes to keep birds out of the engines. Then a scientist named Roxie Laybourne invented a way to classify birds using a tiny piece of feather. She identified the birds from many crashes. Her work helped engineers design engines to reduce bird collisions. She also helped develop bird management programs for major airports. Roxie's work has saved passengers' lives!

Answer the questions below.

1. What did Roxie Laybourne invent?

Feathers

2. Why was her invention so important?

So she could save many lives

▶ PLANET DIARY Go to **Planet Diary** to learn more about classification.

Lab zone ® Do the Inquiry Warm-Up *Can You Organize a Junk Drawer?*

Vocabulary
- classification • taxonomy • binomial nomenclature
- genus • species

Skills
- Reading: Ask Questions
- Inquiry: Observe

Why Do Biologists Classify Organisms?

So far, scientists have identified more than one million kinds of organisms on Earth. That's a large number, and it keeps growing as scientists discover new organisms. Imagine how difficult it would be to find information about one particular organism if you had no idea even where to begin. It would be a lot easier if similar organisms were placed into groups.

Organizing living things into groups is exactly what biologists have done. Biologists group organisms based on similarities, just as grocers group milk with dairy products and tomatoes with other produce. **Classification** is the process of grouping things based on their similarities, as shown in **Figure 1**.

🔑 **Biologists use classification to organize living things into groups so that the organisms are easier to study.** The scientific study of how organisms are classified is called **taxonomy** (tak SAHN uh mee). Taxonomy is useful because once an organism is classified, a scientist knows a lot of information about that organism. For example, if you know that a crow is classified as a bird, then you know that a crow has wings, feathers, and a beak.

Ask Questions Before you read, preview the headings. Ask a *what*, *why*, or *how* question that you would like answered. As you read, write the answer to your question.

Aone

FIGURE 1 ·····················

Classifying Insects

These bees and wasps belong to a large insect collection in a natural history museum. They have been classified according to the characteristics they share.

✏️ **Observe** What characteristics do you think may have been used to group these insects?

_Colors and alikeness
in their body_

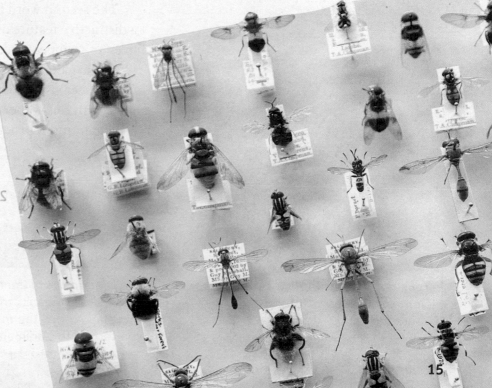

15

Puma concolor (puma)
Concolor means "the same color" in Latin. Notice that this animal's coat is mostly the same color.

FIGURE 2 ···

Binomial Nomenclature
These three different species of cats belong to the same genus. The cats' scientific names share the same first word, *Felis*. The second word of their names describes a feature of the animals.

✏️ **Infer** Suppose someone told you that a jaguarundi is classified in the same genus as house cats. What characteristics and behaviors do you think a jaguarundi might have?

hunts other animals
and hair
_____
_____
_____
_____

The Naming System of Linnaeus

Taxonomy also involves naming organisms. In the 1730s, the Swedish botanist Carolus Linnaeus devised a system of naming organisms that is still used today. Linnaeus placed organisms in groups based on their observable features. Each organism was given a unique, two-part scientific name. This system is called **binomial nomenclature** (by NOH mee ul NOH men klay chur). *Binomial* means "two names."

Genus and Species The first word in an organism's scientific name is its genus. A **genus** (JEE nus; plural *genera*) is a classification grouping that contains similar, closely related organisms. As shown in **Figure 2,** pumas, house cats, and marbled cats are all classified in the genus *Felis*. Organisms that are classified in the genus *Felis* share characteristics such as sharp, retractable claws and behaviors such as hunting other animals.

The second word in a scientific name often describes a distinctive feature of an organism, such as where it lives or its appearance. Together, the two words form the scientific name of a unique kind of organism. A **species** (SPEE sheez) is a group of similar organisms that can mate with each other and produce offspring that can also mate and reproduce.

Felis domesticus (house cat)
Domesticus means "of the house" in Latin.

Felis marmorata (marbled cat)
Marmorata means "marble" in Latin. Notice the marbled pattern of this animal's coat.

Using Binomial Nomenclature A complete scientific name is written in italics. Only the first letter of the first word in a scientific name is capitalized. Notice that scientific names contain Latin words. Linnaeus used Latin words in his naming system because Latin was the language that scientists used during that time.

Binomial nomenclature makes it easy for scientists to communicate about an organism because everyone uses the same scientific name for the same organism. Using different names or common names for the same organism can get very confusing, as **Figure 3** describes.

FIGURE 3 ·······
What Are You Talking About?

Is this animal a groundhog, a woodchuck, a marmot, or a whistlepig? Depending on where you live, all of these names are correct. Luckily, this animal has only one scientific name, *Marmota monax.*

✎ **Describe** How is a scientific name written?

Using latin words

_____

_____

Aristotle and Classification

Aristotle, an ancient Greek scholar, also developed a classification system for animals.

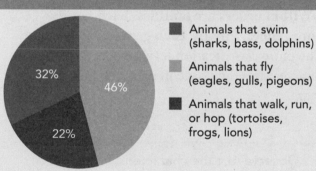

Animals With Blood

- 46% ■ Animals that swim (sharks, bass, dolphins)
- 32% ■ Animals that fly (eagles, gulls, pigeons)
- 22% ■ Animals that walk, run, or hop (tortoises, frogs, lions)

❶ **Read Graphs** Which group made up the largest percentage of animals?

Animals that fly

❷ **Calculate** __78__ percent of these animals either fly or swim.

❸ **Classify** What new categories would you use to make a graph that classifies animals that move in more than one way?

Amphibians and
Mammals

Do the Quick Lab
Classifying Seeds.

🔑 Assess Your Understanding

1a. Define The scientific study of how living things are classified is called

Binomial nomenclature

b. Make Generalizations What is the advantage of using scientific names instead of using common names, like cat or dog?

You can easily classify
them

_____

_____

_____

_____

got it? ·······

○ **I get it!** Now I know that organisms are

classified _____

_____

_____

○ **I need extra help with** _nothing_

_____

Go to **MY SCIENCE** 🅢 **COACH** *online for help with this subject.*

What Are the Levels of Classification?

The classification system that scientists use today is based on the contributions of Linnaeus. But today's classification system uses a series of many levels to classify organisms.

To help you understand the levels of classification, imagine a room filled with everybody who lives in your state. First, all of the people who live in your town raise their hands. Then those who live in your neighborhood raise their hands. Then those who live on your street raise their hands. Finally, those who live in your house raise their hands. Each time, fewer people raise their hands. The more levels you share with others, the more you have in common with them.

The Major Levels of Classification Of course, organisms are not grouped by where they live, but by their shared characteristics. Most biologists today classify organisms into the levels shown in **Figure 4**. First, an organism is placed in a broad group, which in turn is divided into more specific groups.

A domain is the broadest level of organization. Within a domain, there are kingdoms. Within kingdoms, there are phyla (FY luh; singular *phylum*). Within phyla are classes. Within classes are orders. Within orders are families. Each family contains one or more genera. Finally, each genus contains one or more species. The more classification levels two organisms share, the more characteristics they have in common and the more closely related they are.

FIGURE 4 ....

> VIRTUAL LAB **Levels of Classification**

The figure on the facing page shows how the levels of organization apply to a great horned owl.

✎ **Answer the questions.**

1. **Observe** List the characteristics that the organisms share at the kingdom level.
   They are all located at the same trea

2. **Observe** List the characteristics that the organisms share at the class level.
   They are all birds

3. **Observe** List the characteristics that the organisms share at the genus level.
   They are both owls

4. **Draw Conclusions** How does the number of shared characteristics on your list change at each level? It decreases

5. **Interpret Diagrams** Robins have more in common with (lions/owls).

Levels of Classification

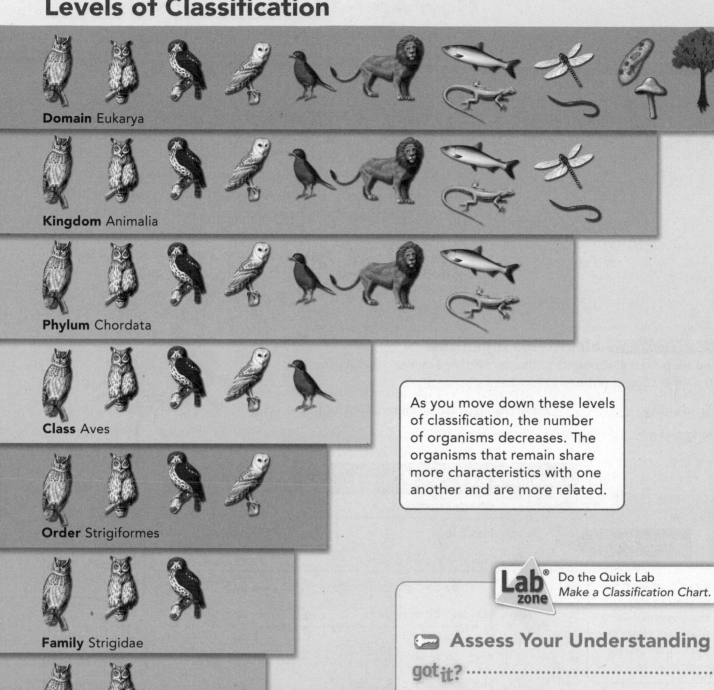

Domain Eukarya

Kingdom Animalia

Phylum Chordata

Class Aves

Order Strigiformes

Family Strigidae

Genus *Bubo*

Species *Bubo virginianus*

As you move down these levels of classification, the number of organisms decreases. The organisms that remain share more characteristics with one another and are more related.

Lab® **zone** Do the Quick Lab *Make a Classification Chart.*

🔑 **Assess Your Understanding**

got it? ⋯⋯⋯⋯⋯⋯⋯⋯⋯⋯⋯⋯⋯⋯⋯⋯⋯

○ **I get it!** Now I know that the levels of classification are _____

_____

_____

○ **I need extra help with** ___ *more* ___

_____

Go to MY SCIENCE ⑤ COACH *online for help with this subject.*

19

How Are Taxonomic Keys Useful?

Why should you care about taxonomy? Suppose that you are watching television and feel something tickling your foot. Startled, you look down and see a tiny creature crawling across your toes. Although it's only the size of a small melon seed, you don't like the looks of its two claws waving at you. Then, in a flash, it's gone.

How could you find out what the creature was? You could use a field guide. Field guides are books with illustrations that highlight differences between similar-looking organisms. You could also use a taxonomic key. **Taxonomic keys are useful tools that help determine the identity of organisms.** A taxonomic key consists of a series of paired statements that describe the various physical characteristics of different organisms. The taxonomic key shown in **Figure 5** can help you identify the mysterious organism.

FIGURE 5 ···

> INTERACTIVE ART **Identifying Organisms**
The six paired statements in this taxonomic key describe physical characteristics of different organisms.

✎ **Identify** _____Use_____ different organisms can be identified using this key. The mysterious organism is a ___mite___

0.4 mm

First: For each set of statements, choose the one that best describes the organism; for example, 1a.

Second: Follow the direction to the next step.

Third: Continue process until organism is identified.

Taxonomic Key			
Step		**Characteristics**	**Organism**
1	1a.	Has 8 legs	Go to Step 2.
	1b.	Has more than 8 legs	Go to Step 3.
2	2a.	Has one oval-shaped body region	Go to Step 4.
	2b.	Has two body regions	Go to Step 5.
3	3a.	Has one pair of legs on each body segment	Centipede
	3b.	Has two pairs of legs on each body segment	Millipede
4	4a.	Is less than 1 millimeter long	Mite
	4b.	Is more than 1 millimeter long	Tick
5	5a.	Has clawlike pincers	Go to Step 6.
	5b.	Has no clawlike pincers	Spider
6	6a.	Has a long tail with a stinger	Scorpion
	6b.	Has no tail or stinger	Pseudoscorpion

Start Here

apply it!

Use the taxonomic key in **Figure 5** to answer the following questions.

1 Interpret Tables Identify each pictured organism.

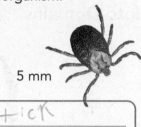

5 mm

tick

64 mm

Scorpion

40 mm

spider

50 mm

Millipede

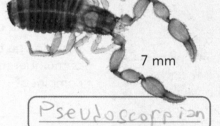

7 mm

Pseudoscorpion

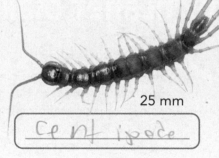

25 mm

centipede

2 Draw Conclusions What other information could have been helpful in identifying these organisms?

color, more precise size

3 CHALLENGE Is this information necessary for the key in **Figure 5?** Explain your answer.

the information I wrote town isnt necessary because you can already figure it out relatively easy

Lab zone Do the Quick Lab *Living Mysteries.*

Assess Your Understanding

got it? ....

○ **I get it!** Now I know that taxonomic keys are used to discover insects and animal

○ **I need extra help with** nothing

Go to **MY SCIENCE** ⑤ **COACH** *online for help with this subject.*

Domains and Kingdoms

🔑 **How Are Organisms Classified Into Domains and Kingdoms?**

my planet diary

Unbeelievable!

If you were classifying organisms, would you expect there to be more bees, more birds, or more mammals in the world? The table below shows the number of species of bees, mammals, and birds that scientists have found so far!

Number of Species		
Bees	**Mammals**	**Birds**
19,200	5,400	10,000

SCIENCE STATS

Answer the question below.

Why do you think that bee species outnumber mammal and bird species combined?

because there arent many bees left so there isnt much to find

▶ PLANET DIARY Go to **Planet Diary** to learn more about domains and kingdoms.

 Do the Inquiry Warm-Up *Which Organism Goes Where?*

How Are Organisms Classified Into Domains and Kingdoms?

Suppose you helped Linnaeus classify organisms. You probably would have identified organisms as either plants or animals. That's because in Linnaeus' time there were no microscopes to see the tiny organisms that are known to exist today. Microscopes helped to discover new organisms and identify differences among cells.

Today, a three-domain system of classification is commonly used. As shown in the table on the top of the next page, the three domains are Bacteria, Archaea, and Eukarya. Within the domains are kingdoms. 🔑 **Organisms are placed into domains and kingdoms based on their cell type, their ability to make food, and the number of cells in their bodies.**

Vocabulary
- prokaryote • nucleus
- eukaryote

Skills
- ⟲ Reading: Identify the Main Idea
- △ Inquiry: Classify

Three Domains of Life					
Bacteria	Archaea	Eukarya			
		Protists	Fungi	Plants	Animals

Domain Bacteria
Although you may not know it, members of the domain Bacteria are all around you. You can find them on the surfaces you touch and inside your body. Some bacteria are autotrophs, while others are heterotrophs.

Members of the domain Bacteria are called prokaryotes (proh KA ree ohtz). **Prokaryotes** are unicellular organisms whose cells lack a nucleus. A **nucleus** (NOO klee us; plural *nuclei*) is a dense area in a cell that contains nucleic acids—the chemical instructions that direct the cell's activities. In prokaryotes, nucleic acids are not contained within a nucleus.

Domain Archaea
Deep in the Pacific Ocean, hot gases and molten rock spew out from a vent in the ocean floor. It is hard to imagine that any living thing could exist in such harsh conditions. Surprisingly, a group of tiny organisms thrives in such a place. They are members of the domain Archaea (ahr KEE uh), whose name comes from the Greek word for "ancient."

Like bacteria, archaea are unicellular prokaryotes. And like bacteria, some archaea are autotrophs and others are heterotrophs. Archaea are classified in their own domain because their chemical makeup differs from that of bacteria. Bacteria and archaea also differ in the structure of their cells. The bacteria in **Figure 1** and the archaea in **Figure 2** have been stained and magnified to make them easier to see.

FIGURE 1 ·······················
Bacteria
Most bacteria, such as *Lactobacillus acidophilus,* are helpful. These bacteria help to produce yogurt and milk for people who are lactose intolerant.

FIGURE 2 ·······················
Archaea
Archaea can be found in extreme environments such as hot springs, very salty water, and the intestines of cows! Scientists think that the harsh conditions in which archaea live are similar to those of ancient Earth.

✎ **Compare and Contrast** How are archaea and bacteria similar? How are they different?

they are both unicellular prokaryotes, they have a different structure

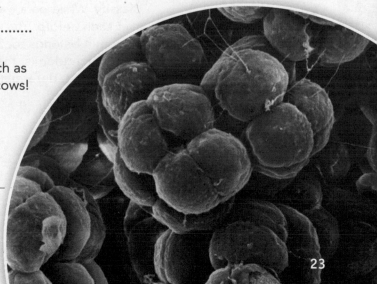

23

FIGURE 3 ·······················

Eukarya
You can encounter organisms from all four kingdoms of Eukarya on a trip to a salt marsh.

Three Domains of Life

Bacteria	Archaea	Eukarya			
		Protists	Fungi	Plants	Animals

Domain Eukarya What do seaweeds, mushrooms, tomatoes, and dogs have in common? They are all members of the domain Eukarya. Organisms in this domain are **eukaryotes** (yoo KA ree ohtz)—organisms with cells that contain nuclei. Scientists classify organisms in the domain Eukarya into one of four kingdoms: protists, fungi, plants, or animals.

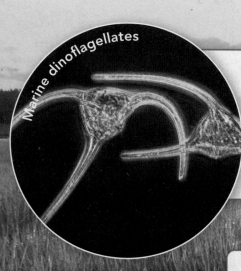

Protists

A protist (PROH tist) is any eukaryotic organism that cannot be classified as a fungus, plant, or animal. Because its members are so different from one another, the protist kingdom is sometimes called the "odds and ends" kingdom. For example, some protists are autotrophs, while others are heterotrophs. Most protists are unicellular, but some, such as seaweeds, are multicellular.

Fungi

If you have eaten mushrooms, then you have eaten fungi (FUN jy). Mushrooms, molds, and mildew are all fungi. The majority of fungi are multicellular eukaryotes. A few, such as the yeast used in baking, are unicellular eukaryotes. Fungi are found almost everywhere on land, but only a few live in fresh water. All fungi are heterotrophs. Most fungi feed by absorbing nutrients from dead or decaying organisms.

apply it!

⚠ **Classify** While on a walk, you find an organism that you've never seen before. You are determined to figure out what kingdom it belongs to. Starting with the first observation below, circle the kingdom(s) the organism could fit into. Using the process of elimination, determine what kingdom the organism belongs to.

❶ There are nuclei present.
(Protists/Fungi/Plants/Animals)

❷ You can count more than one cell.
(Protists/Fungi/Plants/Animals)

❸ The organism cannot make its own food.
(Protists/Fungi/Plants/Animals)

❹ The organism gets nutrients from dead organisms. (Protists/Fungi/Plants/Animals)

❺ Other members of this kingdom can be unicellular. (Protists/Fungi/Plants/Animals)

Plants

Dandelions on a lawn, peas in a garden, and the marsh grass shown here are familiar members of the plant kingdom. Plants are all multicellular eukaryotes, and most live on land. Also, plants are autotrophs that make their own food. Plants provide food for most of the heterotrophs on land.

The plant kingdom includes a great variety of organisms. Some plants produce flowers, while others do not. Some plants, such as giant redwood trees, can grow very tall. Others, like mosses, never grow taller than a few centimeters.

✐ **Identify the Main Idea** In the text under Domain Eukarya, underline the main idea.

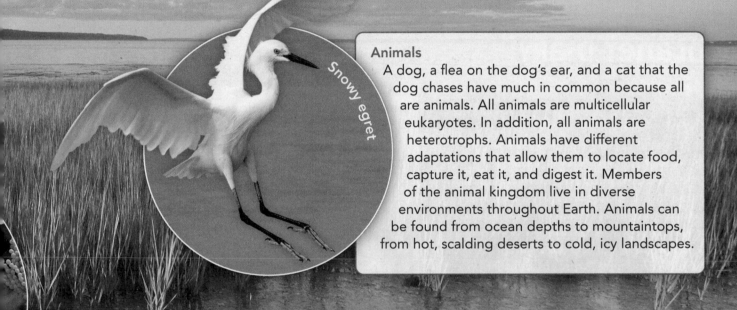

Snowy egret

Animals

A dog, a flea on the dog's ear, and a cat that the dog chases have much in common because all are animals. All animals are multicellular eukaryotes. In addition, all animals are heterotrophs. Animals have different adaptations that allow them to locate food, capture it, eat it, and digest it. Members of the animal kingdom live in diverse environments throughout Earth. Animals can be found from ocean depths to mountaintops, from hot, scalding deserts to cold, icy landscapes.

Lab zone® Do the Quick Lab *Staining Leaves.*

🔑 Assess Your Understanding

1a. Define A cell that lacks a nucleus is called a (eukaryote/prokaryote).

b. List Two ways that the members of the two domains of prokaryotes differ are in the

_____

_____

c. CHALLENGE You learn that a dandelion is in the same kingdom as pine trees. Name three characteristics that these organisms share.

_____

_____

got it?

○ **I get it!** Now I know that organisms are classified into domains and kingdoms based on their _____

_____

_____

○ I need extra help with _____

_____

Go to MY SCIENCE Ⓢ COACH *online for help with this subject.*

Evolution and Classification

🔑 **How Are Evolution and Classification Related?**

MY PLANET DIARY

DISCOVERY

If It Looks Like a Duck...

The first scientist to see the pelt of the platypus thought it was a joke. Could a four-legged, duck-billed, egg-laying mammal exist? How had it evolved? Native people from Australia believed that the first platypus was born when a water rat mated with a duck. But scientists put the platypus into a new group of egg-laying mammals. Then many years later, scientists began to argue. Had the platypus really evolved later with younger marsupials such as kangaroos? Would the platypus have to be reclassified? Scientists studied its DNA and discovered that the platypus was in the right place!

Answer the question below.

How did DNA help classify the platypus?

With DNA scientists were able to classify platypi where they belong.

▷ **PLANET DIARY** Go to **Planet Diary** to learn more about evolution and classification.

 Do the Inquiry Warm-Up *Observing Similarities.*

How Are Evolution and Classification Related?

When Linnaeus developed his classification system, people thought that species never changed. In 1859, a British naturalist named Charles Darwin published an explanation for how species could change over time. Recall that the process of change over time is called **evolution.** Darwin thought that evolution occurs by means of natural selection. Natural selection is the process by which individuals that are better adapted to their environment are more likely to survive and reproduce than other members of the same species.

Vocabulary
- evolution • branching tree diagram
- shared derived characteristic
- convergent evolution

Skills
- ↻ Reading: Summarize
- △ Inquiry: Infer

As understanding of evolution increased, biologists changed how they classify species. Scientists now understand that certain organisms may be similar because they share a common ancestor and an evolutionary history. The more similar the two groups are, the more recent the common ancestor probably is. Today's system of classification considers the history of a species. 🗝 **Species with similar evolutionary histories are classified more closely together.**

Branching Tree Diagrams
Two groups of organisms with similar characteristics may be descended from a common ancestor. A **branching tree diagram,** like the one in **Figure 1,** shows probable evolutionary relationships among organisms and the order in which specific characteristics may have evolved. Branching tree diagrams begin at the base with the common ancestor of all the organisms in the diagram. Organisms are grouped according to their shared derived characteristics.

↻ **Summarize** Name two things that similar organisms share.

a tail, four legs

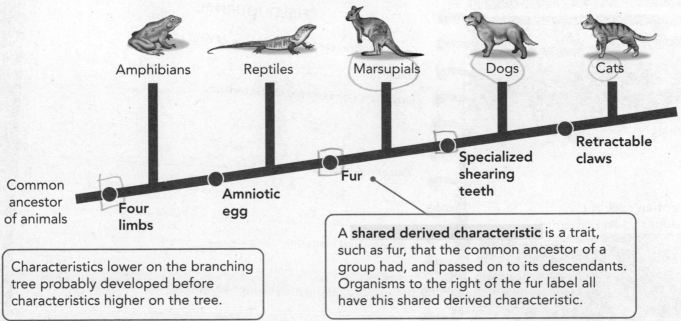

Characteristics lower on the branching tree probably developed before characteristics higher on the tree.

A **shared derived characteristic** is a trait, such as fur, that the common ancestor of a group had, and passed on to its descendants. Organisms to the right of the fur label all have this shared derived characteristic.

FIGURE 1 ••

▶ ART IN MOTION **A Branching Tree**
This branching tree diagram shows how cats have evolved.

✎ **Complete the tasks.**

1. **Interpret Diagrams** Put squares around the shared derived characteristics.

2. **Interpret Diagrams** Circle the animal(s) that belong to the smallest group.

3. **Apply Concepts** Cats are more closely related to (reptiles/marsupials).

apply it!

Note the characteristics of Figures A, B, C, and D.

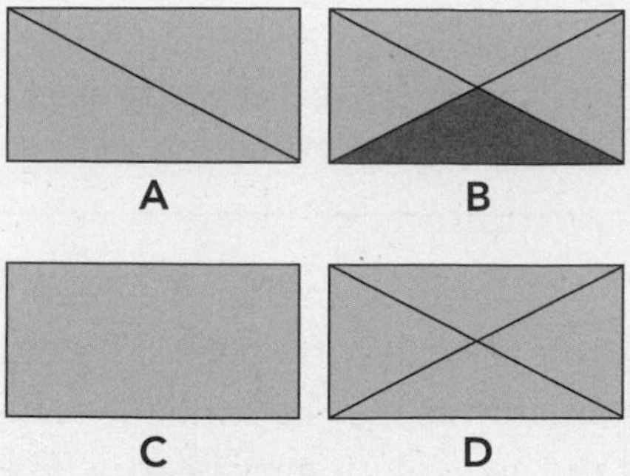

1 **Infer** Which figure is the most similar to Figure B?

D

2 **CHALLENGE** Suppose these shapes are fossils of extinct organisms. Which organism do you think might be the ancestor of all the others? Why?

C be cause it woul't start the shape

A

B

C

D

Finding a New Species

How are living things alike yet different?

FIGURE 2 ··

While on an expedition, you photograph what you think is a new species.

Draw Conclusions Use the camera image of the new species and the photos of organisms previously identified from the same area to record your observations in your field journal.

Laotian rock rat
Laonastes aenigmanus

Golden-crowned flying fox
Acerodon jubatus

FIELD JOURNAL

Location: Greater Mekong region of Asia

Date: 9/17/21

Organism's observable characteristics: 4 limbs
a tail, fur

Observed habitat(s): open fields

Domain and kingdom: marsupials

Additional information needed to determine if organism is a new species: finger like hands

Name (assuming it's a new species): asian black rat

Significance/meaning of name: its black and it was discovered in asia

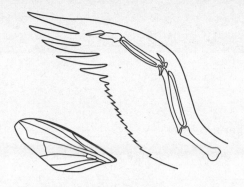

FIGURE 3

Convergent Evolution
Birds and insects both use wings to help them fly. However, these two organisms are not closely related.

Determining Evolutionary Relationships How do scientists determine the evolutionary history of a species? One way is to compare the structure of organisms. Scientists can also use information about the chemical makeup of the organisms' cells.

Sometimes unrelated organisms evolve similar characteristics because they evolved in similar environments, like organisms that move through the water or eat similar foods. Because the organisms perform similar functions, their body structures may look similar. Look at **Figure 3.** The process by which unrelated organisms evolve characteristics that are similar is called **convergent evolution.**

When studying the chemical makeup of organisms, sometimes new information is discovered that results in reclassification. For example, skunks and weasels were classified in the same family for 150 years. When scientists compared nucleic acids from the cells of skunks and weasels, they found many differences. These differences suggest that the two groups are not that closely related. As a result, scientists reclassified skunks into a separate family.

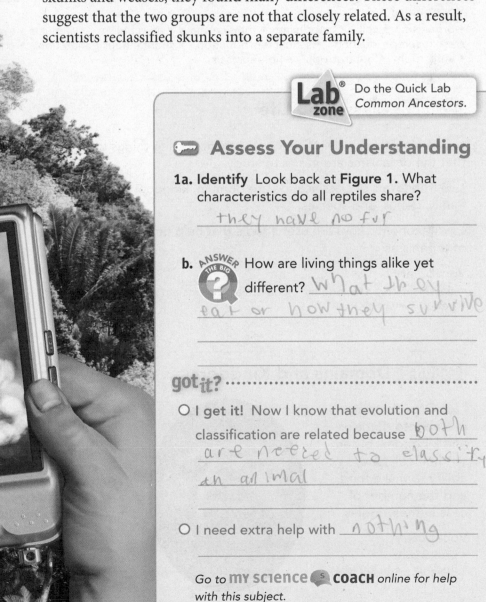

Lab zone® Do the Quick Lab *Common Ancestors.*

🔑 Assess Your Understanding

1a. Identify Look back at **Figure 1.** What characteristics do all reptiles share?

they have no fur

b. ANSWER THE BIG ❓ How are living things alike yet different? _what they eat or how they survive_

got it?

○ I get it! Now I know that evolution and classification are related because _both are need to classify an animal_

○ I need extra help with _nothing_

Go to MY SCIENCE ⑤ COACH *online for help with this subject.*

1 Study Guide

Living things can vary. For example, organisms may be prokaryotes or _____.
Yet all living things are made of _____, which grow, develop, and reproduce.

LESSON 1 What Is Life?

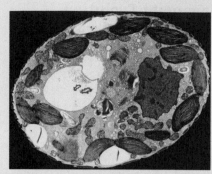

🔑 All living things have a cellular organization, contain similar chemicals, use energy, respond to their surroundings, grow and develop, and reproduce.

🔑 Living things arise from other living things through reproduction.

🔑 All living things must satisfy their basic needs for food, water, living space, and stable internal conditions.

Vocabulary
• organism • cell • unicellular • multicellular • metabolism • stimulus • response • development
• asexual reproduction • sexual reproduction • spontaneous generation • controlled experiment
• autotroph • heterotroph • homeostasis

LESSON 2 Classifying Life

🔑 Biologists use classification to organize living things into groups so that the organisms are easier to study.

🔑 The levels of classification are domain, kingdom, phylum, class, order, family, genus, and species.

🔑 Taxonomic keys are useful tools that help determine the identity of organisms.

Vocabulary
• classification • taxonomy • binomial nomenclature
• genus • species

LESSON 3 Domains and Kingdoms

🔑 Organisms are placed into domains and kingdoms based on their cell type, ability to make food, and the number of cells in their bodies.

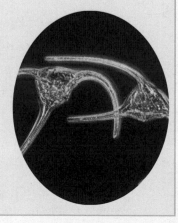

Vocabulary
• prokaryote
• nucleus • eukaryote

LESSON 4 Evolution and Classification

🔑 Species with similar evolutionary histories are classified more closely together.

Vocabulary
• evolution
• branching tree diagram
• shared derived characteristic
• convergent evolution

Review and Assessment

LESSON 1 **What Is Life?**

1. The maintenance of stable internal conditions is called

    a. stimulus.   **b.** autotrophy.

    c. homeostasis.   **d.** response.

2. _____ involves only one parent and produces offspring that are identical to the parent.

3. Apply Concepts Pick an organism in your home and describe how this organism meets the four basic conditions for survival.

_____

_____

_____

_____

_____

_____

4. Control Variables A student is designing a controlled experiment to test whether the amount of water that a plant receives affects its growth. Which variables should the student hold constant and which variable should the student manipulate?

_____

_____

_____

_____

5. Write About It Suppose you are searching for new life forms as part of an expedition in a remote region of Alaska. At one site you find 24 greenish-brown objects, each measuring around 1 cm³. The objects do not appear to have heads, tails, or legs, but you suspect they may be alive. Describe what you would do to determine if the objects are alive.

LESSON 2 **Classifying Life**

6. Which of the following is the broadest level of classification?

    a. genus   **b.** species

    c. domain   **d.** kingdom

7. The two-part naming system called

_____

was devised by Linnaeus in the 1700s.

8. Predict The scientific name for the red maple tree is *Acer rubrum*. Another organism is called *Acer negundo*. Based on its name, what can you predict about this organism? Explain.

_____

_____

_____

_____

_____

9. Make Models Develop a taxonomic key that a person could use to identify each of the plants shown below.

White ash   Red oak   White oak   Pasture rose

1 Review and Assessment

LESSON 3 Domains and Kingdoms

10. Which four kingdoms belong to the domain Eukarya?

    a. prokarya, archaea, eukarya, bacteria

    b. protists, fungi, plants, animals

    c. mite, tick, scorpion, spider

    d. class, order, family, genus

11. All eukaryotes belong to domain Eukarya, while _____ belong to domain Bacteria or domain Archaea.

12. **Compare and Contrast** Both plants and fungi belong to the domain Eukarya. What is one main difference between these organisms?

_____

_____

_____

_____

LESSON 4 Evolution and Classification

13. Which of the following factors is most important when classifying an organism?

    a. size   **b.** shape

    c. habitat   **d.** evolutionary history

14. A diagram that shows probable evolutionary relationships among organisms is called a

_____

15. **Apply Concepts** If you discovered two unrelated organisms that looked very similar, how could you explain it?

_____

_____

_____

_____

 APPLY THE BIG **How are living things alike yet different?**

16. With the advances in commercial space travel, some day you may have the opportunity to visit another planet and see things you've never seen before! How would you go about identifying things on the other planet as being living or nonliving? If an object turns out to be living, what characteristics would you look for in order to classify it? Use four vocabulary terms from the chapter in your answer.

_____

_____

_____

_____

_____

_____

_____

_____

_____

_____

_____

_____

_____

_____

Standardized Test Prep

Multiple Choice

Circle the letter of the best answer.

1. How many kingdoms are represented by the organisms shown below?

   A 1   **B** 2

   C 3   **D** 4

2. Which statement is the correct contrast to the mistaken idea of spontaneous generation?

   A All organisms must take in energy.

   B All organisms must respond to their environments.

   C All organisms reproduce either sexually or asexually.

   D All organisms are made up of cells.

3. Which of the following is an example of a multicellular autotroph?

   A a lion   **B** a tree

   C archaea   **D** a mushroom

4. Which domain does NOT contain prokaryotes?

   A Archaea

   B Bacteria

   C Eukarya

   D None of the above. All three domains contain prokaryotes.

5. How are metabolism and homeostasis related?

   A Homeostasis controls the rate of an organism's metabolism.

   B Both are used to classify organisms.

   C Metabolism involves chemical processes that maintain an organism's internal environment.

   D Homeostasis occurs only in prokaryotes while metabolism occurs in eukaryotes.

Constructed Response

Use the chart below and your knowledge of science to help you answer Question 6. Write your answer on a separate piece of paper.

Some Types of Trees			
Common Name of Tree	**Kingdom**	**Family**	**Species**
Bird cherry	Plants	Rosaceae	*Prunus avium*
Flowering cherry	Plants	Rosaceae	*Prunus serrula*
Smooth-leaved elm	Plants	Ulmaceae	*Ultimus minor*
Whitebeam	Plants	Rosaceae	*Sorbus aria*

6. Which one of the four trees is most different from the other three? Explain your answer.

A RECIPE for Success

Before the 1800s, people thought that living things could appear from nonliving material. But Louis Pasteur did not think that this accepted theory was correct. He suspected that bacteria traveled on particles in the air and reproduced when they landed on biological material—like broth. Pasteur experimented to test his theory. His experiments were successful because they followed a good experimental design. Pasteur tested only one variable, included a control, and repeated his experiments.

Pasteur put broth into two flasks with curved necks. The necks would let in oxygen but keep out bacteria in air. Pasteur boiled the broth in one flask to kill any bacteria in the broth. He did not boil the broth in the other flask.

In a few days, the unboiled broth turned cloudy, showing that new bacteria were growing. The boiled broth remained clear. Pasteur then took the flask with clear broth and broke its curved neck. Bacteria from the air could enter the flask. In a few days, the broth became cloudy. Pasteur's results showed that bacteria were introduced into the broth through the air, and did not grow from the broth itself. He repeated the experiment, and showed that the results were not an accident.

Recipe for a Successful Experiment

1. Make a hypothesis.
2. Write a procedure.
3. Identify the control.
4. Identify the variable.
5. Observe and record data.
6. Repeat.
7. Make a conclusion.

Design It The Dutch scientist Jean-Baptiste van Helmont proposed a recipe for generating mice. He set up an experiment using dirty rags and a few grains of wheat in an open barrel. After about 21 days, mice appeared. The results, he concluded, supported his hypothesis that living things come from nonliving sources. What is wrong with van Helmont's experimental design? Using his hypothesis, design your own experimental procedure. What is your control? What is your variable?

Are you going to Eat That?

Bacteria are everywhere. Most bacteria have no effect on you. Some even help you. But bacteria in your food can be dangerous and can make you sick.

Milk and many juices are treated by a process called pasteurization. The process is named after Louis Pasteur, who invented it. Before the milk or juice reaches the grocery store, it is heated to a temperature that is high enough to kill the most harmful bacteria. Fewer bacteria means slower bacterial growth, giving you enough time to finish your milk before it spoils.

Tips for Keeping Food Safe in Homes and Restaurants

- Keep foods refrigerated until cooking them to prevent any bacteria in the foods from reproducing.

- Cook meat thoroughly, so that the meat reaches a temperature high enough to kill any bacteria that has been growing on it.

- Wash fresh foods, such as fruits and vegetables, to remove bacteria on the surface.

- Do not use the same utensils or cutting board for cutting raw meat and fresh foods, so that any bacteria in raw meat are not transferred to other foods.

Write About It Some champions of raw-food diets suggest that traditional methods of pasteurization reduce the nutritional value of milk and cause milk to spoil rather than to sour. Research the debate about raw dairy products and write a persuasive article that explains whether you support pasteurization of dairy products.

HOW ARE YOU LIKE THIS CREATURE?

THE BIG ?

What are cells made of?

You sure don't see this sight when you look in the mirror! This deep-sea animal does not have skin, a mouth, or hair like yours. It's a young animal that lives in the Atlantic Ocean and may grow up to become a crab or shrimp. Yet you and this creature have more in common than you think.

Infer What might you have in common with this young sea animal?

_____

_____

_____

_____

_____

> UNTAMED SCIENCE Watch the **Untamed Science** video to learn more about cells.

Introduction to Cells 2

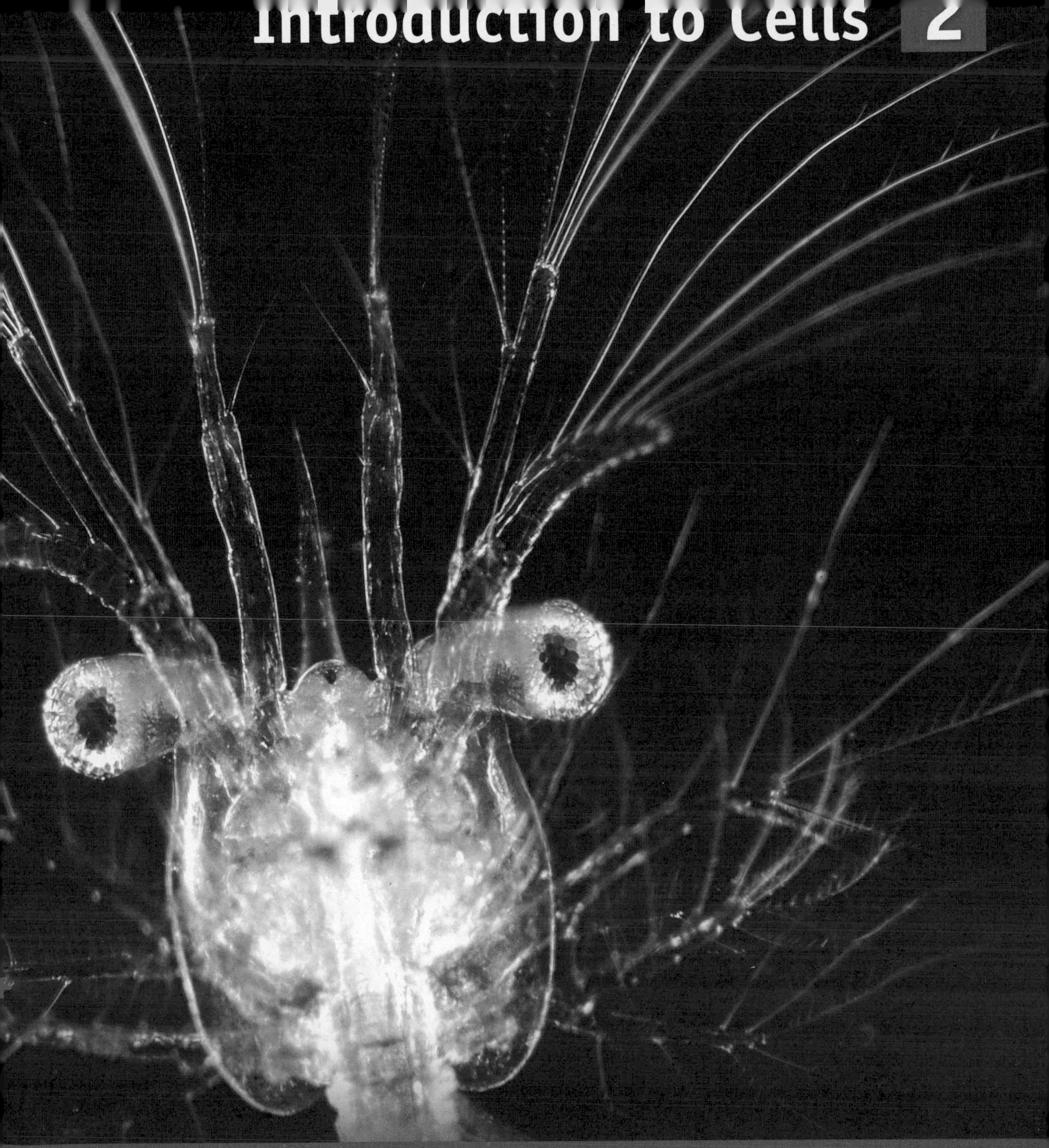

2 Getting Started

Check Your Understanding

1. **Background** Read the paragraph below and then answer the question.

You heard that a pinch of soil can contain millions of **organisms,** and you decide to check it out. Many organisms are too small to see with just your eyes, so you bring a hand **lens.** You see a few organisms, but you think you would see more with greater **magnification.**

> An **organism** is a living thing.
>
> A **lens** is a curved piece of glass or other transparent material that is used to bend light.
>
> **Magnification** is the condition of things appearing larger than they are.

- How does a hand lens help you see more objects in the soil than you can see with just your eyes?

_____

_____

▶ MY READING WEB If you had trouble answering the question above, visit **My Reading Web** and type in *Introduction to Cells.*

Vocabulary Skill

Prefixes Some words can be divided into parts. A root is the part of the word that carries the basic meaning. A prefix is a word part that is placed in front of the root to change the word's meaning. The prefixes below will help you understand some of the vocabulary in this chapter.

Prefix	Meaning	Example
chroma-	color	chromatin, *n.* the genetic material in the nucleus of a cell, that can be colored with dyes
multi-	many	multicellular, *adj.* having many cells

2. **Quick Check** Circle the prefix in the boldface word below. What does the word tell you about the organisms?

- Fishes, insects, grasses, and trees are examples of **multicellular** organisms.

_____

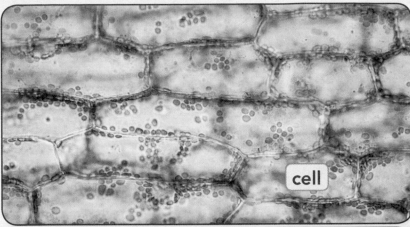

cell

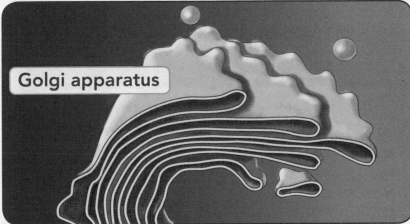

Golgi apparatus

carbohydrate

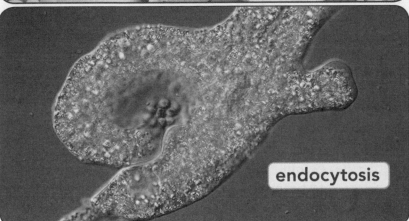

endocytosis

Chapter Preview

LESSON 1

- cell
- microscope
- cell theory
- ↻ Sequence
- △ Measure

LESSON 2

- cell wall   • cell membrane
- nucleus   • organelle   • ribosome
- cytoplasm   • mitochondria
- endoplasmic reticulum
- Golgi apparatus   • vacuole
- chloroplast   • lysosome
- multicellular   • unicellular
- tissue   • organ   • organ system
- ↻ Identify the Main Idea
- △ Make Models

LESSON 3

- element   • compound
- carbohydrate   • lipid   • protein
- enzyme   • nucleic acid   • DNA
- double helix
- ↻ Compare and Contrast
- △ Draw Conclusions

LESSON 4

- selectively permeable
- passive transport   • diffusion
- osmosis   • active transport
- endocytosis   • exocytosis
- ↻ Relate Cause and Effect
- △ Predict

> VOCAB FLASH CARDS For extra help with vocabulary, visit **Vocab Flash Cards** and type in **Introduction to Cells.**

Discovering Cells

- 🔑 **What Are Cells?**

- 🔑 **What Is the Cell Theory?**

- 🔑 **How Do Microscopes Work?**

my planet Diary

VOICES FROM HISTORY

Read the quote, and answer the question below.

Why do you think Leeuwenhoek was so excited about what he saw?

_____

_____

▶ PLANET DIARY Go to **Planet Diary** to learn more about studying cells.

Life at First Sight

Anton van Leeuwenhoek was the first researcher to see bacteria under a microscope. In his journal, he described how he felt after discovering this new and unfamiliar form of life.

"For me . . . no more pleasant sight has met my eye than this of so many thousand of living creatures in one small drop of water."

A modern view of bacteria similar to those seen by Leeuwenhoek

 Do the Inquiry Warm-Up *What Can You See?*

What Are Cells?

What do you think a mushroom, a tree, a spider, a bird, and you have in common? All are living things, or organisms. Like all organisms, they are made of cells. **Cells** form the parts of an organism and carry out all of its functions. 🔑 **Cells are the basic units of structure and function in living things.**

Cells and Structure When you describe the structure of an object, you describe what it is made of and how its parts are put together. For example, the structure of a building depends on the way bricks, steel beams, or other materials are arranged. The structure of a living thing is determined by the amazing variety of ways its cells are put together.

Vocabulary

- cell
- microscope
- cell theory

Skills

- ↻ Reading: Sequence
- △ Inquiry: Measure

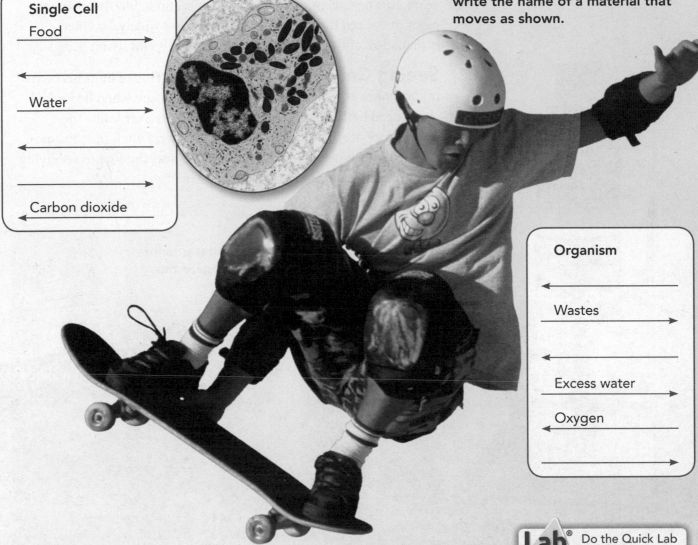

Single Cell

Food ⟶

⟵

Water ⟶

⟵

Carbon dioxide ⟵

FIGURE 1 ....

Needs of Cells

A single cell has the same needs as an entire organism.

✎ **Classify** On each blank arrow, write the name of a material that moves as shown.

Organism

⟵

Wastes ⟶

⟵

Excess water ⟶

Oxygen ⟵

⟶

Cells and Function An organism's functions are the processes that enable it to live, grow, and reproduce. Those functions include obtaining oxygen, food, and water and getting rid of wastes. Cells are involved in all these functions. For example, cells in your digestive system absorb food. The food provides your body with energy and materials needed for growth. Cells in your lungs help you get oxygen. Your body's cells work together, keeping you alive. And for each cell to stay alive, it must carry out many of the same functions as the entire organism.

Lab ® Do the Quick Lab
zone *Comparing Cells.*

🔓 Assess Your Understanding

got it? ....

- ⭘ **I get it!** Now I know that a cell is the basic unit of_____

_____

- ⭘ **I need extra help with** _____

Go to **my science** Ⓢ **coach** *online for help with this subject.*

What Is the Cell Theory?

Until the 1600s, no one knew cells existed because there was no way to see them. Around 1590, the invention of the first microscope allowed people to look at very small objects. A **microscope** is an instrument that makes small objects look larger. Over the next 200 years, this new technology revealed cells and led to the development of the cell theory. The **cell theory** is a widely accepted explanation of the relationship between cells and living things.

Seeing Cells English scientist Robert Hooke built his own microscopes and made drawings of what he saw when he looked at the dead bark of certain oak trees. Hooke never knew the importance of what he saw. A few years later, Dutch businessman Anton van Leeuwenhoek (LAY von hook) was the first to see living cells through his microscopes.

FIGURE 2

Growth of the Cell Theory

The cell theory describes how cells relate to the structure and function of living things. ✎ **Review** Answer the questions in the spaces provided.

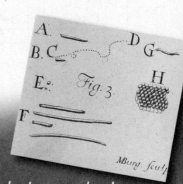

Drawing by Leeuwenhoek

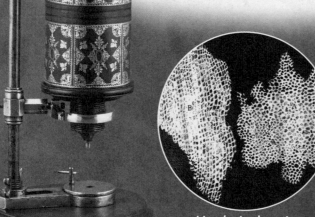

Hooke's drawing of cork

Hooke's Microscope

In 1663, Robert Hooke used his microscope to observe a thin slice of cork. Cork, the bark of the cork oak tree, is made up of cells that are no longer alive. To Hooke, the empty spaces in the cork looked like tiny rectangular rooms. Therefore, Hooke called the empty spaces cells, which means "small rooms."

What was important about Hooke's work?

Leeuwenhoek's Microscope

Leeuwenhoek built microscopes in his spare time. Around 1674, he looked at drops of lake water, scrapings from teeth and gums, and water from rain gutters. Leeuwenhoek was surprised to find a variety of one-celled organisms. He noted that many of them whirled, hopped, or shot through water like fast fish. He called these moving organisms animalcules, meaning "little animals."

What did Leeuwenhoek's observations reveal?

What the Cell Theory Says

Figure 2 highlights people who made key discoveries in the early study of cells. Their work and the work of many others led to the development of the cell theory. The cell theory states the following:

- **All living things are composed of cells.**
- **Cells are the basic units of structure and function in living things.**
- **All cells are produced from other cells.**

Living things differ greatly from one another, but all are made of cells. The cell theory holds true for all living things, no matter how big or how small. Because cells are common to all living things, cells can provide clues about the functions that living things perform. And because all cells come from other cells, scientists can study cells to learn about growth and reproduction.

Sequence Fill in the circle next to the name of the person who was the first to see living cells through a microscope.

- ◯ Matthias Schleiden
- ◯ Robert Hooke
- ◯ Anton van Leeuwenhoek
- ◯ Rudolf Virchow
- ◯ Theodor Schwann

Schleiden, Schwann, and Virchow

In 1838, using his own research and the research of others, Matthias Schleiden concluded that all plants are made of cells. A year later, Theodor Schwann reached the same conclusion about animals. In 1855, Rudolf Virchow proposed that new cells are formed only from cells that already exist. "All cells come from cells," wrote Virchow.

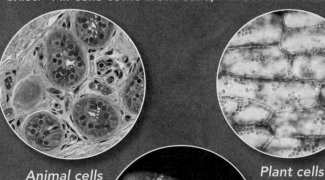

Animal cells

Plant cells

A cell reproducing

To which part of the cell theory did Virchow contribute?

_____

_____

Lab zone Do the Quick Lab *Observing Cells.*

Assess Your Understanding

1a. Relate Cause and Effect Why would Hooke's discovery have been impossible without a microscope?

_____

_____

_____

b. Apply Concepts Use Virchow's ideas to explain why plastic plants and stuffed animals are not alive.

_____

_____

_____

_____

got it?

◯ **I get it!** Now I know that the cell theory describes _____

_____

_____

◯ **I need extra help with** _____

Go to MY SCIENCE ⓢ COACH *online for help with this subject.*

How Do Microscopes Work?

The cell theory could not have been developed without microscopes. ▭ **Some microscopes focus light through lenses to produce a magnified image, and other microscopes use beams of electrons.** Both light microscopes and electron microscopes do the same job in different ways. For a microscope to be useful, it must combine two important properties—magnification and resolution.

Magnification and Lenses Have you ever looked at something through spilled drops of water? If so, did the object appear larger? Magnification is the condition of things appearing larger than they are. Looking through a magnifying glass has the same result. A magnifying glass consists of a convex lens, which has a center that is thicker than its edge. When light passes through a convex lens and into your eye, the image you see is magnified. Magnification changes how you can see objects and reveals details you may not have known were there, as shown in **Figure 3**.

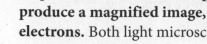

Vocabulary Prefixes The prefix *magni-* means "great" or "large." Underline all the words in the paragraph at the right that you can find with this prefix.

❶ Leaf; green color and veins

❷ _____

❸ _____

❹ _____

FIGURE 3 ·······················

Magnification

The images above have all been magnified, which makes them look unfamiliar. ✎ **Infer On the lines, write what you think each photograph shows, and explain your reasoning. (One answer is completed for you.)**

Magnification With a Compound Microscope

Figure 4 shows a microscope that is similar to one you may use in your classroom. This type of instrument, called a compound microscope, magnifies the image using two lenses at once. One lens is fixed in the eyepiece. A second lens is chosen from a group of two or three lenses on the revolving nosepiece. Each of these lenses has a different magnifying power. By turning the nosepiece, you can select the lens you want. A glass slide on the stage holds the object to be viewed.

A compound microscope can magnify an object more than a single lens can. Light from a lamp (or reflecting off a mirror) passes through the object on the slide, the lower lens, and then the lens in the eyepiece. The total magnification of the object equals the magnifications of the two lenses multiplied together. For example, suppose the lower lens magnifies the object 10 times, and the eyepiece lens also magnifies the object 10 times. The total magnification of the microscope is 10 × 10, or 100 times, which is written as "100×."

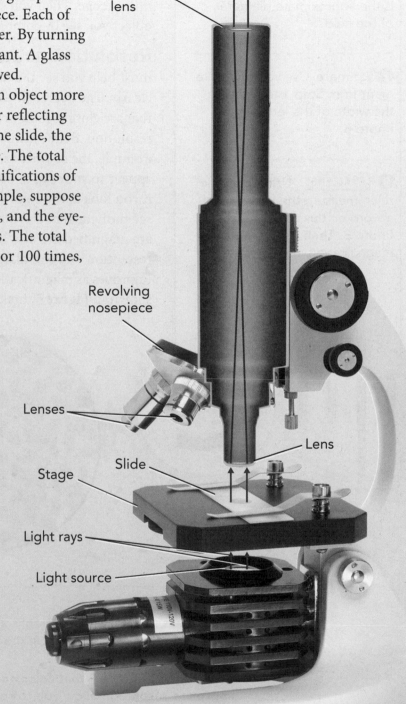

Eyepiece lens

Revolving nosepiece

Lenses

Lens

Slide

Stage

Light rays

Light source

FIGURE 4 ·············

> VIRTUAL LAB **A Compound Microscope**

This microscope has a 10× lens in the eyepiece. The revolving nosepiece holds three different lenses: 4×, 10×, and 40×.

✏ **Complete these tasks.**

1. **Calculate** Calculate the three total magnifications possible for this microscope.

_____

_____

_____

2. **Predict** What would happen if the object on the slide were too thick for light to pass through it?

_____

_____

_____

45

apply it!

1 ⚠ **Measure** In Photo A, you can see the millimeter markings of a metric ruler in the field of the microscope. What is the approximate diameter of the field?

_____

2 **Estimate** Use your measurement from Step 1 to estimate the width of the letter in Photo B.

_____

3 CHALLENGE Using a metric ruler, measure the letter **e** in a word on this page and in Photo B. Then calculate the magnification in the photo.

_____

_____

A   B

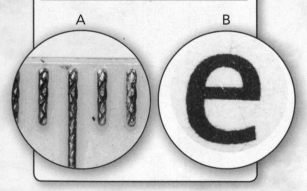

Measuring Microscopic Objects

When you see objects through a microscope, they look larger than they really are. How do you know their true size? One way is to use a metric ruler to measure the size of the circular field in millimeters as you see it through the microscope. Then you can estimate the size of the object you see by comparing it to the width of the field.

Resolution To create a useful image, a microscope must help you see the details of the object's structure clearly. The degree to which two separate structures that are close together can be distinguished is called resolution. Better resolution shows more details. For example, the colors of a newspaper photograph may appear to your eye to be solid patches of color. However, if you look at the colors through a microscope, you will see individual dots. You see the dots not only because they are magnified but also because the microscope improves resolution. In general, for light microscopes, resolution improves as magnification increases. Good resolution, as shown in **Figure 5**, makes it easier to study cells.

FIGURE 5 ·······························

Resolution
The images in colorful photographs actually consist of only a few ink colors in the form of dots.

✏ **Interpret Photos** What color dots does improved resolution allow you to see?

_____

_____

_____

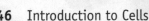

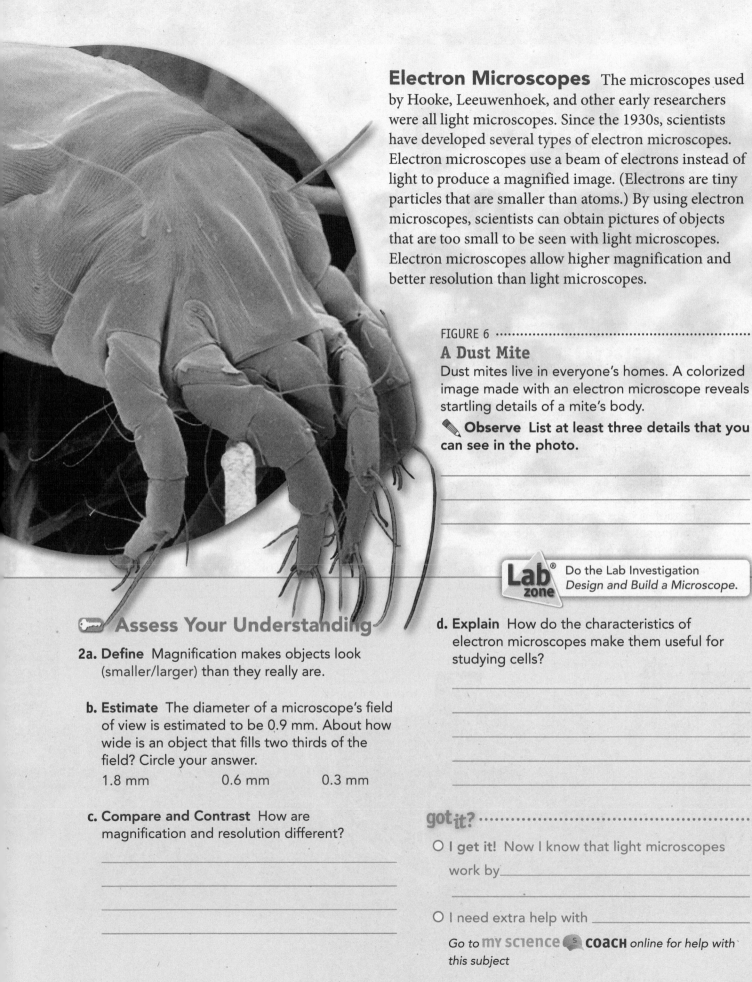

Electron Microscopes

The microscopes used by Hooke, Leeuwenhoek, and other early researchers were all light microscopes. Since the 1930s, scientists have developed several types of electron microscopes. Electron microscopes use a beam of electrons instead of light to produce a magnified image. (Electrons are tiny particles that are smaller than atoms.) By using electron microscopes, scientists can obtain pictures of objects that are too small to be seen with light microscopes. Electron microscopes allow higher magnification and better resolution than light microscopes.

FIGURE 6 ··

A Dust Mite

Dust mites live in everyone's homes. A colorized image made with an electron microscope reveals startling details of a mite's body.

✎ **Observe** List at least three details that you can see in the photo.

_____

_____

_____

Lab zone Do the Lab Investigation
Design and Build a Microscope.

Assess Your Understanding

2a. Define Magnification makes objects look (smaller/larger) than they really are.

b. Estimate The diameter of a microscope's field of view is estimated to be 0.9 mm. About how wide is an object that fills two thirds of the field? Circle your answer.

1.8 mm   0.6 mm   0.3 mm

c. Compare and Contrast How are magnification and resolution different?

_____

_____

_____

_____

d. Explain How do the characteristics of electron microscopes make them useful for studying cells?

_____

_____

_____

_____

_____

got it? ··

○ **I get it!** Now I know that light microscopes work by_____

_____

○ **I need extra help with** _____

Go to MY SCIENCE ⓢ COACH *online for help with this subject*

47

Looking Inside Cells

UNLOCK
THE BIG
?

🔑 **How Do the Parts of a Cell Work?**

🔑 **How Do Cells Work Together in an Organism?**

MY PLANET DIARY

Glowing Globs

Do these cells look as if they're glowing? This photograph shows cells that have been stained with dyes that make cell structures easier to see. Scientists view such treated cells through a fluorescent microscope, which uses strong light to activate the dyes and make them glow. Here, each green area is a cell's nucleus, or control center. The yellow "fibers" form a kind of support structure for the cell.

 Lab ® Do the Inquiry Warm-Up
zone *How Large Are Cells?*

TECHNOLOGY

Communicate Discuss these questions with a partner. Then write your answers below.

1. Why is staining useful when studying cells through a microscope?

_____

_____

2. If you had a microscope, what kinds of things would you like to look at? Why?

_____

_____

_____

▷ PLANET DIARY Go to **Planet Diary** to learn more about cell parts.

Vocabulary

- cell wall • cell membrane • nucleus • organelle
- ribosome • cytoplasm • mitochondria
- endoplasmic reticulum • Golgi apparatus • vacuole
- chloroplast • lysosome • multicellular • unicellular
- tissue • organ • organ system

Skills

🔁 Reading: Identify the Main Idea

△ Inquiry: Make Models

How Do the Parts of a Cell Work?

When you look at a cell through a microscope, you can usually see the outer edge of the cell. Sometimes you can also see smaller structures within the cell. **Each kind of cell structure has a different function within a cell.** In this lesson, you will read about the structures that plant and animal cells have in common. You will also read about some differences between the cells.

Cell Wall The **cell wall** is a rigid layer that surrounds the cells of plants and some other organisms. The cells of animals, in contrast, do not have cell walls. A plant's cell wall helps protect and support the cell. The cell wall is made mostly of a strong material called cellulose. Still, many materials, including water and oxygen, can pass through the cell wall easily.

Cell Membrane Think about how a window screen allows air to enter and leave a room but keeps insects out. One of the functions of the cell membrane is something like that of a screen. The **cell membrane** controls which substances pass into and out of a cell. Everything a cell needs, such as food particles, water, and oxygen, enters through the cell membrane. Waste products leave the same way. In addition, the cell membrane prevents harmful materials from entering the cell.

All cells have cell membranes. In plant cells, the cell membrane is just inside the cell wall. In cells without cell walls, the cell membrane forms the border between the cell and its environment.

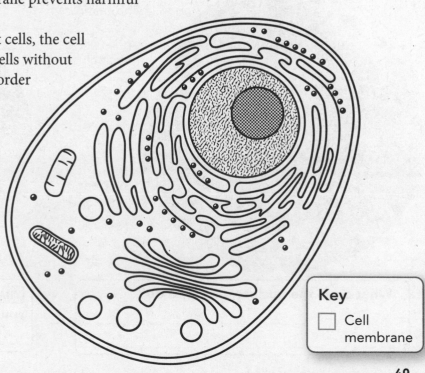

FIGURE 1 ·····················

A Typical Animal Cell
You will see this diagram of a cell again in this lesson.

✏️ **Identify** Use a colored pencil to shade the cell membrane and fill in the box in the key.

Key

☐ Cell membrane

Nucleus

A cell doesn't have a brain, but it has something that functions in a similar way. A large oval structure called the **nucleus** (NOO klee us) acts as a cell's control center, directing all of the cell's activities. The nucleus is the largest of many tiny cell structures, called **organelles,** that carry out specific functions within a cell. Notice in **Figure 2** that the nucleus is surrounded by a membrane called the nuclear envelope. Materials pass in and out of the nucleus through pores in the nuclear envelope.

Chromatin

You may wonder how the nucleus "knows" how to direct the cell. Chromatin, thin strands of material that fill the nucleus, contains information for directing a cell's functions. For example, the instructions in the chromatin ensure that leaf cells grow and divide to form more leaf cells.

Nucleolus

Notice the small, round structure in the nucleus. This structure, the nucleolus, is where ribosomes are made. **Ribosomes** are small grain-shaped organelles that produce proteins. Proteins are important substances in cells.

FIGURE 2 ·················

Organelles of a Cell

The structures of a cell look as different as their functions.

✏ **Complete each task.**

1. **Review** Answer the questions in the boxes.

2. **Relate Text and Visuals** In the diagram on the facing page, use different-colored pencils to color each structure and its matching box in the color key.

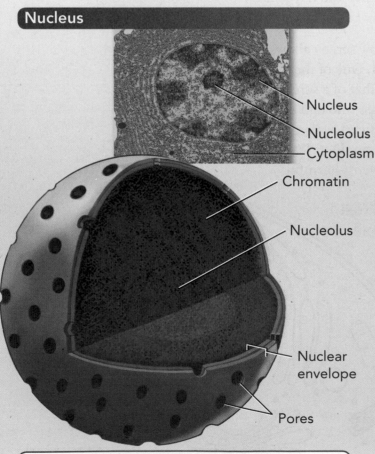

Nucleus

- Nucleus
- Nucleolus
- Cytoplasm
- Chromatin
- Nucleolus
- Nuclear envelope
- Pores

Mitochondrion

What does the nuclear envelope do?

_____

_____

[CHALLENGE] In what types of cells would you expect to find a lot of mitochondria?

_____

Organelles in the Cytoplasm

Most of a cell consists of a thick, clear, gel-like fluid. The **cytoplasm** fills the region between the cell membrane and the nucleus. The fluid of the cytoplasm moves constantly within a cell, carrying along the nucleus and other organelles that have specific jobs.

Mitochondria Floating in the cytoplasm are rod-shaped structures that are nicknamed the "powerhouses" of a cell. Look again at **Figure 2. Mitochondria** (myt oh KAHN dree uh; singular *mitochondrion*) convert energy stored in food to energy the cell can use to live and function.

Endoplasmic Reticulum and Ribosomes In **Figure 2,** you can see what looks something like a maze of passageways. The **endoplasmic reticulum** (en doh PLAZ mik rih TIK yuh lum), often called the ER, is an organelle with a network of membranes that produces many substances. Ribosomes dot some parts of the ER, while other ribosomes float in the cytoplasm. The ER helps the attached ribosomes make proteins. These newly made proteins and other substances leave the ER and move to another organelle.

Vocabulary Prefixes The prefix *endo-* is Greek for "within." If the word part *plasm* refers to the "body" of the cell, what does the prefix *endo-* tell you about the endoplasmic reticulum?

_____

_____

Endoplasmic Reticulum and Ribosomes

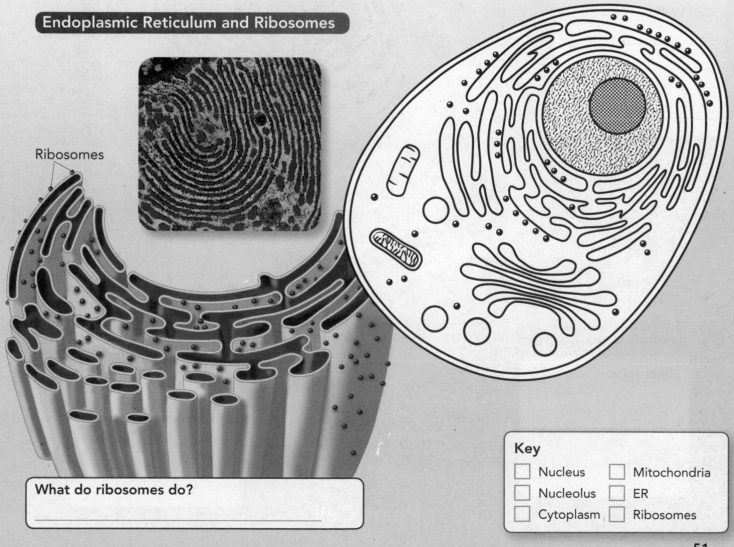

Ribosomes

What do ribosomes do?

_____

Key

- ☐ Nucleus
- ☐ Nucleolus
- ☐ Cytoplasm
- ☐ Mitochondria
- ☐ ER
- ☐ Ribosomes

CELLS IN LIVING THINGS

What are cells made of?

FIGURE 3 ···

> **INTERACTIVE ART** These illustrations show typical structures found in plant and animal cells. Other living things share many of these structures, too. ✎ **Describe** Describe the function of each structure in the boxes provided.

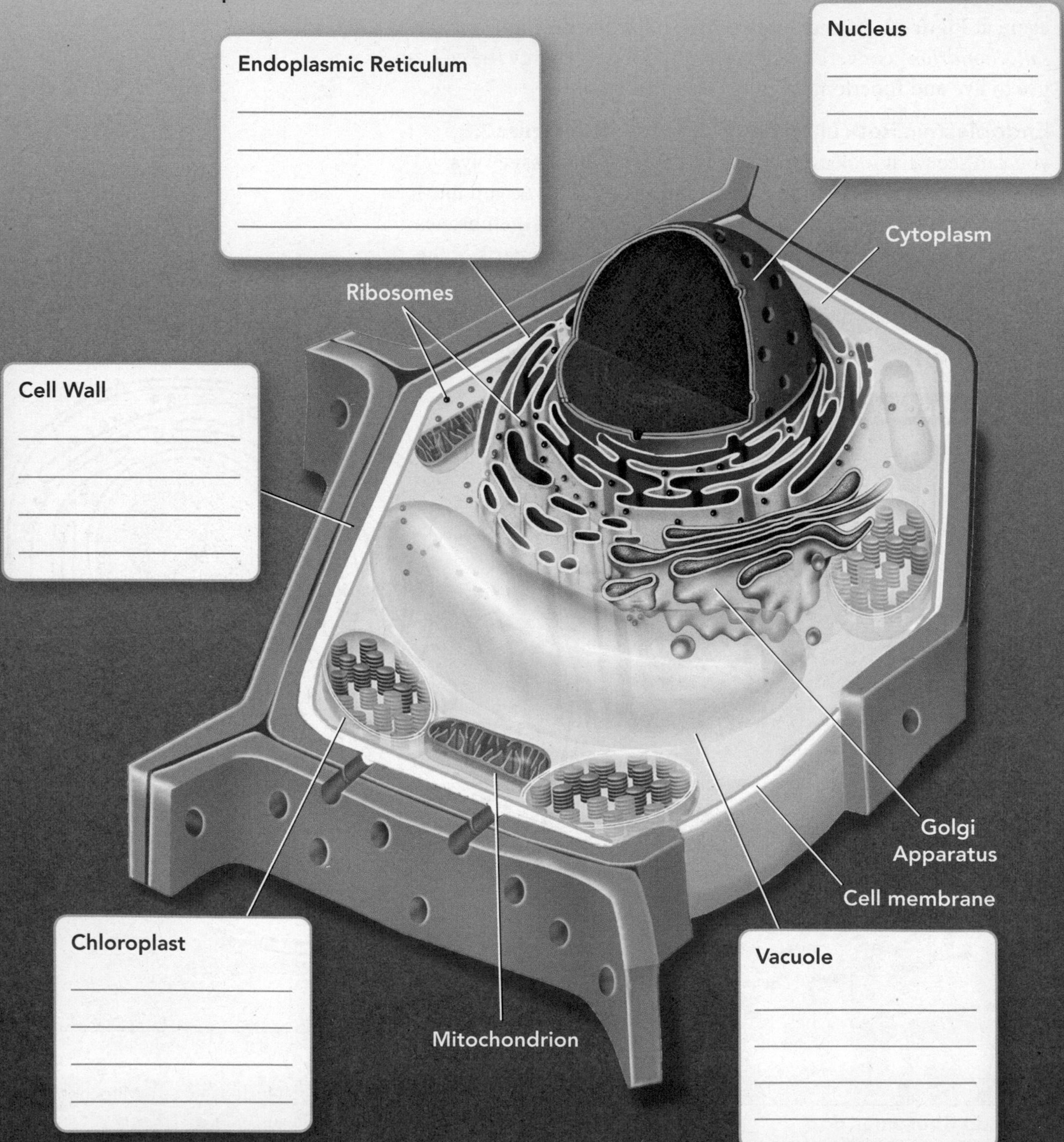

Endoplasmic Reticulum
_____
_____
_____
_____

Nucleus
_____
_____
_____

Cytoplasm

Ribosomes

Cell Wall
_____
_____
_____
_____

Golgi
Apparatus

Cell membrane

Chloroplast
_____
_____
_____

Vacuole
_____
_____
_____
_____

Mitochondrion

Plant Cell

Check the box for each structure present in plant cells or animal cells.

Structure	Cell wall	Cell membrane	Cytoplasm	Nucleus	Mitochondria	Chloroplasts	Ribosomes	Endoplasmic reticulum	Vacuoles	Golgi apparatus	Lysosomes
Plant cells											
Animal cells											

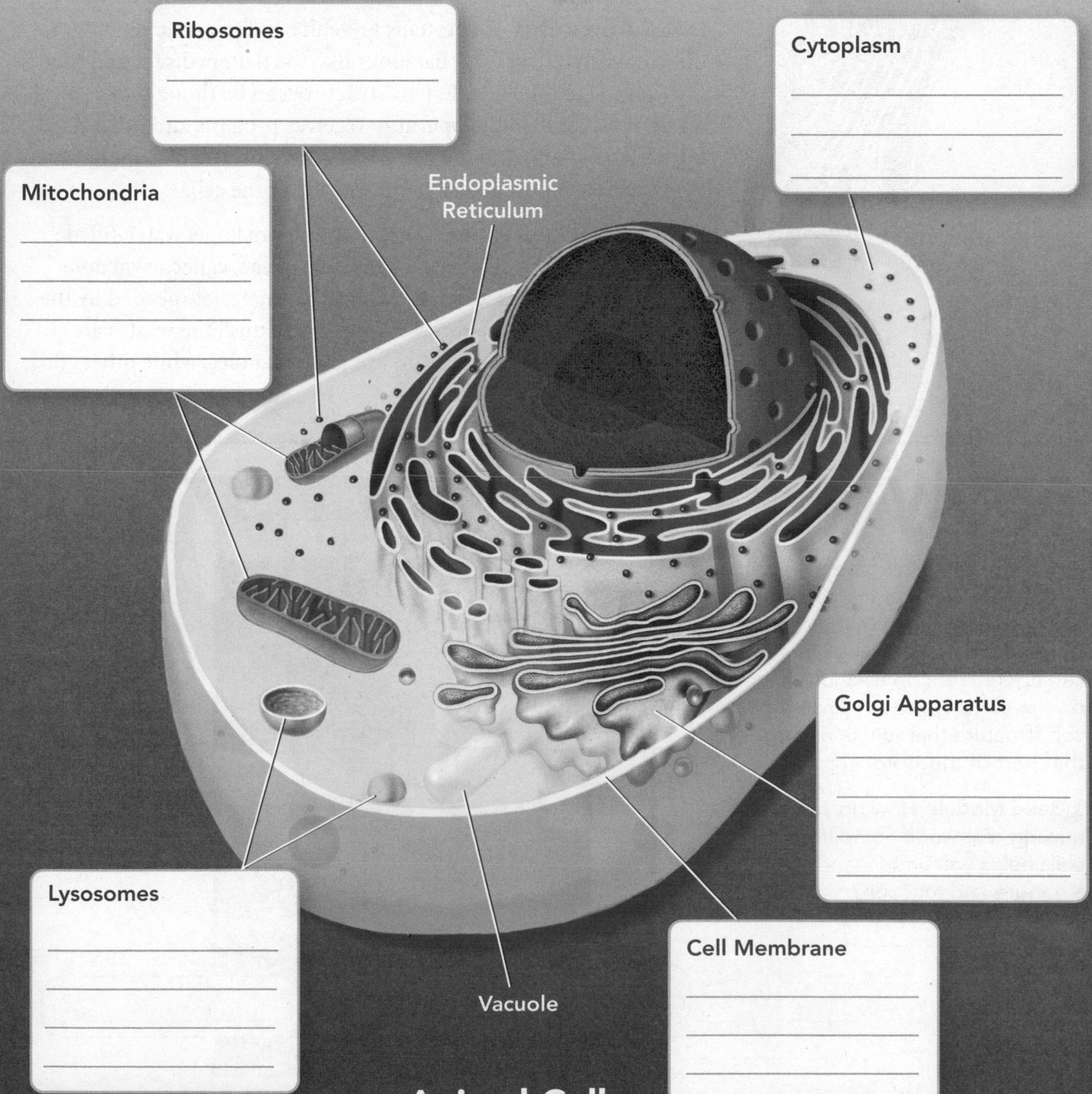

Ribosomes

_____

_____

Cytoplasm

_____

_____

_____

Mitochondria

_____

_____

_____

Endoplasmic
Reticulum

Golgi Apparatus

_____

_____

_____

_____

Lysosomes

_____

_____

_____

Vacuole

Cell Membrane

_____

_____

_____

Animal Cell

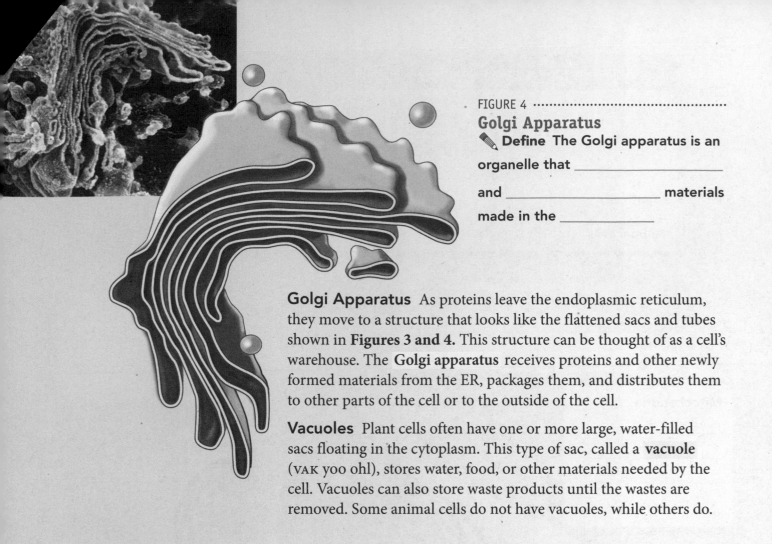

FIGURE 4 ···

Golgi Apparatus

✎ **Define** The Golgi apparatus is an organelle that _____ and _____ materials made in the _____

Golgi Apparatus As proteins leave the endoplasmic reticulum, they move to a structure that looks like the flattened sacs and tubes shown in **Figures 3 and 4.** This structure can be thought of as a cell's warehouse. The **Golgi apparatus** receives proteins and other newly formed materials from the ER, packages them, and distributes them to other parts of the cell or to the outside of the cell.

Vacuoles Plant cells often have one or more large, water-filled sacs floating in the cytoplasm. This type of sac, called a **vacuole** (VAK yoo ohl), stores water, food, or other materials needed by the cell. Vacuoles can also store waste products until the wastes are removed. Some animal cells do not have vacuoles, while others do.

apply it!

Can a store's building be a model for a cell? If so, how do the parts of a cell function in ways that are similar to the parts of a building? See if you can figure it out. In each blank space on the picture, write the name of a cell structure that functions most like that part of the store.

⚠ **Make Models** How do you think making real-world comparisons with cells helps you understand cell structure and function?

_____

_____

_____

_____

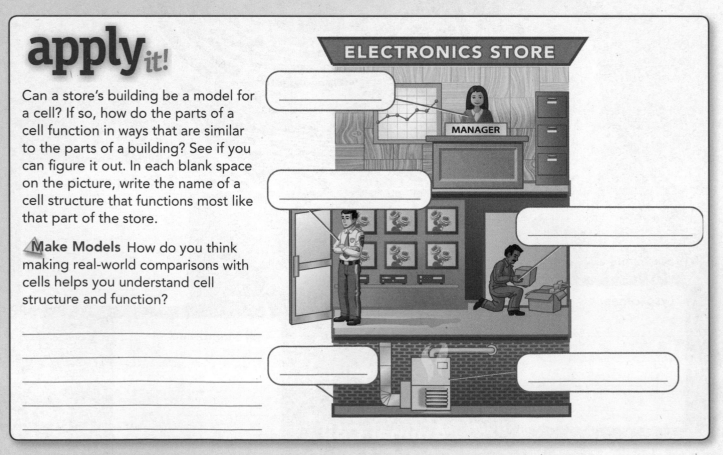

Chloroplasts A typical plant cell contains green structures, called chloroplasts, in the cytoplasm. A **chloroplast,** shown in **Figure 5,** captures energy from sunlight and changes it to a form of energy cells can use in making food. Animal cells don't have chloroplasts, but the cells of plants and some other organisms do. Chloroplasts make leaves green because leaf cells contain many chloroplasts.

Lysosomes Look again at the animal cell in **Figure 3**. Notice the saclike organelles, called **lysosomes** (LY suh sohmz), which contain substances that break down large food particles into smaller ones. Lysosomes also break down old cell parts and release the substances so they can be used again. You can think of lysosomes as a cell's recycling centers.

FIGURE 5 ···

A Chloroplast

✎ **Infer** In which part of a plant would you NOT expect to find cells with chloroplasts?

_____

_____

Do the Quick Lab
Gelatin Cell Model.

🗝 **Assess Your Understanding**

1a. Interpret Tables Use the table you completed in **Figure 3** to summarize the differences between a plant cell and an animal cell.

_____

_____

_____

b. Make Generalizations How are the functions of the endoplasmic reticulum and the Golgi apparatus related?

_____

_____

_____

_____

c. CHALLENGE A solar panel collects sunlight and converts it to heat or electrical energy. How is a solar panel similar to chloroplasts?

_____

_____

_____

d. ANSWER THE BIG ? What are cells made of?

_____

_____

_____

gotit? ··

○ I get it! Now I know that different kinds of organelles in a cell_____

○ I need extra help with _____

Go to MY SCIENCE ⓢ COACH *online for help with this subject.*

How Do Cells Work Together in an Organism?

Plants and animals (including you) are **multicellular,** which means "made of many cells." Single-celled organisms are called **unicellular.** In a multicellular organism, the cells often look quite different from one another. They also perform different functions.

Specialized Cells All cells in a multicellular organism must carry out key functions, such as getting oxygen, to remain alive. However, cells also may be specialized. That is, they perform specific functions that benefit the entire organism. These specialized cells share what can be called a "division of labor." One type of cell does one kind of job, while other types of cells do other jobs. For example, red blood cells carry oxygen to other cells that may be busy digesting your food. Just as specialized cells differ in function, they also differ in structure. **Figure 6** shows specialized cells from plants and animals. Each type of cell has a distinct shape. For example, a nerve cell has thin, fingerlike extensions that reach toward other cells. These structures help nerve cells transmit information from one part of your body to another. The nerve cell's shape wouldn't be helpful to a red blood cell.

✐ **Identify the Main Idea**
Reread the paragraph about specialized cells. Then underline the phrases or sentences that describe the main ideas about specialized cells.

FIGURE 6 ....

▷ INTERACTIVE ART **The Right Cell for the Job**

Many cells in plants and animals carry out specialized functions.
✎ **Draw Conclusions** Write the number of each kind of cell in the circle of the matching function.

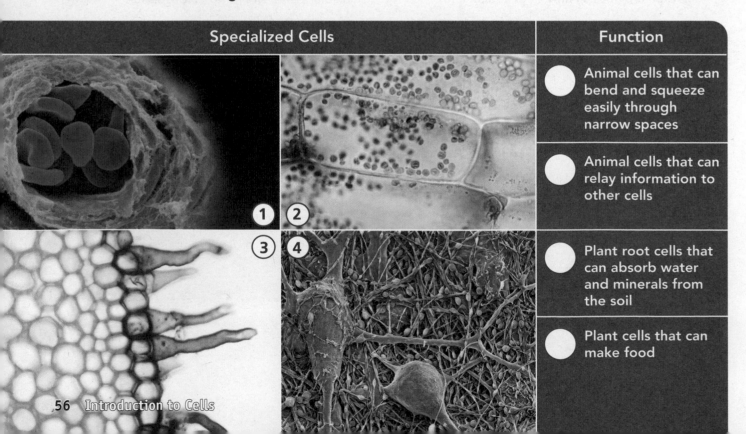

Specialized Cells	Function
① ② ③ ④	○ Animal cells that can bend and squeeze easily through narrow spaces
	○ Animal cells that can relay information to other cells
	○ Plant root cells that can absorb water and minerals from the soil
	○ Plant cells that can make food

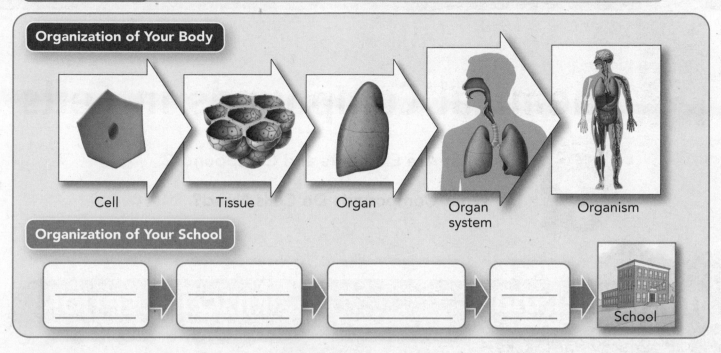

Organization of Your Body

Cell ➤ Tissue ➤ Organ ➤ Organ system ➤ Organism

Organization of Your School

School

Cells Working Together
A division of labor occurs among specialized cells in an organism. It also occurs at other levels of organization. 🔑 **In multicellular organisms, cells are organized into tissues, organs, and organ systems.** A **tissue** is a group of similar cells that work together to perform a specific function. For example, your brain is made mostly of nerve tissue, which consists of nerve cells that relay information to other parts of your body. An **organ,** such as your brain, is made of different kinds of tissues that function together. For example, the brain also has blood vessels that carry the blood that supplies oxygen to your brain cells. Your brain is part of your nervous system, which directs body activities and processes. An **organ system** is a group of organs that work together to perform a major function. As **Figure 7** shows, the level of organization in an organism becomes more complex from cell, to tissue, to organ, to organ systems.

FIGURE 7 ·········
Levels of Organization
Living things are organized in levels of increasing complexity. Many nonliving things, like a school, have levels of organization, too.

✏️ **Apply Concepts** On the lines above, write the levels of organization of your school building, from the simplest level, such as your desk, to the most complex.

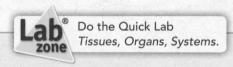

Do the Quick Lab
Tissues, Organs, Systems.

🔑 Assess Your Understanding

2a. Describe What does the term *division of labor* mean as it is used in this lesson?

b. Infer Would a tissue or an organ have more kinds of specialized cells? Explain your answer.

got**it?** ·········

○ **I get it!** Now I know that the levels of organization in a multicellular organism include _____

○ **I need extra help with** _____

Go to MY SCIENCE ⬢ᔆ COACH online for help with this subject.

Chemical Compounds in Cells

What Are Elements and Compounds?

What Compounds Do Cells Need?

my PLANET DiARY

Energy Backpacks

Some people think a camel's humps carry water. Not true! They actually store fat. A hump's fatty tissue supplies energy when the camel doesn't eat. When a camel has enough food, the hump remains hard and round. But when food is scarce, the hump gets smaller and may sag to the side. If the camel then gets more food, the hump can regain its full size and shape in about three or four months.

MISCONCEPTION

Communicate Discuss this question with a group of classmates. Then write your answer below.

How do you think the camel might be affected if it didn't have humps?

_____

_____

_____

▷ PLANET DIARY Go to **Planet Diary** to learn more about chemical compounds in cells.

 Do the Inquiry Warm-Up *Detecting Starch.*

What Are Elements and Compounds?

You are made of many substances. These substances supply the raw materials that make up your blood, bones, muscles, and more. They also take part in the processes carried out by your cells.

Elements You have probably heard of carbon, hydrogen, oxygen, and nitrogen—maybe phosphorus and sulfur, too. All of these are examples of **elements** found in your body. **An element is any substance that cannot be broken down into simpler substances.** The smallest unit of an element is a particle called an atom. Any single element is made up of only one kind of atom.

Vocabulary

- element • compound • carbohydrate • lipid
- protein • enzyme • nucleic acid • DNA
- double helix

Skills

↻ **Reading:** Compare and Contrast

△ **Inquiry:** Draw Conclusions

How many atoms form a water molecule?

_____

_____

Name the elements in a molecule of carbon dioxide.

_____

_____

Compounds Carbon dioxide and water are examples of **compounds**. 🔑 **Compounds form when two or more elements combine chemically.** Most elements in living things occur in the form of compounds. For example, carbon dioxide is a compound made up of the elements carbon and oxygen.

The smallest unit of many compounds is a molecule. A molecule of carbon dioxide consists of one carbon atom and two oxygen atoms. Compare the diagrams of the carbon dioxide molecule and the water molecule in **Figure 1**.

FIGURE 1 ·····················

Molecules and Compounds
Carbon dioxide, in the air exhaled from the swimmer's lungs, is a compound. So is water.

✎ **Interpret Diagrams Answer the questions in the boxes provided.**

Lab zone® Do the Quick Lab
What Is a Compound?

🔑 **Assess Your Understanding**

got it? ·····················

○ **I get it!** Now I know that compounds form when _____

_____

○ **I need extra help with** _____

Go to **MY SCIENCE** ⑤ **COACH** *online for help with this subject.*

What Compounds Do Cells Need?

Many of the compounds in living things contain the element carbon. Most compounds that contain carbon are called organic compounds. Organic compounds that you may have heard of include nylon and polyester. Compounds that don't contain carbon are called inorganic compounds. Water and table salt are familiar examples of inorganic compounds.

🔑 **Some important groups of organic compounds that living things need are carbohydrates, lipids, proteins, and nucleic acids. Water is a necessary inorganic compound.** Many of these compounds are found in the foods you eat. This fact makes sense because the foods you eat come from living things.

Carbohydrates

You have probably heard of sugars and starches. They are examples of **carbohydrates,** energy-rich organic compounds made of the elements carbon, hydrogen, and oxygen.

The food-making process in plants produces sugars. Fruits and some vegetables have a high sugar content. Sugar molecules can combine, forming larger molecules called starches, or complex carbohydrates. Plant cells store excess energy in molecules of starch. Many foods, such as potatoes, pasta, rice, and bread, come from plants and contain starch. When you eat these foods, your body breaks down the starch into glucose, a sugar your cells can use to get energy.

Carbohydrates are important components of some cell parts. For example, the cellulose found in the cell walls of plants is a type of carbohydrate. Carbohydrates are also found on cell membranes.

did you
know? ....
Did you know that your body needs a new supply of proteins every day because protein cannot be stored for later use, as fat or carbohydrates can?

FIGURE 2 ·····································
Energy-Rich Compounds
Cooked pasta served with olive oil, spices, and other ingredients makes an energy-packed meal.
✏️ **Classify** Label each food a starch or a lipid. Next to the label, write another example of a food that contains starch or lipids.

Lipids

Have you ever seen a cook trim fat from a piece of meat before cooking it? The cook is trimming away one kind of lipid. **Lipids** are compounds that are made mostly of carbon and hydrogen and some oxygen. Cell membranes consist mainly of lipids.

Fats, oils, and waxes are all lipids. Gram for gram, fats and oils contain more energy than carbohydrates. Cells store energy from fats and oils for later use. For example, during winter, an inactive bear lives on the energy stored in its fat cells. Foods high in fats include whole milk, ice cream, and fried foods.

Proteins

What do a bird's feathers, a spider's web, and a hamburger have in common? They consist mainly of proteins. **Proteins** are large organic molecules made of carbon, hydrogen, oxygen, nitrogen, and, in some cases, sulfur. Foods that are high in protein include meat, dairy products, fish, nuts, and beans.

Much of a cell's structure and function depends on proteins. Proteins form part of a cell's membrane. Proteins also make up parts of the organelles within a cell. A group of proteins known as **enzymes** speed up chemical reactions in living things. Without enzymes, the many chemical reactions that are necessary for life would take too long. For example, an enzyme in your saliva speeds up the digestion of starch. The starch breaks down into sugars while still in your mouth.

FIGURE 3 ··

Proteins
A parrot's beak, feathers, and claws are made of proteins.

✎ **Apply Concepts** What part of your body most likely consists of proteins similar to those of a parrot's claws?

_____

_____

↻ **Compare and Contrast**
As you read, complete the table below to compare carbohydrates, lipids, and proteins.

Type of Compound	Elements	Functions
Carbohydrate		
Lipid		
Protein		

FIGURE 4 ······································

DNA

Smaller molecules connect in specific patterns and sequences, forming DNA.

✏️ **Interpret Diagrams** In the diagram below, identify the pattern of colors. Then color in the ones that are missing.

Nucleic Acids

Nucleic acids are very long organic molecules. These molecules consist of carbon, oxygen, hydrogen, nitrogen, and phosphorus. Nucleic acids contain the instructions that cells need to carry out all the functions of life. Foods high in nucleic acids include red meat, shellfish, mushrooms, and peas.

One kind of nucleic acid is deoxyribonucleic acid (dee AHK see RY boh noo KLEE ik), or DNA. **DNA** is the genetic material that carries information about an organism and is passed from parent to offspring. This information directs a cell's functions. Most DNA is found in a cell's nucleus. The shape of a DNA molecule is described as a **double helix.** Imagine a rope ladder that's been twisted around a pole, and you'll have a mental picture of the double helix of DNA. The double helix forms from many small molecules connected together. The pattern and sequence in which these molecules connect make a kind of chemical code the cell can "read."

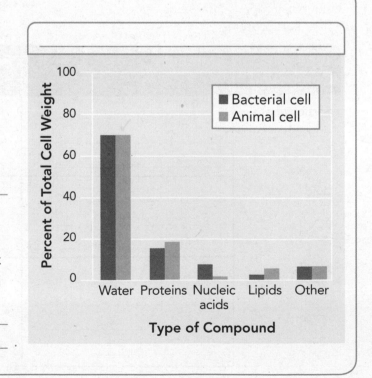

do the math!

Most cells contain the same compounds. The graph compares the percentages of some compounds found in a bacterial cell and in an animal cell. Write a title for the graph and answer the questions below.

❶ **Read Graphs** Put a check above the bar that shows the percentage of water in an animal cell. How does this number compare to the percentage of water in a bacterial cell?

_____

❷ **Read Graphs** (Proteins/Nucleic acids) make up a larger percentage of an animal cell.

❸ △ **Draw Conclusions** In general, how do you think a bacterial cell and an animal cell compare in their chemical composition?

_____

_____

FIGURE 5 ···

Mostly Water
About two thirds of the human body is water. But you know you don't really look like a tank of water with a fish! ✎ **Graph Complete and label the circle graph to show the percentage of water in your body.**

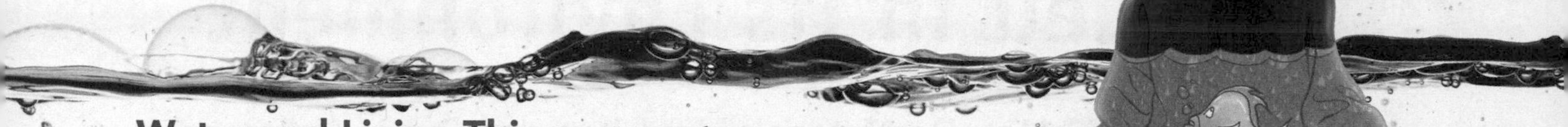

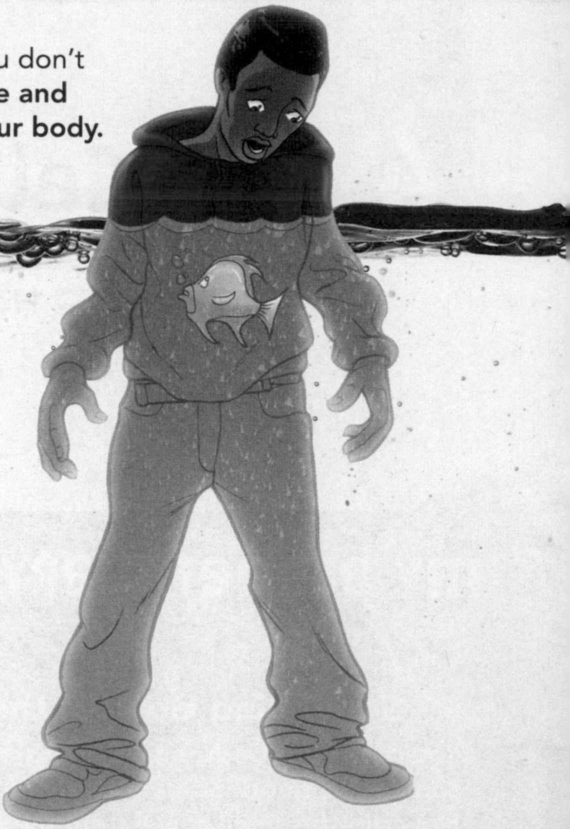

Water and Living Things
Water plays many important roles in cells. For example, most chemical reactions in cells depend on substances that must be dissolved in water to react. And water itself takes part in many chemical reactions in cells.

Water also helps cells keep their shape. A cell without water would be like a balloon without air! Think about how the leaves of a plant wilt when the plant needs water. After you add water to the soil, the cells absorb the water, and the leaves perk up.

Water changes temperature slowly, so it helps keep the temperature of cells from changing rapidly—a change that can be harmful. Water also plays a key role in carrying substances into and out of cells. Without water, life as we know it would not exist on Earth.

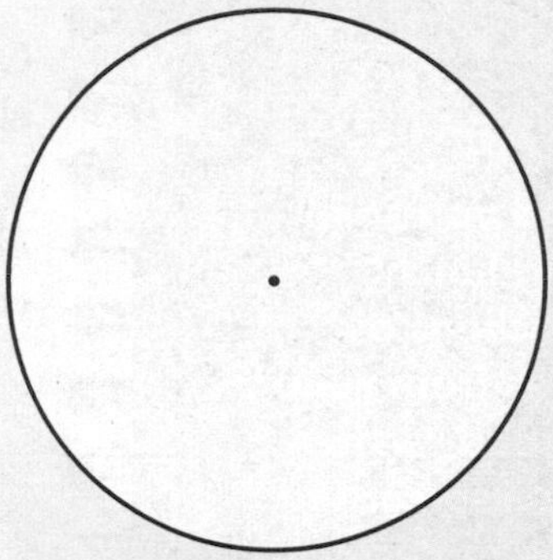

Lab zone® Do the Quick Lab
What's That Taste?

🔑 Assess Your Understanding

1a. Describe An organic compound that contains only the elements carbon, hydrogen, and oxygen is most likely (a carbohydrate/ a protein/DNA). Explain your answer.

_____

_____

_____

b. Classify Which groups of organic compounds found in living things are NOT energy rich?

_____

c. Review What is the function of DNA?

_____

_____

_____

d. CHALLENGE Describe ways a lack of water could affect cell functions.

_____

_____

_____

got it? ··

○ **I get it!** Now I know that the important compounds in living things include _____

_____

○ I need extra help with _____

Go to MY SCIENCE ⓢ COACH *online for help with this subject.*

The Cell in Its Environment

🔑 How Do Materials Move Into and Out of Cells?

my planet Diary

Something Good in the Air

You're in your bedroom studying, and you smell something good. Someone is cooking lunch! How did the smell travel from the kitchen to your nose? During cooking, molecules from soup and many other foods diffuse, or spread farther and farther apart. The molecules are also carried by air currents. Your nose sniffs in the molecules and sends a message to your brain. Even if only one molecule in ten million carries the odor, your nose will send a "smell" message! Amazingly, your brain can identify about ten thousand different smells.

FUN FACTS

Communicate Discuss this question with a classmate and write your answers below.

If the kitchen door is closed, how will that affect your ability to smell cooking odors in your room?

_____

_____

_____

_____

_____

_____

> PLANET DIARY Go to **Planet Diary** to learn more about cells in their environments.

Lab zone® Do the Inquiry Warm-Up *Diffusion in Action.*

How Do Materials Move Into and Out of Cells?

Cells have structures that protect their contents from the world outside the cell. To live and function, however, cells must let certain materials enter and leave. Oxygen and water and particles of food must be able to move into a cell, while carbon dioxide and other waste materials must move out. Much as a gatekeeper controls the flow of traffic into and out of a parking lot, the cell membrane controls how materials move into or out of a cell.

Vocabulary
- selectively permeable
- osmosis
- exocytosis
- passive transport
- active transport
- diffusion
- endocytosis

Skills
- Reading: Relate Cause and Effect
- Inquiry: Predict

Importance of the Cell Membrane Every cell is surrounded by a cell membrane. In **Figure 1** you can see that the cell membrane consists of a double layer of lipid molecules lined up side by side. Remember that lipids are a group of organic compounds found in living things. Here and there in the double layer of lipid molecules, you can see proteins, some with chains of carbohydrates attached. Other carbohydrate chains sit on the surface of the membrane. All these molecules play important roles in helping materials move through the cell membrane.

Some materials move freely across the cell membrane. Others move less freely or not at all. The cell membrane is **selectively permeable,** which means that some substances can cross the membrane while others cannot. 🔑 **Substances that can move into and out of a cell do so by means of one of two processes: passive transport or active transport.**

FIGURE 1 ....

> **ART IN MOTION** **A Selective Barrier**

✏️ **Make Models** In what way is the cell membrane like a gatekeeper?

_____

_____

Cell membrane

Inside of cell

Carbohydrate chain

Protein

Lipid molecule

Outside of cell

Diffusion and Osmosis: Forms of Passive
Transport If you have ever ridden a bicycle down a hill, you know that it takes hardly any of your energy to go fast. But you do have to use energy to pedal back up the hill. Moving materials across the cell membrane sometimes requires the cell to use its own energy. At other times, the cell uses no energy. The movement of dissolved materials across a cell membrane without using the cell's energy is called **passive transport.**

FIGURE 2 ···

Diffusion
A drop of food coloring in a plate of gelatin gradually spreads as molecules of the dye diffuse. ✎ **Predict In the third plate, draw how you think the plate would look if diffusion continues.**

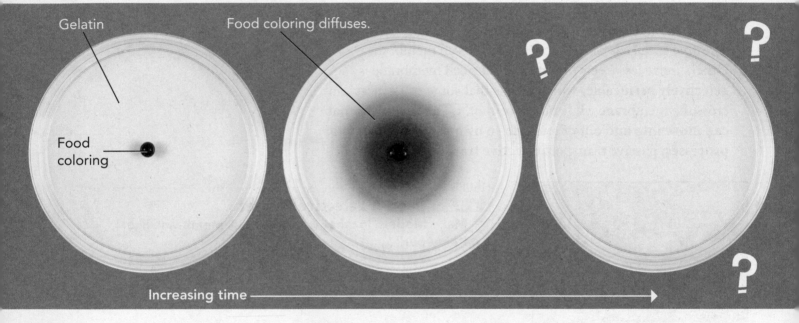

Gelatin

Food coloring diffuses.

Food coloring

Increasing time ⟶

Diffusion Molecules are always moving. As they move, they bump into one another. The more molecules there are in a space, the more they are said to be concentrated in that space. So they collide more often. Collisions cause molecules to push away from one another. Over time, as molecules continue colliding and moving apart, they become less concentrated. Eventually, they spread evenly throughout the space. **Diffusion** (dih FYOO zhun) is the process by which molecules move from an area of higher concentration to an area of lower concentration. See **Figure 2.**

Consider a unicellular organism that lives in pond water. It gets oxygen from that water. Many more molecules of oxygen are dissolved in the water outside the cell than inside the cell. In other words, the concentration of oxygen is higher outside the cell. What happens? Oxygen moves easily into the cell. The diffusion of oxygen into the cell does not require the cell to use any of its energy. Diffusion is one form of passive transport.

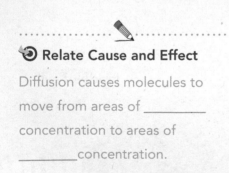

⟲ **Relate Cause and Effect**

Diffusion causes molecules to move from areas of _____ concentration to areas of _____ concentration.

Osmosis Like oxygen, water passes easily into and out of a cell across the cell membrane. **Osmosis** is the diffusion of water molecules across a selectively permeable membrane. Because cells cannot function properly without adequate water, many cellular processes depend on osmosis. Osmosis is a form of passive transport.

Osmosis can have important effects on cells and entire organisms. The plant cells in the top photo of **Figure 3** have a healthy flow of water both into and out of each cell. Under certain conditions, osmosis can cause water to move out of the cells more quickly than it moves in. When that happens, the cytoplasm shrinks and the cell membrane pulls away from the cell wall, as shown in the bottom photo. If conditions do not change, the cells can die.

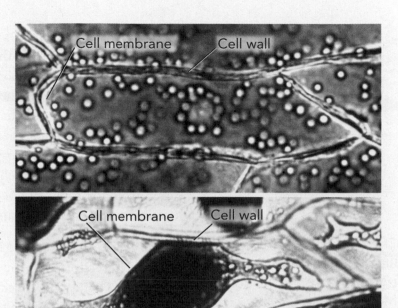

FIGURE 3 ·······································

Effects of Osmosis
Cells shrink and die when they lose too much water.

✎ **Infer** Using a colored pencil, shade the cells in the bottom photo to show how they would change if the flow of water was reversed.

apply it!

Most cells are too small to be seen without a microscope. What does cell size have to do with moving materials into and out of a cell? Suppose the diagrams at the right represent two cells. One cell is three times the width of the other cell. Think about how this difference could affect processes in the cells.

❶ Infer Cytoplasm streams within a cell, moving materials somewhat as ocean currents move a raft. In which cell will materials move faster from the cell membrane to the center of the cell? Why?

_____

_____

❷ Predict Wastes are poisonous to a cell and must be removed from the cytoplasm. Predict how cell size could affect the removal process and the survival of a cell.

_____

_____

_____

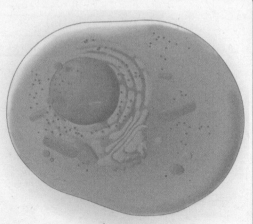

Large cell

Small cell

Facilitated Diffusion Oxygen and carbon dioxide diffuse freely across a cell membrane. Other molecules, such as sugar, do not. Sugars cannot cross easily through the membrane's lipid molecules. In a process called facilitated diffusion, proteins in the cell membrane form channels through which the sugars can pass. The word *facilitate* means "to make easier." As shown in **Figure 4,** these proteins provide a pathway for the sugars to diffuse. The proteins function much the way downspouts guide water that flows from the roof of a house to the ground. Facilitated diffusion uses no cell energy and is another form of passive transport.

Active Transport Molecules in cells must often move in the opposite direction from the way they would naturally move due to diffusion. That is, the molecules move from a place of *lower* concentration to a place of *higher* concentration. Cells have to supply the energy to do this work—just as you would supply the energy to pedal a bike uphill. **Active transport** is the movement of materials across a cell membrane using cellular energy.

As in facilitated diffusion, proteins within the cell membrane play a key role in active transport. Using the cell's energy, transport proteins "pick up" specific molecules and carry them across the membrane. Substances that are carried into and out of cells by this process include calcium, potassium, and sodium.

FIGURE 4 ·······························
> ART IN MOTION **Crossing the Cell Membrane**
✎ Molecules move into and out of a cell by means of passive or active transport.

1. **Name** Fill in the words missing in the boxes.
2. **CHALLENGE** On the diagram, write an "H" where the concentration of each substance is high and an "L" where the concentration is low.

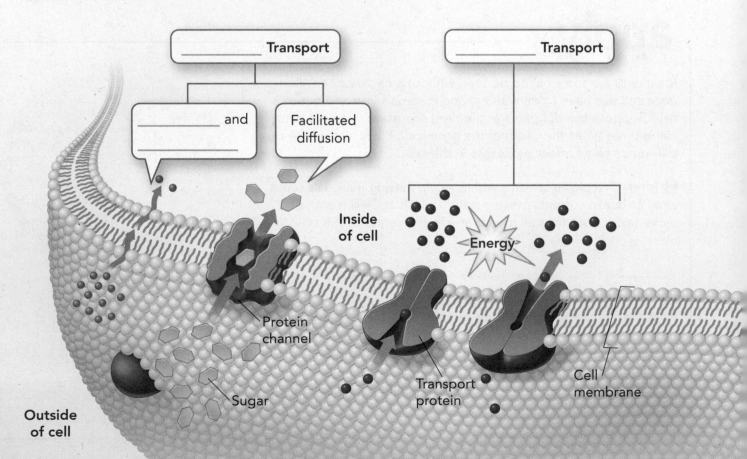

_____ Transport

_____ and

Facilitated diffusion

_____ Transport

Inside of cell

Energy

Protein channel

Sugar

Transport protein

Cell membrane

Outside of cell

Moving Large Particles

Some materials, such as food particles, are too large to cross the cell membrane. In a process called **endocytosis** (ehn doh sigh TOH sihs), the cell membrane changes shape and engulfs the particle. You can see this process happening in **Figure 5**. Once the food particle is engulfed, the cell membrane fuses, pinching off a vacuole within the cell. The reverse process, called **exocytosis** (ehk soh sigh TOH sihs), allows large particles to leave a cell. During exocytosis, a vacuole first fuses with the cell membrane. Then the cell membrane forms an opening to the outside and spills out the contents of the vacuole. Both endocytosis and exocytosis require energy from the cell.

FIGURE 5 ·
Amoeba Engulfing Food
A single-celled amoeba slowly surrounds bits of food.

✎ **Observe** Look at these photographs. They show (endocytosis/exocytosis).

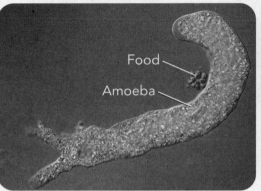

1 Amoeba's cytoplasm streams toward food particles.

Food — Amoeba —

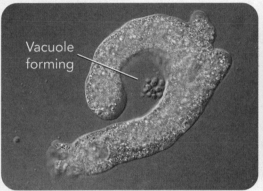

2 Cytoplasm surrounds food particles as vacuole begins to form.

Vacuole forming —

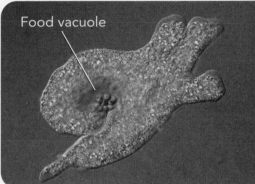

3 Cell membrane fuses, trapping food particles in new vacuole.

Food vacuole —

Lab zone® Do the Quick Lab *Effect of Concentration on Diffusion.*

🔑 Assess Your Understanding

1a. Review Use diffusion to tell what happens when you drop a sugar cube into water.

_____

_____

_____

b. ✐ **Predict** Draw an arrow to show the overall direction water will travel as a result of osmosis. (The yellow line is the cell membrane.)

Water molecule

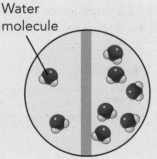

c. Identify Active transport depends on (sugars/proteins) to move molecules across the cell membrane.

d. Compare and Contrast How does active transport differ from passive transport?

_____

_____

_____

_____

got **it?** ·

○ **I get it!** Now I know that a key function of the cell membrane is to _____

_____

○ I need extra help with _____

Go to MY SCIENCE ⓢ COACH *online for help with this subject.*

69

CHAPTER

2 Study Guide

All living things are made of _____, which are the smallest units of _____

and _____

LESSON 1 Discovering Cells

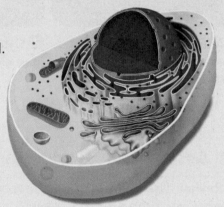

🔑 Cells are the basic units of structure and function in living things.

🔑 All living things are composed of cells, and all cells come from other cells.

🔑 Some microscopes focus light through lenses to produce a magnified image, and other microscopes use beams of electrons.

Vocabulary
• cell • microscope • cell theory

LESSON 2 Looking Inside Cells

🔑 Each kind of cell structure has a different function within a cell.

🔑 In multicellular organisms, cells are organized into tissues, organs, and organ systems.

Vocabulary
• cell wall • cell membrane • nucleus • organelle
• ribosome • cytoplasm • mitochondria
• endoplasmic reticulum • Golgi apparatus • vacuole
• chloroplast • lysosome • multicellular • unicellular
• tissue • organ • organ system

LESSON 3 Chemical Compounds in Cells

🔑 Elements are the simplest substances. Compounds form when elements combine.

🔑 Important compounds in living things include carbohydrates, lipids, proteins, nucleic acids, and water.

Vocabulary
• element • compound • carbohydrate
• lipid • protein • enzyme
• nucleic acid • DNA • double helix

LESSON 4 The Cell in Its Environment

🔑 Substances move into and out of a cell by one of two processes: passive transport or active transport.

Vocabulary
• selectively permeable • passive transport
• diffusion • osmosis • active transport
• endocytosis • exocytosis

---

70 Introduction to Cells

Review and Assessment

LESSON 1 Discovering Cells

1. Which tool could help you see a plant cell?

a. a filter **b.** a microscope

c. a microwave **d.** an electromagnet

2. The _____ states that all living things are made of cells.

3. Classify Your cells take in oxygen, water, and food. What is one waste product that leaves your cells?

_____

_____

4. Compare and Contrast How is a light microscope similar to an electron microscope? How do the two types of microscopes differ?

_____

_____

_____

5. Estimate Using a microscope, you see the one-celled organism shown below. The diameter of the microscope's field of view is 0.8 mm. Estimate the cell's length and width, and write your answer in the space provided.

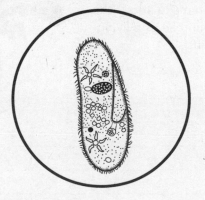

_____

_____

_____

LESSON 2 Looking Inside Cells

6. Which cellular structures are found in plant cells but NOT in animal cells?

a. chloroplast and cell wall

b. Golgi apparatus and vacuole

c. mitochondrion and ribosome

d. endoplasmic reticulum and nucleus

7. Mitochondria and chloroplasts are two types

of _____

8. Interpret Diagrams What is the function of the cell structure shown in purple in the cell at the right?

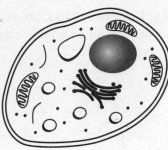

_____

_____

9. Sequence Arrange the following, from smallest to largest level of organization: organ system, tissue, cell, organ.

_____

_____

_____

10. Infer A certain cell can no longer package and release materials out of the cell. Which of the cell's organelles is not working?

_____

_____

11. Write About It Imagine you are a tour guide. You and the tour group have shrunk to the size of water molecules. You are now ready to start a tour of the cell! Write a narrative of your tour that you could give a new tour guide to use.

LESSON 3 Chemical Compounds in Cells

12. Starch is an example of a

a. lipid. b. protein.

c. nucleic acid. d. carbohydrate.

13. Which type of organic molecule is found primarily in a cell's nucleus?

_____

14. Compare and Contrast What is the difference between an element and a compound?

_____

_____

_____

15. Infer How may a lack of proteins in a person's diet affect the body?

_____

_____

_____

16. math! The graph below shows the amounts of different compounds that make up an animal cell. What percentage of the total cell weight is made up of lipids?

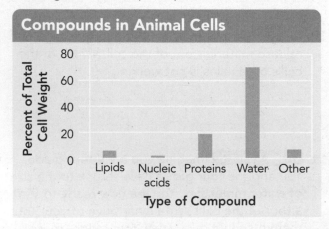

Compounds in Animal Cells

y-axis: Percent of Total Cell Weight — 0, 20, 40, 60, 80

x-axis: Type of Compound — Lipids, Nucleic acids, Proteins, Water, Other

_____

LESSON 4 The Cell in Its Environment

17. The process by which water moves across a cell's membrane is called

a. osmosis. b. exocytosis.

c. resolution. d. active transport.

18. Some substances but not others can cross the

_____ membrane of

a cell.

19. Compare and Contrast How are facilitated diffusion and active transport similar? How are they different?

_____

_____

_____

_____

APPLY THE BIG Q

What are cells made of?

20. At right is a photograph of a multicellular plant called a primrose. List three conclusions you can make about the primrose as a living thing.

_____

_____

_____

_____

_____

_____

_____

Standardized Test Prep

Multiple Choice

Circle the letter of the best answer.

1. Which transport process is shown in the illustration below?

A osmosis	**B** diffusion
C endocytosis	**D** exocytosis

2. Which of the following types of cells have cell walls?

A plant cells	**B** muscle cells
C blood cells	**D** animal cells

3. In order for an organism to develop specialized tissues, the organism must be which of the following?

A a plant	**B** an animal
C unicellular	**D** multicellular

4. Which of the following is the most complex level of cell organization?

A cell	**B** organ
C organism	**D** tissue

5. The cell membrane is made mostly of a double layer of molecules called

A lipids.	**B** proteins.
C nucleic acids.	**D** carbohydrates.

Constructed Response

Use the diagram below and your knowledge of cells to help you answer Question 6 on a separate sheet of paper.

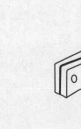

6. Identify this drawing as a plant cell or an animal cell. Justify your answer by describing how the structures of this cell compare to those of plant cells and animal cells.

ElectronEYES

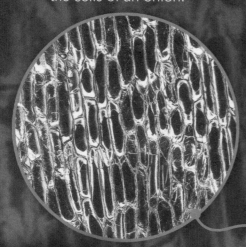

▼ Looking through a TEM gives a close-up view of the cells of an onion.

The invention of the optical microscope around the year 1600 caused a revolution in science. For the first time, scientists were able to see the cells that make up living things. However, even the most modern optical microscopes that focus light through lenses to produce an enlarged image can magnify an object only about 1,000 times.

Beginning in the early 1930s, new kinds of microscopes have caused new revolutions in science. The electron microscope uses electrons, instead of light, to make very detailed images of specimens. Today, powerful microscopes can magnify images up to 1,000,000 times—enough to enable scientists to see individual atoms!

Scientists use three main types of very powerful microscopes:

Transmission Electron Microscope (TEM) A TEM focuses a beam of electrons so that they pass through a very thinly sliced specimen. They are very useful for studying the interior structures of cells.

Scanning Electron Microscope (SEM) An SEM uses an electron beam to scan the surface of the specimen. The electron beam excites the electrons on the object's surface. The excited electrons are used to make a three-dimensional image of the specimen.

Scanning Tunneling Microscope (STM) An STM works by passing an electrically charged probe very close to the surface of a specimen. As the probe passes over the specimen, the probe moves up and down to keep the current in the probe constant. The path of the probe is recorded and is used to create an image of the specimen's surface.

▼ Samples of bread mold as captured by an SEM

Design It Research to find images taken by electron or scanning tunneling microscopes. Create a gallery or slide presentation of amazing microscope images to share with your class. See if your classmates can guess what object is shown in each image!

THE GENOGRAPHIC PROJECT

Have you ever wondered where your earliest ancestors came from? Archaeologists have worked for years to uncover evidence of ancient human migrations. They study the things people left behind, such as arrowheads, beads, and tools. Yet some of the most promising evidence is not found in archaeological sites. It is found in the cells that make up our bodies! The Genographic Project is a research project that uses DNA samples to help uncover the history of the human species.

Participants in the Genographic Project receive a kit that allows them to provide a DNA sample. To give a sample, participants use a cotton swab to gather cells from the inside of their cheek. This sample is mailed to a lab that analyzes the DNA contained in the cells. The DNA in the cells is compared with other DNA samples from around the world.

Then participants receive a report that describes the history of their earliest ancestors. The report includes a map that shows the migration route that these ancestors may have followed. Participants may choose to have their genetic information anonymously added to a genetic database. This database will help researchers build a very detailed map of ancient and modern human migration.

Explore It What has the Genographic Project discovered so far? Research the project, and create a map that shows what it has revealed about ancient human migration.

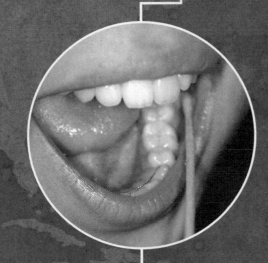

▲ People who want to help the Genographic Project collect cells from their cheeks.

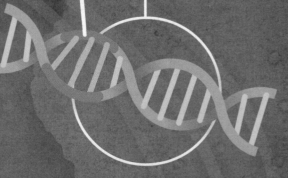

▲ Scientists trace ancestry by determining which individuals share specific genes or sequences of genes called genetic markers.

HOW DO THESE GIANTS GROW?

How do living things get energy?

Looking straight up into the sky from the ground, you can see the tallest trees on Earth. These giant California redwoods can grow up to 110 meters tall, about the size of a 35-story skyscraper! To grow this big takes energy and raw materials from food. These trees don't eat food as you do. But they do get water through their roots, gases from the air, and lots of sunlight. ✎**Develop Hypotheses** How do these trees get the energy they need to grow?

_____

_____

_____

_____

_____

▶ **UNTAMED SCIENCE** Watch the **Untamed Science** video to learn more about living things and energy.

Cell Processes and Energy

Getting Started

Check Your Understanding

1. **Background** Read the paragraph below and then answer the question.

In science class, we looked at both plant and animal cells under the microscope. I could see the **nucleus** in many cells. In plant cells, we could see green-colored **chloroplasts.** Both plant and animal cells have **mitochondria,** but they were too small for us to see with the microscopes we had.

> The **nucleus** is the organelle that acts as the cell's control center and directs the cell's activities.
>
> **Chloroplasts** are organelles that capture energy from sunlight and use it to produce food for the cell.
>
> **Mitochondria** are organelles that convert energy in food to energy the cell can use to carry out its functions.

- Circle the names of the organelles found only in plant cells. Underline the organelles found in both plant and animal cells.

  nucleus   mitochondria   chloroplasts

> MY READING WEB If you had trouble completing the question above, visit **My Reading Web** and type in *Cell Processes and Energy.*

Vocabulary Skill

Greek Word Origins The table below shows English word parts that have Greek origins. Learning the word parts can help you understand some of the vocabulary in this chapter.

Greek Word Part	Meaning	Example
auto-	self	**autotroph,** *n.* an organism that makes its own food; a producer
hetero-	other, different	**heterotroph,** *n.* an organism that cannot make its own food; a consumer

2. **Quick Check** The word part -*troph* comes from the Greek word *trophe,* which means "food." Circle the word part in two places in the chart above. How does the Greek word relate to the meaning of the terms?

_____

_____

heterotroph

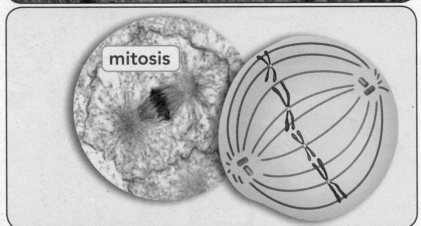

fermentation

mitosis

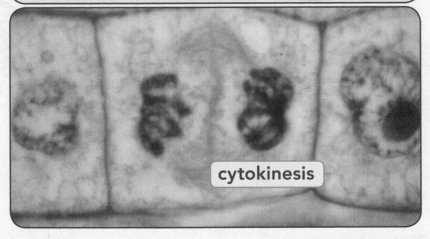

cytokinesis

Chapter Preview

LESSON 1
- photosynthesis
- autotroph
- heterotroph
- chlorophyll
- ⟳ **Sequence**
- △ **Classify**

LESSON 2
- cellular respiration
- fermentation
- ⟳ **Summarize**
- △ **Control Variables**

LESSON 3
- cell cycle
- interphase
- replication
- chromosome
- mitosis
- cytokinesis
- ⟳ **Ask Questions**
- △ **Interpret Data**

> VOCAB FLASH CARDS For extra help with vocabulary, visit **Vocab Flash Cards** and type in *Cell Processes and Energy.*

Photosynthesis

🔑 **How Do Living Things Get Energy From the Sun?**

🔑 **What Happens During Photosynthesis?**

my planet DiaRy

MISCONCEPTION

When Is Food Not Food?

Misconception: Some people think that the plant food they give to house and garden plants is food for the plants. It isn't.

Plants make their own food—in the form of sugars—using water, carbon dioxide, and sunlight. So what is the "food" that people add to plants? It's fertilizer. Fertilizer is a mixture of minerals, such as potassium, calcium, and phosphorus. It helps plants grow but doesn't supply them with energy as food does. Farmers add fertilizer to soil to grow better quality crops. People do the same to grow bigger and healthier plants at home.

Communicate Write your answers to the questions below. Then discuss Question 2 with a partner.

1. What is "plant food"?

_____

_____

2. What do you think would happen if you put a small seedling in complete darkness for a month but kept all other environmental conditions the same?

_____

▶ PLANET DIARY Go to **Planet Diary** to learn more about photosynthesis.

Lab zone Do the Inquiry Warm-Up *Where Does the Energy Come From?*

Vocabulary
- photosynthesis   • autotroph
- heterotroph   • chlorophyll

Skills
- ⟳ Reading: Sequence
- △ Inquiry: Classify

How Do Living Things Get Energy From the Sun?

On a plain in Africa, a herd of zebras peacefully eats grass. But watch out! A group of lions is about to attack the herd. The lions will kill one of the zebras and eat it.

Both the zebras and the lion you see in **Figure 1** use the food they eat to obtain energy. Every living thing needs energy. All cells need energy to carry out their functions, such as making proteins and transporting substances into and out of the cell. The more cells an organism has, the more energy the organism will require for survival. Like the raw materials used within a cell, energy used by living things comes from their environment. Plant and animal cells obtain their energy differently. Zebra meat supplies the lion's cells with energy. Similarly, grass provides the zebra's cells with energy. But where does the energy in the grass come from? Plants and certain other organisms, such as algae and some bacteria, use the energy in sunlight to make their own food.

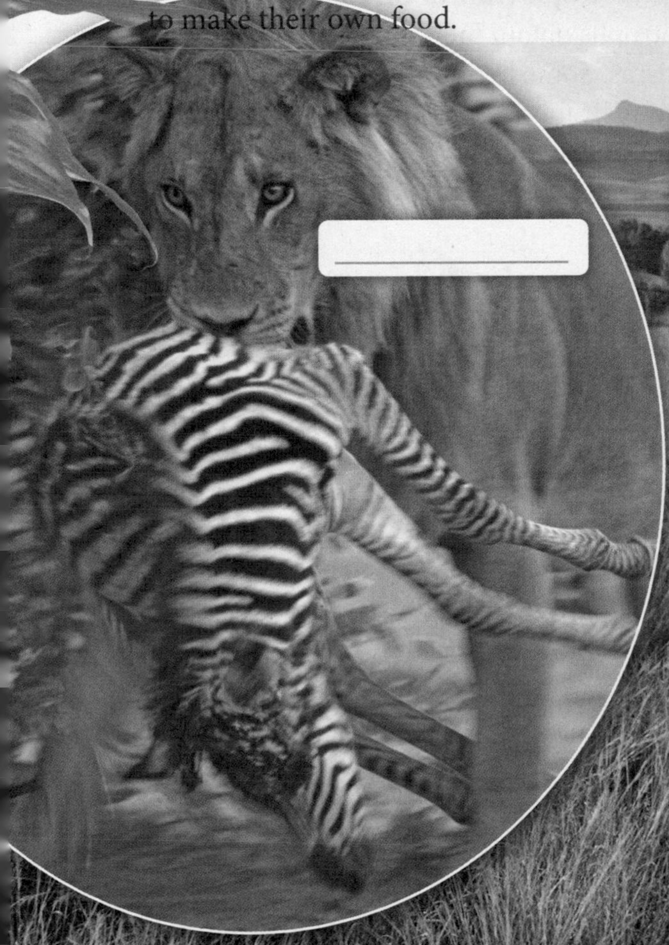

FIGURE 1 ••••••••••••••••••••••••••••••••••

An Energy Chain
All living things need energy.

✎ **Interpret Photos** In the boxes, write the direct source of energy for each organism. Which organism shown does not depend on another organism for food?

81

apply it!

A spider catches and eats a caterpillar that depends on plant leaves for food.

1 🔄 **Sequence** Draw a diagram of your own that tracks how the sun's energy gets to the spider.

2 ⚠ **Classify** In your diagram, label each organism as a heterotroph or an autotroph.

The Sun as an Energy Source

The process by which a cell captures energy in sunlight and uses it to make food is called **photosynthesis** (foh toh SIN thuh sis). The term *photosynthesis* comes from the Greek words *photos*, which means "light," and *syntithenai*, which means "putting together."

🔑 **Nearly all living things obtain energy either directly or indirectly from the energy of sunlight that is captured during photosynthesis.** Grass obtains energy directly from sunlight because grass makes its own food during photosynthesis. When the zebra eats grass, it gets energy from the sun that has been stored in the grass. Similarly, the lion obtains energy stored in the zebra. The zebra and lion both obtain the sun's energy indirectly from the energy that the grass obtained through photosynthesis.

Producers and Consumers

Plants make their own food through the process of photosynthesis. An organism that makes its own food is called a producer, or an **autotroph** (AWT oh trohf). An organism that cannot make its own food, including animals such as the zebra and the lion, is called a consumer, or a **heterotroph** (HET ur oh trohf). Many heterotrophs obtain food by eating other organisms. Some heterotrophs, such as fungi, absorb their food from other organisms.

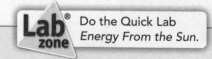

Lab zone® Do the Quick Lab *Energy From the Sun.*

🔑 Assess Your Understanding

1a. Identify An organism that makes its own food is a(n) (autotroph/heterotroph).

b. Explain Why do living things need energy?

_____

c. Apply Concepts Give an example of how energy from the sun gets into your cells.

_____

_____

_____

got it? ....

O **I get it!** Now I know that living things get energy directly from the sun by _____

or indirectly by _____

O **I need extra help with** _____

Go to **MY SCIENCE** 🔗 **COACH** online for help with this subject.

What Happens During Photosynthesis?

You've just read that plants make their own food. So how do they do that? 🔑 **During photosynthesis, plants and some other organisms absorb energy from the sun and use the energy to convert carbon dioxide and water into sugars and oxygen.** You can think of photosynthesis as taking place in two stages. First, plants capture the sun's energy. Second, plants produce sugars.

Stage 1: Capturing the Sun's Energy In the first stage of photosynthesis, energy from sunlight is captured. In plants, this process occurs mostly in the leaves. Recall that chloroplasts are green organelles inside plant cells. The green color comes from pigments, colored chemical compounds that absorb light. The main pigment for photosynthesis in chloroplasts is **chlorophyll**.

Chlorophyll functions something like the solar cells in a solar-powered calculator. Solar cells capture the energy in light and convert it to a form that powers the calculator. Similarly, chlorophyll captures light energy and converts it to a form that is used in the second stage of photosynthesis.

During Stage 1, water in the chloroplasts is split into hydrogen and oxygen, as shown in **Figure 2**. The oxygen is given off as a waste product. The hydrogen is used in Stage 2.

Vocabulary Greek Word Origins The Greek word part *chloros-* means "pale green." Circle two words in the text that begin with this word part. Which word means "a green compound that absorbs light"?

○ Chloroplast
○ Chlorophyll

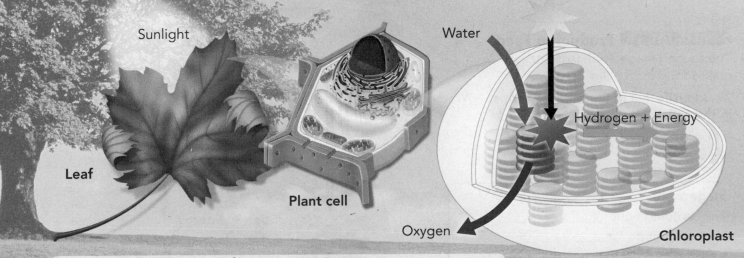

Light energy

Sunlight

Water

Hydrogen + Energy

Leaf

Plant cell

Oxygen

Chloroplast

FIGURE 2 ·····························

▶ VIRTUAL LAB **First Stage of Photosynthesis**
You might say the first stage of photosynthesis powers the "energy engine" of the living world.

✏ **Make Generalizations** What do you think this sentence means?

_____

_____

Sequence Complete the flowchart to show the process of photosynthesis.

Photosynthesis

> Sunlight strikes leaf.

⬇

> _____
> _____
> _____

⬇

> _____
> _____
> _____

Stage 2: Using Energy to Make Food

In the second stage of photosynthesis, cells produce sugars. As shown in **Figure 3**, cells use hydrogen (H) that came from the splitting of water in Stage 1. Cells also use carbon dioxide (CO_2) from the air. Carbon dioxide enters the plant through small openings on the undersides of the leaves and moves into the chloroplasts.

Powered by the energy captured in Stage 1, hydrogen and carbon dioxide undergo a series of reactions that result in sugars. One important sugar produced is glucose. It has the chemical formula $C_6H_{12}O_6$. You may know that sugars are a type of carbohydrate. Cells can use the energy in glucose to carry out vital cell functions.

The other product of photosynthesis is oxygen gas (O_2). Recall that oxygen forms during the first stage when water molecules are split apart. Oxygen gas exits a leaf through the openings on its underside. Almost all the oxygen in Earth's atmosphere is produced by living things through the process of photosynthesis.

FIGURE 3 ·······················

▶ **INTERACTIVE ART** **Producing Food**

The second stage of photosynthesis makes food for a plant.

✎ **Identify** Fill in the missing terms in the spaces provided.

Stage 2
The captured light _____, hydrogen, and _____ are used to produce _____

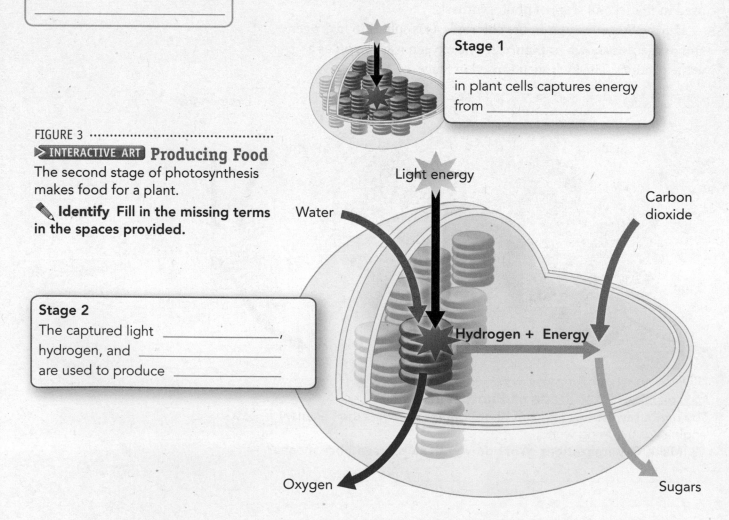

Stage 1
_____
in plant cells captures energy from _____

Light energy

Water

Carbon dioxide

Hydrogen + Energy

Oxygen

Sugars

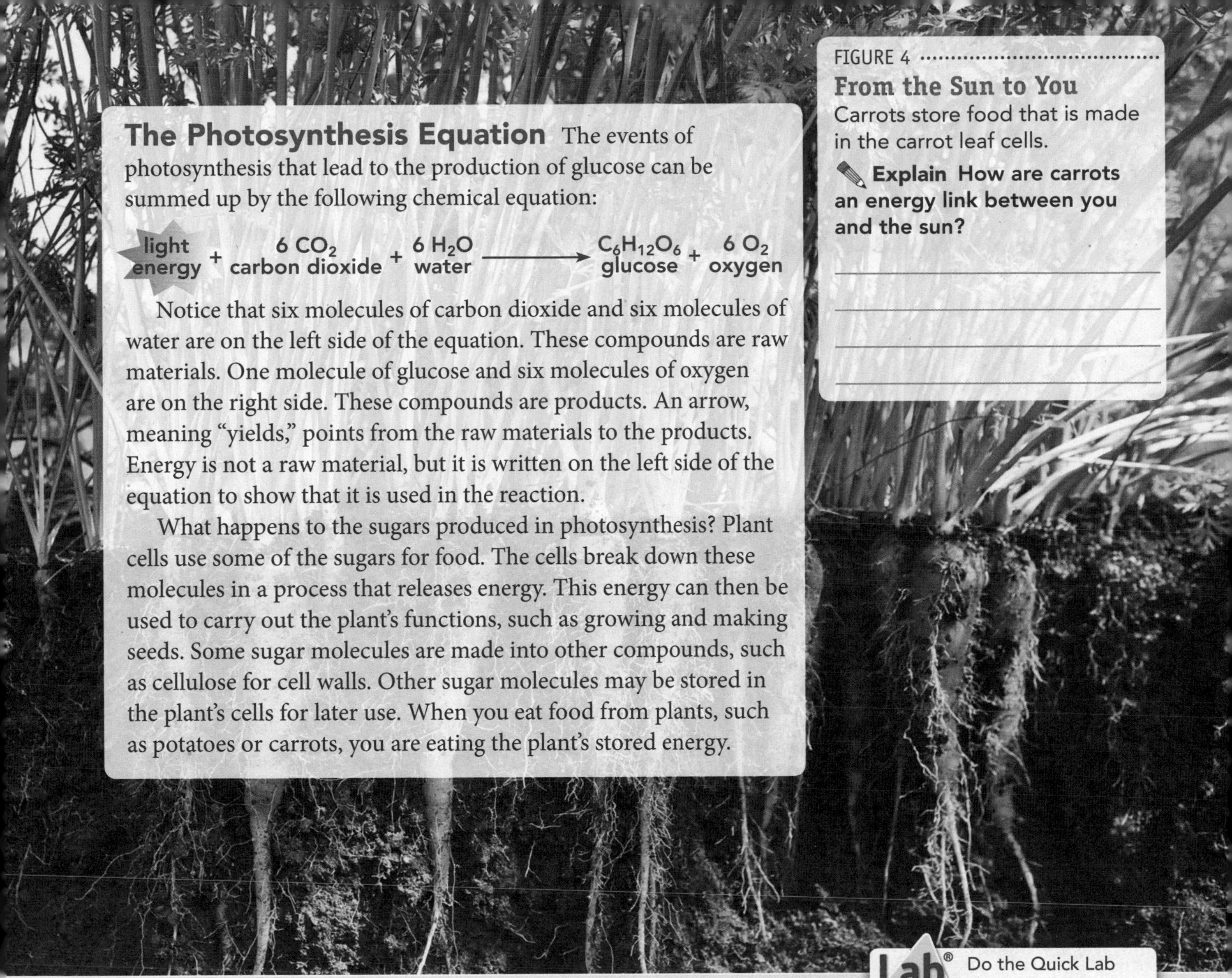

The Photosynthesis Equation
The events of photosynthesis that lead to the production of glucose can be summed up by the following chemical equation:

$$\text{light energy} + 6\,CO_2\ (\text{carbon dioxide}) + 6\,H_2O\ (\text{water}) \longrightarrow C_6H_{12}O_6\ (\text{glucose}) + 6\,O_2\ (\text{oxygen})$$

Notice that six molecules of carbon dioxide and six molecules of water are on the left side of the equation. These compounds are raw materials. One molecule of glucose and six molecules of oxygen are on the right side. These compounds are products. An arrow, meaning "yields," points from the raw materials to the products. Energy is not a raw material, but it is written on the left side of the equation to show that it is used in the reaction.

What happens to the sugars produced in photosynthesis? Plant cells use some of the sugars for food. The cells break down these molecules in a process that releases energy. This energy can then be used to carry out the plant's functions, such as growing and making seeds. Some sugar molecules are made into other compounds, such as cellulose for cell walls. Other sugar molecules may be stored in the plant's cells for later use. When you eat food from plants, such as potatoes or carrots, you are eating the plant's stored energy.

FIGURE 4
From the Sun to You
Carrots store food that is made in the carrot leaf cells.

✎ **Explain** How are carrots an energy link between you and the sun?

_____

_____

_____

_____

Lab zone® Do the Quick Lab *Looking at Pigments.*

⚷ Assess Your Understanding

2a. Name Circle two products of photosynthesis.
glucose/carbon dioxide/oxygen/chlorophyll

b. Interpret Diagrams Refer to **Figure 3** on the facing page. Where does the hydrogen that is used in Stage 2 of photosynthesis come from?

_____

_____

c. [CHALLENGE] Would you expect a plant to produce more oxygen on a sunny day or a cloudy day? Explain your answer.

_____

_____

_____

_____

got it? ....

○ **I get it!** Now I know that during photosynthesis _____

_____

○ **I need extra help with** _____

Go to MY SCIENCE ⓢ COACH online for help with this subject.

85

Cellular Respiration

UNLOCK THE BIG

🔑 What Happens During Cellular Respiration?

🔑 What Happens During Fermentation?

my planet diary

FUN FACTS

Going to Extremes

You may not know it, but there are organisms living in rocks deep below Earth's surface. Other organisms hang out in steaming hot lakes, like Grand Prismatic Spring in Yellowstone National Park, shown here. The water in this lake can be as hot as 86°C! Still other organisms nestle inside nuclear waste. All of these organisms are extremophiles, organisms that thrive in extreme habitats. These life forms can get energy in strange ways. Some make food from ocean minerals. Others break down compounds in radioactive rocks!

Pose Questions Write a question about something else you would like to learn about extremophiles.

_____

_____

_____

_____

▶ PLANET DIARY Go to **Planet Diary** to learn more about extremophiles.

Lab zone® Do the Inquiry Warm-Up Cellular Respiration.

What Happens During Cellular Respiration?

You and your friend have been hiking all morning. You look for a flat rock to sit on, so you can eat the lunch you packed. The steepest part of the trail is ahead. You'll need a lot of energy to get to the top of the mountain! That energy will come from food.

Vocabulary
- cellular respiration
- fermentation

Skills
- Reading: Summarize
- Inquiry: Control Variables

What Is Cellular Respiration?

After you eat a meal, your body breaks down the food and releases the sugars in the food. The most common sugar in foods is glucose ($C_6H_{12}O_6$). **Cellular respiration** is the process by which cells obtain energy from glucose. **During cellular respiration, cells break down glucose and other molecules from food in the presence of oxygen, releasing energy.** Living things need a constant supply of energy. The cells of living things carry out cellular respiration continuously.

Storing and Releasing Energy

Imagine you have money in a savings account. If you want to buy something, you withdraw some money. Your body stores and uses energy in a similar way, as shown in **Figure 1**. When you eat a meal, you add to your body's energy savings account by storing glucose. When cells need energy, they "withdraw" it by breaking down glucose through cellular respiration.

Breathing and Respiration

You may have already heard of the word *respiration*. It can mean "breathing"—or moving air in and out of your lungs. Breathing brings oxygen into your lungs, which is then carried to cells for cellular respiration. Breathing also removes the waste products of cellular respiration from your body.

FIGURE 1 ·····················

Getting Energy
Your body runs on the energy it gets from food.

✎ **Complete each task.**

1. **Infer** Color in the last three energy scales to show how the hiker's energy changes.

2. [CHALLENGE] How do you think the hiker's breathing rate changes as she climbs?

_____

_____

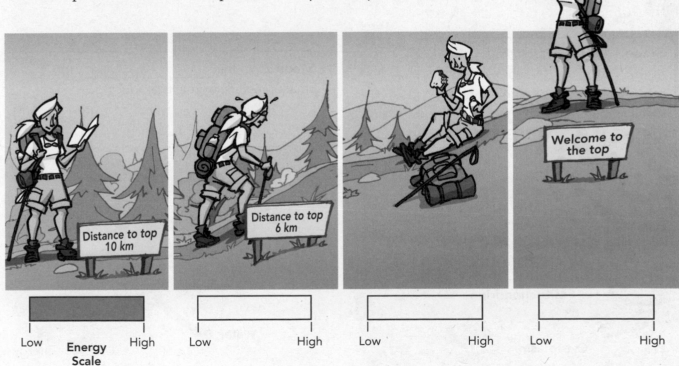

Distance to top 10 km

Distance to top 6 km

Welcome to the top

| Low | Energy Scale | High | Low | High | Low | High | Low | High |

Summarize
Complete the concept map below about cellular respiration.

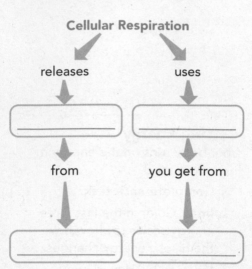

Cellular Respiration

releases → [_____] → from → [_____]

uses → [_____] → you get from → [_____]

The Two Stages of Cellular Respiration
Like photosynthesis, cellular respiration is a two-stage process. See **Figure 2.** The first stage occurs in the cytoplasm of a cell. There, molecules of glucose are broken down into smaller molecules. Oxygen is not involved in this stage, and only a small amount of energy is released.

The second stage takes place in the mitochondria. There, the small molecules are broken down even more. This change requires oxygen and releases a great deal of energy that the cell can use for all its activities. No wonder mitochondria are sometimes called the "powerhouses" of the cell!

The Cellular Respiration Equation
Although respiration occurs in a series of complex steps, the overall process can be summarized in the following equation:

$$\underset{\text{glucose}}{C_6H_{12}O_6} + \underset{\text{oxygen}}{6\,O_2} \longrightarrow \underset{\text{carbon dioxide}}{6\,CO_2} + \underset{\text{water}}{6\,H_2O} + energy$$

Notice that the raw materials for cellular respiration are glucose and oxygen. Animals get glucose from the foods they consume. Plants and other organisms that carry out photosynthesis are able to produce their own glucose. The oxygen needed for cellular respiration is in the air or water surrounding the organism.

FIGURE 2 ···

> INTERACTIVE ART **Releasing Energy**
Cellular respiration takes place in two stages.

Identify Fill in the missing terms in the spaces provided.

Stage 1 In the cytoplasm, _____ is broken down into smaller molecules, releasing a small amount of _____

Stage 2 In the _____, the smaller molecules react, producing _____, water, and large amounts of _____

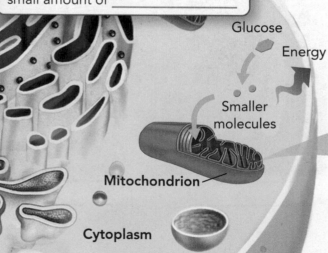

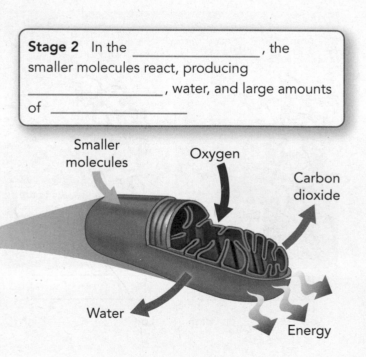

Glucose

Energy

Smaller molecules

Mitochondrion

Cytoplasm

Smaller molecules

Oxygen

Carbon dioxide

Water

Energy

Comparing Two Energy Processes

If you think the equation for cellular respiration is the opposite of the one for photosynthesis, you're right! Photosynthesis and cellular respiration can be thought of as opposite processes. Together, these two processes form a cycle that keeps the levels of oxygen and carbon dioxide fairly constant in Earth's atmosphere. As you can see from **Figure 3**, living things cycle both gases over and over again. The energy released through cellular respiration is used or lost as heat.

FIGURE 3 ....

Opposite Processes

Producers carry out photosynthesis, but producers and consumers both carry out cellular respiration.

✎ **Name** Use the word bank to fill in the missing terms. Words can be used more than once.

Word Bank	
Oxygen	Energy
Carbon dioxide	Glucose
Water	

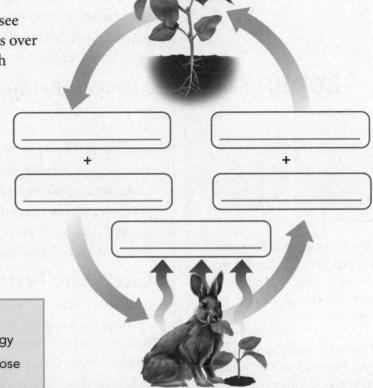

Photosynthesis

+

+

Cellular Respiration

Lab® zone Do the Lab Investigation *Exhaling Carbon Dioxide.*

🔑 Assess Your Understanding

1a. Interpret Diagrams Look at **Figure 2** on the facing page. How does Stage 2 of cellular respiration benefit a cell?

_____

_____

_____

b. Relate Cause and Effect Why does cellular respiration add carbon dioxide to the atmosphere, but photosynthesis does not?

_____

_____

_____

got it? ....

○ **I get it!** Now I know that during cellular respiration, cells _____

_____

○ I need extra help with _____

Go to **my science** ⬤ᔆ **coach** online for help with this subject.

What Happens During Fermentation?

Some organisms can live in the presence or absence of oxygen. If not enough oxygen is present to carry out cellular respiration, these organisms switch to another process. **Fermentation** is an energy-releasing process that does not require oxygen. 🔑 **During fermentation, cells release energy from food without using oxygen.** One drawback to fermentation is that it releases far less energy than cellular respiration does.

Alcoholic Fermentation

Did you know that when you eat a slice of bread, you are eating a product of fermentation? Alcoholic fermentation occurs in yeast and other single-celled organisms. This type of fermentation produces alcohol, carbon dioxide, and a small amount of energy. These products are important to bakers and brewers. Carbon dioxide produced by yeast creates gas pockets in bread dough, causing it to rise. Carbon dioxide is also the source of bubbles in alcoholic drinks such as beer and sparkling wine.

Lactic Acid Fermentation

Think of a time when you ran as fast and as long as you could. Your leg muscles were pushing hard against the ground, and you were breathing quickly. But, no matter how quickly you breathed, your muscle cells used up the oxygen faster than it could be replaced. Because your cells lacked oxygen, fermentation occurred. Your muscle cells got energy, but they did so by breaking down glucose without using oxygen. One product of this type of fermentation is a compound known as lactic acid. When lactic acid builds up, you may feel a painful burning sensation in your muscles.

Lactic acid was once thought to be the cause of muscle soreness. Scientists have learned that lactic acid is gone from muscles shortly after exercising and is not responsible for the soreness you feel in the days after you exercise. Instead, the soreness is likely caused by microscopic damage to muscles that occurred during the exercise.

apply it!

A ball of bread dough mixed with yeast is left in a bowl at room temperature. As time passes, the dough increases in size.

❶ Compare and Contrast How does fermentation that causes dough to rise differ from fermentation in muscles?

_____

_____

_____

_____

_____

❷ Control Variables How would you show that yeast was responsible for making the dough rise?

_____

_____

_____

_____

_____

EXPLORE THE BIG ?

Energy for Life

How do living things get energy?

FIGURE 4

ART IN MOTION Energy processes in living things include photosynthesis, cellular respiration, and fermentation.

Review **Circle the correct answers and complete the sentences in the spaces provided.**

Producers

Plant cells capture energy by way of (photosynthesis/fermentation/cellular respiration).

Plants are autotrophs because

____

____

Plant cells release energy for cell function by way of (photosynthesis/fermentation/cellular respiration).

Plants get this energy when oxygen reacts with

____

____

Consumers

A runner on an easy jog through the woods gets energy by way of (photosynthesis/fermentation/cellular respiration).

The runner is a heterotroph because she gets energy from

____

If the runner makes a long, fast push to the finish, her muscle cells may get energy by way of (photosynthesis/fermentation/cellular respiration).

This process releases less energy and _______________

____

Lab zone Do the Quick Lab *Observing Fermentation.*

Assess Your Understanding

2a. Develop Hypotheses When a race ends, why do you think runners continue to breathe quickly and deeply for a few minutes?

____

____

b. ANSWER THE BIG ? How do living things get energy?

____

____

____

____

____

____

got it?

O **I get it!** Now I know fermentation is a way for cells to _______________

____

____

O I need extra help with _______________

____

____

Go to MY SCIENCE COACH *online for help with this subject.*

3 Cell Division

🔑 **What Are the Functions of Cell Division?**

🔑 **What Happens During the Cell Cycle?**

my planeT DiaRY

Cycling On

How long do you think it takes a cell to grow and reproduce, that is, to complete one cell cycle? The answer depends on the type of cell and the organism. Some cells, such as the frog egg cells shown here, divide every 30 minutes, and others take as long as a year! The table below compares the length of different cell cycles.

Comparing Cell Cycles			
Frog Egg Cells	**Yeast Cells**	**Fruit Fly Wing Cells**	**Human Liver Cells**
30 minutes	90 minutes	9–10 hours	Over 1 year

SCIENCE STATS

Interpret Data Use the table to help you answer the following questions.

1. Which type of cell completes a cell cycle fastest?

_____

2. With each cell cycle, two cells form from one cell. In three hours, how many cells could form from one frog egg cell?

_____

▶ **PLANET DIARY** Go to **Planet Diary** to learn more about cell division.

 Lab zone Do the Inquiry Warm-Up *What Are the Yeast Cells Doing?*

What Are the Functions of Cell Division?

How do tiny frog eggs become big frogs? Cell division allows organisms to grow larger. One cell splits into two, two into four, and so on, until a single cell becomes a multicellular organism.

How does a broken bone heal? Cell division produces new healthy bone cells that replace the damaged cells. Similarly, cell division can replace aging cells and those that die from disease.

Vocabulary

- cell cycle
- interphase
- replication
- chromosome
- mitosis
- cytokinesis

Skills

- ↻ Reading: Ask Questions
- △ Inquiry: Interpret Data

Growth and repair are two functions of cell division. A third function is reproduction. Some organisms reproduce simply through cell division. Many single-celled organisms, such as amoebas, reproduce this way. Other organisms can reproduce when cell division leads to the growth of new structures. For example, a cactus can grow new stems and roots. These structures can then break away from the parent plant and become a separate plant.

Most organisms reproduce when specialized cells from two different parents combine, forming a new cell. This cell then undergoes many divisions and grows into a new organism.

Cell division has more than one function in living things, as shown in **Figure 1.** 🔑 **Cell division allows organisms to grow, repair damaged structures, and reproduce.**

FIGURE 1 ·····················

Cell Division

Each photo represents at least one function of cell division.

✏️ **Answer these questions.**

1. **Identify** Label each photo as
   (A) growth,
   (B) repair, or
   (C) reproduction.

2. [CHALLENGE] Which photo(s) represents more than one function and what are they?

_____

_____

Lab® zone | Do the Quick Lab *Observing Mitosis.*

🔑 Assess Your Understanding

got it? ···

- ○ **I get it!** Now I know the functions of cell division are _____

- ○ **I need extra help with** _____

  Go to my science ⑤ **coach** *online for help with this subject.*

What Happens During the Cell Cycle?

The regular sequence of growth and division that cells undergo is known as the **cell cycle**. 🔑 **During the cell cycle, a cell grows, prepares for division, and divides into two new cells, which are called "daughter cells."** Each of the daughter cells then begins the cell cycle again. The cell cycle consists of three main stages: interphase, mitosis, and cytokinesis.

Stage 1: Interphase

The first stage of the cell cycle is **interphase.** This stage is the period before cell division. During interphase, the cell grows, makes a copy of its DNA, and prepares to divide into two cells.

Growing Early during interphase, a cell grows to its full size and produces the organelles it needs. For example, plant cells make more chloroplasts. And all cells make more ribosomes and mitochondria. Cells also make more enzymes, substances that speed up chemical reactions in living things.

Copying DNA Next, the cell makes an exact copy of the DNA in its nucleus in a process called **replication.** You may know that DNA holds all the information that a cell needs to carry out its functions. Within the nucleus, DNA and proteins form threadlike structures called **chromosomes.** At the end of replication, the cell contains two identical sets of chromosomes.

Preparing for Division Once the DNA has replicated, preparation for cell division begins. The cell produces structures that will help it to divide into two new cells. In animal cells, but not plant cells, a pair of centrioles is duplicated. You can see the centrioles in the cell in **Figure 2.** At the end of interphase, the cell is ready to divide.

FIGURE 2 ....
Interphase: Preparing to Divide
The changes in a cell during interphase prepare the cell for mitosis.

✏️ **List** **Make a list of the events that occur during interphase.**

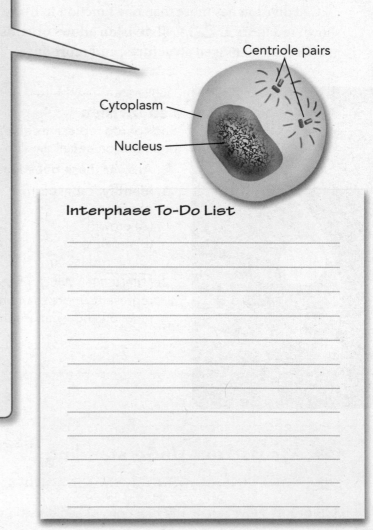

Centriole pairs

Cytoplasm

Nucleus

Interphase To-Do List

_____

_____

_____

_____

_____

_____

_____

_____

_____

_____

apply it!

When one cell splits in half during cell division, the result is two new cells. Each of those two cells can divide into two more, and so on.

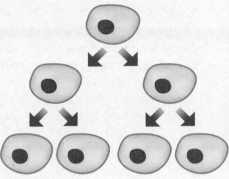

1 **Calculate** How many cell divisions would it take to produce at least 1,000 cells from one cell?

_____

2 **Describe** What happens to the number of cells after each division?

_____

3 CHALLENGE Do you think all human cells divide at the same rate throughout life? Justify your answer.

_____

_____

Stage 2: Mitosis

Once interphase ends, the second stage of the cell cycle begins. During **mitosis** (my TOH sis), the cell's nucleus divides into two new nuclei and one set of DNA is distributed into each daughter cell.

Scientists divide mitosis into four parts, or phases: prophase, metaphase, anaphase, and telophase. During prophase, the chromosomes condense into shapes that can be seen under a microscope. In **Figure 3** you can see that a chromosome consists of two rod-like parts, called chromatids. Each chromatid is an exact copy of the other, containing identical DNA. A structure known as a centromere holds the chromatids together until they move apart later in mitosis. One copy of each chromatid will move into each daughter cell during the final phases of mitosis. When the chromatids separate they are called chromosomes again. Each cell then has a complete copy of DNA. **Figure 4** on the next page summarizes the events of mitosis.

FIGURE 3 ·································

Mitosis: Prophase

Mitosis begins with prophase, which involves further changes to the cell.

✎ **Compare and Contrast** How does prophase look different from interphase?

_____

_____

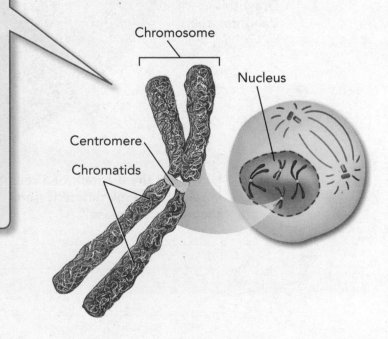

Chromosome

Nucleus

Centromere

Chromatids

FIGURE 4

> INTERACTIVE ART **The Cell Cycle**

Cells undergo an orderly sequence of events as they grow and divide. The photographs show cells of a developing whitefish.

✎ **Interpret Diagrams** Answer the questions and draw the missing parts of the stages in the spaces provided.

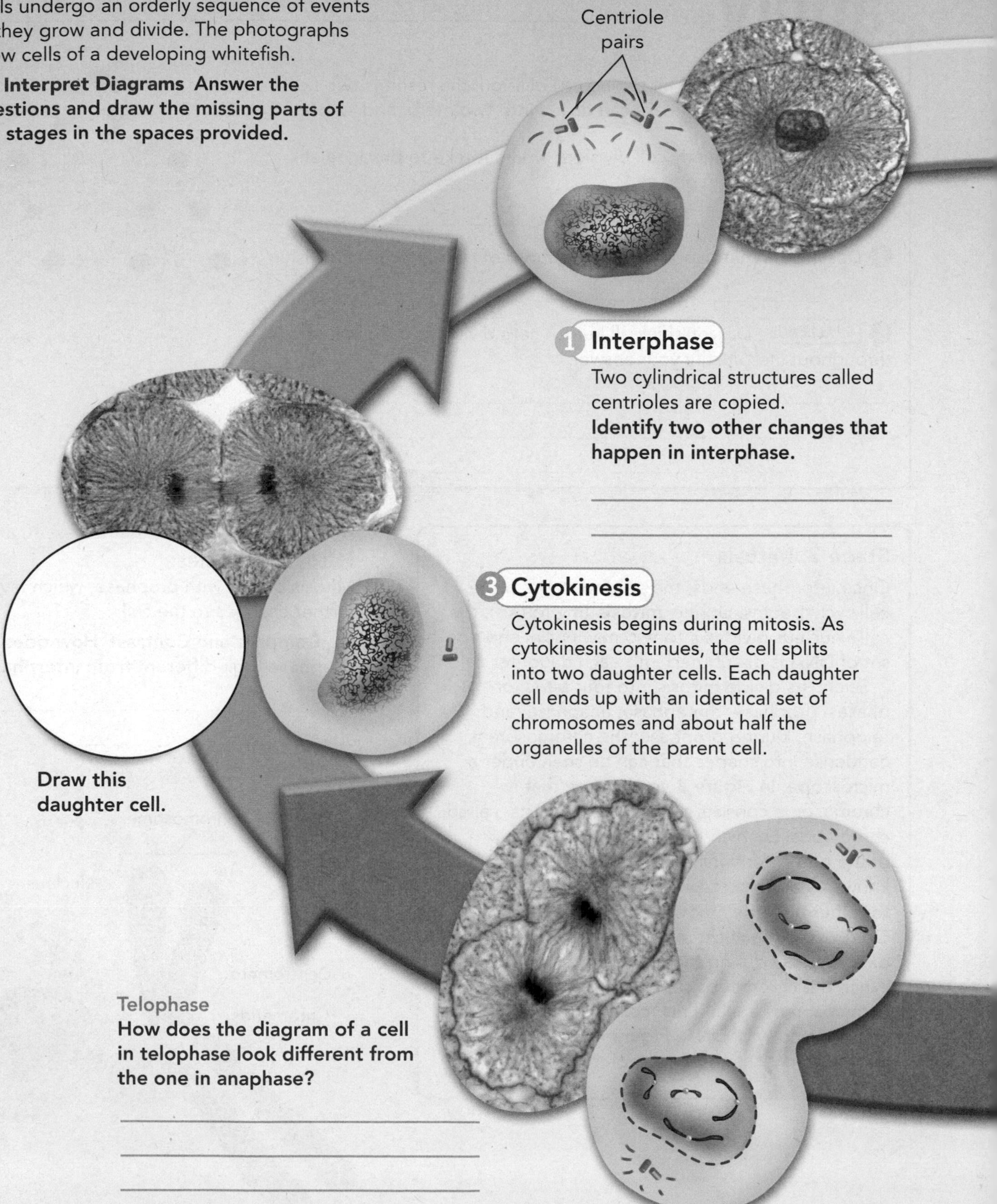

Centriole pairs

1 Interphase

Two cylindrical structures called centrioles are copied.
Identify two other changes that happen in interphase.

_____

_____

3 Cytokinesis

Cytokinesis begins during mitosis. As cytokinesis continues, the cell splits into two daughter cells. Each daughter cell ends up with an identical set of chromosomes and about half the organelles of the parent cell.

Draw this daughter cell.

Telophase
How does the diagram of a cell in telophase look different from the one in anaphase?

_____

_____

_____

_____

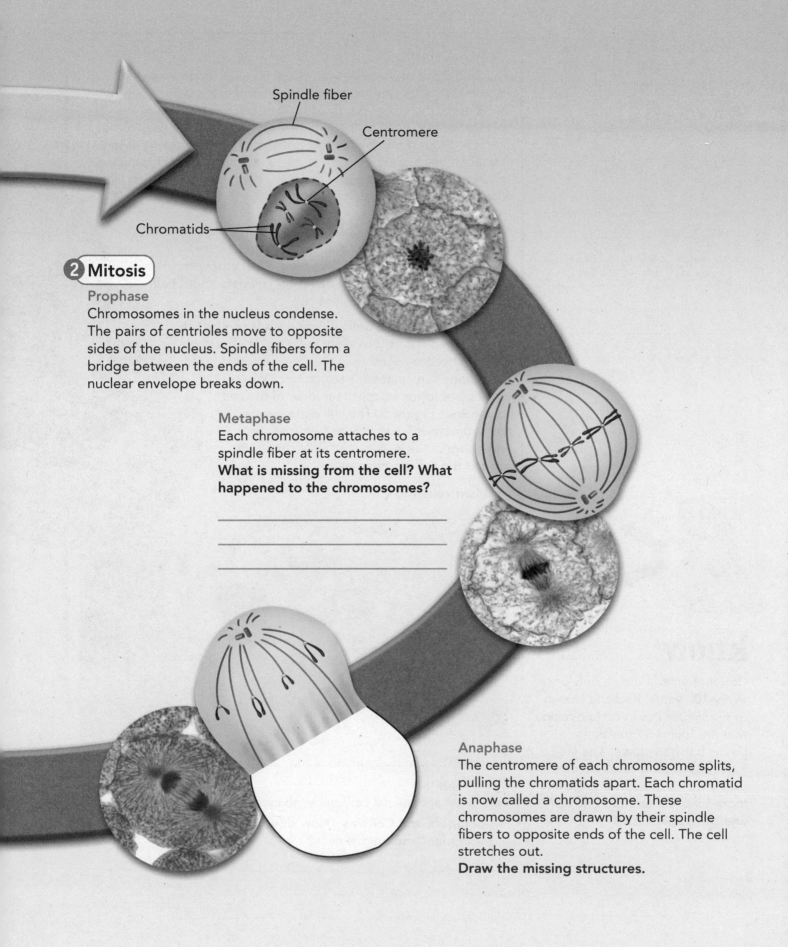

Spindle fiber

Centromere

Chromatids

② **Mitosis**

Prophase
Chromosomes in the nucleus condense. The pairs of centrioles move to opposite sides of the nucleus. Spindle fibers form a bridge between the ends of the cell. The nuclear envelope breaks down.

Metaphase
Each chromosome attaches to a spindle fiber at its centromere.
What is missing from the cell? What happened to the chromosomes?

_____

_____

_____

Anaphase
The centromere of each chromosome splits, pulling the chromatids apart. Each chromatid is now called a chromosome. These chromosomes are drawn by their spindle fibers to opposite ends of the cell. The cell stretches out.
Draw the missing structures.

Stage 3: Cytokinesis

The final stage of the cell cycle, which is called **cytokinesis** (sy toh kih NEE sis), completes the process of cell division. During cytokinesis, the cytoplasm divides. The structures are then distributed into each of the two new cells. Cytokinesis usually starts at about the same time as telophase. When cytokinesis is complete, each daughter cell has the same number of chromosomes as the parent cell. At the end of cytokinesis, each cell enters interphase, and the cycle begins again.

Cytokinesis in Animal Cells During cytokinesis in animal cells, the cell membrane squeezes together around the middle of the cell, as shown here. The cytoplasm pinches into two cells. Each daughter cell gets about half of the organelles of the parent cell.

Cytokinesis in Plant Cells Cytokinesis is somewhat different in plant cells. A plant cell's rigid cell wall cannot squeeze together in the same way that a cell membrane can. Instead, a structure called a cell plate forms across the middle of the cell, as shown in **Figure 5**. The cell plate begins to form new cell membranes between the two daughter cells. New cell walls then form around the cell membranes.

Plant cells ▼   **Animal cells ▶**

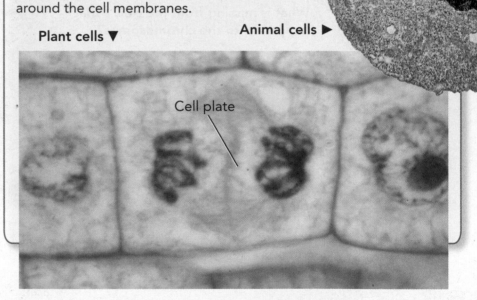

Cell plate

FIGURE 5 ···

Cytokinesis
Both plant and animal cells undergo cytokinesis.

✎ **Compare and Contrast** How does cytokinesis differ in plant and animal cells?

_____

_____

_____

✎ **Ask Questions** Before you read details about cytokinesis, write a question that asks something you would like to learn.

_____

_____

_____

_____

_____

_____

did you
know?·····················

Certain bacteria divide only once every 100 years! Bacteria known as *Firmicutes* live in certain rocks that are found 3 kilometers below Earth's surface. The life functions of *Firmicutes* occur so slowly that it takes 100 years or more for them to store enough energy to split in two.

do the math! Analyzing Data

Length of a liver cell cycle

How long does it take for a cell to go through one cell cycle? It depends on the cell. Human liver cells generally reproduce less than once per year. At other times, they can complete one cell cycle in about 22 hours, as shown in the circle graph. Study the graph and answer the following questions.

1 **Read Graphs** What do the three curved arrows outside of the circle represent?

_____

_____

2 **Read Graphs** The wedge representing growth is in which stage of the cell cycle?

_____

3 **Interpret Data** About what percentage of the cell cycle is shown for DNA replication?

_____

4 **Interpret Data** What stage in the cell cycle takes the shortest amount of time? How do you know?

_____

_____

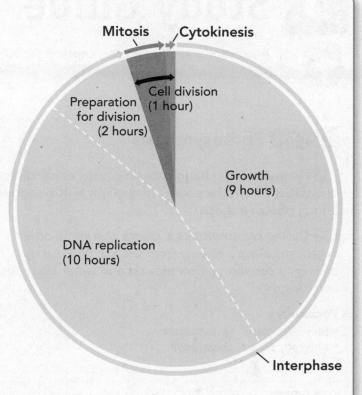

Mitosis   Cytokinesis

Cell division (1 hour)

Preparation for division (2 hours)

Growth (9 hours)

DNA replication (10 hours)

Interphase

Lab zone® Do the Quick Lab *Modeling Mitosis.*

🔑 Assess Your Understanding

1a. List What are the three stages of the cell cycle?

_____

b. Sequence Put the following terms in correct order: anaphase, telophase, metaphase, prophase.

_____

_____

c. Predict What do you think would happen if a cell's DNA did not replicate correctly?

_____

_____

_____

_____

_____

got it? ....

○ **I get it!** Now I know that during the cell cycle _____

_____

○ **I need extra help with** _____

   Go to **MY SCIENCE COACH** *online for help with this subject.*

3 Study Guide

Autotrophs, such as plants, capture the sun's energy and make their food through

_____, while _____ get energy by eating food.

LESSON 1 Photosynthesis

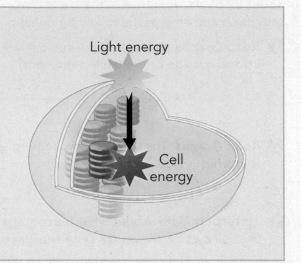

Light energy

Cell energy

🔑 Nearly all living things obtain energy either directly or indirectly from the energy of sunlight that is captured during photosynthesis.

🔑 During photosynthesis, plants and some other organisms absorb energy from the sun and use the energy to convert carbon dioxide and water into sugars and oxygen.

Vocabulary
- photosynthesis
- autotroph
- heterotroph
- chlorophyll

LESSON 2 Cellular Respiration

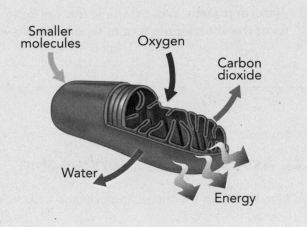

Smaller molecules

Oxygen

Carbon dioxide

Water

Energy

🔑 During cellular respiration, cells break down glucose and other molecules from food in the presence of oxygen, releasing energy.

🔑 During fermentation, cells release energy from food without using oxygen.

Vocabulary
- cellular respiration
- fermentation

LESSON 3 Cell Division

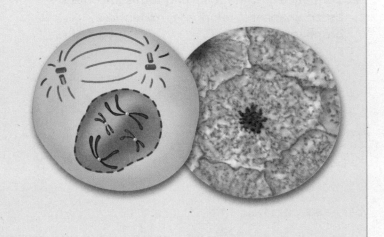

🔑 Cell division allows organisms to grow, repair damaged structures, and reproduce.

🔑 During the cell cycle, a cell grows, prepares for division, and divides into two new cells, which are called "daughter cells."

Vocabulary
- cell cycle
- interphase
- replication
- chromosome
- mitosis
- cytokinesis

Review and Assessment

LESSON 1 Photosynthesis

1. Which of the following organisms are autotrophs?

   a. fungi   **b.** rabbits

   c. humans   **d.** oak trees

2. Plants are green because of

_____, the main

photosynthetic pigment in chloroplasts.

3. Interpret Diagrams Fill in the missing labels in the diagram below.

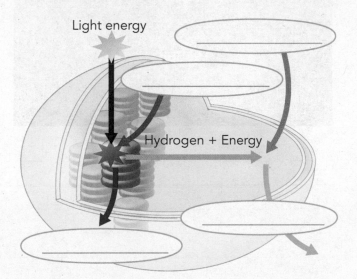

Light energy

Hydrogen + Energy

4. Predict Suppose a volcano threw so much ash into the air that it blocked much of the sunlight. How might this event affect the ability of animals to obtain energy to live?

_____

_____

_____

_____

5. **Write About It** How do you get energy? Describe the path of energy from the sun to you, using at least two vocabulary terms you learned in this lesson.

LESSON 2 Cellular Respiration

6. In which organelle does cellular respiration take place?

   a. nucleus   **b.** chloroplast

   c. chlorophyll   **d.** mitochondrion

7. _____ is a process that releases energy in cells without using oxygen.

8. What is one common food that is made with the help of fermentation?

_____

9. Explain Write a word equation for cellular respiration in cells.

_____

_____

_____

_____

10. Summarize In one or two sentences, summarize what happens during each of the two stages of cellular respiration.

_____

_____

_____

_____

_____

_____

_____

_____

11. Apply Concepts How is breathing related to cellular respiration?

_____

_____

_____

_____

LESSON 3 Cell Division

12. During which phase of the cell cycle does DNA replication occur?

    a. mitosis   **b.** division

    c. interphase   **d.** cytokinesis

13. During _____, a cell's nucleus divides into two new nuclei.

14. **Make Generalizations** Why is cell division a necessary function of living things?

_____

_____

_____

15. **Relate Cause and Effect** Why is replication a necessary step in cell division?

_____

_____

_____

16. **Sequence** Fill in the diagram below with descriptions of each part of the cell cycle.

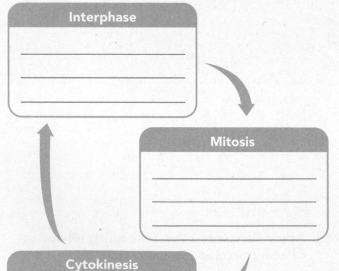

Interphase

_____

_____

Mitosis

_____

_____

_____

Cytokinesis

_____

_____

_____

 How do living things get energy?

17. All living things need energy. Use the terms *autotroph* and *heterotroph* to describe how each of the organisms in the illustration below obtains energy.

_____

_____

_____

_____

_____

_____

_____

_____

_____

_____

_____

_____

Standardized Test Prep

Multiple Choice

Circle the letter of the best answer.

1. Choose the name and cellular process that match the organelle shown below.

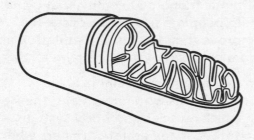

   A   chloroplast; cellular respiration
   B   mitochondrion; cellular respiration
   C   chloroplast; photosynthesis
   D   mitochondrion; photosynthesis

2. What is the result of cell division?

   A   one daughter cell with double the DNA of the parent cell
   B   two daughter cells with double the DNA of the parent cell
   C   one daughter cell with half the DNA of the parent cells
   D   two daughter cells with the same DNA as the parent cell

3. What is the source of energy used in photosynthesis?

   A   glucose
   B   sunlight
   C   chlorophyll
   D   DNA

4. What is one main difference between fermentation and cellular respiration?

   A   Fermentation does not require oxygen, while cellular respiration does.
   B   Fermentation does not release energy, while cellular respiration does.
   C   Fermentation does not occur in animals, while cellular respiration does.
   D   Fermentation does not depend on the sun, while cellular respiration does.

5. Which statement best applies to chromosomes?

   A   They carry out respiration.
   B   They consist mostly of the pigment chlorophyll.
   C   Their structure is visible only during interphase.
   D   They become visible during the mitosis stage of the cell cycle.

Constructed Response

Copy the table below onto a separate piece of paper. Use your table to answer Question 6.

	Photosynthesis	Cellular Respiration
Raw materials	Water and carbon dioxide	a. _____ _____
Products	b. _____ _____	c. _____ _____
Energy released?	d. _____	e. _____

6. Complete the table to compare and contrast photosynthesis and cellular respiration.

Athletic Trainer

Research It Find out about an athletic trainer, and create a profile of that person. Describe where he or she works, why he or she chose this career, and whether the trainer performs any research. Then, identify where in your community an athletic trainer might be able to help people.

Athletic trainers at commercial gyms help people perform exercises to improve their health. But athletic trainers do more than play at the gym all day.

In reality, athletic trainers are professionals who understand the ways in which muscles and body systems work together. Many athletic trainers who work with elite athletes study biology, anatomy and physiology, or physical education in college. They are often athletes too, and may gain experience as a trainer at a commercial gym.

An athletic trainer must apply scientific discoveries to people's fitness training. For example, have you ever felt a burning sensation in your muscles after a workout? People sometimes think this feeling is caused by a buildup of lactic acid in the muscles. However, scientists think that cells use lactic acid to produce energy when glucose supplies are low. An athletic trainer may suggest that an athlete use endurance training. Endurance training helps train muscles to efficiently burn lactic acid, which improves the athlete's performance.

Athletic trainers work in an exciting and constantly changing field. As scientists learn more about human biology, athletic trainers apply these lessons. They help athletes continue to push the limits of human performance.

WHY HEARTS
Don't Get Cancer

You've probably heard of heartburn and heart attacks, and even heartbreak. But have you heard of heart cancer? Heart cancer occurs very rarely, and the tumors usually do not grow the way most cancer tumors do. So why doesn't the heart usually develop cancer? The answer may lie with cell division.

Every moment of your life, cells in your body are dividing. During cell division, a cell's genetic material is copied, and a new cell forms. However, mistakes in how genes are copied can occur during cell division. Occasionally, these mistakes can lead to certain forms of cancer.

In a healthy heart, cell division slows significantly by the time a person reaches adulthood. Cell division is slow and rare in the adult heart because the cells of the heart are active every minute of life. Therefore, heart cells do not mutate very often, so the risk of a mutation causing cancer is very low.

Present It Find out more about rare cancers. Then, create a multimedia presentation that describes why these types of cancer are uncommon. Be sure to cite your sources of information.

This colored transmission electron micrograph (TEM) shows muscle cells from a healthy heart. The hardworking cells in your heart rarely rest long enough for cell division to occur. ▶

WHAT MAKES THIS BABY KOALA DIFFERENT?

Why don't offspring always look like their parents?

Even though this young koala, or joey, has two fuzzy ears, a long nose, and a body shaped like its mom's, you can see that the two are different. You might expect a young animal to look exactly like its parents, but think about how varied a litter of kittens or puppies can look. This joey is an albino—an animal that lacks the usual coloring in its eyes, fur, and skin.

 Observe **Describe how this joey looks different from its mom.**

_____

_____

_____

_____

▶ UNTAMED SCIENCE Watch the **Untamed Science** video to learn more about heredity.

Genetics: The Science of Heredity

Check Your Understanding

1. **Background** Read the paragraph below and then answer the question.

Kent's cat just had six kittens. All six kittens look different from one another—and from their two parents! Kent knows each kitten is unique because cats reproduce through **sexual reproduction,** not **asexual reproduction.** Before long, the kittens will grow bigger and bigger as their cells divide through **mitosis.**

- In what way are the two daughter cells that form by mitosis and cell division identical?

_____

> **Sexual reproduction** involves two parents and combines their genetic material to produce a new organism that differs from both parents.

> **Asexual reproduction** involves only one parent and produces offspring that are identical to the parent.

> During **mitosis,** a cell's nucleus divides into two new nuclei, and one copy of DNA is distributed into each daughter cell.

> **MY READING WEB** If you had trouble completing the question above, visit **My Reading Web** and type in *Genetics: The Science of Heredity.*

Vocabulary Skill

Suffixes A suffix is a word part that is added to the end of a word to change its meaning. For example, the suffix -*tion* means "process of." If you add the suffix -*tion* to the verb *fertilize,* you get the noun *fertilization.* *Fertilization* means "the process of fertilizing." The table below lists some other common suffixes and their meanings.

Suffix	Meaning	Example
-*ive*	performing a particular action	recessive allele, *n.* an allele that is masked when a dominant allele is present
-*ance* or -*ant*	state, condition of	codominance, *n.* occurs when both alleles are expressed equally

2. **Quick Check** Fill in the blank with the correct suffix.

- A domin_____ allele can mask a recessive allele.

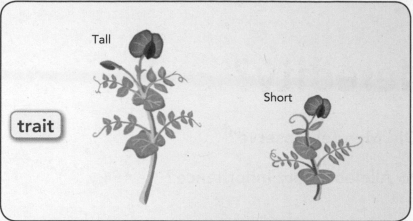

trait

Tall

Short

phenotype

incomplete dominance

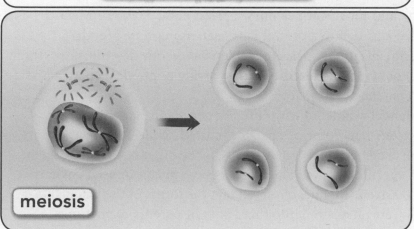

meiosis

Chapter Preview

LESSON 1
- heredity
- trait
- genetics
- fertilization
- purebred
- gene
- allele
- dominant allele
- recessive allele
- hybrid
- ⊙ **Identify Supporting Evidence**
- △ **Predict**

LESSON 2
- probability
- Punnett square
- phenotype
- genotype
- homozygous
- heterozygous
- ⊙ **Identify the Main Idea**
- △ **Draw Conclusions**

LESSON 3
- incomplete dominance
- codominance
- multiple alleles
- polygenic inheritance
- ⊙ **Compare and Contrast**
- △ **Interpret Data**

LESSON 4
- meiosis
- ⊙ **Relate Cause and Effect**
- △ **Design Experiments**

▷ VOCAB FLASH CARDS   For extra help with vocabulary, visit **Vocab Flash Cards** and type in *Genetics: The Science of Heredity.*

What Is Heredity?

🔑 **What Did Mendel Observe?**

🔑 **How Do Alleles Affect Inheritance?**

MY PLANET DIARY

BIOGRAPHY

Almost Forgotten

When scientists make great discoveries, sometimes their work is praised, criticized, or even forgotten. Gregor Mendel was almost forgotten. He spent eight years studying pea plants, and he discovered patterns in the way characteristics pass from one generation to the next. For almost 40 years, people overlooked Mendel's work. When it was finally rediscovered, it unlocked the key to understanding heredity.

Communicate Discuss the question below with a partner. Then write your answer.

Did you ever rediscover something of yours that you had forgotten? How did you react?

_____

_____

_____

▷ **PLANET DIARY** Go to **Planet Diary** to learn more about heredity.

 Do the Inquiry Warm-Up *What Does the Father Look Like?*

What Did Mendel Observe?

In the mid-nineteenth century, a priest named Gregor Mendel tended a garden in a central European monastery. Mendel's experiments in that peaceful garden would one day transform the study of heredity. **Heredity** is the passing of physical characteristics from parents to offspring.

Mendel wondered why different pea plants had different characteristics. Some pea plants grew tall, while others were short. Some plants produced green seeds, while others had yellow seeds. Each specific characteristic, such as stem height or seed color, is called a **trait.** Mendel observed that the forms of the pea plants' traits were often similar to those of their parents. Sometimes, however, the forms differed.

Vocabulary
- heredity • trait • genetics • fertilization
- purebred • gene • allele • dominant allele
- recessive allele • hybrid

Skills
- ⤵ Reading: Identify Supporting Evidence
- △ Inquiry: Predict

Mendel's Experiments Mendel experimented with thousands of pea plants. Today, Mendel's discoveries form the foundation of **genetics,** the scientific study of heredity. **Figure 1** shows the parts of a pea plant's flower. The pistil produces female sex cells, or eggs. The stamens produce pollen, which contains the male sex cells, or sperm. A new organism begins to form when egg and sperm cells join in the process called **fertilization.** Before fertilization can happen in pea plants, pollen must reach the pistil of a pea flower. This process is called pollination.

Pea plants are usually self-pollinating. In self-pollination, pollen from a flower lands on the pistil of the same flower. Mendel developed a method by which he cross-pollinated, or "crossed," pea plants. **Figure 1** shows his method.

Mendel decided to cross plants that had contrasting forms of a trait—for example, tall plants and short plants. He started with purebred plants. A **purebred** organism is the offspring of many generations that have the same form of a trait. For example, purebred tall pea plants always come from tall parent plants.

FIGURE 1 ....

Crossing Pea Plants
Mendel devised a way to cross-pollinate pea plants.

✎ **Use the diagram to answer the questions about Mendel's procedure.**

1. **Observe** How does flower B differ from flower A?

_____

_____

2. **Infer** Describe how Mendel cross-pollinated pea plants.

_____

_____

_____

_____

B

A

Pistil

Stamens

Pollen

111

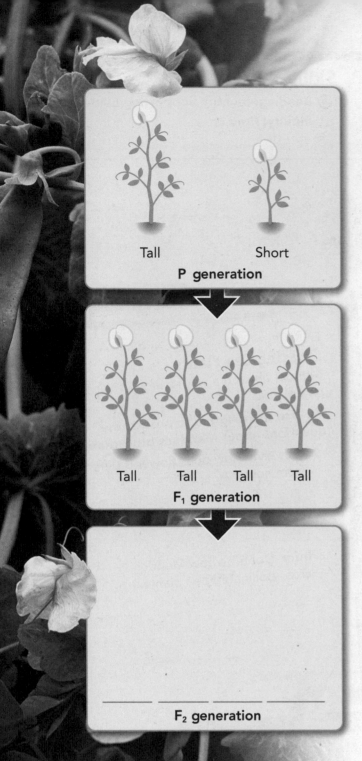

Tall   Short
P generation

Tall   Tall   Tall   Tall
F₁ generation

_____ _____ _____
F₂ generation

The F₁ and F₂ Offspring

Mendel crossed purebred tall plants with purebred short plants. Today, scientists call these plants the parental, or P, generation. The resulting offspring are the first filial (FIL ee ul), or F₁, generation. The word *filial* comes from *filia* and *filius*, the Latin words for "daughter" and "son."

Look at **Figure 2** to see the surprise Mendel found in the F₁ generation. All the offspring were tall. The shortness trait seemed to have disappeared!

When these plants were full-grown, Mendel allowed them to self-pollinate. The F₂ (second filial) generation that followed surprised Mendel even more. He counted the plants of the F₂ generation. About three fourths were tall, while one fourth were short.

Experiments With Other Traits

Mendel repeated his experiments, studying other pea-plant traits, such as flower color and seed shape. ⚷ **In all of his crosses, Mendel found that only one form of the trait appeared in the F₁ generation. However, in the F₂ generation, the "lost" form of the trait always reappeared in about one fourth of the plants.**

FIGURE 2 ···
Results of a Cross
In Mendel's crosses, some forms of a trait were hidden in one generation but reappeared in the next.

✎ **Interpret Diagrams** Draw and label the offspring in the F₂ generation.

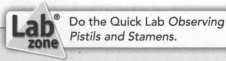 Do the Quick Lab *Observing Pistils and Stamens.*

⚷ Assess Your Understanding

1a. Define What happens during fertilization?

_____

_____

b. Compare and Contrast In Mendel's cross for stem height, how did the plants in the F₂ generations differ from the F₁ plants?

_____

got it?

○ **I get it!** Now I know that Mendel found that one form of a trait _____

_____

_____

○ **I need extra help with** _____

Go to MY SCIENCE ⓢ COACH online for help with this subject.

How Do Alleles Affect Inheritance?

Mendel reached several conclusions from his experimental results. He reasoned that individual factors, or sets of genetic "information," must control the inheritance of traits in peas. The factors that control each trait exist in pairs. The female parent contributes one factor, while the male parent contributes the other factor. Finally, one factor in a pair can mask, or hide, the other factor. The tallness factor, for example, masked the shortness factor.

Genes and Alleles Today, scientists use the word **gene** to describe the factors that control a trait. **Alleles** (uh LEELZ) are the different forms of a gene. The gene that controls stem height in peas has one allele for tall stems and one allele for short stems. Each pea plant inherits two alleles—one from the egg and the other from the sperm. A plant may inherit two alleles for tall stems, two alleles for short stems, or one of each.

🔑 **An organism's traits are controlled by the alleles it inherits from its parents. Some alleles are dominant, while other alleles are recessive.** A **dominant allele** is one whose trait always shows up in the organism when the allele is present. A **recessive allele,** on the other hand, is hidden whenever the dominant allele is present. **Figure 3** shows dominant and recessive alleles of the traits in Mendel's crosses.

FIGURE 3 ·······················

Alleles in Pea Plants
Mendel studied the inheritance of seven different traits in pea plants.

✏️ **Use the table to answer the questions.**

1. **Draw Conclusions** Circle the picture of each dominant form of the trait in the P generation.

2. **Predict** Under what conditions would the recessive form of one of these traits reappear?

_____

_____

Inheritance of Pea Plants Studied by Mendel							
	Seed Shape	**Seed Color**	**Pod Shape**	**Pod Color**	**Flower Color**	**Flower Position**	**Stem Height**
P	Wrinkled	Yellow	Pinched	Green	Purple	Tip of stem	Tall
	X	X	X	X	X	X	X
	Round	Green	Smooth	Yellow	White	Side of stem	Short
F₁	Round	Yellow	Smooth	Green	Purple	Side of stem	Tall

Alleles in Mendel's Crosses

In Mendel's cross for stem height, the purebred tall plants in the P generation had two alleles for tall stems. The purebred short plants had two alleles for short stems. But each F_1 plant inherited one allele for tall stems and one allele for short stems. The F_1 plants are called hybrids. A **hybrid** (HY brid) organism has two different alleles for a trait. All the F_1 plants are tall because the dominant allele for tall stems masks the recessive allele for short stems.

Symbols for Alleles

Geneticists, scientists who study genetics, often use letters to represent alleles. A dominant allele is symbolized by a capital letter. A recessive allele is symbolized by the lowercase version of the same letter. For example, T stands for the allele for tall stems, and t stands for the allele for short stems. When a plant has two dominant alleles for tall stems, its alleles are written as TT. When a plant has two recessive alleles for short stems, its alleles are written as tt. These plants are the P generation shown in **Figure 4.** Think about the symbols that would be used for F_1 plants that all inherit one allele for tall stems and one for short stems.

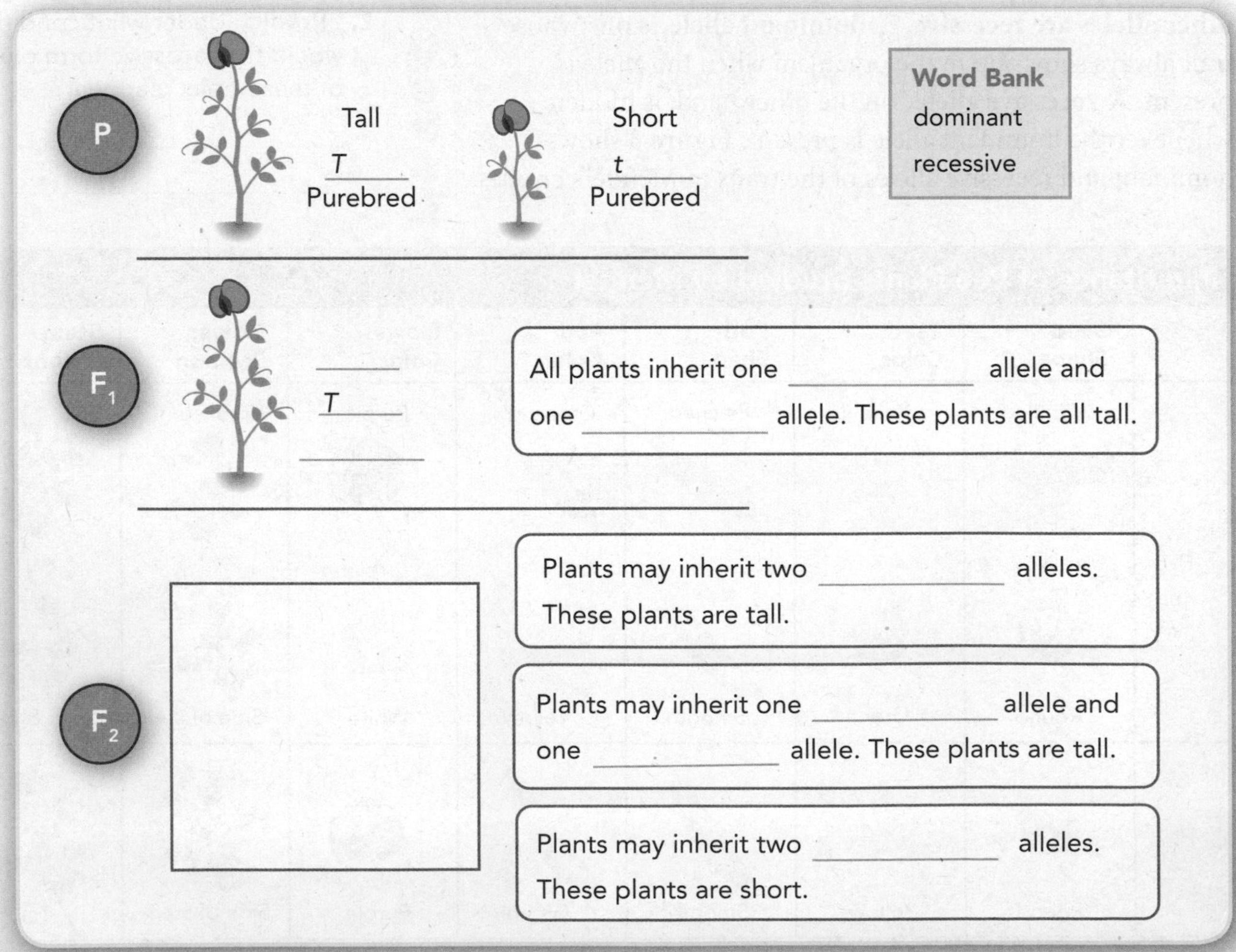

FIGURE 4 ·············
> VIRTUAL LAB **Dominant and Recessive Alleles**
Symbols serve as a shorthand way to identify alleles.

✎ **Complete each row of the diagram.**

1. **Identify** Fill in the missing allele symbols and descriptions.

2. **Summarize** Use the word bank to complete the statements. (Terms will be used more than once.)

3. **Relate Cause and Effect** Draw the two possible ways the F_2 offspring could look.

P — Tall T Purebred   Short t Purebred

Word Bank
dominant
recessive

F_1 — T ____

All plants inherit one _____ allele and one _____ allele. These plants are all tall.

F_2 —

Plants may inherit two _____ alleles. These plants are tall.

Plants may inherit one _____ allele and one _____ allele. These plants are tall.

Plants may inherit two _____ alleles. These plants are short.

apply it!

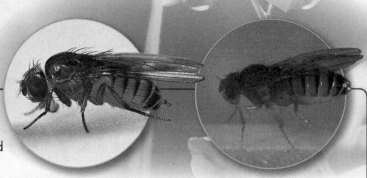

In fruit flies, long wings are dominant over short wings. A scientist crossed a purebred long-winged fruit fly with a purebred short-winged fruit fly.

1 If *W* stands for long wings, write the symbols for the alleles of each parent fly.

_____

2 ◢Predict What will be the wing length of the F_1 offspring?

_____

3 ◢Predict If the scientist crosses a hybrid male F_1 fruit fly with a hybrid F_1 female, what will their offspring probably be like?

_____

_____

_____

Significance of Mendel's Contribution
Mendel's discovery of genes and alleles eventually changed scientists' ideas about heredity. Before Mendel, most people thought that the traits of an individual organism were simply a blend of the parents' characteristics. Mendel showed that offspring traits are determined by individual, separate alleles inherited from each parent. Unfortunately, the value of Mendel's discovery was not known during his lifetime. But when scientists in the early 1900s rediscovered Mendel's work, they quickly realized its importance. Because of his work, Mendel is often called the Father of Genetics.

✎ **Identify Supporting Evidence** What evidence showed Mendel that traits are determined by separate alleles?

_____

_____

_____

_____

 Lab zone® Do the Quick Lab *Inferring the Parent Generation.*

🔑 Assess Your Understanding

2a. Relate Cause and Effect Why is a pea plant that is a hybrid for stem height tall?

_____

_____

_____

b. ⌈CHALLENGE⌋ Can a short pea plant be a hybrid for the trait of stem height? Why or why not?

_____

_____

_____

_____

got it?

○ **I get it!** Now I know that an organism's traits are controlled by _____

_____

_____

_____

○ **I need extra help with** _____

Go to MY SCIENCE ⑤ COACH *online for help with this subject.*

Probability and Heredity

UNLOCK THE BIG Q?

🔑 How Is Probability Related to Inheritance?

🔑 What Are Phenotype and Genotype?

MY PLANET DIARY

FIELD TRIP

Storm on the Way?

Have you ever watched a hurricane form? Weather forecasters at the National Hurricane Center (NHC) in Miami, Florida, have. From May 15 to November 30, the NHC Operations Area is staffed around the clock with forecasters. They study data from aircraft, ocean buoys, and satellites to develop computer models. These models predict the probable paths of a storm. If the probability of a certain path is high, the NHC issues a warning that helps save lives and reduce damage.

Communicate Answer the question below. Then discuss your answer with a partner.

Local weather forecasters often talk about the percent chance for rainfall. What do you think they mean?

_____

_____

_____

_____

_____

▶ **PLANET DIARY** Go to **Planet Diary** to learn more about probability and weather.

 Lab zone Do the Inquiry Warm-Up *What's the Chance?*

How Is Probability Related to Inheritance?

Before the start of a football game, the team captains stand with the referee for a coin toss. The team that wins the toss chooses whether to kick or receive the ball. As the referee tosses the coin, the visiting team captain calls "heads." What is the chance that the visitors will win the toss? To answer this question, you need to understand the principles of probability.

Vocabulary
- probability
- phenotype
- homozygous
- Punnett square
- genotype
- heterozygous

Skills
- ↪ Reading: Identify the Main Idea
- △ Inquiry: Draw Conclusions

What Is Probability?
Each time you toss a coin, there are two possible ways it can land—heads up or tails up. **Probability** is a number that describes how likely it is that an event will occur. In mathematical terms, you can say the probability that a tossed coin will land heads up is 1 in 2. There's also a 1 in 2 probability that the coin will land tails up. A 1 in 2 probability is expressed as the fraction $\frac{1}{2}$ or as 50 percent.

The laws of probability predict what is *likely* to occur, not what *will* occur. If you toss a coin 20 times, you may expect it to land heads up 10 times and tails up 10 times. But you may get 11 heads and 9 tails, or 8 heads and 12 tails. The more tosses you make, the closer your actual results will be to those predicted by probability.

Do you think the result of one toss affects the result of the next toss? Not at all. Each event occurs independently. Suppose you toss a coin five times and it lands heads up each time. What is the probability that it will land heads up on the next toss? If you said the probability is still 1 in 2, or 50 percent, you're right. The results of the first five tosses do not affect the result of the sixth toss.

do the math!

Percentage

One way to express probability is as a percentage. A percentage is a number compared to 100. For example, 50 percent, or 50%, means 50 out of 100. Suppose you want to calculate percentage from the results of a series of basketball free throws in which 3 out of 5 free throws go through the hoop.

STEP 1 Write the comparison as a fraction.

$$3 \text{ out of } 5 = \frac{3}{5}$$

STEP 2 Calculate the number value of the fraction.

$$3 \div 5 = 0.6$$

STEP 3 Multiply this number by 100%.

$$0.6 \times 100\% = 60\%$$

················· Practice! ·················

❶ **Calculate** Suppose 5 out of 25 free throws go through the hoop. Write this result as a fraction.

_____

❷ **Calculate** Express your answer in Question 1 as a percentage.

_____

_____

_____

_____

Probability and Genetics How is probability related to genetics? Think back to Mendel's experiments. He carefully counted the offspring from every cross. When he crossed two plants that were hybrid for stem height (*Tt*), about three fourths of the F_2 plants had tall stems. About one fourth had short stems.

Each time Mendel repeated the cross, he observed similar results. He realized that the principles of probability applied to his work. He found that the probability of a hybrid cross producing a tall plant was 3 in 4. The probability of producing a short plant was 1 in 4. Mendel was the first scientist to recognize that the principles of probability can predict the results of genetic crosses.

Punnett Squares

A tool that can help you grasp how the laws of probability apply to genetics is called a Punnett square. A **Punnett square** is a chart that shows all the possible ways alleles can combine in a genetic cross. Geneticists use Punnett squares to see these combinations and to determine the probability of a particular outcome, or result. 🗝 **In a genetic cross, the combination of alleles that parents can pass to an offspring is based on probability.**

Figure 1 shows how to make a Punnett square. In this case, the cross is between two hybrid pea plants with round seeds (*Rr*). The allele for round seeds (*R*) is dominant over the allele for wrinkled seeds (*r*). Each parent can pass either one allele or the other to an offspring. The boxes in the Punnett square show the possible combinations of alleles that the offspring can inherit.

FIGURE 1 ···
▶ INTERACTIVE ART **How to Make a Punnett Square**
You can use a Punnett square to find the probabilities of a genetic cross.

✎ **Follow the steps in the figure to fill in the Punnett square.**

1. **Predict** What is the probability that an offspring will have wrinkled seeds?

_____

2. **Interpret Tables** What is the probability that an offspring will have round seeds? Explain your answer.

_____

_____

_____

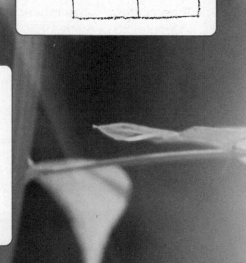

2 The male parent's alleles are written along the top of the square. Fill in the female parent's alleles along the left side.

1 Start by drawing a box and dividing it into four squares.

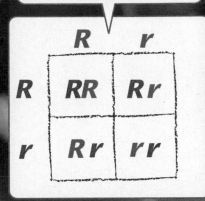

5 The completed square shows all the possible allele combinations the offspring can have.

4 Copy the male parent's alleles into the boxes beneath them.

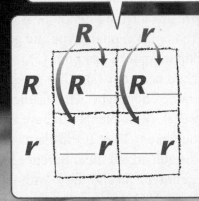

3 Copy the female parent's alleles into the boxes to their right. The first one is done for you.

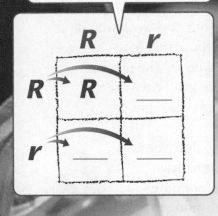

Identify the Main Idea In your own words, describe what a Punnet square shows you about combinations of alleles.

_____

_____

_____

_____

_____

Relating Punnett Squares to Mendel Mendel did not know about alleles. But a Punnett square shows why he got the results he saw in the F$_2$ generations. Plants with alleles *RR* would have round seeds. So would plants with alleles *Rr*. Only plants with alleles *rr* would have wrinkled seeds.

Do the Quick Lab *Coin Crosses.*

🔑 Assess Your Understanding

1a. Review What is probability?

_____

_____

b. Apply Concepts What is the probability that a cross between a hybrid pea plant with round seeds and one with wrinkled seeds will produce offspring with wrinkled seeds? (Draw a Punnett square on other paper to find the answer.)

_____

got it?

○ **I get it!** Now I know that the combination of alleles parents can pass to offspring _____

_____

_____

○ **I need extra help with** _____

Go to **MY SCIENCE COACH** online for help with this subject.

What Are Phenotype and Genotype?

Two terms that geneticists use are **phenotype** (FEE noh typ) and **genotype** (JEE noh typ). 🔑 **An organism's phenotype is its physical appearance, or visible traits. An organism's genotype is its genetic makeup, or alleles.** In other words, genotype is an organism's alleles. Phenotype is how a trait looks or is expressed.

To compare phenotype and genotype, look at **Figure 2**. The allele for smooth pea pods (*S*) is dominant over the allele for pinched pea pods (*s*). All the plants with at least one *S* allele have the same phenotype. That is, they all produce smooth pods. However, these plants can have two different genotypes—*SS* or *Ss*. If you were to look at the plants with smooth pods, you would not be able to tell the difference between those that have the genotype *SS* and those with the genotype *Ss*. The plants with pinched pods, on the other hand, would all have the same phenotype—pinched pods—as well as the same genotype—*ss*.

Geneticists use two additional terms to describe an organism's genotype. An organism that has two identical alleles for a trait is said to be **homozygous** (hoh moh ZY gus) for that trait. A smooth-pod plant that has the alleles *SS* and a pinched-pod plant with the alleles *ss* are both homozygous. An organism that has two different alleles for a trait is **heterozygous** (het ur oh ZY gus) for that trait. A smooth-pod plant with the alleles *Ss* is heterozygous. Recall that Mendel used the term *hybrid* to describe heterozygous pea plants.

Vocabulary Suffixes The suffix *-ous* means "having." Circle this suffix in the highlighted terms *homozygous* and *heterozygous* in the paragraph at the right. These terms describe the organism as having

_____

_____

_____

FIGURE 2 ······················

Describing Inheritance

An organism's phenotype is its physical appearance. Its genotype is its genetic makeup.

✏️ **Based on what you have read, answer these questions.**

1. **Classify** Fill in the missing information in the table.

2. **Interpret Tables** How many genotypes are there for the smooth-pod phenotype?

_____

Phenotypes and Genotypes

Phenotype	Genotype	Homozygous or Heterozygous
Smooth pods 	_____	_____
Smooth pods 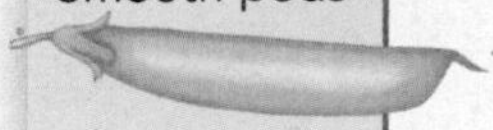	_____	_____
Pinched pods 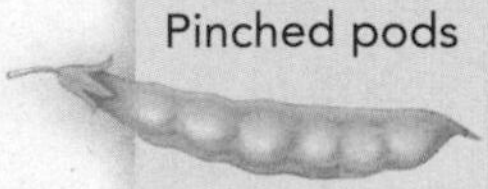	_____	_____

apply it!

Mendel's principles of heredity apply to many other organisms. For example, in guinea pigs, black fur color (*B*) is dominant over white fur color (*b*). Suppose a pair of black guinea pigs produces several litters of pups during their lifetimes. The graph shows the phenotypes of the pups. Write a title for the graph.

1 **Read Graphs** How many black pups were produced? How many white pups were produced?

_____

2 **Infer** What are the possible genotypes of the offspring?

_____

3 **Draw Conclusions** What can you conclude about the genotypes of the parent guinea pigs? Explain your answer.

_____
_____
_____
_____
_____

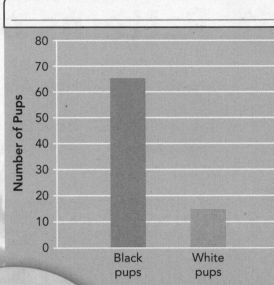

Phenotype of Offspring

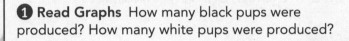
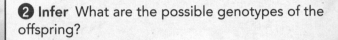
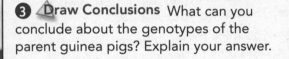

Lab zone® Do the Lab Investigation *Make the Right Call!*

🔑 Assess Your Understanding

2a. Relate Cause and Effect Explain how two organisms can have the same phenotype but different genotypes.

_____
_____
_____

b. |CHALLENGE| In their lifetimes, two guinea pigs produce 40 black pups and 40 white pups. On a separate paper, make a Punnett square and find the likely genotypes of these parents.

_____
_____

got it?

○ **I get it!** Now I know that phenotype and genotype are terms that describe _____

_____
_____
_____

○ **I need extra help with** _____

Go to my science ⑤ COACH *online for help with this subject.*

Patterns of Inheritance

🔑 **How Are Most Traits Inherited?**

🔑 **How Do Genes and the Environment Interact?**

MY PLANET DiARY

DISCOVERY

Cold, With a Chance of Males

Is it a male or a female? If you're a red-eared slider turtle, the answer might depend on the temperature! These slider turtles live in the calm, fresh, warm waters of the southeastern United States. For these turtles and some other reptiles, the temperature of the environment determines the sex of their offspring. At 26°C, the eggs of red-eared slider turtles all hatch as males. But at 31°C, the eggs all hatch as females. Only at about 29°C is there a 50% chance of hatching turtles of either sex.

Predict Discuss the question below with a partner. Then write your answer.

What do you think might happen to a population of red-eared slider turtles in a place where the temperature remains near or at 26°C?

_____

_____

_____

_____

> **PLANET DIARY** Go to **Planet Diary** to learn more about patterns of inheritance.

Lab zone® Do the Inquiry Warm-Up *Observing Traits.*

How Are Most Traits Inherited?

The traits that Mendel studied are controlled by genes with only two possible alleles. These alleles are either dominant or recessive. Pea flower color is either purple or white. Peas are either yellow or green. Can you imagine if all traits were like this? If people were either short or tall? If cats were either black or yellow?

Studying two-allele traits is a good place to begin learning about genetics. But take a look around at the variety of living things in your surroundings. As you might guess, most traits do not follow such a simple pattern of inheritance. 🔑 **Most traits are the result of complex patterns of inheritance.** Four complex patterns of inheritance are described in this lesson.

Vocabulary
- incomplete dominance
- codominance • multiple alleles
- polygenic inheritance

Skills
↻ Reading: Compare and Contrast
△ Inquiry: Interpret Data

Incomplete Dominance

Some traits result from a pattern of inheritance known as incomplete dominance. **Incomplete dominance** occurs when one allele is only partially dominant. For example, look at **Figure 1.** The flowers shown are called snapdragons. A cross between a plant with red flowers and one with white flowers produces pink offspring.

Snapdragons with alleles *RR* produce a lot of red color in their flowers. It's no surprise that their flowers are red. A plant with two white alleles (*WW*) produces no red color. Its flowers are white. Both types of alleles are written as capital letters because neither is totally dominant. If a plant has alleles *RW*, only enough color is produced to make the flowers just a little red. So they look pink.

Codominance

The chickens in **Figure 1** show a different pattern of inheritance. **Codominance** occurs when both alleles for a gene are expressed equally. In the chickens shown, neither black feathers nor white feathers are dominant. All the offspring of a black hen and a white rooster have both black and white feathers.

Here, F^B stands for the allele for black feathers. F^W stands for the allele for white feathers. The letter *F* tells you the trait is feathers. The superscripts *B* for black and *W* for white tell you the color.

FIGURE 1 ·····················
Other Patterns of Inheritance
Many crosses do not follow the patterns Mendel discovered.

✎ **Apply Concepts** Fill in the missing pairs of alleles.

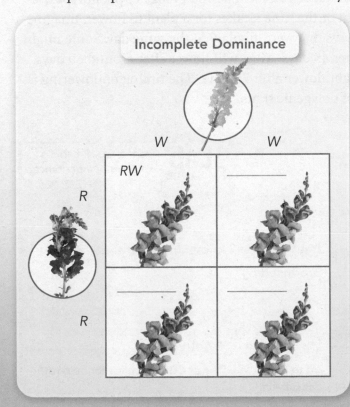

Incomplete Dominance

W   W

R | RW | ____ |

R | ____ | ____ |

Codominance

F^W F^W

F^B | F^BF^W | ____ |

F^B | ____ | ____ |

apply it!

An imaginary insect called the blingwing has three alleles for wing color: *R* (red), *B* (blue), and *Y* (yellow).

1 List If an organism can inherit only two alleles for a gene, what are the six possible allele pairs for wing color in blingwings? One answer is given.

RB,

_____

2 Interpret Data Suppose wing color results from incomplete dominance. What wing color would each pair of alleles produce? One answer is given.

RB: purple

_____

_____

_____

_____

_____

Multiple Alleles Some genes have **multiple alleles,** which means that three or more possible alleles determine the trait. Remember that an organism can only inherit two alleles for a gene—one from each parent. Even if there are four, five, or more possible alleles, an individual can only have two. However, more genotypes can occur with multiple alleles than with just two alleles. For example, four alleles control the color of fur in some rabbits. Depending on which two alleles a rabbit inherits, its coat color can range from brownish gray to all white.

Polygenic Inheritance The traits that Mendel studied were each controlled by a single gene. **Polygenic inheritance** occurs when more than one gene affects a trait. The alleles of the different genes work together to produce these traits.

Polygenic inheritance results in a broad range of phenotypes, like human height or the time it takes for a plant to flower. Imagine a field of sunflowers that were all planted the same day. Some might start to flower after 45 days. Most will flower after around 60 days. The last ones might flower after 75 days. The timing of flowering is a characteristic of polygenic traits.

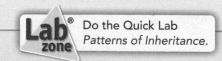

Do the Quick Lab
Patterns of Inheritance.

🔑 Assess Your Understanding

1a. Describe How are the symbols written for alleles that share incomplete dominance?

_____

_____

b. CHALLENGE How is polygenic inheritance different from the patterns described by Mendel?

_____

_____

got it?

○ **I get it!** Now I know that most traits are produced by _____

_____

○ **I need extra help with** _____

Go to **MY SCIENCE COACH** online for help with this subject.

How Do Genes and the Environment Interact?

You were not born knowing how to skateboard, but maybe you can skateboard now. Many traits are learned, or acquired. Unlike inherited traits, acquired traits are not carried by genes or passed to offspring. Although inherited traits are determined by genes, they also can be affected by factors in the environment. The phenotypes you observe in an organism result both from genes and from interactions of the organism with its environment.

Inherited and Acquired Traits Humans are born with inherited traits, such as vocal cords and tongues that allow for speech. But humans are not born speaking Spanish, or Mandarin, or English. The languages that a person speaks are acquired traits. Do you have a callus on your finger from writing with your pencil? That is an acquired trait. Skills you learn and physical changes that occur, such as calluses and haircuts, are aquired traits. See if you can tell the inherited traits from the acquired traits in **Figure 2**.

FIGURE 2 ·····························

Inherited or Acquired?
Which traits shown are carried in the genes, and which are not?

✎ **Classify** Identify each trait shown as inherited or acquired.

Fish body color

Dyed hair color

Their heights

These hedge shapes

Her freckles

Genes and the Environment Think again about sunflowers. Genes control when the plants flower. But sunlight, temperature, soil nutrients, and water also affect a plant's flowering time. 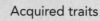 **Environmental factors can influence the way genes are expressed.** Like sunflowers, you have factors in your environment that can affect how your genes are expressed. For example, you may have inherited the ability to play a musical instrument. But without an opportunity to learn, you may never develop the skill.

Some environmental factors can change an organism's genes. For example, tobacco smoke and other pollutants can affect genes in a person's body cells in a way that may result in lung cancer and other cancers. Still other genetic changes happen by chance.

Changes in body cells cannot be passed to offspring. Only changes in the sex cells—eggs and sperm—can be passed to offspring. Not all genetic changes have negative effects. Genetic change in sex cells is an important source of life's variety.

⟳ **Compare and Contrast**
Underline two sentences that tell how changes to genes in body cells differ from changes to genes in egg and sperm cells.

EXPLORE THE BIG **?**

Patterns of Inheritance

Why don't offspring always look like their parents?

FIGURE 3 ....

▶ INTERACTIVE ART The traits you see in organisms result from their genes and from interactions of genes with the environment.

✎ **Summarize** Match the terms in the word bank with the examples shown.

Word Bank

Incomplete dominance	Dominant and recessive traits
Environmental factors	Polygenic inheritance
Multiple alleles	Codominance
Acquired traits	

_____

_____

_____

_____

_____

_____

Lab® zone Do the Quick Lab
Is It All in the Genes?

Assess Your Understanding

2a. Review Only genetic changes in (sex cells/ body cells) can be passed to offspring.

b. Describe Give one example of how environmental factors affect gene expression.

_____

_____

_____

c. ANSWER THE BIG ? Why don't offspring always look like their parents?

_____

_____

_____

_____

_____

got it? ....

○ **I get it!** Now I know that the environment can affect _____

_____

○ **I need extra help with** _____

_Go to_ MY SCIENCE ⓢ COACH _online for help with this subject._

Chromosomes and Inheritance

UNLOCK THE BIG ?

🔑 **How Are Chromosomes, Genes, and Inheritance Related?**

🔑 **What Happens During Meiosis?**

my planet Diary

Chromosome Sleuth

Finding answers about how chromosomes relate to disease is one job of genetic technologists. These scientists analyze chromosomes from cells. The analysis may pinpoint genetic information that can cause disease or other health problems. In their work, genetic technologists use microscopes, computer-imaging photography, and lab skills. They report data that are used in research and in treating patients affected by genetic diseases.

CAREER

Communicate Answer these questions. Then discuss Question 2 with a partner.

1. Would you like to be a genetic technologist? Why or why not?

_____

_____

_____

2. If you were a genetic technologist, what would you like to research?

_____

_____

_____

▶ PLANET DIARY Go to **Planet Diary** to learn more about genetic technologists.

Lab® zone Do the Inquiry Warm-Up *Which Chromosome Is Which?*

Vocabulary
- meiosis

Skills
- Reading: Relate Cause and Effect
- Inquiry: Design Experiments

How Are Chromosomes, Genes, and Inheritance Related?

Mendel's work showed that genes exist. (Remember that he called them "factors.") But scientists in the early twentieth century did not know what structures in cells contained genes. The search for the answer was something like a mystery story. The story could be called "The Clue in the Grasshopper's Cells."

At the start of the 1900s, Walter Sutton, an American geneticist, studied the cells of grasshoppers. He wanted to understand how sex cells (sperm and eggs) form. Sutton focused on how the chromosomes moved within cells during the formation of sperm and eggs. He hypothesized that chromosomes are the key to learning how offspring have traits similar to those of their parents.

apply it!

Design Experiments Different types of organisms have different numbers of chromosomes, and some organisms are easier to study than others. Suppose you are a scientist studying chromosomes and you have to pick an organism from those shown below to do your work. Which one would you pick and why?

_____

_____

_____

_____

_____

did you know?

The organism with the highest known number of chromosomes is a plant in the fern family. The netted adderstongue fern has more than 1,200 chromosomes!

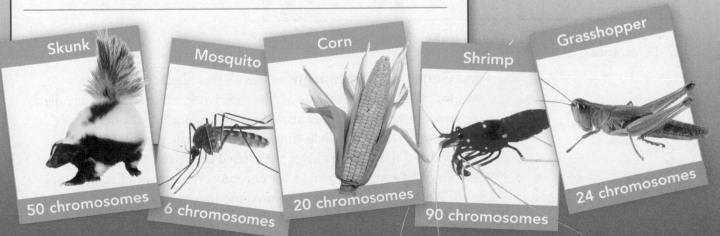

Skunk — 50 chromosomes

Mosquito — 6 chromosomes

Corn — 20 chromosomes

Shrimp — 90 chromosomes

Grasshopper — 24 chromosomes

Chromosomes and Inheritance
Sutton needed evidence to support his hypothesis. Look at **Figure 1** to see how he found this evidence in grasshopper cells. To his surprise, he discovered that grasshopper sex cells have exactly half the number of chromosomes found in grasshopper body cells.

Chromosome Pairs Sutton observed what happened when a sperm cell and an egg cell joined. The fertilized egg that formed had 24 chromosomes. It had the same number of chromosomes as each parent. These 24 chromosomes existed as 12 pairs. One chromosome in each pair came from the male parent. The other chromosome came from the female parent.

FIGURE 1 ·······················

Paired Up
Sutton studied grasshopper cells through a microscope. He concluded that genes are carried on chromosomes.

✎ **Relate Text and Visuals** Answer the questions in the spaces provided.

1 **Body Cell**

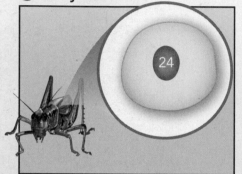

Each grasshopper body cell has 24 chromosomes.

2 **Sex Cells**

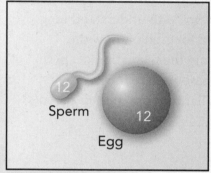

Sperm

Egg

Sutton found that grasshopper sex cells each have 12 chromosomes.

1. How does the number of chromosomes in grasshopper sex cells compare to the number in body cells?

_____

_____

_____

_____

3 **Fertilization**

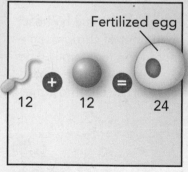

Fertilized egg

12 ➕ 12 ➖ 24

The fertilized egg cell has 24 chromosomes.

4 **Grasshopper Offspring**

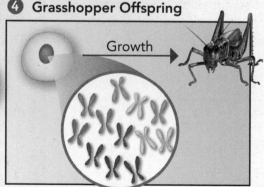

Growth

The 24 chromosomes exist as 12 pairs.

2. How is the inheritance of chromosomes similar to what you know about alleles?

_____

_____

_____

_____

Genes on Chromosomes Recall that alleles are different forms of a gene. Because of Mendel's work, Sutton knew that alleles exist in pairs in an organism. One allele comes from the female parent. The other allele comes from the male parent. Sutton realized that paired alleles are carried on paired chromosomes. His idea is now known as the chromosome theory of inheritance. 🔑 **According to the chromosome theory of inheritance, genes pass from parents to their offspring on chromosomes.**

A Lineup of Genes
The body cells of humans contain 46 chromosomes that form 23 pairs. Chromosomes are made up of many genes joined together like beads on a string. Although you have only 23 pairs of chromosomes, your body cells each contain between 20,000 and 25,000 genes. Genes control traits.

Figure 2 shows a pair of chromosomes from an organism. One chromosome is from the female parent. The other chromosome is from the male parent. Notice that each chromosome has the same genes. The genes are lined up in the same order on both chromosomes. However, the alleles for some of the genes are not identical. For example, one chromosome has allele *A*, and the other chromosome has allele *a*. As you can see, this organism is heterozygous for some traits and homozygous for others.

✎

⊕ Relate Cause and Effect
Suppose gene A on the left chromosome is damaged and no longer functions. What form of the trait would show? Why?

_____

_____

_____

_____

_____

FIGURE 2 ·······················

A Pair of Chromosomes
Chromosomes in a pair may have different alleles for some genes and the same alleles for others.

✎ **Interpret Diagrams** For each pair of alleles, tell whether the organism is homozygous or heterozygous. The first two answers are shown.

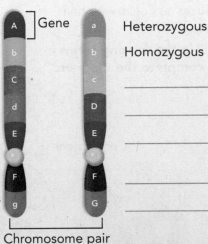

Chromosome pair

Heterozygous

Homozygous

_____

_____

_____

_____

_____

_____

Lab® **Do the Quick Lab** *Chromosomes*
zone *and Inheritance.*

🔑 Assess Your Understanding

1a. Describe When two grasshopper sex cells join, the chromosome number in the new cell is (half/double) the number in the sex cells.

b. Summarize Describe the arrangement of genes on a pair of chromosomes.

_____

_____

_____

c. Relate Evidence and Explanation How do Sutton's observations support the chromosome theory of inheritance?

_____

_____

_____

_____

_____

got it? ·······························

O **I get it!** Now I know that genes are passed from parents to offspring _____

_____

O **I need extra help with** _____

Go to MY SCIENCE ⓢ COACH online for help with this subject.

What Happens During Meiosis?

How do sex cells end up with half the number of chromosomes as body cells? The answer to this question is a form of cell division called meiosis. **Meiosis** (my OH sis) is the process by which the number of chromosomes is reduced by half as sex cells form. You can trace the events of meiosis in **Figure 3**. Here, the parent cell has four chromosomes arranged in two pairs. 🔑 **During meiosis, the chromosome pairs separate into two different cells. The sex cells that form later have only half as many chromosomes as the other cells in the organism.**

FIGURE 3 ···

▷ INTERACTIVE ART **Meiosis**

During meiosis, a cell produces sex cells with half the number of chromosomes.

✏️ **Interpret Diagrams** Fill in the missing terms in the spaces provided, and complete the diagram.

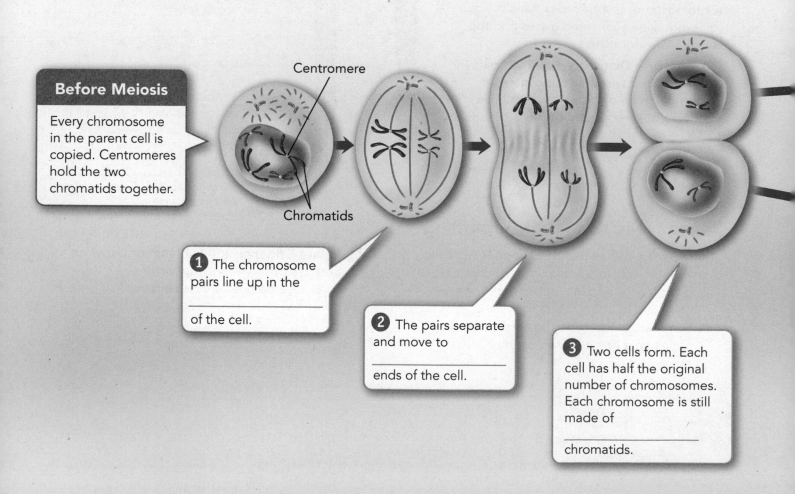

Centromere

Before Meiosis

Every chromosome in the parent cell is copied. Centromeres hold the two chromatids together.

Chromatids

1 The chromosome pairs line up in the

_____

of the cell.

2 The pairs separate and move to

_____

ends of the cell.

3 Two cells form. Each cell has half the original number of chromosomes. Each chromosome is still made of

_____

chromatids.

During meiosis, a cell divides into two cells. Then each of these cells divides again, forming a total of four cells. The chromosomes duplicate only before the first cell division.

Each of the four sex cells shown below receives two chromosomes—one chromosome from each pair in the original cell. When two sex cells join at fertilization, the new cell that forms has the full number of chromosomes. In this case, the number is four. The organism that grows from this cell got two of its chromosomes from one parent and two from the other parent.

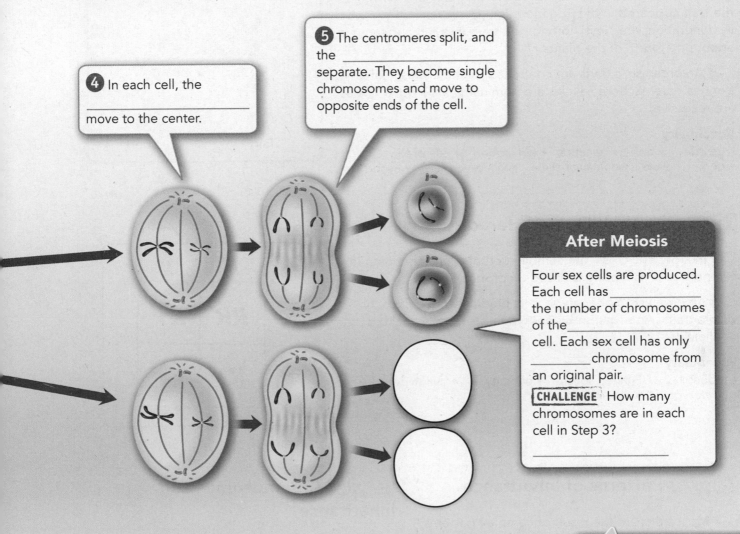

5 The centromeres split, and the _____ separate. They become single chromosomes and move to opposite ends of the cell.

4 In each cell, the _____ move to the center.

After Meiosis

Four sex cells are produced. Each cell has _____ the number of chromosomes of the_____ cell. Each sex cell has only _____chromosome from an original pair.

CHALLENGE How many chromosomes are in each cell in Step 3?

_____

Lab zone®   Do the Quick Lab *Modeling Meiosis.*

Assess Your Understanding

got it? ....

○ I get it! Now I know that during meiosis, the number of chromosomes_____

_____

○ I need extra help with _____

Go to MY SCIENCE COACH online for help with this subject.

4 Study Guide

Offspring inherit different forms of genes called _____ from each parent. Traits are affected by patterns of inheritance and interactions with the _____.

LESSON 1 What Is Heredity?

🗝 In all of his crosses, Mendel found that only one form of the trait appeared in the F_1 generation. However, in the F_2 generation, the "lost" form of the trait always reappeared in about one fourth of the plants.

🗝 An organism's traits are controlled by the alleles it inherits from its parents. Some alleles are dominant, while other alleles are recessive.

Vocabulary
- heredity • trait • genetics • fertilization • purebred
- gene • allele • dominant allele • recessive allele • hybrid

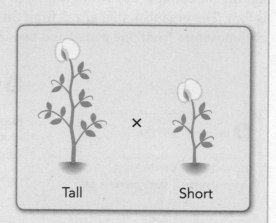

Tall   Short

LESSON 2 Probability and Heredity

🗝 In a genetic cross, the combination of alleles that parents can pass to an offspring is based on probability.

🗝 An organism's phenotype is its physical appearance, or visible traits. An organism's genotype is its genetic makeup, or alleles.

Vocabulary
- probability • Punnett square • phenotype • genotype
- homozygous • heterozygous

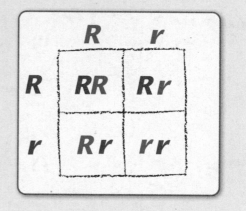

LESSON 3 Patterns of Inheritance

🗝 Most traits are the result of complex patterns of inheritance.

🗝 Environmental factors can influence the way genes are expressed.

Vocabulary
- incomplete dominance
- codominance
- multiple alleles
- polygenic inheritance

LESSON 4 Chromosomes and Inheritance

🗝 The chromosome theory of inheritance states that genes pass from parents to their offspring on chromosomes.

🗝 Meiosis produces sex cells that have half as many chromosomes as body cells.

Vocabulary
- meiosis

Review and Assessment

LESSON 1 What Is Heredity?

1. Different forms of a gene are called

   a. alleles.   **b.** hybrids.

   c. genotypes.   **d.** chromosomes.

2. _____ is the scientific

study of heredity.

3. Explain Mendel crossed two pea plants:
one with green pods and one with yellow
pods. The F_1 generation all had green pods.
What color pods did the F_2 generation have?
Explain your answer.

_____

_____

_____

_____

4. Predict The plant below is purebred for height
(tall). Write the alleles of this plant. In any cross
for height, what kind of offspring will this plant
produce? Why?

_____

_____

_____

_____

_____

5. Compare and Contrast How do dominant
alleles and recessive alleles differ?

_____

_____

_____

_____

6. Write About It Write a diary entry as if you are
Gregor Mendel. You may describe any part of
his experiences, experiments, or observations.

LESSON 2 Probability and Heredity

7. Which of the following represents a
heterozygous genotype?

   a. YY **b.** yy

   c. Yy **d.** $Y^H Y^H$

8. An organism's _____

is the way its genotype is expressed.

9. Make Models Fill in the Punnett square below
to show a cross between two guinea pigs that
are heterozygous for coat color. B is for black
coat color, and b is for white coat color.

10. Interpret Tables What is the probability that
an offspring from the cross above has each
of the following genotypes?

BB _____

Bb _____

bb _____

11. Apply Concepts What kind of cross might tell
you if a black guinea pig is BB or Bb? Why?

_____

_____

_____

12. do the **math!** A garden has 80 pea plants.
Of this total, 20 plants have short stems and
60 plants have tall stems. What percentage of
the plants have short stems? What percentage
have tall stems?

CHAPTER

LESSON 3 Patterns of Inheritance

13. Which of the following terms describes a pattern of inheritance in which one allele is only partially dominant?

    a. codominance

    b. acquired traits

    c. multiple alleles

    d. incomplete dominance

14. Traits that have three or more phenotypes may be the result of _____ alleles.

15. Compare and Contrast How is codominance different from incomplete dominance?

_____

_____

_____

_____

_____

16. Relate Cause and Effect Human height is a trait with a very broad range of phenotypes. Which pattern of inheritance could account for human height? Explain your answer.

_____

_____

_____

_____

_____

17. Identify Faulty Reasoning Neither of Josie's parents plays a musical instrument. Josie thinks that she won't be able to play an instrument because her parents can't. Is she right? Why or why not?

_____

_____

_____

_____

LESSON 4 Chromosomes and Inheritance

18. Genes are carried from parents to offspring on structures called

    a. alleles.   **b.** chromosomes.

    c. phenotypes.   **d.** genotypes.

19. The process of _____ results in the formation of sex cells.

20. Summarize If an organism's body cells have 12 chromosomes, how many chromosomes will the sex cells have? Explain your answer.

_____

_____

_____

_____

_____

Why don't offspring always look like their parents?

21. A species of butterfly has three alleles for wing color: blue, orange, and pale yellow. A blue butterfly mates with an orange butterfly. The following offspring result: about 25% are blue and 25% are orange. However, another 25% are speckled blue and orange, and 25% are yellow. Explain how these results could occur.

Offspring of blue butterfly and orange butterfly

_____

_____

_____

_____

Standardized Test Prep

Multiple Choice

Circle the letter of the best answer.

1. The Punnett square below shows a cross between two pea plants, each with round seeds. What is the missing genotype in the empty square?

	R	R
R	RR	
r	Rr	Rr

   A rr
   B rR
   C Rr
   D RR

2. A particular trait has multiple alleles: A, B, and C. How many different genotypes are possible?

   A 2
   B 3
   C 4
   D 6

3. A sperm and an egg cell join during the process of

   A meiosis.
   B fertilization.
   C probability.
   D genetics.

4. For a particular plant, leaf texture is either fuzzy or smooth. A purebred fuzzy plant is crossed with a purebred smooth plant. All offspring are smooth. Which sentence best describes the alleles for this trait?

   A Fuzzy is dominant over smooth.
   B Smooth is dominant over fuzzy.
   C The alleles are codominant.
   D The alleles have incomplete dominance.

5. Which of the following traits is acquired?

   A the number of petals that grow in a plant's flowers
   B the wing shape of a wild bird
   C the ability of some gorillas to use sign language
   D a cheetah's ability to run faster than any other land animal

Constructed Response

Use the diagram below and your knowledge of genetics to answer Question 6. Write your answer on a separate piece of paper.

A. 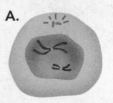 B.  C.

6. One of the cells shown is a parent cell about to undergo meiosis. Another cell is in the process of meiosis. A third cell is a sex cell that results from meiosis. Identify which cell is which, and explain your reasoning.

Nature vs. Nurture

In 1990, the Monterey Bay Aquarium in Monterey, California, released a young otter into the wild. Wildlife rehabilitators at the aquarium raised the otter and taught her how to find food. But, because she was used to receiving food and affection from people at the aquarium, she did not know to avoid other humans. After the otter pestered some local divers, she had to be returned to live at the aquarium.

So, which behaviors do animals learn, and which behaviors "just come naturally"? Actually, the line between inherited behaviors and learned behaviors is rarely clear. Although wild otters are naturally shy around humans, the otter at the Monterey Bay Aquarium had learned to expect food and affection from humans. As a result, wildlife rehabilitators commonly use puppets or animal costumes to keep the animals they care for from becoming too familiar with humans.

▼ This photograph shows a pair of otters, one of the species wildlife rehabilitators try to reintroduce into the wild.

Design It Choose a species, such as deer, otter, or panda, that is raised in captivity and returned to the wild. Design a rehabilitation activity to help orphaned animals learn a skill that they will need to survive in the wild. Explain the features of your rehabilitation activity to your class.

Seeing
Spots

You would probably recognize a Dalmatian if you saw one—Dalmatians typically have white coats with distinctive black or brown spots. Spots are a defining characteristic of the Dalmatian breed. These spots can be large or small, but all Dalmatians have them.

In Dalmatians, spots are a dominant trait. When two Dalmatians breed, each parent contributes a gene for spots. The trait for spots is controlled by one set of genes with only two possible alleles. No matter how many puppies are in a litter, they will all develop spots.

But what if a Dalmatian breeds with another dog that isn't a Dalmatian? While the puppies won't develop the distinctive Dalmatian pattern, they will have spots, because the allele for spots is dominant. Some puppies will have many tiny spots and some will have large patches! Dalmatians, like leopards, cannot change their spots.

Newborn Dalmatian puppies are white—their spots develop when the puppies are about a week old. ▼

Predict It! Dalmatians' spots may be black or liver (brown), but never both on the same dog. Liver is a recessive allele. Use a Punnett square to predict the color of the spots on the offspring of a liver Dalmatian and a black Dalmatian with a recessive liver allele. Display your prediction on a poster.

139

WHY IS THIS LOBSTER BLUE?

What does DNA do?

American lobsters are usually dark green in color. But, most people see only red lobsters. Lobsters turn red after they have been cooked. The chance of finding a blue lobster is about one in a million.

Infer **Why might a lobster have a blue shell?**

_____

_____

_____

_____

_____

_____

_____

_____

> **UNTAMED SCIENCE** Watch the **Untamed Science** video to learn more about DNA.

DNA: The Code of Life

5 Getting Started

Check Your Understanding

1. Background Read the paragraph below and then answer the question.

Leo's sister likes to joke that Leo inherited his dad's **genes** for playing the piano. Leo knows that **heredity** may not be that simple. But there are other **traits** —like the widow's peak on his forehead—that he did inherit from his father.

> A segment of DNA on a chromosome that codes for a specific trait is a **gene**.
>
> **Heredity** is the passing of traits from parent to offspring.
>
> A **trait** is a characteristic that an organism can pass on through its genes.

- Why couldn't Leo inherit his dad's piano skills?

_____

_____

▶ MY READING WEB If you had trouble completing the question above, visit **My Reading Web** and type in *DNA: The Code of Life.*

Vocabulary Skill

Latin Word Parts Some vocabulary in this chapter contains word parts with Latin origins. Look at the Latin words below, and the example derived from each word.

Latin Word	Meaning of Latin Word	Example
mutare	to change	mutation, *n.* any change in the DNA of a gene or chromosome
tumere	to swell	tumor, *n.* a mass of abnormal cells that develops when cells divide and grow uncontrollably

2. Quick Check The meaning of the Latin word *mutare* appears in the definition of *mutation.* Circle the word in both places that it appears in the table above.

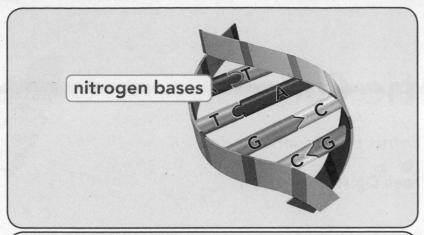

nitrogen bases

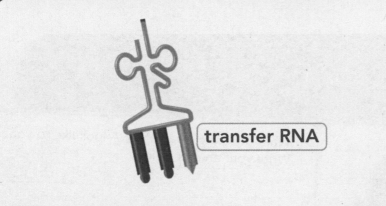

transfer RNA

mutation

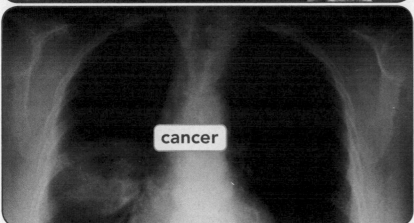

cancer

Chapter Preview

LESSON 1
- nitrogen bases
- DNA replication
- ↻ **Identify the Main Idea**
- △ **Infer**

LESSON 2
- messenger RNA
- transfer RNA
- ↻ **Summarize**
- △ **Design Experiments**

LESSON 3
- mutation
- cancer
- tumor
- chemotherapy
- ↻ **Relate Cause and Effect**
- △ **Calculate**

LESSON 4
- sex chromosomes
- sex-linked gene
- carrier
- ↻ **Relate Cause and Effect**
- △ **Infer**

LESSON 5
- selective breeding
- inbreeding
- hybridization
- clone
- genetic engineering
- gene therapy
- ↻ **Ask Questions**
- △ **Draw Conclusions**

> **VOCAB FLASH CARDS** For extra help with vocabulary, visit **Vocab Flash Cards** and type in *DNA: The Code of Life.*

The Genetic Code

UNLOCK THE BIG ?

🔑 **What Forms the Genetic Code?**

🔑 **How Does DNA Copy Itself?**

MY PLANET DIARY   BIOGRAPHY

DNA Debut

In 1951, English scientist Rosalind Franklin discovered that DNA could exist in a dry form and a wet form. Franklin made an image of the wet form of DNA by exposing it to X-rays. The X-rays bounced off the atoms in the DNA to make the image. The image (see the background on the next journal page) was so clear that it helped scientists understand the structure of DNA for the first time. Her discovery was important for figuring out how genetic information is passed from parent to offspring. Franklin's contribution to science was not only in her research, but also in that she succeeded at a time when many people thought women shouldn't be scientists.

▷ PLANET DIARY Go to **Planet Diary** to learn more about the genetic code.

What does the X-ray of DNA look like to you? Write your answer below.

_____

_____

_____

_____

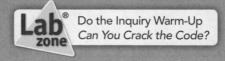

Lab® zone

Do the Inquiry Warm-Up *Can You Crack the Code?*

Vocabulary
- nitrogen bases
- DNA replication

Skills
- ↻ Reading: Identify the Main Idea
- △ Inquiry: Infer

What Forms the Genetic Code?

It took almost 100 years after the discovery of DNA for scientists to figure out that it looks like a twisted ladder. When James Watson and Francis Crick published the structure of DNA in 1953, they added another clue to how traits are passed from parent to offspring. DNA contains the genetic information for cells to make proteins. Proteins determine a variety of traits, from hair color to an organism's ability to digest food.

The Structure of DNA Parents pass traits to offspring through chromosomes. Chromosomes are made of DNA and proteins and are located in a cell's nucleus. Look at **Figure 1.** The twisted ladder structure of DNA is also known as a "double helix." The sides of the double helix are made up of sugar molecules called deoxyribose, alternating with phosphate molecules. The name DNA, or deoxyribonucleic acid (DEE ahk see ry boh noo klee ik), comes from this structure.

The rungs of DNA are made of nitrogen bases. **Nitrogen bases** are molecules that contain nitrogen and other elements. DNA has four kinds of nitrogen bases: adenine (AD uh neen), thymine (THY meen), guanine (GWAH neen), and cytosine (SY tuh seen). The capital letters *A, T, G,* and *C* are used to represent the bases.

FIGURE 1 ··················
> ART IN MOTION **Genetic Structures**
Hummingbirds, like all organisms, contain all of the genetic structures below.
✎ **Sequence** Put the structures in order from largest to smallest by writing the numbers two through five in the blank circles.

DNA

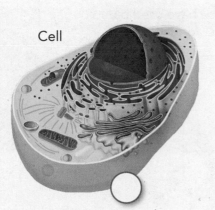

Cell

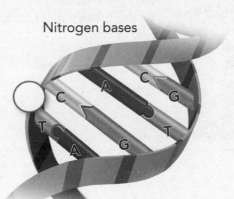

Nitrogen bases

Chromosome

✎

⟳ Identify the Main Idea
Underline the sentence that explains the role of genes in making proteins.

FIGURE 2 ••••••••••••••••••••••••
Chromosomes and Genes
Humans have between 20,000 and 25,000 genes on their chromosomes. The corals that make up ocean reefs are thought to have as many as 25,000 genes too!

Chromosomes, Genes, and DNA In **Figure 2,** you can see the relationship among chromosomes, genes, and DNA. A gene is a section of a DNA molecule that contains the information to code for one specific protein. A gene is made up of a series of bases in a row. The bases in a gene are arranged in a specific order—for example, ATGACGTAC. A single gene on a chromosome may contain anywhere from several hundred to a million or more of these bases. Each gene is located at a specific place on a chromosome.

Because there are so many possible combinations of bases and genes, each individual organism has a unique set of DNA. DNA can be found in all of the cells of your body except for red blood cells. DNA can be found in blood samples, however, because white blood cells do contain DNA.

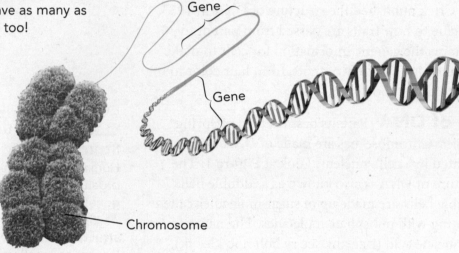

Gene

Gene

Chromosome

apply it!

Can you help solve the crime?

Someone robbed a jewelry store. The robber's DNA was extracted from skin cells found on the broken glass of a jewelry case. The police collected DNA samples from three suspects. The letters below represent the sequences of nitrogen bases in the DNA. Based on the DNA found at the crime scene, circle the DNA of the guilty suspect.

Robber: GACCAGTTAGCTAAGTCT

Suspect 1: TAGCTGA

Suspect 2: GACGAGT

Suspect 3: CTAAGTC

❶ **Explain** Why can you solve crimes using DNA?

_____

_____

_____

❷ **Infer** Could the police have used blood on the broken glass to test for DNA? Why or why not?

_____

_____

_____

Order of the Bases

A gene contains the code that determines the structure of a protein. 🔑 **The order of the nitrogen bases along a gene forms a genetic code that specifies what type of protein will be produced.** Remember that proteins are long-chain molecules made of individual amino acids. In the genetic code, a group of three DNA bases codes for one specific amino acid. For example, the three-base sequence CGT (cytosine-guanine-thymine) always codes for the amino acid alanine. The order of the three-base code units determines the order in which amino acids are put together to form a protein.

did you know?

If you took all the DNA from the cells in the average adult human body and stretched it out, it would reach to the sun and back again multiple times!

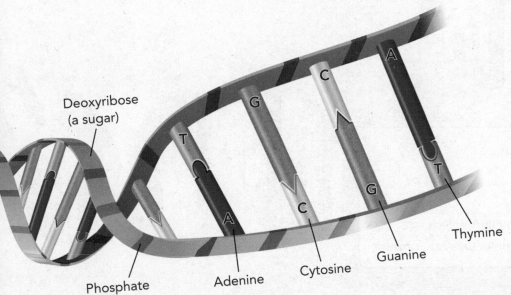

Deoxyribose (a sugar)

Phosphate

Adenine

Cytosine

Guanine

Thymine

FIGURE 3 ·····················

DNA Bases

Notice the pattern in the DNA bases.

✎ **Interpret Diagrams**
Which base always pairs with cytosine?

_____

_____

Lab zone® Do the Lab Investigation
Guilty or Innocent?

🔑 Assess Your Understanding

1a. Identify These letters represent the nitrogen bases on one strand of DNA: GGCTATCCA. What letters would form the other strand of the helix?

_____

_____

b. Explain How can a parent pass a trait such as eye color to its offspring?

_____

_____

_____

got it?

◯ **I get it!** Now I know that the genetic code of nitrogen bases specifies _____

_____

_____

◯ **I need extra help with** _____

Go to **MY SCIENCE** ⓢ **COACH** *online for help with this subject.*

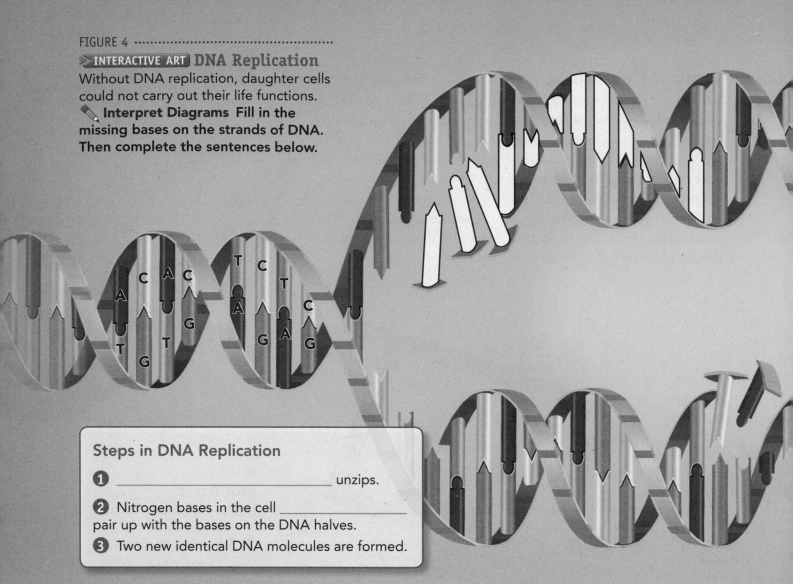

FIGURE 4

> INTERACTIVE ART) DNA Replication

Without DNA replication, daughter cells could not carry out their life functions.

✎ **Interpret Diagrams** Fill in the missing bases on the strands of DNA. Then complete the sentences below.

Steps in DNA Replication

❶ _____ unzips.

❷ Nitrogen bases in the cell _____ pair up with the bases on the DNA halves.

❸ Two new identical DNA molecules are formed.

How Does DNA Copy Itself?

Two new cells, or daughter cells, result when a cell divides. To ensure that each daughter cell has the genetic information it needs to carry out its activities, DNA copies itself. **DNA replication** is the process in which an identical copy of a DNA strand is formed for a new cell. Replication is very important, since daughter cells need a complete set of DNA to survive.

DNA replication begins when the two sides of a DNA molecule unwind and separate, like a zipper unzipping, between the nitrogen bases. Next, nitrogen bases in the nucleus pair up with the bases on each half of the DNA. 🗝 **Because of the way the nitrogen bases pair up, the order of the bases in each new DNA strand exactly matches the order in the original DNA strand.** This pattern is key to understanding how DNA replication occurs. Adenine always pairs with thymine, while guanine always pairs with cytosine. At the end of replication, two identical DNA molecules are formed.

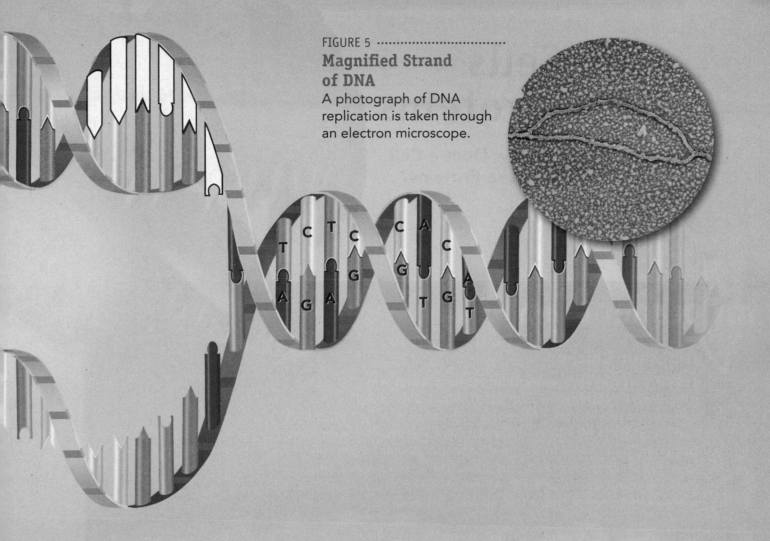

FIGURE 5 ·····················
Magnified Strand of DNA
A photograph of DNA replication is taken through an electron microscope.

Lab zone® Do the Quick Lab *Modeling the Genetic Code.*

🔑 **Assess Your Understanding**

2a. Review The (nitrogen base pattern/ number of genes/size of DNA) determines how DNA is replicated.

b. Describe Where in the cell does DNA replication take place?

_____

_____

_____

c. CHALLENGE What do you think would happen if the DNA code in a daughter cell did not match the code in the parent cell?

_____

_____

_____

_____

_____

got it? ···

○ **I get it!** Now I know that DNA replication is the process in which_____

○ **I need extra help with** _____

Go to MY SCIENCE ⓢ COACH online for help with this subject.

How Cells Make Proteins

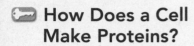 **How Does a Cell Make Proteins?**

my planeT DiaRY

DISCOVERY

Dinosaur Chicken?

In 2007, a 68-million-year-old dinosaur protein was discovered by Harvard scientists. The protein, called *collagen,* was extracted from the soft tissue of a *Tyrannosaurus rex* that died in Montana. Collagen is an important component of bone. The protein from the dinosaur is similar to protein found in modern-day chickens, supporting the connection between dinosaurs and birds. With this discovery, scientists have more evidence that these two species are related.

Communicate Discuss the question with a group of classmates. Write your answer below.

What other information about the two species would you want to

compare? _____

_____

▶ PLANET DIARY Go to **Planet Diary** to learn more about how cells make proteins.

 Do the Inquiry Warm-Up *What Is RNA?*

How Does a Cell Make Proteins?

The production of proteins in a cell is called protein synthesis. **During protein synthesis, the cell uses information from a gene on a chromosome to produce a specific protein.** Proteins help determine the size, shape, color, and other traits of an organism by triggering cellular processes. The protein code passes from parent to offspring through DNA, resulting in inherited traits.

Vocabulary
messenger RNA
transfer RNA

Skills
↻ Reading: Summarize
△ Inquiry: Design Experiments

The Structure of Proteins Proteins are made up of molecules called amino acids, as shown in **Figure 1.** Although there are only 20 amino acids, cells can combine them in different ways to form thousands of different proteins. You can think of the 20 amino acids as being like the 26 letters of the alphabet. Those 26 letters can form thousands of words. The letters you use and their order determine the words you form. A change in just one letter, for example, from *rice* to *mice*, creates a new word. Similarly, a change in the type or order of amino acids can result in a different protein.

The Role of RNA Protein synthesis takes place in the cytoplasm outside the cell's nucleus. The chromosomes are found inside the nucleus, so a messenger must carry the genetic code from the DNA inside the nucleus to the cytoplasm. This genetic messenger is called RNA, or ribonucleic acid (ry boh noo KLEE ik).

Although both RNA and DNA are nucleic acids, they have some differences. RNA has only one strand and contains a different sugar molecule than DNA. Another difference is in the nitrogen bases. Like DNA, RNA contains adenine, guanine, and cytosine. However, instead of thymine, RNA contains uracil (YOOR uh sil).

Types of RNA Two types of RNA take part in protein synthesis. **Messenger RNA** (mRNA) copies the message from DNA in the nucleus and carries the message to the ribosome in the cytoplasm. **Transfer RNA** (tRNA) carries amino acids to the ribosome and adds them to the growing protein.

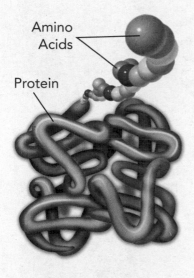

Amino Acids

Protein

FIGURE 1 ·······················
Proteins
Proteins help determine what you look like.
✎ **Interpret Diagrams**
Complete the sentence.
Proteins are made of folded and bundled chains of

_____

_____

apply it!

RNA

DNA

While working in the lab, your assistant accidentally mixes one beaker of DNA into a beaker containing RNA. You need to separate the molecules before doing your experiments.

△**Design Experiments** How could you test each molecule to determine if it was DNA or RNA? _____

_____

_____

_____

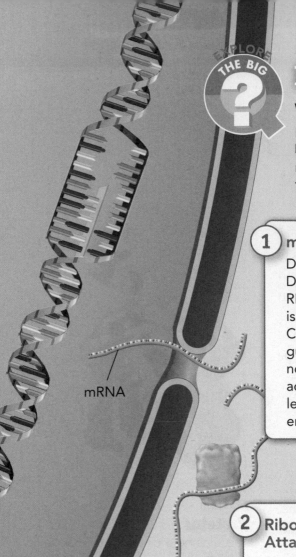

Protein Synthesis

What does DNA do?

EXPLORE THE BIG ?

FIGURE 2 ···
> INTERACTIVE ART The steps of protein synthesis are shown in the numbered boxes. Notice that the bases in the steps align with the bases in the summary chart on the far right.

1 mRNA Enters the Cytoplasm

DNA unzips between its base pairs. Then one of the strands of DNA directs the production of a strand of mRNA. To form the RNA strand, RNA bases pair up with the DNA bases. The process is similar to DNA replication. Cytosine always pairs with guanine. However, uracil, not thymine, pairs with adenine. The mRNA leaves the nucleus and enters the cytoplasm.

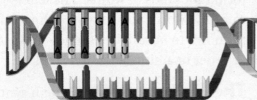

2 Ribosomes Attach to mRNA

A ribosome attaches to mRNA in the cytoplasm. On the ribosome, the mRNA provides the code for the protein that will be made. In the cytoplasm, specific amino acids are attached to specific molecules of tRNA.

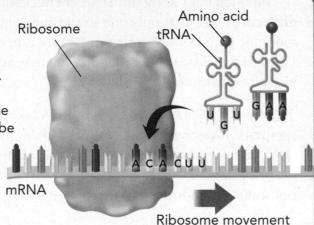

Ribosome

Amino acid

tRNA

mRNA

Ribosome movement

3 tRNA Attaches to mRNA

Molecules of tRNA and their amino acids attach to the mRNA. The bases on tRNA "read" the message and pair with bases on mRNA.

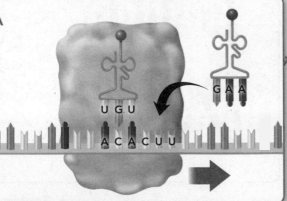

mRNA

Nucleus

4 Amino Acids Join in the Ribosome

Transfer molecules attach one at a time to the ribosome and continue to read the message. The amino acids are linked together and form a growing chain. The order of the amino acids is determined by the order of the three-base codes on the mRNA.

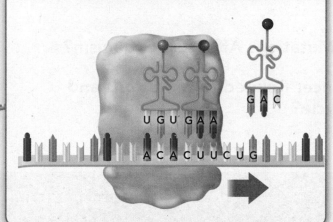

✏️ **Summarize** The chart below summarizes protein synthesis. Read the chart and fill in the blank labels.

DNA

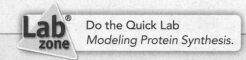

Protein

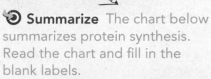

5 Protein Chain Forms

As the ribosome continues to move along the mRNA adding amino acids, the protein grows. Once an amino acid is added, the tRNA is released and picks up another amino acid of the same kind. The protein continues to grow until the ribosome reaches a three-base code that signals it to stop. The protein is then released.

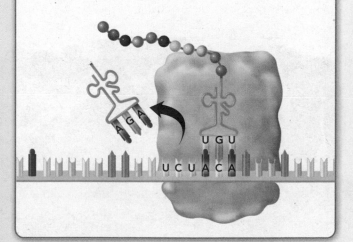

Lab ® zone
Do the Quick Lab
Modeling Protein Synthesis.

🔑 Assess Your Understanding

1a. Review (Messenger RNA/Transfer RNA) carries the genetic information in DNA from the nucleus to the cytoplasm.

b. 🅰 **ANSWER THE BIG Q** What does DNA do?

_____

_____

_____

_____

got it? ....

⭕ **I get it!** I now know that protein

synthesis is the process in which _____

_____

_____

⭕ **I need extra help with** _____

_____

Go to **MY SCIENCE ⓢ COACH** *online for help with this subject.*

Mutations

UNLOCK THE BIG ?

🔑 **How Can Mutations Affect an Organism?**

🔑 **How Is Cancer Related to Mutations and the Cell Cycle?**

my planet diary

Dairy DNA

Every mammal, from mice to monkeys to whales, drinks milk as a baby. But humans are the only mammals that can digest milk and other dairy products throughout their lifetime. Humans have a mutation (a change in DNA) that allows their bodies to break down lactose, a sugar in dairy products. However, not all people can digest dairy products. Many people are lactose intolerant, meaning their bodies cannot break down lactose. Lactose-intolerant people have the original DNA without the mutation. While many other mutations are considered harmful, this mutation is helpful to humans. And just think—ice cream might never have been invented if humans couldn't break down lactose!

MISCONCEPTION

Communicate Discuss these questions with a group of classmates. Write your answers below.

1. Do you think lactose intolerance is a serious condition? Explain.

_____

_____

2. Do you think people with this condition can *never* have milk?

_____

_____

_____

▷ **PLANET DIARY** Go to **Planet Diary** to learn more about mutations.

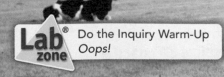

Lab zone® Do the Inquiry Warm-Up *Oops!*

Vocabulary
- mutation • cancer • tumor
- chemotherapy

Skills
↻ Reading: Relate Cause and Effect
△ Inquiry: Calculate

How Can Mutations Affect an Organism?

Some traits are not inherited from parent organisms. Traits can also be a result of a change in DNA. A **mutation** is any change in the DNA of a gene or chromosome. For example, instead of the base sequence AAG, the DNA might have the sequence ACG. **Mutations can cause a cell to produce an incorrect protein during protein synthesis. As a result, the organism's trait may be different from what it normally would be.**

If a mutation occurs in a body cell, such as a skin cell, the mutation will not be passed on to the organism's offspring. But if a mutation occurs in a sex cell (egg or sperm), the mutation can be passed on to an offspring and affect the offspring's traits.

Types of Mutations Some mutations are the result of small changes in an organism's DNA. For example, a base pair may be added, a base pair may be substituted for another, or one or more bases may be deleted from a section of DNA. These types of mutations can occur during the DNA replication process. Other mutations may occur when chromosomes don't separate correctly during the formation of sex cells. When this type of mutation occurs, a cell can end up with too many or too few chromosomes. The cell can also end up with extra segments of chromosomes.

Vocabulary Latin Word Origins *Mutation* comes from the Latin word *mutare*, meaning "to change." How can mutations change an organism's traits?

_____

_____

_____

FIGURE 1 ·······················

Mutations
The types of mutations of DNA include deletion, addition, and substitution.
✎ **Interpret Diagrams** Circle the added base pair on the third piece of DNA. Fill in the nitrogen bases on the fourth piece of DNA to illustrate a substitution.

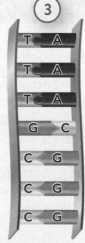

Original DNA sequence

One base pair is removed (deletion).

One base pair is added (addition).

One base pair is switched for another (substitution).

155

Effects of Mutations Mutations introduce changes in an organism. Mutations can be harmful, helpful, or neither harmful nor helpful. A mutation is harmful if it reduces the organism's chances for survival and reproduction.

Whether a mutation is harmful or not depends partly on the organism's environment. The mutation that led to this alligator's white color would probably be harmful to it in the wild. A white alligator is more visible to its prey. This alligator may find it difficult to catch prey and may not get enough food to survive. A white alligator in a zoo has the same chance for survival as a green alligator because it does not hunt. In a zoo, the mutation neither helps nor harms the alligator.

Helpful mutations increase an organism's ability to survive and reproduce. Mutations have allowed some bacteria that are harmful to humans to become resistant to drugs. The drugs do not kill the bacteria with the mutations, so they continue to survive and reproduce.

FIGURE 2 ···

✎ Review Check the phrase that best completes the sentence.

▶ VIRTUAL LAB **Alligator Mutation**
A white alligator does not blend into its natural habitat, but this color change may be a beneficial mutation for an organism if it

- ⬤ reduces its chances for survival.
- ⬤ increases its chances for survival.
- ⬤ decreases its chances for reproduction.

🔑 Assess Your Understanding

1a. Explain Mutations that occur in body cells (can/cannot) be passed on to offspring. Mutations that occur in sex cells (can/cannot) be passed on to offspring.

b. Apply Concepts Drug resistance in bacteria is a beneficial mutation for the bacteria, but how can it be harmful for humans?

_____

_____

_____

_____

Labzone® Do the Quick Lab *Effects of Mutations.*

got it?

- ◯ **I get it!** Now I know that mutations affect an organism's traits by_____

_____

- ◯ **I need extra help with** _____

_____

Go to MY SCIENCE ⬤ˢ COACH *online for help with this subject.*

How Is Cancer Related to Mutations and the Cell Cycle?

Did you know cancer is not just one disease? There are more than 100 types of cancer, and they can occur in almost any part of the body. Cancer affects many people around the world, regardless of age, race, or gender. Cancers are often named for the place in the body where they begin. For example, lung cancer begins in lung tissues, as shown in **Figure 3**.

What Is Cancer?   **Cancer** is a disease in which cells grow and divide uncontrollably, damaging the parts of the body around them. Cancer cells are like weeds in a garden. Weeds can overrun a garden by robbing plants of the space, sunlight, and water they need. Similarly, cancer cells can overrun normal cells.

Different factors work together in determining if a person gets cancer. Because of their inherited traits, some people are more likely than others to develop certain cancers. A woman with a mother or grandmother who had breast cancer has an increased chance of developing breast cancer herself. Some substances in the environment may also lead to cancer, like the tar in cigarettes or ultraviolet light from the sun or tanning beds. People who have a high-fat diet may also be more likely to develop cancer.

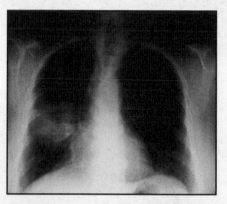

FIGURE 3 ·····························
Lung Tumor X-Ray
Tumors can be visible in X-rays.
✎ **Interpret Photos** Circle the tumor in the X-ray above.

do the math!

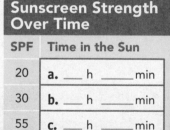

You may have noticed labels like SPF 15 on your sunscreen. *SPF* stands for "sun protection factor," and the number lets you know how long the sunscreen works. For example, a person who burns in the sun after 10 minutes could use sunscreen with an SPF of 15 and stay in the sun for as long as 150 minutes (10 × 15 = 150). This time can vary greatly and sunscreen should be reapplied often to prevent damaging sunburns.

Sunscreen Strength Over Time		
SPF	**Time in the Sun**	
20	**a.** ___ h	_____min
30	**b.** ___ h	_____min
55	**c.** ___ h	_____min

❶ Fill in the table with the length of time for sun protection each SPF rating offers for someone who burns in 10 minutes without sunscreen.

❷ ◢**Calculate** At the beach, you put on SPF 25 at 8:00 A.M. and your friend puts on SPF 15 at 9:00 A.M. You both would burn in 10 minutes without sunscreen. Who should reapply their sunscreen first? When?

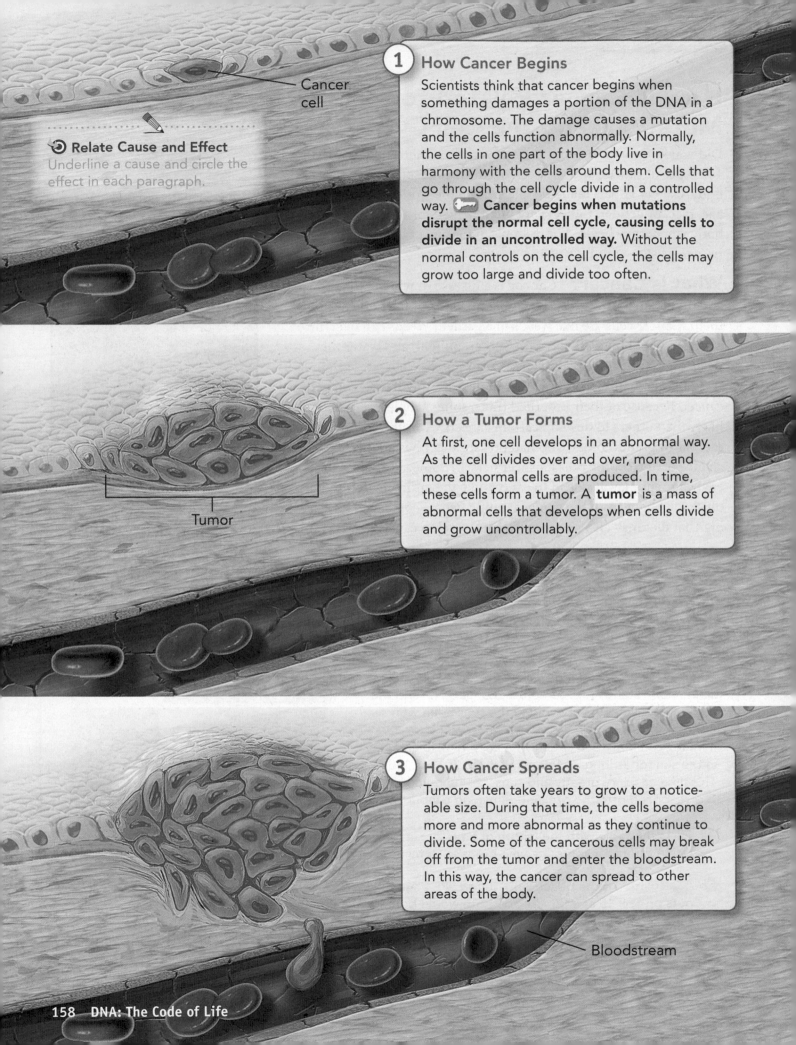

Cancer cell

✏️ **Relate Cause and Effect**
Underline a cause and circle the effect in each paragraph.

1 How Cancer Begins

Scientists think that cancer begins when something damages a portion of the DNA in a chromosome. The damage causes a mutation and the cells function abnormally. Normally, the cells in one part of the body live in harmony with the cells around them. Cells that go through the cell cycle divide in a controlled way. 🔑 **Cancer begins when mutations disrupt the normal cell cycle, causing cells to divide in an uncontrolled way.** Without the normal controls on the cell cycle, the cells may grow too large and divide too often.

Tumor

2 How a Tumor Forms

At first, one cell develops in an abnormal way. As the cell divides over and over, more and more abnormal cells are produced. In time, these cells form a tumor. A **tumor** is a mass of abnormal cells that develops when cells divide and grow uncontrollably.

3 How Cancer Spreads

Tumors often take years to grow to a noticeable size. During that time, the cells become more and more abnormal as they continue to divide. Some of the cancerous cells may break off from the tumor and enter the bloodstream. In this way, the cancer can spread to other areas of the body.

Bloodstream

How Cancer Is Treated

People with cancer can undergo a variety of treatments. Treatments include surgery, radiation, and drugs that destroy the cancer cells.

When cancer is detected before it has spread to other parts of the body, surgery is usually the best treatment. If doctors can completely remove a cancerous tumor, the person may be cured. If the cancer cells have spread or the tumor cannot be removed, doctors may use radiation. Radiation treatment uses beams of high-energy waves. The beams are more likely to destroy the fast-growing cancer cells than normal cells.

Chemotherapy is another treatment option. **Chemotherapy** is the use of drugs to treat a disease. Cancer-fighting drugs are carried throughout the body by the bloodstream. The drugs can kill cancer cells or slow their growth. Many of these drugs, however, destroy some normal cells as well, producing nausea and other side effects patients often experience with chemotherapy treatments.

Scientists are continuing to look for new ways to treat cancer. If scientists can better understand how the cell cycle is controlled, they may find ways to stop cancer cells from multiplying.

apply it!

Drugs are one cancer treatment option.

1 If you were a cancer researcher working on a cure, would you want to design a chemotherapy drug that would speed up the cell cycle or slow it down? Why?

_____

_____

_____

_____

2 [CHALLENGE] Based on what you have learned about cancer and chemotherapy, explain why you think cancer patients who are treated with chemotherapy drugs can lose their hair.

_____

_____

_____

_____

_____

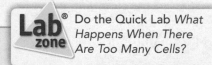 **Lab zone**® Do the Quick Lab *What Happens When There Are Too Many Cells?*

🔑 Assess Your Understanding

2a. List What are the options for treating cancer?

_____

_____

b. Draw Conclusions Based on the fact that people can get cancer regardless of their genetics, what are some things you can do to lower your risk of getting cancer?

_____

_____

_____

_____

got it?

○ **I get it!** Now I know that cancer is related to mutations and the cell cycle because _____

_____

_____

_____

○ **I need extra help with** _____

_____

_____

Go to **MY SCIENCE** Ⓢ **COACH** *online for help with this subject.*

🔑 **What Are Some Patterns of Human Inheritance?**

🔑 **What Are the Functions of the Sex Chromosomes?**

my planet diary

BLOG

Posted by: Hannah

Location: Old Tappan, New Jersey

I have many traits and characteristics that my parents have passed down to me. I have brown hair, like my mom's, but it's curly, like my dad's. I also have my dad's dark brown eyes, while my mom has blue. Both my parents have fair skin tone, but I have an olive complexion like my grandfather. I'm an interesting mix of all my relatives.

Write your answer below.

What characteristics do you have that resemble those of your relatives?

_____

_____

_____

_____

_____

▶ PLANET DIARY Go to **Planet Diary** to learn more about human inheritance.

 Do the Inquiry Warm-Up *How Tall Is Tall?*

What Are Some Patterns of Human Inheritance?

Look at the other students in your classroom. Some people have curly hair; others have straight hair. Some people are tall, some are short, and many others are in between. You'll probably see eyes of many different colors, ranging from pale blue to dark brown. The different traits you see are determined by a variety of inheritance patterns. 🔑 **Some human traits are controlled by single genes with two alleles, and others by single genes with multiple alleles. Still other traits are controlled by many genes that act together.**

Vocabulary
- sex chromosomes • sex-linked gene • carrier

Skills
- Reading: Relate Cause and Effect
- Inquiry: Infer

Single Genes With Two Alleles A number of human traits, such as a dimpled chin or a widow's peak, are controlled by a single gene with either a dominant or a recessive allele. These traits have two distinctly different physical appearances, or phenotypes.

Single Genes With Multiple Alleles Some human traits are controlled by a single gene that has more than two alleles. Such a gene is said to have multiple alleles—three or more forms of a gene that code for a single trait. Even though a gene may have multiple alleles, a person can carry only two of those alleles. This is because chromosomes exist in pairs. Each chromosome in a pair carries only one allele for each gene. Recall that an organism's genetic makeup is its genotype. The physical characteristics that result are called the organism's phenotype.

Human blood type is controlled by a gene with multiple alleles. There are four main blood types—A, B, AB, and O. Three alleles control the inheritance of blood types. The allele for blood type A is written as I^A. The allele for blood type B is written as I^B. The allele for blood type A and the allele for blood type B are codominant. This means that both alleles for the gene are expressed equally. A person who inherits an I^A allele from one parent and an I^B allele from the other parent will have type AB blood. The allele for blood type O—written as i—is recessive. **Figure 1** shows the different allele combinations that result in each blood type.

FIGURE 1 ·····
Inheritance of Blood Type
The table below shows which combinations of alleles result in each human blood type.

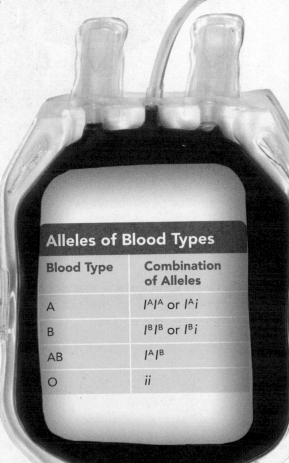

Alleles of Blood Types	
Blood Type	**Combination of Alleles**
A	$I^A I^A$ or $I^A i$
B	$I^B I^B$ or $I^B i$
AB	$I^A I^B$
O	ii

Use what you have learned about blood types and **Figure 1** to answer the following questions.

❶ **Interpret Tables** Genotypes are listed in the (left/right) column of the table, while phenotypes are on the (left/right).

❷ ⚠ **Infer** Why are there more genotypes than phenotypes for blood types?

_____

_____

_____

_____

250 cm

225 cm

200 cm

175 cm

150 cm

125 cm

100 cm

75 cm

50 cm

25 cm

0 cm

Traits Controlled by Many Genes

If you look around your classroom, you'll see that height in humans has more than two distinct phenotypes. In fact, there is an enormous variety of phenotypes for height. Some human traits show a large number of phenotypes because the traits are controlled by many genes. The alleles of the different genes act together as a group to produce a single trait. At least four genes control height in humans. You can see the extreme range of heights in **Figure 2.** Skin color is another human trait that is controlled by many genes.

FIGURE 2 ···

Extreme Heights

Human heights are known to range from the tall Bao Xishun, at 236 cm, to the short He Pingping, at 76 cm.

✏ **On the scale, mark your height and the heights of Bao Xishun and He Pingping.**

1. **Calculate** How many times taller are you than He Pingping?

_____

2. **Predict** Do you think Bao Xishun's parents are also tall? Why?

_____

_____

Do the Quick Lab
The Eyes Have It.

☞ Assess Your Understanding

1a. Explain Why do some traits exhibit a large number of phenotypes?

_____

_____

b. Draw Conclusions Aaron has blood type O. Can either of his parents have blood type AB? Explain your answer.

_____

_____

_____

_____

_____

got it?

○ **I get it!** Now I know that some human traits

are controlled by _____

_____

_____

_____

○ **I need extra help with** _____

_____

_____

Go to MY SCIENCE ⓢ COACH *online for help with this subject.*

What Are the Functions of the Sex Chromosomes?

The body cells of humans contain 23 chromosome pairs, or 46 chromosomes. The **sex chromosomes** are one of the 23 pairs of chromosomes in each body cell. 🔑 **The sex chromosomes carry genes that determine a person's sex as being either male or female. They also carry genes that determine other traits.**

Girl or Boy? The sex chromosomes are the only chromosome pair that do not always match. Girls have two sex chromosomes that match. The two chromosomes are called X chromosomes. Boys have two sex chromosomes that do not match. They have an X chromosome and a Y chromosome. The Y chromosome is much smaller than the X chromosome. To show the size difference, the sex chromosomes in **Figure 3** have been stained and magnified.

Sex Chromosomes and Fertilization When egg cells and sperm cells form, what happens to the sex chromosomes? Since both of a female's sex chromosomes are X chromosomes, all eggs carry one X chromosome. Males, however, have two different sex chromosomes. Therefore, half of a male's sperm cells carry an X chromosome, while half carry a Y chromosome.

When a sperm cell with an X chromosome fertilizes an egg, the egg has two X chromosomes. The fertilized egg will develop into a girl. When a sperm with a Y chromosome fertilizes an egg, the egg has one X chromosome and one Y chromosome. The fertilized egg will develop into a boy.

X Chromosome

Y Chromosome

X Chromosomes

FIGURE 3 ·······················

Male or Female?

The father's chromosome determines the sex of his child.

✏️ **Using the genotypes given for the mother and father, complete the Punnett square to show their child's genotype and phenotype.**

1. **Calculate** What is the probability that the child will be a girl? A boy?

_____

_____

2. **Interpret Diagrams** What sex will the child be if a sperm with a Y chromosome fertilizes an egg? _____

Relate Cause and Effect
Underline the cause of
sex-linked traits in males and
circle the effect of the traits.

Sex-Linked Genes The genes for some human traits are
carried on the sex chromosomes. Genes found on the X and Y
chromosomes are often called **sex-linked genes** because their
alleles are passed from parent to child on a sex chromosome. Traits
controlled by sex-linked genes are called sex-linked traits. One
sex-linked trait is red-green colorblindness. A person with this trait
cannot see the difference between red and green. Normal vision is
dominant, while colorblindness is recessive.

FIGURE 4

> VIRTUAL LAB **X and Y Chromosomes**

The human X chromosome
is larger and carries more
genes than the human
Y chromosome.

Y Chromosome

Recall that a Y chromosome is smaller
than an X chromosome. Females have two
X chromosomes, but males have one
X chromosome and one Y chromosome.
These chromosomes have different genes.

X Chromosome

Most of the genes on the X chromosome
are not on the Y chromosome. So an
allele on an X chromosome may have no
corresponding allele on a Y chromosome.

Like other genes, sex-linked genes can have dominant and
recessive alleles. In females, a dominant allele on an X chromosome
will mask a recessive allele on the other X chromosome. But in
males, there is usually no matching allele on the Y chromosome to
mask the allele on the X chromosome. As a result, any allele on the
X chromosome—even a recessive allele—will produce the trait in
a male who inherits it. This means that males are more likely than
females to express a sex-linked trait that is controlled by a recessive
allele. Individuals with colorblindness may have difficulty seeing
the numbers in **Figure 5.** Test your vision below.

FIGURE 5

Colorblindness
Most colorblind individuals have
difficulty seeing red and green.

✎ **Communicate** Working with a
partner, look at the circles. Write the
number you see in the space below
each circle.

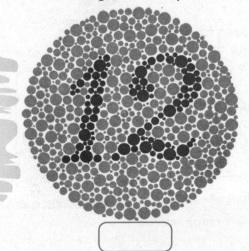

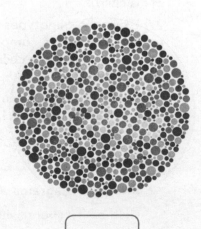

Inheritance of Colorblindness

Colorblindness is a trait controlled by a recessive allele on the X chromosome. Many more males than females have red-green colorblindness. You can understand why this is the case by examining the Punnett square in **Figure 6.** Both parents have normal color vision. Notice that the mother carries the dominant allele for normal vision (X^C) and the recessive allele for colorblindness (X^c). A **carrier** is a person who has one recessive allele for a trait and one dominant allele. A carrier of a trait controlled by a recessive allele does not express the trait. However, the carrier can pass the recessive allele on to his or her offspring. In the case of sex-linked traits, only females can be carriers because they are the only ones who can carry two alleles for the trait.

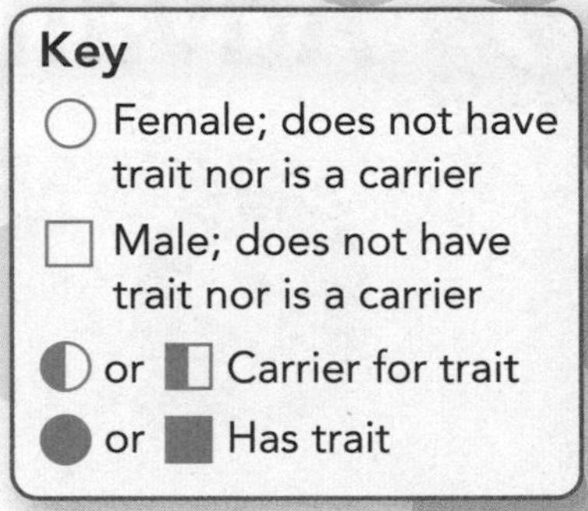

Key

- ○ Female; does not have trait nor is a carrier
- □ Male; does not have trait nor is a carrier
- ◐ or ◨ Carrier for trait
- ● or ■ Has trait

FIGURE 6 ·······························

Colorblindness Punnett Square

Red-green colorblindess is a sex-linked trait.

✎ **Using the parents' information and the key, complete the Punnett square.**

1. **Identify** Complete the Punnett square by filling in the child's genotype, sex, and phenotype. For each child, draw the correct shape, and color it in to match the key.

2. **Calculate** What is the probability that this couple will have a colorblind child?

_____

3. **Apply Concepts** What allele combination would a daughter need to inherit to be colorblind?

_____

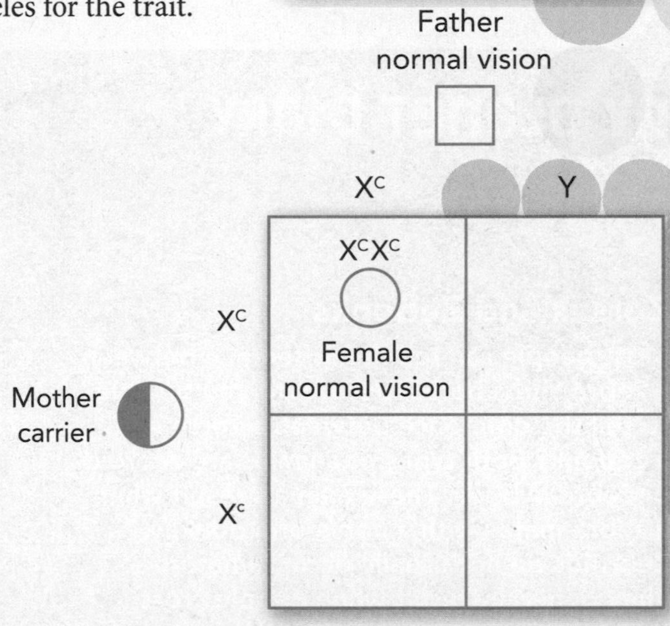

Father normal vision □

Mother carrier ◐

	X^C	Y
X^C	$X^C X^C$ ○ Female normal vision	
X^c		

Lab zone Do the Lab Investigation *How Are Genes on the Sex Chromosomes Inherited?*

🔑 Assess Your Understanding

2a. Review What is the sex of a person who is a carrier for colorblindness?_____

b. CHALLENGE Mary and her mother are both colorblind. Is Mary's father colorblind, too? How do you know?

_____
_____
_____
_____

got it?

○ **I get it!** Now I know that the functions of the sex chromosomes are _____
_____
_____

○ **I need extra help with** _____

Go to MY SCIENCE Ⓢ COACH *online for help with this subject.*

165

How Can Organisms Be Produced With Desired Traits?

my planet Diary

Zorses and Zedonks

Most people can tell the difference between a zebra and a horse. But would you be able to tell the difference between a zorse and a zedonk? Both types of animals are zebroids, or zebra hybrids. These animals result when a zebra mates with a horse or a donkey. Zebroids do not usually occur in nature. They generally result when people cross them on purpose. People may have first crossed zebras and horses in an effort to develop disease-resistant transportation animals for use in Africa. Zebras are resistant to African sleeping sickness. It was hoped that zorses, the offspring of zebras and horses, would have this resistance.

Communicate Discuss these questions with a classmate. Write your answers below.

1. Why may zebras and horses have been first crossed by people?

_____

_____

2. If zebras and horses do not usually mate in nature, should people intentionally cross them? Why or why not?

_____

_____

_____

_____

_____

> PLANET DIARY Go to **Planet Diary** to learn more about advances in genetics.

Lab zone Do the Inquiry Warm-Up *What Do Fingerprints Reveal?*

Vocabulary
- selective breeding • inbreeding • hybridization
- clone • genetic engineering • gene therapy

Skills
- Reading: Ask Questions
- Inquiry: Draw Conclusions

How Can Organisms Be Produced With Desired Traits?

Unless you are an identical twin, your DNA is different from everyone else's. Because of advances in genetics, DNA evidence can show many things, such as family relationships or the ability to produce organisms with desirable traits. **Selective breeding, cloning, and genetic engineering are three different methods for developing organisms with desired traits.**

Selective Breeding The process of selecting organisms with desired traits to be parents of the next generation is called **selective breeding.** Thousands of years ago, in what is now Mexico, the food that we call corn was developed in this way. Every year, farmers saved seeds from the healthiest plants that produced the best food. In the spring, they planted only those seeds. This process was repeated over and over. In time, farmers developed plants that produced better corn. People have used selective breeding with many types of plants and animals. Two techniques for selective breeding are inbreeding and hybridization.

Ask Questions Before you read this lesson, preview the red headings. In the graphic organizer below, ask a question for each heading. As you read, write answers to your questions.

Question	Answer
What is selective breeding?	Selective breeding is

Vocabulary High-Use Academic **Words** Use the word *resistant* to explain how hybridization can be useful.

_____

_____

_____

_____

_____

Inbreeding The technique of **inbreeding** involves crossing two individuals that have similar desirable characteristics. Suppose a male and a female golden retriever are both friendly and have the same coloring. Their offspring will probably also have those qualities. Inbreeding produces organisms that are genetically very similar. When inbred organisms are mated, the chance of their offspring inheriting two recessive alleles increases. This can lead to genetic disorders. For example, inherited hip problems are common in golden retrievers and other types of inbred dogs.

Hybridization In **hybridization** (hy brid ih ZAY shun), breeders cross two genetically different individuals. Recall that a hybrid organism has two different alleles for a trait. The hybrid organism that results is bred to have the best traits from both parents. For example, a farmer might cross corn that produces many kernels with corn that is resistant to disease. The farmer is hoping to produce a hybrid corn plant with both of the desired traits. Roses and other types of flowers are also commonly crossed.

apply it!

Since the late eighteenth century, gardeners and plant breeders have used hybridization to develop roses with certain characteristics.

1 Observe Look at each rose below. One characteristic for each flower is given to you. List any other observable characteristics you see.

2 ▲ Draw Conclusions Based on the characteristics of the two roses, draw with colored pencils or describe what you think the hybrid offspring will look like. Name the flower and list its characteristics.

Parent A

fragrant

_____

_____

Parent B

survives cold temperatures

_____

_____

Hybrid name:_____

_____

_____

_____

Year	Yield
1965	2.04
1970	2.38
1975	2.52
1980	2.75
1985	3.26
1990	3.53
1995	3.66
2000	3.89
2005	4.09

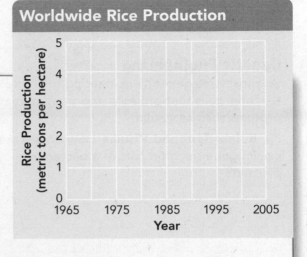

Worldwide Rice Production

Changing Rice Production

This data table shows how worldwide rice production changed between 1965 and 2005. New hybrid varieties of rice plants are one factor that has affected the amount of rice produced.

1 Graph Plot the data from the table and draw a line graph.

2 Interpret Data What is the approximate difference between rice production in 1965 and 2005? _____

3 **CHALLENGE** What other factors might help account for the difference in rice production between 1965 and 2005?

_____

_____

_____

Cloning

For some organisms, such as the dog shown in **Figure 1,** a technique called cloning can be used to produce offspring with desired traits. A **clone** is an organism that has exactly the same genes as the organism from which it was produced. It isn't hard to clone some kinds of plants such as African violets. Just cut a stem from one plant and put the stem in soil. Water it, and soon you will have a whole new plant. The new plant is genetically identical to the plant from which the stem was cut.

Genetic Engineering

Geneticists have developed another powerful technique for producing organisms with desired traits. In this process, called **genetic engineering,** genes from one organism are transferred into the DNA of another organism. Genetic engineering can produce medicines and improve food crops.

FIGURE 1 ....
Cloning
This puppy, Lancelot Encore, is thought to be the first commercially cloned puppy in the United States. His owners paid $150,000 to have him cloned in South Korea.

✏ **Make Judgments** Would you pay $150,000 to clone a pet? Why or why not?

_____

_____

FIGURE 2

Genetic Engineering

Scientists use genetic engineering to create bacterial cells that produce important human proteins such as insulin.

✏ **Relate Text and Visuals** How does a human insulin gene become part of a bacterium's plasmid?

_____

_____

_____

_____

_____

_____

_____

Genetic Engineering in Bacteria One type of bacterium is genetically engineered to produce a human protein called insulin. Many people with diabetes need insulin injections. Bacteria have a single DNA molecule in the cytoplasm. Some bacterial cells also contain small circular pieces of DNA called plasmids. You can see how scientists insert the DNA for the human insulin gene into the plasmid of a bacterium in **Figure 2.** Once the gene is inserted into the plasmid, the bacterial cell and all of its offspring will contain this human gene. As a result, the bacteria produce the protein that the human gene codes for—in this case, insulin. Because bacteria can reproduce quickly, large amounts of insulin can be produced in a short time.

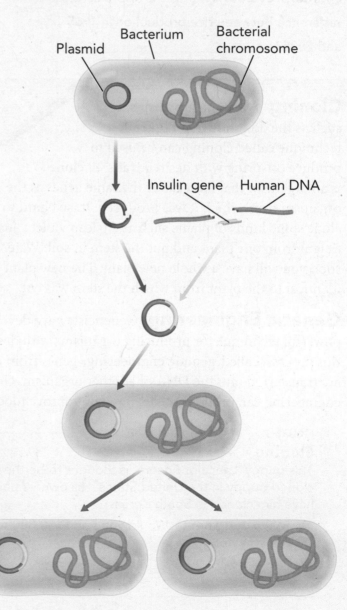

❶ Small rings of DNA, or plasmids, can be found in some bacterial cells.

❷ Scientists remove the plasmid. An enzyme cuts open the plasmid and removes the human insulin gene from its chromosome.

❸ The human insulin gene attaches to the open ends of the plasmid to form a closed ring.

❹ Some bacterial cells take up the plasmids that have the insulin gene.

❺ When the cells reproduce, the new cells will contain copies of the "engineered" plasmid. The foreign gene directs the cells to produce human insulin.

Genetic Engineering in Other Organisms

Scientists can also use genetic engineering techniques to insert genes into animals. For example, human genes can be inserted into the cells of cows. The cows then produce milk containing the human protein coded by the gene. Scientists have used this technique to produce the blood-clotting protein needed by people with hemophilia.

Genes have also been inserted into the cells of plants, such as tomatoes and rice. Some of the genes enable the plants to survive in cold temperatures or in poor soil. Other genetically engineered crops can resist insect pests or contain more nutrients.

Gene Therapy Someday it may be possible to use genetic engineering to correct some genetic disorders in humans. This process, called gene therapy, will involve inserting copies of a gene directly into a person's cells. For example, doctors may be able to treat hemophilia by replacing the defective allele on the X chromosome. The inserted gene would provide the body the correct instructions to clot blood normally.

Concerns About Genetic Engineering

Some people are concerned about the long-term effects of genetic engineering. For example, some people think that genetically engineered crops may not be entirely safe. People fear that these crops may harm the environment or cause health problems in humans. To address such concerns, scientists are studying the effects of genetic engineering.

FIGURE 3 ·······························
> ART IN MOTION Glow Cats
A fluorescent protein was added to the cells of the cat below. This protein allows the cat to glow red when exposed to ultraviolet light. The cat above lacks this protein.

Lab® zone Do the Quick Lab
Selective Breeding.

🗝 Assess Your Understanding

1a. Identify The technique of crossing two individuals with similar characteristics is (inbreeding/hybridization).

b. Explain Why are identical twins not clones according to the text definition?

_____

_____

c. Apply Concepts Lupita has a houseplant. Which method would be the best way of producing a similar plant for a friend? Explain your answer.

_____

_____

_____

_____

got it? ···

○ **I get it!** Now I know that the three ways of producing organisms with desired traits are

_____

_____

○ **I need extra help with** _____

_____

Go to MY SCIENCE COACH online for help with this subject.

Study Guide

DNA passes information to _____ which passes the information to _____, the source of amino acids that make up _____.

LESSON 1 The Genetic Code

🔑 The order of the nitrogen bases along a gene forms a genetic code that specifies what type of protein will be produced.

🔑 Because of the way the nitrogen bases pair up, the order of the bases in each new DNA strand exactly matches the order in the original DNA strand.

Vocabulary
• nitrogen bases
• DNA replication

LESSON 2 How Cells Make Proteins

🔑 During protein synthesis, the cell uses information from a gene on a chromosome to produce a specific protein.

Vocabulary
• messenger RNA
• transfer RNA

LESSON 3 Mutations

🔑 Mutations can cause a cell to produce an incorrect protein during protein synthesis. This may result in abnormal traits.

🔑 Cancer begins when mutations disrupt the normal cell cycle, causing cells to divide in an uncontrolled way.

Vocabulary
• mutation • cancer • tumor • chemotherapy

LESSON 4 Human Inheritance

🔑 Human traits may be controlled by single genes with two alleles, by single genes with multiple alleles, or by many genes that act together.

🔑 Sex chromosomes carry genes that determine whether a person is male or female as well as other traits.

Vocabulary
• sex chromosomes   • sex-linked gene
• carrier

LESSON 5 Advances in Genetics

🔑 Selective breeding, cloning, and genetic engineering are three methods for developing organisms with desired traits.

Vocabulary
• selective breeding
• inbreeding
• hybridization
• clone
• genetic engineering
• gene therapy

Review and Assessment

LESSON 1 The Genetic Code

1. DNA has four bases: A, C, G, and T. The base A always pairs with _____, and C always pairs with _____.

- **a.** A, C
- **b.** C, G
- **c.** C, T
- **d.** T, G

2. A _____ is a section of DNA within a chromosome that codes for a specific protein.

- **a.** double helix
- **b.** ribosome
- **c.** gene
- **d.** amino acid

3. Interpret Diagrams A DNA molecule is shaped like a double helix. Label the structures of the molecule. Draw in the missing bases and label each base with its code letter.

_____

_____

_____

_____

LESSON 2 How Cells Make Proteins

4. Proteins are made up of molecules called

- **a.** RNA.
- **b.** ribosomes.
- **c.** nitrogen bases.
- **d.** amino acids.

5. _____ carries the information from the genetic code out of the nucleus and into the cytoplasm.

LESSON 3 Mutations

6. A mass of cancer cells is called a

- **a.** tumor.
- **b.** chromosome.
- **c.** mutation.
- **d.** phenotype.

7. A mutation is a change in _____.

8. Interpret Diagrams Circle the mutation shown in the illustration below.

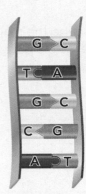 

Original DNA   After mutation

9. Relate Cause and Effect What is the relationship between the cell cycle and cancer?

_____

_____

_____

_____

10. Apply Concepts How can cancer spread from one part of the body to another?

_____

_____

_____

11. Infer Why does chemotherapy cause side effects such as nausea?

_____

_____

_____

5 Review and Assessment

LESSON 4 Human Inheritance

12. Which human trait is controlled by a single gene with multiple alleles?

    a. height   **b.** dimples

    c. skin color   **d.** blood type

13. Colorblindness is carried on the X chromosome and is more common in males than in females because it is a _____

_____

14. Compare and Contrast Describe the main differences between the inheritance patterns for a dimpled chin and for height.

_____

_____

_____

_____

_____

_____

_____

_____

LESSON 5 Advances in Genetics

15. An organism that has the same genes as the organism that produced it is called a

    a. clone.   **b.** hybrid.

    c. genome.   **d.** pedigree.

16. Inbreeding and hybridization are two different

types of _____

17. 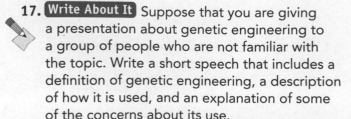 **Write About It** Suppose that you are giving a presentation about genetic engineering to a group of people who are not familiar with the topic. Write a short speech that includes a definition of genetic engineering, a description of how it is used, and an explanation of some of the concerns about its use.

 APPLY THE BIG Q

How can genetic information be used?

18. Genetic information can be applied in healthcare, agriculture, forensics, and many other fields. Using at least three vocabulary terms from this chapter, describe a situation in which genetic information such as this karyotype could have either a positive or negative impact on your daily life. Explain your reasoning.

_____

_____

_____

_____

_____

_____

_____

_____

_____

_____

_____

_____

Standardized Test Prep

Multiple Choice

Circle the letter of the best answer.

1. What determines a single inherited trait of an individual?

   A   one pair or many pairs of genes

   B   a disrupted cell cycle

   C   one half of the replicated DNA strand

   D   amino acids joined to form proteins

2. What is the main function of messenger RNA?

   A   It adds amino acids to a growing protein chain.

   B   It carries the information necessary for protein synthesis.

   C   It carries the information necessary for DNA replication.

   D   It carries information that causes deletions and other mutations.

3. What is the sequence of events that results in the growth of a tumor?

   A   cancer, mutation, disrupted cell cycle, tumor

   B   disrupted cell cycle, protein change, mutation, tumor

   C   mutation, disrupted cell cycle, cancer, tumor

   D   DNA, cancer, mutation, tumor

4. Which of the following is a selective breeding technique that can produce organisms more likely to survive in a given environment?

   A   mutation

   B   forensics

   C   inbreeding

   D   gene therapy

5. When DNA replicates, the genes in the new strand are _____ the original strand.

   A   similar to

   B   larger than

   C   different from

   D   identical to

Constructed Response

Use the diagram below and your knowledge of science to help you answer Question 6. Write your answer on a separate piece of paper.

6. The drawing below shows half of a DNA molecule. Write the letters of the bases that would form the other half. Then explain the relationship between DNA and your traits. What could happen if the base C were substituted for the first base T?

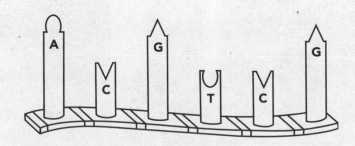

The Frozen ZOO

In addition to habitat loss, gorillas in Africa are threatened by the trade in bushmeat. Bushmeat is meat that comes from killing wild animals, such as gorillas. Catching people who sell gorilla meat is difficult because gorilla meat looks like other types of meat that are legal. Fortunately, researchers at the Frozen Zoo are developing genetic tools to catch people who sell gorilla meat.

The Frozen Zoo is a resource center that stores biological material to aid in the conservation of threatened and endangered animals. Researchers at the Frozen Zoo are building a database of genetic material from gorillas. They hope that this database will help conservation officers identify gorilla meat by using DNA barcoding. DNA barcoding is a method that uses a short DNA sequence, found in a cell's mitochondria, to identify an organism as belonging to a particular species.

Students at High Tech High in San Diego recently used DNA barcoding to identify samples of beef, ostrich meat, and turkey meat. Students in New York have also used this tool to identify the fish in their sushi. Now, researchers would like to teach this technique to conservation officers in Nigeria, where gorillas are severely threatened by the trade in bushmeat.

▲ Western Lowland Gorillas are one of the species that is most at risk from illegal hunting and the sale of bushmeat.

▼ Preserved DNA from many animals, including the Western Lowland Gorillas, is kept at the Frozen Zoo.

Research It Find out more about the Frozen Zoo. How do researchers use the biological material stored there? Create a concept map that shows the main ways that the Frozen Zoo aids in the conservation of threatened and endangered animals.

Fighting Cancer

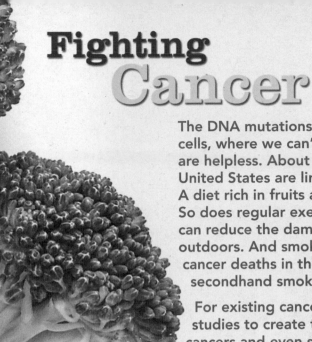

The DNA mutations that cause cancer happen deep inside cells, where we can't see them, but that doesn't mean we are helpless. About one third of all cancer deaths in the United States are linked to poor diet and lack of exercise. A diet rich in fruits and vegetables reduces your cancer risk. So does regular exercise. Sunscreen or protective clothing can reduce the damage to DNA caused by sunlight when outdoors. And smoking is the largest cause of preventable cancer deaths in the world—by avoiding smoking and secondhand smoke, you are doing your cells a favor!

For existing cancer cases, scientists are using DNA studies to create treatments for specific types of cancers and even specific individuals! Scientists are also developing drugs that repair the damaged DNA.

Write About It Create a poster explaining one thing your classmates can do to reduce their risk of cancer. Use facts and other appropriate information to persuade your classmates.

There's Something Fishy About This Sushi!

Do restaurant menus always tell the truth? High school students Kate Stoeckle and Louisa Strauss asked themselves this question while eating sushi in New York City. They decided to identify the fish in their sushi. Kate and Louisa gathered 60 fish samples from local restaurants and grocery stores. They sent the samples to a lab that used DNA barcoding to test the samples.

The tests showed that 25 percent of the samples were mislabeled! Often, inexpensive fish was labeled as more expensive fish. For example, a sample labeled "red snapper" was actually Atlantic cod. Another sample was from an endangered fish.

In the future, DNA barcoding could be done by using a handheld device. Such a device might look similar to a supermarket barcode scanner. Then, anyone could quickly solve a DNA mystery at the dinner table or beyond!

Research It Find out more about DNA barcoding. Identify a question you could answer by using this technology. Describe how you could use DNA barcoding to answer your question.

DOES THIS FISH HAVE LEGS?

How do life forms change over time?

This is not your average fish. Besides having bright red lips, the rosy-lipped batfish is a poor swimmer. Instead of using its pectoral fins for swimming, the batfish uses them to crawl along the seafloor.

△ Develop Hypotheses How do you think the batfish's leglike fins help it survive?

_____

_____

_____

_____

_____

_____

> UNTAMED SCIENCE Watch the **Untamed Science** video to learn more about adaptations.

Change Over Time

6 Getting Started

Check Your Understanding

1. **Background** Read the paragraph below and then answer the question.

Last fall, Jerome collected more than 100 seeds from a single sunflower in his garden. In the spring, he planted all the seeds. He was not surprised that the new plants all varied in many **traits.** Jerome knows that, because of **sexual reproduction,** each plant's **DNA** is different.

> A **trait** is a characteristic that an organism passes to offspring through its genes.
>
> **Sexual reproduction** results in offspring that are genetically different from each parent.
>
> **DNA** is genetic material that carries information about an organism and is passed from parent to offspring.

- How are the plants' different traits related to sexual reproduction?

_____

_____

> **▶ MY READING WEB** If you had trouble completing the question above, visit **My Reading Web** and type in *Change Over Time.*

Vocabulary Skill

Identify Multiple Meanings Familiar words may mean something else in science. Look at the different meanings of the words below.

Word	Everyday Meaning	Scientific Meaning
theory	*n.* a guess **Example:** Sue has a theory that soccer is harder to play than basketball.	*n.* a well-tested concept that explains a wide range of observations **Example:** The cell theory says that all organisms are made of cells.
adaptation	*n.* a change in an individual's behavior **Example:** Talia's adaptation to her new school was hard, but she did it.	*n.* a trait that helps an individual survive and reproduce **Example:** Fur is an adaptation to cold.

2. **Quick Check** Circle the sentence that uses the scientific meaning of the word *theory.*

- Evolutionary *theory* describes change over time.

- Do you have a *theory* about why Sarah is a vegetarian?

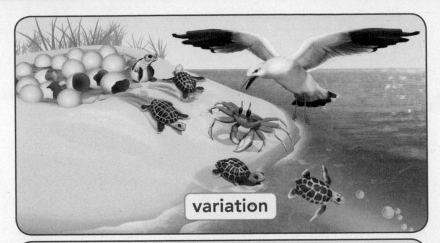

variation

Chapter Preview

LESSON 1
- species
- fossil
- adaptation
- evolution
- scientific theory
- natural selection
- variation
- ◎ Relate Cause and Effect
- △ Develop Hypotheses

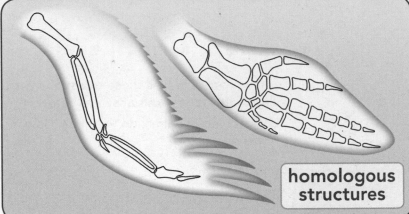

homologous structures

LESSON 2
- homologous structures
- ◎ Identify the Main Idea
- △ Communicate

LESSON 3
- gradualism
- punctuated equilibrium
- ◎ Compare and Contrast
- △ Make Models

> **VOCAB FLASH CARDS** For extra help with vocabulary, visit **Vocab Flash Cards** and type in *Change Over Time.*

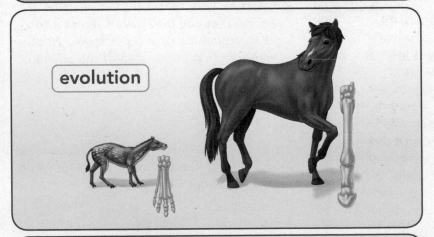

evolution

adaptation

UNLOCK
THE BIG
?

🔑 **What Was Darwin's Hypothesis?**

🔑 **What Is Natural Selection?**

my planet Diary

Charles Darwin

In 1839, Charles Darwin published his book *The Voyage of the Beagle*. Read the following excerpt about an animal Darwin encountered while in the Galápagos Islands.

The inhabitants believe that these animals are absolutely deaf; certainly they do not overhear a person walking close behind them. I was always amused when overtaking one of these great monsters, as it was quietly pacing along, to see how suddenly, the instant I passed, it would draw in its head and legs, and uttering a deep hiss fall to the ground with a heavy sound, as if struck dead. I frequently got on their backs, and then giving a few raps on the hinder part of their shells, they would rise up and walk away; — but I found it very difficult to keep my balance.

VOICES FROM HISTORY

Communicate Discuss these questions with a classmate. Write your answers below.

1. What kind of animal do you think Darwin was describing?

_____

_____

2. Describe your reaction to an unusual animal that you may have seen at a zoo, at an aquarium, or in a pet store. What was your first impression of the animal?

_____

_____

_____

▶ PLANET DIARY Go to **Planet Diary** for more information about Charles Darwin.

Lab zone® Do the Inquiry Warm-Up *How Do Living Things Vary?*

Vocabulary
- species
- fossil
- adaptation
- evolution
- scientific theory
- natural selection
- variation

Skills
- ➲ Reading: Relate Cause and Effect
- △ Inquiry: Develop Hypotheses

What Was Darwin's Hypothesis?

In 1831, the British ship HMS *Beagle* set sail from England on a five-year trip around the world. Charles Darwin was on board. Darwin was a naturalist—a person who observes and studies the natural world.

Diversity Darwin was amazed by the diversity of living things that he saw during the voyage. He wondered why they were so different from those in England. Darwin saw insects that looked like flowers. He also observed sloths, slow-moving animals that spent much of their time hanging in trees. Today, scientists know that organisms are even more diverse than Darwin thought. In fact, scientists have identified more than 1.6 million species of organisms on Earth. A **species** is a group of similar organisms that can mate with each other and produce fertile offspring. The exact number of species is unknown because many areas of Earth have not yet been studied.

Fossils Darwin saw fossils of animals that had died long ago. A **fossil** is the preserved remains or traces of an organism that lived in the past. Darwin was puzzled by some of the fossils he observed. For example, he saw fossils that resembled the bones of living sloths but were much larger in size. He wondered what had happened to the ancient, giant ground sloths. See **Figure 1**.

FIGURE 1 ·····················
Sloth Similarities
Darwin thought that the fossil bones of the giant ground sloths (left) resembled the bones of modern-day sloths (above).

✎ **Observe** List two similarities that you notice between the two sloths.

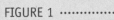

Similarities
_____
_____
_____
_____

did you know?

The Galápagos penguin is the northernmost penguin in the world! It lives on the equator and is kept cool by ocean currents. The Galápagos penguin is the rarest penguin species and is endangered.

Galápagos Organisms

The *Beagle* made many stops along the Atlantic and Pacific coasts of South America. From the Pacific coast, the ship traveled west to the Galápagos Islands. Darwin observed many unusual life forms there. He compared organisms from the Galápagos Islands to organisms that lived elsewhere. He also compared organisms living on the different islands.

Comparisons to South American Organisms Darwin discovered many similarities between Galápagos organisms and those found in South America. Many of the birds and plants on the islands resembled those on the mainland. However, he also noted important differences between the organisms. For instance, you can see differences between island and mainland iguanas in **Figure 2.**

Darwin became convinced that species do not always stay the same. Instead, he thought species could change and even produce new species over time. Darwin began to think that maybe the island species were somehow related to South American species. Perhaps, he thought, the island species had become different from their mainland relatives over time.

FIGURE 2 ·········

Comparing Iguanas

The iguanas on the Galápagos Islands have large claws that allow them to grip slippery rocks so they can feed on seaweed.

The iguanas on the mainland have smaller claws that allow them to climb trees so they can eat leaves.

✎ **Infer** The color of each iguana is an adaptation to its

○ food.   ○ habitat.

○ predators.   ○ climate.

Explain your answer.

_____

_____

_____

FIGURE 3 ··

> INTERACTIVE ART Galápagos Finches
The structure of each bird's beak is an adaptation
to the type of food the bird eats. Birds with long,
pointed, sharp beaks pick at cacti. Those with
short, thick beaks crush seeds.

Birds with narrow, pointed beaks grasp insects.
Those with short, hooked beaks tear open fruit.

✎ **Interpret Diagrams Look at the different
beak structures. Draw a line from each finch to
the type of food you think it eats.**

Comparisons Among the Islands Darwin also discovered
many differences among organisms on the different Galápagos
Islands. For example, the tortoises on one island had dome-shaped
shells. Those on another island had saddle-shaped shells. A government official in the islands told Darwin that he could tell which
island a tortoise came from just by looking at its shell.

Adaptations Birds were also different from one island to the
next. Look at **Figure 3.** When Darwin returned to England, he
learned that the different birds were all finches. Darwin
concluded that the finch species were all related to a single ancestor
species that came from the mainland. Over time, different finches
developed different beak shapes and sizes that were well suited to
the food that they ate. Beak shape is an example of an **adaptation,**
a trait that increases an organism's ability to survive and reproduce.

✎
**Vocabulary Identify Multiple
Meanings** Write a sentence
using the everyday meaning of
the word *adapt*.

_____

_____

_____

_____

_____

_____

Darwin's Hypothesis Darwin thought about what he had seen during his voyage on the *Beagle*. By this time, Darwin was convinced that organisms change over time. The process of change over time is called **evolution.** Darwin, however, wanted to know *how* organisms change. Over the next 20 years, he consulted with other scientists and gathered more information. Based on his observations, Darwin reasoned that plants or animals that arrived on the Galápagos Islands faced conditions that were different from those on the nearby mainland. 🔑 **Darwin hypothesized that species change over many generations and become better adapted to new conditions.**

Darwin's ideas are often referred to as a theory of evolution. A **scientific theory** is a well-tested concept that explains a wide range of observations. From the evidence he collected, Darwin concluded that organisms on the Galápagos Islands had changed over time.

Standard poodle   Labrador retriever   Labradoodle

apply it!

The first labradoodle dog was bred in 1989. A labradoodle is a cross between a standard poodle and a Labrador retriever. The poodle is very smart and has fur that sheds very little. The poodle may be less irritating for people allergic to dogs. Labradors are gentle, easily trained, and shed seasonally.

❶ Make Generalizations Why do you think people breed these two dogs together?

_____

_____

❷ Develop Hypotheses Would you expect the first labradoodle puppies to be the same as puppies produced several generations later? Explain.

_____

_____

Artificial Selection Darwin studied the offspring of domesticated animals that were produced by artificial selection in an effort to understand how evolution might occur. In artificial selection, only the organisms with a desired characteristic, such as color, are bred. Darwin himself had bred pigeons with large, fan-shaped tails. By repeatedly allowing only those pigeons with many tail feathers to mate, Darwin produced pigeons with two or three times the usual number of tail feathers. Darwin thought that a process similar to artificial selection might happen in nature. But he wondered what natural process selected certain traits.

FIGURE 4 ·······································

Artificial Selection

The pigeons that Darwin bred were all descended from the rock dove (left). Pigeons can be bred for characteristics such as color, beak shape, wingspan, and feather patterns.

✏ **Describe** If you were to breed an animal, what would it be and what traits would you want it to have?

_____
_____
_____

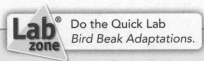
Do the Quick Lab
Bird Beak Adaptations.

🗝 Assess Your Understanding

1a. List Make a list of three observations that Darwin made during the *Beagle's* voyage.

_____
_____
_____

b. Describe An adaptation is a trait that increases an organism's ability to _____ and _____.

c. △Develop Hypotheses How does artificial selection support Darwin's hypothesis?

_____
_____
_____
_____
_____

got it? ·······································

○ **I get it!** Now I know that Darwin's hypothesis was _____ .

○ **I need extra help with** _____

Go to **MY SCIENCE** ⓢ **COACH** *online for help with this subject.*

What Is Natural Selection?

In 1858, Darwin and Alfred Russel Wallace, another British biologist, both proposed the same explanation for how evolution occurs. The next year, Darwin described his explanation in his book *The Origin of Species*. In this book, Darwin proposed that evolution occurs by means of natural selection. **Natural selection** is the process by which individuals that are better adapted to their environment are more likely to survive and reproduce more than other members of the same species. Darwin identified factors that affect the process of natural selection: overproduction, variation, and competition. **Figure 5** shows how natural selection might happen in a group of sea turtles.

Overproduction Darwin knew that most species produce far more offspring than can possibly survive. In many species, so many offspring are produced that there are not enough resources—food, water, and living space—for all of them.

Factors That Affect Natural Selection
How do life forms change over time?

FIGURE 5 ·······

> **REAL-WORLD INQUIRY** Overproduction, variation, and competition are factors that affect the process of natural selection.

✏ **Summarize** Examine the sequence below that shows how natural selection could affect a group of sea turtles over time. Label each factor in the illustration and write a brief caption explaining what is occurring.

Variation Members of a species differ from one another in many of their traits. Any difference between individuals of the same species is called a **variation.** For example, sea turtles may differ in color, size, the ability to swim quickly, and shell hardness.

Competition Since food, space, and other resources are limited, the members of a species must compete with one another to survive. Competition does not always involve physical fights between members of a species. Instead, competition is usually indirect. For example, some turtles may not find enough to eat. A slower turtle may be caught by a predator, while a faster turtle may escape. Only a few turtles will survive to reproduce.

Selection Darwin observed that some variations make individuals better adapted to their environment. Those individuals are more likely to survive and reproduce. Their offspring may inherit the helpful characteristic. The offspring, in turn, will be more likely to survive and reproduce, and pass the characteristic to their offspring. After many generations, more members of the species will have the helpful characteristic.

In effect, the environment selects organisms with helpful traits to become parents of the next generation. ⚷ **Darwin proposed that, over a long time, natural selection can lead to change. Helpful variations may accumulate in a species, while unfavorable ones may disappear.**

✎ **Relate Cause and Effect**
Fill in the graphic organizer to identify the factors that cause natural selection.

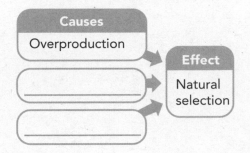

Causes
Overproduction

_____

_____

Effect
Natural selection

_____
_____
_____

Environmental Change A change in the environment can affect individuals, organisms with specific traits, or entire species. Changes that affect an organism's ability to survive, and therefore reproduce, lead to natural selection. For example, monkey flowers are plants that do not normally grow in soil that has a high concentration of copper. However, because of genetic variation, some varieties of monkey flower now grow near copper mines. In **Figure 6** you can see how natural selection might have resulted in monkey flowers that can grow in copper-contaminated soil.

Genes and Natural Selection Without variations, all the members of a species would have the same traits and the same chance of surviving and reproducing. But where do variations come from? How are they passed on from parents to offspring?

Darwin could not explain what caused variations or how they were passed on. As scientists later learned, variations can result from changes in genes and the shuffling of different forms of genes when egg and sperm join. Genes, such as those for hair color and height, are passed from parents to their offspring. Only traits that are inherited, or controlled by genes that are passed on to offspring, can be acted upon by natural selection.

do the math!

The typical clutch size, or number of eggs, a loggerhead sea turtle can lay at once is around 113. Even with producing so many offspring, the loggerhead sea turtle is endangered in many areas. Suppose that scientists counted the number of eggs laid at seven different nesting sites along the southeast coast of the United States. The following year, scientists check the nesting sites to see how many offspring survived and returned.

Loggerhead Sea Turtle Data							
Site	A	B	C	D	E	F	G
Clutch Size	114	103	121	118	107	103	104
Returning Turtles	45	35	55	53	40	66	38

❶ Calculate Determine the mean for the clutch sizes of the seven nesting sites in the table. _____ How does the mean compare to the typical clutch size for loggerheads? _____

_____

_____

❷ Interpret Data Do you think clutch size influences the survival rates of the offspring? Use the data to support your answer.

_____

_____

_____

_____

❸ CHALLENGE Hypothesize why Site F had the largest number of returning turtles.

_____

_____

_____

_____

Monkey flowers grow successfully in healthy, unpolluted soil.

Copper seeps into the soil around the copper mine. Most monkey flowers cannot grow in this polluted soil, and they begin to die.

Some monkey flowers have genetic variations that allow them to survive and reproduce in copper-contaminated soil.

FIGURE 6 ....

Environmental Change

When copper contaminated the soil surrounding the monkey flowers, the environment changed. Due to a genetic variation, some varieties of monkey flower are now able to survive in that soil.

✎ **Draw Conclusions** In the last circle, draw what you think the area will look like in ten years' time. Write a caption describing what has taken place.

Do the Lab Investigation
Nature at Work.

🔑 Assess Your Understanding

2a. Define A variation is any (similarity/difference) between individuals of the same species.

b. ANSWER THE BIG ❓ How do life forms change over time?

_____

_____

_____

c. 🔄 **Relate Cause and Effect** Explain how unfavorable traits can disappear in a species.

_____

_____

_____

_____

_____

got**it?** ....

○ **I get it!** Now I know that natural selection occurs _____

_____

○ **I need extra help with** _____

Go to **MY SCIENCE** 🔵 **COACH** online for help with this subject.

Evidence of Evolution

🔑 **What Evidence Supports Evolution?**

my pLaneT DiaRY

DISCOVERY

Moving On Up

In 2004, researchers on Ellesmere Island, Nunavut, in the Canadian Arctic, found a fossil that provides information about when fish first came onto land. The fossil, called *Tiktaalik*, is 375 million years old. *Tiktaalik* has characteristics of both fish and four-legged animals. Like other fish, it has fins. However, the fins have interior bones that helped push the animal up in the shallow waters close to shore to find food. The discovery of *Tiktaalik* has provided new fossil evidence to help scientists understand the relationship between marine vertebrates and land vertebrates.

Researcher from
Ellesmere Island

Communicate Discuss these questions with a partner. Write your answers below.

1. Do you think the discovery of *Tiktaalik* is important to understanding evolution? Why?

_____

_____

_____

_____

2. Do you think *Tiktaalik* spent most of its time on land or in water? Why?

_____

_____

_____

> **PLANET DIARY** Go to **Planet Diary** to learn more about fossil evidence.

This model of *Tiktaalik* shows what it may have looked like 375 million years ago.

 Lab zone Do the Inquiry Warm-Up
How Can You Classify a Species?

Vocabulary
- homologous structures

Skills
- ⟳ Reading: Identify the Main Idea
- △ Inquiry: Communicate

What Evidence Supports Evolution?

Since Darwin's time, scientists have found a great deal of evidence that supports the theory of evolution. ⟲ **Fossils, patterns of early development, similar body structures, and similarities in DNA and protein structures all provide evidence that organisms have changed over time.**

Fossils By examining fossils, scientists can infer the structures of ancient organisms. Fossils show that, in many cases, organisms that lived in the past were very different from organisms alive today. The millions of fossils that scientists have collected are called the fossil record. The fossil record provides clues about how and when new species evolved and how organisms are related. Rock layers that were deposited more recently are more likely to contain fossils of organisms that resemble current species.

Similarities in Early Development Scientists also infer evolutionary relationships by comparing the early development of different organisms. For example, the organisms in **Figure 1** look similar during the early stages of development. All four organisms have a tail. They also have a row of tiny slits along their throats. The similarities suggest that these vertebrate species are related and share a common ancestor.

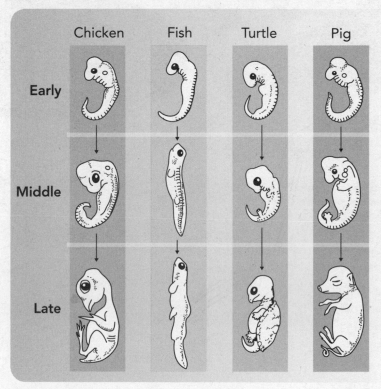

FIGURE 1 ·······················

Similarities in Development
These four organisms all look similar during their early development.

✎ **Complete each task.**

1. **Observe** Circle at least two similarities shared by all four organisms.

2. **Describe** What are some differences between the organisms?

_____

_____

_____

_____

Similarities in Body Structure

An organism's body structure is its basic body plan, which in vertebrates includes how its bones are arranged. Fishes, amphibians, reptiles, birds, and mammals all have an internal skeleton with a backbone. This similarity provides evidence that these animal groups all evolved from a common ancestor.

Similar structures that related species have inherited from a common ancestor are known as **homologous structures** (hoh MAHL uh gus). In **Figure 2,** you can see some examples of homologous structures. These include a bird's wing, a dolphin's flipper, and a dog's leg.

Sometimes fossils show structures that are homologous with structures in living species. For example, scientists have recently found fossils of ancient whalelike creatures. The fossils show that the ancestors of today's whales had legs and walked on land. This evidence supports other evidence that whales and other vertebrates share a common ancestor that had a skeleton with a backbone.

✏️ **Identify the Main Idea**
Describe the main idea on this page.

_____

_____

_____

_____

_____

FIGURE 2 ···

> INTERACTIVE ART **Homologous Structures**
The bones in a bird's wing, a dolphin's flipper, and a dog's leg have similar structures.

✏️ **Interpret Diagrams** Use the drawing of the dog's leg as a guide. Color in the matching bones in the bird's wing and the dolphin's flipper with the appropriate colors.

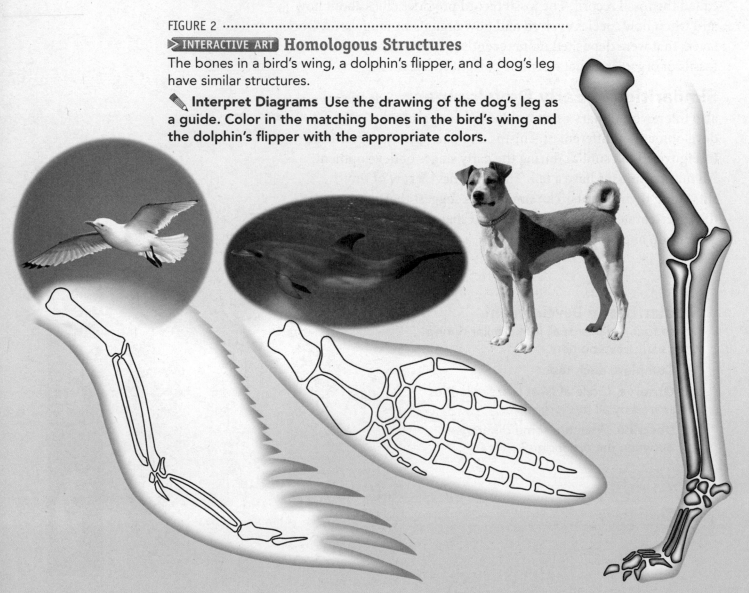

Similarities in DNA and Protein Structure

Why do some species have similar body structures and development patterns? Scientists infer that the species inherited many of the same genes from a common ancestor.

Recall that genes are segments of DNA. Scientists compare the sequence of nitrogen bases in the DNA of different species to infer how closely related the two species are. The more similar the DNA sequences, the more closely related the species are. The DNA bases along a gene specify what type of protein will be produced. Therefore, scientists can also compare the order of amino acids in a protein to see how closely related two species are.

In most cases, evidence from DNA and protein structure has confirmed conclusions based on fossils, embryos, and body structure. For example, DNA comparisons show that dogs are more similar to wolves than to coyotes. Scientists had already reached this conclusion based on similarities in the structure and development of these three species.

apply it!

The table shows the sequence of amino acids in one region of a protein, cytochrome c, for five different animals. Each letter corresponds to a different amino acid in the protein.

Section of Cytochrome c Protein in Animals

Animal	Amino Acid Position in the Sequence											
	39	40	41	42	43	44	45	46	47	48	49	50
Horse	N	L	H	G	L	F	G	R	K	T	G	Q
Donkey	N	L	H	G	L	F	G	R	K	T	G	Q
Rabbit	N	L	H	G	L	F	G	R	K	T	G	Q
Snake	N	L	H	G	L	F	G	R	K	T	G	Q
Turtle	N	L	N	G	L	I	G	R	K	T	G	Q

❶ Interpret Tables Which species is most distantly related to the horse? _____

❷ Communicate Explain how amino acid sequences provide information about evolutionary relationships among organisms.

_____
_____
_____
_____
_____
_____

Lab zone Do the Quick Lab *Finding Proof.*

Assess Your Understanding

1a. Define _____ structures are structurally similar body parts in related species.

b. CHALLENGE Insects and birds both have wings. What kinds of evidence might show whether or not insects and birds are closely related? Explain.

_____
_____
_____

got it?

○ **I get it!** Now I know that the theory of evolution is supported by evidence that includes _____

_____
_____
_____

○ **I need extra help with** _____

Go to **my science coach** online for help with this subject.

3 Rate of Change

🔑 How Do New Species Form?

🔑 What Patterns Describe the Rate of Evolution?

my planet diary

Crickets, Maggots, and Flies, Oh My!

A male cricket chirps to attract a mate. Unfortunately, chirping also attracts a parasitic fly. Parasitic flies listen for chirping crickets. When a cricket is located, a female fly deposits larvae onto the cricket's back. The larvae, or maggots, burrow into the cricket. The maggots come out seven days later, killing the cricket in the process. Parasitic flies reduced the cricket population on the Hawaiian island of Kauai between 1991 and 2001. By 2003, the cricket population on Kauai had increased. The male crickets were silent! In about 20 cricket generations, the crickets had evolved into an almost silent population.

Lab Do the Inquiry Warm-Up
zone *Making a Timeline.*

FUN FACT

Communicate Discuss these questions with a classmate. Write your answers below.

1. Why do you think the crickets on Kauai evolved so quickly?

_____

_____

2. If most of the male crickets can no longer chirp, how do you think it might affect the size of the cricket population?

_____

_____

_____

> PLANET DIARY Go to **Planet Diary** to learn more about evolution.

How Do New Species Form?

Natural selection explains how variations can lead to changes in a species. But how could an entirely new species form? 🔑 **A new species can form when a group of individuals remains isolated from the rest of its species long enough to evolve different traits that prevent reproduction.** Isolation, or complete separation, occurs when some members of a species become cut off from the rest of the species. One way this can happen is when a natural barrier, such as a river, separates group members.

Vocabulary
- gradualism
- punctuated equilibrium

Skills
- ⟳ Reading: Compare and Contrast
- △ Inquiry: Make Models

FIGURE 1 ·············

Kaibab and Abert's Squirrels

The Kaibab squirrel (left) and the Abert's squirrel (right) have been isolated from each other for a long time. Eventually, this isolation may result in two different species.

✎ **Identify** What conditions might differ from one side of the Grand Canyon to the other that would cause the squirrels to be different colors?

_____

_____

_____

As you can see in **Figure 1,** the populations of Kaibab and Abert's squirrels are separated by the Grand Canyon. The two kinds of squirrels are the same species, but they have slightly different characteristics. For example, the Kaibab squirrel has a black belly, while Abert's squirrel has a white belly. It is possible that one day these squirrels will become so different that they will no longer be able to mate with each other and will become separate species.

Key

| | Range of Kaibab squirrel | | Range of Abert's squirrel |

Lab zone® Do the Quick Lab *Large-Scale Isolation.*

🗝 Assess Your Understanding

got it? ···

○ **I get it!** Now I know that new species form when _____

_____

○ **I need extra help with** _____

Go to **MY SCIENCE** ⑤ **COACH** online for help with this subject.

What Patterns Describe the Rate of Evolution?

The fossil record has provided scientists with a lot of important information about past life on Earth. For example, fossils show a great variety of species that became extinct as their environments changed. Scientists also have found many examples of the appearance of new species as older species vanish. Sometimes the new species appear rapidly, and at other times they are the result of more gradual change.

🔑 **Scientists have developed two patterns to describe the pace of evolution: gradualism and punctuated equilibrium.**

Gradual Change Some species in the fossil record seem to change gradually over time. **Gradualism** involves small changes that add up to major changes over a long period of time. Since the time scale of the fossil record involves hundreds, thousands, or even millions of years, there is plenty of time for gradual changes to produce new species. The fossil record contains many examples of species that are intermediate between two others. One example is the horse relative, *Merychippus*, shown in **Figure 2**. Many such intermediate forms seem to be the result of gradual change.

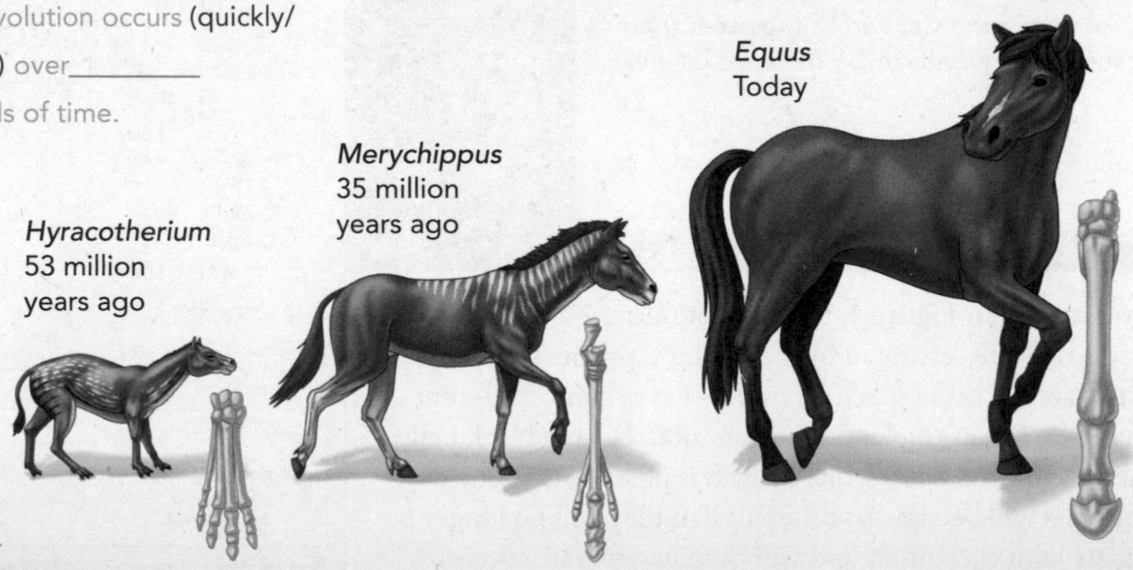

✏️
⟳ Compare and Contrast
Identify the similarity and the key differences between gradualism and punctuated equilibrium.

- Both describe the

  _____

- Gradualism states that evolution occurs (quickly/slowly) and (steadily/in short bursts).

- Punctuated equilibrium states that evolution occurs (quickly/slowly) over_____ periods of time.

Equus
Today

Merychippus
35 million
years ago

Hyracotherium
53 million
years ago

FIGURE 2 ···

▷ ART IN MOTION **Horse Evolution**

Horses left a rich and detailed fossil record of their evolution. Many intermediate forms have been found between modern horses and their four-toed ancestors. *Merychippus* is shown here.

✏️ **Answer these questions.**

1. List Name two differences between the horses.

_____
_____

2. **CHALLENGE** How could the evolution of the shape of the leg and the number of toes have benefited *Equus*?

_____
_____
_____
_____

Rapid Change Scientists have also found that many species remain almost unchanged during their existence. Then, shortly after they become extinct, related species often appear in the fossil record. This pattern, in which species evolve during short periods of rapid change and then don't change much, is called **punctuated equilibrium.** Today most scientists think that evolution can occur rapidly at some times, and more gradually at others. Scientists have observed that some species of insects and bacteria have undergone significant change in just a few years.

Two patterns that describe the rate of evolution are modeled at the right.

⚠️ **Make Models** Look at the shells in the key. For each pattern, decide if—and at what point—each shell belongs on the timelines. Using colored pencils, draw and color in the shells at their correct locations to show how they have evolved over time.

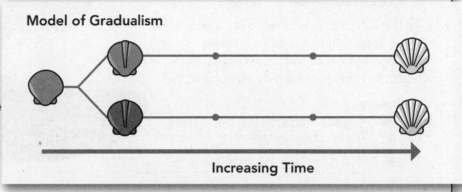

Model of Gradualism

Increasing Time

Key

A   B
C   D

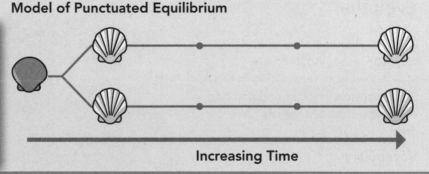

Model of Punctuated Equilibrium

Increasing Time

Lab zone® Do the Quick Lab *Slow or Fast?*

🔑 **Assess Your Understanding**

1a. Identify The _____ has given scientists information about past life on Earth.

b. Infer Why are fossils of intermediate life forms likely to be rare if the pattern of punctuated equilibrium explains how evolution occurs?

_____

_____

_____

got it?

○ I get it! Now I know that two patterns of

evolution are _____

_____

_____

○ I need extra help with _____

_____

Go to my science ⑤ coach *online for help with this subject.*

Living things change over time, or _____, through a process called _____.

LESSON 1 Darwin's Theory

🔑 Darwin hypothesized that species change over many generations and become better adapted to new conditions.

🔑 Darwin proposed that, over a long time, natural selection can lead to change. Helpful variations may accumulate in a species, while unfavorable ones may disappear.

Vocabulary
- species • fossil • adaptation • evolution
- scientific theory • natural selection • variation

LESSON 2 Evidence of Evolution

🔑 Fossils, patterns of early development, similar body structures, and similarities in DNA and protein structures all provide evidence that organisms have changed over time.

Vocabulary
- homologous structures

LESSON 3 Rate of Change

🔑 A new species can form when a group of individuals remains isolated from the rest of its species long enough to evolve different traits that prevent reproduction.

🔑 Scientists have developed two patterns to describe the pace of evolution: gradualism and punctuated equilibrium.

Vocabulary
- gradualism
- punctuated equilibrium

Review and Assessment

LESSON 1 Darwin's Theory

1. A trait that helps an organism to survive and reproduce is called a(n)

   a. variation.   **b.** adaptation.

   c. species.   **d.** selection.

2. Two organisms that can mate and produce fertile offspring are members of the same

_____

3. Infer Why are Darwin's ideas classified as a scientific theory?

_____
_____
_____
_____

4. Apply Concepts What is one factor that affects natural selection? Give an example.

_____
_____
_____
_____
_____

5. Compare and Contrast Identify one similarity and one difference between natural selection and artificial selection.

_____
_____
_____
_____
_____
_____

6. Write About It You are a reporter in the 1800s interviewing Charles Darwin about his theory of evolution. Write three questions you would ask him. Then write answers that Darwin might have given.

LESSON 2 Evidence of Evolution

7. Similar structures that related species have inherited from a common ancestor are called

   a. adaptations.

   b. fossils.

   c. ancestral structures.

   d. homologous structures.

8. The more _____ the DNA sequences between two organisms are, the more closely related the two species are.

9. Draw Conclusions Look at the drawing, at the right, of the bones in a crocodile's leg. Do you think that crocodiles share a common ancestor with birds, dolphins, and dogs? Support your answer with evidence.

Crocodile

_____
_____
_____
_____

10. Make Judgments What type of evidence is the best indicator of how closely two species are related? Explain your answer.

_____
_____
_____
_____
_____
_____
_____
_____

LESSON 3 **Rate of Change**

11. The pattern of evolution that involves short periods of rapid change is called

   a. adaptation.

   b. gradualism.

   c. isolation.

   d. punctuated equilibrium.

12. _____ involves tiny changes in a species that slowly add up to major changes over time.

13. **Apply Concepts** A population of deer lives in a forest. Draw a picture that illustrates how a geographic feature could isolate this deer population into two separate groups. Label the geographic feature.

14. **Develop Hypotheses** Describe the conditions that could cause these two groups of deer to become separate species over time.

   _____

   _____

   _____

   _____

   _____

 APPLY **THE BIG** **?**

How do life forms change over time?

15. Suppose that over several years, the climate in an area becomes much drier than it was before. How would plants, like the ones shown below, be affected? Using the terms *variation* and *natural selection*, predict what changes you might observe in the plants as a result of this environmental change.

   _____

   _____

   _____

   _____

   _____

   _____

   _____

   _____

   _____

   _____

   _____

   _____

Standardized Test Prep

Multiple Choice

Circle the letter of the best answer.

1. The illustration below has no title. Which of the following titles would best describe the concept shown in this drawing?

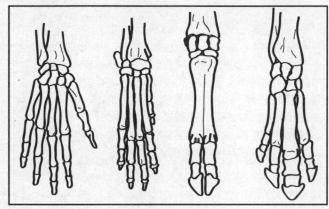

   A Wrist Bone Adaptations
   B Similarities in Wrist Bone Development
   C Evolutionary Change Through Gradualism
   D Homologous Structures in Four Animals

2. Which of the following has provided scientists with evidence about the changes in species over time?

   A fossil record
   B equilibrium record
   C evolution record
   D adaptation record

3. Which of the following is the best example of an adaptation that helps organisms survive in their environment?

   A green coloring in lizards living on gray rocks
   B a thick coat of fur on animals that live in the desert
   C an extensive root system in desert plants
   D thin, delicate leaves on plants in a cold climate

4. Which of the following sets of factors did Darwin identify as affecting natural selection?

   A adaptations, gradualism, and evolution
   B overproduction, variation, and competition
   C adaptations, traits, and variations
   D predation, competition, and mutualism

5. Evolution that occurs slowly is described by the pattern of _____, while rapid changes are described by

   _____.

   A gradualism; natural selection
   B homologous structures; fossils
   C gradualism; punctuated equilibrium
   D natural selection; punctuated equilibrium

Constructed Response

Use the diagram below and your knowledge of science to help you answer Question 6. Write your answer on a separate piece of paper.

6. This drawing shows variations in wing size within a species of fly. Describe a situation in which natural selection might favor flies with the smallest wings.

THE INCREDIBLE SHRINKING FISH

For years, fishers have followed a simple rule: keep the big fish and release the small fish. This practice aims to keep fish populations stable by allowing young fish to reach reproductive age. However, a scientist named David Conover thinks that this practice of throwing back small fish might be affecting the evolution of fish species.

Not all small fish are young. Like humans, adult fish come in different sizes. Conover hypothesized that removing the largest fish from fish populations might result in populations of smaller fish because smaller adult fish would survive to reproduce more often than larger adult fish. To test this hypothesis, Conover's team divided a population of 6,000 fish into different groups. Over four generations, the scientists selectively removed 90 percent of the fish in each group before they could reproduce.

The results showed that over just a few generations, selection pressures can influence not only the size of fish, but also the health of fish populations. Currently, Conover is researching ways to change fishing regulations so fish populations can recover.

▲ The practice of commercial fishing may be leading to populations of smaller and smaller fish.

This diagram shows how Dr. Conover and his team set up and performed their experiment. It also shows the results. ▶

Design It If current policies are causing the average size of fish to decrease, what is the best way to help fish populations recover? Design an experiment that would test your method for helping fish populations recover.

	Group 1	Group 2	Control Group
Starting population			
Fish removed from the population			
Ending population			
	Only small fish remain in the population.	Only big fish remain in the population.	A mixture of small and big fish remain in the population.

WALKING WHALES?

If you could visit Earth 50 million years ago, you would see many amazing sights. One of the strangest things you might see is the ancestor of modern whales—walking on land!

For years, scientists have thought that whales evolved from land-dwelling mammals. About 50 million years ago, the ancestors of modern whales had four legs and were similar to large dogs. Over 50 million years, whales evolved to become the giant marine mammals we recognize today. However, scientists have had difficulty finding fossils of whales that show how this dramatic change occurred. These missing links could reveal how whales lost their legs.

Now, several new discoveries are helping scientists fill in the blanks in the evolutionary history of whales. A fossil whale skeleton discovered in Washington State has a pelvis with large cuplike sockets. These sockets likely held short legs that enabled the whale to move on land. Other whale fossils, found in Alabama, include large hind limbs that probably helped the animals swim. Researchers have also discovered the gene mutation that could have been responsible for whales losing their legs about 35 million years ago.

Design It Find out more about the evolutionary history of whales. How is a whale flipper similar to a bat wing and a human hand? Design a poster that shows the evolutionary history of whales.

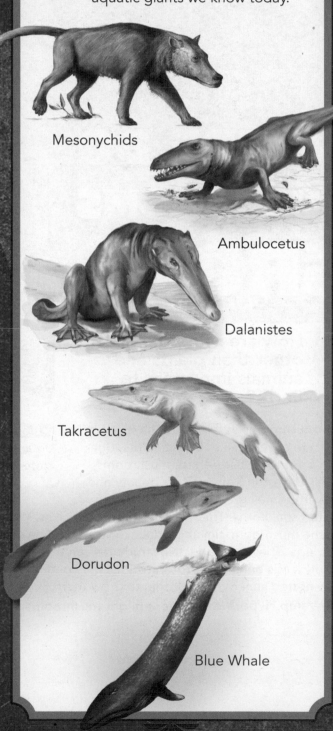

Over 50 million years, whales evolved from a species of doglike land mammals to the aquatic giants we know today.

Mesonychids

Ambulocetus

Dalanistes

Takracetus

Dorudon

Blue Whale

WHERE DO MUSHROOMS GROW?

How are living things other than plants and animals important to Earth?

The mushrooms in this photo have a lacy, delicate covering and bright colors. But don't get too close—these mushrooms smell like rotting meat! Their beauty and powerful smell gives them the name netted stinkhorns. The rotting smell attracts flies. When a fly lands on the mushroom, tiny reproductive structures may stick to the fly's legs. These reproductive structures can then drop off when the fly lands on another rotting surface. If conditions are right, a new netted stinkhorn will begin to grow there.

⚠️**Develop Hypotheses** Where might mushrooms grow?

_____

_____

_____

▶ UNTAMED SCIENCE Watch the **Untamed Science** video to learn more about mushrooms.

Viruses, Bacteria, Protists, and Fungi

Check Your Understanding

1. **Background** Read the paragraph below and then answer the question.

"Yes, it is a **prokaryote**!" said Lena, pulling her head away from the microscope. "No, it's not!" said Kiera. "Stop fighting!" said their friend Isa. "Let me see." Isa looked. "It's not a prokaryote; that's for sure. First of all, it is too large. More importantly, you can clearly see its **nucleus.** It is obviously a **eukaryote.**"

> A **prokaryote** is an organism whose single cell lacks a nucleus.
>
> A **nucleus** is a large oval organelle that contains the cell's genetic material in the form of DNA and controls many of the cell's activities.
>
> A **eukaryote** is an organism with cells that contain nuclei.

• Which organisms have nuclei—prokaryotes or eukaryotes?

_____

> MY READING WEB If you had trouble completing the question above, visit **My Reading Web** and type in *Viruses, Bacteria, Protists, and Fungi.*

Vocabulary Skill

Prefixes Some words can be divided into parts. A root is the part of the word that carries the basic meaning. A prefix is a word part that is placed in front of the root to change the word's meaning. The prefixes below will help you understand some of the vocabulary in this chapter.

Prefix	Meaning	Example
endo-	inside, within	endospore, *n.* a small, rounded, thick-walled cell that forms inside of a bacterial cell
pseudo-	false	pseudopod, *n.* a "false foot"; a structure used by certain protozoans for movement

2. **Quick Check** Which part of the word *endospore* tells you it is something that forms inside a bacterial cell?

_____

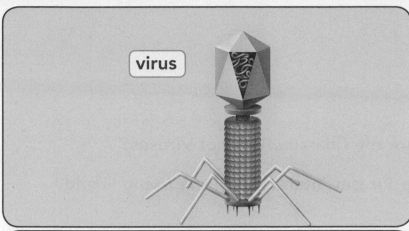

virus

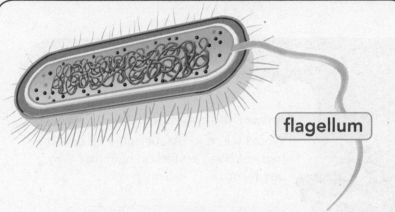

flagellum

algae

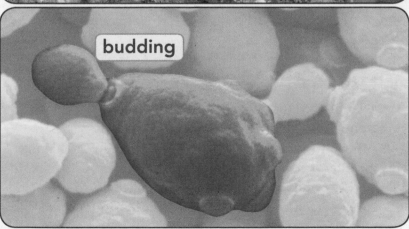

budding

Chapter Preview

LESSON 1
- virus
- host
- parasite
- vaccine
- ⟳ Identify the Main Idea
- △ Infer

LESSON 2
- bacteria
- cytoplasm
- ribosome
- flagellum
- cellular respiration
- binary fission
- conjugation
- endospore
- pasteurization
- decomposer
- ⟳ Compare and Contrast
- △ Predict

LESSON 3
- protist
- protozoan
- pseudopod
- contractile vacuole
- cilia
- algae
- pigment
- spore
- ⟳ Summarize
- △ Graph

LESSON 4
- fungus
- hyphae
- fruiting body
- budding
- lichen
- ⟳ Identify Supporting Evidence
- △ Observe

> **VOCAB FLASH CARDS** For extra help with vocabulary, visit **Vocab Flash Cards** and type in **Viruses, Bacteria, Protists, and Fungi.**

Viruses

UNLOCK
THE BIG
?

🔑 **What Are the Characteristics of Viruses?**

🔑 **How Do Viruses Interact With the Living World?**

MY PLANET DIARY

VOICES FROM HISTORY

A Mad Choice

Have you ever seen a snarling dog on TV? Chances are this "mad dog" was supposed to have rabies. Rabies is a virus that affects the brain, causing "mad" behaviors and spasms of the throat. Infected animals avoid water, giving the disease the nickname *hydrophobia*, meaning "fear of water."

In the 1800s, if people were bitten by a mad dog, they would likely die. Then, in 1884, the scientist Louis Pasteur said he had a cure. He claimed, "Whoever gets bitten by a mad dog has only to submit to my three little inoculations, and he need not have the slightest fear of hydrophobia."

Answer the question below.

Would you try Pasteur's cure, even if it had not been tested on humans? Why or why not?

_____

_____

_____

_____

_____

_____

▶ PLANET DIARY Go to **Planet Diary** to learn more about viruses.

 Lab® Do the Inquiry Warm-Up
zone *Which Lock Does the Key Fit?*

What Are the Characteristics of Viruses?

Have you ever noticed that when you spent time with a friend suffering from a cold, you sometimes felt sick a few days later? You were probably infected by a virus. A **virus** is a tiny, nonliving particle that enters and then reproduces inside a living cell. 🔑 **Viruses are nonliving, have a protein coat that protects an inner core of genetic material, and cannot reproduce on their own.**

Vocabulary
- virus • host
- parasite • vaccine

Skills

⟳ Reading: Identify the Main Idea

△ Inquiry: Infer

Virus Needs Why are viruses considered nonliving? They lack most of the characteristics of living things. Viruses are not cells and do not use their own energy to grow or to respond to their surroundings. Viruses also cannot make food, take in food, or produce wastes. Although viruses can multiply like organisms, they can only do so when they are inside a living cell.

The organism that a virus enters and multiplies inside of is called a host. A **host** is an organism that provides a source of energy for a virus or another organism. A virus acts like a **parasite** (PA ruh syt), an organism that lives on or in a host and causes it harm. Almost all viruses destroy the cells in which they multiply.

Influenza virus

Tobacco mosaic virus

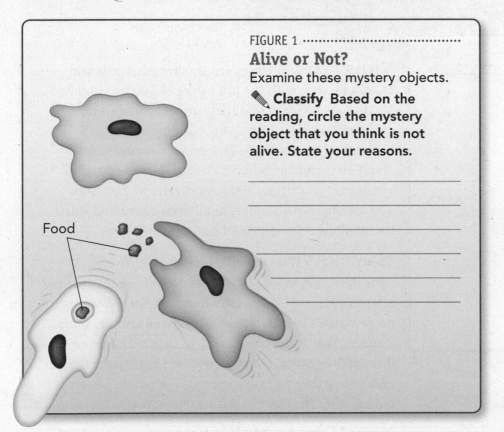

FIGURE 1 ···

Alive or Not?
Examine these mystery objects.

✏ **Classify** Based on the reading, circle the mystery object that you think is not alive. State your reasons.

_____
_____
_____
_____
_____
_____

Food

T4 bacteriophage

Virus Shapes As you can see in **Figure 2,** viruses vary widely in shape. Some viruses are round, and some are rod-shaped. Other viruses are shaped like bricks, threads, or bullets. There are even viruses that have complex, robotlike shapes, such as the bacteriophage. A bacteriophage (bak TEER ee oh fayj) is a virus that infects bacteria. In fact, its name means "bacteria eater."

FIGURE 2 ·······························

Virus Shapes
The leglike structures on the bottom of the T4 bacteriophage keep the virus firmly in place as it infects a cell.

211

FIGURE 3 ······························

Virus Sizes

The *Streptococcus* bacterium is a round organism that causes the infection strep throat.

✎ **Read the text about virus sizes and then complete each task.**

1. **Calculate** A *Streptococcus* bacterium is 10 times larger than a cold virus. Calculate the size of the bacterium.

_____

2. **Measure** Use your calculation from Step 1 to mark and label on the scale the size of the *Streptococcus* bacterium.

3. **Make Models** Draw the bacterium to scale in the box provided.

All measurements represent approximate diameters.

 Smallpox virus 250 nm

 Cold sore virus 130 nm

 Influenza virus 90 nm

Cold virus 75 nm

 Yellow fever virus 22 nm

Red blood cell
7,500 nm

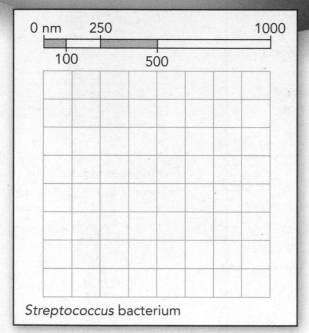

0 nm   250   1000
   100   500

Streptococcus bacterium

Virus Sizes Viruses are smaller than cells and cannot be seen with the microscopes you use in school. Viruses are so small that they are measured in units called nanometers (nm). One nanometer is one billionth of a meter (m). The smallest viruses are about 20 nanometers in diameter, while the largest viruses are more than 200 nanometers in diameter. The average virus is quite small even compared with the smallest cells—those of bacteria.

Naming Viruses Because viruses are not considered organisms, scientists do not use the two-part scientific naming system to identify them. Scientists name viruses in a variety of ways. For example, some viruses, such as the poliovirus, are named after the disease they cause. Other viruses are named for the area where they were discovered. The West Nile virus is named after the place in Africa where it was first found.

How Viruses Multiply After a virus attaches to a host cell, it enters the cell. Once inside a cell, the virus's genetic material takes over many of the cell's functions. It instructs the cell to produce the virus's proteins and genetic material. These proteins and genetic material then assemble into new viruses. Some viruses take over cell functions immediately. Other viruses wait for a while.

The Structure of Viruses

Although viruses have many different shapes and sizes, they all have a similar structure. All viruses have two basic parts: an inner core containing genetic material and a protein coat that protects the virus. A virus's genetic material contains the instructions for making new viruses.

Each virus contains unique surface proteins. These surface proteins play an important role during the invasion of a host cell. The shape of the surface proteins allows a virus to attach only to certain cells in the host. Like keys, a virus's proteins fit only into specific "locks," or proteins, on the surface of a host's cells. So a particular virus can attach only to one or a few types of host cells. For example, most cold viruses infect cells only in the nose and throat of humans. Those cells have proteins on their surfaces that complement or fit the proteins on cold viruses. **Figure 4** shows how the lock-and-key system works.

FIGURE 4 ·····················

> INTERACTIVE ART **Virus Structure and Invasion** Some viruses are surrounded by an outer membrane envelope.

✎ **Interpret Diagrams** For the virus on the right, draw a line from the virus surface proteins to the matching cell surface proteins. Circle any of the cell proteins that do not match.

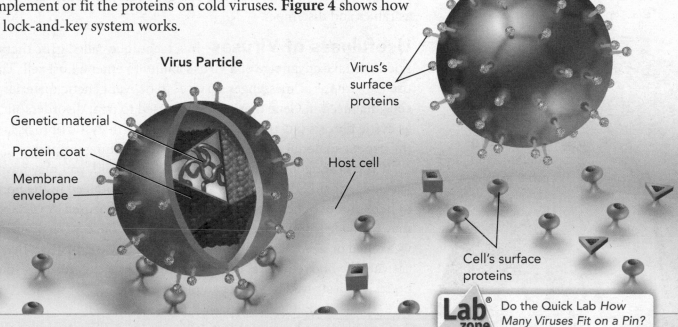

Virus Particle

Genetic material

Protein coat

Membrane envelope

Virus's surface proteins

Host cell

Cell's surface proteins

Lab zone Do the Quick Lab *How Many Viruses Fit on a Pin?*

🔑 Assess Your Understanding

1a. Define A virus is a (living/nonliving) particle that enters a cell and uses it to reproduce.

b. Relate Cause and Effect How do the surface proteins on a virus help it to invade a host cell?

_____

_____

c. CHALLENGE Scientists hypothesize that viruses could not have existed on Earth before organisms appeared. Do you agree? Explain.

_____

_____

_____

_____

got it? ··

○ **I get it!** Now I know that the characteristics of viruses are _____

_____

○ **I need extra help with** _____

Go to MY SCIENCE ⓢ COACH *online for help with this subject.*

How Do Viruses Interact With the Living World?

You may have only heard of viruses causing colds and diseases. But sometimes viruses help rather than harm. 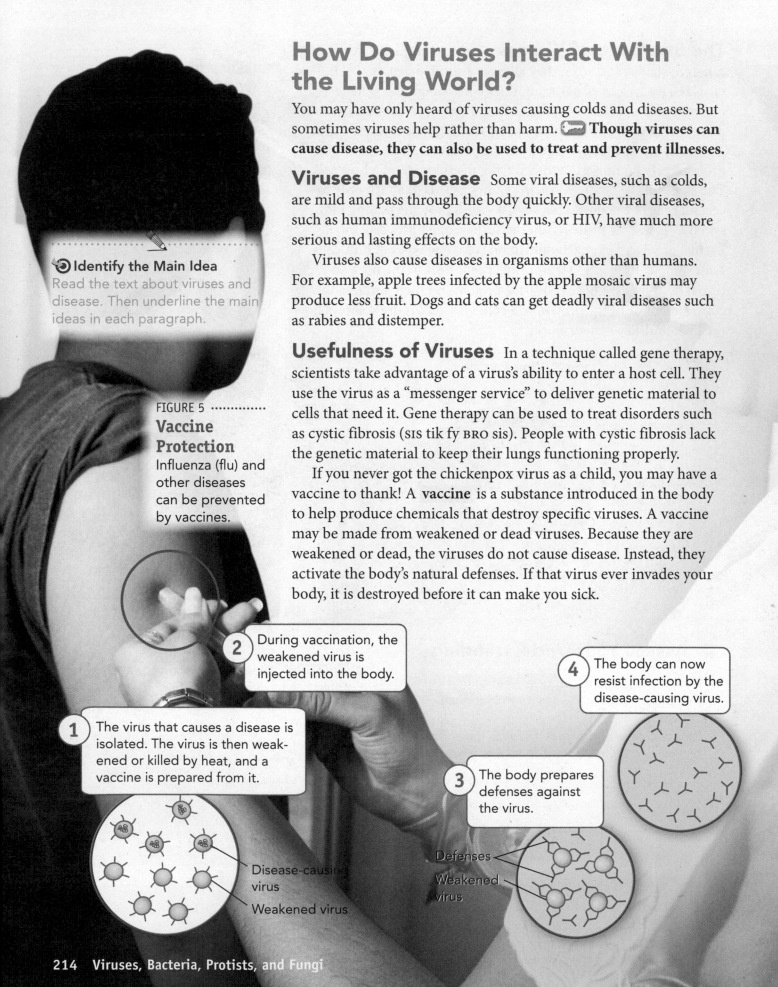 **Though viruses can cause disease, they can also be used to treat and prevent illnesses.**

Viruses and Disease Some viral diseases, such as colds, are mild and pass through the body quickly. Other viral diseases, such as human immunodeficiency virus, or HIV, have much more serious and lasting effects on the body.

Viruses also cause diseases in organisms other than humans. For example, apple trees infected by the apple mosaic virus may produce less fruit. Dogs and cats can get deadly viral diseases such as rabies and distemper.

Usefulness of Viruses In a technique called gene therapy, scientists take advantage of a virus's ability to enter a host cell. They use the virus as a "messenger service" to deliver genetic material to cells that need it. Gene therapy can be used to treat disorders such as cystic fibrosis (SIS tik fy BRO sis). People with cystic fibrosis lack the genetic material to keep their lungs functioning properly.

If you never got the chickenpox virus as a child, you may have a vaccine to thank! A **vaccine** is a substance introduced in the body to help produce chemicals that destroy specific viruses. A vaccine may be made from weakened or dead viruses. Because they are weakened or dead, the viruses do not cause disease. Instead, they activate the body's natural defenses. If that virus ever invades your body, it is destroyed before it can make you sick.

⊙ **Identify the Main Idea**
Read the text about viruses and disease. Then underline the main ideas in each paragraph.

FIGURE 5 ··············

Vaccine Protection
Influenza (flu) and other diseases can be prevented by vaccines.

1 The virus that causes a disease is isolated. The virus is then weakened or killed by heat, and a vaccine is prepared from it.

2 During vaccination, the weakened virus is injected into the body.

3 The body prepares defenses against the virus.

4 The body can now resist infection by the disease-causing virus.

Disease-causing virus

Weakened virus

Defenses

Weakened virus

apply it!

Viruses can cause disease around the world. Use the world map below to answer the questions about dengue (DEN gay) fever, a viral disease.

1 Interpret Maps Which continents have outbreaks of dengue fever?

_____

_____

2 Draw Conclusions Why do you think dengue fever only occurs in warm places?

_____

_____

_____

3 ⚠ **Infer** Suppose people in South America are getting sick with an influenza virus. A few days earlier, there were reports of the same virus infecting people in Africa. How could the influenza virus have spread so quickly?

_____

_____

_____

_____

_____

_____

Arctic Ocean

Dengue Fever
The virus is spread by mosquitoes. Mosquitoes cannot spread the virus in temperatures below 16°C.

NORTH AMERICA

EUROPE

ASIA

Atlantic Ocean

AFRICA

Equator

SOUTH AMERICA

Pacific Ocean

Indian Ocean

AUSTRALIA

Lab zone® Do the Quick Lab
How Viruses Spread.

🔑 Assess Your Understanding

got it? ....

○ **I get it!** Now I know that viruses interact in the living world by both _____

_____

○ **I need extra help with** _____

Go to **MY SCIENCE** ⓢ **COACH** *online for help with this subject.*

Bacteria

🔑 **What Are Bacteria?**

🔑 **How Do Bacteria Get Food, Get Energy, and Reproduce?**

🔑 **What Is the Role of Bacteria in Nature?**

MY PLANET DIARY

"Good" Germs

Misconception: All bacteria are harmful.

Many bacteria are harmless or even good for you! Your intestines are full of good bacteria. Some types of helpful bacteria, often called probiotics, are found in foods like yogurt, smoothies, and even cereal! Scientists have found that eating foods containing probiotics keeps you healthy. These foods put good bacteria into your body to help fight off the harmful bacteria that can cause disease.

MISCONCEPTION

Communicate Discuss these questions with a classmate. Write your answers below.

1. Why do people often think all bacteria are bad for you?

_____

_____

2. Can you think of some products you have used at home or at school to kill harmful bacteria?

_____

_____

_____

_____

▶ PLANET DIARY Go to **Planet Diary** to learn more about bacteria.

 Do the Inquiry Warm-Up *How Quickly Can Bacteria Multiply?*

What Are Bacteria?

They thrive in your cup of yogurt. They coat your skin and swarm inside your nose. You cannot escape them because they live almost everywhere—under rocks, in the ocean, and all over your body. In fact, there are more of these organisms in your mouth than there are people on Earth! You don't notice them because they are very small. These organisms are bacteria.

Vocabulary

- bacteria • cytoplasm • ribosome • flagellum
- cellular respiration • binary fission • conjugation
- endospore • pasteurization • decomposer

Skills

- Reading: Compare and Contrast
- Inquiry: Predict

Cell Structures Bacteria were first discovered in the late 1600s by a Dutch merchant named Anton von Leeuwenhoek (LAY vun hook). He made microscopes as a hobby. One day, while looking at scrapings of his teeth, he noticed small wormlike organisms. If Leeuwenhoek had owned a modern high-powered microscope, he would have seen that the single-celled organisms were **bacteria** (singular *bacterium*). **Bacteria are prokaryotes. The genetic material in their cells is not contained in a nucleus.** In addition to lacking a nucleus, the cells of bacteria also lack many other structures that are found in the cells of eukaryotes. Recall that eukaryotes include protists, fungi, and animals.

Figure 1 shows the structures in a typical bacterial cell. Most bacterial cells are surrounded by a rigid cell wall that protects the cell. Just inside the cell wall is the cell membrane, which controls what materials pass in and out of the cell. The region inside the cell membrane, called the **cytoplasm** (SY toh plaz um), contains a gel-like fluid that moves structures throughout the cell. Located in the cytoplasm are tiny structures called **ribosomes** (RY bo sohmz), chemical factories where proteins are produced. The cell's genetic material, which looks like a tangled string, is also found in the cytoplasm. It contains the instructions for all of the cell's functions. A bacterial cell may also have a **flagellum** (fluh JEL um; plural *flagella*), a long, whiplike structure that helps a cell to move.

Bacteria as seen through Anton von Leeuwenhoek's microscope

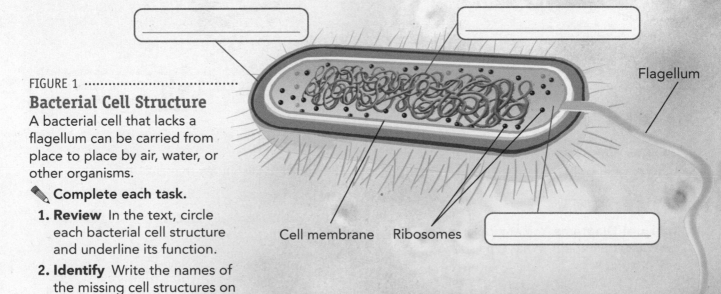

FIGURE 1 ·····························

Bacterial Cell Structure

A bacterial cell that lacks a flagellum can be carried from place to place by air, water, or other organisms.

✏ **Complete each task.**

1. **Review** In the text, circle each bacterial cell structure and underline its function.

2. **Identify** Write the names of the missing cell structures on the lines provided.

Flagellum

Cell membrane   Ribosomes

Cell Shapes If you were to look at bacteria under a microscope, you would notice that most bacterial cells have one of three basic shapes: spherical, rodlike, or spiral. The chemical makeup of the cell wall determines the shape of a bacterial cell. The shape of the cell helps scientists identify the type of bacteria.

Cell Sizes Bacteria vary greatly in size. The largest known bacterium is about as big as the period at the end of this sentence. An average bacterium, however, is much smaller. For example, the spherical strep throat bacteria are about 0.5 to 1 micrometer in diameter. A micrometer is one millionth of a meter.

FIGURE 2 ·······································

Bacteria Shapes and Names

Bacteria are sometimes named for their shape.

✏ **Classify** Use the key to match the scientific names in the word bank to the correct bacteria. Write your answers in the boxes.

Word Bank

Leptospira interrogans   Bacillus anthracis

Stella vacuolata   Streptococcus thermophilus

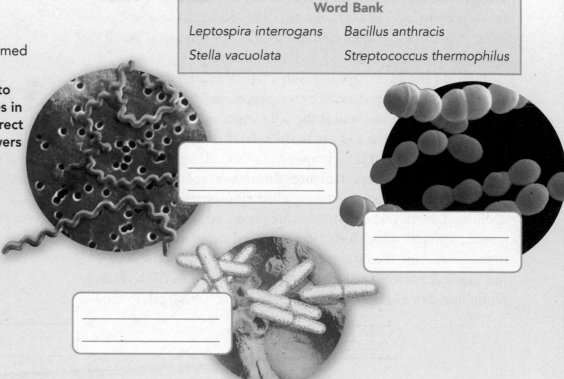

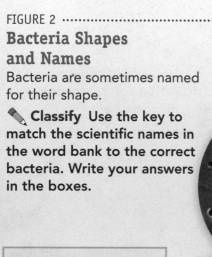

Key to Scientific Names

Stella: star

Spira: coil or spiral

Kokkos: sphere

Bacillus: rod

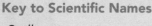

🔑 **Assess Your Understanding**

1a. Identify Where is the genetic material located in a bacterial cell?

_____

b. Interpret Diagrams You are looking at a *Stella vacuolata* bacterium. What is its shape and how do you know?

_____

_____

Lab Do the Quick Lab
zone *Classifying Bacteria.*

got it?

○ I get it! Now I know that bacteria are _____

_____

_____

○ I need extra help with _____

Go to **MY SCIENCE** ⬤ **COACH** online for help with this subject.

How Do Bacteria Get Food, Get Energy, and Reproduce?

From the bacteria that live in soil to those that live in the pores of your skin, all bacteria need certain things to survive and reproduce. **Bacteria get energy by either making food or eating other organisms, and can reproduce asexually or sexually.**

Obtaining Food
Some bacteria are autotrophs, meaning they make their own food. Some capture and use the sun's energy as plants do. Others, such as bacteria that live deep in mud, do not use the sun's energy. Instead, these bacteria use the energy from chemical substances in their environment to make their food.

Some bacteria are heterotrophs, and cannot make their own food. These bacteria must consume other organisms or the food that other organisms make. Heterotrophic bacteria consume a variety of foods—from milk and meat, which you might also eat, to decaying leaves on a forest floor.

⊃ Compare and Contrast How do autotrophic and heterotrophic bacteria differ in the way they obtain food?

_____

_____

_____

_____

_____

_____

FIGURE 3 ·········

Obtaining Food
Autotrophic bacteria in hot springs use chemical energy to make food. Heterotrophic bacteria in compost get energy from decaying food.

Compost ▼

Autotrophic bacteria

▲ Trained researcher permitted to work at hot springs in Yellowstone National Park

Heterotrophic bacteria

219

FIGURE 4

Bacteria Buffet
These bacteria break down pollutants in this biopile to get energy.

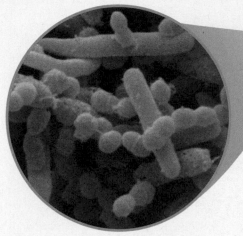

Respiration Like all organisms, bacteria need a constant supply of energy to carry out their functions. This energy comes from food. The process of breaking down food to release energy is called **cellular respiration.** Like many other organisms, most bacteria need oxygen to break down their food. But a few kinds of bacteria do not need oxygen for respiration. In fact, those bacteria die if oxygen is present in their surroundings. For them, oxygen is a poison that kills!

apply it!

Suppose you are a scientist studying disease-causing bacteria. You make a table that lists how the bacteria get energy and whether they need oxygen. One day, some of your data are accidentally erased.

❶ **Create Data Tables** Use what you know about bacteria to fill in the first two columns in the table.

❷ **Draw Conclusions** How would you destroy these dangerous bacteria? Use the information in the table to fill in the last column.

Food Source	Type of Bacterium	Need Oxygen?	How to Destroy
Decaying leaves	_____	Yes	_____
_____	Autotrophic	No	_____
Chemicals	_____	No	_____

Reproduction One of the characteristics of living things is that they are able to reproduce, or make more copies of themselves. When bacteria have plenty of food, the right temperature, and other suitable conditions, they thrive and reproduce often. Bacteria can reproduce asexually or sexually.

FIGURE 5 ·······························

Bacterial Reproduction

Some bacteria are able to reproduce every 20 minutes.

✏️ **Relate Text and Visuals** In the diagrams, label each reproductive process and answer the questions.

Asexual Reproduction

Bacteria sometimes reproduce asexually by a process called **binary fission,** in which one cell divides to form two identical cells. To prepare for binary fission, a bacterial cell grows to almost twice its size. Then it duplicates its genetic material and splits into two separate cells. Each new cell receives a complete copy of the parent's genetic material. As a result, the offspring are genetically identical to the parent. Binary fission increases the number of bacteria.

Asexual process called

Why are all the bacteria the same color?

Sexual Reproduction

Sometimes bacteria reproduce sexually by a process called **conjugation.** During conjugation, one bacterium transfers some of its genetic material into another bacterium through a thin, threadlike bridge. After the transfer, the bacteria separate. Conjugation results in bacteria with new combinations of genetic material. When the bacteria divide by binary fission, the new genetic material passes to the offspring. Conjugation does not increase the number of bacteria, as binary fission does. However, it does result in bacteria that are genetically different from the parent cells.

Sexual process called

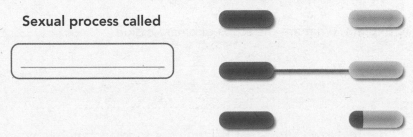

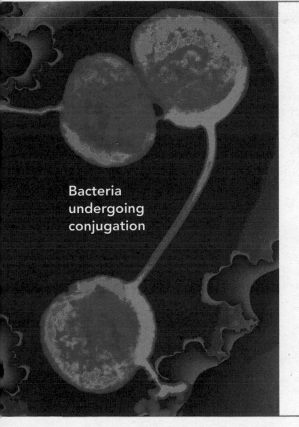

Bacteria undergoing conjugation

Why is the bacterium on the bottom right colored red and yellow?

Endospore Formation

Endospore Formation Sometimes, conditions in the environment become unfavorable for the growth of bacteria. For example, food sources can disappear, water can dry up, or the temperature can fall or rise dramatically. Some bacteria can survive harsh conditions by forming endospores. An **endospore** is a small, rounded, thick-walled resting cell that forms inside a bacterial cell. It encloses the cell's genetic material and some of its cytoplasm.

Because endospores can resist freezing, heating, and drying, they can survive for many years in harsh conditions. Endospores are also light—a breeze can lift and carry them to new places. If an endospore lands in a place where conditions are suitable, it opens up. Then the bacterium can begin to grow and multiply.

FIGURE 6 ·····················

Endospore Formation
The panels below illustrate endospore formation.

✎ **Sequence** Based on the reading, draw and label the last panel.

Increasing time

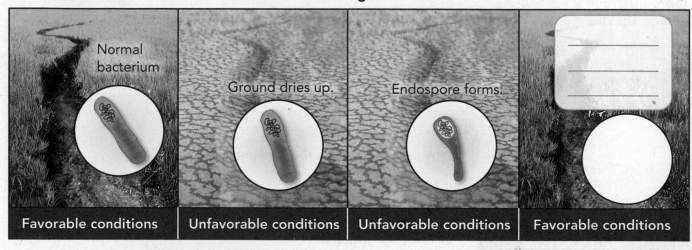

| Normal bacterium | Ground dries up. | Endospore forms. | |
| Favorable conditions | Unfavorable conditions | Unfavorable conditions | Favorable conditions |

Lab zone® Do the Lab Investigation *Comparing Disinfectants.*

🔑 Assess Your Understanding

2a. Name What are three ways bacteria get food?

_____

_____

_____

b. Explain What are the steps of binary fission?

_____

_____

c. [CHALLENGE] Why might bacteria that undergo conjugation be better able to survive in unfavorable conditions?

_____

_____

_____

_____

got it? ··

○ **I get it!** Now I know that bacteria get food and energy by _____

_____ and reproduce _____

○ I need extra help with _____

Go to **MY SCIENCE ⓢ COACH** online for help with this subject.

What Is the Role of Bacteria in Nature?

When you hear the word *bacteria*, you may think about getting sick. After all, strep throat, many ear infections, and other diseases are caused by bacteria. However, most bacteria are either harmless or helpful to people. In fact, in many ways, people depend on bacteria. **Bacteria are involved in oxygen and food production, in health maintenance and medicine production, and in environmental cleanup and recycling.**

Oxygen Production Would it surprise you to learn that the air you breathe depends in part on bacteria? As autotrophic bacteria use the sun's energy to produce food, they release oxygen into the air. Billions of years ago, Earth had very little oxygen. Scientists think that autotrophic bacteria were responsible for first adding oxygen to Earth's atmosphere. Today, the distant offspring of those bacteria help keep oxygen levels in the air stable.

FIGURE 7 ....

Early Earth

Conditions on early Earth were very different than conditions today. There were frequent volcanic eruptions, storms, and earthquakes.

✎ **Infer** Could today's organisms have survived on early Earth? Why or why not?

_____

_____

_____

_____

---

apply it!

Predict Imagine you are growing a colony of autotrophic bacteria in the laboratory. What might happen to the level of oxygen as each of the three events listed below occurs? Read all three events, then draw your prediction on the graph.

❶ First event: The colony of autotrophic bacteria grows quickly under a sun lamp.

❷ Second event: The size of the bacterial colony stays stable.

❸ Third event: You accidentally put the bacteria in the shade.

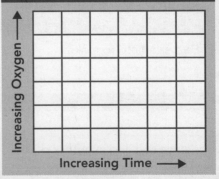

Level of Oxygen

Increasing Oxygen →

Increasing Time →

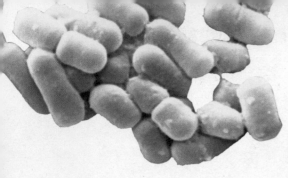

Food Production

Do you like cheese, sauerkraut, or pickles? The activities of helpful bacteria produce all of these foods and more. For example, bacteria that grow in milk produce dairy products such as buttermilk, yogurt, sour cream, and cheeses.

However, some bacteria cause food to spoil when they break down the food's chemicals. Spoiled food usually smells or tastes foul and can make you very sick. Refrigerating and heating foods are two ways to slow down food spoilage. Another method, called pasteurization, is most often used to treat beverages such as milk and juice. During **pasteurization,** the food is heated to a temperature that is high enough to kill most harmful bacteria without changing the taste of the food. As you might have guessed, this process was named after Louis Pasteur, its inventor.

Health and Medicine

Did you know that many of the bacteria living in your body actually keep you healthy? In your digestive system, for example, your intestines teem with bacteria. Some help you digest your food. Some make vitamins that your body needs. Others compete for space with disease-causing organisms. They prevent the harmful bacteria from attaching to your intestines and making you sick.

Scientists use certain bacteria to make medicines and other substances. By manipulating the bacteria's genetic material, scientists can cause bacteria to produce human insulin. Although healthy people can make their own insulin, those with some types of diabetes cannot. Many people with diabetes need to take insulin daily. Thanks to bacteria's fast rate of reproduction, large numbers of insulin-making bacteria can be grown in huge vats. The human insulin they produce is then purified and made into medicine.

did you know?

Did you know that one to two kilograms of your body weight are bacteria in your digestive system? Up to 1,000 species of bacteria are crowded into your stomach and intestines.

FIGURE 8

> ART IN MOTION **Bacteria and the Environment**

The *Deinococcus* bacteria pictured are named for their spherical shape.

✎ **Summarize** Fill in this graphic organizer to summarize the role of bacteria in nature.

Bacteria help to make
_____

_____
delays spoiling in milk and juice.

Bacteria can help plants by
_____
_____
_____

Bacteria that break down dead organisms are
_____

Bacteria are used to make large amounts of medicine because
_____

Bacteria

Food Production

Health and Medicine

Environmental Recycling

Environmental Cleanup

Some bacteria help to clean up Earth's land and water. Certain bacteria can convert the poisonous chemicals in oil into harmless substances. Scientists have put these bacteria to work cleaning up oil spills in oceans and gasoline leaks in the soil under gas stations.

Environmental Recycling

Do you recycle? So do bacteria! Some bacteria that live in soil are **decomposers**—organisms that break down large, complex chemicals in dead organisms into small, simple chemicals.

Decomposers are "nature's recyclers." They return basic chemicals to the environment for other living things to reuse. For example, in autumn, the leaves of many trees die and drop to the ground. Decomposing bacteria spend the next months breaking down the chemicals in the dead leaves. The broken-down chemicals mix with the soil and can then be absorbed by the roots of nearby plants.

Another type of recycling bacteria, called nitrogen-fixing bacteria, help plants survive. Nitrogen-fixing bacteria live in the roots of certain plants, such as peanuts, peas, and soybeans. These helpful bacteria change nitrogen gas from the air into nitrogen products that plants need to grow. Plants are unable to make this conversion on their own. Therefore, nitrogen-fixing bacteria are vital to the plants' survival.

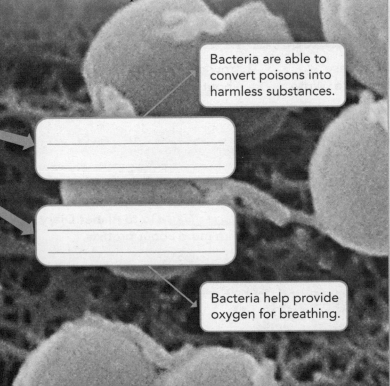

Bacteria are able to convert poisons into harmless substances.

Bacteria help provide oxygen for breathing.

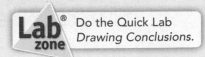

🔑 Assess Your Understanding

3a. Review How can certain bacteria in food make you sick?

_____

_____

b. List A friend says that all bacteria are harmful to people. List three reasons this statement is incorrect.

_____

_____

_____

_____

_____

c. Relate Cause and Effect How would life on Earth change if all autotrophic bacteria died off?

_____

_____

_____

_____

d. Apply Concepts How can bacteria acting as decomposers help plants grow?

_____

_____

_____

_____

got it? ···

○ **I get it!** Now I know that the role of

bacteria in nature includes _____

_____

_____

_____

○ **I need extra help with** _____

_____

Go to MY SCIENCE 🅢 COACH *online for help with this subject.*

225

Protists

UNLOCK THE BIG **?**

🔑 **What Are the Characteristics of Animal-Like Protists?**

🔑 **What Are the Characteristics of Plant-Like Protists?**

🔑 **What Are the Characteristics of Fungus-Like Protists?**

MY PLANET DIARY

PROFILE

Dancin' for a Cause

The protist *Plasmodium* causes malaria, a disease of the blood that can kill people. *Plasmodium* is carried by mosquitoes and is spread by their bites.

Malaria claims the life of a child in Africa every 30 seconds. Nets like these may help to prevent malaria infections.

When Allyson Brown from Melbourne, Florida, learned about malaria, she took action. She turned a school dance into a fundraiser, named Stayin' Alive, to buy mosquito nets for people in Africa. The nets keep mosquitoes away while people sleep. Since then, Allyson has teamed with the organization, *Malaria No More*, to help other schools to do the same.

Communicate Discuss these questions with a classmate. Write your answers below.

1. Why did Allyson donate mosquito nets to people in Africa?

_____

_____

_____

_____

2. How could you raise awareness about malaria at your school?

_____

_____

_____

_____

▷ PLANET DIARY Go to **Planet Diary** to learn more about protists.

Lab zone® Do the Inquiry Warm-Up *What Lives in a Drop of Pond Water?*

Vocabulary
- protist • protozoan • pseudopod
- contractile vacuole • cilia • algae
- pigment • spore

Skills
- Reading: Summarize
- Inquiry: Graph

What Are the Characteristics of Animal-Like Protists?

The beautiful and diverse organisms in **Figure 1** below are protists. **Protists** are eukaryotes that cannot be classified as animals, plants, or fungi. The word that best describes protists is *diverse*. For example, most protists are unicellular, but some are multicellular. Some are heterotrophs, some are autotrophs, and others are both. Some protists cannot move, while others zoom around their habitats. However, all protists are eukaryotes, and all protists live in moist surroundings. Recall that eukaryotes are cells in which the genetic material is contained in a nucleus.

Because protists are so different from each other, scientists divide them into three categories based on characteristics they share with organisms in other kingdoms. These categories are: animal-like protists, plant-like protists, and fungus-like protists.

What image pops into your head when you think of an animal? Most people immediately associate animals with movement. In fact, movement is often involved with an important characteristic of animals—obtaining food. All animals that obtain food by eating other organisms are heterotrophs.

🔑 **Like animals, animal-like protists are heterotrophs, and most can move to get food.** But unlike animals, animal-like protists, or **protozoans** (proh tuh ZOH unz), are unicellular.

Vocabulary Prefixes The Greek word *proton* means "first" or "early." If the Greek word *zoia* means "animal," what do you think *protozoan* means?

FIGURE 1 ·························
Diversity of Protists
Protists come in many sizes and forms. Slime molds, amoebas, and euglenoids are just some of the many types of protists.

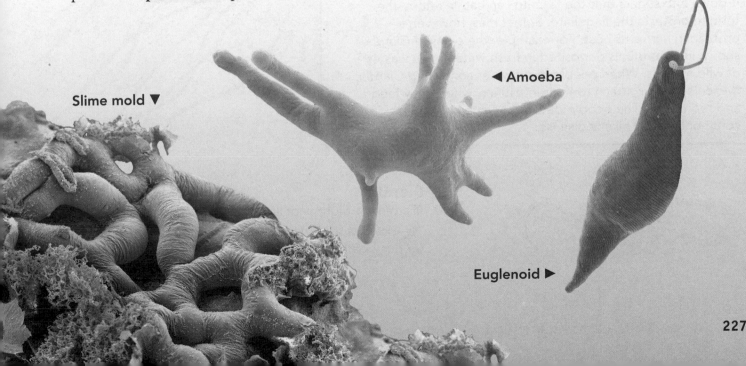

Slime mold ▼

◄ Amoeba

Euglenoid ►

The Four Groups of Protozoans—How They Move and Live

Protozoans With Pseudopods

The amoeba in **Figure 2** belongs to the first group of protozoans called sarcodines. Sarcodines move and feed by forming **pseudopods** (SOO duh pahdz)—temporary bulges of the cell. The word *pseudopod* means "false foot." Pseudopods form when cytoplasm flows toward one location and the rest of the organism follows. Pseudopods enable sarcodines to move away from bright light. Sarcodines also use pseudopods to trap food by extending one on each side of a food particle. When the two pseudopods join together, the food is trapped inside the cell, as shown in **Figure 2**. Protozoans that live in fresh water have a problem. If excess water builds up inside the cell, the amoeba will burst. But amoebas have a **contractile vacuole** (kun TRAK til VAK yoo ohl), a structure that collects and expels excess water from the cell.

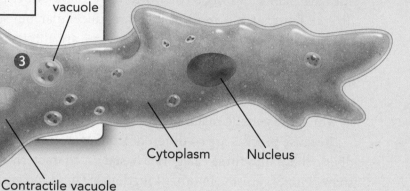

FIGURE 2 ·····················
Amoeba
This amoeba's pseudopods surround and trap a food particle.

✏ **Interpret Diagrams** Draw the second step of this process in the box on the left.

Food vacuole

Pseudopod

Contractile vacuole

Cytoplasm   Nucleus

Protozoans With Flagella

The second group of protozoans are the flagellates. Flagellates (FLAJ uh lits) are protozoans that use long, whiplike flagella to move. Some live inside the bodies of other organisms. One type of flagellate lives in the intestines of termites. When the termite eats wood, the flagellate breaks it down into sugars that the termite can eat. In return, the termite protects the flagellate. Sometimes, however, a protozoan harms its host. For example, the parasite *Giardia*, shown in **Figure 3**, is deposited in fresh water in the wastes of wild animals. When people drink water containing *Giardia*, these flagellates attach to their intestines, where they feed and reproduce. The people develop an intestinal condition commonly called hiker's disease.

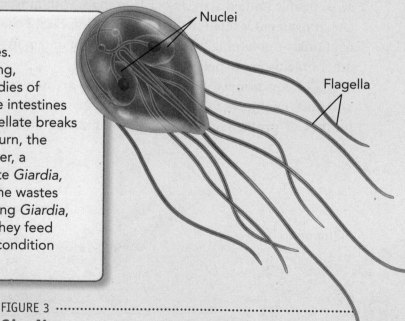

Nuclei

Flagella

FIGURE 3 ·····················
Giardia
Giardia has eight flagella and two nuclei.

✏ **Make Models** How is the movement of the oar on this boat similar to the movement of a flagellum?

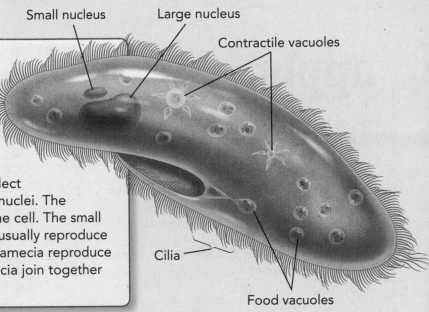

Small nucleus

Large nucleus

Contractile vacuoles

Cilia

Food vacuoles

Protozoans With Cilia

The third group of protozoans are the ciliates. Ciliates have structures called **cilia** (SIL ee uh). These hairlike projections beat with a wavelike motion, moving the organism. The cilia also sweep food into the organism. Notice that the paramecium in **Figure 4** has two contractile vacuoles that collect and expel water from the cell. It also has two nuclei. The large nucleus controls the everyday tasks of the cell. The small nucleus functions in reproduction. Paramecia usually reproduce asexually by binary fission. But sometimes paramecia reproduce by conjugation. This occurs when two paramecia join together and exchange some of their genetic material.

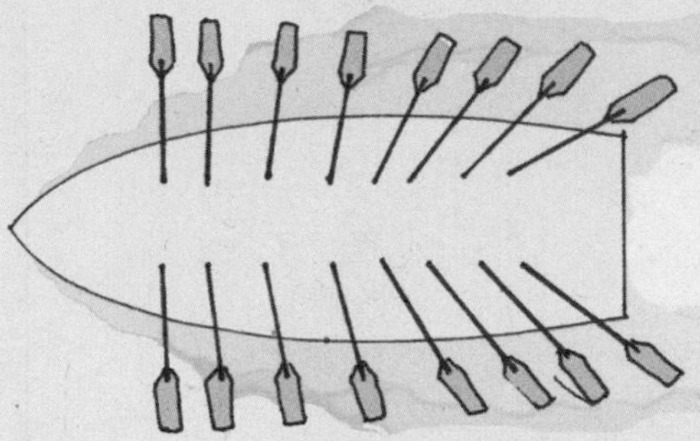

FIGURE 4 ·······························

> **INTERACTIVE ART** **Paramecium**

Paramecia use cilia to move through water.

✎ **Make Models** How is the movement of oars on this boat similar to the movement of cilia?

Protozoans That Are Parasites

The fourth group of protozoans are characterized more by the way they live than by the way they move. They are all parasites that feed on the cells and body fluids of their hosts. These protozoans move in a variety of ways. Some have flagella, and some depend on hosts for transport. One even produces a layer of slime that allows it to slide from place to place! Many of these parasites have more than one host. *Plasmodium,* shown in **Figure 5,** is a protozoan that causes malaria, a disease of the blood. Two hosts are involved in *Plasmodium's* life cycle—humans and a species of mosquitoes found in tropical areas. The disease spreads when a mosquito bites a person with malaria, becomes infected, and then bites a healthy person. Symptoms of malaria include high fevers that alternate with severe chills. These symptoms can last for weeks, then disappear, only to reappear a few months later. Malaria can be fatal.

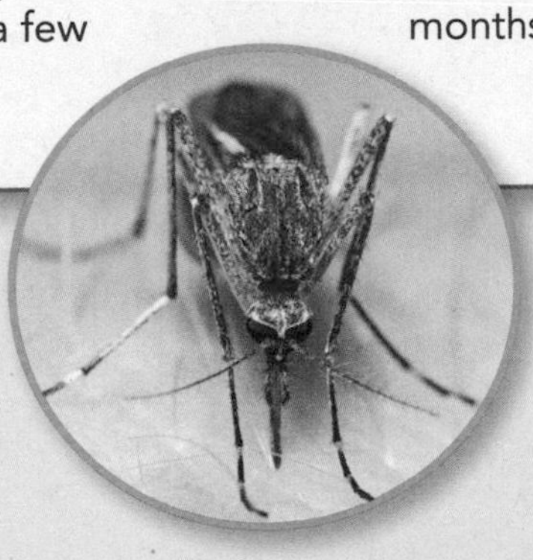

FIGURE 5 ·······························

Plasmodium

Plasmodium is transmitted through mosquito saliva.

✎ **Apply Concepts** If you lived in a tropical area, how could you reduce the risk of being infected with malaria?

229

apply it!

Suppose you fill a container with a culture of amoebas. Then you shine a bright light on one half of the container.

① Predict How do you think the amoebas will respond to bright light? Draw your prediction in the empty container below.

② Explain How were the amoebas able to respond to the light?

_____

_____

_____

③ Infer Why do you think it is important for amoebas to respond to bright light?

_____

_____

_____

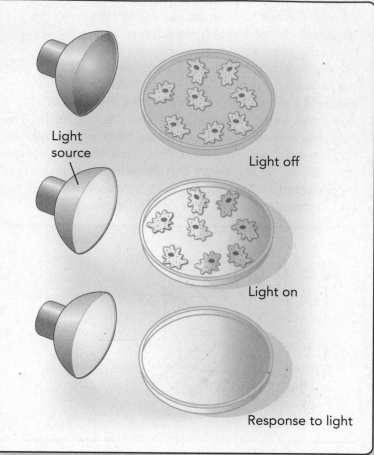

Light source

Light off

Light on

Response to light

🔑 Assess Your Understanding

1a. Review What are the three ways that animal-like protists move?

_____

b. Classify You observe a protist under a microscope. It moves by forming temporary bulges of the cytoplasm. What type of protist is it? Explain your answer.

_____

_____

c. Draw Conclusions Why should you filter water from a stream before drinking it?

_____

_____

Do the Quick Lab *Observing Pseudopod Movement.*

got it?

○ **I get it!** Now I know that the characteristics of animal-like protists are _____

_____

_____

_____

_____

○ **I need extra help with** _____

_____

Go to **MY SCIENCE** 🅢 **COACH** *online for help with this subject.*

What Are the Characteristics of Plant-Like Protists?

Plant-like protists, which are commonly called **algae** (AL jee; singular *alga*), are extremely diverse. 🔑 **Algae are autotrophs, can be unicellular or multicellular, and use pigments to capture the sun's energy.** Most are able to use the sun's energy to make their own food.

Algae play a significant role in many environments. For example, algae that live near the surface of ponds, lakes, and oceans are an important food source for other organisms. In addition, much of the oxygen in Earth's atmosphere is made by these algae.

Algae vary greatly in size and color. Some algae are unicellular, while others are multicellular. Still others are groups of unicellular organisms that live together in colonies. Algae exist in a wide variety of colors because they contain many types of **pigments** — chemicals that produce color. Depending on their pigments, algae can be green, yellow, red, brown, orange, or even black.

✏️

⟳ Summarize Read the text about plant-like protists. Then summarize three characteristics of algae on the lines below.

_____

_____

_____

_____

Euglenoids

Euglenoids (yoo GLEE noydz) are green, unicellular algae that are usually found in fresh water. Most euglenoids are autotrophs that produce food using the sun's energy. However, when sunlight is not available, euglenoids will act as heterotrophs and obtain food from their environment. The euglena on the right is a common euglenoid. Notice the long, whiplike flagellum that helps the organism move. Locate the red eyespot near the flagellum. The eyespot is not really an eye, but it contains pigments that are sensitive to light. It helps the euglena recognize the direction of a light source. Think how important this response is to an organism that needs light to make food.

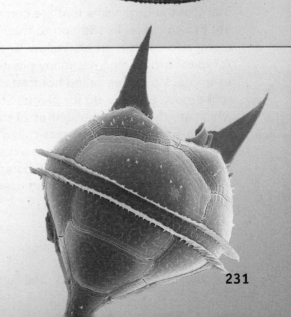

Dinoflagellates

Dinoflagellates (dy noh FLAJ uh lits) are unicellular algae surrounded by stiff plates that look like a suit of armor. Dinoflagellates exist in a variety of colors because they have different amounts of green, orange, and other pigments. All dinoflagellates have two flagella held in grooves between their plates. When the flagella beat, the dinoflagellates twirl like toy tops as they move through the water. Many glow in the dark. They can light up an ocean's surface when disturbed by a passing boat or swimmer at night.

Diatoms

Diatoms are unicellular protists with beautiful glasslike cell walls. Some float near the surface of lakes or oceans or attach to rocks in shallow water. Diatoms are also a source of food for heterotrophs in the water. Many diatoms can move by oozing chemicals out of slits in their cell walls and gliding in the slime. When diatoms die, their cell walls collect on the bottoms of oceans and lakes. Over time, they form layers of a coarse substance called diatomaceous (dy uh tuh MAY shus) earth. Diatomaceous earth makes a good polishing agent and is used in household scouring products. It is even used as an insecticide—the diatoms' sharp cell walls puncture the bodies of insects.

Red Algae

Almost all red algae are multicellular seaweeds. Divers have found red algae growing more than 260 meters below the ocean's surface. Their red pigments are especially good at absorbing the small amount of light that is able to reach deep ocean waters. People use red algae in a variety of ways. Substances extracted from red algae, such as carrageenan (ka ruh JEE nun) and agar, are used in products such as ice cream and hair conditioner. Red algae is a nutrient-rich food that is eaten fresh, dried, or toasted by many people in Asian cultures.

Brown Algae

Many of the organisms that are commonly called seaweeds are brown algae. In addition to their brown pigment, brown algae also contain green, yellow, and orange pigments. A typical brown alga has many plant-like structures. For example, structures called holdfasts anchor the alga to rocks much as roots do for plants. Stalks support the blades, which are the leaflike structures of the alga. Many brown algae also have gas-filled sacs called bladders that allow the algae to float upright in ocean water. Some people eat brown algae. In addition, substances called algins are extracted from brown algae and used as thickeners in puddings and other foods.

Blade

Stalk

Holdfast

FIGURE 6 ··

Functions of Algae

Algae play important roles in the environment.

✎ **Complete each task.**

1. **Classify** Label the type of algae in each of these photos.

2. **Explain** Check off the functions for each type of algae in the table below.

_____ _____

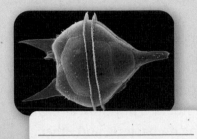

_____ _____ _____

Function	Type of Algae				
	Euglenoids	Dinoflagellates	Diatoms	Red Algae	Brown Algae
Produce oxygen					
Food source for other aquatic organisms					
Eaten by people					
Used in insecticides					
Used in polishing products					
Used in hair conditioner					

Lab zone® Do the Quick Lab Predicting.

🔑 Assess Your Understanding

2a. Review Why is sunlight important to plant-like protists?

_____

_____

b. Compare and Contrast What are some ways that algae are different from each other?

_____

_____

c. CHALLENGE How are euglenoids similar to animal-like protists?

_____

got it?

○ **I get it!** Now I know that the characteristics of plant-like protists are _____

_____

_____

_____

○ **I need extra help with** _____

_____

Go to **MY SCIENCE COACH** online for help with this subject.

What Are the Characteristics of Fungus-Like Protists?

You can think of the fungus-like protists as the "sort of like" organisms. Fungus-like protists are sort of like animals because they are heterotrophs. They are sort of like plants because their cells have cell walls. 🔑 **Fungus-like protists are heterotrophs, have cell walls, and use spores to reproduce.** A **spore** is a tiny cell that is able to grow into a new organism. All fungus-like protists are able to move at some point in their lives. Three types of fungus-like protists are slime molds, water molds, and downy mildews.

Slime Molds Slime molds are often brilliantly colored. They live in moist, shady places like forest floors. They ooze along the surfaces of decaying materials, feeding on bacteria and other microorganisms. Some slime molds are so small that you need a microscope to see them. Others may span several meters!

Slime molds begin their life cycle as tiny, amoeba-like individual cells. The cells use pseudopods to feed and creep around. If food is scarce, the cells grow bigger or join together to form a giant, jellylike mass. In some species, the giant mass is multicellular. In others, the giant mass is actually one giant cell with many nuclei.

The mass oozes along as a single unit. When environmental conditions become harsh, spore-producing structures grow out of the mass, as shown in **Figure 8,** and release spores. Eventually the spores develop into a new generation of slime molds.

Water Molds and Downy Mildews Most water molds and downy mildews live in water or moist places. These organisms often grow as tiny threads that look like fuzz.

Water molds and downy mildews attack many food crops, such as potatoes, corn, and grapes. A water mold impacted history when it destroyed the Irish potato crops in 1845 and 1846. The loss of these crops led to a famine. More than 1 million people in Ireland died.

FIGURE 7 ·······································

A Slime Mold

This slime mold, *Diachea leucopodia*, is producing spores.

✏️ **Interpret Photos** What conditions might have changed in the slime mold's environment to cause spore production?

_____

_____

_____

_____

_____

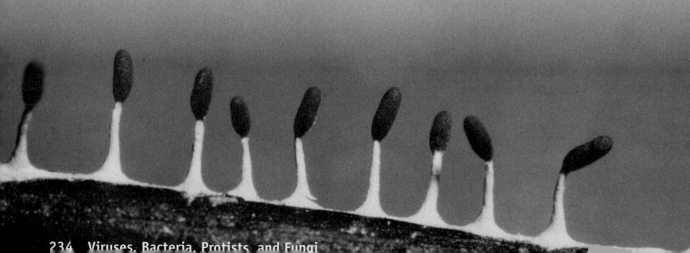

do the math! Analyzing Data

Soybean Crop Loss

Soybean plants can be infected and ruined by a water mold called *Phytophthora sojae*. The graph shows crop loss in metric tons in the United States between 2002 and 2005.

1 Graph Create a title for the graph. Then label the vertical axis.

2 Read Graphs In which year were the most soybeans lost?

_____

3 Read Graphs Describe how the soybean crop loss changed between 2002 and 2005.

_____

_____

_____

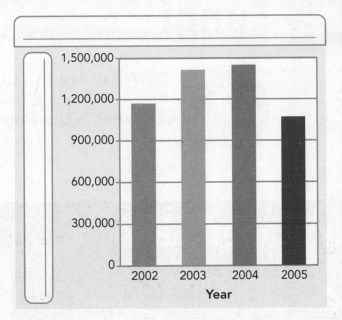

Year

Lab zone Do the Quick Lab *Observing Slime Mold.*

Assess Your Understanding

3a. List What are three types of fungus-like protists?

_____

_____

b. Describe What are two ways that fungus-like and animal-like protists are similar?

_____

_____

c. Apply Concepts A forest loses its trees and the forest floor dries up. How would slime molds be affected?

_____

_____

_____

_____

_____

got it? ....

O **I get it!** Now I know that the characteristics of fungus-like protists are _____

O **I need extra help with** _____

Go to MY SCIENCE COACH online for help with this subject.

235

4 Fungi

🗝 **What Are the Characteristics of Fungi?**

🗝 **What Is the Role of Fungi in Nature?**

my PLANET DiaRY

Fungus Farmers

You may have heard of an "ant farm," but have you ever heard of ant farmers? Leafcutter ants act like farmers, growing fungus for food. First, the ants cut pieces of leaves from trees. Then the ants carry the leaves to an underground nest, where the leaves are crushed and chewed to make a mulch. Surprisingly, the ants don't eat the mulched leaves. They place them in a special growing chamber or "garden." Then they move strands of fungus from an existing garden to the new chamber, where it grows on the leaves. The ants help the fungus grow by removing harmful bacteria and mold. Finally, the ants eat the fungus!

FUN FACTS

Write your answer to each question below.

1. How do the ants act like farmers?

_____

_____

_____

2. How do the leafcutter ants and the fungus benefit from their relationship?

_____

_____

_____

_____

▶ PLANET DIARY Go to **Planet Diary** to learn more about fungi.

Lab zone® Do the Inquiry Warm-Up
There's a Fungus Among Us.

What Are the Characteristics of Fungi?

You accidentally left an orange in your backpack. When you find it, it is covered in white fuzz! The orange is being digested by a mold, which is a type of fungus. You may be familiar with other kinds of fungi, too. For example, the molds that grow on stale bread and the mushrooms that sprout in forests are also fungi.

Vocabulary
- fungus
- hyphae
- fruiting body
- budding
- lichen

Skills
- ↻ Reading: Identify Supporting Evidence
- △ Inquiry: Observe

Most **fungi** (singular *fungus*) share several important characteristics. 🔑 **Fungi are eukaryotes that have cell walls, are heterotrophs that feed by absorbing their food, and use spores to reproduce.** In addition, fungi need moist, warm places in which to grow. They thrive on damp tree barks, moist foods, lawns coated with dew, damp forest floors, and even wet bathroom tiles.

Cell Structure
Fungi range in size from tiny unicellular yeasts to large multicellular fungi. The cells of all fungi are surrounded by cell walls. Except for the simplest fungi, such as unicellular yeasts, the cells of most fungi are arranged in structures called **hyphae** (HY fee; singular *hypha*), shown in **Figure 1**. Hyphae are the branching, threadlike tubes that make up the bodies of multicellular fungi. The hyphae of some fungi are continuous threads of cytoplasm that contain many nuclei. Substances move quickly and freely through the hyphae. What a fungus looks like depends on how its hyphae are arranged. In fuzzy-looking molds, the threadlike hyphae are loosely tangled. In other fungi, the hyphae are packed tightly together.

Obtaining Food
Although fungi are heterotrophs, they do not take food into their bodies as you do. Instead, fungi absorb food through hyphae that grow into the food source.

First, the fungus grows hyphae into a food source. Then digestive chemicals ooze from the hyphae into the food. The chemicals break down the food into small substances that can be absorbed by the hyphae. Some fungi feed on dead organisms. Other fungi are parasites that break down the chemicals in organisms.

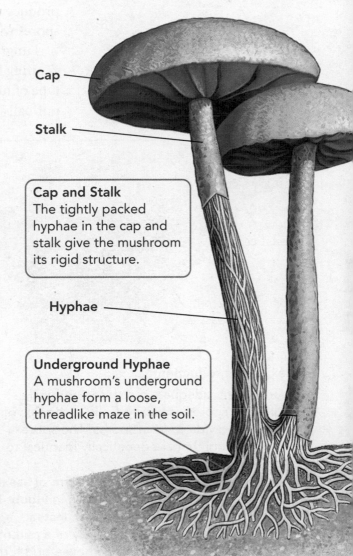

Cap

Stalk

Cap and Stalk
The tightly packed hyphae in the cap and stalk give the mushroom its rigid structure.

Hyphae

Underground Hyphae
A mushroom's underground hyphae form a loose, threadlike maze in the soil.

FIGURE 1 ·················
Structure of a Mushroom
The largest known organism on Earth is an underground fungus that is larger than a thousand football fields.

✎ **Infer** What function might the underground hyphae in this mushroom perform?

_____

_____

_____

Reproduction in Fungi

The way that fungi reproduce guarantees their survival and spread. Most fungi reproduce both asexually and sexually. Fungi usually reproduce by making spores. The lightweight spores are surrounded by a protective covering and can be carried easily through air or water to new sites. Fungi produce millions of spores, more than can ever survive. Only a few spores will fall where conditions are right for them to grow.

Fungi produce spores in reproductive structures called **fruiting bodies.** The appearance of a fruiting body varies from one type of fungus to another. In some fungi, such as mushrooms and puffballs, the visible part of the fungus is the fruiting body. In other fungi, such as bread molds, the fruiting bodies are tiny, stalklike hyphae that grow upward from the other hyphae. A knoblike spore case at the tip of each stalk contains the spores.

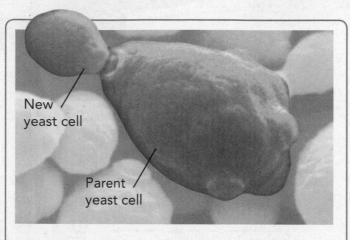

New
yeast cell

Parent
yeast cell

Asexual Reproduction

When there is adequate moisture and food, fungi make spores asexually. Cells at the tips of the hyphae divide to form spores. The spores grow into fungi that are genetically identical to the parent.

Unicellular yeast cells undergo a form of asexual reproduction called **budding,** shown in **Figure 2.** In budding, no spores are produced. Instead, a small yeast cell grows from the body of a parent cell in a way somewhat similar to how a bud forms on a tree branch. The new cell then breaks away and lives on its own.

FIGURE 2 ·
Yeast Reproduction
The smaller structure in the photo above is a new yeast cell budding from its parent.

✏ **Interpret Photos** How is this new yeast cell similar to its parent?

_____

_____

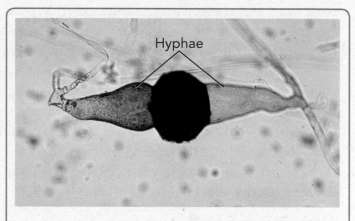

Hyphae

Sexual Reproduction

Most fungi can also reproduce sexually, especially when growing conditions become unfavorable. In sexual reproduction, the hyphae of two fungi grow together and genetic material is exchanged. Eventually, a new reproductive structure grows from the joined hyphae and produces spores. The spores develop into fungi that differ genetically from either parent.

FIGURE 3 ·
Bread Mold Reproduction
Two hyphae in this bread mold have joined together to undergo sexual reproduction. The round object between the hyphae will eventually produce spores.

Classification of Fungi

Three major groups of fungi are the club, sac, and zygote fungi. These groups are classified by the appearance of their reproductive structures. Additional groups include water species that produce spores with flagella and those that form tight associations with plant roots. **Figure 4** shows an example from one of the major groups of fungi.

FIGURE 4 ·······································

Club Fungus

The reproductive structures of this chanterelle look like tiny clubs. You can see spherical spores forming at the end of one of the club-shaped reproductive structures.

✎ **Predict** What will happen after these spores are released?

_____

_____

_____

_____

Do the Quick Lab *Do All Molds Look Alike?*

🔑 Assess Your Understanding

1a. Define What are hyphae?

_____

b. Review What role do spores play in the reproduction of fungi?

_____

_____

c. Sequence Outline the steps by which fungi produce spores during sexual reproduction.

_____

_____

_____

_____

_____

_____

got it? ·······································

○ **I get it!** Now I know that the characteristics of fungi are _____

_____

○ **I need extra help with** _____

Go to **MY SCIENCE COACH** online for help with this subject.

What Is the Role of Fungi in Nature?

Fungi affect humans and other organisms in many ways. **Fungi may act as decomposers and recyclers, or provide foods for people. Fungi may help fight or cause disease. Some fungi live in a beneficial relationship with other organisms.**

Environmental Recycling Like bacteria, many fungi are decomposers—organisms that break down the chemicals in dead organisms. For example, many fungi live in the soil and break down the chemicals in dead plant matter. This process returns important nutrients to the soil. Without fungi and bacteria, Earth would be buried under dead plants and animals!

Food and Fungi When you eat a slice of bread, you benefit from the work of yeast, a type of fungus. Bakers add yeast to bread dough to make it rise. Yeast cells use the sugar in the dough for food and produce carbon dioxide gas as they feed. The gas forms bubbles, which cause the dough to rise. You see these bubbles as holes in a slice of bread. Without yeast, bread would be flat and solid. Yeast is also used to make wine from grapes. Yeast cells feed on the sugar in the grapes and produce carbon dioxide and alcohol.

Other fungi are also important sources of foods. The blue streaks in blue cheese, for example, are actually growths of mold. People enjoy eating mushrooms in salads and soups and on pizza. Because some mushrooms are extremely poisonous, however, you should never pick or eat wild mushrooms.

FIGURE 5 ·····················
Wanted: A Fungus!
Fungi are useful in many ways.

✎ **Communicate** Create a want ad for a fungus. Include a title for your ad. Then list at least two things that the fungus can help you do.

Classifieds

FUNGUS NEEDED
to decompose dead organisms in my garden and return nutrients to the soil

Disease-Fighting Fungi

In 1928, a Scottish biologist named Alexander Fleming was examining petri dishes in which he was growing bacteria. To his surprise, Fleming noticed a spot of bluish green mold growing in one dish. Curiously, no bacteria were growing near the mold. Fleming hypothesized that the mold, a fungus named *Penicillium*, produced a substance that killed the bacteria near it.

Fleming's work contributed to the development of the first antibiotic, penicillin. It has saved the lives of millions of people with bacterial infections. Since the discovery of penicillin, many other antibiotics have been isolated from both fungi and bacteria.

Disease-Causing Fungi

Many fungi are parasites that cause serious diseases in plants. The sac fungus that causes Dutch elm disease is responsible for killing millions of elm trees in North America and Europe. Corn smut and wheat rust are two club fungi that cause diseases in important food crops. Fungal plant diseases also affect other crops, including rice, cotton, and soybeans, resulting in huge crop losses every year.

Some fungi cause diseases in humans. Athlete's foot is an itchy irritation in the damp places between toes. Ringworm shows up as a circular rash on the skin. Because the fungus that causes these diseases produces spores at the site of infection, the diseases spread easily from person to person. Both diseases can be treated with antifungal medications.

Identify Supporting Evidence Underline the evidence in the text that supports the conclusion that *Penicillium* mold kills bacteria.

apply it!

Suppose you are a scientist studying two dishes of the same bacteria. One day, you notice that two dots of mold have started growing in the middle of each dish. The next day you observe what happened.

❶ **Observe** How were the two dishes of bacteria affected by the mold?

_____

_____

❷ **CHALLENGE** Are the two dots of mold the same type of fungus? Explain your answer.

_____

_____

Day One
Mold
Bacteria
Dish A   Dish B

Day Two
Mold
Bacteria
Dish A   Dish B

Fungus-Plant Root Associations Some fungi help plants grow larger and healthier when their hyphae grow into, or on, the plants' roots. The hyphae spread out underground and absorb water and nutrients from the soil for the plant. With more water and nutrients, the plant grows larger than it would have grown without its fungal partner. The plant is not the only partner that benefits. The fungus gets to feed on the extra food that the plant makes and stores.

Most plants have fungal partners. Many plants are so dependent on the fungi that they cannot survive without them. For example, orchid seeds cannot develop without their fungal partners.

Rico arrives at a dairy factory in Europe. How are bacteria and fungi being used to make dairy products?

_____

_____

_____

_____

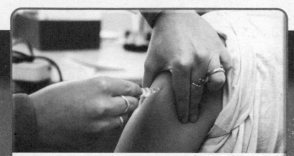

Before he starts his trip, Rico receives a vaccine. What will this vaccine protect him against?

_____

_____

_____

EXPLORE THE BIG ?

What in the world?

How are living things other than plants and animals important to Earth?

FIGURE 6 ·····················

▶ **REAL-WORLD INQUIRY** Rico is taking a trip around the world. Follow him as he encounters viruses, bacteria, protists, and fungi in the environment.

✎ **Interpret Photos** Answer the question in each box on the lines provided.

During Rico's first stop in South America, he steps over a rotting tree trunk. What are the roles of bacteria and fungi?

_____

_____

_____

Lichens A **lichen** (LY kun) consists of a fungus and either algae or autotrophic bacteria that live together in a relationship that benefits both organisms. You have probably seen some familiar lichens—irregular, flat, crusty patches that grow on tree barks or rocks. The fungus benefits from the food produced by the algae or bacteria. The algae or bacteria, in turn, obtain shelter, water, and minerals from the fungus.

Do the Quick Lab
Considering Fungi as Decomposers.

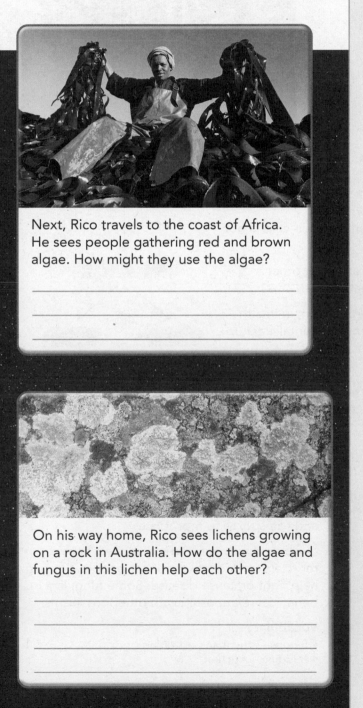

Next, Rico travels to the coast of Africa. He sees people gathering red and brown algae. How might they use the algae?

_____

_____

_____

On his way home, Rico sees lichens growing on a rock in Australia. How do the algae and fungus in this lichen help each other?

_____

_____

_____

Assess Your Understanding

2a. Name What are some foods that are made with fungi?

_____

b. Explain How can fungi be used to treat disease?

_____

_____

_____

c. ANSWER THE BIG ? How are living things other than plants and animals important to Earth?

_____

_____

_____

_____

got**it?**..

○ **I get it!** Now I know the roles of fungi in

the environment are _____

_____

_____

_____

○ **I need extra help with** _____

_____

Go to MY SCIENCE ⓢ COACH *online for help with this subject.*

REVIEW THE BIG **?**

_____ are nonliving. Some protists, such as _____,

produce oxygen. Bacteria and fungi both play roles as _____.

LESSON 1 Viruses

🔑 Viruses are nonliving, have a protein coat that protects an inner core of genetic material, and cannot reproduce on their own.

🔑 Though viruses can cause disease, they can also be used to treat and prevent illnesses.

Vocabulary
• virus • host • parasite • vaccine

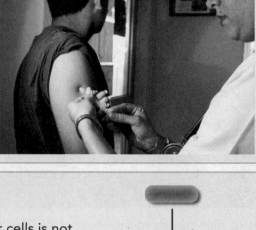

LESSON 2 Bacteria

🔑 Bacteria are prokaryotes. The genetic material in their cells is not contained in a nucleus.

🔑 Bacteria get energy by either making food or eating other organisms, and can reproduce asexually or sexually.

🔑 Bacteria are involved in oxygen and food production, in health maintenance and medicine production, and in environmental cleanup and recycling.

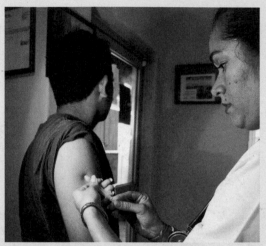

Vocabulary
• bacteria • cytoplasm • ribosome • flagellum • cellular respiration
• binary fission • conjugation • endospore • pasteurization • decomposer

---

LESSON 3 Protists

🔑 Like animals, animal-like protists are heterotrophs, and most can move to get food.

🔑 Algae are autotrophs, can be unicellular or multicellular, and use pigments to capture the sun's energy.

🔑 Fungus-like protists are heterotrophs, have cell walls, and use spores to reproduce.

Vocabulary
• protist • protozoan • pseudopod • contractile vacuole • cilia • algae • pigment • spore

LESSON 4 Fungi

🔑 Fungi are eukaryotes that have cell walls, are heterotrophs that feed by absorbing their food, and use spores to reproduce.

🔑 Fungi may act as decomposers and recyclers, or provide foods for people. Fungi may help fight or cause disease. Some fungi live in a beneficial relationship with other organisms.

Vocabulary
• fungus • hyphae • fruiting body
• budding • lichen

Review and Assessment

LESSON 1 Viruses

1. Bacteriophages are viruses that attack and destroy

   a. plants.   **b.** bacteria.

   c. humans.   **d.** other viruses.

2. A _____ is an organism that lives on or in a host and causes it harm.

3. Interpret Diagrams Label the following structures in the diagram below: protein coat, surface proteins, and genetic material.

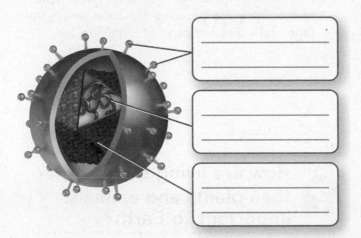

4. Predict Chickenpox is a disease caused by a virus. The chickenpox vaccine began to be recommended for children in 1995. How do you think the rate of chickenpox infections changed after 1995?

_____

_____

_____

_____

5. **Write About It** Bacteria will grow in agar, a substance containing nutrients. Viruses do not grow in agar. If you needed to grow viruses in the laboratory, what kind of substances would you have to use? Explain your reasoning.

LESSON 2 Bacteria

6. Which process is used to kill bacteria in foods such as milk and juice?

   a. conjugation   **b.** pasteurization

   c. binary fission   **d.** decomposition

7. Bacteria reproduce sexually through

_____

8. Classify Look at the photos below. Classify the bacteria according to their shape.

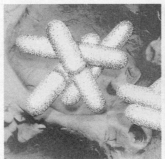 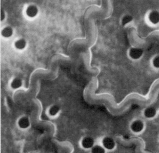

_____

9. Compare and Contrast Fill in the chart below to describe how bacteria obtain energy.

Type of Bacteria	Methods of Obtaining Energy	
Autotrophic	_____ _____ _____	Use chemical energy to make food
Heterotrophic	Consume decaying leaves	_____ _____ _____

10. Infer How do bacteria "recycle" Earth's nutrients?

_____

_____

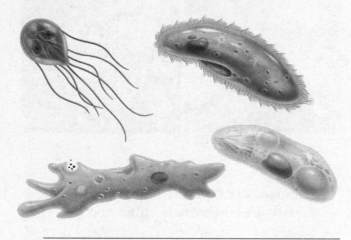

LESSON 3 Protists

11. Protozoans, such as ciliates and flagellates, are

   a. animal-like protists. **b.** plant-like protists.

   c. fungus-like protists. **d.** bacteria-like protists.

12. Algae may be green, orange, red, yellow, brown, or black depending on the _____ they contain.

13. Make Generalizations Four different groups of protists are classified as "animal-like." What characteristics do these groups share?

_____

_____

14. Predict If all algae suddenly disappeared from Earth's waters, how would other living things be affected? Explain your answer.

_____

_____

_____

_____

15. **Write About It** Write a pamphlet describing how homeowners can prevent the growth of slime molds in their basements. Be sure to explain why the suggested action will be effective.

LESSON 4 Fungi

16. Which of the following is a characteristic of fungi?

   a. They are autotrophic.

   b. They lack cell walls.

   c. They are eukaryotes.

   d. They reproduce with seeds.

17. Spores are produced in reproductive structures called _____

18. Apply Concepts A fungicide is a substance that kills fungi and may be used in crop fields where plants are growing. Describe an advantage and a disadvantage of fungicide use.

_____

_____

_____

_____

APPLY THE BIG ?

How are living things other than plants and animals important to Earth?

19. Viruses, bacteria, protists, and fungi are neither plants nor animals. In fact, viruses are not even alive! Still, each plays important roles on Earth. Describe at least three ways in which viruses, bacteria, protists, or fungi are important in your daily life.

_____

_____

_____

_____

_____

_____

_____

_____

Standardized Test Prep

Multiple Choice

Circle the letter of the best answer.

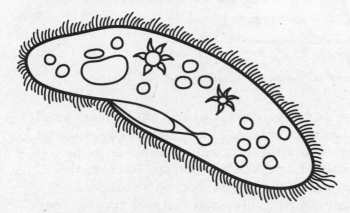

1. Identify the organism shown above and the structure it uses to move.

   A paramecium; cilia

   B protozoan; flagella

   C amoeba; pseudopod

   D parasite; contractile vacuole

2. Which of the following statements about fungus reproduction is true?

   A Fungi only reproduce asexually.

   B Fungi can reproduce by making spores.

   C Fungi reproduce sexually by budding.

   D Fungi reproduce asexually by joining hyphae and exchanging genetic material.

3. Which part of a virus determines which host cell it can infect?

   A nucleus   B protein coat

   C ribosomes   D surface proteins

4. Which statement is correct about plant-like and fungus-like protists?

   A Plant-like protists are all parasitic, while fungus-like protists are not.

   B Plant-like protists are unicellular, while fungus-like protists are multicellular.

   C Plant-like protists are usually autotrophs, while fungus-like protists are heterotrophs.

   D Plant-like protists live on land, while fungus-like protists live on land and in water.

5. Yogurt is produced with the help of _____ while bread rises because of _____.

   A viruses; fungi.   B fungi; protists.

   C bacteria; fungi.   D protists; bacteria.

Constructed Response

Use the diagram below and your knowledge of science to help you answer Question 6. Write your answer on a separate piece of paper.

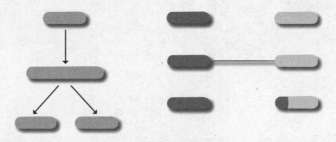

6. Name each process in the drawings of bacteria shown above. Then describe the main differences between these processes.

VIRUS TRACKERS

An epidemiologist wearing a hazardous materials (hazmat) "bunny suit," which insulates the wearer from infectious diseases ▽

When an illness breaks out and affects an unusual number of people in an area, most people want to be as far away as possible. However, some scientists, called epidemiologists, travel to the front lines of these breakouts to investigate. Epidemiologists study how diseases spread. They identify a breakout or epidemic's cause, locate its source, and track how it is spreading. Then they help health officials develop strategies to slow or stop the spread of the disease.

Some of an epidemiologist's most dangerous work occurs in labs, where teams of scientists study disease-causing organisms called pathogens. There are only six labs in the world where epidemiologists can study deadly pathogens such as the Ebola and Marburg viruses. These labs feature multiple airlocks, which prevent unfiltered, infected air from leaving the lab. Epidemiologists must wear pressurized suits and use oxygen tanks. This type of work is dangerous, but epidemiologists are helping us to understand how to protect groups of people from deadly infectious diseases.

Research It Find out more about the history of epidemiology. Learn about the spread of one major disease. What have epidemiologists learned about that disease? Create a timeline showing the first reported cases, the major events in the epidemic, and major events in the treatment of the disease.

Experimenting With Human Subjects

Sometimes researchers need to use human subjects in order to understand how a new treatment will work on people. How do they weigh whether a decision is appropriate? The research must be unlikely to hurt the subjects. The subjects must also understand the risks and join the study voluntarily.

Debate It Newspapers, buses, and the radio often have advertisements for research studies. These studies may offer volunteers money to try an experimental medicine, such as pain medicine, during recovery from surgery. These advertisements often appeal to college students and unemployed people. With a group of three or four classmates, discuss any ethical issues in advertising for research subjects. With your group, organize a debate about the ethics of these advertisements and studies.

page 3

January 1, 2009   The Science Daily

MUSHROOMS WORTH THEIR WEIGHT IN GOLD

A mushroom that attracts wild pigs? That's a delicacy? Absolutely! One of these mushrooms even sold for $330,000 at a charity auction.

Truffles live on the roots of certain trees. They feed on the trees, and in turn help the roots of the trees absorb minerals. Animals such as rodents or wild pigs eat the truffles, and their spores are spread around in the animals' feces. Some truffles release an odor that pigs find irresistible. Truffle hunters use pigs to sniff for these tasty underground fungi.

Evaluate It Research efforts to farm truffles using trees that have had truffle spores pumped into them. Were the sources written for young students, scientists, or someone else? Write a paragraph or two explaining your conclusion.

WHAT'S UNUSUAL ABOUT THESE TREES?

How do you know a plant when you see it?

With its wide trunk and short stubby branches, the baobab tree looks like a sweet potato or an upside-down tree. Seen for miles across the dry African savannah, the baobab can live for over 1,000 years and can grow to over 23 meters high and 27 meters around the trunk. It would take about 18 teenagers with arms spread wide and fingertips touching to encircle a tree that wide!

△ Draw Conclusions Why do you think the baobab tree has such a wide trunk and short branches only at the very top?

_____

_____

_____

_____

_____

▷ UNTAMED SCIENCE Watch the **Untamed Science** video to learn more about plants.

Plants

Check Your Understanding

1. Background Read the paragraph below and then answer the question.

Rahim and Malika were in the park after school. "Plants are such cool **organisms,**" said Rahim. "Can you imagine if humans had green **pigment** in their skin?" "Yeah," said Malika. "If we were **autotrophs,** I'd never have to get up early to pack my lunch!"

> An **organism** is a living thing.
>
> A **pigment** is a colored chemical compound that absorbs light.
>
> An **autotroph** is an organism that makes its own food.

- Give an example of an autotrophic organism that has green pigment.

_____

_____

▶ MY READING WEB If you had trouble completing the question above, visit **My Reading Web** and type in *Plants.*

Vocabulary Skill

Greek Word Origins Many science words come to English from ancient Greek. Learning the Greek word parts can help you understand some of the vocabulary in this chapter.

Greek Word Part	Meaning	Example Word
chloros	pale green	chloroplast, *n.* green cellular structure in which photosynthesis occurs
petalon	leaf	petal, *n.* colorful, leaflike flower structure

2. Quick Check *Chlorophyll* is a pigment found in plants. Which part of the word *chlorophyll* tells you that it is a green pigment?

_____

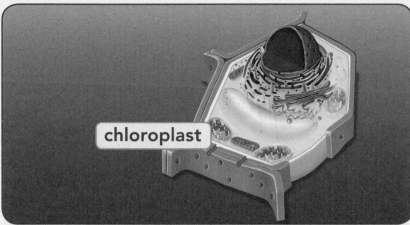
chloroplast

monocot

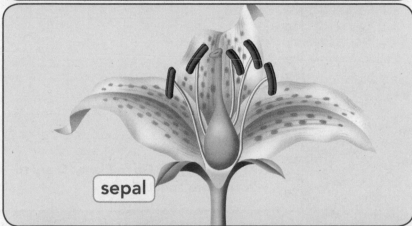
sepal

fruit

Chapter Preview

LESSON 1
- chlorophyll - photosynthesis
- tissue - chloroplast - vacuole
- cuticle - vascular tissue
- Compare and Contrast
- Predict

LESSON 2
- nonvascular plant - rhizoid
- vascular plant - phloem
- xylem - frond - pollen - seed
- gymnosperm - angiosperm
- cotyledon - monocot
- dicot
- Outline
- Communicate

LESSON 3
- root cap - cambium - stoma
- transpiration - embryo
- germination - flower
- pollination - sepal - petal
- stamen - pistil - ovary
- Relate Cause and Effect
- Observe

LESSON 4
- sporophyte - gametophyte
- annual - biennial - perennial
- fertilization - zygote
- cone - ovule - fruit
- Summarize
- Infer

LESSON 5
- tropism - hormone
- auxin - photoperiodism
- critical night length
- short-day plant - long-day plant
- day-neutral plant - dormancy
- Relate Text and Visuals
- Draw Conclusions

LESSON 6
- peat
- Identify the Main Idea
- Pose Questions

253

What Is a Plant?

🔑 **What Characteristics Do All Plants Share?**

🔑 **What Do Plants Need to Live Successfully on Land?**

my planet diary

PROFILE

How Does Your Garden Grow?

Students at The Hilldale School in Daly City, California, get to play in the dirt during class. The students planted and maintain a garden filled with native species. Native plants, or plants that have been in an area for a long time, can struggle to survive if new plants are introduced. This creates problems for the insects, animals, and other organisms that rely on the native plants. The students spent three months removing nonnative plants before creating a garden that will help local organisms right outside their school.

Communicate Discuss the question with a group of classmates. Write your answer below.

Describe a plant project you would like to do at your school.

_____

_____

_____

_____

_____

_____

_____

> **PLANET DIARY** Go to **Planet Diary** to learn more about plants.

 Do the Inquiry Warm-Up *What Do Leaves Reveal About Plants?*

What Characteristics Do All Plants Share?

Which organisms were the ancestors of today's plants? In search of answers, biologists studied fossils, the traces of ancient life forms preserved in rock and other substances. The oldest plant fossils are about 400 million years old. These fossils show that even at that early date, plants already had many adaptations for life on land.

Vocabulary

- chlorophyll • photosynthesis • tissue • chloroplast
- vacuole • cuticle • vascular tissue

Skills

- Reading: Compare and Contrast
- Inquiry: Predict

Better clues to the origin of plants came from comparing the chemicals in modern plants to those in other organisms. Biologists studied a pigment called chlorophyll. **Chlorophyll** (KLAWR uh fil) is a green pigment found in the chloroplasts of plants, algae, and some bacteria. Land plants and green algae contain the same forms of chlorophyll. Further comparisons of genetic material clearly showed that plants and green algae are very closely related. Today, green algae are classified as plants.

Members of the plant kingdom share several characteristics. **Nearly all plants are autotrophs, organisms that produce their own food. With the exception of some green algae, all plants contain many cells. In addition, all plant cells are surrounded by cell walls.**

Plants Are Autotrophs
You can think of a typical plant as a sun-powered, food-making factory. Sunlight provides the energy for this food-making process, called **photosynthesis.** During photosynthesis, a plant uses carbon dioxide gas and water to make food and oxygen.

Compare and Contrast
How do you think the ancient environment of the leaf in the fossil differed from that of the modern leaf in the pictures below?

_____

_____

_____

_____

_____

_____

_____

_____

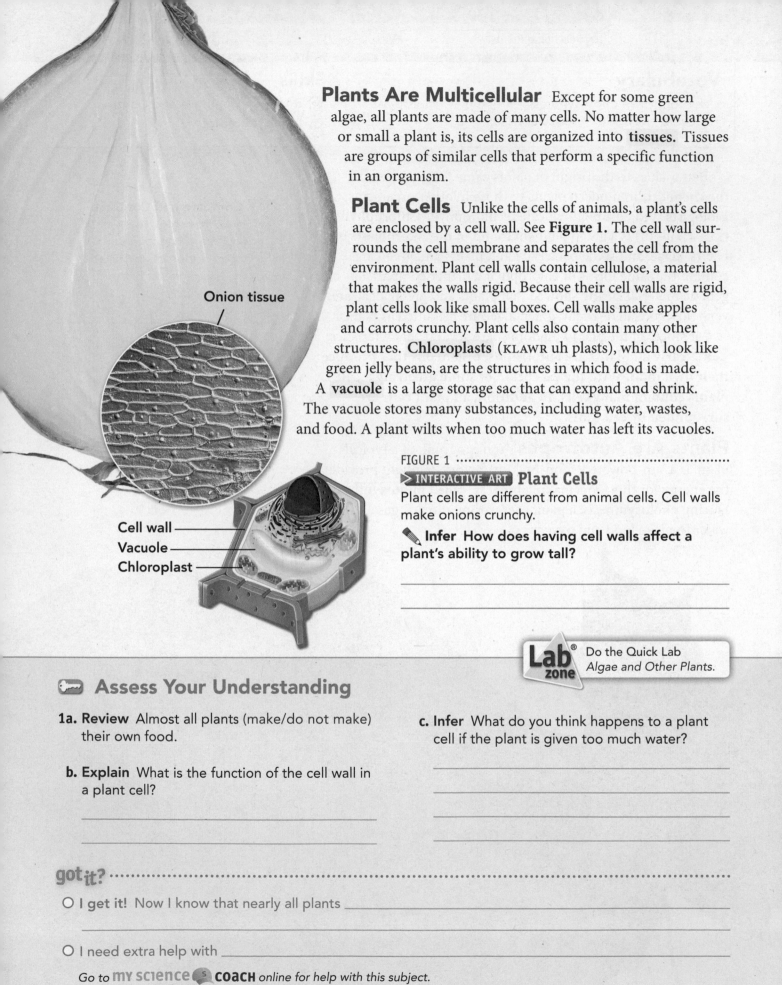

Plants Are Multicellular

Except for some green algae, all plants are made of many cells. No matter how large or small a plant is, its cells are organized into **tissues.** Tissues are groups of similar cells that perform a specific function in an organism.

Plant Cells

Unlike the cells of animals, a plant's cells are enclosed by a cell wall. See **Figure 1.** The cell wall surrounds the cell membrane and separates the cell from the environment. Plant cell walls contain cellulose, a material that makes the walls rigid. Because their cell walls are rigid, plant cells look like small boxes. Cell walls make apples and carrots crunchy. Plant cells also contain many other structures. **Chloroplasts** (KLAWR uh plasts), which look like green jelly beans, are the structures in which food is made. A **vacuole** is a large storage sac that can expand and shrink. The vacuole stores many substances, including water, wastes, and food. A plant wilts when too much water has left its vacuoles.

Onion tissue

Cell wall
Vacuole
Chloroplast

FIGURE 1 ··

> **INTERACTIVE ART** **Plant Cells**

Plant cells are different from animal cells. Cell walls make onions crunchy.

✎ **Infer** How does having cell walls affect a plant's ability to grow tall?

_____

_____

Lab zone® Do the Quick Lab
Algae and Other Plants.

🔑 Assess Your Understanding

1a. Review Almost all plants (make/do not make) their own food.

b. Explain What is the function of the cell wall in a plant cell?

_____

_____

c. Infer What do you think happens to a plant cell if the plant is given too much water?

_____

_____

_____

got it? ···

○ **I get it!** Now I know that nearly all plants _____

_____

○ **I need extra help with** _____

Go to MY SCIENCE COACH online for help with this subject.

What Do Plants Need to Live Successfully on Land?

Imagine multicellular algae floating in the ocean. The algae obtain water and other materials directly from the water around them. They are held up toward the sunlight by the water. Now imagine plants living on land. What adaptations would help them meet their needs without water all around them? **For plants to survive on land, they must have ways to obtain water and other nutrients from their surroundings, retain water, support their bodies, transport materials, and reproduce.**

Obtaining Water and Other Nutrients Recall that all organisms need water to survive. Obtaining water is easy for algae because water surrounds them. To live on land, plants need adaptations for obtaining water from the soil. One adaptation is the way the plant produces its roots, as shown in **Figure 2**. Plants must also have ways of obtaining other nutrients from the soil.

Saguaro cactus

Acacia tree

FIGURE 2 ·····················
Getting Water in the Desert
The saguaro cactus and the acacia tree both live in deserts with limited water. Saguaro roots spread out horizontally. When it rains, the roots quickly absorb water over a wide area. Acacia trees in the Negev Desert of Israel get their water from deep underground instead of at the surface.

✎ **Interpret Diagrams** Draw the roots of the acacia tree. Then describe how the growth of the roots differs between the plants.

_____

_____

257

FIGURE 3 ....

Waterproof Leaves

The waxy cuticle of many leaves, like the one below, looks shiny under light.

Retaining Water When there is more water in plant cells than in the air, the water leaves the plant and enters the air. The plant could dry out if it cannot hold onto water. One adaptation that helps a plant reduce water loss is a waxy, waterproof layer called the **cuticle.** You can see the cuticle on the leaf in **Figure 3.**

Support A plant on land must support its own body. It's easier for small, low-growing plants to support themselves. In larger plants, the food-making parts must be exposed to as much sunlight as possible. Cell walls and tissue strengthen and support the large bodies of these plants.

Transporting Materials A plant needs to transport water, minerals, food, and other materials from one part of its body to another. In general, water and minerals are taken up by the bottom part of the plant, while food is made in the top part. But all of the plant's cells need water, minerals, and food.

In small plants, materials can simply move from one cell to the next. Larger plants need a more efficient way to transport materials from one part of the plant to another. These plants have tissue for transporting materials called vascular tissue. **Vascular tissue** is a system of tubelike structures inside a plant through which water, minerals, and food move. See vascular tissue in action in **Figure 4.**

apply it!

This graph shows how much water a plant loses during the day. Give the graph a title.

❶ **Interpret Graphs** During what part of the day did the plant lose the most water?

_____

❷ **Predict** How might the line in the graph look from 10 P.M. to 8 A.M.? Why?

_____

_____

_____

_____

_____

_____

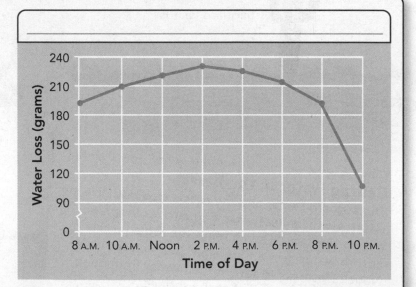

❸ **CHALLENGE** Do you think this graph would be the same for plants all around the world? Why?

_____

_____

_____

_____

Reproduction For algae and some other plants, reproduction can only occur if there is water in the environment. This is because the sperm cells of these plants swim through the water to the egg cells. Land plants need to have adaptations that make reproduction possible in dry environments.

FIGURE 4 ••
Colorful Carnations
These three carnations were left overnight in glasses of water. Blue dye was added to the glass in the middle. The stem of the flower on the right was split in half. Part of the stem was placed in water with blue dye and the other part was placed in water with red dye.

✎ **Draw Conclusions** Why did the flowers in the glasses with dye change color?

_____

_____

_____

_____

_____

_____

Lab zone ® Do the Quick Lab
Local Plant Diversity.

🔑 Assess Your Understanding

2a. Define What is a cuticle?

_____

_____

_____

b. Apply Concepts Describe the pros and cons of being a tall land plant.

_____

_____

_____

_____

_____

got it?

○ **I get it!** Now I know that to live on land, plants need to _____

_____

_____

_____

_____

○ **I need extra help with** _____

_____

_____

Go to MY SCIENCE ⓢ COACH *online for help with this subject.*

259

Classifying Plants

🔑 **What Are the Characteristics of Nonvascular Plants?**

🔑 **What Are the Characteristics of Seedless Vascular Plants?**

🔑 **What Are the Characteristics of Seed Plants?**

my planet Diary

CAREER

The Moss Is Greener on the Other Side

Tired of mowing the lawn? Never want to pull out another weed? Hire a moss landscaper! Landscapers design beautiful yards, usually planting trees, flowers, bushes, and grasses. These plants need a lot of care. Moss doesn't. Moss grows in the shade where other plants can't. Landscapers can use moss to cover an entire yard if the conditions are right. Mosses are also better for the environment. People don't have to put toxic chemicals on their moss lawns to kill weeds or keep it green.

Write your answer below.

Do you think people should use moss instead of grass for their lawns? Why?

_____

_____

_____

_____

▶ **PLANET DIARY** Go to **Planet Diary** to learn more about plant classification.

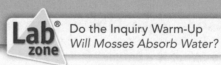 Do the Inquiry Warm-Up
Will Mosses Absorb Water?

What Are the Characteristics of Nonvascular Plants?

Plants that lack vascular tissue for transporting materials are known as **nonvascular plants.** 🔑 **Nonvascular plants are low-growing, have thin cell walls, and do not have roots for absorbing water from the ground.** Instead, they obtain water and materials directly from their surroundings. The materials then pass from one cell to the next. This means that materials do not travel far or quickly. This slow method helps explain why most nonvascular plants live in damp, shady places. The thin cell walls are why these plants cannot grow more than a few centimeters tall.

Vocabulary

- nonvascular plant • rhizoid • vascular plant • phloem
- xylem • frond • pollen • seed • gymnosperm
- angiosperm • cotyledon • monocot • dicot

Skills

↻ **Reading: Outline**
△ **Inquiry: Communicate**

Mosses Have you ever seen mosses growing in the cracks of a sidewalk or in a shady spot? With more than 10,000 species, mosses are by far the most diverse group of nonvascular plants.

If you were to look closely at a moss, you would see a plant that looks something like **Figure 1.** Structures that look like tiny leaves grow off a small, stemlike structure. Thin, rootlike structures called **rhizoids** anchor the moss and absorb water and nutrients. Moss grows a long, slender stalk with a capsule at the end. The capsule contains spores for reproduction.

FIGURE 1 ·······

Moss Structure

Diagrams can be easier to read than photographs, but photographs are more realistic.

✎ **Relate Diagrams and Photos** Label the capsule, stalk, and leaflike structure in the photo. Draw lines from your labels to the structure itself, like in the diagram below.

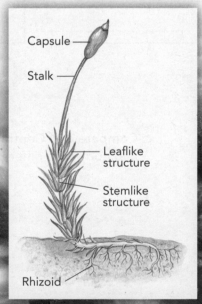

Capsule

Stalk

Leaflike structure

Stemlike structure

Rhizoid

Liverwort ▲

Liverworts and Hornworts Liverworts and hornworts are two other groups of nonvascular plants. There are more than 8,000 species of liverworts. This group of plants is named for the shape of the plant's body, which looks somewhat like a human liver. *Wort* is an old English word for "plant." Liverworts are often found growing as a thick crust on moist rocks or soil along the sides of a stream. There are fewer than 100 species of hornworts. If you look closely at a hornwort, you can see slender, curved structures that look like horns growing out of the plant. Unlike mosses or liverworts, hornworts are seldom found on rocks or tree trunks. Instead, hornworts usually live in moist soil, often mixed in with grass plants.

●**Outline** Fill in the table to the right with what you have learned about liverworts and hornworts.

Hornwort ▶

Nonvascular Plants

Plant	Identifiable Physical Characteristic	Where Found
Mosses	Fuzzy appearance	Shady spots, rocks, tree trunks
Liverworts		
Hornworts		

Lab zone® Do the Quick Lab *Masses of Mosses.*

🔑 Assess Your Understanding

1a. Review (Vascular tissues/Rhizoids) anchor moss and absorb water and nutrients.

b. Explain Why are most nonvascular plants short?

_____

_____

c. Compare and Contrast How are liverworts and hornworts different?

_____

_____

_____

_____

got it? ....

○ **I get it!** Now I know the characteristics of nonvascular plants are _____

_____

○ **I need extra help with** _____

Go to **MY SCIENCE** 💬 **COACH** *online for help with this subject.*

What Are the Characteristics of Seedless Vascular Plants?

If you could have walked through the ancient forests that existed long before the dinosaurs lived, they would have looked very strange to you. You might have recognized the mosses and liverworts that carpeted the moist soil, but you would have seen very tall, odd-looking trees. Among the trees grew huge, tree-sized ferns. Other trees resembled giant sticks with leaves up to one meter long. The odd-looking plants in the ancient forests are the ancestors of the ferns, clubmosses, and horsetails of today. **Ferns, club mosses, and horsetails share two characteristics. They have vascular tissue and they do not produce seeds. Instead of seeds, these plants reproduce by releasing spores.**

Vascular Tissue Ancient trees were vascular plants. **Vascular plants** are plants with true vascular tissue. Vascular plants can grow tall because their vascular tissue provides an effective way of transporting materials throughout the plant. The vascular tissue also strengthens the plants' bodies. You can see vascular tissue in **Figure 2.** The cells making up the vascular tissue have strong cell walls. Imagine a handful of drinking straws bundled together with rubber bands. The bundle of straws is stronger and more stable than a single straw would be. Arranged similarly, the strong, tubelike structures in vascular plants give the plants strength and stability.

There are two types of vascular tissue. **Phloem** (FLOH um) is the vascular tissue through which food moves. After food is made in the leaves, it enters the phloem and travels to other parts of the plant. Water and minerals, on the other hand, travel in the vascular tissue called **xylem** (ZY lum). The roots absorb water and minerals from the soil. These materials enter the root's xylem and move upward into the stems and leaves.

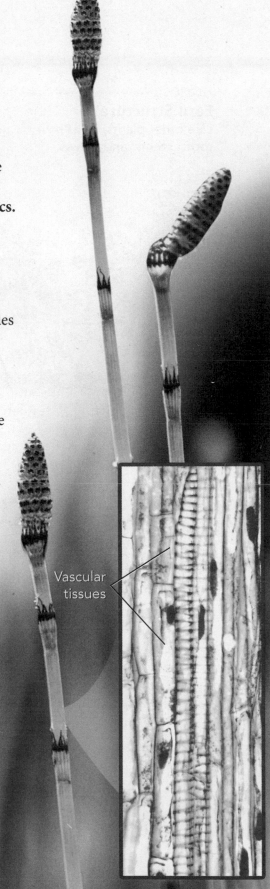

Vascular tissues

FIGURE 2 ·····················

Vascular Tissue
Vascular plants have xylem and phloem.

✏️ **Identify** In the text, underline the roles of vascular tissue.

FIGURE 3

Fern Structure

Like other plants, ferns have roots, stems, and leaves.

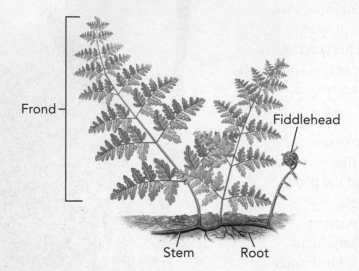

Frond

Fiddlehead

Stem   Root

Ferns

There are more than 12,000 species of ferns alive today. They range in size from tiny plants about the size of this letter *M* to tree ferns that grow up to five meters tall. Ferns thrive in shaded areas with moist soil. Some remain green year-round while others turn brown in the fall and regrow in spring.

The Structure of Ferns

Like other vascular plants, ferns have stems, roots, and leaves. The stems of most ferns are underground. Leaves grow upward from the top side of the stems, while roots grow downward from the bottom of the stems. Water and nutrients enter the root's vascular tissue and travel through the tissue into the stems and leaves.

Figure 3 shows a fern's structure. Notice that the fern's leaves, or **fronds,** are divided into many smaller parts that look like small leaves. The upper surface of each frond is coated with a cuticle that helps the plant retain water. In many ferns, the developing leaves are coiled at first. Because they resemble the top of a violin, these young leaves are often called fiddleheads. Fiddleheads uncurl as they mature.

apply it!

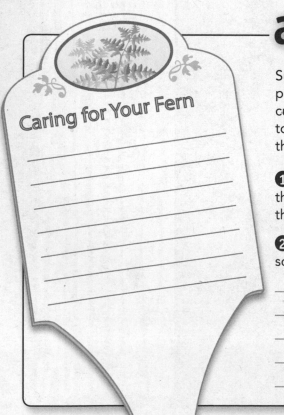

Caring for Your Fern

_____

_____

_____

_____

_____

_____

Suppose you ran a flower shop that sold cut flowers and potted plants. You have just received a shipment of potted ferns and several customers are interested in purchasing them. Before they are ready to be sold, you need to make sure your customers can take care of the ferns so they won't regret their purchase.

1 **Communicate** On the tag at left, write the care instructions that will be given to your customers who buy potted ferns. Include the conditions that the fern needs for light and water.

2 [CHALLENGE] Florists recommend not putting plants like ferns in south- or west-facing windows. Why?

_____

_____

_____

_____

_____

◀ Horsetail

Club Mosses and Horsetails Like ferns, club mosses and horsetails have true stems, roots, and leaves. However, there are relatively few species of club mosses and horsetails alive today.

Do not be confused by the name *club moss*. Unlike true mosses, club mosses have vascular tissue. You may be familiar with the club moss in **Figure 4.** The plant, which looks a little like a small branch of a pine tree, is sometimes called ground pine or princess pine. Club mosses usually grow in moist woodlands and near streams.

There are about 30 species of horsetails on Earth today. The whorled pattern of growth somewhat resembles the appearance of a horse's tail. The stems contain silica, a gritty substance also found in sand. During colonial times, Americans used the plants to scrub their pots and pans. Another common name for horsetails is scouring brushes.

Club moss ▼

FIGURE 4 ···
Moss Imposter?
A club moss is pictured at left.

✎ **Describe** Why is a club moss not a true moss?

_____

_____

_____

_____

_____

Lab zone® Do the Quick Lab *Examining a Fern.*

🗝 Assess Your Understanding

2a. Identify In plants, water moves through (phloem/xylem). Food moves through (phloem/xylem).

b. Infer Why do you think the developing leaves of a fern are coiled?

_____

c. Develop Hypotheses Why do you think there are more ferns than club mosses?

_____

_____

_____

got it? ··

○ **I get it!** Now I know the characteristics of seedless vascular plants include _____

_____

○ **I need extra help with** _____

Go to **MY SCIENCE** Ⓢ **COACH** online for help with this subject.

What Are the Characteristics of Seed Plants?

Seed plants outnumber seedless plants by more than ten to one. You eat many seed plants—rice, peas, and squash, for example. You wear clothes made from seed plants, such as cotton and flax. You may live in a home built from seed plants—oak, pine, or maple trees. In addition, seed plants produce much of the oxygen you breathe.

Seed plants share two important characteristics.  **Seed plants have vascular tissue, and they use pollen and seeds to reproduce.** In addition, the bodies of all seed plants have roots, stems, and leaves. Most seed plants live on land. Recall that land plants face many challenges, including standing upright and supplying all their cells with food and water. Like ferns, seed plants meet these two challenges with vascular tissue.

Pollen and Seeds Unlike seedless plants, seed plants can live in a wide variety of environments. Recall that seedless plants need water in their surroundings for fertilization to occur. Seed plants do not need water for sperm to swim to the eggs. Instead, seed plants produce **pollen,** tiny structures that contain the cells that will later become sperm cells. Pollen deliver sperm cells directly near the eggs. After sperm cells fertilize the eggs, seeds develop. A **seed** is a structure that contains a young plant inside a protective covering. Seeds protect the young plant from drying out.

Gymnosperms The giant sequoia trees belong to the group of seed plants known as gymnosperms. A **gymnosperm** (JIM noh spurm) is a seed plant that produces naked seeds. The seeds of gymnosperms are referred to as "naked" because they are not enclosed by a protective fruit.

Many gymnosperms have needlelike or scalelike leaves and deep-growing root systems. Gymnosperms are the oldest type of seed plant. According to fossil evidence, gymnosperms first appeared on Earth about 360 million years ago. Fossils also indicate that there were many more species of gymnosperms on Earth in the past than there are today. Four types of gymnosperms exist today, as shown in **Figure 5.**

Vocabulary Greek Word Origins The word *gymnosperm* comes from the Greek words *gumnos,* meaning "naked," and *sperma,* meaning "seed." Why are the seeds of gymnosperms considered to be naked?

_____

_____

_____

_____

GYMNOSPERM	DESCRIPTION/FUNCTION
Cycads 	About 175 million years ago, the majority of plants were cycads (SY kadz). Today, cycads grow mainly in tropical and subtropical areas. Cycads look like palm trees with cones that can grow as large as a football!
Conifers 	Conifers (KAHN uh furz), or cone-bearing plants, are the largest and most diverse group of modern gymnosperms. Most conifers are evergreens, meaning they keep their leaves or needles year-round.
Ginkgoes 	Ginkgoes (GING kohz) also grew hundreds of millions of years ago. Today, only one species, *Ginkgo biloba*, exists. It probably survived because the Chinese and Japanese cared for it in their gardens. Today, ginkgo trees are planted along city streets because they can tolerate air pollution.
Gnetophytes 	Gnetophytes (NEE tuh fyts) live in hot deserts and in tropical rain forests. Some are trees, some are shrubs, and others are vines. The *Welwitschia* (shown at left) of West Africa can live for more than 1,000 years!

FIGURE 5 ·······························

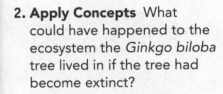

Types of Gymnosperms
The chart describes the four main groups of gymnosperms.

✎ **Answer these questions.**

1. **Name** Which group of gymnosperms has the most species?

_____

2. **Apply Concepts** What could have happened to the ecosystem the *Ginkgo biloba* tree lived in if the tree had become extinct?

_____

_____

_____

_____

_____

_____

_____

_____

_____

Angiosperms

You probably associate the word *flower* with a sweet-smelling plant growing in a garden. You certainly wouldn't think of something that smells like rotting meat. That's exactly what the corpse flower, or rafflesia, smells like. This flower, which grows in Asia, produces a meat smell, which attracts flies that spread the flower's pollen. You won't be seeing rafflesia in your local florist shop any time soon! Rafflesia belongs to the group of seed plants known as angiosperms (AN jee uh spurmz). **Angiosperms,** or flowering plants, share two important characteristics. First, they produce flowers. Second, in contrast to gymnosperms, which produce uncovered seeds, angiosperms produce seeds that are enclosed in fruits.

Angiosperms live almost everywhere on Earth. They grow in frozen areas in the Arctic, tropical jungles, and barren deserts. A few angiosperms, such as mangrove trees, live at the ocean's edge.

Types of Angiosperms

Angiosperms are divided into two major groups: monocots and dicots. "Cot" is short for cotyledon (kaht uh LEED un). The **cotyledon,** or seed leaf, provides food for the embryo. *Mono-* means "one" and *di-* means "two." **Monocots** are angiosperms that have only one seed leaf. Grasses, including corn, wheat, and rice, and plants such as lilies and tulips, are monocots. **Dicots,** on the other hand, produce seeds with two seed leaves. Dicots include plants such as roses and violets, as well as dandelions. Both oak and maple trees are dicots, as are food plants such as beans and apples. **Figure 6** shows the characteristics of monocots and dicots.

_____

FIGURE 6 ·······························

> VIRTUAL LAB **Monocots and Dicots**

Use the table below to find your answers.

✎ **Interpret Photos** Label the rafflesia (top) and the other flowers on this page as *monocots* or *dicots.*

_____

Characteristics of Monocots and Dicots

	Seeds	Leaves	Flowers	Stems	Roots
Monocots	Single cotyledon	Parallel veins	Floral parts often in multiples of 3	Vascular tissue bundles scattered throughout stem	Many roots spread out
Dicots	Two cotyledons	Branched veins	Floral parts often in multiples of 4 or 5	Vascular tissue bundles arranged in a ring	One main root

do the
math!

Use the graph of known plant species to answer the questions.

❶ Interpret Graphs Which plant group has the fewest species?

_____

❷ Calculate Figure out the percentage that each of the following plant groups represents. Round your answer to the nearest tenth.

Green algae _____

Ferns and relatives _____

Angiosperms _____

❸ CHALLENGE Why do you think angiosperms are the largest group?

_____

_____

_____

_____

_____

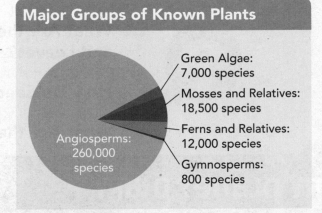

Major Groups of Known Plants

Green Algae:
7,000 species

Mosses and Relatives:
18,500 species

Ferns and Relatives:
12,000 species

Angiosperms:
260,000
species

Gymnosperms:
800 species

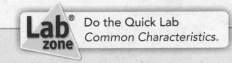
Do the Quick Lab
Common Characteristics.

🔑 Assess Your Understanding

3a. Define What are pollen?

_____

_____

_____

_____

b. Draw Conclusions Why do you think angiosperms enclose their seeds in fruits?

_____

_____

_____

_____

got it? ·

○ **I get it!** Now I know the characteristics of seed plants include _____

_____

○ **I need extra help with** _____

Go to MY SCIENCE 🄢 COACH *online for help with this subject.*

Plant Structures

UNLOCK
THE BIG

🔑 **What Are the Functions of Roots, Stems, and Leaves?**

🔑 **How Do Seeds Become New Plants?**

🔑 **What Are the Structures of a Flower?**

my planeT DiaRY

SCIENCE STATS

Plant Giants

- The aroid plant (as shown here) on the island of Borneo in Asia has leaves that can grow three meters long! These are the largest undivided leaves on Earth!

- The rafflesia flower can grow up to one meter wide and weigh seven kilograms.

- The jackfruit can weigh up to 36 kilograms. That's the world's largest fruit that grows on trees!

Write your answer below.
Why do you think the aroid plant has such big leaves?

_____

_____

_____

▷ PLANET DIARY Go to **Planet Diary** to learn more about plant structures.

 Do the Inquiry Warm-Up
Which Plant Part Is It?

What Are the Functions of Roots, Stems, and Leaves?

Each part of a plant plays an important role in its structure and function. Roots, stems, and leaves are just three structures we will look into further.

Roots Have you ever tried to pull a dandelion out of the soil? It's not easy, is it? That is because most roots are good anchors. Roots have three main functions. 🔑 **Roots anchor a plant in the ground, absorb water and minerals from the soil, and sometimes store food.** The more root area a plant has, the more water and minerals it can absorb.

Vocabulary

- root cap • cambium • stoma • transpiration
- embryo • germination • flower • pollination
- sepal • petal • stamen • pistil • ovary

Skills

↺ Reading: Relate Cause and Effect

△ Inquiry: Observe

Types of Roots The two main types of root systems are shown in **Figure 1.** A fibrous root system consists of many similarly sized roots that form a dense, tangled mass. Plants with fibrous roots take a lot of soil with them when you pull them out of the ground. Lawn grass, corn, and onions have fibrous root systems. In contrast, a taproot system has one long, thick main root. Many smaller roots branch off the main root. A plant with a taproot system is hard to pull out of the ground. Carrots, dandelions, and cacti have taproots.

FIGURE 1 ·······························

Root Systems and Structure

There are two main root systems with many structures.

✎ **Interpret Photos** Label the taproot *T* and the fibrous roots *F*.

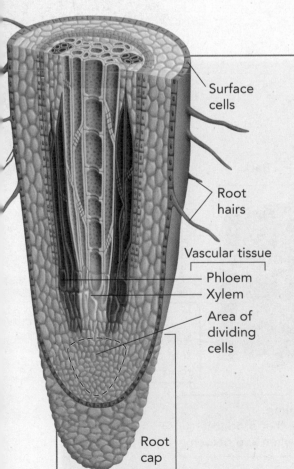

Surface cells

Root hairs

Vascular tissue

Phloem
Xylem

Area of dividing cells

Root cap

Root Structure

In **Figure 2,** you can see the structure of a typical root. The tip of the root is rounded and is covered by the root cap. The **root cap** protects the root from injury as the root grows through the soil. Behind the root cap are the cells that divide to form new root cells.

Root hairs grow out of the root's surface. These tiny hairs can enter the spaces between soil particles, where they absorb water and minerals. The root hairs also help to anchor the plant in the soil.

Locate the vascular tissue in the center of the root. The water and nutrients that are absorbed from the soil quickly move into the xylem. From there, these substances are transported upward to the plant's stems and leaves. Phloem transports food manufactured in the leaves to the root. The root tissues then use the food for growth or store it for future use by the plant.

FIGURE 2 ·······························

Root Structure

Roots have many structures.

✎ **Define** What is the function of the root cap?

_____

_____

Stems

The stem of a plant has two main functions. 🔑 **The stem carries substances between the plant's roots and leaves. The stem also provides support for the plant and holds up the leaves so they are exposed to the sun.** In addition, some stems, such as those of asparagus, store food.

The Structure of a Stem Stems can be either woody or herbaceous (hur BAY shus). Woody stems are hard and rigid, such as in maple trees. Herbaceous stems contain no wood and are often soft. Plants with herbaceous stems include daisies, ivy, and asparagus (pictured left).

Herbaceous and woody stems consist of phloem and xylem tissue as well as many other supporting cells. As you can see in **Figure 3,** a woody stem contains many layers of tissue. The outermost layer is bark. Bark includes an outer protective layer and an inner layer of living phloem, which transports food through the stem. Next is a layer of cells called the **cambium** (KAM bee um), which divides to produce new phloem and xylem. It is xylem that makes up most of what you call "wood." Sapwood is active xylem that transports water and minerals through the stem. The older, darker, heartwood is inactive but provides support.

FIGURE 3 ···

Stem Structure

The woody stem of a tree contains many different structures.

✎ **Interpret Diagrams** Label the active xylem and phloem on the tree trunk below.

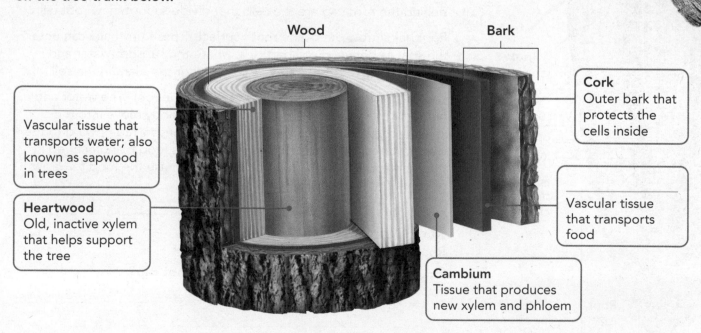

Wood

Bark

Cork
Outer bark that protects the cells inside

Vascular tissue that transports water; also known as sapwood in trees

Vascular tissue that transports food

Heartwood
Old, inactive xylem that helps support the tree

Cambium
Tissue that produces new xylem and phloem

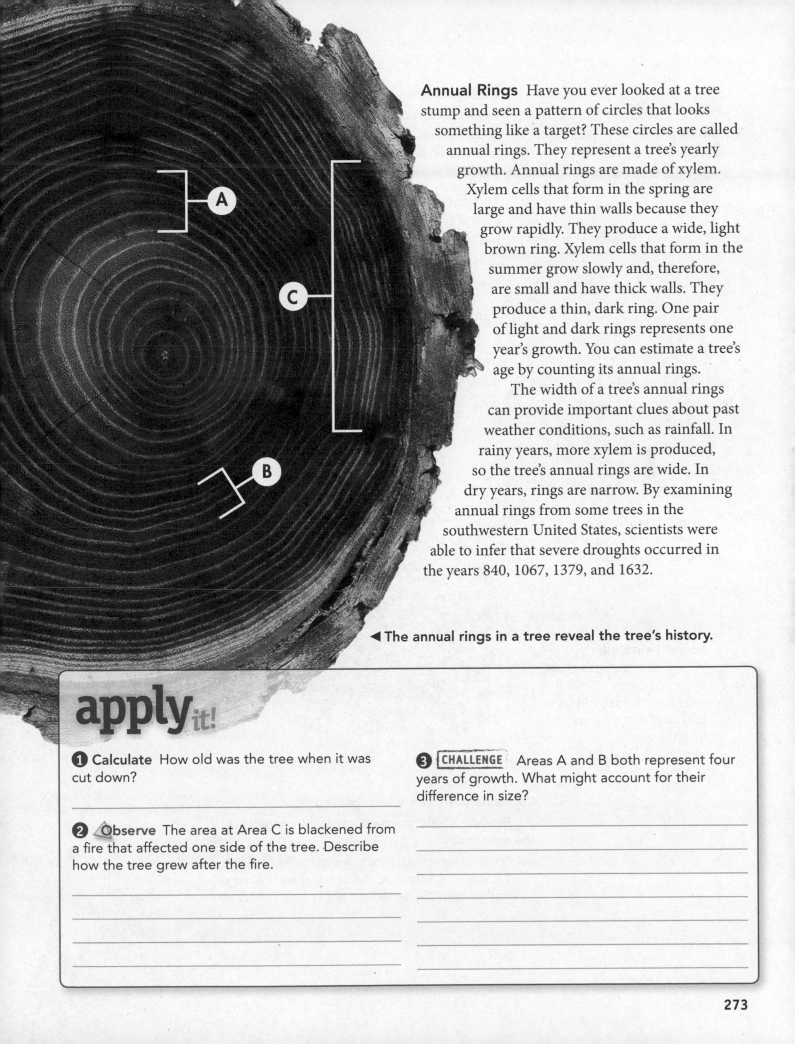

Annual Rings Have you ever looked at a tree stump and seen a pattern of circles that looks something like a target? These circles are called annual rings. They represent a tree's yearly growth. Annual rings are made of xylem. Xylem cells that form in the spring are large and have thin walls because they grow rapidly. They produce a wide, light brown ring. Xylem cells that form in the summer grow slowly and, therefore, are small and have thick walls. They produce a thin, dark ring. One pair of light and dark rings represents one year's growth. You can estimate a tree's age by counting its annual rings.

The width of a tree's annual rings can provide important clues about past weather conditions, such as rainfall. In rainy years, more xylem is produced, so the tree's annual rings are wide. In dry years, rings are narrow. By examining annual rings from some trees in the southwestern United States, scientists were able to infer that severe droughts occurred in the years 840, 1067, 1379, and 1632.

◀ The annual rings in a tree reveal the tree's history.

apply it!

❶ Calculate How old was the tree when it was cut down?

_____

_____

❷ Observe The area at Area C is blackened from a fire that affected one side of the tree. Describe how the tree grew after the fire.

_____

_____

_____

_____

❸ CHALLENGE Areas A and B both represent four years of growth. What might account for their difference in size?

_____

_____

_____

_____

_____

_____

Vocabulary Greek Word Origins The Greek word *stoma* means "mouth." How are the stomata of a plant like mouths?

_____

_____

_____

_____

_____

_____

Leaves

Leaves vary greatly in size and shape. Pine trees have needle-shaped leaves. Birch trees have small rounded leaves with jagged edges. Regardless of their shape, leaves play an important role in a plant. ⚷ **Leaves capture the sun's energy and carry out the food-making process of photosynthesis.**

The Structure of a Leaf If you were to cut through a leaf and look at the edge under a microscope, you would see the structures in **Figure 4.** The leaf's top and bottom surface layers protect the cells inside. Between the layers of cells are veins that contain xylem and phloem.

The surface layers of the leaf have small openings, or pores, called stomata (stoh MAH tuh; *singular* stoma). The stomata open and close to control when gases enter and leave the leaf. When the stomata are open, carbon dioxide enters the leaf, and oxygen and water vapor exit.

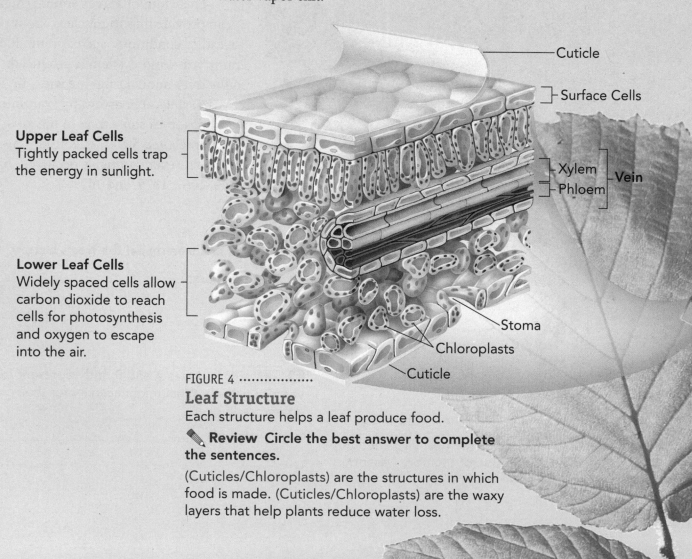

Upper Leaf Cells
Tightly packed cells trap the energy in sunlight.

Lower Leaf Cells
Widely spaced cells allow carbon dioxide to reach cells for photosynthesis and oxygen to escape into the air.

Cuticle

Surface Cells

Xylem — **Vein**
Phloem —

Stoma

Chloroplasts

Cuticle

FIGURE 4 ·················
Leaf Structure
Each structure helps a leaf produce food.

✏ **Review** Circle the best answer to complete the sentences.

(Cuticles/Chloroplasts) are the structures in which food is made. (Cuticles/Chloroplasts) are the waxy layers that help plants reduce water loss.

The Leaf and Photosynthesis The structure of a leaf is ideal for carrying out photosynthesis. The cells that contain the most chloroplasts are located near the leaf's upper surface, where they get the most light. The chlorophyll in the chloroplasts traps the sun's energy.

Carbon dioxide enters the leaf through open stomata. Water, which is absorbed by the plant's roots, travels up the stem to the leaf through the xylem. During photosynthesis, sugar and oxygen are produced from the carbon dioxide and water. Oxygen passes out of the leaf through the open stomata. The sugar enters the phloem and then travels throughout the plant.

Controlling Water Loss Because such a large area of a leaf is exposed to the air, water can quickly evaporate from a leaf into the air. The process by which water evaporates from a plant's leaves is called **transpiration.** A plant can lose a lot of water through transpiration. A corn plant, for example, can lose almost 4 liters of water on a hot summer day. Without a way to slow down the process of transpiration, a plant would shrivel up and die.

Fortunately, plants have ways to slow down transpiration. One way plants retain water is by closing the stomata. The stomata often close when leaves start to dry out.

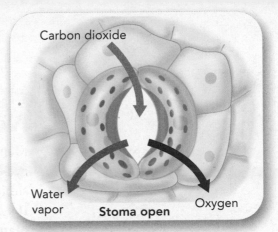

Carbon dioxide

Water vapor **Stoma open** Oxygen

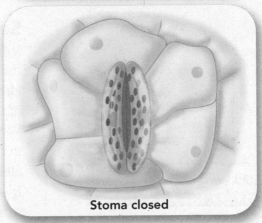

Stoma closed

FIGURE 5 ·······························

Stomata
Stomata can slow water loss.

✎ **Name** What three substances enter and leave a plant through stomata?

_____

_____

Lab zone® Do the Lab Investigation *Investigating Stomata.*

🗝 Assess Your Understanding

1a. List What are the functions of a stem?

_____

_____

_____

_____

_____

b. Infer If you forget to water a houseplant for a few days, would its stomata be open or closed? Why?

_____

_____

_____

_____

got it? ··

○ **I get it!** Now I know that roots, stems, and leaves perform functions like _____

_____

○ **I need extra help with** _____

Go to **MY SCIENCE** 🔊 **COACH** *online for help with this subject.*

How Do Seeds Become New Plants?

Many plants begin their life cycle as a seed. You can follow the cycle from seed to plant in **Figure 6**. All seeds share important similarities. 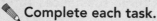 **Inside a seed is a partially developed plant. If a seed lands in an area where conditions are favorable, the plant sprouts out of the seed and begins to grow.**

Seed Structure A seed has three main parts—an embryo, stored food, and a seed coat. The young plant that develops from the zygote, or fertilized egg, is called the **embryo.** The embryo already has the beginnings of roots, stems, and leaves. In the seeds of most plants, the embryo stops growing when it is quite small. When the embryo begins to grow again, it uses the food stored in the seed until it can make its own food by photosynthesis. In all seeds, the embryo has one or more seed leaves, or cotyledons. In some seeds, food is stored in the cotyledons. In others, food is stored outside the embryo.

The outer covering of a seed is called the seed coat. The seed coat acts like plastic wrap, protecting the embryo and its food from drying out. This allows a seed to remain inactive for a long time. In many plants, the seeds are surrounded by a structure called a fruit.

FIGURE 6 ··························

▶ **INTERACTIVE ART** **Story of a Seed**

Read the text on this page and the next page. Then complete the activities about seeds becoming new plants.

✏ **Complete each task.**

1. **Review** On the diagram, label the seed's embryo, cotyledons, and seed coat.

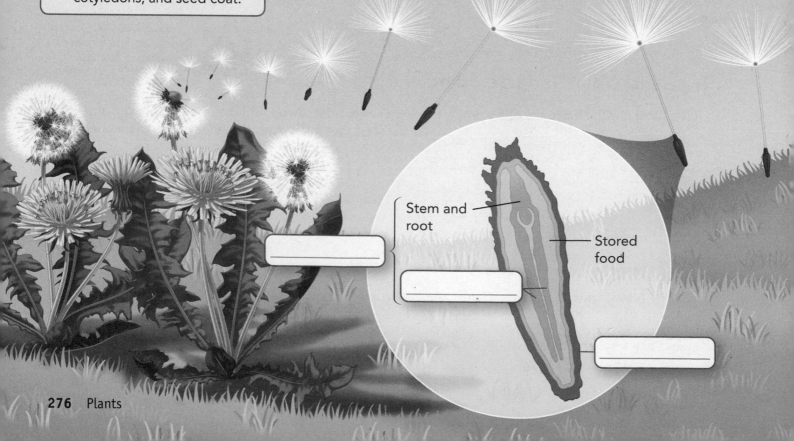

Stem and root

Stored food

Seed Dispersal After seeds form, they are usually scattered. The scattering of seeds is called seed dispersal. Seeds can be dispersed in many different ways. When animals eat fruit, the seeds inside the fruit pass through the animal's digestive system and are deposited in new areas. Other seeds are enclosed in barblike structures that hook onto fur or clothing. The seeds fall off in a new area. Water also disperses seeds that fall into oceans and rivers. Wind disperses lightweight seeds, such as those of dandelions and maple trees. Some plants eject their seeds. The force scatters the seeds in many directions. A seed that is dispersed far from its parent plant has a better chance of survival. Far away, a seed does not have to compete with its parent for light, water, and nutrients.

Germination After a seed is dispersed, it may remain inactive for a while before it germinates. **Germination** (jur muh NAY shun) occurs when the embryo begins to grow again and pushes out of the seed. Germination begins when the seed absorbs water. Then the embryo uses stored food to begin to grow. The roots first grow downward. Then its stem and leaves grow upward.

⟲ **Relate Cause and Effect**
Underline a cause of seed dispersal and circle its effect in the text on this page.

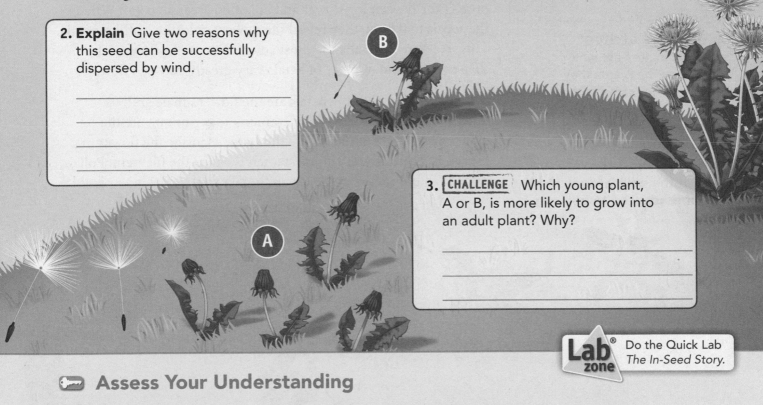

2. **Explain** Give two reasons why this seed can be successfully dispersed by wind.

_____

_____

_____

B

A

3. **CHALLENGE** Which young plant, A or B, is more likely to grow into an adult plant? Why?

_____

_____

_____

Lab zone ® Do the Quick Lab
The In-Seed Story.

🔑 **Assess Your Understanding**

got it?

○ **I get it!** Now I know that a seed becomes a new plant when _____

_____

○ **I need extra help with** _____

Go to **my science** ⓢ **COACH** *online for help with this subject.*

What Are the Structures of a Flower?

Flowers come in all sorts of shapes, sizes, and colors. But, despite their differences, all flowers have the same function—reproduction. A **flower** is the reproductive structure of an angiosperm. 🔑 **A typical flower contains sepals, petals, stamens, and pistils.**

The colors and shapes of most flower structures and the scents produced by most flowers attract insects and other animals. These organisms ensure that pollination occurs. **Pollination** is the transfer of pollen from male reproductive structures to female reproductive structures. Pollinators, such as those shown in **Figure 7,** include birds, bats, and insects such as bees and flies. As you read, keep in mind that some flowers lack one or more of the parts. For example, some flowers have only male reproductive parts, and some flowers do not have petals.

Sepals and Petals When a flower is still a bud, it is enclosed by leaflike structures called **sepals** (SEE pulz). Sepals protect the developing flower and are often green in color. When the sepals fold back, they reveal the flower's colorful, leaflike **petals.** The petals are generally the most colorful parts of a flower. The shapes, sizes, and number of petals vary greatly between flowers.

Stamens Within the petals are the flower's male and female reproductive parts. The **stamens** (STAY munz) are the male reproductive parts. Locate the stamens inside the flower in **Figure 8.** The thin stalk of the stamen is called the filament. Pollen is made in the anther, at the top of the filament.

FIGURE 7 ·······································

Pollinator Matchup
Some pollinators are well adapted to the plants they pollinate. For example, the long tongue of the nectar bat helps the bat reach inside the agave plant, as shown below.

✎ **Apply Concepts** Write the letter of the pollinator on the plant it is adapted to pollinate.

Pistils The female parts, or **pistils** (PIS tulz), are found in the center of most flowers, as shown in **Figure 8.** Some flowers have two or more pistils; others have only one. The sticky tip of the pistil is called the stigma. A slender tube, called a style, connects the stigma to a hollow structure at the base of the flower. This hollow structure is the **ovary,** which protects the seeds as they develop. An ovary contains one or more ovules.

FIGURE 8 ·····················

> INTERACTIVE ART **Structures of a Typical Flower**
Flowers have many structures.

✎ **Relate Text and Visuals**
Use the word bank to fill in the missing labels.

_____ are the small, leaflike parts of a flower. They protect the developing flower.

_____ are usually the most colorful parts of a flower. Pollinators are attracted by their color and scent.

_____ are the male reproductive parts of a flower. Pollen is produced in the anther, at the top of the stalklike filament.

_____ are the female reproductive parts of a flower. They consist of a sticky stigma, a slender tube called the style, and a hollow structure called the ovary at the base.

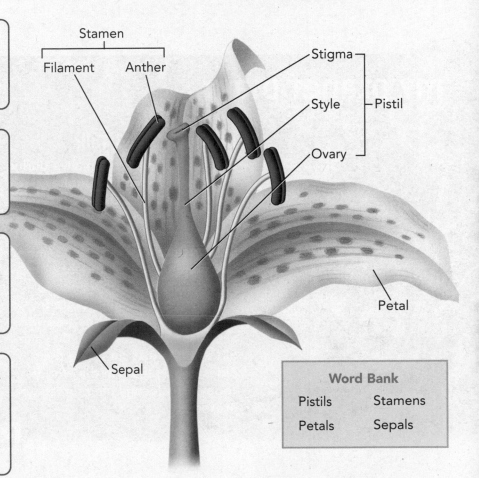

Word Bank

Pistils	Stamens
Petals	Sepals

Lab® Do the Quick Lab
zone *Modeling Flowers.*

🔑 **Assess Your Understanding**

got it? ···

○ **I get it!** Now I know that the structures of a flower include _____

_____

○ **I need extra help with** _____

Go to MY SCIENCE ⒮ COACH *online for help with this subject.*

Plant Reproduction

🗝 **What Are the Stages of a Plant Life Cycle?**

🗝 **How Do Plants Reproduce?**

MY PLANET DiARY

FUN FACT

If Trees Could Talk

Suppose you had been alive during the ancient Egyptian Empire, the Middle Ages, the American Revolution, and both World Wars. Think of the stories you could tell! Bristlecone pine trees can be this old. In 1964, a student got permission to cut down one of these trees. He counted the tree rings to see how old the tree was, and discovered it was 4,900 years old. He had just cut down the oldest living thing in the world! Today, Bristlecone pine forests are protected.

Write your answer below.
What could you learn from a 5,000-year-old tree?

_____

_____

_____

_____

_____

▷ **PLANET DIARY** Go to **Planet Diary** to learn more about plant reproduction.

Do the Inquiry Warm-Up
Make the Pollen Stick.

What Are the Stages of a Plant's Life Cycle?

Like other living things, plants develop and reproduce through life stages. 🗝 **Plants have complex life cycles that include two different stages, the sporophyte stage and the gametophyte stage.** In the **sporophyte** (SPOH ruh fyt) stage, the plant produces spores. The spore develops into the plant's other stage, called the gametophyte. In the **gametophyte** (guh MEE tuh fyt) stage, the plant produces two kinds of sex cells: sperm cells and egg cells. See **Figure 1.**

Vocabulary

- sporophyte • gametophyte • annual • biennial
- perennial • fertilization • zygote • cone
- ovule • fruit

Skills

↻ Reading: Summarize

△ Inquiry: Infer

FIGURE 1 ....

Plant Life Cycle

All plants go through two stages in their life cycle.

✎ **Interpret Diagrams** Label the sporophyte and gametophyte stages.

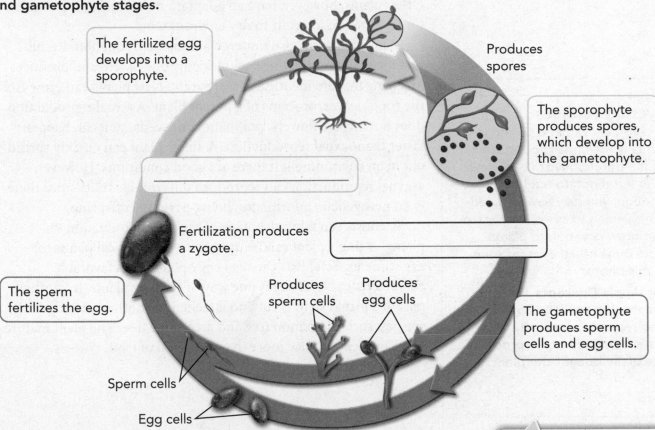

The fertilized egg develops into a sporophyte.

Produces spores

The sporophyte produces spores, which develop into the gametophyte.

Fertilization produces a zygote.

The sperm fertilizes the egg.

Produces sperm cells

Produces egg cells

The gametophyte produces sperm cells and egg cells.

Sperm cells

Egg cells

Angiosperms are classified based on the length of their life cycles. Flowering plants that complete a life cycle within one growing season are called **annuals.** Annuals include marigolds, petunias, wheat, and cucumbers. Angiosperms that complete their life cycle in two years are called **biennials** (by EN ee ulz). In the first year, biennials germinate and grow roots, very short stems, and leaves. During their second year, biennials lengthen their stems, grow new leaves, and then produce flowers and seeds. Parsley, celery, and foxglove are biennials. Flowering plants that live for more than two years are called **perennials.** Most perennials flower every year.

Lab zone® Do the Quick Lab *Plant Life Cycles.*

⌕ Assess Your Understanding

got it? ....

○ **I get it!** Now I know that the stages of a plant's life cycle include _____

_____

_____

○ **I need extra help with** _____

_____

Go to MY SCIENCE ⑤ COACH *online for help with this subject.*

281

How Do Plants Reproduce?

Plants reproduce in different ways depending on their structures and the environment they live in.  **All plants undergo sexual reproduction that involves fertilization. Fertilization** occurs when a sperm cell unites with an egg cell. The fertilized egg is called a **zygote.** For algae and some plants, fertilization can only occur if there is water in the environment. This is because the sperm cells of these plants swim through the water to the egg cells. Other plants, however, have an adaptation that makes it possible for fertilization to occur in dry environments.

Many plants can also undergo asexual reproduction. Recall that asexual reproduction includes only one parent and produces offspring that are identical to the parent. New plants can grow from the roots, leaves, or stems of a parent plant. Asexual reproduction does not involve flowers, pollination, or seeds, so it can happen faster than sexual reproduction. A single plant can quickly spread out in an environment if there are good conditions. However, asexual reproduction can reproduce unfavorable traits since there is no new genetic information being passed to offspring.

Scientists can take advantage of asexual reproduction in plants. A single plant can be used to create identical plants for experiments. Scientists can also copy plants with favorable characteristics. Grafting is one way of copying plants. In grafting, part of a plant's stem is cut and attached to another related plant species, such as a lemon tree and an orange tree. The plant matures and can then produce more than one kind of fruit.

FIGURE 2

Eyes on Potatoes

Did you know that a potato is actually the underground stem of the potato plant? If you have ever left a potato out long enough, you may have noticed it beginning to sprout. A potato can grow new potato plants from buds called eyes, as seen in this photo.

✎ **Apply Concepts** Potato plants also produce flowers and reproduce sexually. How does being able to reproduce asexually benefit the plant?

_____

_____

_____

_____

_____

_____

_____

apply it!

A citrus farmer was able to graft a lemon tree branch onto an orange tree. Now the same tree produces lemons and oranges! The farmer plans to use branches from the same lemon trees to create other combined fruit trees.

1 Review The farmer used the lemon tree's ability to (sexually/asexually) reproduce.

2 ⚠Infer Name at least one negative effect of using the same lemon tree to create new trees the farmer should know about.

_____

_____

3 CHALLENGE Why might the public be opposed to using this method to create new fruit trees?

_____

_____

Nonvascular and Seedless Vascular Plants

Mosses, liverworts, hornworts, ferns, club mosses, and horsetails need to grow in moist environments. This is because the plants release spores into their surroundings, where they grow into gametophytes. When the gametophytes produce egg cells and sperm cells, there must be enough water available for the sperm to swim toward the eggs.

For example, the familiar fern, with its visible fronds, is the sporophyte stage of the plant. On the underside of mature fronds, spores develop in tiny spore cases. Wind and water can carry the spores great distances. If a spore lands in moist, shaded soil, it develops into a gametophyte. Fern gametophytes are tiny plants that grow low to the ground.

Spore cases on the fronds of a fern

283

Gymnosperms You can follow the process of gymnosperm reproduction in **Figure 3.**

1 Cone Production

Most gymnosperms have reproductive structures called **cones.** Cones are covered with scales. Most gymnosperms produce two types of cones: male cones and female cones. Usually, a single plant produces both male and female cones. In some types of gymnosperms, however, individual trees produce either male cones or female cones. A few gymnosperms produce no cones.

2 Pollen Production and Ovule Development

(A) Male cones produce pollen grains. Cells in the pollen will mature into sperm cells. (B) The female gametophyte develops in structures called ovules. An **ovule** (OH vyool) is a structure that contains an egg cell. Female cones contain at least one ovule at the base of each scale. The ovule later develops into the seed.

3 Egg Production

Two egg cells form inside each ovule on the female cone.

4 Pollination

The transfer of pollen from a male reproductive structure to a female reproductive structure is called pollination. In gymnosperms, wind often carries the pollen from the male cones to the female cones. The pollen collect in a sticky substance produced by each ovule.

5 Fertilization

Once pollination has occurred, the ovule closes and seals in the pollen. The scales also close, and a sperm cell fertilizes an egg cell inside each ovule. The zygote then develops into the embryo part of the seed.

6 Seed Development

Female cones remain on the tree while the seeds mature. As the seeds develop, the female cone increases in size. It can take up to two years for the seeds of some gymnosperms to mature. Male cones, however, usually fall off the tree after they have shed their pollen.

7 Seed Dispersal

When the seeds are mature, the scales open. The wind shakes the seeds out of the cone and carries them away. Only a few seeds will land in suitable places and grow into new plants.

FIGURE 3 ·····························

Gymnosperm Reproduction Cycle

The reproduction cycle of a gymnosperm is shown at right.

✎ **Complete each task.**

1. **Identify** Underline the sentence(s) on this page that use the vocabulary terms *cone* and *ovule.*

2. **Describe** What is the relationship between cones and ovules?

_____

_____

_____

_____

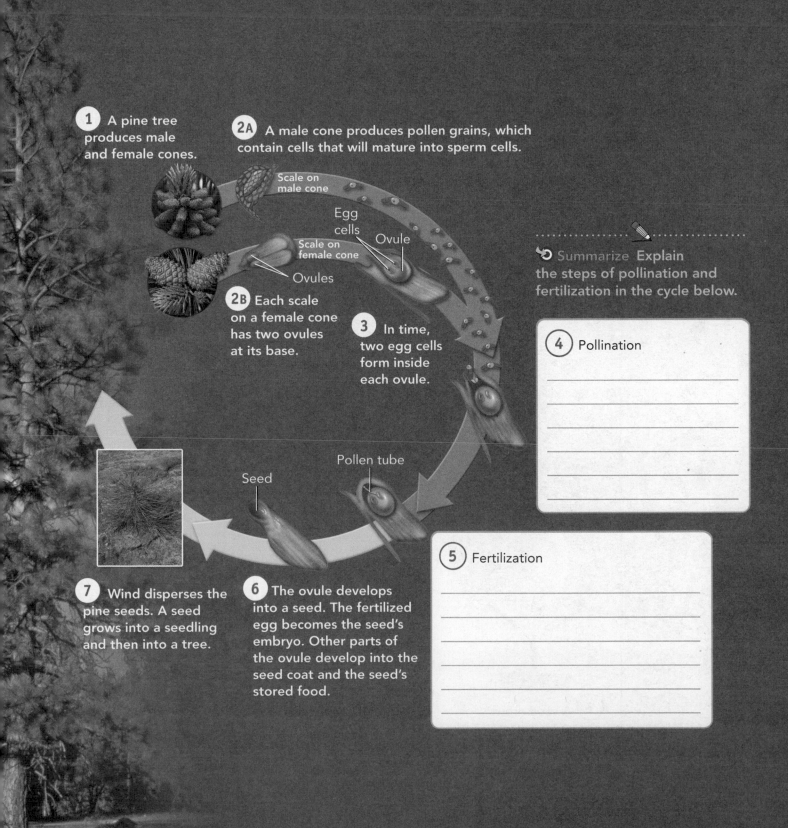

1 A pine tree produces male and female cones.

2A A male cone produces pollen grains, which contain cells that will mature into sperm cells.

Scale on male cone

Scale on female cone

Egg cells

Ovule

Ovules

2B Each scale on a female cone has two ovules at its base.

3 In time, two egg cells form inside each ovule.

↶ **Summarize Explain** the steps of pollination and fertilization in the cycle below.

4 Pollination

_____

5 Fertilization

_____

Seed

Pollen tube

7 Wind disperses the pine seeds. A seed grows into a seedling and then into a tree.

6 The ovule develops into a seed. The fertilized egg becomes the seed's embryo. Other parts of the ovule develop into the seed coat and the seed's stored food.

FIGURE 4 ·······························

Angiosperm Reproduction

Reproduction in angiosperms begins with flowers.

✎ **Relate Text and Visuals**
Look back at the plant life and gymnosperm reproduction cycles in this lesson. What do the yellow and purple colors of the arrows represent?

_____

_____

_____

_____

_____

Angiosperms

You can follow angiosperm reproduction in **Figure 4.** First, pollen fall on a flower's stigma. In time, the sperm cell and egg cell join together in the flower's ovule. The zygote develops into the embryo part of the seed.

Pollination A flower is pollinated when a grain of pollen falls on the stigma. Some angiosperms are pollinated by the wind, but most rely on other organisms. When an organism enters a flower to obtain food, it becomes coated with pollen. Some of the pollen can drop onto the flower's stigma as the animal leaves. The pollen can also be brushed onto the stigma of the next flower the animal visits.

Fertilization If the pollen fall on the stigma of a similar plant, fertilization can occur. A sperm cell joins with an egg cell inside an ovule within the ovary at the base of the flower. The zygote then begins to develop into the seed's embryo. Other parts of the ovule develop into the rest of the seed.

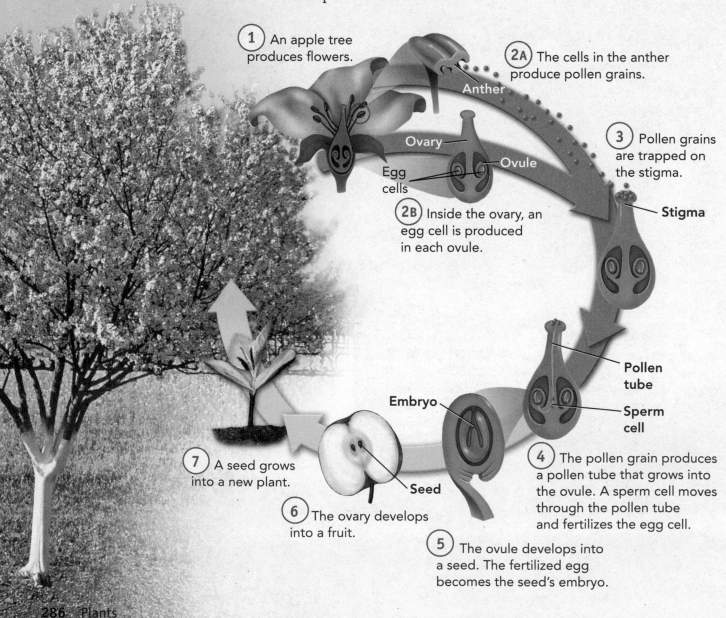

1. An apple tree produces flowers.

2A. The cells in the anther produce pollen grains.

Anther

Ovary

Egg cells

Ovule

2B. Inside the ovary, an egg cell is produced in each ovule.

3. Pollen grains are trapped on the stigma.

Stigma

Pollen tube

Sperm cell

Embryo

Seed

4. The pollen grain produces a pollen tube that grows into the ovule. A sperm cell moves through the pollen tube and fertilizes the egg cell.

5. The ovule develops into a seed. The fertilized egg becomes the seed's embryo.

6. The ovary develops into a fruit.

7. A seed grows into a new plant.

Fruit Development and Seed Dispersal As the seed develops, the ovary changes into a **fruit.** A fruit is the ripened ovary and other structures that enclose one or more seeds. Fruits include apples, cherries, tomatoes, squash, and many others. Fruits are the means by which angiosperm seeds are dispersed. Animals that eat fruits help to disperse their seeds by depositing them in new areas.

did you know? ....

The *Arabidopsis* plant became the first plant to flower and produce seeds in the zero-gravity environment of outer space on a Soviet space station in 1982.

FIGURE 5 ....
Flower to Fruit
Flowers eventually develop into fruit.

✎ **Sequence** Write the numbers 1 through 4 in the blank circles to show the progression from flower to fruit.

Lab zone ® Do the Quick Lab
Where Are the Seeds?

🔑 Assess Your Understanding

1a. Review (Fertilization/Asexual reproduction) occurs when a sperm cell unites with an egg cell.

b. Explain Why do plants like liverworts need to live in moist environments?

_____

_____

c. Relate Cause and Effect Underline the cause and circle the effect in the sentences below.

Pollination can occur when pollen on an insect is dropped onto the stigma.

Animals eating fruit is one way seeds are dispersed.

got it? ....

○ I get it! Now I know that all of the major plant groups reproduce _____

_____

○ I need extra help with _____

Go to **MY SCIENCE** Ⓢ **COACH** online for help with this subject.

287

Plant Responses and Growth

🔑 **What Are Three Stimuli That Produce Plant Responses?**

🔑 **How Do Plants Respond to Seasonal Changes?**

my planet diary

DISCOVERY

Flower Power

What makes a plant flower? Plants detect the amount of light each day. When there is just enough light, the plant sends a signal to the flower. But what is this signal? For almost 80 years, the answer remained a mystery. In 2008, scientists discovered the protein that was responsible. They linked the protein they thought controlled flowering to a fluorescent, or glowing, protein they obtained from a jellyfish. Then they watched the bright green protein travel with the flowering protein through the stem to make the plant bloom. Why does this experiment matter?

Global climate change is starting to hurt crops. Some places near the equator are becoming too warm to farm. Areas closer to Earth's poles may be needed to grow more crops as they warm. These areas, however, do not get as much sunlight. Scientists could use the flowering protein to encourage plants to flower without direct sunlight.

Communicate Discuss the question with a group of classmates. Then write your answer below.

In addition to getting the plants to flower with no light, what other challenges might scientists have to overcome when trying to get plants to succeed in a new area?

_____

_____

_____

_____

_____

▷ **PLANET DIARY** Go to **Planet Diary** to learn more about plant responses and growth.

Lab zone® Do the Inquiry Warm-Up *Can a Plant Respond to Touch?*

The green you see in these plant cells is from a fluorescent protein like the one used in the flowering experiment.

Vocabulary
- tropism • hormone • auxin • photoperiodism
- critical night length • short-day plant • long-day plant
- day-neutral plant • dormancy

Skills
- Reading: Relate Text and Visuals
- Inquiry: Draw Conclusions

What Are Three Stimuli That Produce Plant Responses?

You may be one of those people who close their window shades at night because the morning light wakes you up. People respond to many stimuli each day. Did you know plants also respond to some of the same stimuli, including light?

Tropisms Animals usually respond to stimuli by moving. Unlike animals, plants usually respond by growing either toward or away from a stimulus. A plant's growth response toward or away from a stimulus is called a **tropism** (TROH piz um). If a plant grows toward the stimulus, it is said to show a positive tropism. If a plant grows away from a stimulus, it shows a negative tropism. 🔑 **Touch, gravity, and light are three important stimuli that trigger growth responses, or tropisms, in plants.**

Touch

Some plants show a response to touch called thigmotropism. The prefix *thigmo-* comes from a Greek word that means "touch." The stems of many vines, such as morning glories, sweet peas, and grapes, show a positive thigmotropism. As the vines grow, they coil around any object they touch.

FIGURE 1 ....

Plant Responses to Stimuli
The stimuli in space are not always the same as those on Earth.

✎ **Develop Hypotheses** How might the roots of a plant grow in space without the influence of gravity?

_____

_____

_____

_____

_____

Gravity

Plants can respond to gravity. This response is called gravitropism. Roots show positive gravitropism if they grow downward. Stems, on the other hand, show negative gravitropism. Stems grow upward against gravity.

⟳ Relate Text and Visuals Use what you have read to label the side of the plant with more auxin and the side with less auxin.

Light

All plants exhibit a response to light called phototropism. The leaves, stems, and flowers of plants grow toward light. This shows a positive phototropism. A plant receives more energy for photosynthesis by growing toward the light.

Plants are able to respond to stimuli because they produce hormones. A **hormone** produced by a plant is a chemical that affects how the plant grows and develops. One important plant hormone is named **auxin** (AWK sin). Auxin speeds up the rate at which a plant's cells grow and controls a plant's response to light. When light shines on one side of a plant's stem, auxin builds up in the shaded side of the stem. The cells on the shaded side begin to grow faster. The cells on the stem's shaded side are longer than those on its sunny side. The stem bends toward the light.

Lab® Do the Quick Lab
zone *Watching Roots Grow.*

🔑 Assess Your Understanding

1a. Define What is a tropism?

_____

_____

_____

_____

b. Predict What do you think would happen if a plant did not create enough of the hormone that controlled flower formation?

_____

_____

_____

got it? ••

○ **I get it!** Now I know that plants respond to _____

_____

○ I need extra help with _____

Go to **MY SCIENCE COACH** online for help with this subject.

How Do Plants Respond to Seasonal Changes?

People have long observed that plants respond to the changing seasons. Some plants bloom in early spring, while others don't bloom until summer. The leaves on some trees change color in autumn and then fall off by winter.

Photoperiodism What triggers a plant to flower?
🔑 **The amount of darkness a plant receives determines the time of flowering in many plants.** A plant's response to seasonal changes in the length of night and day is called **photoperiodism.**

Plants respond differently to the length of nights. Some plants will only bloom when the nights last a certain length of time. This length, called the **critical night length,** is the number of hours of darkness that determines whether or not a plant will flower. For example, if a plant has a critical night length of 11 hours, it will flower only when nights are longer than 11 hours. You can read more on how different plants respond to night length in **Figure 2.**

Photoperiodism

Plants and Night Length		Examples
Short-day plants flower when the nights are longer than a critical length. They bloom in fall or winter.	Midnight / Noon	Chrysanthemums, poinsettias
Long-day plants flower when nights are shorter than a critical length. They bloom in spring or summer.	Midnight / Noon	Irises, lettuce
Day-neutral plants have a flowering cycle that is not sensitive to periods of light and dark. They can bloom year-round depending on weather.	Midnight / Noon Midnight / Noon	Dandelions, rice, tomatoes

FIGURE 2 ·········
Photoperiodism
Flowering plants can be grouped as short-day plants, long-day plants, and day-neutral plants.

✎ **Infer** Suppose you are a farmer in a climate that supports plant growth all year-round but night length varies. Based on the categories in the chart, would you plant mostly one type of plant or a mixture of all three? Explain.

_____

_____

_____

_____

_____

Winter Dormancy Some plants prepare differently than others for certain seasons. As winter draws near, many plants prepare to go into a state of **dormancy.** Dormancy is a period when an organism's growth or activity stops. 🔑 **Dormancy helps plants survive freezing temperatures and the lack of liquid water.**

With many trees, the first visible change is that the leaves begin to turn color. Cooler weather and shorter days cause the leaves to stop making chlorophyll. As chlorophyll breaks down, yellow and orange pigments become visible. In addition, the plant begins to produce new red pigments. This causes the brilliant colors of autumn leaves. Over the next few weeks, sugar and water are transported out of the tree's leaves. When the leaves fall to the ground, the tree is ready for winter.

apply it!

One hundred radish seeds were planted in two identical trays of soil. One tray was kept at 10°C. The other tray was kept at 20°C. The trays received equal amounts of sun and water. The graph shows how many seeds germinated over time at each temperature.

❶ **Read Graphs** About how many seeds in the 20°C tray germinated on Day 13?

_____

_____

❷ **Draw Conclusions** Based on the graph, what can you conclude about the relationship between the two temperatures and germination?

_____

_____

_____

❸ **CHALLENGE** After the experiment, a fellow scientist concludes that more seeds will *always* germinate at higher temperatures. Is the scientist right? Why?

_____

_____

_____

_____

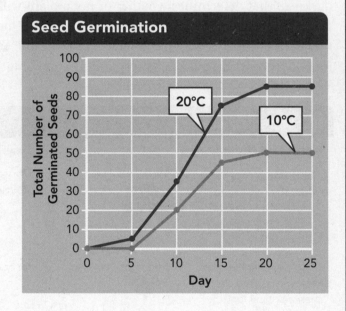

Seed Germination

Total Number of Germinated Seeds vs. Day

20°C

10°C

Roving for Life in Space

How do you know a plant when you see it?

FIGURE 3 ···

> **ART IN MOTION** You are a scientist researching distant planets. You have sent a rover to collect samples from one of the planets and you get some exciting results. The rover has found three living things, and one of them is a plant! But, on the way back to Earth, the rover has a rough landing and the samples get mixed up. You run some tests in your lab to find which sample is the plant. The results are shown below.

✏ Circle the sample that is a plant. Then answer the question below.

Lab Findings on Rover Life-Form Samples

	Sample 1	Sample 2	Sample 3
Reproduces sexually	Yes	Yes	No
Cells have cell walls	No	Yes	Yes
Contains vascular tissue	Yes	No	No
Multicellular	Yes	Yes	No
Autotroph	No	Yes	Yes
Responds to light	Yes	Yes	No

Choose one of the samples you did not circle. Why is this sample not a plant?

_____

_____

_____

_____

 Lab zone® Do the Quick Lab *Seasonal Changes.*

🔑 Assess Your Understanding

2a. Review (Short-day/Long-day) plants flower when nights are shorter than a critical length.

b. Explain Why do the leaves of some trees change color in autumn?

_____

_____

c. 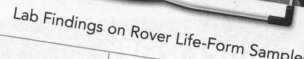 **ANSWER THE BIG ?** How do you know a plant when you see it?

_____

_____

_____

got it? ···

○ **I get it!** Now I know that plants respond to seasonal changes because_____

_____

○ **I need extra help with** _____

Go to **MY SCIENCE ⓢ COACH** online for help with this subject.

Plants in Everyday Life

UNLOCK THE BIG Q 🔑 **How Are Plants Important to Everyday Life?**

my planeT DiaRY

BLOG

Posted by: George

Location: Tacoma, Washington

I never really thought much about how important trees are until my dad and I planted a plum tree in our yard. I've watched it grow over the last couple of years. The first year we didn't get any plums. The next year, we had tons of plums and they were good! This made me think more about all that we get from plants —food to eat, wood to build houses, and cotton to make clothes!

Communicate Discuss the question with a group of classmates. Then write your answer below.

Describe a plant that is important to your everyday life.

_____

_____

_____

_____

_____

_____

▶ PLANET DIARY Go to **Planet Diary** to learn more about plants in everyday life.

 Lab zone® Do the Inquiry Warm-Up *Feeding the World.*

Vocabulary
- peat

Skills
- ⟳ Reading: Identify the Main Idea
- △ Inquiry: Pose Questions

How Are Plants Important to Everyday Life?

What did you have for breakfast today? Cereal? Toast? Orange juice? Chances are you have already eaten something today that came from plants. Besides providing food, plants play many roles on Earth. 🔑 **In addition to food, plants provide habitats. Plants can clean the water and protect the soil in an environment. Plants are also the base of many products important to human life, such as medicines, paper, and clothing.**

The Role of Plants in an Ecosystem Plants play many roles in an ecosystem. You can see some of these roles in **Figure 1.** Recall that an ecosystem contains living things and the nonliving surroundings. People are included in ecosystems too!

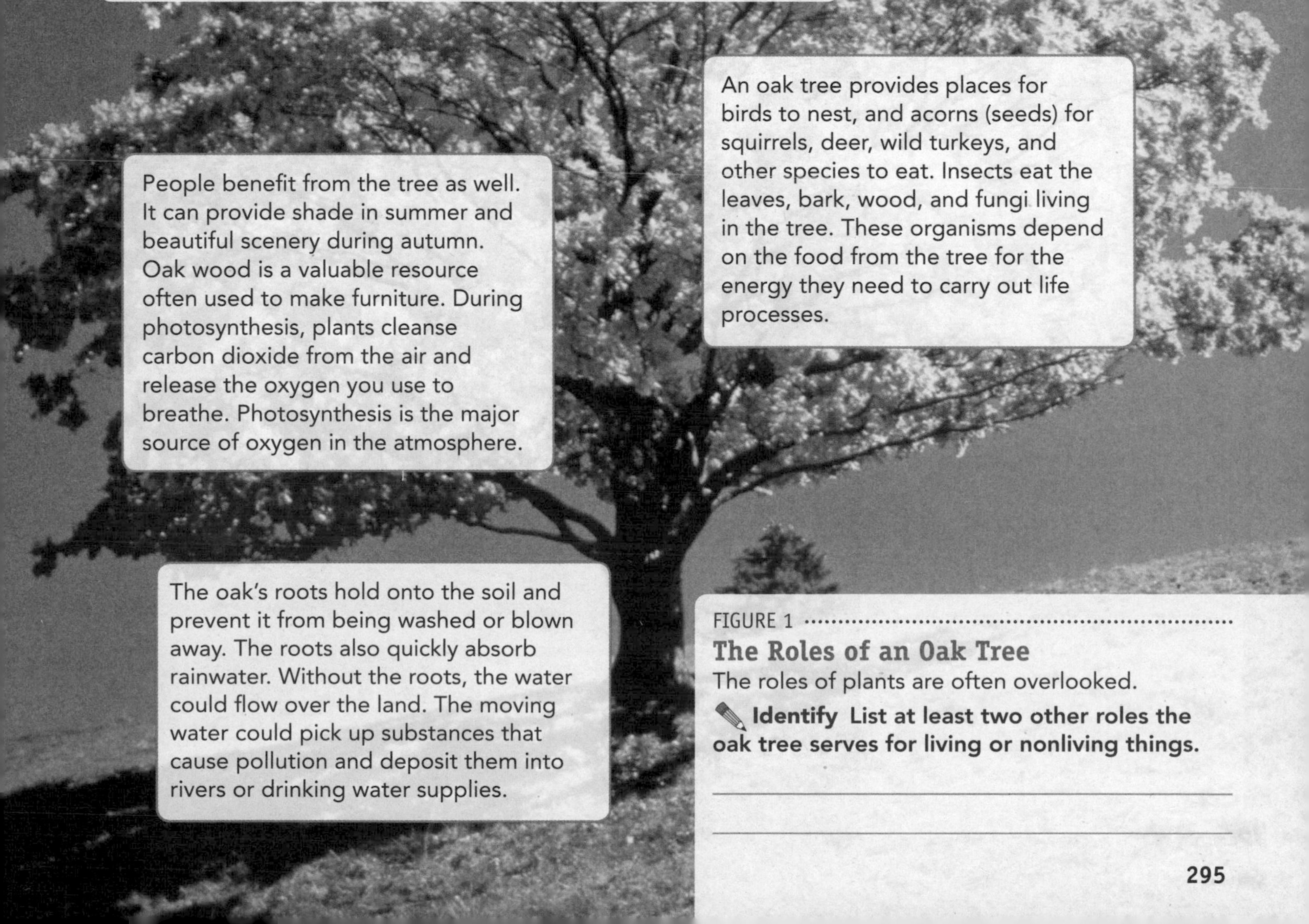

People benefit from the tree as well. It can provide shade in summer and beautiful scenery during autumn. Oak wood is a valuable resource often used to make furniture. During photosynthesis, plants cleanse carbon dioxide from the air and release the oxygen you use to breathe. Photosynthesis is the major source of oxygen in the atmosphere.

An oak tree provides places for birds to nest, and acorns (seeds) for squirrels, deer, wild turkeys, and other species to eat. Insects eat the leaves, bark, wood, and fungi living in the tree. These organisms depend on the food from the tree for the energy they need to carry out life processes.

The oak's roots hold onto the soil and prevent it from being washed or blown away. The roots also quickly absorb rainwater. Without the roots, the water could flow over the land. The moving water could pick up substances that cause pollution and deposit them into rivers or drinking water supplies.

FIGURE 1 ....
The Roles of an Oak Tree
The roles of plants are often overlooked.

✎ **Identify** List at least two other roles the oak tree serves for living or nonliving things.

_____

_____

295

✎

> **Identify the Main Idea** In the text under the heading How People Use Plants, underline at least three plant groups and circle one product made from each.

apply it!

You are at a grocery store buying cleaning products to clean your bathroom. You can choose a cleaner made from chemicals made in a lab or one made from plant-derived chemicals.

1 **Pose Questions** What questions should you ask before making your decision?

_____

_____

_____

_____

_____

_____

_____

2 **CHALLENGE** What could be some disadvantages of the plant-based cleaner?

_____

_____

_____

_____

_____

_____

_____

How People Use Plants People have found ways to directly use almost all plants. Green algae is often used in scientific research and as a thickening agent in some foods. Liverworts, club mosses, and other plants are used in parts of the world to treat conditions from fevers to itchy skin.

Many people use moss in agriculture and gardening. The moss that gardeners use contains sphagnum (SFAG num) moss. Sphagnum moss grows in a type of wetland called a bog. The still water in a bog is so acidic that decomposers cannot live in the water. When the plants die, they do not decay. Instead, the dead plants accumulate at the bottom of the bog. Over time, the mosses become compressed into layers and form a blackish-brown material called **peat.** In some parts of Europe and Asia, people use peat as a fuel to heat homes and to cook food.

Peat drying after being extracted from a bog

Gymnosperms provide many useful products. Paper and the lumber used to build homes come from conifers. The rayon fibers in clothes as well as the cellophane wrappers on some food also come from conifers. Turpentine and the rosin used by baseball pitchers, gymnasts, and musicians are made from conifer sap.

Angiosperms are an important source of food, clothing, and medicine. People eat a variety of vegetables, fruits, and cereals, all of which are angiosperms. The seeds of cotton plants are covered with cotton fibers. The stems of flax plants provide linen fibers. The sap of rubber trees is used to make rubber for tires and other products. Furniture is often made from the wood of maple, cherry, and oak trees. Some important medications come from angiosperms, too. For example, the heart medication digitalis comes from the leaves of the foxglove plant.

FIGURE 2 ·······························
Plants in Your Life

You may not have realized how many things, like clothes and sports equipment, are made of plants!

✎ **Name** List at least five things in your everyday life that come from plants.

_____
_____
_____
_____

Lab zone® Do the Quick Lab *Everyday Plants.*

🔑 Assess Your Understanding

1a. List Give two uses of moss.

_____

b. Describe Why is conifer sap important?

_____
_____
_____
_____

c. Make Judgments Should governments spend more money on plant research than they currently do? Why?

_____
_____
_____
_____

got it? ··

○ **I get it!** Now I know that plants provide many useful things, such as _____

_____

○ **I need extra help with** _____

Go to MY SCIENCE ⑤ COACH *online for help with this subject.*

8 Study Guide

Nearly all plants have cells surrounded by _____, are _____ that photosynthesize, and are made of many cells.

LESSON 1 What Is a Plant?

🔑 Nearly all plants are autotrophs and contain many cells surrounded by cell walls.

🔑 For plants to survive on land, they must have ways to obtain water and nutrients, retain water, support their bodies, transport materials and reproduce.

Vocabulary
- chlorophyll
- photosynthesis   • tissue
- chloroplast   • vacuole
- cuticle   • vascular tissue

LESSON 2 Classifying Plants

🔑 Nonvascular plants are low-growing, have thin cell walls, and do not have roots.

🔑 Seedless vascular plants have vascular tissue and produce spores.

🔑 Seed plants have vascular tissue and seeds.

Vocabulary
- nonvascular plant   • rhizoid   • vascular plant
- phloem   • xylem   • frond   • pollen   • seed
- gymnosperm   • angiosperm
- cotyledon   • monocot   • dicot

LESSON 3 Plant Structures

🔑 A plant's roots, stems, and leaves anchor the plant, absorb water and minerals, capture the sun's energy, and make food.

🔑 A seed contains a partially developed plant.

🔑 A typical flower contains sepals, petals, stamens, and pistils.

Vocabulary
- root cap   • cambium   • stoma   • transpiration
- embryo   • germination   • flower   • pollination
- sepal   • petal   • stamen   • pistil   • ovary

LESSON 4 Plant Reproduction

🔑 Plants have complex life cycles that include a sporophyte stage and a gametophyte stage.

🔑 All plants undergo sexual reproduction that involves fertilization.

Vocabulary
- sporophyte   • gametophyte   • annual   • biennial
- perennial   • fertilization   • zygote   • cone
- ovule   • fruit

LESSON 5 Plant Responses and Growth

🔑 Plants show growth responses, or tropisms, toward touch, gravity, and light.

🔑 The amount of darkness a plant receives determines the time of flowering in many plants. Dormancy helps plants survive winter.

Vocabulary
- tropism   • hormone   • auxin   • photoperiodism
- critical night length   • short-day plant
- long-day plant   • day-neutral plant   • dormancy

LESSON 6 Plants in Everyday Life

🔑 In addition to food, plants provide habitats, clean water, and protect soil. Plants are also the base of many products, including medicine, paper, and clothing.

Vocabulary
- peat

Review and Assessment

LESSON 1 What Is a Plant?

1. In which cellular structure do plants store water and other substances?

   a. cuticle   **b.** vacuole

   c. cell wall   **d.** chloroplast

2. The pigment _____ is found in chloroplasts.

3. Make Generalizations Complete the table below to describe plant adaptions for life on land.

Structure	Function
Roots	Help obtain water and nutrients
Cuticle	_____ _____
Vascular tissue	_____ _____

LESSON 2 Classifying Plants

4. Which of the following are seedless vascular plants?

   a. ferns   **b.** liverworts

   c. gymnosperms   **d.** angiosperms

5. Nonvascular plants have rootlike structures called _____

6. Compare and Contrast How are gymnosperms and angiosperms alike and different?

_____

_____

_____

_____

_____

LESSON 3 Plant Structures

7. A plant absorbs water and minerals through

   a. roots.   **b.** stems.

   c. leaves.   **d.** stomata.

8. Transpiration slows down when _____ are closed.

9. Relate Cause and Effect When a strip of bark is removed all the way around the trunk of a tree, the tree dies. Explain why.

_____

_____

_____

10. **Write About It** Plant structures do not look the same among all plants. For example, some leaves are short and others long. Explain why you think there is so much variation.

LESSON 4 Plant Reproduction

11. A zygote is the direct result of

   a. pollination.

   b. fertilization.

   c. biennial growth.

   d. the sporophyte stage.

12. _____ complete their life cycles within one growing season.

13. Sequence Describe the major events in the plant life cycle. Use the terms *zygote*, *sperm*, *sporophyte*, *spores*, *gametophyte*, and *egg*.

_____

_____

_____

_____

_____

LESSON 5 Plant Responses and Growth

14. A plant's response to gravity is an example of a

    a. dormancy.   **b.** hormone.

    c. tropism.   **d.** critical night length.

15. The plant hormone _____ affects the rate of cell growth.

16. Predict A particular short-day plant has a critical night length of 15 hours. Fill in the chart below to predict when this plant would flower.

Day Length	Night Length	Will It Flower?
9 h	15 h	_____
10 h	14 h	_____
7.5 h	16.5 h	_____

17. Develop Hypotheses Suppose climate change alters the environment of an oak tree from one with cold and snowy winters to one with warmer winters. Will the tree still go into a state of dormancy? Explain.

_____

_____

_____

_____

_____

_____

_____

_____

LESSON 6 Plants in Everyday Life

18. Which of the following is *not* a way that people use plants?

    a. for food   **b.** for clothing

    c. for medicines   **d.** for metal extracts

19. Over time, mosses may compact into _____

20. Make Judgments Should the government put as much effort into protecting plants as they do animals? Why or why not?

_____

_____

_____

_____

_____

_____

APPLY THE BIG ? How do you know a plant when you see it?

21. Plants are all around us. Describe a plant that you see often and then explain what makes it a plant.

_____

_____

_____

_____

_____

_____

_____

_____

_____

Standardized Test Prep

Multiple Choice

Circle the letter of the best answer.

1. The diagram below shows the parts of a flower. In which flower part does pollination take place?

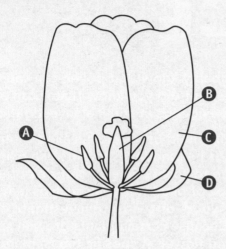

   A part A   **B** part B
   C part C   **D** part D

2. You examine plant cells under a microscope and notice many round, green structures within the cells. The structures are most likely

   A tissues.   **B** vacuoles.
   C cell walls.   **D** chloroplasts.

3. In order to reproduce, most gymnosperms produce _____, while most angiosperms produce _____.

   A sperm, eggs   **B** pollen, cones
   C cones, flowers   **D** flowers, fruits

4. What kind of tropism do roots display when they respond to the environment by growing downward into the soil?

   A gravitropism   **B** phototropism
   C thigmotropism   **D** photoperiodism

5. The vegetables, fruits, and cereals that people eat all come from which type of producer?

   A peat   **B** angiosperms
   C moss   **D** nonvascular plants

Constructed Response

Use the diagrams below to help you answer Question 6. Write your answer on a separate piece of paper.

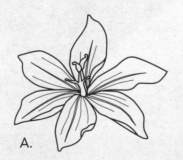 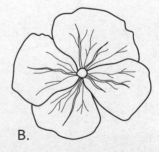

A.   B.

6. Which of the plants above is a monocot? Which is a dicot? Explain your answers.

GRAINS
OF EVIDENCE

You probably know that pollen can cause allergies, but did you know that it can also be used as evidence in criminal investigations?

A growing field of research, called forensic botany, is helping investigators use plant evidence to solve crimes. Forensic botany is the study of plant material, such as leaves, pollen, wood, or seeds, to investigate a crime. Because certain plants grow in specific areas and flower at specific times, plant material can help identify the time or place that a crime occurred.

Seeds or pollen found on a suspect's clothing can be used to link a suspect to a crime scene. Botanical evidence can also be found in a victim's stomach. Because certain plant parts cannot be digested, forensic botanists can even determine a victim's last meal!

Write About It Find out more about the life cycle of a plant described in this chapter. Draw a life cycle for the plant. Then describe how investigators could use knowledge of the plant's life cycle to solve a crime.

◀ Back in 1997 in New Zealand, pollen grains such as this one were used as the evidence to prove that a suspect was involved in a struggle at the crime scene.

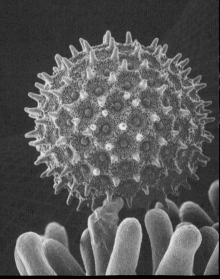

PLANTING
ROOTS IN OUTER
SPACE

Far from farms and greenhouses on Earth, future space explorers will need to grow their own food, and recycle and purify their air and water. Astronauts from the National Aeronautics and Space Administration (NASA) have been experimenting with plants in space for many years.

Which Way Is Up?

On Earth, plant roots grow downward and outward in response to Earth's gravity, while plant shoots grow upward. In space, where there is no clear up or down, roots and shoots both grow toward the light! In order to grow with the roots at the bottom and the stems at the top, plants need gravity. So space stations need special plant chambers that rotate continuously to create artificial gravity for plants.

Tomatoes From Outer Space

To study whether radiation in space will affect the ability of seeds to grow, NASA scientists placed 12.5 million tomato seeds in a satellite that orbited Earth for six years! Students around the world then planted the seeds, which grew normally and produced normal tomatoes. So scientists now know that seeds will survive for a long time in orbit.

Design It Scientists are still learning about how to grow plants to support space travel. Find out about current NASA research on plants in space. Identify one question you have about plant growth in space. Then write a proposal for an experiment to investigate your question.

A researcher holds tiny *Arabidopsis* seedlings. *Arabidopsis* plants are related to the cabbage plant, and are often used as model plants in research projects. ▽

303

HOW ARE THESE TWO LIVING THINGS DIFFERENT?

THE BIG
?

How do you know an animal when you see it?

These living things look alike and are both green. Each needs water and energy to grow. Yet one makes food, and the other has to find food.

⚠ Infer **What is different about these living things?**

_____

_____

_____

_____

_____

_____

_____

_____

▷ UNTAMED SCIENCE Watch the **Untamed Science** video to learn more about animals.

Introduction to Animals

Getting Started

Check Your Understanding

1. **Background** Read the paragraph below and then answer the question.

Mei's birthday present is a bird. She knows that to **survive**, an **organism** needs food, water, and oxygen. So at home she chooses a stable **environment** in a warm place, away from drafts. Here, she sets up a cage with dishes for food and paper for waste removal. Under Mei's care, her bird will have what it needs to live and grow.

> To **survive** is to manage to stay alive, especially in difficult situations.
>
> An **organism** is a living thing.
>
> An **environment** is all the surrounding factors that affect the organism's life.

• What does an organism need to survive?

_____

_____

> **MY READING WEB** If you had trouble completing the question above, visit **My Reading Web** and type in *Introduction to Animals.*

Vocabulary Skill

Prefixes A prefix is a word part that is added to the beginning of a word to change its meaning. The table below lists prefixes that will help you learn terms used in this chapter.

Prefix	Meaning of Prefix	Example
endo-	inner	endoskeleton, *n.* internal skeleton
exo-	outer	exoskeleton, *n.* outer skeleton

2. **Quick Check** Complete the following sentence with the correct terms from the table above.

• The _____ of a crab, which is a tough outer shell, differs from the _____ of a cat, which is internal.

vertebrate

bilateral symmetry

mollusk

endotherm

Chapter Preview

LESSON 1
- homeostasis • adaptation
- vertebrate • invertebrate
- 🔁 **Relate Text and Visuals**
- 🔺 **Classify**

LESSON 2
- tissue • organ • radial symmetry
- bilateral symmetry
- 🔁 **Relate Cause and Effect**
- 🔺 **Make Models**

LESSON 3
- cnidarian • mollusk
- arthropod • exoskeleton
- echinoderm • endoskeleton
- 🔁 **Identify the Main Idea**
- 🔺 **Classify**

LESSON 4
- chordate • notochord
- vertebra • ectotherm
- endotherm
- 🔁 **Summarize**
- 🔺 **Draw Conclusions**

LESSON 5
- fish • cartilage • amphibian
- reptile • bird • mammal
- mammary gland
- monotreme • marsupial
- placental mammal • placenta
- 🔁 **Compare and Contrast**
- 🔺 **Interpret Data**

▸ **VOCAB FLASH CARDS** For extra help with vocabulary, visit **Vocab Flash Cards** and type in *Introduction to Animals.*

What Is an Animal?

UNLOCK
THE BIG
?

🔑 **What Are the Functions of Animals?**

🔑 **How Are Animals Classified?**

my planet Diary

Animal Discoveries

What would a mammal never before seen look like? The answer lies in the mountains of Tanzania, Africa. There, scientists discovered a new species of mammal in 2005. The animal, which has been named *Rhynchocyon udzungwensis*, is a species of giant elephant shrew. It weighs about 700 grams and measures about 30 centimeters in length, which is just a little longer than this book. This newly discovered mammal is larger than other elephant shrews, and it has its own distinctive color.

Other animals have also been discovered in the mountains of Tanzania. Unknown amphibians and reptiles have been discovered there as well. Each discovery reveals more of the diversity of the animals living on Earth.

DISCOVERY

Read the following question. Then write your answer below.

Do you think it is important to protect areas such as these mountains? Why?

_____

_____

_____

_____

_____

▶ **PLANET DIARY** Go to **Planet Diary** to learn more about animals.

Lab zone® Do the Inquiry Warm-Up *Is It an Animal?*

What Are the Functions of Animals?

Like plants, animals live almost everywhere on Earth. Animals may have scales, feathers, shells, or fins. They may be brightly colored or completely see-through. Some animals do not have limbs. Others have too many limbs to count. You may wonder if animals have anything in common. Well, they do.

Vocabulary
- homeostasis • adaptation
- vertebrate • invertebrate

Skills
- ↪ Reading: Relate Text and Visuals
- △ Inquiry: Classify

Functions   All animals are multicellular organisms that feed on other organisms and perform the same basic functions. 🔑 The main functions of an animal are to obtain food and oxygen, keep internal conditions stable, move in some way, and reproduce. Keeping internal body conditions stable is called **homeostasis** (hoh mee oh stay sis).

Adaptations   Structures and behaviors that allow animals to perform their functions are called **adaptations.** Teeth and limbs are adaptations that allow animals to obtain food and move. The pouch of a kangaroo is an adaptation for reproduction.

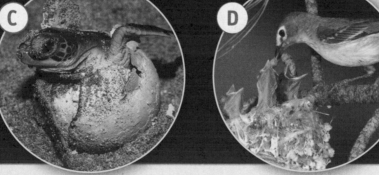

↪ **Relate Text and Visuals**
Match each animal to the function(s) it is performing.

Obtaining Food _____
Animals eat other organisms and raw materials for energy and for growth.

Reproducing _____
Animals make new individuals like themselves.

Moving _____
Animals move to perform other functions as well.

Do the Quick Lab
Get Moving.

🔑 **Assess Your Understanding**

got it?

O **I get it!** Now I know that the functions of animals are _____

_____

O **I need extra help with** _____

Go to **my science** s **coach** *online for help with this subject.*

How Are Animals Classified?

There are more than 1.6 million species of animals, and more are discovered each year. So far, biologists have classified animals into about 35 major groups. In **Figure 1,** you can see some of the major groups. Notice how the groups are arranged on branches. Animal groups on nearby branches are more closely related than groups on branches farther apart. For example, birds are more closely related to reptiles than they are to mammals.

Animals are classified according to how they are related to other animals. These relationships are determined by an animal's body structure, the way the animal develops, and its DNA. DNA is a chemical in cells that controls an organism's inherited characteristics.

All animals are either vertebrates or invertebrates. **Vertebrates** are animals with a backbone. **Invertebrates** are animals without a backbone.

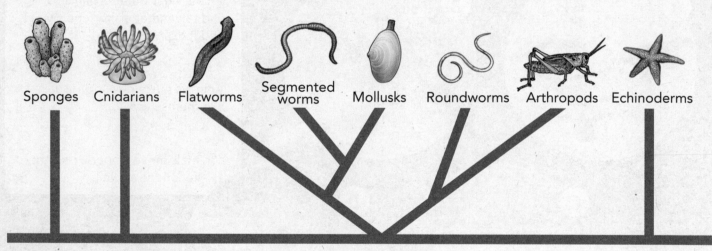

Sponges   Cnidarians   Flatworms   Segmented worms   Mollusks   Roundworms   Arthropods   Echinoderms

Invertebrates

FIGURE 1 ···

> VIRTUAL LAB **Major Animal Groups**
✎ Complete these tasks.

1. **Interpret Diagrams** Are flatworms more closely related to segmented worms or to roundworms? Circle your answer on the diagram.

2. **CHALLENGE** What do you think the bird branch coming off of the reptile branch indicates?

_____

_____

_____

apply it!

Use the information in **Figure 1** to help you classify the animals at the right.

① **Classify** Write the name of each animal's group in the box provided.

② **Identify** Which animals are vertebrates? Which animals are invertebrates?

_____

_____

_____

_____

_____

Fishes

Amphibians

Reptiles

Birds

Mammals

Vertebrates

Assess Your Understanding

1a. Define What is a vertebrate?

_____

_____

b. Compare and Contrast How are vertebrates and invertebrates alike? How do they differ?

_____

_____

Lab® **zone** Do the Quick Lab *Classifying Animals.*

got it?

○ **I get it!** Now I know that animals are classified based on _____

_____

○ **I need extra help with** _____

Go to **MY SCIENCE** 🔊 **COACH** online for help with this subject.

311

Animal Body Plans

UNLOCK THE BIG

🔑 **How Are Animal Bodies Organized?**

🔑 **How Is Symmetry Related to Body Structure?**

my planet diary

DISCOVERY

Spiny Sea Animals

What animal do you think of when you hear the word *spiny*? You might think of a porcupine, but sea urchins are spiny, too. These small, colorful creatures live in the ocean. Just by looking at them, you can't tell that studying sea urchins would lead to a major discovery about how animals reproduce.

In 1875, biologist Oskar Hertwig was studying a transparent egg of a sea urchin under a microscope. He saw a sperm, the male sex cell, enter the egg, the female sex cell, and fuse with the nucleus of the egg. He had discovered how sexual reproduction occurs.

Answer the question below.

How do you think a sea urchin's transparent egg was important to the discovery of how sexual reproduction occurs?

_____

_____

_____

_____

▶ PLANET DIARY Go to **Planet Diary** to learn more about animal body plans.

Lab zone® Do the Inquiry Warm-Up *How Many Ways Can You Fold It?*.

How Are Animal Bodies Organized?

Animals are diverse organisms. But the animals within each phylum have uniquely organized body structures. This organization is called a body plan. 🔑 **The organization of an animal's cells into higher levels of structure, including tissues, organs, and organ systems, helps to describe an animal's body plan.**

Vocabulary

- tissue • organ • radial symmetry
- bilateral symmetry

Skills

- Reading: Relate Cause and Effect
- Inquiry: Make Models

Cells and Tissues All animals are made up of many cells. Their cells are usually specialized and organized as tissues. A **tissue** is a group of similar cells that performs a specific function. Muscle tissue, nervous tissue, and connective tissue are all animal tissues. Bone and blood are examples of kinds of connective tissues.

Organs and Organ Systems In most animals, tissues combine to form organs and organ systems. An **organ** is made up of different tissues. For example, the leg bone of a frog shown in **Figure 1** is an organ composed of bone tissue, nervous tissue, and blood. An organ performs more complex functions than the tissues that make it up could perform alone. Groups of organs make up organ systems. These systems perform the animal's broadest functions.

FIGURE 1 ·····························

A Skeletal System's Organization

Different levels of organization are found in a frog's skeleton.

✎ **Describe** Tell what makes up each level of organization in this frog's skeletal system.

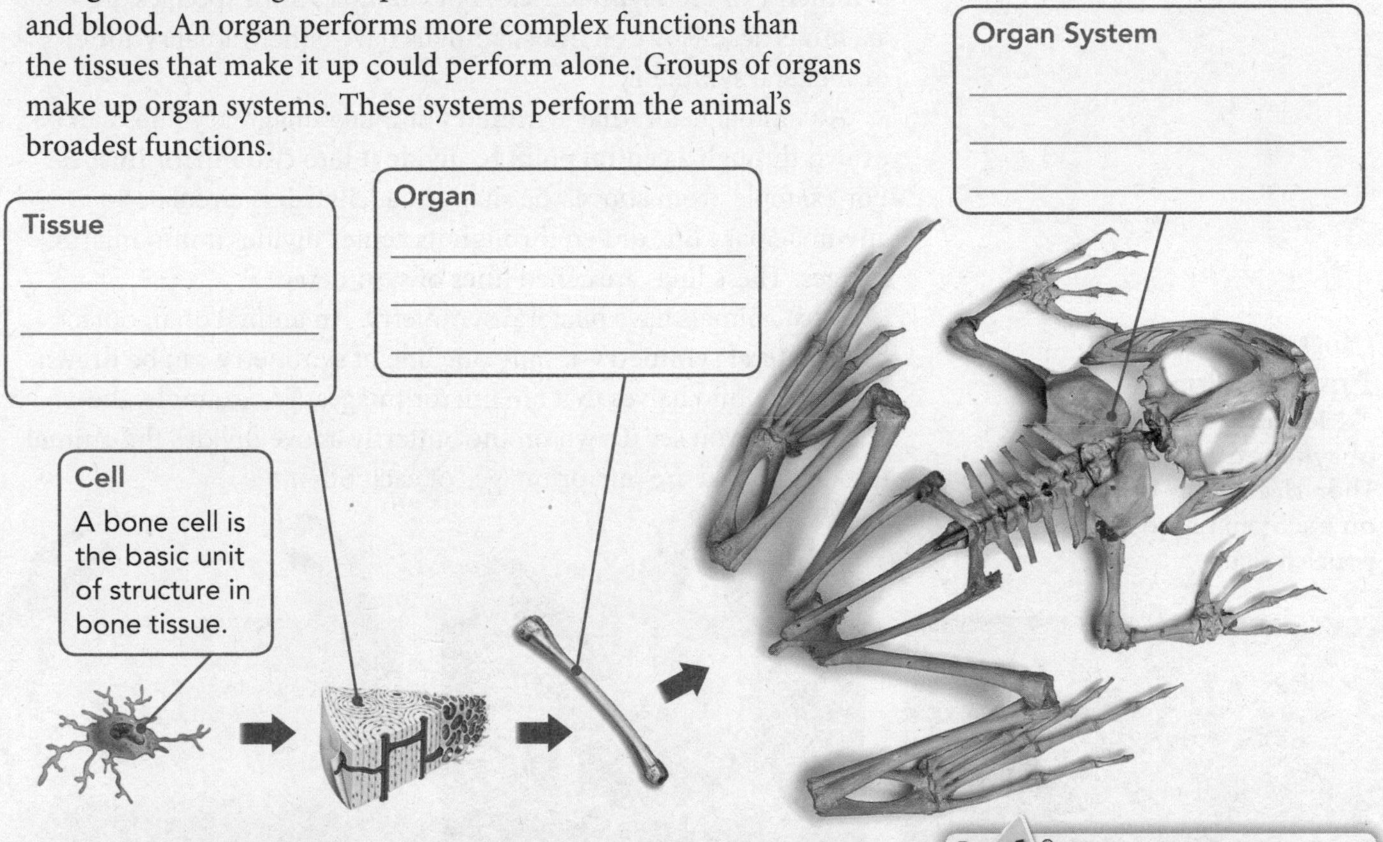

Organ System
_____
_____
_____

Tissue
_____
_____
_____

Organ
_____
_____
_____

Cell
A bone cell is the basic unit of structure in bone tissue.

Lab zone® Do the Quick Lab *Organizing Animal Bodies.*

Assess Your Understanding

got it? ··

○ I get it! Now I know that animal bodies are organized into _____

_____.

○ I need extra help with _____

Go to MY SCIENCE ⓢ COACH online for help with this subject.

How Is Symmetry Related to Body Structure?

A butterfly with bilateral symmetry

Have you ever noticed a butterfly perched on a flower? You probably saw its colors and wing patterns. Did you also see that the pattern on the left side is a mirror image of the pattern on the right side? Many organisms and objects have this balanced display of body parts called symmetry.

Types of Symmetry Animals have different types of symmetry, as you can see in **Figure 2.** Some animals have no symmetry, or are asymmetrical. For example, most sponges are asymmetrical. However, most animals have either radial symmetry or bilateral symmetry.

An animal has **radial symmetry** if many imaginary lines can be drawn through a central point to divide it into two mirror images. For example, from above, the shape of a jellyfish is circular. So any imaginary line drawn through its center divides it into mirror images. These lines are called lines of symmetry.

Most animals have bilateral symmetry. An animal or an object has **bilateral symmetry** if only one line of symmetry can be drawn to divide it into halves that are mirror images. For example, the dashed line you see drawn on the butterfly above divides the animal into halves that are mirror images of each other.

FIGURE 2 ·······································

Types of Symmetry
✏ **Identify** Write the type of symmetry each animal has. Then draw lines of symmetry on each animal to support your choice.

Symmetry and Body Structure
The structures of animals are related to their symmetry. **The bodies of animals without symmetry are organized simply, with some specialized cells but no tissues. In contrast, animals with radial symmetry have complex body plans with tissues and usually with organ systems. Animals with bilateral symmetry have organ systems.**

Radial Symmetry All animals with radial symmetry live in water. Some creep slowly along the ocean floor. Others stay in one spot as adults. A few can move quickly. Most animals with radial symmetry do not have front or back ends. Also, they do not have heads with specialized sense organs. This kind of symmetry allows them to take in information about their surroundings from all directions. This is an advantage for animals that usually move slowly.

Relate Cause and Effect
In the second paragraph, underline an effect of having radial symmetry.

apply it!

Many objects you see have symmetry, but some do not.

❶ **Interpret Photos** Under each picture, write the type of symmetry shown by the object.

❷ **Explain** Draw lines of symmetry on each object to support your choice.

❸ **Make Models** Draw a common object not pictured here that has radial symmetry. Draw lines of symmetry to support your choice.

Bilateral Symmetry

In general, animals with bilateral symmetry are larger and more complex than animals with radial symmetry. They have complex organ systems that help them function efficiently. Also, most animals with bilateral symmetry have streamlined bodies, which help them move quickly.

Most animals with bilateral symmetry have heads at their front ends. Having a head is important to an animal. Most of an animal's specialized sense organs, such as its eyes, are in its head, as you can see in **Figure 3.** In addition, a concentration of nervous tissue is found in an animal's head. Nervous tissue processes information for the animal and coordinates the animal's responses. In fact, an animal usually moves into a new area with its head first.

CHALLENGE Why is it an advantage for an animal to have its head be the first part of its body to enter a new area?

_____

_____

_____

_____

FIGURE 3

A Coral Reef

Many animals with bilateral and radial symmetry live in coral reefs.

✎ **Compare and Contrast** In the Venn diagram, write how a sea star and a fish are alike and how they are different.

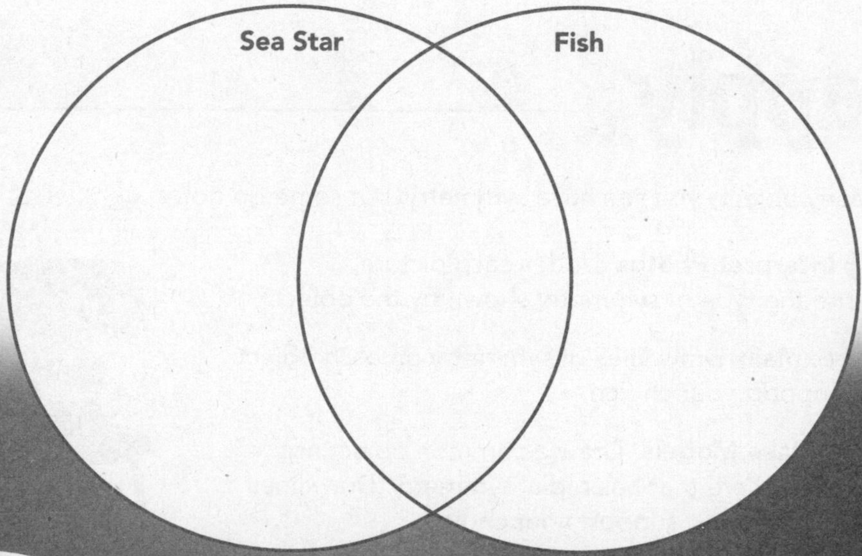

EXPLORE THE BIG Q

Animal or Not?

How do you know an animal when you see it?

FIGURE 4 ....

All animals have functions they perform. Most animals have some type of symmetry and an organization that includes organ systems.

Apply Concepts Answer the questions in the boxes.

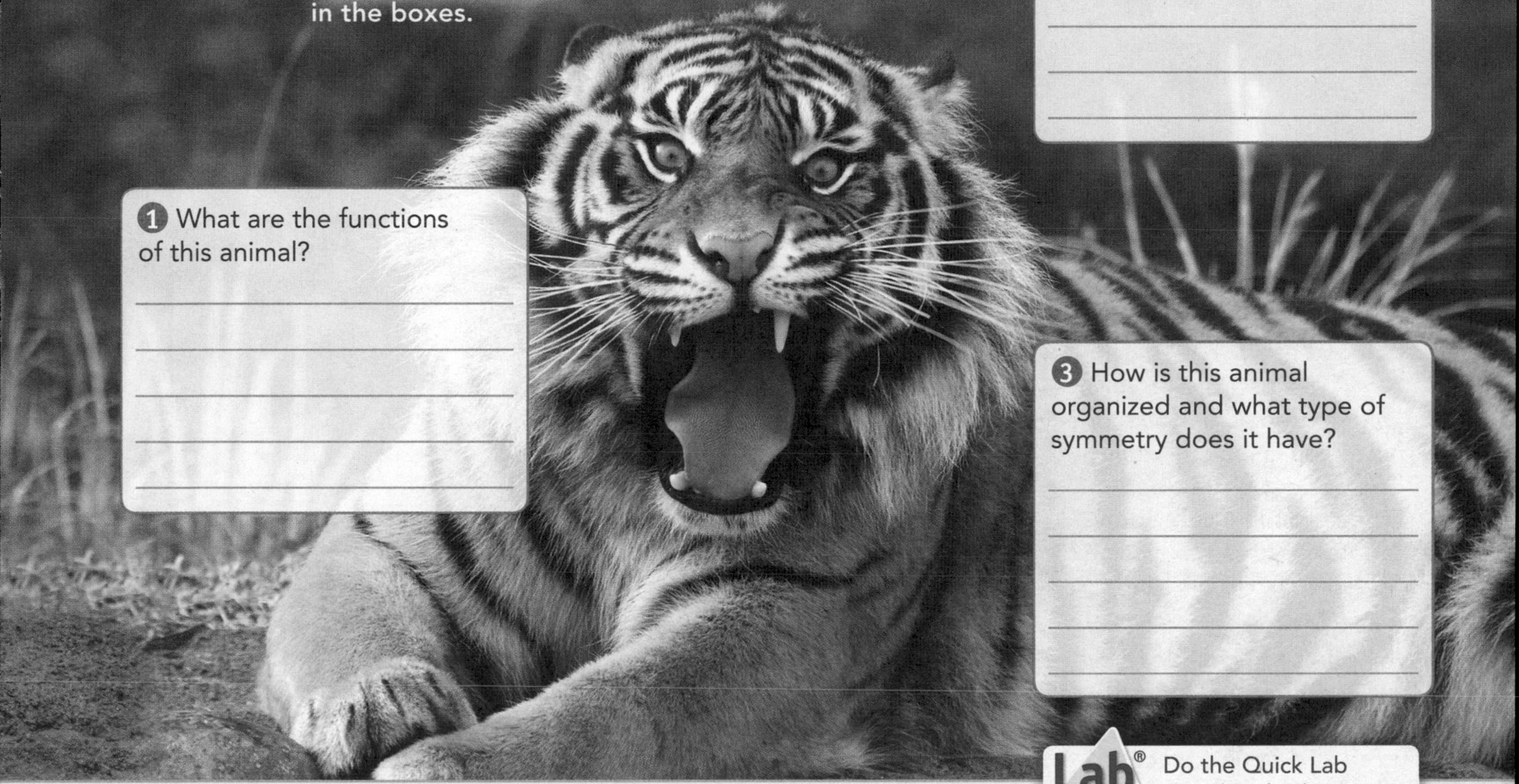

1 What are the functions of this animal?

2 What adaptations does this animal have for obtaining food?

3 How is this animal organized and what type of symmetry does it have?

Lab zone® Do the Quick Lab *Front-End Advantages.*

Assess Your Understanding

1a. Infer Why do you think bilateral symmetry is an advantage for an animal?

b. ANSWER THE BIG Q How do you know an animal when you see it?

got it? ....

O **I get it!** Now I know that symmetry relates to body structure because

O I need extra help with

Go to **MY SCIENCE COACH** *online for help with this subject.*

Introduction to Invertebrates

🔑 **What Are Invertebrates?**

my planeT DiaRY

FUN FACTS

Ready, Aim, Fire!

To *bombard* is to "attack with materials that explode." This action is exactly what the bombardier beetle does. This incredible insect sprays predators with an explosion of deadly chemicals from its own body!

Why don't the chemicals kill the beetle? The chemicals needed for the spray are stored in different places in the beetle's body. When the beetle defends itself, the chemicals are combined into a deadly mixture. The mixture is sprayed on a predator at a temperature of 100°C!

Communicate Discuss the following question with a partner. Then write your answer below.

What other animals do you know about that have unique forms of self defense? Describe their defenses.

_____

_____

_____

▶ **PLANET DIARY** Go to **Planet Diary** to learn more about invertebrates.

 Lab zone Do the Inquiry Warm-Up *How Do Natural and Synthetic Sponges Compare?*

What Are Invertebrates?

At dusk near the edge of a meadow, a grasshopper leaps through the grass. Nearby, a hungry spider waits in its web. The grasshopper leaps into the web. It's caught! The spider bites the grasshopper to stun it and quickly wraps it in silk. The grasshopper will soon become a tasty meal for the spider.

Vocabulary
- cnidarian • mollusk • arthropod • exoskeleton
- echinoderm • endoskeleton

Skills
↩ Reading: Identify the Main Idea
△ Inquiry: Classify

Invertebrate Characteristics
A grasshopper and a spider are both invertebrates. 🔑 **Animals that do not have backbones are invertebrates. The main invertebrate groups are sponges, cnidarians, flatworms, roundworms, segmented worms, mollusks, arthropods, and echinoderms.** About 96 percent of known animals are invertebrates. They live in every climate.

Sponges
Sponges, such as the one shown in **Figure 1,** are asymmetrical invertebrates. They have some specialized cells but no tissues or organs. Unlike most animals you know, adult sponges stay in one place, like plants. But, like other animals, sponges take food into their bodies to get energy.

Cnidarians
Jellyfishes and corals are examples of **cnidarians** (ny DEHR ee unz), invertebrates that have stinging cells and take food into a central body cavity. Cnidarians have radial symmetry. Although they lack organs, they do have some tissues.

FIGURE 1 ·······························
▶ INTERACTIVE ART **Sponges and Cnidarians**
Both sponges and cnidarians are animals that live in water.

✏ **Interpret Photos** Based on symmetry, label these animals as sponges or cnidarians. Then write how sponges and cnidarians are alike and different.

_____
_____
_____
_____
_____
_____
_____

Worms If you have ever worked in a garden, you have probably seen some worms. The three major phyla of worms are flatworms, roundworms, and segmented worms, which you can see in **Figure 2.** All worms have bilateral symmetry, with head and tail ends. They also have tissues, organs, and organ systems. Flatworms have flat, soft bodies. Some have eye spots on their heads that detect light. Roundworms look like smooth, thin tubes. They have two body openings: a mouth and an anus. Segmented worms have bodies made up of many linked sections called segments. They are the simplest animals with a brain. Their brains help them detect food and predators.

FIGURE 2 ···
Worms
The three major phyla of worms are flatworms, roundworms, and segmented worms.

Classify In the boxes, write the phylum of each worm. Then write notes that describe each worm.

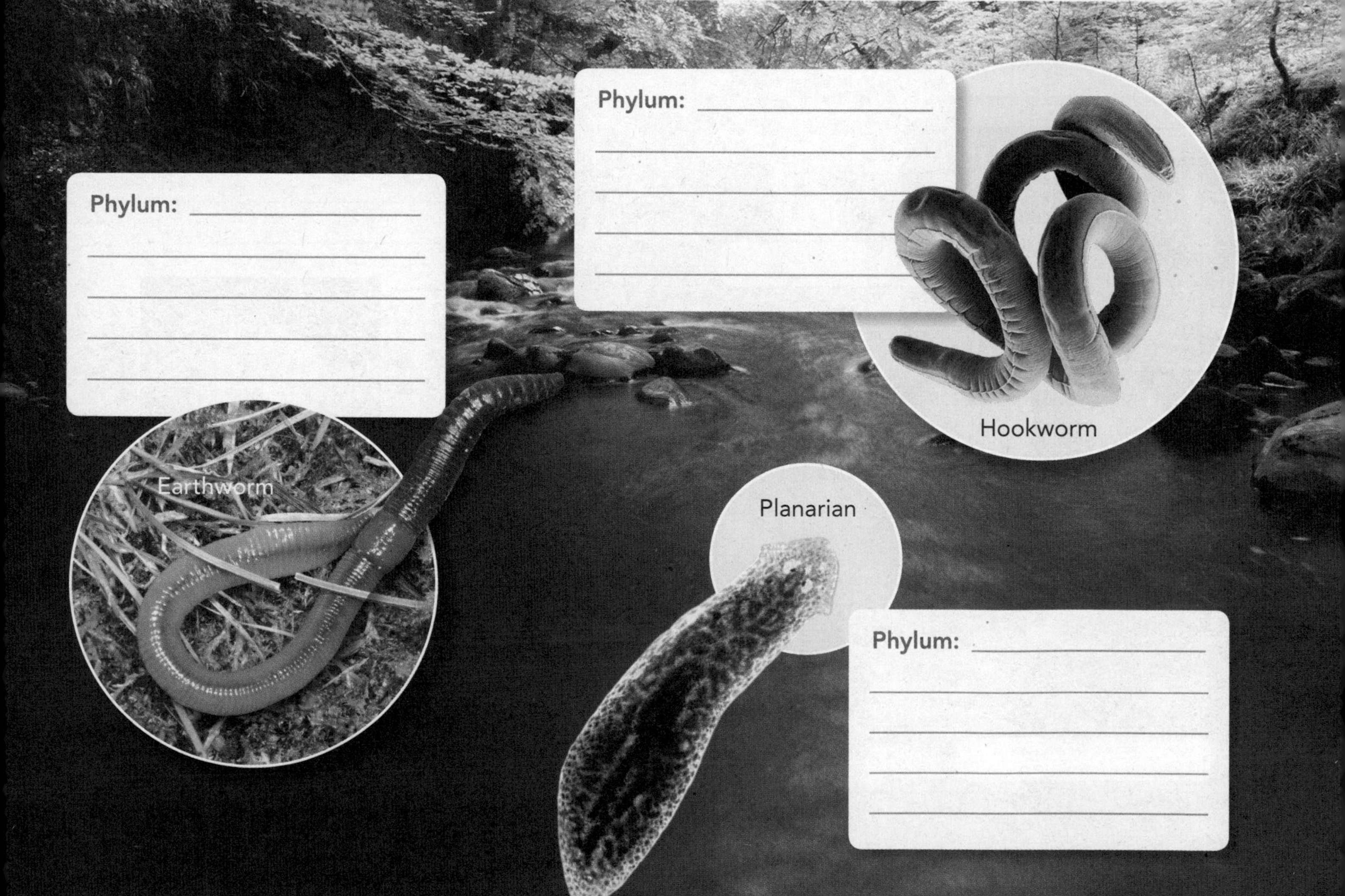

Phylum: _____
_____
_____
_____

Phylum: _____
_____
_____
_____

Hookworm

Earthworm

Planarian

Phylum: _____
_____
_____
_____
_____

Mollusks Have you ever picked up seashells on the beach? Those seashells probably belonged to a mollusk. Invertebrates with soft, unsegmented bodies that are often protected by a hard shell are called **mollusks.** All mollusks have a thin layer of tissue called a mantle that covers their internal organs and an organ called a foot. Depending on the type of mollusk, the foot might be used for crawling, digging, or catching prey. **Figure 3** shows some mollusks.

The three major groups of mollusks are gastropods, bivalves, and cephalopods (SEF uh luh pahdz). Gastropods, such as snails, have a single shell or no shell, and a distinct head. Bivalves, such as clams, have two shells and a simple nervous system. Cephalopods may have an external or internal shell or no shell at all. They have good vision and large brains to help them remember what they've learned. A squid is a cephalopod with an internal shell.

Identify the Main Idea
Underline the main idea in the second paragraph. Then circle the supporting details.

FIGURE 3 ·······································

Mollusks
A snail, clam, and squid do not look alike, but they have the same basic structure.

Summarize Fill in each box in the chart for each organism. Then write a title for the chart.

Characteristics	Gastropod	Bivalve	Cephalopod
	Snail	Clam	Squid
Number of Shells			
Internal or External Shells			
Uses Foot to ...			

321

Smaller than a paper clip, honeybees are important insects. They collect nectar from flowers to make honey and pollinate some plants. Without the honey bee, an apple tree might not produce the apples you eat.

do the math! **Analyzing Data** ....

This circle graph shows a distribution of animal groups.

Distribution of Animal Groups

- ■ Insects
- ■ Noninsect arthropods
- ■ Nonarthropod invertebrates
- ■ Vertebrates

❶ **Read Graphs** What percentage of animals are not insects?

_____

❷ [CHALLENGE] What percentage of animals are invertebrates that are not insects?

_____
_____

Arthropods At first you may not think that a crab and a spider have anything in common. But look at the spider and crab in **Figure 4.** Crabs and spiders are **arthropods,** or invertebrates that have hard outer coverings, segmented bodies, and pairs of jointed appendages. Legs, wings, and antennae are appendages. The outer covering is called an **exoskeleton,** or outer skeleton. At times, the exoskeleton is shed and replaced as the animal grows. One arthropod group, crustaceans, includes animals such as crabs. A second group, arachnids, includes animals such as spiders. A third group includes centipedes, millipedes, and insects, such as bees and ants.

Insect

Arachnid

FIGURE 4 ....
Arthropods
Members of the three arthropod groups have different characteristics.

✎ **Observe** Tell how the number of pairs of legs of a spider and a bee differ.

_____
_____
_____
_____
_____
_____

Crustacean

Echinoderms An **echinoderm** is an invertebrate that has an internal skeleton and a system of fluid-filled tubes. An internal skeleton is called an **endoskeleton.** Echinoderms, shown in **Figure 5,** have radial symmetry. They use their system of tubes to move and obtain food and oxygen. Sea cucumbers, sea stars, sea urchins, and brittle stars are the major echinoderm groups.

Sea cucumber

Sea star

Sea urchins

Brittle stars

FIGURE 5 ·······················

> **ART IN MOTION** **Echinoderms**
Echinoderms are diverse animals, but all live in salt water.

✎ **Compare and Contrast** In the chart, write a brief description of the shape and symmetry of each echinoderm.

	Sea Cucumber	Sea Star	Sea Urchin	Brittle Star
Shape				
Symmetry				

Lab zone ® Do the Lab Investigation *Earthworm Responses.*

🔑 **Assess Your Understanding**

1a. Identify How are all cnidarians alike?

_____

_____

b. Explain If you saw a worm, how would you identify its phylum?

_____

_____

got it?

○ I get it! Now I know that invertebrates _____

_____

_____

○ I need extra help with _____

Go to MY SCIENCE ⑤ COACH online for help with this subject.

Introduction to Vertebrates

🔑 **What Are the Characteristics of Chordates and Vertebrates?**

🔑 **How Do Vertebrates Control Body Temperature?**

my pLANET DiaRY

BRRRR! It's Freezing!

How can anything survive in Antarctica, the coldest and windiest place on Earth? Emperor penguins have many physical characteristics that help them live there. For example, they have a layer of fat that helps them stay warm. They also have short, stiff feathers that help to insulate and protect them from the freezing air.

However, the penguins' physical characteristics are not enough to stay warm in Antarctica during the winter. Emperor penguins cooperate to keep warm. They huddle together in groups and take turns standing on the outside of the huddle where it is the coldest. This way, every penguin gets a chance to stand in the middle of the huddle where it is the warmest. Now that's teamwork!

FUN FACTS

Read the following questions. Then write your answers below.

1. Why don't emperor penguins freeze to death in Antarctica?

_____

_____

_____

2. What are other ways you know about that animals use to stay warm?

_____

_____

_____

▶ PLANET DIARY Go to **Planet Diary** to learn more about vertebrates.

 Lab zone® Do the Inquiry Warm-Up *How Is an Umbrella Like a Skeleton?*

Vocabulary
- chordate • notochord • vertebra
- ectotherm • endotherm

Skills
↻ Reading: Summarize
△ Inquiry: Draw Conclusions

What Are the Characteristics of Chordates and Vertebrates?

The animals you are probably most familiar with are members of the phylum Chordata. Members of this phylum are called chordates (KAWR dayts). Most chordates, including all fishes, amphibians, reptiles, birds, and mammals, are vertebrates. A few chordates, such as sea squirts and lancelets, do not have backbones.

Chordate Characteristics 🗝 **At some point in their lives, all chordates have three characteristics: a notochord, a nerve cord, and pouches in the throat area. Most chordates also have a backbone.**

Notochord A **notochord** is a flexible rod that supports a chordate's back. The name *Chordata* comes from this structure's name.

Nerve Cord All chordates have a nerve cord that runs down their back. Your spinal cord is such a nerve cord. The nerve cord connects the brain to nerves in other parts of the body.

Throat Pouches At some point in their lives, chordates have pouches in their throat area. In fishes and lancelets, like the one shown in **Figure 1**, grooves between these pouches become gill slits. In most other vertebrates, the pouches disappear before birth.

FIGURE 1 ·····················

Chordates
Lancelets show the three characteristics shared by all chordates at some point in their lives.

✎ **Relate Text and Visuals** Circle the labels of the three chordate characteristics. Then explain how a lancelet is different from a fish.

_____
_____
_____
_____
_____

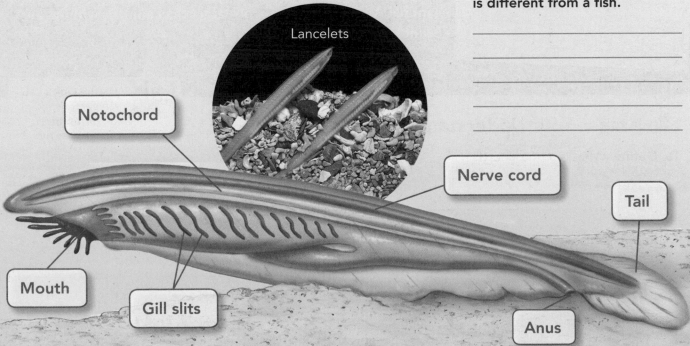

Lancelets

Notochord

Nerve cord

Tail

Mouth

Gill slits

Anus

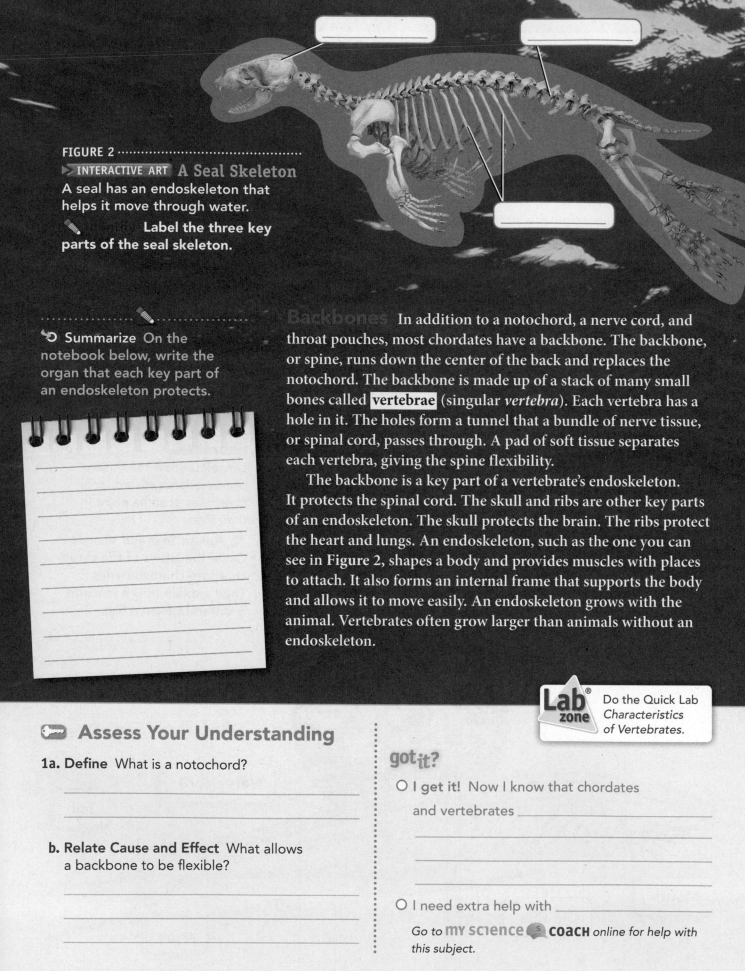

FIGURE 2 ·······················
▶ INTERACTIVE ART A Seal Skeleton
A seal has an endoskeleton that helps it move through water.

Label the three key parts of the seal skeleton.

✎ Summarize On the notebook below, write the organ that each key part of an endoskeleton protects.

Backbones In addition to a notochord, a nerve cord, and throat pouches, most chordates have a backbone. The backbone, or spine, runs down the center of the back and replaces the notochord. The backbone is made up of a stack of many small bones called **vertebrae** (singular *vertebra*). Each vertebra has a hole in it. The holes form a tunnel that a bundle of nerve tissue, or spinal cord, passes through. A pad of soft tissue separates each vertebra, giving the spine flexibility.

The backbone is a key part of a vertebrate's endoskeleton. It protects the spinal cord. The skull and ribs are other key parts of an endoskeleton. The skull protects the brain. The ribs protect the heart and lungs. An endoskeleton, such as the one you can see in **Figure 2**, shapes a body and provides muscles with places to attach. It also forms an internal frame that supports the body and allows it to move easily. An endoskeleton grows with the animal. Vertebrates often grow larger than animals without an endoskeleton.

Lab zone®
Do the Quick Lab
Characteristics of Vertebrates.

🔑 **Assess Your Understanding**

1a. Define What is a notochord?

_____

_____

b. Relate Cause and Effect What allows a backbone to be flexible?

_____

_____

_____

got it?

○ **I get it!** Now I know that chordates and vertebrates _____

_____

_____

_____

○ **I need extra help with** _____

Go to MY SCIENCE 🔵 COACH online for help with this subject.

How Do Vertebrates Control Body Temperature?

The major groups of vertebrates differ in how they control body temperature. **Some vertebrates do not produce much internal heat. Therefore, their body temperatures change with the environment. Other vertebrates control their internal heat and maintain a constant body temperature.**

Amphibians, reptiles, and most fishes are ectotherms. An animal that produces little internal body heat is called an **ectotherm.** Its body temperature changes with temperature changes in its environment.

Birds and mammals are endotherms. An **endotherm** is an animal that controls the internal heat it produces and regulates its own temperature. An endotherm's body temperature is always fairly constant. Endotherms have adaptations such as sweat glands, fur, and feathers for maintaining body temperature.

Vocabulary Prefixes The prefix ecto- means "outside." What do you think the prefix endo- means?

_____

apply it!

Animals control body temperature in different ways.

❶ **Draw Conclusions** Write whether you think each animal is an endotherm or ectotherm.

❷ **CHALLENGE** Would it be more difficult for a penguin to live in a desert or a snake to live in a polar region? Explain.

_____
_____
_____
_____

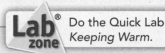
Do the Quick Lab
Keeping Warm.

Assess Your Understanding

got it? ....

○ I get it! Now I know that vertebrates' body temperature _____

_____

○ I need extra help with _____

Go to **my science COACH** *online for help with this subject.*

Vertebrate Diversity

🔑 **What Are the Major Groups of Vertebrates?**

my PLANET DIARY

FUN FACTS

Sending Messages

Have you ever felt like stomping your feet to show your frustration? People aren't the only ones who stomp their feet to express themselves. Researchers think that elephants communicate by stomping. For example, they think elephants stomp their feet to greet one another and send warnings.

What if an animal has no feet to stomp? It can sing! Many species of whales communicate with one another through song. They make different sounds to communicate different messages. Who knows what else researchers will discover about animal communication!

Communicate Discuss the following question with a partner. Then write your answers below.

What are three ways you communicate with others without using words?

_____

_____

_____

_____

_____

> **PLANET DIARY** Go to **Planet Diary** to learn more about vertebrate diversity.

Lab zone Do the Inquiry Warm-Up Exploring Vertebrates.

What Are the Major Groups of Vertebrates?

Vertebrates, like all other animals, are diverse. They live in almost all types of environments on Earth and vary in shape, size, and color. 🔑 **There are five major groups of vertebrates. They are fishes, amphibians, reptiles, birds, and mammals.** Members of each group share certain characteristics.

Vocabulary

- fish • cartilage • amphibian • reptile • bird
- mammal • mammary gland • monotreme • marsupial
- placental mammal • placenta

Skills

↻ **Reading: Compare and Contrast**
△ **Inquiry: Interpret Data**

Fishes A **fish** is a vertebrate that lives in water and uses fins to move. Most fishes are ectotherms. They have scales and obtain oxygen through gills. They make up the largest group of vertebrates. Based on certain characteristics, fishes are organized into three major groups, which are shown in **Figure 1.**

Jawless fishes have no jaws or scales. They scrape, suck, and stab their food. Their skeletons are made of **cartilage,** a tissue more flexible than bone. Fish with jaws, scales, and skeletons made of cartilage are cartilaginous fishes (kahr tuh LAJ uh nuhs). Bony fishes have jaws, scales, and a pocket on each side of the head that holds the gills. Their skeletons are made of hard bone.

FIGURE 1 ·····························

Types of Fishes

The three groups of fishes are jawless fishes, cartilaginous fishes, and bony fishes.

✎ **Summarize** Write on the notebook the characteristics of each group of fishes.

Lamprey

Lamprey's mouth

Jawless fish

Gray reef shark

Cartilaginous fish

Bony fish

Goldfish

Gill pocket

Amphibians

You may know that some amphibians such as frogs can be noisy neighbors. Frogs, toads, and salamanders are examples of amphibians. An **amphibian** is a vertebrate that is ectothermic and spends its early life in water and its adult life on land. In fact, the word *amphibian* means "double life." Most amphibians spend their adult lives on land. But they return to water to lay eggs and reproduce. Look at the amphibians in **Figure 2**.

FIGURE 2 ....

Amphibian Diversity

Adult salamanders have tails, but almost all adult frogs and toads do not.

✎ **Interpret Photos**
Label each type of amphibian. Explain the evidence in each picture that helped you decide.

_____

_____

_____

_____

_____

_____

_____

_____

do the math!

Vertebrate Diversity

The table shows the estimated number of species in each vertebrate group. Use the table to answer the questions.

❶ **Calculate** About how many vertebrate species are there in all?

_____

❷ ⚠ **Interpret Data** Which group has the greatest number of species? The least?

_____

_____

Estimated Number of Species of Vertebrates	
Vertebrate Group	Number of Species
Fishes	30,700
Amphibians	6,347
Reptiles	8,734
Birds	9,990
Mammals	5,488

Reptiles The alligator, snake, and chameleon shown in **Figure 3** are all reptiles. A **reptile** is an ectothermic vertebrate that has scaly skin and lungs and lays eggs on land. Some reptiles, such as sea turtles, live in water but still breathe air. Most reptiles live on land even though some swim a lot. To live on land, an animal must have adaptations that keep water in its cells. The skin of reptiles is thick and helps keep water inside their bodies. Reptiles also have organs called kidneys that conserve water. Most young reptiles develop inside tough-shelled eggs. The eggshell helps keep water inside the egg.

Chameleon

FIGURE 3 ·······························

Reptile Diversity

Reptiles are adapted to life on land.

✎ **Complete these tasks.**

1. **Draw Conclusions** In each box, describe how you know that the animal is a reptile.

2. CHALLENGE Explain how a shell keeps water inside an egg.

_____

_____

Alligator

This ibis wades through water with its tall, thin legs. It uses its long bill to find small prey.

Birds If you have ever watched birds at a feeder, you know how fascinating they are. A **bird** is an endothermic vertebrate that lays eggs and has feathers and a four-chambered heart. Birds are adapted for flight. They have wings and lightweight, nearly hollow bones. Shown in **Figure 4,** birds are the only modern animals with feathers.

FIGURE 4 ···

Birds

Different adaptations allow birds to live in different environments.

✎ **Make Generalizations** In each box, underline adaptations the bird has that help it survive. Then explain how you think feathers help birds survive.

_____

_____

_____

This rainbow bee-eater uses its pointed bill to feed on bees and other insects, which it catches as it flies.

Sharp vision and keen hearing help owls like this tawny owl hunt at night. They use razor-sharp claws to grab prey.

◑ **Compare and Contrast** In the Venn diagram, list how reptiles and birds are alike and different.

Birds   Reptiles

Mammals There are three main groups of mammals. **Mammals** are endothermic vertebrates that have skin covered with fur or hair, and a four-chambered heart. The young are fed with milk produced by organs, called **mammary glands,** in the mother's body.

The mammal groups differ in how their young develop. **Monotremes** lay eggs. **Marsupials** are born at an early stage of development, and they usually continue to develop in a pouch on the mother's body. A **placental mammal** develops inside its mother's body until its body systems can function independently. Materials are exchanged between the mother and the embryo through an organ called the **placenta.**

Giraffe

FIGURE 5 ·····················
Mammals
The main groups of mammals are monotremes, marsupials, and placental mammals.

✏ **Review** In each box, write a note about how the young of the group develops.

Kangaroo

Placental Mammal
_____
_____

Marsupial
_____
_____
_____
_____

Platypus

Monotreme
_____
_____

Lab® Do the Quick Lab
zone *It's Plane to See.*

🔑 **Assess Your Understanding**

1a. Name Name the three groups of fishes.
_____
_____

b. Relate Cause and Effect Why can mammals live in colder environments than reptiles?
_____
_____

got it? ···

○ **I get it!** Now I know that the major groups of vertebrates are _____
_____

○ **I need extra help with** _____

Go to **MY SCIENCE** ⑤ **COACH** *online for help with this subject.*

REVIEW
THE BIG
?

I would know an animal by its _____, _____, and _____.

LESSON 1 What Is an Animal?

🔑 The main functions of an animal are to obtain food and oxygen, keep internal conditions stable, move in some way, and reproduce.

🔑 Animals are classified according to how they are related to other animals. These relationships are determined by an animal's body structure, the way the animal develops, and its DNA.

Vocabulary
- homeostasis • adaptation
- vertebrate • invertebrate

LESSON 2 Animal Body Plans

🔑 The organization of an animal's cells into higher levels of structure helps to describe an animal's body plan.

🔑 Animals without symmetry have no tissues. Animals with radial symmetry have tissues and usually have organ systems. Animals with bilateral symmetry have organ systems.

Vocabulary
- tissue • organ • radial symmetry
- bilateral symmetry

LESSON 3 Introduction to Invertebrates

🔑 Animals that do not have backbones are invertebrates.

Vocabulary
- cnidarian
- mollusk
- arthropod
- exoskeleton
- echinoderm
- endoskeleton

LESSON 4 Introduction to Vertebrates

🔑 At some point in their lives, all chordates have three characteristics: a notochord, a nerve cord, and pouches in the throat area.

🔑 The body temperatures of some vertebrates change with the environment. Other vertebrates maintain a constant body temperature.

Vocabulary
- chordate • notochord
- vertebra • ectotherm
- endotherm

LESSON 5 Vertebrate Diversity

🔑 There are five major groups of vertebrates. They are fishes, amphibians, reptiles, birds, and mammals.

Vocabulary
- fish • cartilage • amphibian
- reptile • bird
- mammal • mammary gland
- monotreme • marsupial
- placental mammal
- placenta

Review and Assessment

LESSON 1 What Is an Animal?

1. The process that the body uses to maintain a stable internal environment is called

   a. adaptation.   **b.** endothermic.

   c. homeostasis.   **d.** sweating.

2. The presence of a _____ determines whether an animal is a vertebrate or an invertebrate.

3. **Identify the Main Idea** What are the five main functions of animals?

   _____

   _____

   _____

   _____

   _____

4. **Draw Conclusions** Suppose a book titled *Earth's Animals* is about vertebrates. Is its title a good one? Explain your answer.

   _____

   _____

   _____

   _____

5. **Apply Concepts** Some insects and birds can fly. Despite this similarity, why are insects and birds classified as different groups?

   _____

   _____

   _____

6. **Write About It** Choose an animal that you know well and describe a day in its life. Include the functions it carries out and the adaptations it uses to survive in its environment.

LESSON 2 Animal Body Plans

7. What is the highest level of organization an animal can have?

   a. cells   **b.** organ systems

   c. organs   **d.** tissues

8. An animal with many lines of symmetry has _____ symmetry.

9. **Compare and Contrast** Describe how the symmetry of a sea star, a sponge, and a fish differ.

   _____

   _____

   _____

   _____

LESSON 3 Introduction to Invertebrates

10. Mollusks with two shells are called

    a. cephalopods.   **b.** sea stars.

    c. bivalves.   **d.** gastropods.

11. An _____ has a system of fluid-filled tubes for obtaining food and oxygen.

12. **Make Generalizations** Suppose you see an animal. You wonder if it is an arthropod. What characteristics would you look for?

    _____

    _____

    _____

    _____

13. **Write About It** Explain whether a snail or a sponge has a higher level of organization and how this organization helps the invertebrate.

9 Review and Assessment

Introduction to Vertebrates

14. All vertebrates are

    a. chordates.   **b.** invertebrates.

    c. fishes.   **d.** reptiles.

15. A _____ is replaced by a backbone in many vertebrates.

16. Make Generalizations Why is the endoskeleton important?

_____

_____

_____

_____

17. Relate Cause and Effect Whales, polar bears, and seals are endotherms. How might their thick layer of fat help them?

_____

_____

_____

18. Infer Would an ectotherm or an endotherm be more active on a cold night? Explain.

_____

_____

_____

_____

_____

19. [**Write About It**] Your friend has both a hamster and a lizard as pets. She wants to buy a heat lamp for each of them to keep them warm. Tell her whether each pet needs a heat lamp to stay warm. Include the two ways animals maintain their body temperatures in your answer.

Vertebrate Diversity

20. A reptile

    a. is an endotherm.   **b.** lives only in water.

    c. has gills.   **d.** has scaly skin.

21. _____ are the only animals with feathers.

22. Classify Into which group of fishes would you classify a fish with jaws and a skeleton made of cartilage?

_____

_____

23. Summarize What is the main difference between the three mammal groups?

_____

_____

_____

APPLY THE BIG ?

How do you know an animal when you see it?

24. Look at the squid below. Describe how you know it is an animal. Include details about its functions and its adaptations to survive.

_____

_____

_____

_____

_____

_____

_____

_____

Standardized Test Prep

Multiple Choice

Circle the letter of the best answer.

1. A lancelet is shown below. Which of its characteristics belong to a chordate?

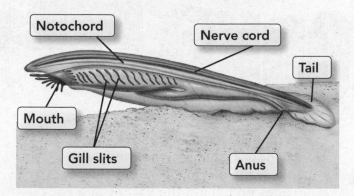

    A the mouth, gill slits, and nerve cord
    B the gill slits, notochord, and nerve cord
    C the notochord, nerve cord, and tail
    D the gill slits, notochord, and mouth

2. Which characteristics do birds and mammals have in common?

    A Both are endothermic vertebrates.
    B Both have fur or hair.
    C Both have a three-chambered heart.
    D Both are vertebrates that produce milk.

3. Which of the following best describes the function of the placenta?

    A delivers oxygen to the body's cells
    B stores food inside the body before swallowing and digesting it
    C directs and coordinates a mammal's complex movements
    D passes materials between a mother and her offspring before it is born

4. What kind of evidence is used to determine the relationships between animals?

    A evidence from the way an animal develops
    B evidence from an animal's DNA
    C evidence from an animal's body structure
    D all of the above

5. Which describes an ectothermic animal?

    A an animal that has a thick coat of fur
    B an animal that sweats when the environment is too hot
    C an animal that depends on the sun to raise its body temperature
    D an animal that maintains its body temperature when walking through snow

Constructed Response

Use the photos below and your knowledge of science to help you answer Question 6. Write your answer on a separate sheet of paper.

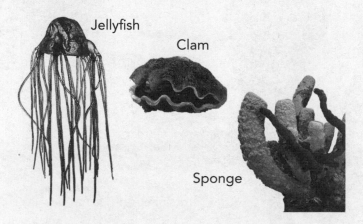

6. Invertebrates are animals without a backbone. Identify the group each of the invertebrates above belongs to. Then, for each group, name three characteristics that all its members share.

JUNIOR ZOOKEEPERS

What is a lemur's favorite snack? Are baboons grumpy when they wake up in the morning? What, exactly, goes on behind the scenes at a zoo? If you want to know the answers to these questions, find out about Junior Zookeeper programs.

Many zoos throughout the country have volunteer programs for teenagers. Junior Zookeepers' tasks can include caring for zoo animals and assisting in zoo research. At some zoos, volunteers even help design and run educational programs. These volunteers serve as guides to help the public learn more from the zoo exhibits.

Some jobs are a little messy. You might have to help clean up the elephant cages! But the rewards can be just as big—taking care of animals can be a life-changing experience.

Design It Find out more about how zoo habitats are designed. How do zookeepers simulate an animal's habitat? How do they design exhibits that educate the public? Then choose an animal and design a model zoo exhibit that simulates its habitat and educates the public about the animal.

A Slimy Defense

If there were a contest for the most disgusting animal in the sea, the hagfish would probably win. This eel-like creature is almost blind, and it feeds by burrowing into the flesh of dead animals on the ocean floor. If a hagfish is attacked, it releases large amounts of thick slime, which can suffocate any predator foolish enough to attack! This thick gooey slime contains threads that are almost as strong as spider silk. Studies of hagfish slime may one day help scientists make materials that are stronger than the fabric we now use in bulletproof vests!

Write About It Find examples of how biological research has inspired the development of technology. Then make a poster that describes three examples. Explain how the technology affected society.

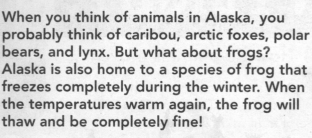

SUPERCOOLING FROGS

When you think of animals in Alaska, you probably think of caribou, arctic foxes, polar bears, and lynx. But what about frogs? Alaska is also home to a species of frog that freezes completely during the winter. When the temperatures warm again, the frog will thaw and be completely fine!

The wood frog has several adaptations that allow it to freeze. Much of the water from the frog's cells moves into its body cavity before the water freezes. This prevents the ice from damaging tissues. High levels of glucose protect the frog's cells from freezing. Finally, the wood frog may even ingest bacteria that allow it to control the rate at which freezing occurs!

Research It Find out about other animals that have adapted to live in extreme conditions. Then create an illustrated guide that shows how three of these animals survive in extreme environments.

WHAT MAKES A BAT AGILE IN FLIGHT?

How do animals move?

Bats are the only mammals that can truly fly. The wings of a bat are made of a thin skin that stretches from its shoulders to the tips of its long, flexible finger bones. When the bat moves its wings up and down, the skin billows out like a balloon. As a bat flies, its wings are more flexible than your hand waving because the wing bones bend. This little brown bat can reach speeds of 35 km/h as it flies, swoops, or dives after a moth.

Develop Hypotheses How can a bat alter its course so quickly?

_____

_____

_____

_____

▶ **UNTAMED SCIENCE** Watch the **Untamed Science** video to learn more about how animals move.

Animal Life Processes

10 Getting Started

Check Your Understanding

1. **Background** Read the paragraph below and then answer the question.

Why can you not leap like a frog? Like a frog, you are a **vertebrate.** But frogs have **adaptations** for leaping. A frog's powerful hind legs and sturdy **endoskeleton** allow it to leap and land without injury.

> An animal that has a backbone is a **vertebrate.**
>
> An **adaptation** is a characteristic that enables an animal to live successfully in its environment.
>
> An **endoskeleton** is an internal skeleton.

• What adaptations do frogs have that enable them to leap?

_____

_____

_____

_____

▶ MY READING WEB If you had trouble completing the question above, visit **My Reading Web** and type in *Animal Life Processes.*

Vocabulary Skill

Identify Multiple Meanings Some words have different meanings in science and in everyday use. The table below lists the multiple meanings for some words in this chapter.

Word	Everyday Meaning	Scientific Meaning
impulse	*n.* a sudden desire, urge, or inclination	*n.* an electrical message that moves from one neuron to another
stimulus	*n.* something that encourages an activity to begin	*n.* a change that an animal detects in its environment

2. **Quick Check** In the table above, circle the meaning of the word *stimulus* as it is used in the following sentence.

• The smell of pancakes was the *stimulus* that made Theo's mouth water.

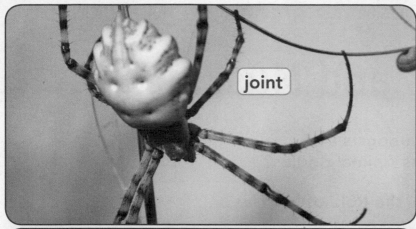
joint

response

carnivore

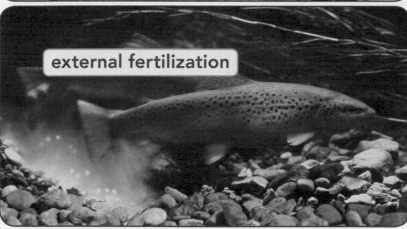
external fertilization

Chapter Preview

> VOCAB FLASH CARDS For extra help with vocabulary, visit **Vocab Flash Cards** and type in *Animal Life Processes.*

Skeletons and Muscles

🔑 **What Supports and Protects Animal Bodies?**

🔑 **What Is the Role of Muscles?**

MY PLANET DIARY

Fast Felines

Which animal is the fastest sprinter? It is a cheetah. The cheetah's body structure and muscles allow it to reach speeds of up to 112 km/h in only three seconds. Its flexible spine enables the cheetah to extend its limbs to great lengths. This ability allows the cheetah to cover as much ground in one stride as a racehorse. The cheetah also has a high percentage of fast-twitch muscle fibers. These fibers provide power and allow the cheetah to reach its incredible speed faster than a race car can reach the same speed. It's no wonder that the cheetah holds the title of "World's Fastest Land Animal."

FUN FACTS

Read the following questions. Then write your answers below.

1. What are two parts of a cheetah's body that help it run fast?

_____

_____

_____

2. Why do you think a cheetah's speed is an advantage to the animal?

_____

_____

_____

_____

▶ PLANET DIARY Go to **Planet Diary** to learn more about skeletons and muscles.

 Lab zone® Do the Inquiry Warm-Up *Will It Bend and Move?*

Vocabulary
- molting
- cartilage
- joint
- muscle

Skills
- ↻ Reading: Compare and Contrast
- △ Inquiry: Infer

What Supports and Protects Animal Bodies?

Imagine you are watching lions moving slowly through tall grass. They are surrounding a young zebra that has wandered away from its mother. Flies buzz, and beetles chew on grass blades. Buzzards circle in the distance. Nearby, a snake slithers away from one of the lions. Unaware, the zebra continues to graze.

Think about all these different animals. Do they have anything in common? The answer is yes. All of their bodies are supported by skeletons, which have similar functions. **A skeleton is a framework that shapes and supports an animal, protects its internal organs, and allows it to move in its environment.**

Types of Skeletons Most animals have one of three types of skeletons: skeletons without hard parts, exoskeletons, and endoskeletons. An exoskeleton is a hard outer covering, while an endoskeleton is a framework inside the body. Some animals, such as sponges, do not have skeletons. However, most sponges have hard, spikelike structures scattered among their cells. These structures help support and protect them.

Endoskeleton   Exoskeleton

Both

✎
↻ **Compare and Contrast**
Complete the Venn diagram to show how endoskeletons and exoskeletons are alike and how they are different.

345

Skeletons Without Hard Parts Have you ever seen blobs that look like clear gelatin washed up on beach sand? These blobs are the bodies of jellyfish. They still have some shape because of their skeleton. Jellyfish and other cnidarians, as well as earthworms and some other annelids, have skeletons without hard parts. These skeletons have fluid-filled cavities surrounded by muscle, a tissue used in movement. Like all skeletons, this type of skeleton helps an animal keep its shape and move about.

Exoskeletons Mollusks and arthropods have exoskeletons. Clam and scallop shells are mollusk exoskeletons made of calcium-containing compounds. The exoskeletons of arthropods are made of a different substance. Exoskeletons have some disadvantages. First, exoskeletons have no cells, so they cannot grow the way organisms grow. A mollusk's shell does get larger over time as the animal secretes calcium. But to grow, arthropods must shed their exoskeletons periodically and produce new ones in a process called **molting**. Second, an exoskeleton can be heavy. This weight prevents an animal from growing very large. Look at the skeletons in **Figure 1**.

did you **know?** ....

Before this Pacific lobster shed its old exoskeleton, a new one grew right under it. Once the new exoskeleton was ready, the lobster began drinking lots of seawater. As its body swelled with seawater, the old exoskeleton started to split. All the lobster had to do was back out of it, pulling its legs out last. Until its new exoskelton hardens a bit, this lobster will not be able to move.

FIGURE 1 ·······························
▷ **INTERACTIVE ART** **Two Types of Skeletons**
Some animals have skeletons without hard parts, while others have exoskeletons.

✏ **Relate Text and Visuals**
In each box, write a description of the type of the animal's skeleton.

Cicada

Old skeleton

Earthworm

Scallop

Endoskeletons Echinoderms and vertebrates have endoskeletons. Like exoskeletons, endoskeletons may contain different materials. For example, a sea star's endoskeleton is made of plates that contain calcium. Sharks and some other fishes have endoskeletons made of **cartilage**, a tissue that is more flexible than bone. The endoskeletons of most other vertebrates are made of mostly bone with some cartilage.

Bone and cartilage contain living cells. As a result, a vertebrate's endoskeleton can grow. In addition, because endoskeletons are relatively light, vertebrates with endoskeletons can grow larger than animals with exoskeletons. Some animals with endoskeletons are shown in **Figure 2**.

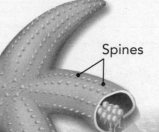

Polar Bear

Foot and leg skeleton

FIGURE 2 ···

Endoskeletons

Endoskeletons are made of different materials.

✎ **Complete these tasks.**

1. **Relate Text and Visuals** In the table, identify the material that each animal's endoskeleton is made of.

Animal	Material in Endoskeleton
Sea Star	
Shark	
Bear	

2. **Draw Conclusions** Why is having an endoskeleton an advantage to a bird?

_____

_____

Sea Star

Spines

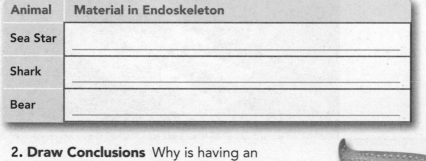

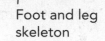

Spine

Skeletal plates

Tube foot

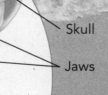

Great White Shark

Skull

Jaws

Joint

Costa Rican Spider

Joints

Joints Have you ever tried to run without bending your legs? If you have, then you know it is difficult. Fortunately, most exoskeletons and endoskeletons have joints. A **joint** is a place where two or more parts of a skeleton meet. The way the parts are held together in a joint determines how the joint can move.

Both arthropods and vertebrates have joints. An arthropod's appendages, or jointed attachments, enable the arthropod to move these appendages in different ways. For example, an insect's mouthparts may move from side to side and crush blades of grass. Its legs, however, may move forward and backward, enabling the insect to crawl. Vertebrates also have jointed appendages. As with arthropods, different joints enable vertebrates to move their appendages in different ways.

apply it!

Joints provide flexibility for animals. Look at the picture of the lemur on the right. Then answer the questions.

1 Interpret Photos Circle the joints you see.

2 ⚠ Infer Describe how the leg joints enable the lemur to move.

_____

_____

_____

_____

Lab zone ® Do the Quick Lab *Comparing Bone and Cartilage.*

🔑 Assess Your Understanding

1a. Define What is cartilage?

_____

_____

b. **CHALLENGE** Why is a lobster more vulnerable to predators when it molts?

_____

_____

_____

got it? ....

○ **I get it!** Now I know that a skeleton is a framework that _____

_____

○ I need extra help with _____

Go to MY SCIENCE ⓢ COACH online for help with this subject.

What Is the Role of Muscles?

Muscles help animals move their body parts. Tissues that contract or relax to create movement are **muscles.** Some muscles are part of an organ. For example, muscles make up most of the walls of some blood vessels. When these muscles contract, or get shorter, they squeeze blood through the vessels.

Other muscles attach to parts of skeletons. Muscles attach to the inside of exoskeletons. In an endoskeleton, muscles attach to the outsides of the bones or cartilage. For both types of skeletons, movement occurs when muscles pull on skeletons.

Muscles attached to skeletons always work in pairs, as shown in **Figure 3.** When one muscle contracts, the other muscle relaxes, or returns to its original length. The contracted muscle pulls on the skeleton and causes it to move in a certain direction. Then, as the contracted muscle relaxes, the relaxed muscle contracts. This action causes the skeleton to move in the opposite direction.

FIGURE 3 ···

Muscle Pairs

✎ **Complete these tasks.**

1. **Use Context to Determine Meaning** In the text above, underline key phrases that help you understand the terms *relaxed* and *contracted*.

2. **Interpret Diagrams** Label each muscle as *relaxed* or *contracted* for both types of skeletons.

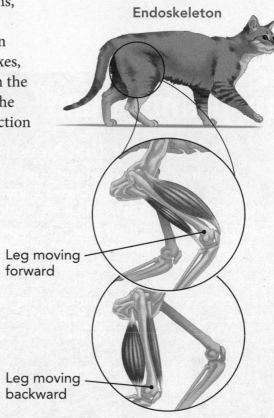

Endoskeleton

Leg moving forward

Leg moving backward

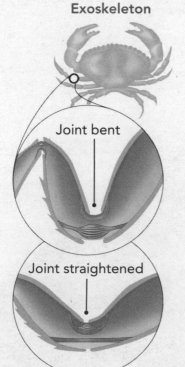

Exoskeleton

Joint bent

Joint straightened

Lab zone® Do the Quick Lab
What Do Muscles Do?

Assess Your Understanding

got it? ···

○ **I get it!** Now I know that muscles help animals _____

○ **I need extra help with** _____

Go to MY SCIENCE ⓈCOACH *online for help with this subject.*

The Nervous System

UNLOCK
THE BIG

🔑 **What Is the Role of the Nervous System?**

🔑 **How Do Nervous Systems Differ?**

MY PLANET DiARY

DISCOVERY

The Nerve of That Newt!

What happens when a newt loses a limb? It grows back! So a newt that loses a limb is not necessarily doomed to having a life on three legs.

In 2007, a team of British scientists made an intriguing discovery. They learned that a protein called nAG is needed for a newt to regrow a missing limb. If the nerve that triggers the production of nAG is removed, the newt cannot regrow its limb. However, the scientists developed a way to make the newt's cells artificially produce nAG. When they did this, the newt was able to regrow its limbs, even without the nerve.

Read the following questions. Write your answers below.

1. What role does a nerve play in the newt's ability to regrow a missing limb?

_____

_____

_____

_____

2. Why do you think the discovery of nAG is important?

_____

_____

_____

_____

> PLANET DIARY Go to **Planet Diary** to learn more about the nervous system of different animals.

Lab ® Do the Inquiry Warm-Up
zone *Sending Signals.*

Vocabulary
- nervous system
- stimulus
- response
- neuron
- impulse
- sensory neuron
- interneuron
- motor neuron
- brain

Skills
⟳ Reading: Identify Supporting Evidence
△ Inquiry: Draw Conclusions

What Is the Role of the Nervous System?

You are in the yard studying. Your dog, Rugger, is lying beside you. Suddenly, Rugger lifts his head and perks his ears. A few seconds later, a car pulls into the driveway.

Interactions Rugger's actions resulted from interactions of his nervous system. A **nervous system** receives information from the environment and coordinates a response. In this way, it acts like the body's control panel. ⟳ **A nervous system allows animals to detect signals in their environments, process the signals, and react to them.**

A signal that causes an animal to react in some way is called a **stimulus** (plural *stimuli*). Touch, sound, and the things animals smell, taste, or see are stimuli. After a nervous system detects a stimulus, it processes the information. For animals like Rugger, this process happens in the brain. Processing information results in a response. A **response** is an animal's reaction to a stimulus. Rugger's response to hearing the car was to lift his head and perk his ears. Rugger could have also responded by barking or running.

A chameleon eats insects. When it sees an insect, a chameleon snaps out its long, sticky tongue, which traps the insect on the end.

❶ **Identify** What is the stimulus for this chameleon? What is the response?

_____

_____

❷ △ **Draw Conclusions** Why is this response important to the chameleon?

_____

_____

Types of Cells

Types of Cells Animals often respond to a stimulus in fractions of seconds. If they didn't, they might not eat, or they might be eaten. The basic unit of the nervous system, a neuron, enables speedy responses. A **neuron** is a nerve cell with a unique structure for receiving and passing on information. In a nerve cell, information travels as an electrical message called an **impulse**.

Complex animals have three kinds of neurons that work together to take in information, process it, and enable an animal to respond. **Sensory neurons** are nerve cells that detect stimuli. Organs, such as eyes and ears, contain many sensory neurons. **Interneurons** are nerve cells that pass information between neurons. **Motor neurons** are nerve cells that carry response information to muscles and other organs.

Identify Supporting Evidence In the second paragraph, underline three examples of supporting evidence for the statement, "Complex animals have three kinds of neurons."

apply it!

In complex animals, different kinds of neurons work together to transfer information.

❶ **Classify** Under each picture, write the type of neuron the mouse is using.

❷ **Describe** Based on these pictures, what stimulus is the mouse receiving? What is its response?

_____

_____

_____

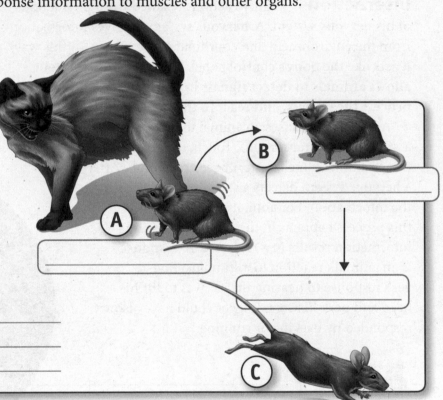

A

B

C

Lab zone ® Do the Quick Lab *Design a Nervous System.*

Assess Your Understanding

1a. Review What is a stimulus?

_____

_____

b. Apply Concepts What kind of stimulus would produce a response from a hungry animal?

_____

_____

got it?

○ **I get it!** Now I know that a nervous system allows animals to _____

_____

○ **I need extra help with** _____

Go to **MY SCIENCE** Ⓢ **COACH** *online for help with this subject.*

How Do Nervous Systems Differ?

It is hard to imagine an animal without a nervous system. This is because most familiar animals have complex nervous systems. But sponges don't have a nervous system, and many other animals have very simple ones. 🔑 **The simplest nervous systems are a netlike arrangement of neurons throughout the body. The most complex systems have a nerve cord and a brain.**

Types of Nervous Systems A cnidarian's nervous system consists of neurons arranged like a net, as you can see in **Figure 1.** This type of nervous system is called a nerve net. Animals with nerve nets have no specialized neurons. Therefore, a stimulus to one neuron sends impulses in all directions.

Many animals have more organized nervous systems than those of cnidarians. For example, a planarian's nervous system has nerve cords formed from groups of interneurons. Arthropods, mollusks, and vertebrates have nervous systems with brains. A **brain** is an organized grouping of neurons in the head of an animal with bilateral symmetry. A brain receives information, interprets it, and controls an animal's response. A complex animal with a brain and nerve cord may have billions of neurons.

A hydra has a nerve net with no specialized neurons.

Cnidarian

Neurons

Groups of interneurons

FIGURE 1 ···

⟩ ART IN MOTION **Nervous Systems**
Different types of nervous systems have different functions.

✏️ **Identify In the table, write the structures that make up each animal's nervous system.**

Nerve cord

Flatworm

A planarian has two small structures in its head that are formed from groups of interneurons.

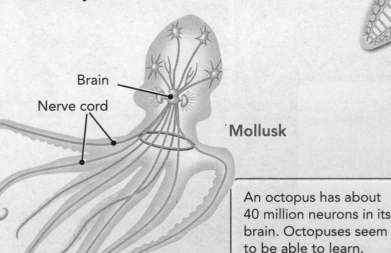

Brain

Nerve cord

Mollusk

An octopus has about 40 million neurons in its brain. Octopuses seem to be able to learn.

Nervous System Structures	
Cnidarian	_____
	_____
Flatworm	_____
	_____
Mollusk	_____
	_____

353

Sense Organs The more complex an animal's nervous system is, the more specialized its sense organs are. Sense organs such as ears, eyes, and noses detect stimuli in the form of sound, light, odor, and touch. Many, but not all, sense organs are located in the head. For example, a grasshopper has compound eyes and antennae on its head, which detect chemicals and touch. It also has membranes on its body that detect vibrations.

Animals with many sense organs can process many stimuli at the same time. This is because different areas of the brain respond to different stimuli at the same time. For example, when an animal such as your dog is around food, its brain processes messages about the food's color, smell, taste, and temperature all at the same time. Look at Figure 2 to learn about some animals' sense organs.

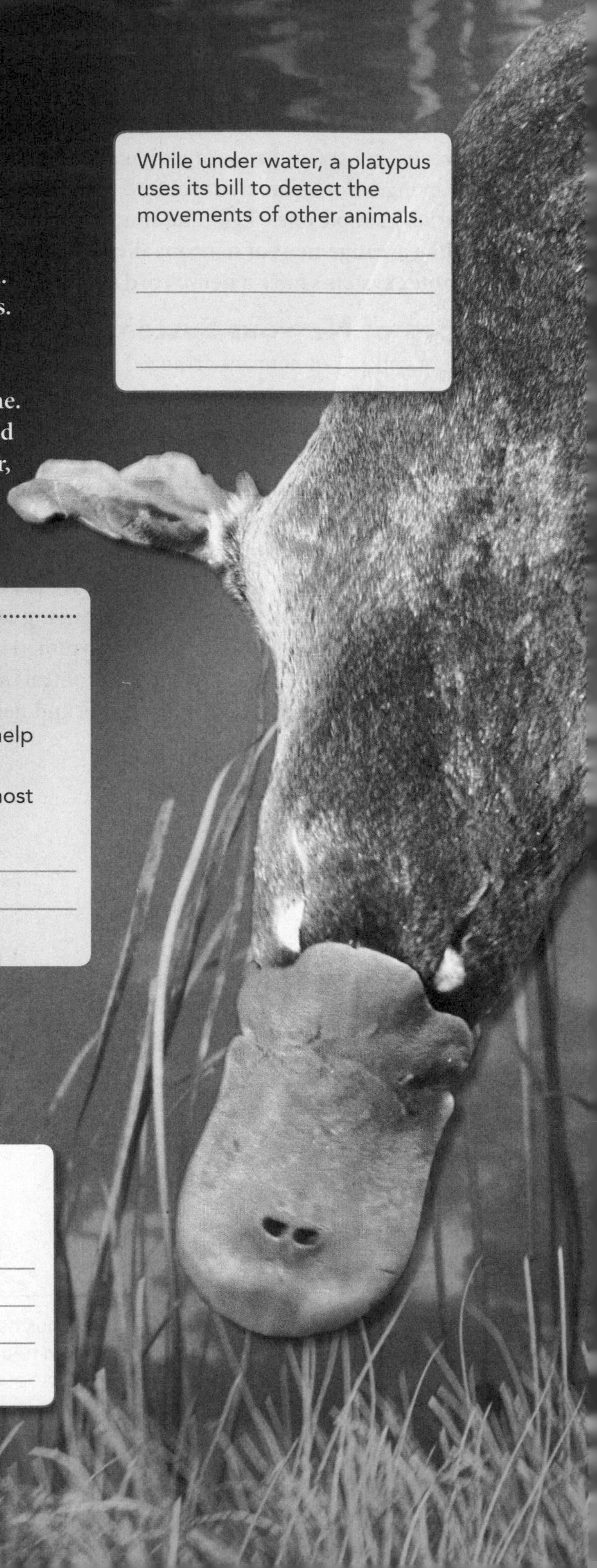

While under water, a platypus uses its bill to detect the movements of other animals.

_____

_____

_____

_____

FIGURE 2 ···

Sense Organs

✎ **Read about each animal. Then answer the questions below.**

1. **Infer** Write in the boxes how the sense organ might help the animal.

2. CHALLENGE Where are the sense organs located on most animals with bilateral symmetry? Why?

_____

_____

A frog detects vibrations in the air with its tympanic membrane.

_____

_____

_____

_____

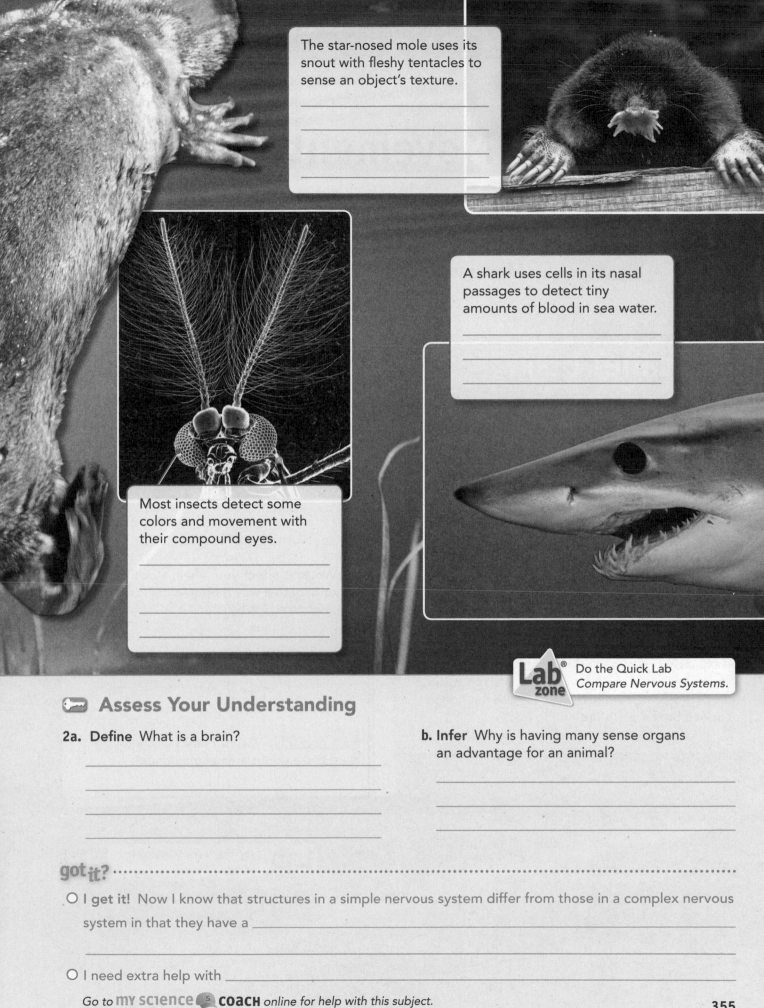

The star-nosed mole uses its snout with fleshy tentacles to sense an object's texture.

_____
_____
_____

A shark uses cells in its nasal passages to detect tiny amounts of blood in sea water.

_____
_____
_____

Most insects detect some colors and movement with their compound eyes.

_____
_____
_____
_____

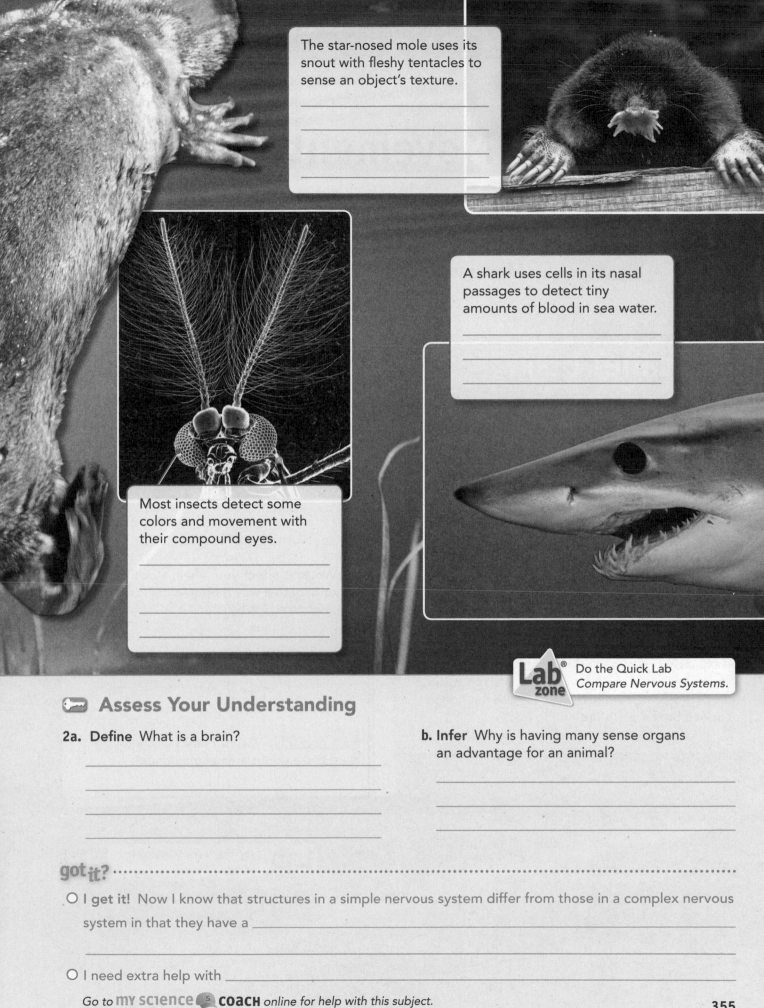

Lab zone® Do the Quick Lab
Compare Nervous Systems.

🔑 Assess Your Understanding

2a. Define What is a brain?

_____
_____
_____

b. Infer Why is having many sense organs an advantage for an animal?

_____
_____
_____

got it? ···

○ **I get it!** Now I know that structures in a simple nervous system differ from those in a complex nervous system in that they have a _____

_____

○ I need extra help with _____

Go to **MY SCIENCE** 🅂 **COACH** online for help with this subject.

Animal Movement

What Causes Animals to Move?

How Do Adaptations for Movement Compare?

MY PLANET DiARY

Posted by Emily

Location Bronxville, NY

If I could choose one thing to do that I can't do today, it would be flying. I look at birds in New York and imagine the great adventures they must have.

I imagined taking off from my roof and heading south to the Atlantic Ocean. As I soared over Long Island, I decided I wanted to see the ocean all around me, so I flew east to Montauk Point. I perched on top of a lighthouse and looked at the view below me. Then I flew over Fire Island without stopping because I didn't want to miss the concert at Jones Beach before returning home.

Communicate Discuss the following questions with a partner. Then write your answers below.

1. In what ways can people fly today?

   _____

   _____

   _____

2. Would it affect your life in a positive or negative way if people could fly unassisted? Why?

   _____

   _____

   _____

   _____

 Go to **Planet Diary** to learn more about animal movement.

 Do the Inquiry Warm-Up *Hydra Doing?*

Vocabulary
- water vascular system
- swim bladder

Skills
- Reading: Relate Text and Visuals
- Inquiry: Calculate

What Causes Animals to Move?

All animals move about in certain ways during their lives. They may swim, walk, slither, crawl, run, hop, fly, soar, jump, or swing through trees. However, all animal movements have something in common. **An animal moves about when its nervous system, muscular system, and skeletal system work together to make movement happen.** First, an animal's nervous system receives a signal from the environment. Second, its nervous system processes the signal. Finally, its nervous system signals the muscles, which contract, causing the skeleton to move.

Animals move for many reasons. They move to obtain food, defend and protect themselves, maintain homeostasis, and find mates.

Relate Text and Visuals For each photo, write a reason why the animal might be moving.

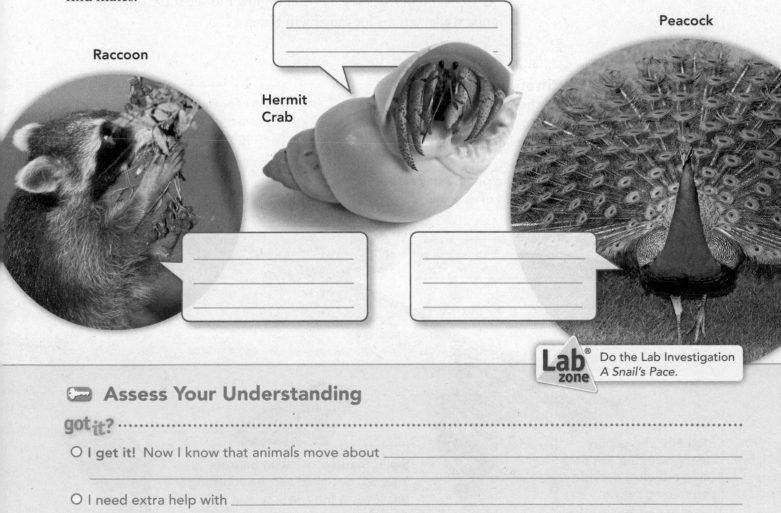

Raccoon

Hermit Crab

Peacock

Lab zone Do the Lab Investigation *A Snail's Pace.*

Assess Your Understanding

got it?

○ **I get it!** Now I know that animals move about _____

_____

○ **I need extra help with** _____

Go to **my science coach** *online for help with this subject.*

How Do Adaptations for Movement Compare?

Animals live nearly everywhere on Earth. **Animals that live in water, on land, or in the air have different adaptations for movement.**

Moving in Water If you have ever tried to walk in a swimming pool, you know that moving in water is more difficult than moving on land. This is because water is resistant to movement through it. Many animals that swim, such as fishes, dolphins, and penguins, have streamlined bodies that help them move through water. They also have appendages for swimming. Fishes have fins, dolphins have flippers, and penguins have wings.

Some animals that live in water do not swim but move through water in other ways. For example, sea stars and other echinoderms have a **water vascular system,** a system of fluid-filled tubes. The tubes produce suction, which enables an echinoderm to grip surfaces and move along. Look at **Figure 1** to see some different animal adaptations for moving in water.

FIGURE 1 ···

> **INTERACTIVE ART** Moving Through Water

✎ **Complete the activity and then answer the question.**

1. **Summarize** In the table on the next page, identify each animal's adaptation for moving. Then describe how the animal moves.

2. **Make Judgments** How is a fish helped by staying at a certain depth without using a lot of energy?

_____

_____

_____

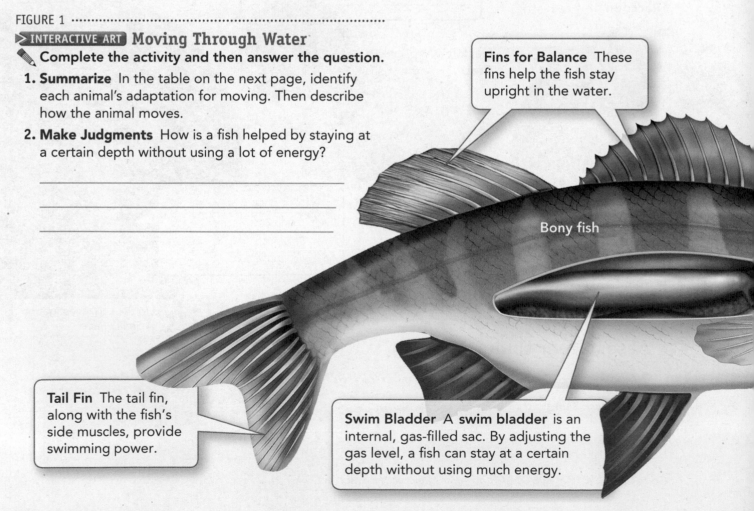

Fins for Balance These fins help the fish stay upright in the water.

Bony fish

Tail Fin The tail fin, along with the fish's side muscles, provide swimming power.

Swim Bladder A **swim bladder** is an internal, gas-filled sac. By adjusting the gas level, a fish can stay at a certain depth without using much energy.

Sea Star

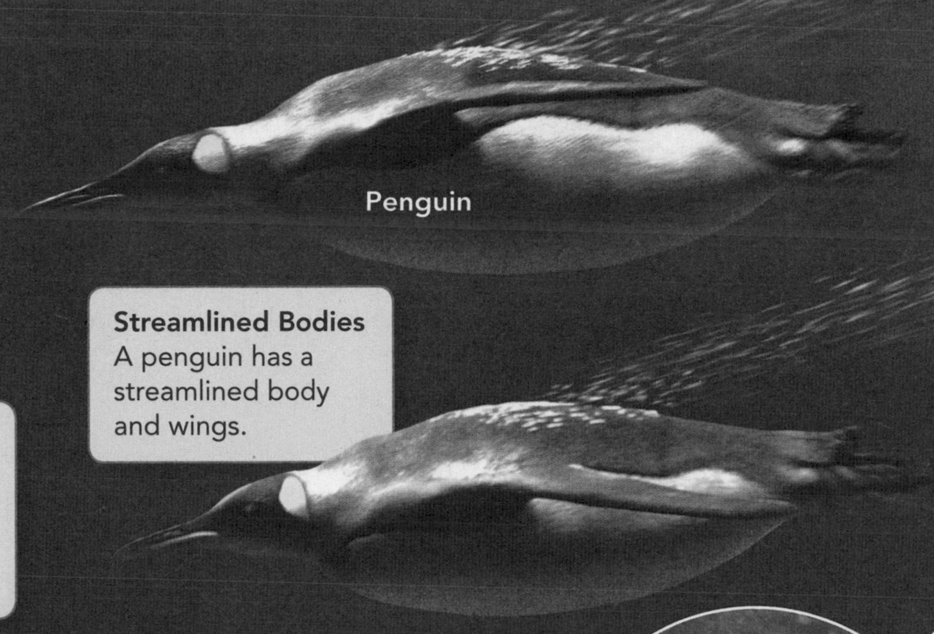

Penguin

Water Vascular System A sea star has tube feet on the under sides of its arms. They are part of the water vascular system and grip surfaces with suction.

Streamlined Bodies A penguin has a streamlined body and wings.

Frog

Jet Propulsion A squid moves by jet propulsion. It uses muscles to pull water into its body, and then shoots it out through a narrow tube. This shoots the squid in the opposite direction.

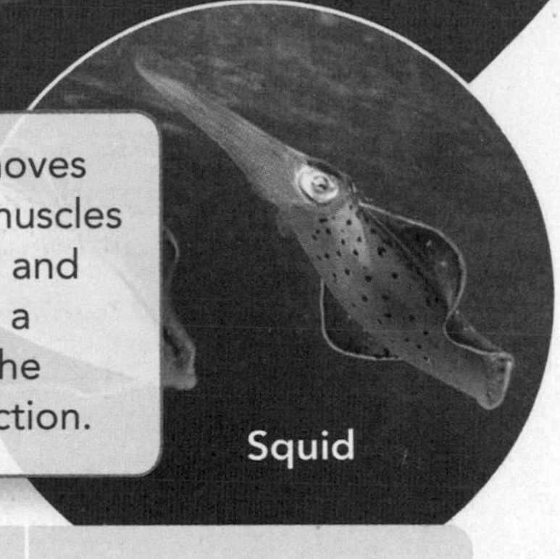

Squid

Webbed Feet Webbed feet help a frog push itself through water.

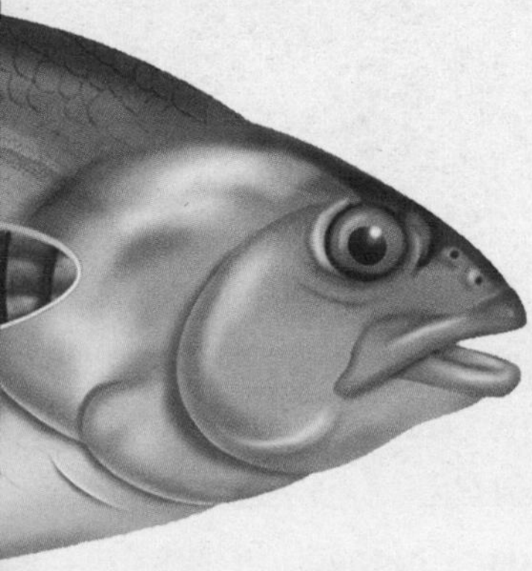

Animal	Movement Adaptations	How It Moves
Bony Fish		
Penguin		
Sea Star		
Frog		
Squid		

Muscles and Bristles
A segmented worm, such as this fireworm, has muscles that contract to extend the worm forward. It also has bristles that grip the soil.

Moving on Land

Have you ever watched a snake slither through the grass? Perhaps you've watched ants walk across the ground. Both snakes and ants move on land, but their adaptations for moving on land are different. A snake contracts its muscles and pushes against the ground with its body. An ant uses its jointed appendages to walk. **Figure 2** shows some of the many adaptations that animals have for moving on land.

Body Muscles This sidewinding adder snake uses its muscles to lift loops of its body off the hot desert sand as it moves along.

FIGURE 2 ······························

Moving on Land

The different adaptations of these animals allow them to move in different ways.

✎ **Complete these activities.**

1. **Apply Concepts** In the graphic organizer on the next page, describe an adaptation for moving that three other animals you know have.

2. **CHALLENGE** Describe the adaptations that a kangaroo has for movement.

_____

_____

_____

_____

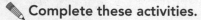

Vocabulary Identify Multiple Meanings The word *foot* has other meanings besides appendage. Write another meaning for *foot* below.

_____

_____

Foot and Mucus To move, a snail contracts its muscular foot. The foot oozes slippery mucus, which makes it easier for the snail to move along.

Foot

Long Arms An orangutan grasps branches with its long arms and swings from place to place.

Muscular Legs A grasshopper's muscular hind legs enable it to push off a surface. An adult grasshopper can travel 20 times its body length in a single jump!

Land Animal Movements

Long Legs and Two Toes An ostrich has long legs with only two toes on each foot. These traits help it run as fast as 60 km/h.

Moving in Air What do beetles, birds, and bats have in common? The answer, of course, is that they can fly. When you think of animals that fly, you probably first think about birds. Birds are uniquely adapted for flight, as shown in **Figure 3.** But many insects are also flight experts. Their wings grow from their exoskeletons and can move up, down, forward, and backward. A few insects can even twist their wings. Some insects warm up their flight muscles before flying by vibrating their wings, much like a pilot warms up an airplane's engines before taking off.

Skin and Bones A bat is the only mammal that flies. A bat wing is made of thin skin stretched over the bat's long finger bones.

Feathers This hawk's long, broad wing feathers provide lift, enabling it to fly very high. Also, the large surface area of its feathers help the hawk soar.

FIGURE 3 ·······························

> INTERACTIVE ART **Moving Through Air**

✎ **Compare and Contrast** Choose two animals on these pages. Then, in the table, write how their wings are alike and different.

Wings	Animals
Alike	
Different	

Paired Wings A dragonfly has two wings on each side of its body. The wings enable it to fly a long time and change direction quickly.

Wings for Hovering The small, narrow wings of this hummingbird can flap rapidly. This allows hummingbirds to fly forward, backward, and even hover like a helicopter.

Short, Round Wings Some forest birds, such as this pheasant, have short, rounded wings that enable them to take off rapidly.

Front and Hind Wings Butterflies have front and hind wings that are linked by a thin layer of cells. This helps the butterfly flap both pairs of wings at the same time.

do the math!

Different insects beat their wings at different rates, which are measured in beats per second (bps).

Insect	Wing bps
Housefly	190
Horsefly	96
Large white butterfly	12

1 Interpret Data How many times does a housefly beat its wings in one minute?

_____

_____

2 Calculate How many times faster does a horsefly beat its wings than a large white butterfly?

_____

_____

EXPLORE THE BIG ?

A MOVING STORY

How do animals move?

FIGURE 4 ···

▷ **REAL-WORLD INQUIRY** A raccoon scurries over rocks as a bald eagle soars above it looking for a meal. Nearby, dragonflies skim over a stream where trout surface to snatch a meal. Movement is everywhere.

✎ Answer the questions in the boxes.

Summarize What adaptations does an eagle have for moving?

Describe What kind of wings does a dragonfly have and how do they help it fly?

List What structures enable a trout to move?

Explain What are the skeletons of earthworms like?

Summarize How does a raccoon's nervous system work with its muscular system to escape an eagle?

_____

_____

_____

_____

Identify When a moose smells a leafy plant, what kinds of neurons are involved? What roles do the neurons serve?

_____

_____

_____

_____

_____

Lab zone® Do the Quick Lab
Webbing Along.

🔑 Assess Your Understanding

1a. Explain What adaptation does a grasshopper have to move on land?

_____

_____

_____

b. ANSWER THE BIG ? How do animals move?

_____

_____

_____

got it? ....

○ **I get it!** Now I know that animals have different adaptations for movement depending on _____

_____

○ **I need extra help with** _____

Go to **MY SCIENCE** 🔵 **COACH** _online for help with this subject._

Obtaining Energy

UNLOCK THE BIG ?

🔑 **How Do Animals Obtain and Digest Food?**

🔑 **How Do Animals Obtain Oxygen?**

🔑 **What Are the Two Types of Circulatory Systems?**

my planet diary

Owl Pellets

You chew your food before you swallow it using your teeth. Owls, however, do not have teeth. They swallow their food whole. Their food includes mice and insects. After an owl swallows, the food travels into its digestive system to be digested.

What happens to the body parts that an owl cannot digest? Any bones, teeth, and fur travel to the gizzard, a part of an owl's digestive system. Then the owl regurgitates, or spits up, the undigested parts as a pellet. Scientists can examine a pellet to find out what an owl eats.

Owl pellet

FUN FACTS

Read the following questions. Write your answers below.

1. What happens to the food that an owl eats?

_____

_____

_____

2. What might you learn about an owl's environment by looking at its pellet?

_____

_____

_____

▶ **PLANET DIARY** Go to **Planet Diary** to learn more about how animals obtain and digest food.

Lab zone® Do the Inquiry Warm-Up *How Do Snakes Feed?*

How Do Animals Obtain and Digest Food?

Think about the last time you had pizza and how good it tasted. That pizza was more than just a great meal. It also gave you the energy you needed to ride a bike or use a computer. All animals—including you—need food to provide the raw materials and energy that their cells need to carry out their functions.

Vocabulary
- carnivore • herbivore • omnivore • filter feeder • digestion
- digestive system • cellular respiration • diffusion
- respiratory system • circulatory system

Skills
- Reading: Compare and Contrast
- Inquiry: Classify

What Animals Eat

The different ways that an animal obtains food depends on what it eats and its adaptations for getting food. Animals may be grouped based on what type of food they eat. Most animals, like those in **Figure 1,** are carnivores, herbivores, or omnivores. Animals that eat only other animals are **carnivores.** Animals that eat only plant material are **herbivores.** Animals that eat both plant material and other animals are **omnivores.** A few types of animals—such as earthworms, snails, and crabs—eat decaying plants and animals.

Caterpillar

FIGURE 1 ·······················

Animal Diets

All animals need food, but they differ in what they eat and how they get it.

🖉 **Infer** Choose one animal from each of the three groups and write in the box what you think it eats.

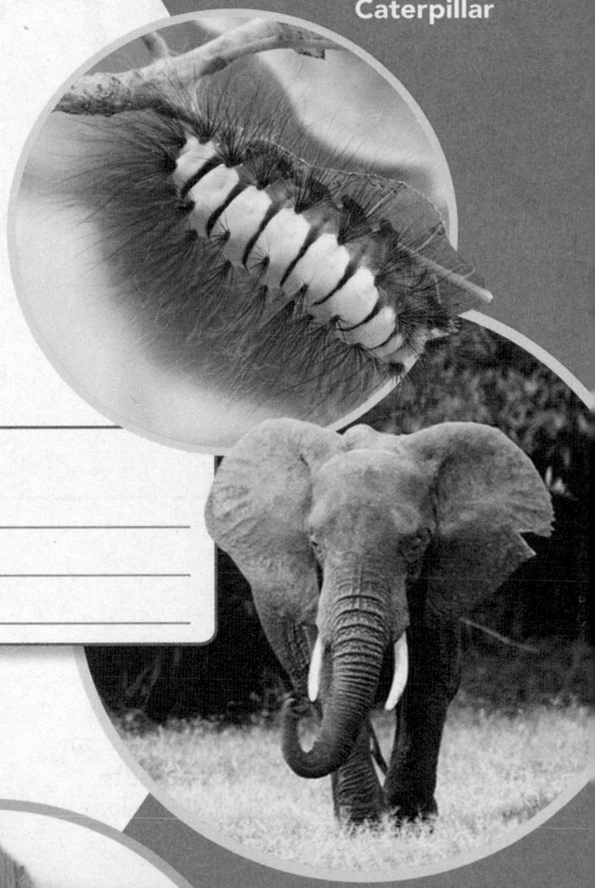

Herbivores
_____
_____
_____

Elephant

Raccoon

Lion

Omnivores
_____
_____
_____

Carnivores
_____
_____
_____

Bear

Jellyfish

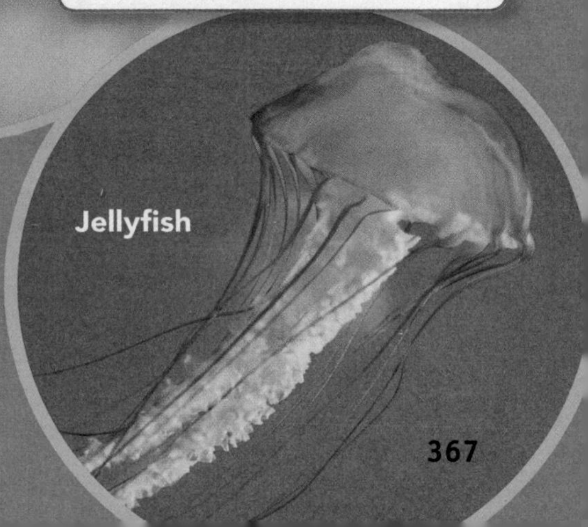

Animal Mouthparts

If you have ever watched animals eating, you may have noticed some of the different adaptations that animals have for eating. Some animals have mouthparts that are specialized for tearing, chewing, or sucking food. For example, grasshoppers have sharp mouthparts that tear and chew leaves. Hummingbirds and butterflies have mouthparts that enable them to suck plant juices from flowers, stems, and leaves.

Other animals have teeth that are specialized for eating certain types of food. Carnivores, such as wolves, have pointed teeth used for tearing meat. Herbivores, such as rabbits, have flat teeth for grinding plant material. Omnivores usually have both pointed and flat teeth for eating their food.

Some animals that live in water strain their food from the water. They are called **filter feeders.** Some filter feeders include baleen whales and clams. Most filter feeders trap and eat microscopic organisms that live in the water.

apply it!

Many animals use teeth to eat.

1 Classify Look at the teeth of each animal. Based on its teeth, classify each animal as a carnivore, herbivore, or omnivore.

2 Relate Evidence and Explanation In each box, explain why you classified the animal as you did.

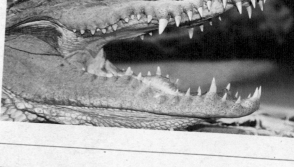

Adaptations for Obtaining Food

Animals have an amazing variety of adaptations for obtaining food. These adaptations include structures and behaviors. For example, animals have an opening through which food enters their bodies. This opening is usually called a mouth. Structures such as beaks and claws enable animals to get food into their mouths. Behaviors also help animals obtain food. For example, most spiders make webs that help them capture their prey. In **Figure 2,** you can see some adaptations that animals have for obtaining food.

FIGURE 2 ·······································

▶ **INTERACTIVE ART** **Obtaining Food**

Adaptations help organisms such as a grasshopper and a spider obtain food.

✏ **Study the photos and read the description about how each animal obtains food. Then answer the questions in the boxes.**

Grasshopper   Spider

Insects have different mouthparts. Grasshoppers have mouthparts for chewing grass.

✏ **Develop Hypotheses** This spider is a carnivore. Describe how you think it uses its fangs.

_____

_____

Hawk

Birds use their beaks to obtain food. The shapes of beaks are specialized for eating different kinds of food.

✏ **Communicate** Look at the beaks of the hawk and pileated woodpeckers. With a partner, decide which beak shape is best for probing soft material and which is best for eating meat.

_____

_____

_____

_____

Pileated Woodpeckers

This type of snake stretches its jaws, opens its mouth very wide, and swallows its food whole.

✏ **CHALLENGE** Explain how this adaptation might help this type of snake survive.

_____

_____

_____

Egg-Eating Snake

369

Animal Digestion

Animal Digestion You already know that the food animals eat provides needed materials to their cells. However, the food that animals eat is too large to enter the cells. It must be broken down first. The process that breaks down food into small molecules is called **digestion.** Some types of animals digest food mainly inside their cells, but most animals digest food outside their cells.

Digestion Inside Cells Sponges and a few other animals digest food inside specialized cells in their bodies. The digested food then diffuses into other cells, where it is used. This process is called intracellular digestion. **Figure 3** shows how intracellular digestion occurs in sponges.

Digestion Outside Cells Most animals digest their food outside their cells. This process is called extracellular digestion. Digestion outside cells occurs in a digestive system. A **digestive system** is an organ system that has specialized structures for obtaining and digesting food. Most carnivores, herbivores, and omnivores have digestive systems.

Internal Body Cavity The simplest kind of digestive system has only one opening. Food enters the body and wastes exit the body through the same opening. Cnidarians and flatworms have this type of digestive system.

FIGURE 3 ·······················

Intracellular Digestion

Structures surrounding the central cavity of a sponge are adapted for digestion.

✎ **Sequence** Read each box carefully. Then write a number in each circle to show the order in which intracellular digestion occurs in sponges.

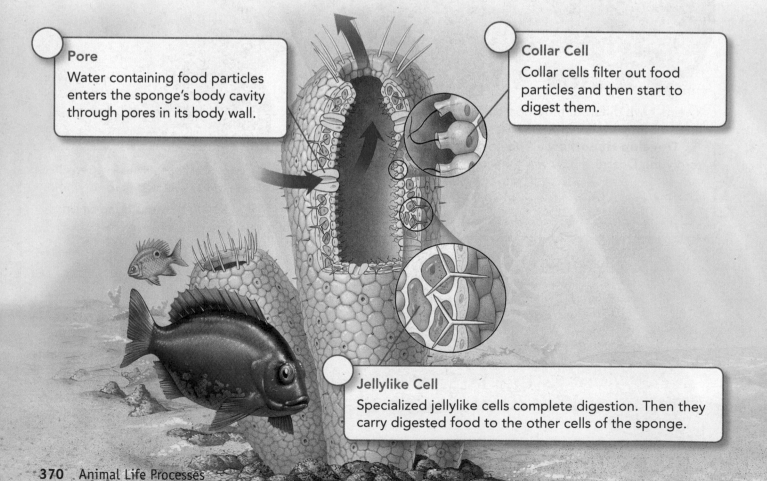

Pore
Water containing food particles enters the sponge's body cavity through pores in its body wall.

Collar Cell
Collar cells filter out food particles and then start to digest them.

Jellylike Cell
Specialized jellylike cells complete digestion. Then they carry digested food to the other cells of the sponge.

Digestive Tube Complex animals have digestive systems that consist of a tube with two openings. One opening is a mouth for taking in food. The other opening is an anus through which wastes leave. A digestive tube has specialized areas where food is processed for digestion, digested, and absorbed. You can see the specialized areas of an earthworm's and a fish's digestive tubes in **Figure 4.** A digestive system with two openings is more efficient than a system with one opening. This is more efficient because digested food does not mix with undigested food.

FIGURE 4 ·····················

Digestive Tubes

The digestive tubes of earthworms and fishes have specialized areas in common. These areas have the same functions.

✎ **Interpret Diagrams** In each box, list the names of each area of the tube in the order through which food passes.

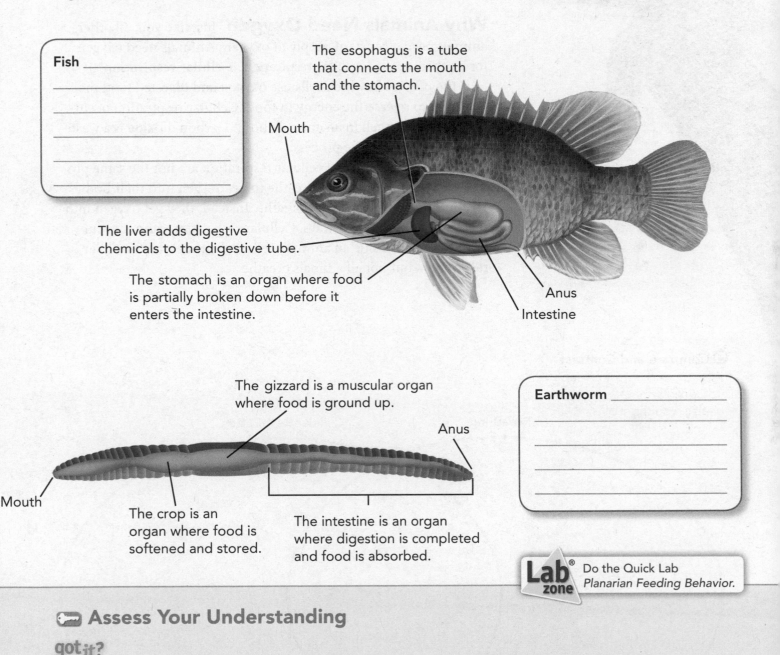

Fish _____

The esophagus is a tube that connects the mouth and the stomach.

Mouth

The liver adds digestive chemicals to the digestive tube.

The stomach is an organ where food is partially broken down before it enters the intestine.

Anus

Intestine

The gizzard is a muscular organ where food is ground up.

Anus

Mouth

The crop is an organ where food is softened and stored.

The intestine is an organ where digestion is completed and food is absorbed.

Earthworm _____

Lab zone Do the Quick Lab *Planarian Feeding Behavior.*

⊶ Assess Your Understanding

got it?

○ **I get it!** Now I know that the way an animal obtains energy depends on _____
_____

○ **I need extra help with** _____
Go to MY SCIENCE ⑤ COACH *online for help with this subject.*

How Do Animals Obtain Oxygen?

What happens when you try to hold your breath? It is not easy after a while, is it? It is difficult because you must breathe to exchange two important gases with your surroundings. Your body cannot function without constantly taking in oxygen and getting rid of carbon dioxide.

Why Animals Need Oxygen Just like you, all other animals need a constant supply of oxygen. Animals need oxygen for a process called cellular respiration. **Cellular respiration** is the process in which cells use oxygen and digested food molecules to release the energy in food. Cellular respiration occurs in every cell in an animal's body. Carbon dioxide is a waste product of the process.

Breathing and cellular respiration are not the same process. Some animals breathe to get oxygen into their bodies. But other animals do not breathe. Instead, they get oxygen into their bodies in different ways. Cellular respiration cannot occur until oxygen is inside an animal's cells. All animals have cellular respiration, but not all animals breathe.

Compare and Contrast
In the Venn diagram, compare and contrast breathing and cellular respiration.

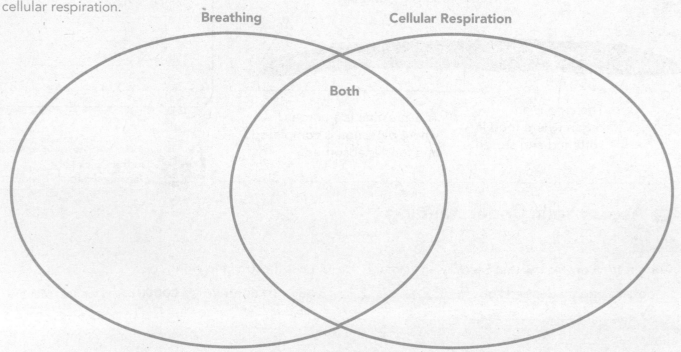

Breathing   Cellular Respiration

Both

Exchanging Gases

Exchanging Gases Animals exchange oxygen and carbon dioxide with their surroundings by diffusion. In the process of **diffusion**, particles move from an area of high concentration to an area of low concentration. 🔑 **Animal cells exchange oxygen and carbon dioxide with their surroundings by diffusion across the outer coverings, or membranes, of cells.** Cell membranes are moist and thin, which enable efficient diffusion.

Cells use oxygen in the process of cellular respiration. Therefore, the concentration of oxygen inside cells is usually lower than it is outside cells. So, oxygen tends to diffuse into cells. Because cellular respiration produces carbon dioxide, there is usually a higher concentration of carbon dioxide inside cells than outside cells. As a result, carbon dioxide tends to diffuse out of cells.

Comparing Animal Respiratory Systems

The structures that an animal uses to exchange gases with its surroundings make up the **respiratory system.** Respiratory systems include structures such as skin, gills, and lungs. The type of respiratory system an animal has depends on how complex the animal is and where it lives.

Animals that exchange gases across their skin live in water or in moist places on land. However, most animals that live in water, which contains dissolved oxygen, have gills. Gills are featherlike structures where gases are exchanged between water and blood. In contrast, most animals that breathe air, which contains oxygen, have lungs. Lungs are saclike structures made up of a thin layer of cells where gases are exchanged between air and blood. Lungs are located inside the body where they can stay moist.

Use this model of an animal's muscle cell to complete the activity.

❶ **Identify** Is the concentration of oxygen greater inside or outside the cell?

_____

❷ **Predict** Draw *X*'s to represent the concentration of carbon dioxide inside and outside the cell. Explain what you drew.

_____

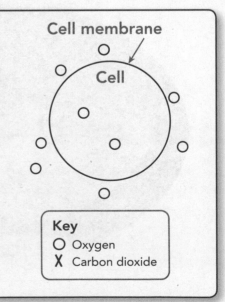

Cell membrane

Cell

Key
O Oxygen
X Carbon dioxide

Animals Living in Water Think about animals that live in water, such as jellyfishes, clams, sharks, and whales. Just as these animals are different, so are their respiratory structures. Most of these animals use either their outer body coverings or gills as respiratory structures, as shown in **Figure 5**. For example, cnidarians use their outer body coverings for gas exchange. Fishes, mollusks, and arthropods use their gills. However, some animals that live in water have lungs and get oxygen from the air. Whales, dolphins, and alligators breathe air at the surface and hold their breath when they dive.

FIGURE 5 ....

Respiration Without Lungs

Animals that live in water and do not have lungs use their outer body covering or gills to exchange gases.

✎ **Relate Text and Visuals** In each box, identify the animal's respiratory structure.

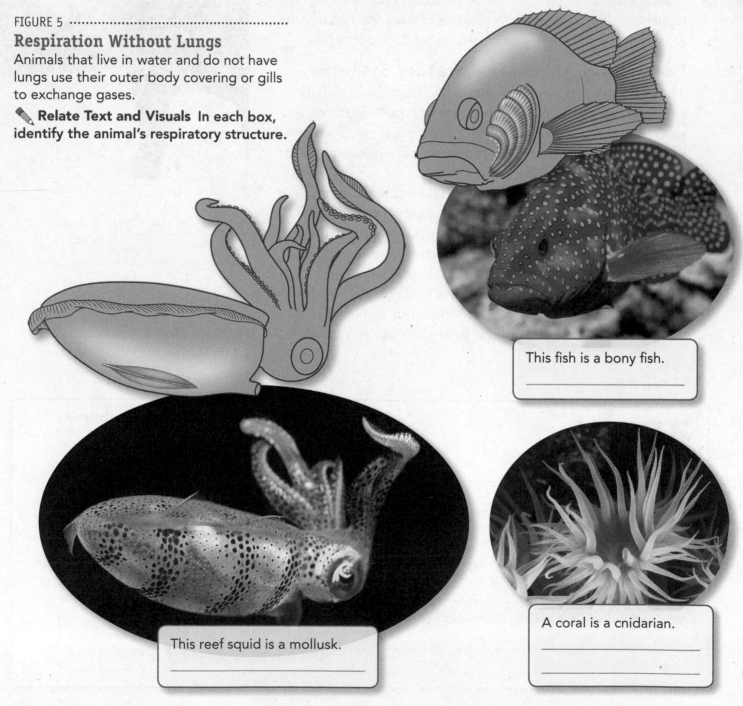

This fish is a bony fish.

_____

This reef squid is a mollusk.

_____

A coral is a cnidarian.

_____

_____

Animals Living on Land

You might think that all animals living on land use their lungs to exchange gases. Some animals do use lungs, but others do not. For example, amphibians may use their skin as their main respiratory structure. Arthropods and other invertebrates have some unique respiratory structures. Although the respiratory structures of land-dwelling animals are diverse, they do have something in common. They all are made up of thin layers of moist cells. In addition, in more complex animals, the layers have folds or pockets that increase the surface area for gas exchange. The respiratory structures of invertebrates and vertebrates are different.

Invertebrate Structures Just a few of the invertebrates that live on land are shown in **Figure 6**. Their respiratory structures include skin, book lungs, and tracheal tubes.

FIGURE 6 ·······························
> ART IN MOTION **Invertebrate Respiration**
Skin, book lungs, and tracheal tubes are respiratory structures of invertebrates.

✎ **Summarize** In the chart, list each animal shown, and write the name of its respiratory structure.

Earthworms exchange gases through their moist skin.

Spiders have structures called book lungs, which are made of thin, stacked cell layers.

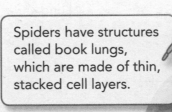

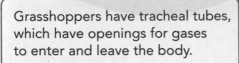

Grasshoppers have tracheal tubes, which have openings for gases to enter and leave the body.

Animal	Respiratory Structure

375

Vertebrate Structures Most vertebrates, including reptiles, birds, mammals, and most adult amphibians, use lungs to breathe. However, lungs are not all the same. Because some lungs have more pockets or folds than others, the amount of surface area for gas exchange differs. For example, adult amphibian lungs are small and do not have many pockets. Therefore, the main respiratory structure for an adult amphibian is its skin. In contrast, the lungs of mammals are large. A mammal's lungs have many more pockets than those of reptiles and adult amphibians. Additional pockets make the lungs of mammals very efficient.

Specialized Respiratory Structures Birds require a lot of energy to fly. Therefore, their cells must receive plenty of oxygen to release the energy contained in food. To obtain more oxygen from each breath of air, birds have a system of air sacs in their bodies. Most birds have nine air sacs. As you can see in **Figure 7**, air sacs connect to the lungs.

FIGURE 7 ···
A Bird's Lungs
In this simplified diagram, you can see how the fresh air a bird inhales flows through a long tube into the lower air sacs. It then flows into the lungs. From there, it flows into the upper air sacs until it is exhaled.

✏️ **Observe** On the diagram, draw arrows to trace the path of air through the bird's respiratory structures.

Upper air sac

Lung

Lower air sac

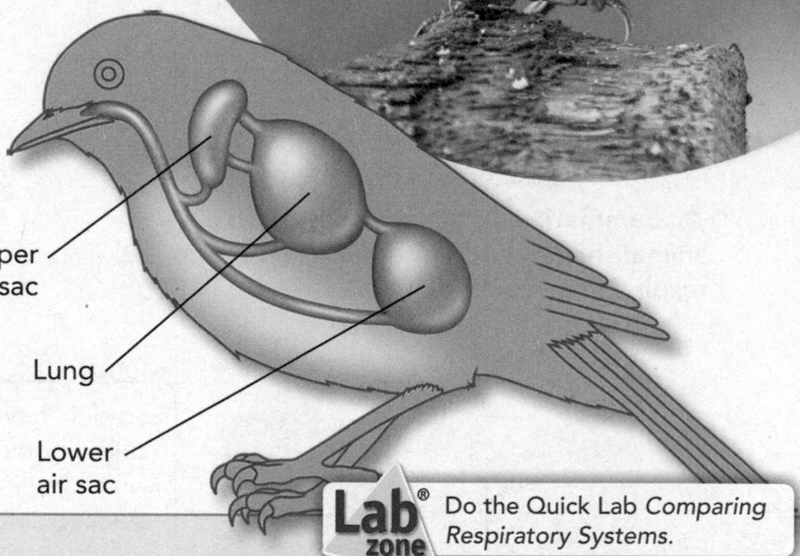

Lab zone Do the Quick Lab *Comparing Respiratory Systems.*

🔑 **Assess Your Understanding**

1a. Explain What do all respiratory structures have in common?

_____

_____

_____

b. Apply Concepts Why is having several air sacs an advantage for a bird?

_____

_____

_____

got it? ···

○ **I get it!** Now I know that the type of respiratory structure an animal has depends on _____

_____

_____

○ I need extra help with _____

Go to **MY SCIENCE COACH** online for help with this subject.

376 Animal Life Processes

What Are the Two Types of Circulatory Systems?

You have probably seen ants coming and going from their nest. Did you know that ants work as a team? Each ant has a specific job. While worker ants are out searching for food, other ants are protecting the nest. A soldier ant may even put its head in the nest's opening to stop enemies from entering. By working together, these ants are able to get food and stay safe. What teamwork!

Getting materials to an animal's cells and taking away wastes also takes teamwork. The circulatory system must work with both the digestive and respiratory systems to do so. The **circulatory system** transports needed materials to cells and takes away wastes.

🔑 **Complex animals have one of two types of circulatory systems: open or closed.** Both types of systems include blood, vessels, and a heart. A heart is a hollow, muscular structure that pumps blood through vessels. Blood vessels are a connected network of tubes that carries blood. Blood transports digested food from the digestive system and oxygen from the respiratory system to the cells. In addition, blood carries carbon dioxide and other wastes from cells to the organs that eliminate them from the body.

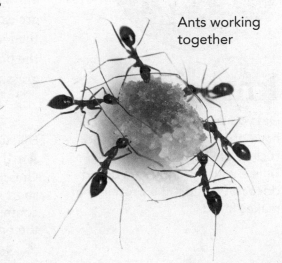

Ants working together

Summarize On the clipboard, write in your own words how the digestive, respiratory, and circulatory systems work as a team.

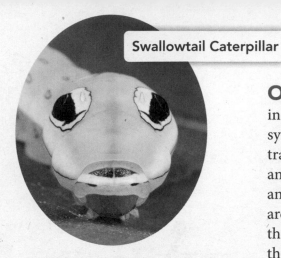

Open Circulatory Systems

Many invertebrates, including arthropods and most mollusks, have open circulatory systems. In an open circulatory system, blood does not always travel inside vessels. One or more hearts pump blood to the head and organs. Then the blood flows into the spaces around the animal's organs. There, food particles, oxygen, water, and wastes are exchanged between the blood and cells directly. Eventually, the blood moves back into the heart or hearts to be pumped out to the body again. You can see this type of circulatory system in the grasshopper shown in **Figure 8.**

did you know?

Did you know that many insects have green blood? Their blood is clear or yellowish green. Unlike your blood, insect blood does not contain the protein that makes it red.

FIGURE 8 ....

An Open Circulatory System

Grasshoppers have several hearts that pump blood into short vessels. These vessels open into the body spaces containing the internal organs. The blood washes over the organs and eventually returns to the hearts.

✎ **Sequence** In the graphic organizer, describe the flow of blood in the grasshopper's body. Start with blood in the hearts.

Hearts

Blood vessels

Step 1	Step 2	Step 3	Step 4

Closed Circulatory Systems

Segmented worms, some mollusks, and all vertebrates have closed circulatory systems. In a closed circulatory system, blood always stays inside vessels and the heart. Large vessels lead away from the heart to the organs. In the organs, vessels called capillaries surround the cells. Capillaries are tiny, thin-walled blood vessels where the blood and body cells exchange substances. Digested food molecules and oxygen in the blood pass through the capillary walls into the cells. At the same time, carbon dioxide and other wastes pass from the cells into the capillaries. The capillaries merge and form large vessels that lead back to the heart. You can see an earthworm's closed circulatory system in **Figure 9**.

CHALLENGE Why is an earth-worm's circulatory system more efficient than that of an insect?

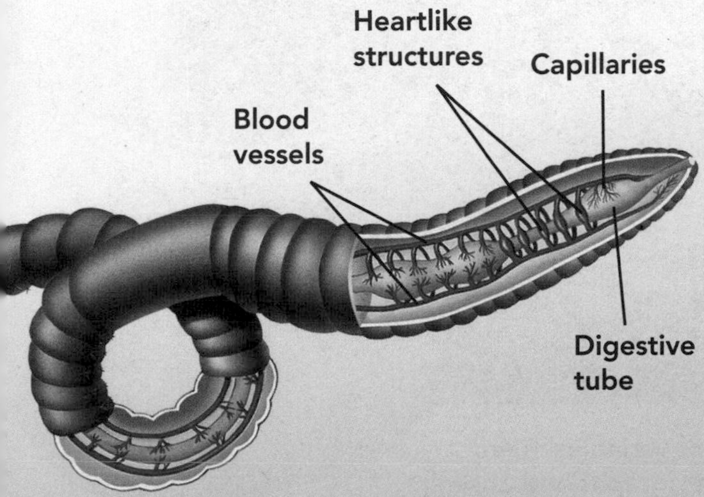

FIGURE 9

A Closed Circulatory System

An earthworm's body is divided into more than 100 segments. The earthworm's circulatory system runs through all of the segments.

Compare and Contrast On the notebook page, write how open and closed circulatory systems are alike and different.

Heartlike structures

Capillaries

Blood vessels

Digestive tube

Lab zone® Do the Quick Lab *Comparing Circulatory Systems.*

🔑 Assess Your Understanding

2a. Describe What are the parts of a circulatory system?

b. Draw Conclusions What happens in a circulatory system if the heart stops functioning?

got it?

○ **I get it!** Now I know that the two types of circulatory systems are _____

○ I need extra help with _____

Go to MY SCIENCE ⑤ COACH online for help with this subject.

379

Animal Reproduction and Fertilization

UNLOCK
THE BIG
?

🔑 **How Do Animals Reproduce?**

🔑 **How Do External and Internal Fertilization Differ?**

MY PLANET DIARY

PROFILE

A Nutty Experiment

Did you know that moths have favorite foods? The navel orangeworm moth lays its eggs inside of nuts, such as pistachios, walnuts, and almonds. The young that hatch out of the eggs look like worms, and eat their way out of the nuts. This causes damage to crops on nut farms.

Navel orangeworm moths were thought to prefer almonds over other nuts—that is, until California middle school student Gabriel Leal found evidence to the contrary. Gabriel conducted a science project to investigate whether the young of navel orangeworm moths preferred pistachios, walnuts, or almonds. He put equal amounts of each type of nut into three different traps. A fourth trap was left empty. All four traps were placed into a cage with young navel orangeworms. Most worms went to the pistachio trap. No worms went to the empty trap. Gabriel's research could help scientists control worm damage to walnut and almond crops.

Control Variables Read the paragraphs and answer the questions below.

1. Write a one-sentence conclusion of Gabriel's research.

_____

_____

_____

2. What was the purpose of the empty trap in Gabriel's experiment?

_____

_____

_____

▶ **PLANET DIARY** Go to **Planet Diary** to learn more about animal reproduction and fertilization.

 Lab® zone Do the Inquiry Warm-Up *Making More.*

Vocabulary
- larva • polyp • medusa • external fertilization
- internal fertilization • gestation period

Skills
- Reading: Compare and Contrast
- Inquiry: Calculate

How Do Animals Reproduce?

Whether they wiggle, hop, fly, or run, have backbones or no backbones—all animal species reproduce. Elephants make more elephants, grasshoppers make more grasshoppers, and sea stars make more sea stars. Some animals produce offspring that are identical to the parent. Most animals, including humans, produce offspring that are different from the parents. **Animals undergo either asexual or sexual reproduction to make more of their own kind or species.** Because no animal lives forever, reproduction is essential to the survival of a species.

Asexual Reproduction

Imagine you are digging in the soil with a shovel, and accidentally cut a worm into two pieces. Most animals wouldn't survive getting cut in two—but the worm might. Certain kinds of worms can form whole new worms from each cut piece. This is one form of asexual reproduction. Another example of asexual reproduction is called budding. In budding, a new animal grows out of the parent and breaks off. In asexual reproduction, one parent produces a new organism identical to itself. This new organism receives an exact copy of the parent's set of genetic material, or DNA. Some animals, including sponges, jellyfish, sea anemones, worms, and the hydra in **Figure 1,** can reproduce asexually.

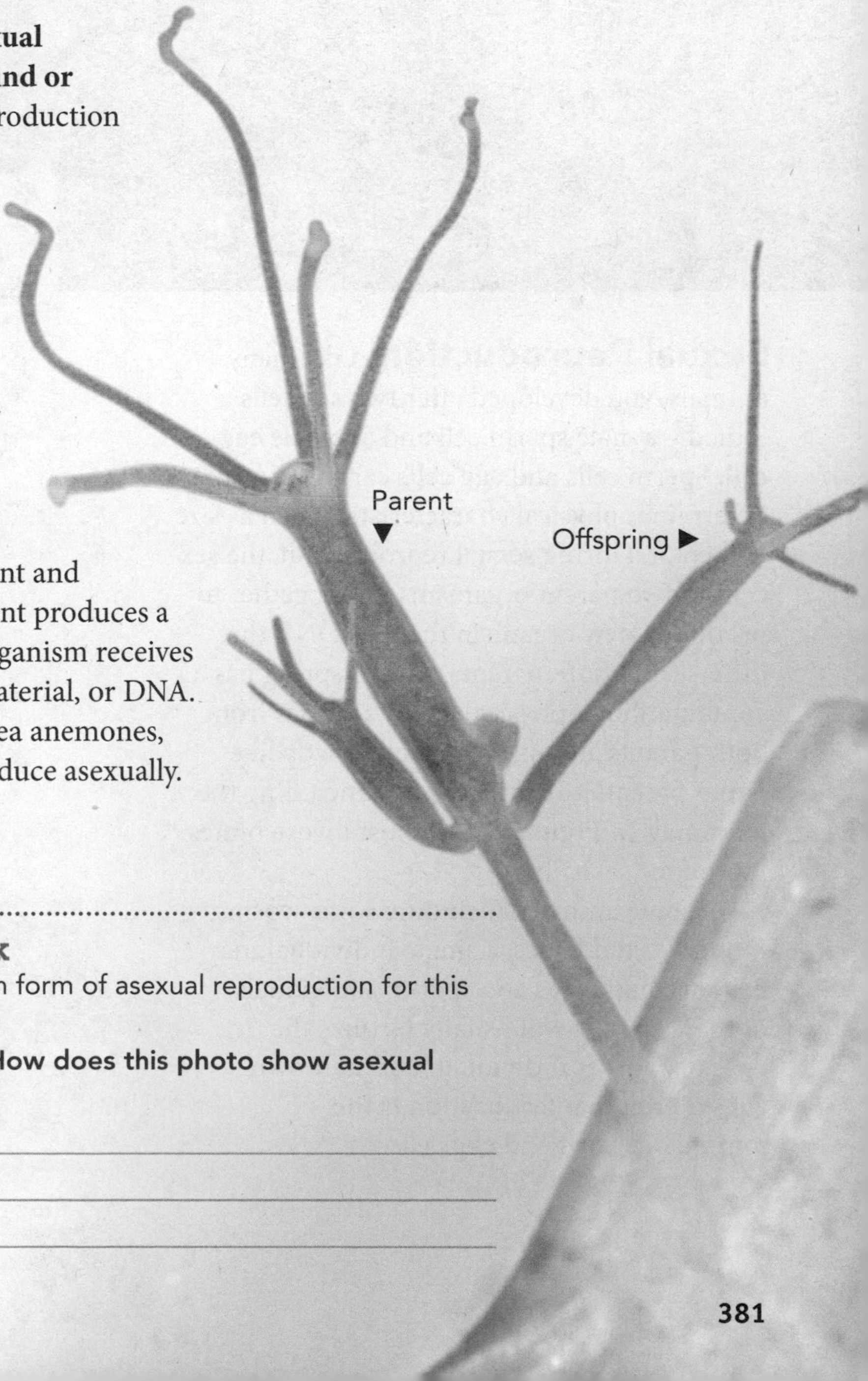

Parent ▼   Offspring ►

FIGURE 1 ·······················

A Chip off the Old Block
Budding is the most common form of asexual reproduction for this hydra, a type of cnidarian.

✎ **Relate Text to Visuals** How does this photo show asexual reproduction?

_____

_____

_____

381

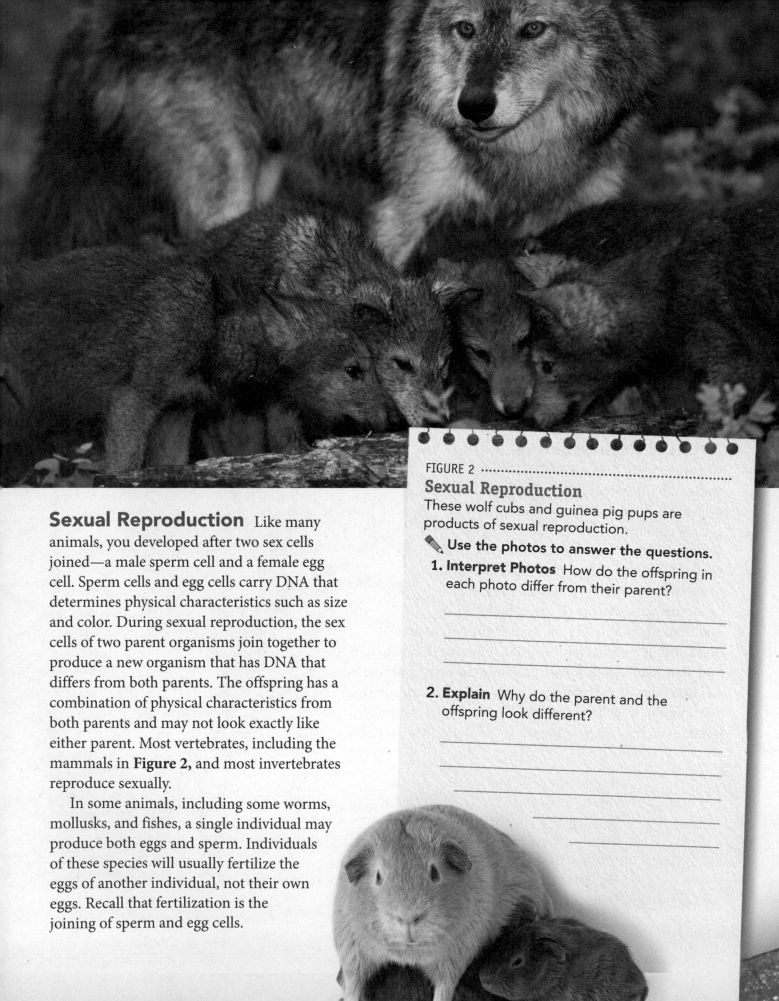

Sexual Reproduction

Sexual Reproduction Like many animals, you developed after two sex cells joined—a male sperm cell and a female egg cell. Sperm cells and egg cells carry DNA that determines physical characteristics such as size and color. During sexual reproduction, the sex cells of two parent organisms join together to produce a new organism that has DNA that differs from both parents. The offspring has a combination of physical characteristics from both parents and may not look exactly like either parent. Most vertebrates, including the mammals in **Figure 2,** and most invertebrates reproduce sexually.

In some animals, including some worms, mollusks, and fishes, a single individual may produce both eggs and sperm. Individuals of these species will usually fertilize the eggs of another individual, not their own eggs. Recall that fertilization is the joining of sperm and egg cells.

FIGURE 2 ....
Sexual Reproduction
These wolf cubs and guinea pig pups are products of sexual reproduction.

✎ **Use the photos to answer the questions.**

1. **Interpret Photos** How do the offspring in each photo differ from their parent?

_____

_____

_____

2. **Explain** Why do the parent and the offspring look different?

_____

_____

_____

_____

Comparing Asexual and Sexual Reproduction

Asexual and sexual reproduction are different survival methods. Each method has advantages and disadvantages. An advantage of asexual reproduction is that one parent can quickly produce many identical offspring. But a major disadvantage is that the offspring have the same DNA as the parent. The offspring have no variation from the parent and may not survive changes in the environment. In contrast, sexual reproduction has the advantage of producing offspring with new combinations of DNA. These offspring may have characteristics that help them adapt and survive changes in the environment. However, a disadvantage of sexual reproduction is that it requires finding a mate, and the development of offspring takes a longer time.

did you know?

Some fishes, such as this anemone clownfish, can change from male to female during their lifetime!

FIGURE 3 ....

Asexual and Sexual Reproduction

Compare and Contrast Write an advantage and a disadvantage of each type of reproduction in the table.

	Asexual Reproduction	Sexual Reproduction
Advantage		
Disadvantage		

These aphids can reproduce asexually and sexually. They reproduce asexually when environmental conditions are favorable. If conditions worsen, they reproduce sexually.

Reproductive Cycles
Several aquatic invertebrates, such as sponges and cnidarians, have life cycles that alternate between asexual and sexual reproduction.

A Sponges

Sponges reproduce both asexually and sexually. Sponges reproduce asexually through budding. Small new sponges grow, or bud, from the sides of an adult sponge. Eventually, the buds break free and begin life on their own. Sponges reproduce sexually, too, but they do not have separate sexes. A sponge can produce both sperm cells and egg cells. After a sponge egg is fertilized by a sperm, a larva develops. A **larva** (plural *larvae*) is an immature form of an animal that looks very different from the adult. **Figure 4** shows sponge reproduction.

B Cnidarians

Many cnidarians alternate between two body forms: a **polyp** (PAHL ip) that looks like an upright vase and a **medusa** (muh DOO suh) that looks like an open umbrella. Some polyps reproduce asexually by budding. Other polyps just pull apart, forming two new polyps. Both kinds of asexual reproduction rapidly increase the number of polyps in a short time. Cnidarians reproduce sexually when in the medusa stage. The medusas release sperm and eggs into the water. A fertilized egg develops into a swimming larva. In time, the larva attaches to a hard surface and develops into a polyp that may continue the cycle. The moon jelly in **Figure 5** undergoes both asexual and sexual reproduction.

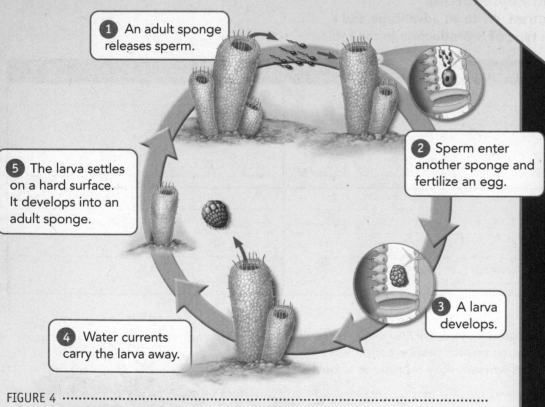

1. An adult sponge releases sperm.

2. Sperm enter another sponge and fertilize an egg.

3. A larva develops.

4. Water currents carry the larva away.

5. The larva settles on a hard surface. It develops into an adult sponge.

FIGURE 4 ···
Reproduction of a Sponge
These sponges are reproducing sexually. ✎ **Complete these tasks.**

1. **Identify** A budded sponge is a product of (asexual/sexual) reproduction and a larva is a product of (asexual/sexual) reproduction.

2. **Interpret Diagrams** How do the sponge larva and adult differ?

_____

_____

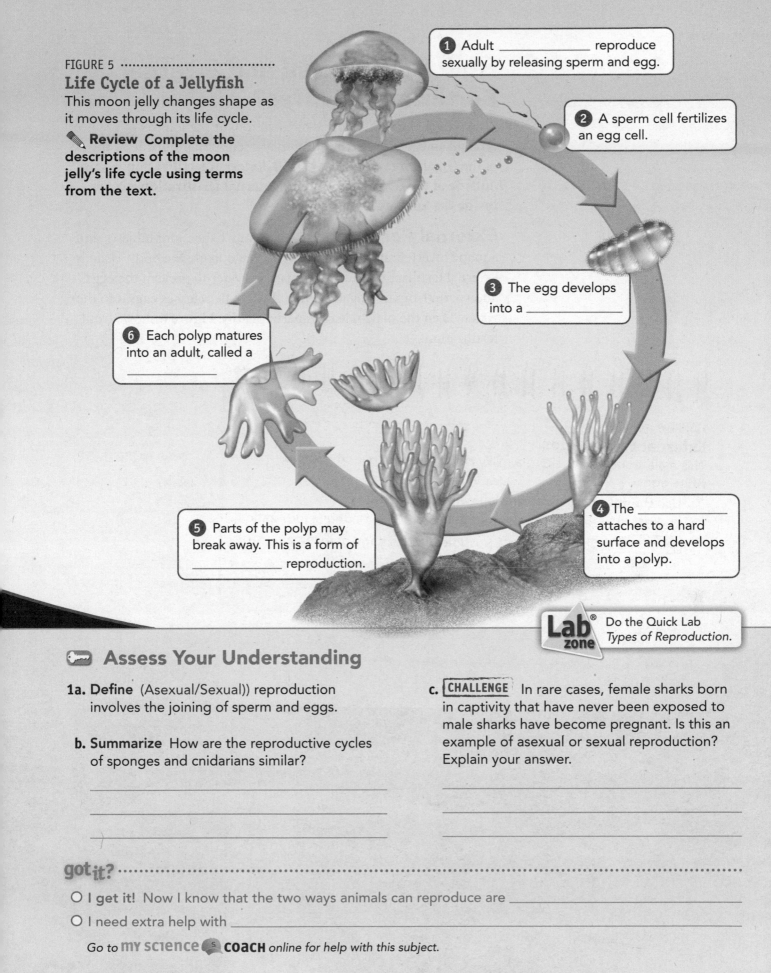

FIGURE 5 ....

Life Cycle of a Jellyfish
This moon jelly changes shape as it moves through its life cycle.

✎ **Review** Complete the descriptions of the moon jelly's life cycle using terms from the text.

1 Adult _____ reproduce sexually by releasing sperm and egg.

2 A sperm cell fertilizes an egg cell.

3 The egg develops into a _____

4 The _____ attaches to a hard surface and develops into a polyp.

5 Parts of the polyp may break away. This is a form of _____ reproduction.

6 Each polyp matures into an adult, called a _____

Lab ® Do the Quick Lab
zone *Types of Reproduction.*

🔑 Assess Your Understanding

1a. Define (Asexual/Sexual)) reproduction involves the joining of sperm and eggs.

b. Summarize How are the reproductive cycles of sponges and cnidarians similar?

_____

_____

_____

c. [CHALLENGE] In rare cases, female sharks born in captivity that have never been exposed to male sharks have become pregnant. Is this an example of asexual or sexual reproduction? Explain your answer.

_____

_____

_____

got it? ....

○ **I get it!** Now I know that the two ways animals can reproduce are _____

○ **I need extra help with** _____

Go to **my science** ⬤ˢ **coach** online for help with this subject.

How Do External and Internal Fertilization Differ?

Sexual reproduction involves fertilization, or the joining of a sperm cell and an egg cell. Fertilization may occur either outside or inside of the female organism's body.  **External fertilization occurs outside of the female's body, and internal fertilization occurs inside the female's body.**

External Fertilization For many fishes, amphibians, and aquatic invertebrates, fertilization occurs outside the body. Usually external fertilization must take place in water to prevent the eggs and sperm from drying out. First, the female releases eggs into the water. Then the male releases sperm nearby. **Figure 6** shows trout fertilization.

FIGURE 6 ···

External Fertilization
This male trout is depositing a milky cloud of sperm over the round, white eggs.

✎ **Use the text to answer the following questions.**

1. **Identify** (Land/Water) is the best environment for external fertilization.

2. CHALLENGE What might be a possible disadvantage of external fertilization?

_____

_____

_____

_____

Internal Fertilization

Internal Fertilization Fertilization occurs inside the body in many aquatic animals and all land animals. The male releases sperm directly into the female's body, where the eggs are located.

Most invertebrates and many fishes, amphibians, reptiles, and birds lay eggs outside the parent's body. The offspring continue to develop inside the eggs. For other animals, including most mammals, fertilized eggs develop inside the female animal. The female then gives birth to live young. The length of time between fertilization and birth is called the **gestation period.** Opossums have the shortest gestation period—around 13 days. African elephants have the longest gestation period—up to 22 months.

✎ **Compare and Contrast**
Describe how external and internal fertilization are alike and different.

_____

_____

_____

_____

_____

_____

_____

_____

do the math!

Study the graph and answer the questions below.

1 ⚠ **Calculate** About how many days longer is the giraffe's gestation period than the fox's?

_____

2 **Make Generalizations** How do you think an animal's size relates to the length of its gestation period?

_____

_____

_____

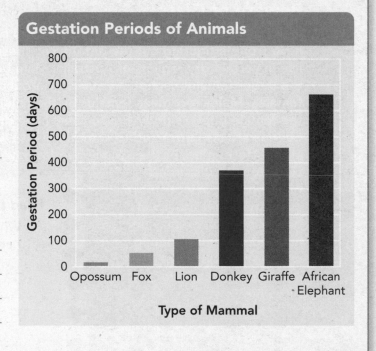

Gestation Periods of Animals

Type of Mammal — Gestation Period (days): Opossum, Fox, Lion, Donkey, Giraffe, African Elephant

---

Lab zone ® Do the Quick Lab *Types of Fertilization.*

🔑 Assess Your Understanding

got it? ·

○ **I get it!** Now I know that external fertilization occurs _____

and internal fertilization occurs _____

○ **I need extra help with** _____

Go to **MY SCIENCE** 💬 **COACH** *online for help with this subject.*

Development and Growth

UNLOCK
THE BIG
Q

🗝 **Where Do Embryos Develop?**

🗝 **How Do Young Animals Develop?**

🗝 **How Do Animals Care for Their Young?**

MY PLANET DiARY

DISCOVERY

Beware of Glass

Is that a beetle or a bottle? Australian jewel beetles seem to have trouble figuring out the difference. These large insects live in certain dry regions of Australia. Male beetles can fly, but the larger females cannot. As males fly around, they look for females. Males recognize females by the color and pattern of the female beetle's body. Researchers have discovered that male beetles are also attracted to something else with a similar color and pattern: glass bottles. Many beetles have been seen trying to mate with discarded glass bottles. Scientists are concerned that the jewel beetle population may be harmed—because mating with bottles does not produce jewel beetle offspring!

Read the paragraph and answer the questions below.

1. Why would the male's attempt to mate with bottles harm the jewel beetle population?

_____

_____

_____

_____

2. What is one way that this problem could be prevented?

_____

_____

▶ **PLANET DIARY** Go to **Planet Diary** to learn more about development and growth.

Lab zone® Do the Inquiry Warm-Up "Eggs-amination."

Vocabulary
- amniotic egg • placenta • metamorphosis
- complete metamorphosis • pupa
- incomplete metamorphosis • nymph • tadpole

Skills
- Reading: Summarize
- Inquiry: Interpret Data

Where Do Embryos Develop?

Turtles, sharks, and mice all reproduce sexually. But after fertilization occurs, the offspring of these animals develop in different ways. **The growing offspring, or embryo, may develop outside or inside of the parent's body.**

Egg-Laying Animals The offspring of some animals develop inside an egg laid outside of the parent's body. Most animals without backbones, including worms and insects, lay eggs. Many fishes, reptiles, and birds lay eggs, too. The contents of the egg provide all the nutrients that the developing embryo needs. The eggs of land vertebrates, such as reptiles and birds, are called **amniotic eggs.** Amniotic eggs are covered with membranes and a leathery shell while still inside the parent's body. **Figure 1** shows some of the structures of an amniotic egg.

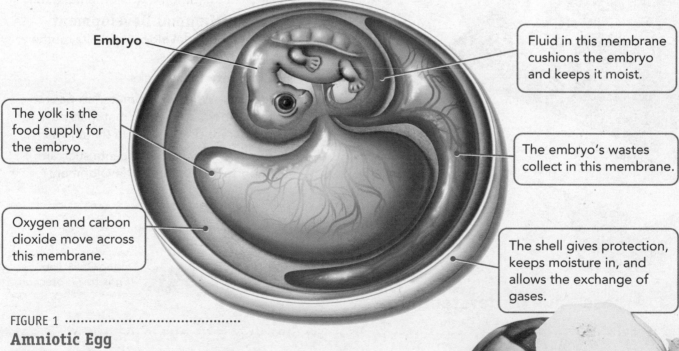

Embryo

Fluid in this membrane cushions the embryo and keeps it moist.

The yolk is the food supply for the embryo.

The embryo's wastes collect in this membrane.

Oxygen and carbon dioxide move across this membrane.

The shell gives protection, keeps moisture in, and allows the exchange of gases.

FIGURE 1 ·····
Amniotic Egg
Reptiles, such as this tortoise, develop inside an amniotic egg. The amniotic egg is a unique adaptation for life on land.

✎ **Relate Text to Visuals** Circle the descriptions of the structures that keep the embryo from drying out.

Summarize Read the text about egg-retaining animals. Then summarize how the embryo develops in these animals.

_____

_____

_____

_____

Egg-Retaining Animals
In certain animals, an embryo develops inside an egg that is kept, or retained, within the parent's body. The developing embryo gets all its nutrients from the egg's yolk, just like the offspring of egg-laying animals. The young do not receive any extra nutrients from the parent. The egg hatches either before or after being released from the parent's body. This type of development is found in fishes, amphibians, and reptiles.

Placental Mammals
In dogs, horses, humans, and other placental mammals, the embryo develops inside the mother's body. The mother provides the embryo with everything it needs during development. Materials are exchanged between the embryo and the mother through an organ called the **placenta,** shown in **Figure 2.** Blood carrying food and oxygen from the mother flows to the placenta and then to the embryo. Blood carrying wastes and carbon dioxide from the embryo flows to the placenta and then to the mother. The mother's blood does not mix with the embryo's blood. A placental mammal develops inside its mother's body until its body systems can function on their own.

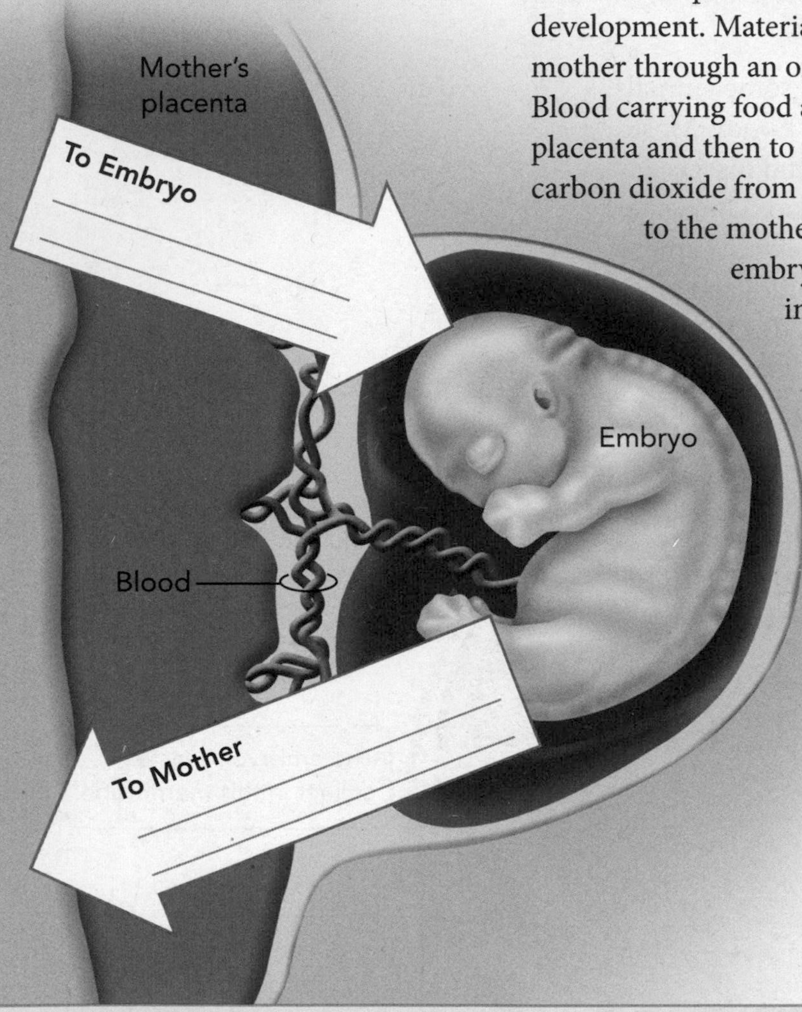

Mother's placenta

To Embryo

Embryo

Blood

To Mother

FIGURE 2 ....
Placental Mammal Development
This cat embryo develops inside its mother for about two months.

Complete these tasks.

1. **Identify** Write which materials pass to the embryo and which materials pass to the parent on the lines in the arrows.

2. **Explain** Why is the placenta such an important structure in development?

_____

_____

Lab zone® Do the Quick Lab "Eggs-tra" Protection.

Assess Your Understanding
got it? ....

O **I get it!** Now I know that the places embryos can develop are _____

_____

O **I need extra help with** _____

Go to MY SCIENCE ⑤ COACH online for help with this subject.

How Do Young Animals Develop?

Living things grow, change, and reproduce during their lifetimes. Some young animals, including most vertebrates, look like small versions of adults. Other animals go through the process of **metamorphosis,** or major body changes, as they develop from young organisms into adults. 🔑 **Young animals undergo changes in their bodies between birth and maturity, when they are able to reproduce.** As you read, notice the similarities and differences among the life cycles of crustaceans, insects, and amphibians.

Crustaceans Most crustaceans, such as lobsters, crabs, and shrimp, begin their lives as tiny, swimming larvae. The bodies of these larvae do not resemble those of adults. Larvae may swim or drift in the water as they grow and change. Eventually, through metamorphosis, crustacean larvae develop into adults. **Figure 3** shows three stages of a lobster's life cycle.

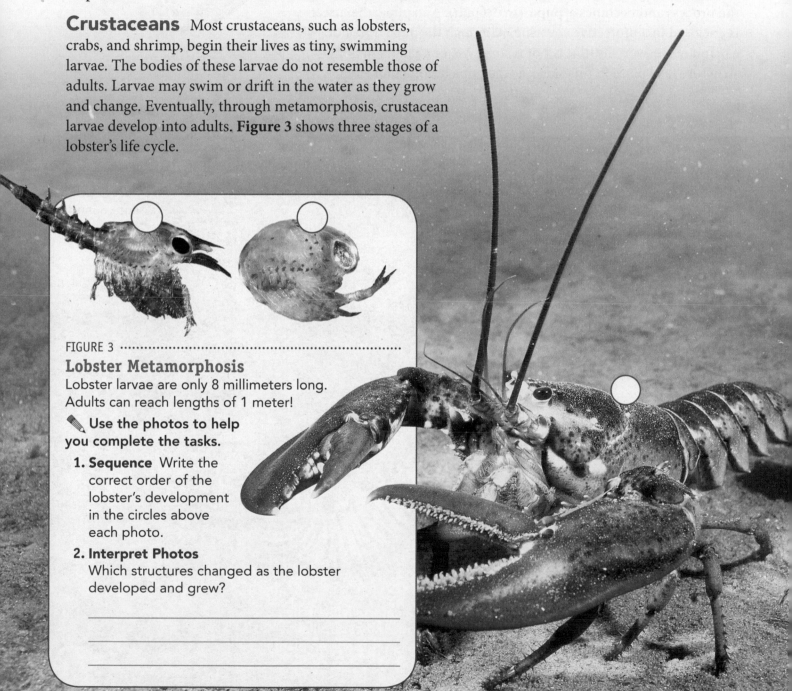

FIGURE 3 ·······················
Lobster Metamorphosis
Lobster larvae are only 8 millimeters long. Adults can reach lengths of 1 meter!

✏ **Use the photos to help you complete the tasks.**

1. **Sequence** Write the correct order of the lobster's development in the circles above each photo.

2. **Interpret Photos** Which structures changed as the lobster developed and grew?

_____

_____

_____

391

Insects Have you ever seen an insect egg? You might find one on the underside of a leaf. After an insect hatches from the egg, it begins metamorphosis as it develops into an adult. Insects such as butterflies, beetles, and grasshoppers undergo complete metamorphosis or incomplete metamorphosis.

Complete Metamorphosis The cycle to the right shows a ladybug going through **complete metamorphosis,** which has four different stages: egg, larva, pupa, and adult. An egg hatches into a larva. A larva usually looks something like a worm. It is specialized for eating and growing. After a time, a larva enters the next stage of the process and becomes a **pupa** (PYOO puh). As a pupa, the insect is enclosed in a protective covering. Although the pupa does not eat and moves very little, it is not resting. Major changes in body structure take place in this stage, as the pupa becomes an adult.

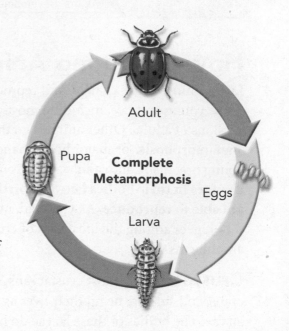

Adult

Pupa · **Complete Metamorphosis** · Eggs

Larva

A monarch butterfly egg develops on a milkweed plant.

A larva, or a caterpillar, hatches from the egg. The caterpillar grows larger as it feeds on plants. Then it enters the pupa stage.

Inside the pupa case, adult structures such as wings, antennae, and legs form.

Incomplete Metamorphosis In contrast, a second type of metamorphosis, called **incomplete metamorphosis,** has no distinct larval stage. Incomplete metamorphosis has three stages: egg, nymph, and adult. An egg hatches into a stage called a **nymph** (nimf), which usually looks like the adult insect without wings. As the nymph grows, it may shed its outgrown exoskeleton several times before becoming an adult. The chinch bug to the right is going through incomplete metamorphosis.

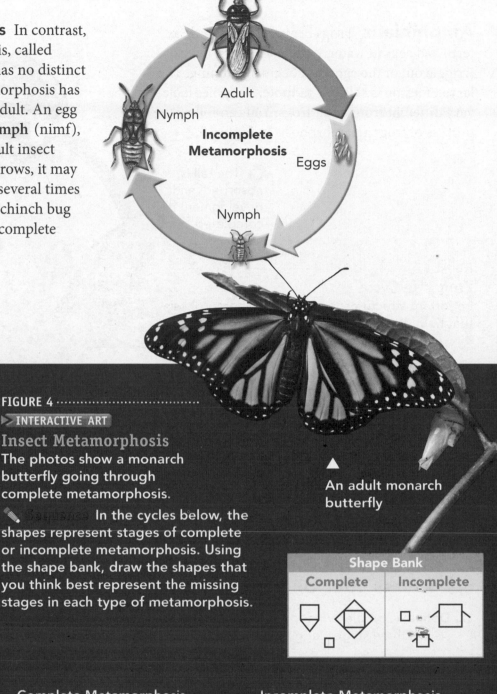

Adult

Nymph

Incomplete Metamorphosis

Eggs

Nymph

An adult monarch butterfly

FIGURE 4 ·····················
▷ **INTERACTIVE ART**

Insect Metamorphosis
The photos show a monarch butterfly going through complete metamorphosis.

✎ Sequence In the cycles below, the shapes represent stages of complete or incomplete metamorphosis. Using the shape bank, draw the shapes that you think best represent the missing stages in each type of metamorphosis.

Shape Bank	
Complete	**Incomplete**

The adult butterfly comes out of the pupa case and the butterfly's wings expand as the blood flows into them.

Complete Metamorphosis

Adult

Egg

Pupa

Larva

Incomplete Metamorphosis

Adult

Egg

Nymph

Nymph

Amphibians Frogs begin their life cycle as fertilized eggs in water. After a few days, larvae wriggle out of the eggs and begin swimming. The larva of a frog is called a **tadpole**. Tadpoles look very different from adult frogs. You can follow the process of frog metamorphosis in **Figure 5**.

1 Adult frogs reproduce sexually.

6 The tail is absorbed, and development is completed.

FIGURE 5 ···

Frog Life Cycle

Important structures form during metamorphosis that help the frog live in water and on land.

✎ **Use the frog life cycle diagram to complete each task.**

5

1. **Name** In the space provided, write the structures that grew at stage 5.

2. **Infer** How do the structures in stages 3, 4, and 5 help the frog live in water and on land?

2 Eggs are fertilized outside of the female's body.

3 A tadpole hatches from an egg.

4 Hind legs develop.

_____

_____

_____

Lab ® Do the Quick Lab
zone *Cycles of Life.*

🔑 **Assess Your Understanding**

1a. Define (Complete/Incomplete) metamorphosis has three stages: egg, nymph, and adult.

b. Apply Concepts Why is a nymph more likely than a larva to eat the same food as an adult?

_____

_____

_____

c. Compare and Contrast How are the life cycles of crustaceans and amphibians similar?

_____

_____

_____

_____

_____

got**it?** ···

○ **I get it!** Now I know that as young animals develop they _____

_____

○ **I need extra help with** _____

Go to **MY SCIENCE** 🔒 **COACH** online for help with this subject.

How Do Animals Care for Their Young?

Have you seen a caterpillar, tadpole, puppy, duckling, or other baby animal recently? You may have noticed that different animals care for their offspring in different ways. ▶ **Most amphibians and reptiles do not provide parental care, while most birds and mammals typically care for their offspring.**

No Parental Care Not all animals take care of their young. Most aquatic invertebrates, fishes, and amphibians release many eggs into water and then completely ignore them! Most amphibian larvae, or tadpoles, develop into adults without parental help. Similarly, the offspring of most reptiles, such as the snakes in **Figure 6,** are independent from the time they hatch. Offspring that do not receive parental care must be able to care for themselves from the time of birth.

FIGURE 6 ....

Checklist for Survival
These bushmaster snakes have just hatched from their eggs. They may stay inside the shell for several days for safety.

✏ **List** Make a list of what you think these snakes must be able to do to survive their first few days of life.

Parental Care You've probably never seen a duckling walking by itself. That's because most birds and all mammals typically spend weeks to years under the care and protection of a parent.

Birds Most bird species lay their eggs in nests that one or both parents build. Then one or both parents sit on the eggs, keeping them warm until they hatch. Some species of birds can move around and find food right after they hatch. Others are helpless and must be fed by the parent, as shown in **Figure 7**. Most parent birds feed and protect their young until they are able to care for themselves.

Mammals Whether a monotreme, a marsupial, or a placental mammal, young mammals are usually quite helpless for a long time after they are born. After birth, all young mammals are fed with milk from the mother's body. One or both parents may continue caring for their offspring until the young animals are independent.

FIGURE 7 ··
Parental Care
The parent bird shown above cares for its hungry offspring until they are ready to fly. The mother polar bear at the right stays with her cubs for up to two years.

✎ **Answer each question.**

1. **Interpret Photos** How are the parents in these two photos caring for their young?

   _____

   _____

   _____

2. **Communicate** What is one way that a family member cares for you?

   _____

   _____

   _____

do the math! Analyzing Data

Suppose that you are a scientist researching how many fox and turtle offspring survive the first year of life. Foxes provide parental care, but turtles do not.

Type of Animal	Number of Offspring	Number That Survive the First Year	Percentage That Survive the First Year
Fox	5	_____	60%
Turtle	20	_____	20%

1 Calculate Using the information in the second and fourth columns of the table, calculate the number of offspring that survive the first year. Put your answer in the third column of the table.

2 Graph Use the data from the table to construct a double bar graph in the space provided. Label the vertical axis. Then provide a key for the data in the graph.

3 ⚠ Interpret Data How do you think parental care is related to the percentage of offspring that survive the first year of life?

_____

_____

_____

_____

4 CHALLENGE Why do you think animals that provide parental care have fewer offspring?

_____

_____

_____

_____

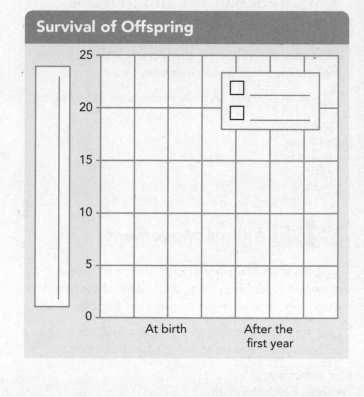

Survival of Offspring

At birth   After the first year

Lab zone® Do the Quick Lab
To Care or Not to Care.

🔑 Assess Your Understanding

got it? ....

○ I get it! Now I know that parental care occurs _____

_____

○ I need extra help with _____

   Go to **MY SCIENCE** 🔵 **COACH** online for help with this subject.

10 Study Guide

An animal's _____, _____, and _____ work together to help the animal move.

LESSON 1 Skeletons and Muscles

🔑 A skeleton is a framework that shapes and supports an animal, protects its internal organs, and allows it to move in its environment.

🔑 Muscles help animals move their body parts.

Vocabulary
- molting
- cartilage
- joint
- muscle

LESSON 2 The Nervous System

🔑 A nervous system allows animals to detect, process, and react to environmental signals.

🔑 The simplest nervous systems are a netlike arrangement of neurons throughout the body. Complex systems have a nerve cord and a brain.

Vocabulary
- nervous system • stimulus • response • neuron
- impulse • sensory neuron • interneuron
- motor neuron • brain

LESSON 3 Animal Movement

🔑 An animal moves about when its nervous system, muscular system, and skeletal system work together to make movement happen.

🔑 Animals that live in water, on land, or in the air have different adaptations for movement.

Vocabulary
- water vascular system
- swim bladder

LESSON 4 Obtaining Energy

🔑 The different ways that an animal obtains energy depends on what and how it eats.

🔑 Animal cells exchange oxygen and carbon dioxide with their surroundings by diffusion.

🔑 Complex animals have one of two types of circulatory systems: open or closed.

Vocabulary
- carnivore • herbivore • omnivore • filter feeder
- digestion • digestive system • cellular respiration
- diffusion • respiratory system • circulatory system

LESSON 5 Animal Reproduction and Fertilization

🔑 Animals undergo either asexual or sexual reproduction to make more of their own kind.

🔑 External fertilization occurs outside of the female's body, and internal fertilization occurs inside the female's body.

Vocabulary
- larva • polyp • medusa
- external fertilization • internal fertilization
- gestation period

LESSON 6 Development and Growth

🔑 The growing offspring, or embryo, may develop outside or inside of the parent's body.

🔑 Young animals undergo changes in their bodies between birth and maturity.

🔑 Most amphibians and reptiles do not provide parental care. Most birds and mammals do.

Vocabulary
- amniotic egg • placenta • metamorphosis
- complete metamorphosis • pupa
- incomplete metamorphosis • nymph • tadpole

Review and Assessment

LESSON 1 **Skeletons and Muscles**

1. A _____ is a place where two or more parts of a skeleton meet.

2. **Relate Cause and Effect** How might an endoskeleton affect the size of an animal?

_____

_____

_____

3. **Sequence** Describe how your muscles work to help you kick a ball.

_____

_____

_____

_____

_____

_____

LESSON 2 **The Nervous System**

4. A signal that causes an animal to react in some way is called a

   a. response.   b. neuron.
   c. stimulus.   d. impulse.

5. The most complex nervous systems have

   a nerve cord and a _____

Use the diagrams below to answer Question 6.

6. **Interpret Diagrams** Explain the stimulus in diagram A and the response in diagram B.

_____

_____

_____

LESSON 3 **Animal Movement**

7. An animal that moves using a water vascular system is a

   a. sea star.   b. penguin.
   c. squid.   d. shark.

8. **Draw Conclusions** What are three reasons why an animal might need to move about?

_____

_____

_____

_____

_____

9. **Write About It** Write a paragraph in which you describe a different adaptation that rabbits, bats, and snakes each have that enables them to move as they do.

LESSON 4 **Obtaining Energy**

10. Animals that eat only plant material are

    a. omnivores.   b. filter feeders.
    c. carnivores.   d. herbivores.

11. The process of breaking down food into small molecules is called _____

12. **Make Generalizations** What type of teeth would you expect an omnivore to have? How do they help the animal eat its food?

_____

_____

_____

_____

_____

_____

_____

10 Review and Assessment

13. The process in which an animal's cells use oxygen and digested food molecules to release the energy in food is

   a. breathing.   **b.** cellular respiration.

   c. diffusion.   **d.** gas exchange.

14. **Write About It** Describe three structures that an animal's respiratory system may have. Name one animal that has each structure.

LESSON 5 Animal Reproduction and Fertilization

15. External fertilization is common for organisms that live in

   a. trees.   **b.** water.

   c. deserts.   **d.** open fields.

16. The _____ is an immature form of an organism that looks very different from the adult.

17. **Write About It** Consider the following statement: *Organisms that reproduce asexually are at a higher risk of extinction than organisms that reproduce sexually.* Do you agree or disagree? Explain your answer.

LESSON 6 Development and Growth

18. Which of the following organisms lays amniotic eggs?

   a. fish   **b.** insect

   c. turtle   **d.** rabbit

19. **Compare and Contrast** How is the development of an embryo in an amniotic egg and in a placental mammal different?

20. **Make Generalizations** Why is parental care so important for newborn birds and mammals?

APPLY THE BIG ?

How do animals move?

21. Suppose this ostrich's nervous system was not receiving signals properly. How might it be dangerous for the ostrich?

Standardized Test Prep

Multiple Choice

Circle the letter of the best answer.

1. Which is true of the endoskeleton of a mammal?

A It grows with the animal.

B It molts as the animal grows.

C It does not have hard parts.

D It is mostly cartilage.

2. The larval form of the frog shown in stage 3 is called a

A nymph.　　　　**B** pupa.

C tadpole.　　　　**D** adult.

3. An amniotic egg is the result of _____ and _____.

A asexual reproduction; external fertilization

B asexual reproduction; internal fertilization

C sexual reproduction; external fertilization

D sexual reproduction; internal fertilization

4. Based on the type of teeth you see in the diagram below, make an inference about what type of animal it is.

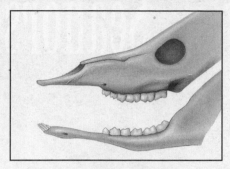

A omnivore　　　　**B** herbivore

C carnivore　　　　**D** filter feeder

5. Animals with nerve nets have

A no specialized neurons.

B sensory neurons, but no interneurons.

C interneurons, but no sensory neurons.

D only motor neurons.

Constructed Response

Use the diagram below and your knowledge of science to help you answer Question 6. Write your answer on a separate sheet of paper.

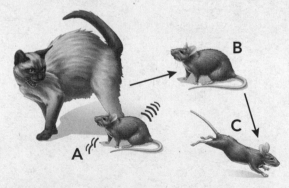

6. Describe how the mouse's nervous system is functioning in this diagram. Include the roles of the sensory neurons, interneurons, and motor neurons.

SPECIAL DELIVERY!

Seahorse Reproduction

In warm, coastal waters all over the world, just after sunrise every day, a dance-like scene takes place. Tails intertwined, pairs of seahorses spin and twirl under water. Some use their long tails to hold onto strands of seaweed. These long tails that are adapted for grabbing and holding things aren't seahorses' only unusual feature. Seahorses also have some unusual reproductive habits!

Seahorses practice sexual reproduction, like other fish do. Unlike fish—or any other vertebrate for that matter—it's the male seahorse that carries fertilized eggs, provides the eggs with oxygen and nutrients, and gives birth. The males can do this because they have pouches, called brood pouches, in their abdomens.

When mating, the female seahorse deposits about 2,000 eggs inside the male's pouch each time, and he does the rest. He fertilizes the eggs, which become embedded in his pouch wall, and carries them for several weeks. During this time, the eggs receive oxygen and nutrients through a network of tiny blood vessels.

In about three weeks, the male seahorse's brood pouch expands until it is almost spherical. It stays this way for several hours, until the seahorse suddenly gives birth to between eight and 200 baby seahorses. These tiny seahorses can swim and feed by themselves, although they will not be ready to mate with their own partners for many months. About an hour after giving birth, the male is ready to mate again.

Design It Pipefish are another species with unusual reproductive habits. Find out about their reproductive cycles. Create a Venn diagram to compare and contrast the pipefish cycle and the seahorse cycle.

▲ The male seahorse's brood pouch expands as the baby seahorses grow.

"feet" of engineering

Geckos are tiny lizards that live in warm climates all over the world, including the southwestern United States. If you've ever seen one, you've probably watched it scale a wall in about the time it takes for you to blink. Or you may have seen a gecko hang from one foot.

How do geckos hang from one foot? The answer is their hair! The gecko's feet are covered in millions of tiny hairs. Molecules in the hairs are attracted to molecules in the wall or on any other surface. These forces of attraction, called van der Waals forces, affect every form of matter, but they are usually so weak that you can't feel them. However, there are so many tiny hairs on a gecko's feet that geckos can cling to nearly any surface!

Gecko feet have inspired scientists to design artificial super-sticky materials that use the same principle. Maybe someday these materials could be used for surgical bandages, wall-crawling robots, or even shoes with incredible grip. For now, scientists will have to see which designs stick!

Design It Technological design inspired by biology is called biomimetic design. Research a few other examples of biomimetic design, and choose a simple problem that one of your examples could solve. Make or draw a model of your solution.

WHAT CAN THESE BODY PARTS DO?

How does your body work?

Your body is an amazingly complex mass of trillions of cells. These cells work together, doing all the functions that keep you alive. On average, an adult has 206 bones, 96,500 kilometers of blood vessels, and a brain with a mass of 1.4 kilograms. Your nerves can send signals at speeds of up to 120 meters per second. Your smallest muscle is in your ear.

⚠ **Infer** **What jobs do some of these body parts do?**

_____

_____

_____

_____

_____

▶ UNTAMED SCIENCE Watch the **Untamed Science** video to learn more about body systems.

Introduction to the Human Body

Check Your Understanding

1. Background Read the paragraph below and then answer the question.

Fara is learning how to build and fix bicycles. First, she learned to change a tire using a tire lever. This tool's **structure**—a lever with a curved end—matches its **function**—to pry a tire off a metal rim. She's also learning about the **interactions** between the different bike parts—how the chain, gears, wheels, and brakes all work together as a **system.**

An object's **structure** is its shape or form.

An object's **function** is the action it performs or the role it plays.

An **interaction** occurs when two or more things work together or affect one another.

A **system** is a group of parts that work together to perform a function or produce a result.

- Circle the structure below that best matches the function of helping a fish to swim.

  scales   gills   fins   eyes

> **MY READING WEB** If you had trouble completing the question above, visit **My Reading Web** and type in *Introduction to the Human Body.*

Vocabulary Skill

Suffixes A suffix is a word part that is added to the end of a word to change its meaning. For example, the suffix *-tion* means "process of." If you add the suffix *-tion* to the verb *digest*, you get the noun *digestion*. *Digestion* means "the process of digesting." The table below lists some other common suffixes and their meanings.

Suffix	Meaning	Example
-al	of, like, or suitable for	epithelial, *adj.* describes a tissue that covers inner and outer surfaces of the body
-ive	of, relating to, belonging to, having the nature or quality of	connective, *adj.* describes a tissue that provides support for the body and connects all of its parts

2. Quick Check Circle the suffix in each of the terms below.

skeletal   digestive   internal

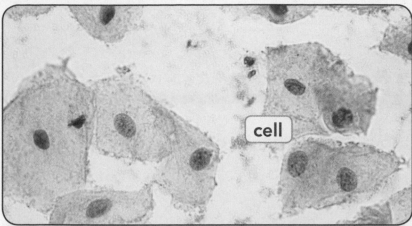

cell

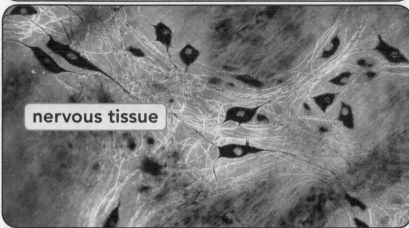

nervous tissue

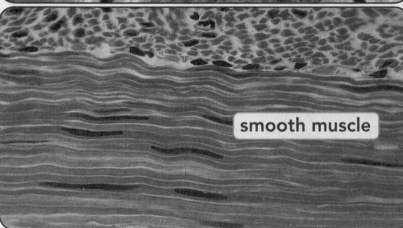

smooth muscle

epidermis

Chapter Preview

LESSON 1
- cell • cell membrane • nucleus
- cytoplasm • tissue
- muscle tissue • nervous tissue
- connective tissue
- epithelial tissue • organ
- organ system
- ⟳ Identify the Main Idea
- △ Make Models

LESSON 2
- skeleton • skeletal muscle • joint
- nutrient • absorption • gland
- stimulus • response • hormone
- ⟳ Summarize
- △ Develop Hypotheses

LESSON 3
- homeostasis • stress
- ⟳ Relate Cause and Effect
- △ Communicate

LESSON 4
- skeleton • vertebrae • joint
- ligament • compact bone
- spongy bone • marrow
- cartilage • osteoporosis
- ⟳ Summarize
- △ Classify

LESSON 5
- involuntary muscle
- voluntary muscle
- skeletal muscle • tendon
- smooth muscle • cardiac muscle
- striated muscle
- ⟳ Compare and Contrast
- △ Infer

LESSON 6
- epidermis • melanin • dermis
- pore • follicle
- ⟳ Relate Cause and Effect
- △ Observe

Body Organization

UNLOCK THE BIG

🔑 **How Is Your Body Organized?**

my planet Diary

CAREER

Medical Illustrator

Who made the colorful drawings of human body structures in this book? The drawings are the work of specialized artists called medical illustrators. These artists use their drawing skills and knowledge of human biology to make detailed images of body structures. Many artists draw images, such as the one on this page, using 3-D computer graphics. The work of medical illustrators appears in textbooks, journals, magazines, videos, computer learning programs, and many other places.

Communicate Answer the question below. Then discuss your answer with a partner.

Why do you think medical illustrations are important to the study of human biology?

_____

_____

_____

_____

> **PLANET DIARY** Go to **Planet Diary** to learn more about body organization.

Lab zone   Do the Inquiry Warm-Up
How Is Your Body Organized?

How Is Your Body Organized?

The bell rings—lunchtime! You hurry to the cafeteria, fill your tray, and pay the cashier. You look around the cafeteria for your friends. Then you walk to the table, sit down, and begin to eat.

Think about how many parts of your body were involved in the simple act of getting and eating your lunch. Every minute of the day, whether you are eating, studying, walking, or even sleeping, your body is busily at work. Each part of the body has a specific job to do. And all these different parts usually work together so smoothly that you don't even notice them.

Vocabulary

- cell • cell membrane • nucleus • cytoplasm • tissue
- muscle tissue • nervous tissue • connective tissue
- epithelial tissue • organ • organ system

Skills

↩ Reading: Identify the Main Idea
△ Inquiry: Make Models

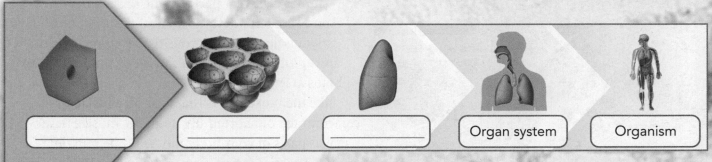

| | | | Organ system | Organism |

FIGURE 1 ....

Body Organization

You will see this diagram three more times in this lesson. It will help you track the levels of organization in the body.

✏ **Name** Fill in the missing terms in the diagram above.

The smooth functioning of your body is due partly to how the body is organized. 🔑 **The levels of organization in the human body consist of cells, tissues, organs, and organ systems.** The smallest unit of organization is a cell. The next largest unit is a tissue, then an organ. Finally, an organ system is the largest unit of organization in an organism. **Figure 1** shows body organization.

Cells
A **cell** is the basic unit of structure and function in a living thing. Complex organisms are made up of many cells in the same way that your school is made up of many rooms. The human body contains about 100 trillion tiny cells. Most cells cannot be seen without a microscope.

Structures of Cells Almost all cells in the human body have the same basic parts, as shown in **Figure 2.** The **cell membrane** forms the outside border of a cell. The **nucleus** directs the cell's activities and holds information that controls a cell's function. The rest of the cell, called the **cytoplasm** (SYT oh plaz um), is made of a clear, jellylike substance that contains many cell structures. Each of these structures has a specific job, or function.

Functions of Cells Cells carry on the processes that keep organisms alive. Inside cells, for example, molecules from digested food undergo changes that release energy that the cells can use. Cells also grow, reproduce, and get rid of the waste products that result from these activities.

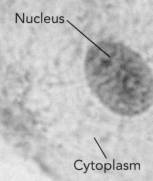

Cell membrane

Nucleus

Cytoplasm

FIGURE 2 ....

Cell Structure
A microscope reveals some of the parts of a human cheek cell.

Muscle tissue

Nervous tissue

Connective tissue

Epithelial tissue

Tissues

The next largest unit of organization in your body is a tissue. A **tissue** is a group of similar cells that perform the same function. Your body contains several types of tissue. Four of these are muscle tissue, nervous tissue, connective tissue, and epithelial tissue. You can see examples in the photos at left.

Like the muscle cells that form it, **muscle tissue** can contract, or shorten. By doing so, muscle tissue makes parts of your body move. While muscle tissue carries out movement, **nervous tissue** directs and controls the process. Nervous tissue carries electrical messages back and forth between the brain and other parts of the body. Another type of tissue, **connective tissue,** provides support for your body and connects all its parts. Bone tissue and fat tissue are examples of connective tissue.

Epithelial tissue (ep uh THEE lee ul) covers the surfaces of your body, inside and out. Some epithelial tissue, such as your skin, protects the delicate structures that lie beneath it. The lining of your digestive system consists of epithelial tissue that allows you to digest and absorb the nutrients in your food.

Identify the Main Idea

Choose the best description of the structure and function of a tissue.

○ A group of different cells that have the same function

○ A group of similar cells that have different functions

○ A group of similar cells that have the same function

FIGURE 3

The Heart

The heart, like your other organs, is made of different kinds of tissues that have different functions.

✎ **Answer the following questions.**

1. **Relate Text and Visuals** In each box, fill in the kind of tissue that matches the function described.

2. **CHALLENGE** Pick one type of tissue shown and describe how the heart would be affected if the tissue did not function properly.

_____ provides strength and flexible support for muscle tissue and other structures inside and outside the heart.

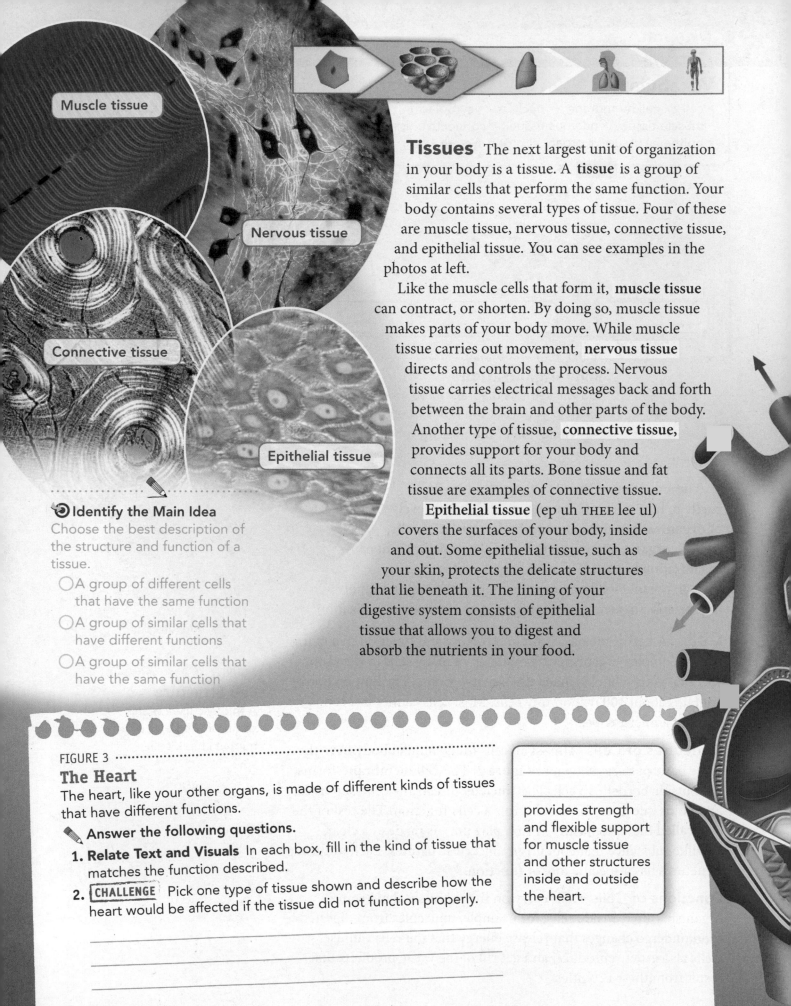

Organs

Your stomach, heart, brain, and lungs are all organs. An **organ** is a structure that is made up of different kinds of tissue. Like a tissue, an organ performs a specific job. The job of an organ, however, is usually more complex than that of a tissue. For example, the heart pumps blood through your body over and over again. The heart contains muscle, connective, and epithelial tissues. In addition, nervous tissue connects to the heart and helps control heart function. **Figure 3** shows a diagram of a human heart and describes how some of the heart's tissues work. Each type of tissue contributes in a different way to the organ's job of pumping blood.

_____ covers the inside surfaces of the heart and of the blood vessels that lead into and out of the heart.

_____ carries electrical messages from the brain to the heart but is not shown in this diagram.

_____ contracts, squeezing the heart so blood moves through the heart's chambers and then into blood vessels that lead to the body.

apply it!

Books are a nonliving model of levels of organization. Find out how a book is organized.

STEP 1 Observe Examine this book to see how its chapters, lessons, and other parts are related.

STEP 2 Make Models Next, compare levels of organization in this book to those in the human body. Draw lines to show which part of this book best models a level in the body.

Organism	Lessons
Organ systems	Book
Organs	Words
Tissues	Chapters
Cells	Paragraphs

STEP 3 Make Models Where in the book model do you think this Apply It fits? What level of organization in the body does the Apply It represent?

_____

_____

_____

_____

_____

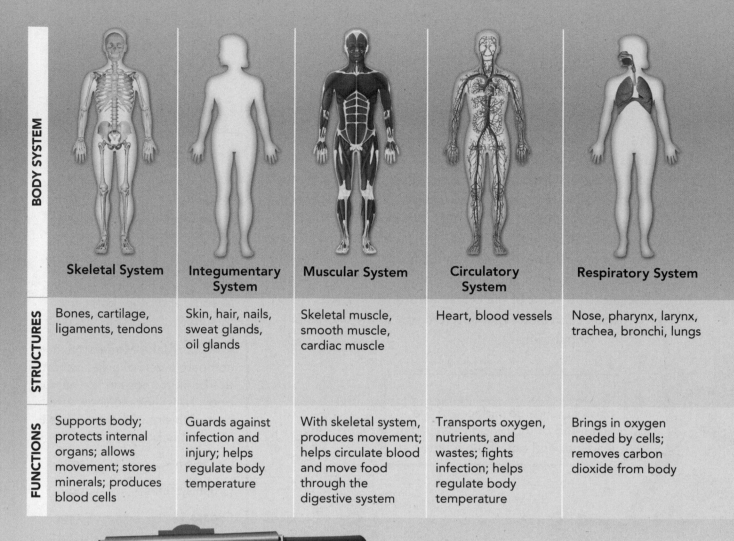

	Skeletal System	Integumentary System	Muscular System	Circulatory System	Respiratory System
STRUCTURES	Bones, cartilage, ligaments, tendons	Skin, hair, nails, sweat glands, oil glands	Skeletal muscle, smooth muscle, cardiac muscle	Heart, blood vessels	Nose, pharynx, larynx, trachea, bronchi, lungs
FUNCTIONS	Supports body; protects internal organs; allows movement; stores minerals; produces blood cells	Guards against infection and injury; helps regulate body temperature	With skeletal system, produces movement; helps circulate blood and move food through the digestive system	Transports oxygen, nutrients, and wastes; fights infection; helps regulate body temperature	Brings in oxygen needed by cells; removes carbon dioxide from body

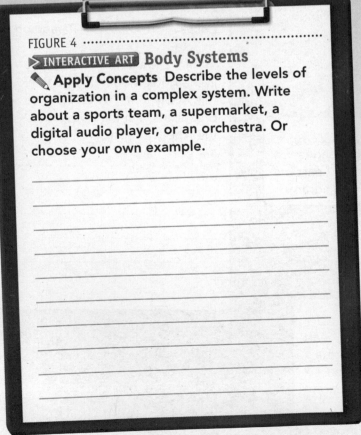

FIGURE 4 ·····································

> **INTERACTIVE ART** **Body Systems**

✎ **Apply Concepts** Describe the levels of organization in a complex system. Write about a sports team, a supermarket, a digital audio player, or an orchestra. Or choose your own example.

_____

_____

_____

_____

_____

_____

_____

_____

_____

_____

Systems

Each organ in your body is part of an **organ system,** which is a group of organs that work together, carrying out major functions. For example, your heart is part of your circulatory system, which carries oxygen and other materials throughout your body. The circulatory system also includes blood vessels and blood. **Figure 4** shows most of the organ systems in the human body.

Organisms

Starting with cells, the levels of organization in an organism become more and more complex. A tissue is more complex than a cell, an organ is more complex than a tissue, and so on. You, as an organism, are the next level of organization. And all organisms are part of levels of organization within the environment.

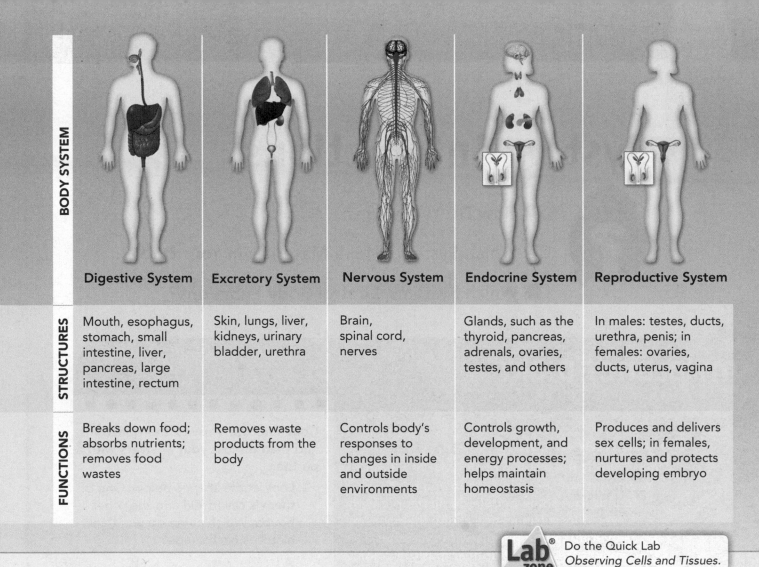

BODY SYSTEM	Digestive System	Excretory System	Nervous System	Endocrine System	Reproductive System
STRUCTURES	Mouth, esophagus, stomach, small intestine, liver, pancreas, large intestine, rectum	Skin, lungs, liver, kidneys, urinary bladder, urethra	Brain, spinal cord, nerves	Glands, such as the thyroid, pancreas, adrenals, ovaries, testes, and others	In males: testes, ducts, urethra, penis; in females: ovaries, ducts, uterus, vagina
FUNCTIONS	Breaks down food; absorbs nutrients; removes food wastes	Removes waste products from the body	Controls body's responses to changes in inside and outside environments	Controls growth, development, and energy processes; helps maintain homeostasis	Produces and delivers sex cells; in females, nurtures and protects developing embryo

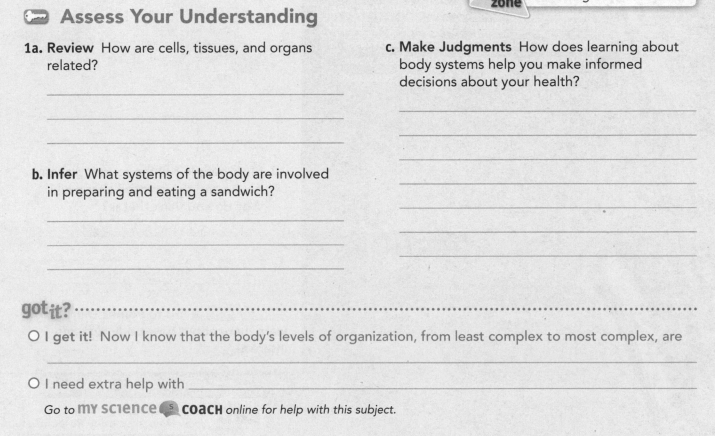

Lab zone ® Do the Quick Lab
Observing Cells and Tissues.

Assess Your Understanding

1a. Review How are cells, tissues, and organs related?

_____

_____

_____

b. Infer What systems of the body are involved in preparing and eating a sandwich?

_____

_____

_____

c. Make Judgments How does learning about body systems help you make informed decisions about your health?

_____

_____

_____

_____

_____

_____

_____

got it? ....

○ **I get it!** Now I know that the body's levels of organization, from least complex to most complex, are

_____

○ I need extra help with _____

Go to **MY SCIENCE COACH** online for help with this subject.

System Interactions

🔑 **How Do You Move?**

🔑 **Which Systems Move Materials in Your Body?**

🔑 **Which Systems Control Body Functions?**

MY PLANET DiARY

FUN FACTS

Do you hear in color?

What color is the letter *b* or the roar of a tiger? You might not see colors when you hear sounds, but some people do. In people with synesthesia (sin us THEE zhuh), their senses overlap. Some people with synesthesia may taste a shape or hear music in colors. Others may hear a sound when they see motion. Even people without synesthesia experience some connections between their senses. You can explore how your own senses overlap in the first question on this page.

Communicate Answer the questions and then discuss your answers with a partner.

1. Look at the shapes below. One of them is called kiki and the other bouba. Which name do you think matches each shape?

   A   B

   _____

   _____

2. Most people call the rounded shape bouba and the pointed shape kiki. Why do you think that is?

   _____

   _____

   _____

▷ **PLANET DIARY** Go to **Planet Diary** to learn more about how body systems interact.

 Lab zone Do the Inquiry Warm-Up *How Does Your Body Respond?*

Vocabulary
- skeleton
- skeletal muscle
- joint
- nutrient
- absorption
- gland
- stimulus
- response
- hormone

Skills
- Reading: Summarize
- Inquiry: Develop Hypotheses

How Do You Move?

Carefully coordinated movements let you thread a needle, ride a bicycle, brush your teeth, and dance. These movements—and all of your body's other movements—happen as a result of the interactions between body systems. Your muscular system is made up of all the muscles in your body. Your skeletal system, or **skeleton**, includes all the bones in your body. ⚷ **Muscles and bones work together, making your body move. The nervous system tells your muscles when to act.**

Muscles and Bones

Skeletal muscles are attached to the bones of your skeleton and provide the force that moves your bones. Muscles contract and relax. When a muscle contracts, it shortens and pulls on the bones to which it is attached, as shown in **Figure 1**.

FIGURE 1 ....

Muscles Moving Bones

As this dancer's muscles pull on his leg bones, he can make rapid, skillful moves.

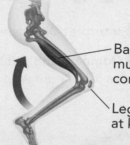

Back thigh muscles contract.

Leg bends at knee.

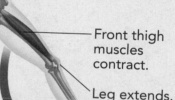

Front thigh muscles contract.

Leg extends.

△ Develop Hypotheses An octopus has no bones. Explain how you think it moves.

_____

_____

_____

415

Summarize In your own words, describe which of your systems work together when you write in this book.

_____

_____

_____

_____

Bones and Joints

What happens when you wiggle your fingers or touch your toes? Even though your bones are rigid, your body can bend in many ways. Your skeleton bends at its joints. A **joint** is a place in the body where two bones come together. For example, your elbow and your shoulder are two joints that move when you raise your hand.

Making Movement Happen

Muscles make bones move at their joints. Try standing on one leg and bending the other leg at the knee. Hold that position. You can feel that you are using the muscles at the back of your thigh. Now straighten your leg. You can feel the muscles in the back of your leg relax, but the muscles in the front of your leg are at work. Your nervous system controls when and how your muscles act on your bones. You will read more about the nervous system later in this lesson.

apply it!

① **Interpret Diagrams** Circle three of the football player's joints.

② **Compare and Contrast** Describe how your shoulder and elbow move in different ways.

_____

_____

_____

③ **CHALLENGE** From a standing position, bend down and grab your ankles. List six places or joints where your skeleton bends.

_____

_____

Lab zone® Do the Lab Investigation
A Look Beneath the Skin.

🔑 Assess Your Understanding

got it? ....

○ **I get it!** Now I know that _____ and _____ work together to make the body move.

○ **I need extra help with** _____

Go to MY SCIENCE ⓢ COACH online for help with this subject.

Which Systems Move Materials in Your Body?

The trillions of cells that make up your body need materials to function. Cells also produce wastes that must be removed. If the processes of moving these materials were made into a movie, your nervous system would be the director. The movie set would include the muscular and skeletal systems. And the main characters would be some of your other systems. **The circulatory, respiratory, digestive, and excretory systems play key roles in moving materials in your body.**

Transporting Materials
Your circulatory system includes your heart, blood vessels, and blood. Blood vessels are found throughout your body. Blood that flows through these vessels carries materials such as water, oxygen, and food to every cell, as shown in **Figure 2**. Materials that your cells must get rid of, such as carbon dioxide and other cell wastes, are also moved through the body in the blood.

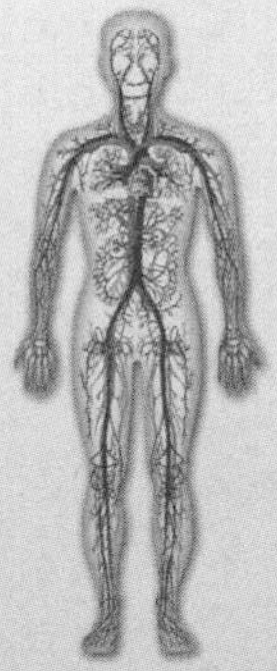

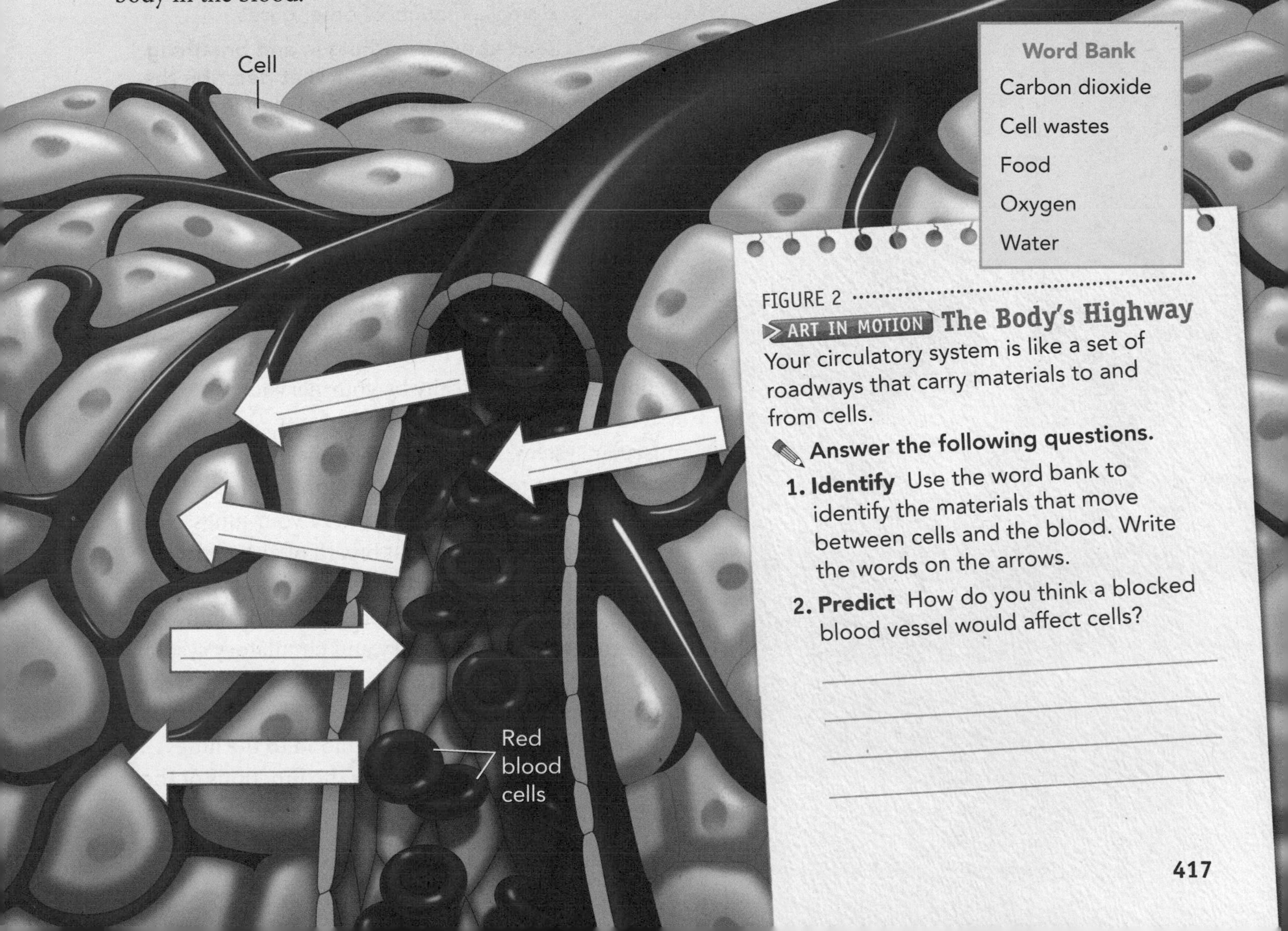

Blood vessel

Cell

Red blood cells

Word Bank

Carbon dioxide

Cell wastes

Food

Oxygen

Water

FIGURE 2 ....
> ART IN MOTION **The Body's Highway**
Your circulatory system is like a set of roadways that carry materials to and from cells.

✎ **Answer the following questions.**

1. **Identify** Use the word bank to identify the materials that move between cells and the blood. Write the words on the arrows.

2. **Predict** How do you think a blocked blood vessel would affect cells?

_____

_____

_____

_____

417

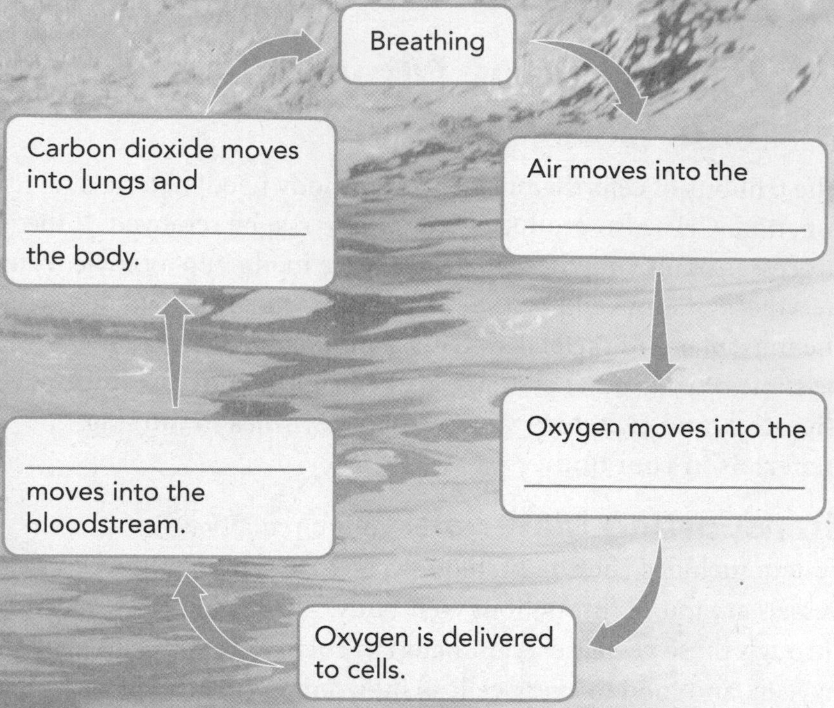

Breathing

Carbon dioxide moves into lungs and

_____

the body.

Air moves into the

_____

_____ moves into the bloodstream.

Oxygen moves into the

_____

Oxygen is delivered to cells.

FIGURE 3 ··

Something in the Air

About 21 percent of air is oxygen gas. The rest is mainly nitrogen gas and small amounts of other gases.

✎ **Sequence Read about breathing in and breathing out. Then complete the steps above that describe the functions of the respiratory system by filling in the missing terms in the boxes.**

Breathing In, Breathing Out

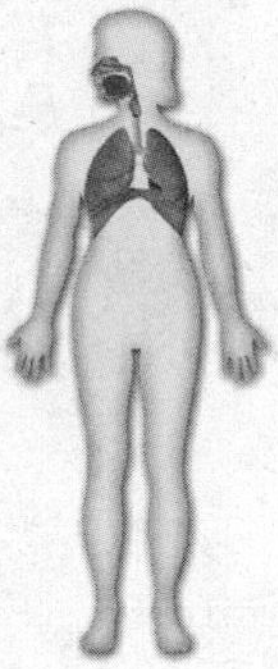

Can you imagine doing something more than 20,000 times a day? Without even realizing it, you already do. You breathe! You don't usually think about breathing, because this process is controlled automatically by your nervous system. Breathing also depends on your muscular system. Muscles in your chest cause your chest area to expand and compress. These changes make air move in and out of your lungs.

When you breathe in, that breath of air goes into your lungs, which are part of your respiratory system. Oxygen from the air moves from your lungs into your bloodstream. Your respiratory and circulatory systems work together, delivering oxygen to all your cells. Your cells give off carbon dioxide as a waste product. Carbon dioxide is carried in the blood to the lungs, where you breathe it out. Review the functions of the respiratory system in **Figure 3.**

Getting Food

Your respiratory system takes in oxygen, and your circulatory system delivers it to your cells. Oxygen is used in cells to release energy from sugar molecules that come from the food you eat. But how do sugar molecules get to your cells? Your digestive system helps to break down foods into sugars and other nutrient molecules that your body can use. A **nutrient** is a substance that you get from food and that your body needs to carry out processes, such as contracting muscles. Through a process called **absorption,** nutrients move from the digestive system into the bloodstream. The circulatory system then delivers the nutrients to all the cells in your body. In this way, your digestive system and circulatory system work together to get food to your cells.

Moving Wastes

The excretory system eliminates wastes from your body. Your respiratory, circulatory, and digestive systems all have roles in the excretory system. You already read that carbon dioxide passes from the circulatory system into the respiratory system and leaves the body when you exhale. Other cellular wastes also pass into the blood. These wastes are filtered out of the blood by the kidneys. This process produces urine, which then carries the wastes out of your body. Materials that are not used by the digestive system leave the body as solid waste.

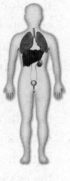

Vocabulary Suffixes The names of three body systems contain the suffix *-atory* or *-etory*, which both mean "of, or pertaining to." Circle the name of each of these systems once in the text on this page. Then underline sentences that describe what these systems do.

Lab zone® Do the Quick Lab *Working Together, Act I.*

🔑 Assess Your Understanding

1a. List Name four body systems that are involved in getting oxygen to your cells.

_____

_____

b. Explain How is absorption an important function of the digestive system?

_____

_____

_____

c. Draw Conclusions How does the circulatory system help other systems function?

_____

_____

_____

_____

_____

_____

got it?

○ **I get it!** Now I know that materials are moved within my body by the _____

_____

○ **I need extra help with** _____

Go to **MY SCIENCE** ⓢ **COACH** *online for help with this subject.*

Which Systems Control Body Functions?

To function properly, each part of your body must be able to communicate with other parts of your body. For example, if you hear a phone ring, that message must be sent to your brain. Your brain then directs your muscles to move your bones so you can answer the phone. These actions are controlled by the nervous system, which is made up of the brain, spinal cord, and nerves. In your nervous system, information travels through nerve cells.

Other messages are sent by chemical signals that are produced by the endocrine system. The endocrine system is made up of organs called **glands** that release chemical signals directly into the bloodstream. For example, when you exercise, your endocrine system sends signals that make you perspire, or sweat. As sweat evaporates, it helps you cool down. **The nervous system and the endocrine system work together to control body functions.**

Nervous System Your eyes, ears, skin, nose, and taste buds send information about your environment to your nervous system. Your senses let you react to bright light, hot objects, and freshly baked cookies. A signal in the environment that makes you react is called a **stimulus** (plural *stimuli*). A **response** is what your body does in reaction to a stimulus. Responses are directed by your nervous system but often involve other body systems. For example, your muscular and skeletal systems help you reach for a cookie. And your digestive system releases saliva before the cookie even reaches your mouth.

did you know?

An optical illusion fools your brain about what you see. Are the horizontal lines in the picture below parallel to one another or slanted?

_____

_____

FIGURE 4 ·······························

Stimulus and Response

Have you ever been startled by something unexpected?

✎ **Use the pictures to complete these tasks.**

1. **Sequence** Use numbers 1, 2, and 3 to put the pictures in order.

2. **Explain** Use the terms *stimulus* and *response* to explain what happened.

_____

_____

_____

_____

apply it!

Among the drugs that affect the nervous system, caffeine is one of the most commonly used worldwide. Caffeine is found in coffee, tea, soda, other beverages, and even in chocolate.

1 Explain How does caffeine reach the brain after someone drinks a cup of coffee or tea? In your answer, be sure to identify the systems involved.

_____

_____

_____

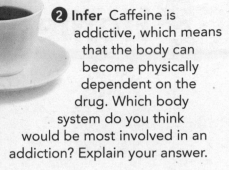

2 Infer Caffeine is addictive, which means that the body can become physically dependent on the drug. Which body system do you think would be most involved in an addiction? Explain your answer.

_____

_____

_____

Endocrine System The chemical signals released by the endocrine system are called **hormones.** Hormones are transported through your body by the circulatory system. These chemicals affect many body processes. For example, one hormone interacts with the excretory system and the circulatory system to control the amount of water in the bloodstream. Another hormone interacts with the digestive system and the circulatory system to control the amount of sugar in the bloodstream. Hormones also affect the reproductive systems of both males and females.

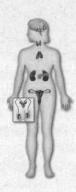

Lab zone Do the Quick Lab *Working Together, Act II.*

🔑 Assess Your Understanding

2a. Compare and Contrast How are the nervous system and the endocrine system different?

_____

_____

_____

_____

b. Apply Concepts Describe an example of a stimulus and response that involves your sense of hearing.

_____

_____

_____

_____

got it? ....

○ **I get it!** Now I know that the _____ system and _____ system work together to _____

○ **I need extra help with** _____

Go to **my science** 🅢 **coach** online for help with this subject.

Homeostasis

UNLOCK THE BIG ?

🔑 **How Does Your Body Stay in Balance?**

my planeT DiaRY

SCIENCE STATS

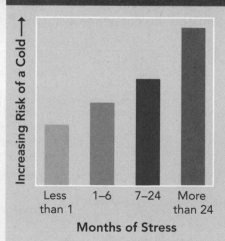

Worried Sick—Not Just an Expression

Starting in the 1980s, scientists began to gather evidence that stress can affect the immune system. For example, the graph below shows the relationship between the length of time a person is stressed and the risk of catching a cold when exposed to a virus. Today, scientists know that high levels of stress and long periods of stress can increase a person's risk for many diseases. Therefore, managing stress is an important part of a healthy lifestyle. Many activities, including hanging out with friends, getting enough sleep, and exercising moderately, can help lower stress levels.

Read Graphs Use the graph to answer the questions.

1. Summarize the information given in the graph.

_____

_____

_____

_____

2. What do you do to manage stress?

_____

_____

_____

▸ PLANET DIARY Go to **Planet Diary** to learn more about homeostasis.

Stress and Catching a Cold

Increasing Risk of a Cold →

Less than 1 | 1–6 | 7–24 | More than 24

Months of Stress

Lab® zone Do the Inquiry Warm-Up
Out of Balance.

Vocabulary
- homeostasis
- stress

Skills
- Reading: Relate Cause and Effect
- Inquiry: Communicate

How Does Your Body Stay in Balance?

It may be summer or winter. You may be indoors or outdoors. You may be running or sitting still. Regardless, your internal body temperature is almost exactly 37°C. The conditions outside your body may change. But the conditions inside your body stay stable, or steady. Most of these conditions, including the chemical makeup of your cells, their water content, and your body temperature, stay about the same.

Homeostasis The condition in which an organism's internal environment is kept stable in spite of changes in the outside environment is called **homeostasis.** Keeping this balance is necessary for an organism to function properly and survive. **All of your body systems working together maintain homeostasis and keep the body in balance.**

FIGURE 1 ....

Keeping Warm in the Cold
The clothes on this snowboarder help keep him warm. But his body is working hard, too. His nervous, circulatory, and muscular systems work together, keeping his body warm.

✎ **Describe** Think of a time when you were really hot or really cold. Describe the changes you felt as your body adjusted to that condition.

_____

_____

_____

_____

_____

_____

_____

_____

Maintaining Homeostasis You experience homeostasis in action when you shiver, sweat, or feel hungry, full, or thirsty. Your nervous and endocrine systems control these responses. Other systems, including the digestive, respiratory, circulatory, and muscular systems, also play roles in your body's responses.

Regulating Temperature When you are cold, your nervous system signals your muscles to make you shiver. Shivering produces heat that helps keep you warm. As explained in the diagram below, when you warm up, shivering stops. When you are too warm, your endocrine system releases hormones that make you perspire. As the sweat evaporates, your body cools. The circulatory system and skin also help regulate temperature. Changes in the amount of blood flow in the skin can help prevent heat loss or carry heat away. In this way, your body temperature stays steady.

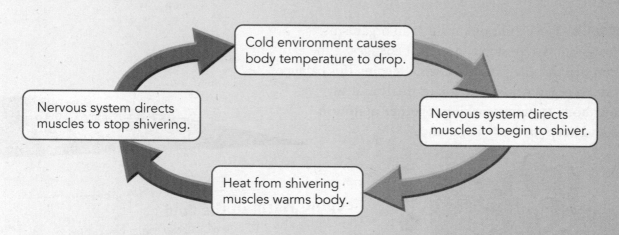

Cold environment causes body temperature to drop.

Nervous system directs muscles to begin to shiver.

Heat from shivering muscles warms body.

Nervous system directs muscles to stop shivering.

Meeting Energy Needs If your body needs more energy, hormones from the endocrine system signal the nervous system to make you feel hungry. After you eat, other hormones tell your brain to make you feel full. Other body systems are also involved. For example, your muscular system helps move food through your digestive system. Your respiratory system takes in the oxygen that is used in cells to release energy from food.

FIGURE 2 ·······························
Hungry or Not?
Signals between your nervous system and your digestive system control your feelings of hunger.

✎ **Sequence Fill in the missing steps in the cycle diagram.**

I feel hungry.

Maintaining Water Balance Life depends on water. All the chemical reactions that keep you alive happen within the watery environment of your cells. If your body needs more water, you feel thirsty. The water you drink passes from your digestive system into your circulatory system. Excess water leaves your body through your excretory system when you exhale, sweat, and urinate.

Keeping Your Balance You know that you hear with your ears. But did you know your ears also help you keep your balance? Structures in your inner ear sense the position of your head. They send this information to your brain, which interprets the signals. If your brain senses that you are losing your balance, it sends messages to your muscles to move in ways that help you stay steady, as in **Figure 3**.

Relate Cause and Effect
Complete the cause-and-effect table below to help you organize what you have learned about homeostasis.

Cause	Effect
_____	Shivers
Body gets overheated.	_____
Body needs more energy.	_____
_____	Thirst

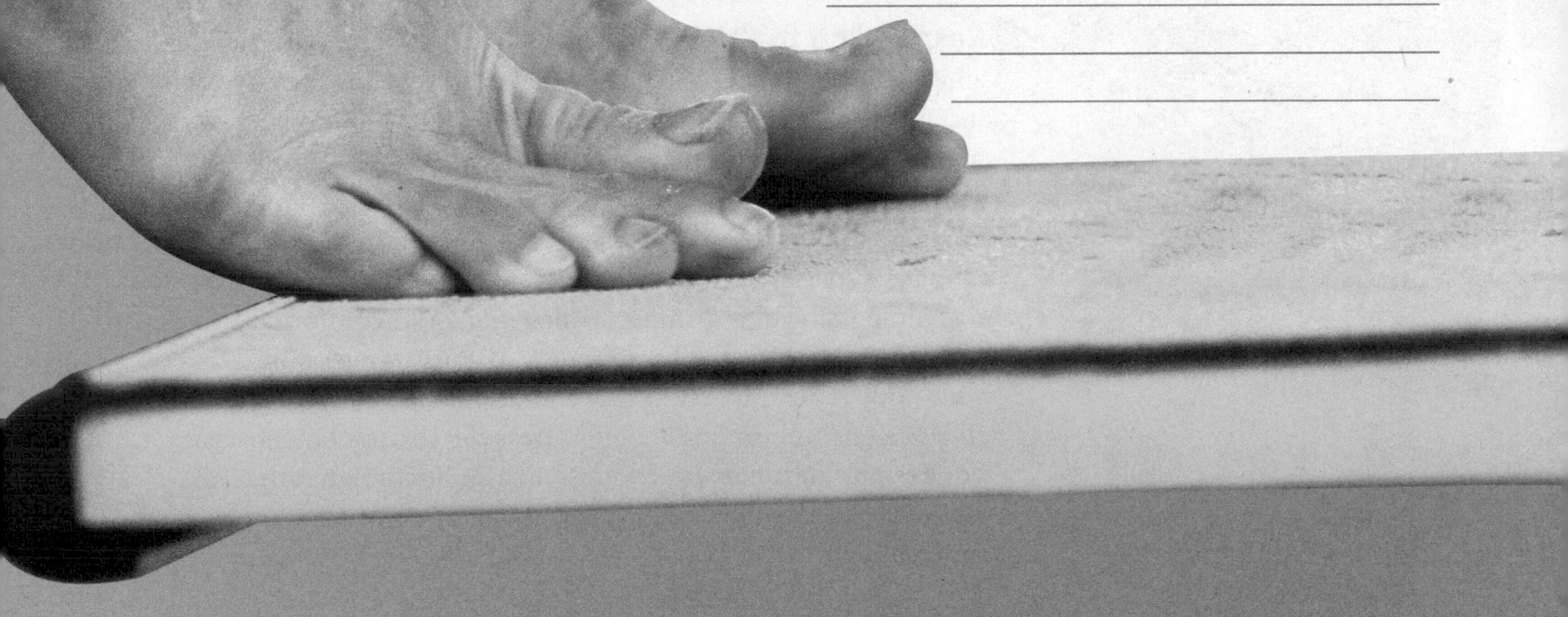

FIGURE 3

Balancing Act
Signals from this diver's ears to her brain lead to movements that help her balance on the edge of the diving board.

✎ **Name** What systems of the diver's body play a role in keeping her balanced on her toes?

_____

_____

_____

425

FIGURE 4 ··

Stressed Out?

Different people view stress differently.

✎ **Use the photos to complete these tasks.**

1. **Interpret Photos** Using numbers 1–4, rank these activities, in your opinion, from least stressful (1) to most stressful (4).

2. **CHALLENGE** Which activity could be very stressful or not stressful at all? Explain.

_____

_____

_____

_____

Responding to Stress Imagine you are out for a walk. Suddenly, a big, snarling dog jumps in front of you! Your endocrine system instantly pumps the hormone adrenaline into your bloodstream, making your heart beat faster and your breathing rate increase. These changes prepare your body for whatever may happen next. You may feel these same changes when you start a race or get ready to make a speech in class. In general, **stress** is the reaction of your body to possibly threatening, challenging, or uncomfortable events.

Some stress is normal and healthy. If stress is over quickly, your body returns to a healthier condition. However, too much stress can be unhealthy. Ongoing stress can disrupt homeostasis. For example, it can disrupt your body's ability to fight disease. It also can cause depression, headaches, digestion problems, heart problems, and other health issues. Managing stress is an important part of a healthy lifestyle.

apply *it!*

△ **Communicate** A soccer game, a music recital, a class presentation, and many other events can cause stress. Think of an event from your life when you felt stress. Describe how your body responded during the event, and then after the event or when the stress went away.

_____

_____

_____

_____

_____

_____

_____

_____

_____

_____

_____

_____

_____

_____

_____

Fighting Disease When your body systems are in balance, you are healthy. However, bacteria and viruses that cause disease can disrupt homeostasis and make you sick. Think about the last time you had a cold or influenza (the flu). You may have had a fever and less energy. You also may have slept more than usual. Over a few days, your immune system probably fought off the disease.

The immune system includes specialized cells that can attack and destroy viruses. When you are sick, these cells temporarily increase in number. Fighting infection sometimes causes your body temperature to go up. It also uses extra energy. As you get well, your fever goes away and your energy comes back. If you are sick for more than a few days, you may need medical attention to help your body fight the infection and become healthy again.

Systems in Action

How does your body work?

FIGURE 5 ....

> REAL-WORLD INQUIRY The body systems of this runner work together as she pushes herself to excel.

✎ **Apply Concepts** Read the descriptions of functions happening in the runner's body. Then identify the main systems involved.

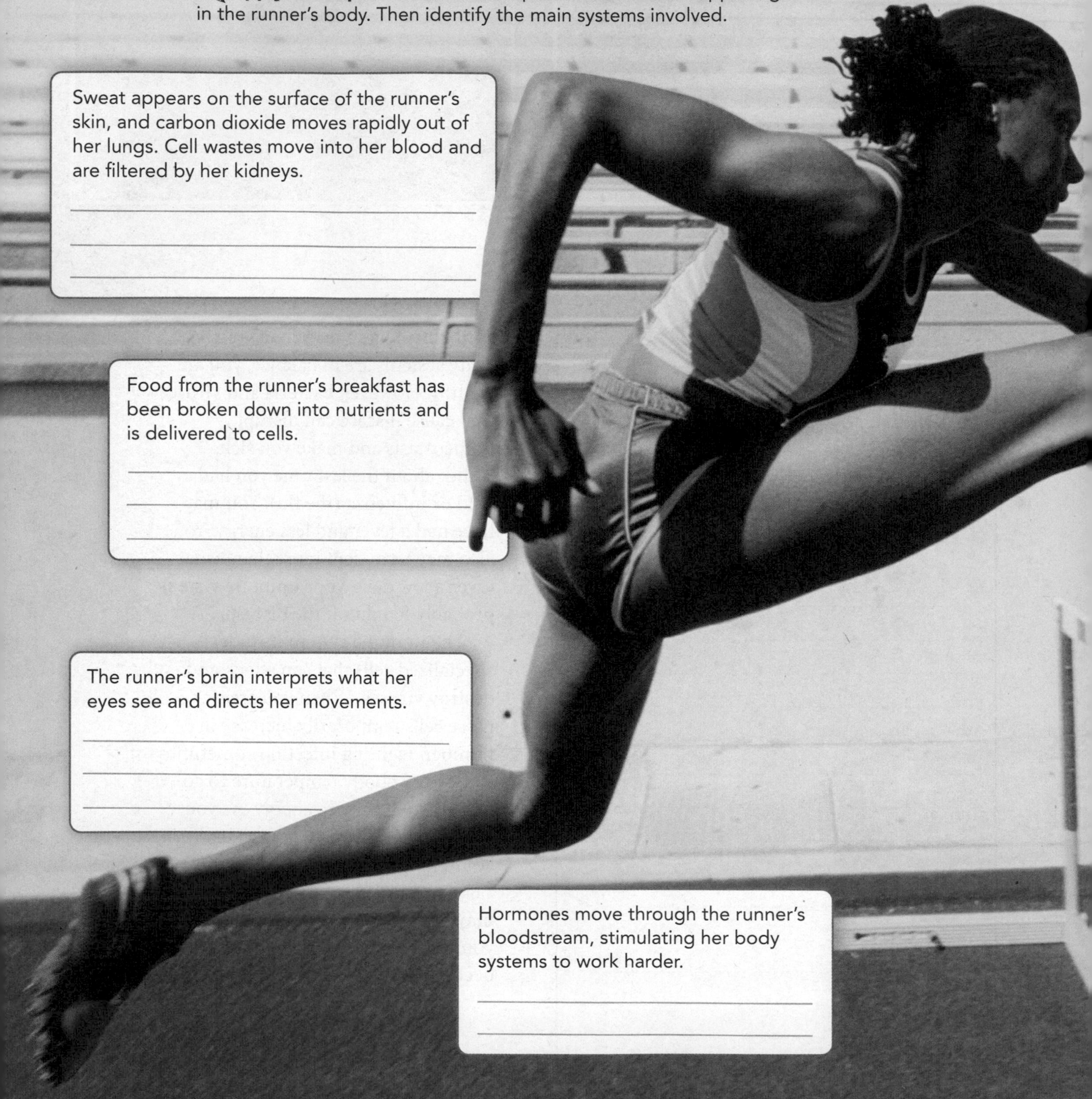

Sweat appears on the surface of the runner's skin, and carbon dioxide moves rapidly out of her lungs. Cell wastes move into her blood and are filtered by her kidneys.

_____
_____
_____

Food from the runner's breakfast has been broken down into nutrients and is delivered to cells.

_____
_____
_____

The runner's brain interprets what her eyes see and directs her movements.

_____
_____
_____

Hormones move through the runner's bloodstream, stimulating her body systems to work harder.

_____
_____

The runner's breathing rate and heart rate increase, supplying more oxygen to her muscle cells.

_____

_____

_____

The runner's legs lift her off the ground and over the hurdle.

_____

_____

_____

🔑 Assess Your Understanding

1a. Define What is homeostasis?

_____

_____

_____

_____

_____

_____

b. List Give four examples of conditions in your body that are related to maintaining homeostasis.

_____

_____

_____

c. Relate Cause and Effect Give an example of how stress can affect homeostasis.

_____

_____

_____

_____

_____

d. ANSWER THE BIG ❓ How does your body work? Use what you have learned about how your body systems function to write your answer.

_____

_____

_____

_____

_____

got it? •

○ **I get it!** Now I know that maintaining homeostasis depends on _____

_____

○ **I need extra help with** _____

Go to MY SCIENCE ⓢ COACH online for help with this subject.

The Skeletal System

UNLOCK THE BIG Q?

🔑 **What Does the Skeleton Do?**

🔑 **What Role Do Joints Play?**

🔑 **What Are the Characteristics of Bones?**

my planeT DiaRY

Know Your Bones!

Here are some fascinating facts you may not know about your bones.

- You have the same number of bones in your neck as a giraffe. However, a single bone in the neck of a giraffe can be as long as 25 centimeters.

- You have 27 bones in each hand and 26 bones in each foot. They account for 106 of the 206 bones in your body.

- You do not have a funny bone. You have a sensitive spot on your elbow where a nerve passes close to the skin. If you hit this spot, the area feels funny.

- No one is truly "double-jointed." People who are able to twist in weird directions have very flexible joints.

FUN FACTS

Communicate Discuss the question with a partner. Then write your answer below.

Why do you think it is helpful for your hand to have 27 bones?

_____

_____

_____

_____

_____

_____

_____

▶ **PLANET DIARY** Go to **Planet Diary** to learn more about bones.

Lab zone® Do the Inquiry Warm-Up *Hard as a Rock?*

Vocabulary
- skeleton • vertebrae • joint • ligament
- compact bone • spongy bone • marrow
- cartilage • osteoporosis

Skills
- ⟳ Reading: Summarize
- △ Inquiry: Classify

What Does the Skeleton Do?

If you have ever visited a construction site, you have seen workers assemble steel pieces into a rigid frame for a building. Once the building is finished, this framework is invisible.

Like a building, you have an inner framework. Your framework, or **skeleton,** is made up of all the bones in your body. Just as a building would fall without its frame, you would collapse without your skeleton. 🔑 **Your skeleton has five major functions. It provides shape and support, enables you to move, and protects your organs. It also produces blood cells and stores minerals and other materials until your body needs them.**

Shape and Support Your skeleton shapes and supports your body. It is made up of about 206 bones of different shapes and sizes. Your backbone, or vertebral column, is the center of your skeleton. A total of 26 small bones, or **vertebrae** (VUR tuh bray) (singular *vertebra*), make up your backbone. **Figure 1** shows how vertebrae connect to form the backbone or vertebral column.

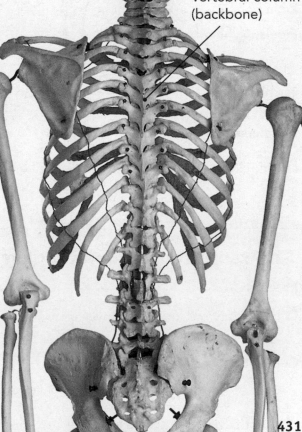

Vertebral column (backbone)

FIGURE 1 ···

The Vertebral Column
Just like a flexible necklace of beads, your vertebrae move against each other, allowing you to bend and twist.

✎ **Use the photo to answer the questions about your vertebrae.**

1. **Interpret Photos** Which body parts does the vertebral column support?

_____

_____

_____

2. CHALLENGE What is the advantage of having large vertebrae at the base of the vertebral column?

_____

_____

_____

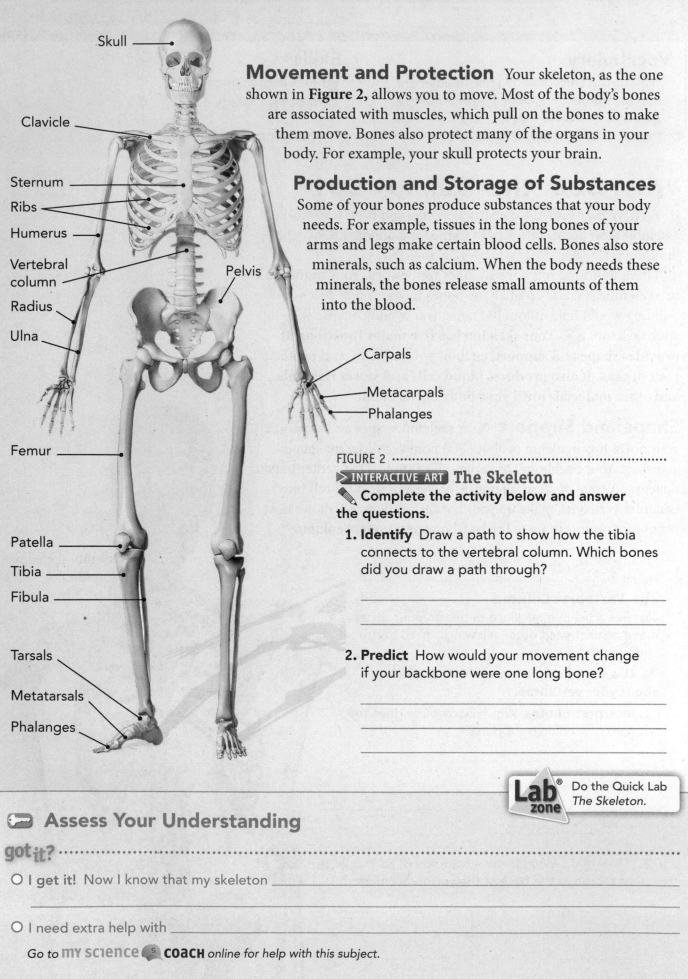

Skull

Clavicle

Sternum

Ribs

Humerus

Vertebral column

Radius

Ulna

Pelvis

Carpals

Metacarpals

Phalanges

Femur

Patella

Tibia

Fibula

Tarsals

Metatarsals

Phalanges

Movement and Protection

Your skeleton, as the one shown in **Figure 2,** allows you to move. Most of the body's bones are associated with muscles, which pull on the bones to make them move. Bones also protect many of the organs in your body. For example, your skull protects your brain.

Production and Storage of Substances

Some of your bones produce substances that your body needs. For example, tissues in the long bones of your arms and legs make certain blood cells. Bones also store minerals, such as calcium. When the body needs these minerals, the bones release small amounts of them into the blood.

FIGURE 2 ··

> INTERACTIVE ART The Skeleton

✎ **Complete the activity below and answer the questions.**

1. **Identify** Draw a path to show how the tibia connects to the vertebral column. Which bones did you draw a path through?

   _____

   _____

2. **Predict** How would your movement change if your backbone were one long bone?

   _____

   _____

   _____

Lab® Do the Quick Lab
zone *The Skeleton.*

⊂⊃ Assess Your Understanding

got it? ···

○ **I get it!** Now I know that my skeleton _____

_____

○ **I need extra help with** _____

Go to MY SCIENCE ⓢ COACH *online for help with this subject.*

What Role Do Joints Play?

If your leg had only one long bone, how would you get out of bed? Luckily, your leg has many bones so you can move it easily. A **joint** is a place where two bones come together. 🔑 **Joints allow bones to move in different ways.** You have two kinds of joints: immovable and movable.

Immovable Joints Immovable joints connect bones but allow little or no movement. The bones of the skull are held together by immovable joints.

Movable Joints Most joints are movable. They allow the body to make many different movements such as those shown in **Figure 3.** The bones in movable joints are held together by **ligaments,** which are made of strong connective tissue.

Infer What would happen if your skull bones had movable joints?

_____

_____

_____

_____

FIGURE 3 ·····················

▷ INTERACTIVE ART **Movable Joints**

Movable joints allow you to move in different ways.

✏️ **Classify Write the name of another joint of each type on the line in each box.**

Hinge Joint

This joint allows forward or backward motion. Your knee is a hinge joint that allows you to bend and straighten your leg.

_____

Ball-and-Socket Joint

This joint allows the greatest range of motion. Your hip has a ball-and-socket joint that allows you to swing your leg in a circle.

_____

Gliding Joint

This joint allows one bone to slide over another. Your wrist has a gliding joint that allows it to bend and flex.

_____

Pivot Joint

This joint allows one bone to rotate around another bone. You use this joint to turn your arm at your elbow side-to-side.

_____

apply it!

Without movable joints, your body would be as stiff as a board.

❶ Observe Perform each activity below. Write the type of joint you use.

Move your arm from the shoulder in a circle. _____

Move your wrist to wave. _____

Turn your head from side to side. _____

❷ Classify In the chart, write the name of the type of joint each object has.

❸ Apply Concepts What type of joint do you have in your toes? Explain your answer.

Object	Type of Joint
Book	_____
Sliding Door	_____
Steering Wheel	_____

_____

_____

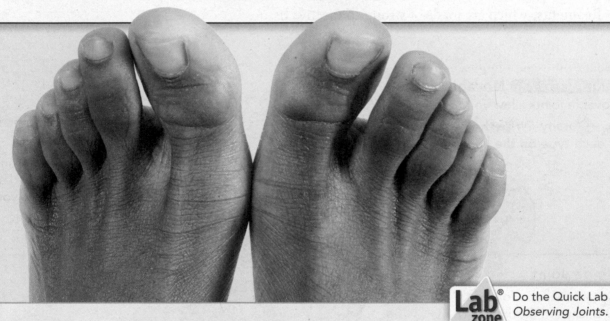

Lab zone® Do the Quick Lab *Observing Joints.*

🔑 Assess Your Understanding

1a. Explain Why does your body need both immovable and movable joints?

_____

_____

_____

_____

b. Relate Cause and Effect How would your legs move if your knees were ball-and-socket joints?

_____

_____

_____

_____

got it?

○ **I get it!** Now I know that joints _____

_____

○ I need extra help with _____

Go to **MY SCIENCE** ⑤ **COACH** online for help with this subject.

What Are the Characteristics of Bones?

The word *skeleton* comes from the Greek words meaning "a dried body." This suggests that a skeleton is dead, but bones are not dead at all. **Bones are complex living structures that grow, develop, and repair themselves. Bones are also strong and lightweight.**

Bones are made up of bone tissue, blood vessels, and nerves. A thin, tough outer membrane covers all of a typical bone except the ends. Beneath the membrane is a thick layer of **compact bone,** which is hard and dense but not solid. Compact bone contains minerals that give bones strength. Small canals in the compact bone carry blood vessels and nerves from the bone's surface to its living cells.

Long bones, such as the femur in **Figure 4,** have a layer of spongy bone at the ends and under the compact bone. The small spaces within **spongy bone** make it lightweight but still strong. Bone also has two types of soft connective tissue called **marrow.** Red bone marrow fills the spaces in some of your spongy bone. It produces most of your blood cells. Yellow bone marrow is found in a space in the middle of the bone. It stores fat.

FIGURE 4 ·······················

Bone Structure

Many tissues make up the femur, the body's longest bone.

✎ **Relate Text and Visuals** Write notes to describe each part of the bone and what it does.

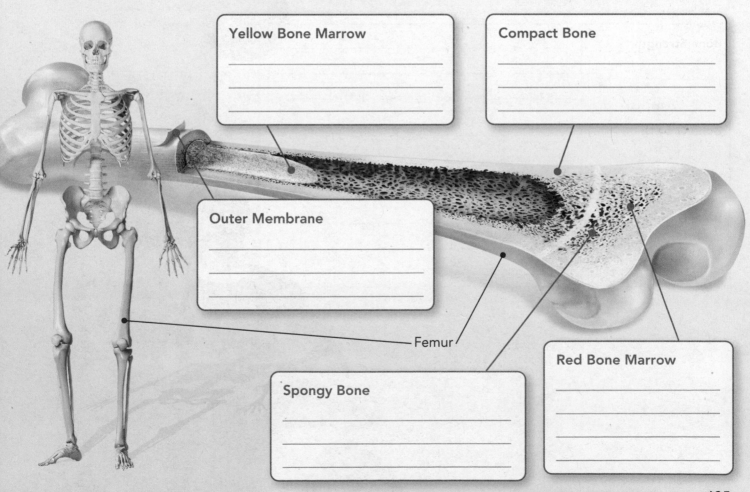

Yellow Bone Marrow
_____
_____
_____

Compact Bone
_____
_____
_____

Outer Membrane
_____
_____
_____

Femur

Spongy Bone
_____
_____
_____

Red Bone Marrow
_____
_____
_____

435

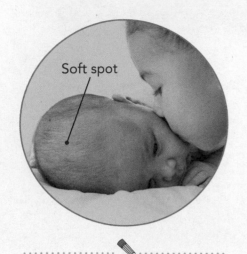

Soft spot

Infer Infants are born with soft spots in their skull made out of cartilage. What do you think happens to softs spot over time?

_____

_____

⟳ Summarize Write a summary about the characteristics of bones.

Bone Strength	
Bone Growth	
Bone Development	

Bone Strength Bone is both strong and lightweight. Bones can absorb more force without breaking than concrete or granite rock can. Yet bones weigh much less than those materials. In fact, only about 20 percent of an average adult's body weight is bone. Bone feels as hard as a rock because it is made of tightly packed minerals—mainly phosphorus and calcium.

Bone Growth Because bones are alive, they form new bone tissue as you grow. Your bones are growing longer now, making you taller. Even after you are fully grown, bone tissue continues to form. For example, every time you play soccer or basketball, some of your bones absorb the force of your weight. They respond by making new bone tissue. New bone tissue also forms when a bone breaks.

Bone Development When you were born, most of your bones were cartilage. **Cartilage** is a strong connective tissue that is more flexible than bone. As you grew, most of that cartilage was replaced with bone. Some cartilage still protects the ends of your bones. You also have cartilage in your ears and at the tip of your nose.

Healthy Bones

A combination of a balanced diet and regular exercise are important for healthy bones. A balanced diet includes foods that contain enough calcium and phosphorus to keep your bones strong while they are growing. You should eat dairy products; meats; whole grains; and green, leafy vegetables.

Exercise helps build and maintain strong bones. During activities such as running and dancing, your bones support the weight of your entire body. These weight-bearing activities help your bones grow stronger. However, to prevent injury, always wear appropriate safety equipment when exercising.

As you age, your bones start to lose some minerals. This mineral loss can lead to **osteoporosis** (ahs tee oh puh ROH sis), a condition in which bones become weak and break easily. You can see how osteoporosis causes the spaces in a bone to become larger, reducing its density and strength in **Figure 5.**

FIGURE 5 ·······················
Osteoporosis
Regular exercise and a diet rich in calcium with vitamin D can help prevent osteoporosis later in life.

✎ **Compare and Contrast** The photos show two bones. Label the healthy bone and the bone with osteoporosis. Then explain your choices.

_____
_____
_____
_____

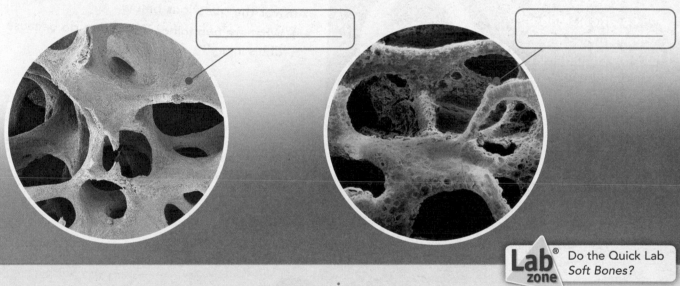

Lab zone® Do the Quick Lab
Soft Bones?

🔑 Assess Your Understanding

2a. Explain How do eating a balanced diet and exercising regularly help your bones?

_____
_____
_____

b. Apply Concepts How do you know that bone is living tissue?

_____
_____
_____
_____

got it?

○ **I get it!** Now I know that my bones are _____

_____
_____
_____
_____
_____
_____

○ **I need extra help with** _____

Go to **MY SCIENCE** 💬 **COACH** *online for help with this subject.*

The Muscular System

🔑 **What Muscles Are in Your Body?**

🔑 **How Do Skeletal Muscles Work?**

UNLOCK THE BIG Q?

MY PLANET DiARY

BLOG

Posted by: Will

Location: Moore, Oklahoma

I hurt my shoulder while participating in tackling drills during football practice. The doctor said I had a deep muscle contusion, which is a bruise deep in a muscle. I was unable to lift my right arm for more than a week because of the injury. I had to take three tablets of ibuprofen every day for two weeks because it helped the swelling go down. I missed playing in only one game, and the pain eventually went away.

Answer the questions below.

1. What are two things Will had to do because of his injury?

_____

_____

_____

2. What can you do to avoid being injured when playing sports?

_____

_____

_____

_____

▷ **PLANET DIARY** Go to **Planet Diary** to learn more about muscles.

Lab zone Do the Inquiry Warm-Up *How Do Muscles Work?*

Vocabulary

- involuntary muscle
- voluntary muscle
- skeletal muscle
- tendon
- smooth muscle
- cardiac muscle
- striated muscle

Skills

↻ Reading: Compare and Contrast

△ Inquiry: Infer

What Muscles Are in Your Body?

Try to sit without moving any muscles. Can you do it? First, you probably need to breathe, so your chest expands to let air in. Then you swallow. Breathing and swallowing involve muscles, so it is impossible to sit still without any muscle movement.

Involuntary and Voluntary Muscles Some body movements, such as smiling, are easy to control. Other movements, such as breathing, are impossible to control completely. That is because some of your muscles are not under your conscious control. Those muscles are **involuntary muscles.** Involuntary muscles are responsible for other activities such as digesting food. The muscles under your conscious control are **voluntary muscles.** Smiling, writing, and getting out of your seat when the bell rings are all actions controlled by voluntary muscles.

FIGURE 1 ·····················

Muscle Use

Some muscles are voluntary and others are involuntary.

✎ **Relate Text and Visuals**
Write how the person in each frame is using involuntary and voluntary muscles.

	Frame 1	Frame 2	Frame 3
Involuntary			
Voluntary			

Types of Muscle Tissue 🔑 Your body has skeletal, smooth, and cardiac muscle tissues. Some of these muscle tissues are involuntary, and some are voluntary.

Skeletal muscles provide the force that moves your bones. A strong connective tissue called a **tendon** attaches the muscle to a bone. Because you have conscious control of skeletal muscles, they are classified as voluntary muscles. In contrast, the inside of many internal body organs, such as the stomach and blood vessels, contain **smooth muscle** tissue. These are involuntary muscles. They work to control certain movements inside your body, such as moving food through your digestive system. The tissue called **cardiac muscle** is found only in your heart. Like smooth muscle, cardiac muscle is involuntary. Look at **Figure 2.**

FIGURE 2 ··

Muscle Tissue

You have three types of muscle tissue: skeletal, smooth, and cardiac.

✎ **Classify** In the table, identify the type of muscle tissue in each body structure.

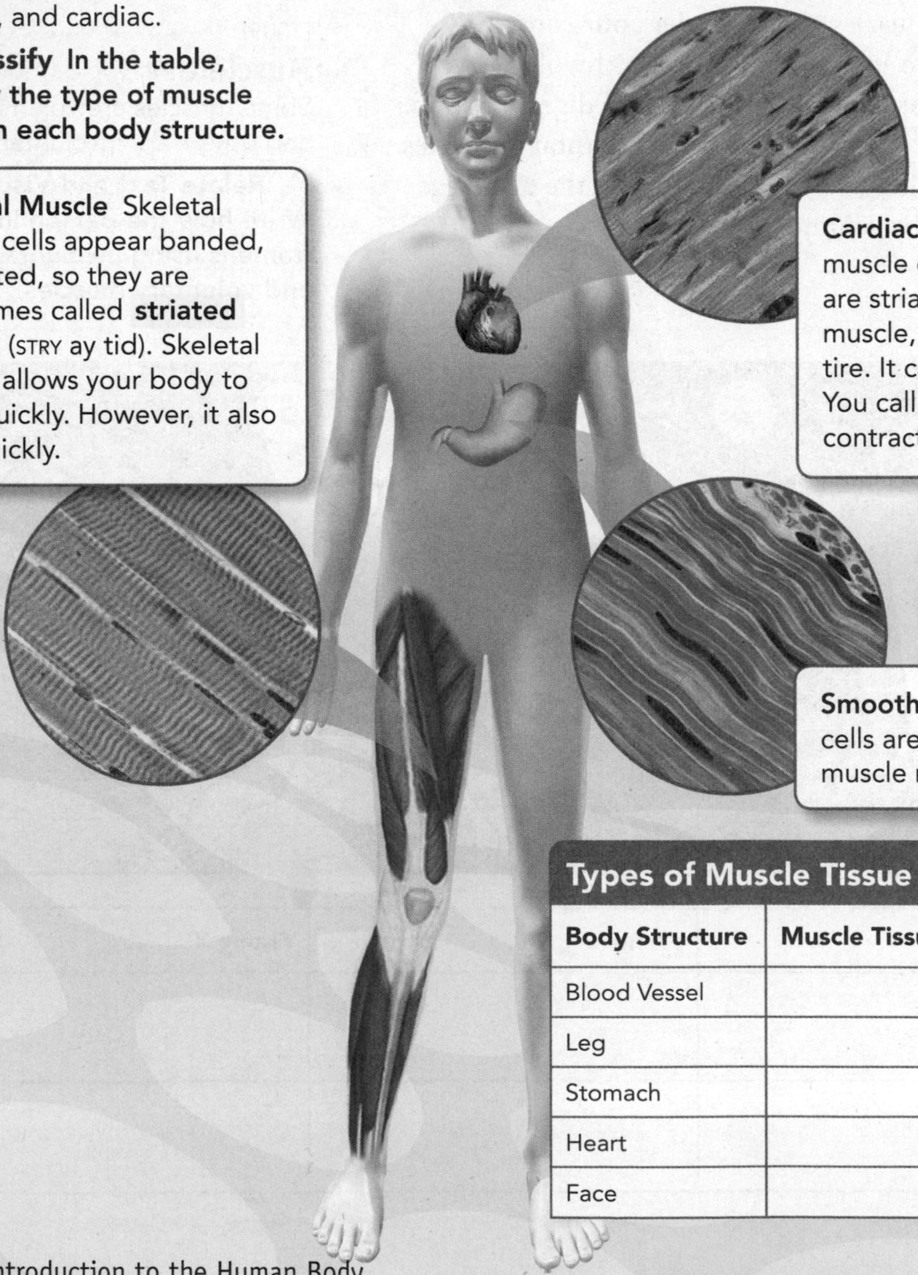

Skeletal Muscle Skeletal muscle cells appear banded, or striated, so they are sometimes called **striated muscle** (STRY ay tid). Skeletal muscle allows your body to react quickly. However, it also tires quickly.

Cardiac Muscle Like skeletal muscle cells, cardiac muscle cells are striated. But unlike skeletal muscle, cardiac muscle does not tire. It can contract repeatedly. You call those repeated contractions heartbeats.

Smooth Muscle Smooth muscle cells are not striated. This type of muscle reacts and tires slowly.

Types of Muscle Tissue

Body Structure	Muscle Tissue
Blood Vessel	
Leg	
Stomach	
Heart	
Face	

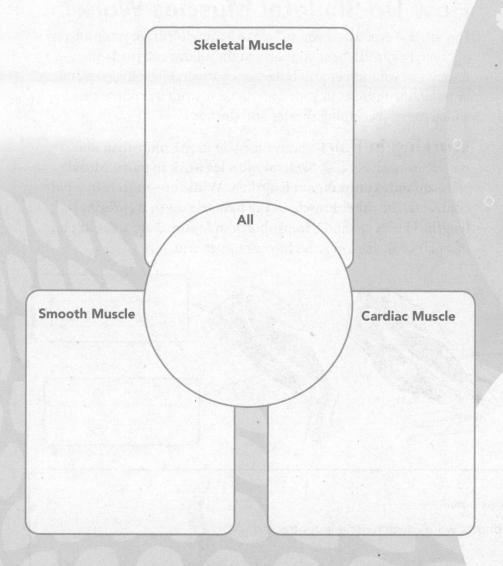

Skeletal Muscle

All

Smooth Muscle

Cardiac Muscle

did you know?

Why do you shiver when you get chilled? You shiver when many of your skeletal muscles contract quickly again and again. When your muscles contract, they produce extra heat. So, by shivering, your body produces heat that warms you.

✐ **Compare and Contrast** In the graphic organizer, write how all three muscle tissues are alike and how each type is different.

Lab zone Do the Quick Lab *Observing Muscle Tissue.*

🔑 Assess Your Understanding

1a. Define What is the difference between voluntary and involuntary muscles?

_____

_____

_____

b. △**Infer** Why is it important that cardiac muscle tissue does not tire?

_____

_____

_____

got it? ....

○ **I get it!** Now I know that the muscles in my body are _____

_____

○ **I need extra help with** _____

Go to **MY SCIENCE COACH** online for help with this subject.

How Do Skeletal Muscles Work?

Has anyone ever asked you to "make a muscle"? If so, you probably tightened your fist, bent your arm at the elbow, and made the muscles in your upper arm bulge, or contract. Like other skeletal muscles, the muscles in your arm do their work by contracting, which means becoming shorter and thicker.

Working in Pairs Each time you move, more than one muscle is involved.  **Skeletal muscles work in pairs. Muscle cells can only contract, not lengthen. While one muscle in a pair contracts, the other muscle in the pair relaxes to its original length.** The biceps and triceps shown in **Figure 3** are an example of a pair of sketetal muscles in your upper arm.

FIGURE 3 ....

> **ART IN MOTION** Muscle Pairs
To bend your arm at the elbow, the biceps contracts while the triceps relaxes.

✎ **Interpret Diagrams** Tell what happens to each muscle as you straighten your arm.

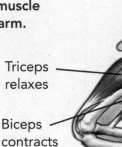

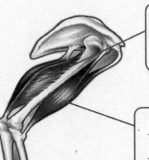

Triceps relaxes

Biceps contracts

apply it!

This girl's biceps and triceps work as a pair.

❶ **Apply Concepts** Below each photo, write which muscle is contracted.

_____   _____

❷ ⚠ **Infer** What might happen if the biceps could not contract?

_____

442 Introduction to the Human Body

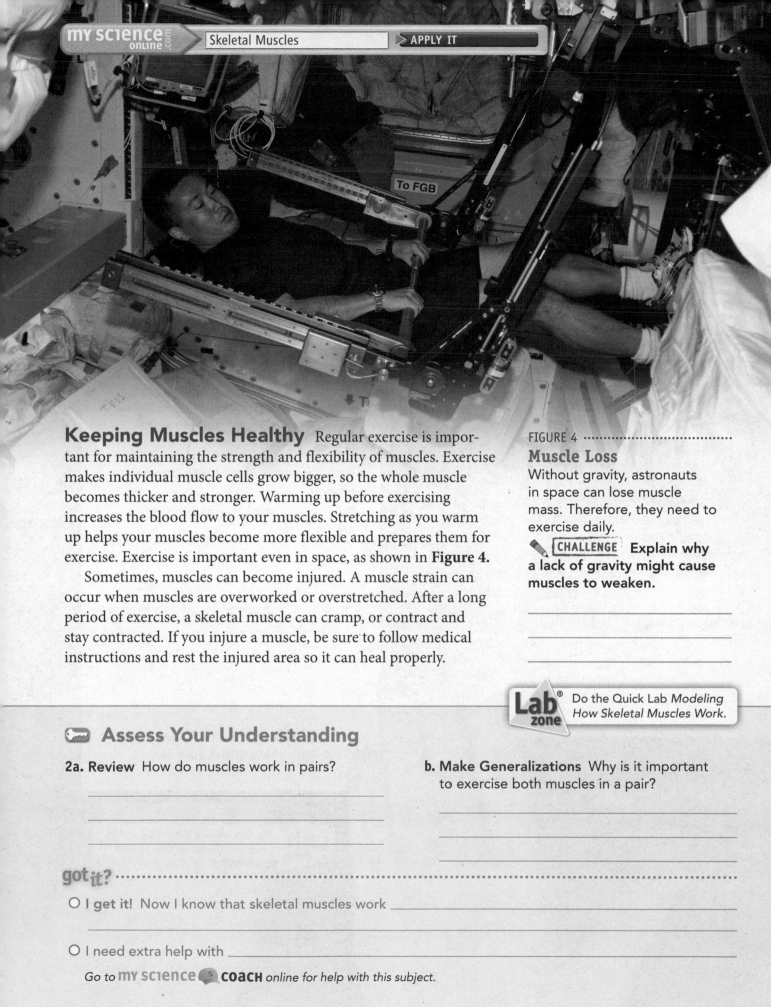

Keeping Muscles Healthy

Regular exercise is important for maintaining the strength and flexibility of muscles. Exercise makes individual muscle cells grow bigger, so the whole muscle becomes thicker and stronger. Warming up before exercising increases the blood flow to your muscles. Stretching as you warm up helps your muscles become more flexible and prepares them for exercise. Exercise is important even in space, as shown in **Figure 4.**

Sometimes, muscles can become injured. A muscle strain can occur when muscles are overworked or overstretched. After a long period of exercise, a skeletal muscle can cramp, or contract and stay contracted. If you injure a muscle, be sure to follow medical instructions and rest the injured area so it can heal properly.

FIGURE 4 ·······························
Muscle Loss
Without gravity, astronauts in space can lose muscle mass. Therefore, they need to exercise daily.

✎ CHALLENGE **Explain why a lack of gravity might cause muscles to weaken.**

_____

_____

_____

Lab® zone | Do the Quick Lab *Modeling How Skeletal Muscles Work.*

🗝 Assess Your Understanding

2a. Review How do muscles work in pairs?

_____

_____

_____

b. Make Generalizations Why is it important to exercise both muscles in a pair?

_____

_____

_____

got it? ·······························

○ **I get it!** Now I know that skeletal muscles work _____

_____

○ I need extra help with _____

Go to **my science** ⓢ **coach** *online for help with this subject.*

UNLOCK THE BIG Q?

🔑 **What Are the Functions and Structures of the Skin?**

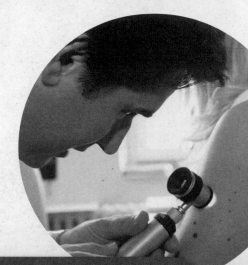

CAREER

my planet diary

Would You Like to Be a Skin Doctor?

Did you know that there is a special type of doctor who studies and treats skin? This type of doctor, a dermatologist, specializes in caring for skin, hair, and nails. Dermatologists diagnose and treat a variety of skin problems ranging from acne to psoriasis to dangerous cancers.

To become a dermatologist, you need a lot of education. You may spend about ten years in schooling and training after you graduate high school. Then you must pass a certification test. Although becoming a dermatologist is not easy, it can be a rewarding career!

Communicate Discuss the question with a partner. Then write down your answer.

Why do you think dermatologists are important?

_____

_____

_____

_____

_____

_____

_____

▶ **PLANET DIARY** Go to **Planet Diary** to learn more about your skin.

Psoriasis

Lab zone Do the Inquiry Warm-Up *What Can You Observe About Skin?*

Vocabulary
- epidermis • melanin • dermis
- pore • follicle

Skills
- Reading: Relate Cause and Effect
- Inquiry: Observe

What Are the Functions and Structures of the Skin?

If an adult's skin were stretched out flat, it would cover an area about the size of a mattress on a twin bed. The skin is part of the integumentary system (in teg yoo MEN tur ee). In addition to the skin, this system includes hair, nails, sweat glands, and oil glands.

Functions of the Skin Your skin helps you in many ways. The skin has two layers that protect the body. Skin helps regulate body temperature, eliminate wastes, gather information about the environment, and produce vitamin D.

Protecting the Body The skin forms a barrier that keeps harmful substances outside the body. It also keeps important substances such as water and other fluids inside the body.

Maintaining Temperature The skin helps the body maintain a steady temperature. When you become too warm, like the runner in **Figure 1,** blood vessels in your skin enlarge. This widening of the vessels allows more blood to flow through them and body heat to escape into the environment. In addition, sweat glands produce perspiration in response to excess heat. As perspiration evaporates from your skin, your skin is cooled. When you get cold, blood vessels in your body contract. This reduces blood flow to the skin and helps your body conserve heat.

FIGURE 1 ....

Amazing Skin

As this runner exercises, his skin helps to cool him off.

✎ **Describe** On the notebook page, describe a time that your skin protected you, maintained your body temperature, or both.

Eliminating Wastes Perspiration contains dissolved waste materials that come from the breakdown of chemical processes. Your skin helps eliminate wastes whenever you perspire.

Gathering Information Nerves in your skin gather information from the environment. They provide information about things such as pressure, temperature, and pain. Pain messages warn you that something in your surroundings can injure you.

Producing Vitamin D Some skin cells produce vitamin D in the presence of sunlight. Vitamin D is important for healthy bones because it helps your body absorb the calcium in your food. Your skin cells need sunlight each day to produce enough vitamin D.

⟳ **Relate Cause and Effect**
Describe the possible effect of not getting enough sunlight each day.

_____

_____

_____

FIGURE 2

Skin at Work
You may not notice that your skin is constantly working.

✏ **Complete the activity and answer the questions below.**

1. **Interpret Photos** Write below each photo the functions that the skin performs.

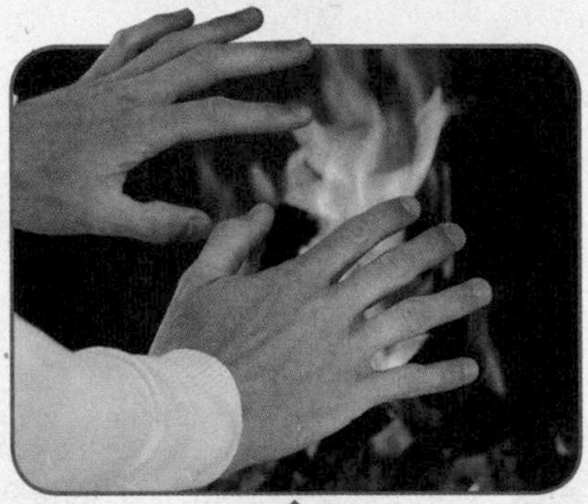

2. ◁**Observe** Press down firmly on your arm with your fingertips. Then lightly pinch yourself. What information did you receive?

_____

_____

_____

3. **CHALLENGE** What might happen if the nerves in your skin did not gather information?

_____

_____

_____

Structures of the Skin The skin has two main layers, as shown in **Figure 3.** Together, these layers—an outer layer and an inner layer—perform all the skin's functions.

The **epidermis** is the outer layer of the skin. Deep in the epidermis, new cells form. As they mature, they move upward until they die. They then become part of the epidermal surface layer. This surface layer helps protect your skin. Cells stay in this layer for about two to three weeks until they are shed. Some cells deep in the epidermis produce **melanin,** a pigment that colors the skin.

The **dermis** is the inner layer of the skin. It is above a layer of fat. This fat layer pads the internal organs and helps keep heat in the body. The dermis includes nerves, blood vessels, sweat glands, hairs, and oil glands. **Pores** are openings that allow sweat to reach the surface. Strands of hair grow within the dermis in **follicles** (FAHL ih kulz). Oil produced in glands around the follicles keeps the surface of the skin moist and the hairs flexible.

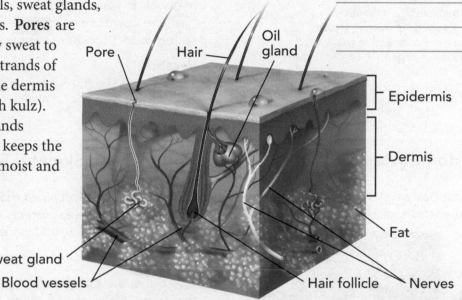

FIGURE 3 ··················

Structures of the Skin
✎ **Relate Text and Visuals** On the lines, write the functions of the epidermis, the nerves, and the sweat gland.

_____
_____
_____
_____
_____
_____
_____

Pore   Hair   Oil gland

Epidermis

Dermis

Fat

Sweat gland
Blood vessels   Hair follicle   Nerves

Lab zone ® Do the Quick Lab *Sweaty Skin.*

🔑 Assess Your Understanding

1a. Describe How does your skin gather information about the environment?

_____
_____
_____

b. Summarize Explain how some structures in the skin protect your body.

_____
_____
_____

got it? ·························

○ **I get it!** Now I know that the skin has two layers that _____
_____
_____

○ **I need extra help with** _____

Go to MY SCIENCE ⓢ COACH *online for help with this subject.*

11 Study Guide

Cells, tissues, and organs make up organ _____ , which constantly interact
to help maintain _____ .

LESSON 1 Body Organization

🔑 The levels of organization in the human body consist of cells, tissues, organs, and organ systems.

Vocabulary
- cell • cell membrane • nucleus
- cytoplasm • tissue • muscle tissue
- nervous tissue • connective tissue
- epithelial tissue • organ • organ system

LESSON 2 System Interactions

🔑 Muscles, bones, and nerves work together to make your body move.
🔑 The circulatory, respiratory, digestive, and excretory systems play key roles in moving materials in your body.
🔑 The nervous system and the endocrine system work together to control body functions.

Vocabulary
- skeleton • skeletal muscle • joint • nutrient
- absorption • gland • stimulus • response
- hormone

LESSON 3 Homeostasis

🔑 All of your body systems working together maintain homeostasis and keep the body in balance.

Vocabulary
- homeostasis
- stress

LESSON 4 The Skeletal System

🔑 Your skeleton provides shape and support, enables you to move, protects your organs, produces blood cells, and stores minerals.

🔑 Joints allow bones to move in different ways.

🔑 Bones are complex living structures that grow, develop, and repair themselves.

Vocabulary
- skeleton • vertebrae • joint • ligament
- compact bone • spongy bone • marrow
- cartilage • osteoporosis

LESSON 5 The Muscular System

🔑 Your body has skeletal, smooth, and cardiac muscle tissues. Some of these muscle tissues are involuntary, and some are voluntary.

🔑 Skeletal muscles work in pairs. Muscle cells only contract, not lengthen. While one muscle in a pair contracts, the other muscle relaxes.

Vocabulary
- involuntary muscle • voluntary muscle
- skeletal muscle • tendon • smooth muscle
- cardiac muscle • striated muscle

LESSON 6 The Skin

🔑 The skin has two layers that protect the body. Skin helps regulate body temperature, eliminate wastes, and produce vitamin D.

Vocabulary
- epidermis
- melanin
- dermis
- pore
- follicle

Review and Assessment

LESSON 1 Body Organization

1. Bone tissue and fat tissue are examples of

   a. muscle tissue.
   b. nervous tissue.
   c. epithelial tissue.
   d. connective tissue.

2. The _____ forms the

   outside border of a cell.

3. **Compare and Contrast** How is a tissue different from an organ? How are they similar?

   _____

   _____

   _____

   _____

   _____

   _____

LESSON 2 System Interactions

4. Signals from the _____

   make skeletal muscles move.

   a. nervous system
   b. digestive system
   c. respiratory system
   d. muscular system

5. _____ occurs when nutrients move from the digestive system into the bloodstream.

6. **Infer** Your knee is called a hinge joint. It is called this because it bends like the hinge on a door. What are some other examples of joints in your body that work like a hinge?

   _____

   _____

   _____

LESSON 3 Homeostasis

7. Under what circumstances would your endocrine system release adrenaline?

   a. sleep
   b. sudden stress
   c. absorption
   d. homeostasis

8. Your body systems work together to maintain internal conditions, or

   _____

9. **Apply Concepts** Imagine you are leading a workshop to help students deal with stress. Explain why it is important to reduce stress.

   _____

   _____

   _____

LESSON 4 The Skeletal System

10. A soft connective tissue found inside bones is

    a. cytoplasm.
    b. marrow.
    c. cartilage.
    d. osteoporosis.

11. The _____ make up your backbone.

12. **Draw Conclusions** Does your body have more immovable or movable joints? Explain.

    _____

    _____

    _____

    _____

    _____

LESSON 5 The Muscular System

13. Muscles that help the skeleton move are

    a. cardiac muscles.   **b.** smooth muscles.

    c. skeletal muscles.   **d.** involuntary muscles.

14. Skeletal muscles must work in pairs because muscle cells can only _____

15. Compare and Contrast Write one similarity and one difference between skeletal muscle and cardiac muscle.

_____

_____

_____

16. Predict What would happen if a tendon in your finger were cut?

_____

_____

LESSON 6 The Skin

17. A pigment that colors the skin is

    a. the dermis.   **b.** the epidermis.

    c. a follicle.   **d.** melanin.

18. Hair grows in _____

19. Make Generalizations What skin layers are affected when a cut on your hand bleeds?

_____

_____

20. **Write About It** You are out running with your friend on a hot day. Your body begins to warm up. Describe how your skin responds to the excess heat.

How does your body work?

21. Describe how the body systems of this boy function during and after the time he eats his lunch. Use at least four different body systems in your answer.

_____

_____

_____

_____

_____

_____

_____

_____

_____

_____

_____

_____

_____

_____

_____

_____

Standardized Test Prep

Multiple Choice

Circle the letter of the best answer.

1. Which term best fits the level of organization pictured in the diagram below?

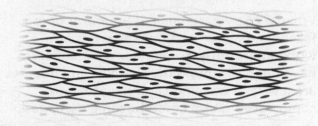

   A organ
   B tissue
   C single cell
   D organ system

2. What is one way that stress can affect homeostasis?

   A disrupts ability to fight disease
   B increases water balance
   C maintains constant internal temperature
   D decreases signals from the inner ear to the brain to help with balance

3. Which two systems work together to respond to internal and external conditions and to control body functions?

   A skeletal and muscular systems
   B endocrine and nervous systems
   C muscular and digestive systems
   D respiratory and circulatory systems

4. When the muscles at the back of your thigh contract, your leg is _____, and when the muscles in the front of your thigh contract, your leg is _____.

   A bent; bent
   B straight; straight
   C bent; straight
   D straight; bent

5. Which body systems are involved in the maintenance of homeostasis?

   A all organ systems
   B nervous and endocrine systems only
   C nervous, endocrine, and respiratory systems only
   D nervous, endocrine, excretory, and respiratory systems only

Constructed Response

Copy the flowchart below on a separate piece of paper. Use your knowledge of body organization to help you answer Question 6.

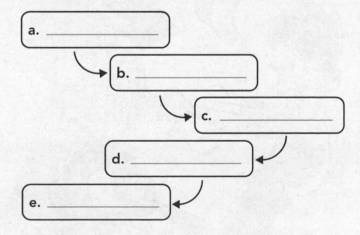

6. Construct a flowchart showing the levels of organization in an organism from the least complex to the most complex. Then explain how the terms in your flowchart are related.

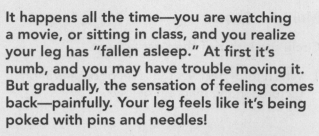

ON PINS AND NEEDLES

It happens all the time—you are watching a movie, or sitting in class, and you realize your leg has "fallen asleep." At first it's numb, and you may have trouble moving it. But gradually, the sensation of feeling comes back—painfully. Your leg feels like it's being poked with pins and needles!

When a body part, such as your arm or leg, falls asleep, your nervous system is not working properly. A nerve or several nerves have been compressed. The pins and needles are a sort of warning sign. Eventually, a compressed nerve could become damaged.

How does this warning sign work? Nerves carry sensory information to your brain. They also carry signals that control the movement of body parts. When your leg or arm is compressed, these signals are disrupted and your limb "falls asleep."

At first, nerve cells send confused sensory information to the brain. But gradually, the nerve cells stop sending signals, making your limb numb. When you move and the pathways between your brain and your limb start working again, your nerves become very excitable. The more you stimulate them—by moving or shaking a sleeping limb—the more excitable the nerves become. The very excitable nerves cause the feeling of "pins and needles."

Research It Pins and needles can sometimes be a sign of more serious nervous system problems. Research one condition, such as carpal tunnel syndrome, that can cause this symptom. Make a pamphlet describing prevention, warning signs, and treatment of the condition.

From One Cell—Many

blastula

Look at your hand or face—you can easily see different tissues. Your skin, nails, hair, eyes, and teeth are all made of different types of cells. Like those of all mammals, our body has more than 200 different types of cells, each with a specialized function or job. Yet all these different cells developed from just one fertilized egg cell.

How does one cell multiply into many specialized cells? When an embryo first starts to develop, the original fertilized cell divides. As cell division continues, a clustered mass organizes into a hollow ball called a blastula. Eventually, the multiplying cells differentiate into three layers. The inner layer becomes the digestive tract and respiratory system. The middle layer gives rise to most of the other organs and internal structures. The outer layer becomes sense organs, nerves, and skin.

Cells that have the ability to divide into other, more specialized cells are called stem cells. The processes that stimulate stem cells to change involve chemicals, enzymes, and hormones, and those processes are directed by an organism's DNA.

Scientists have tracked many stages of the growth of embryos and the process of one kind of cell differentiating into different types of cells. Yet many of the exact causes of cell differentiation remain unknown. The process is the subject of intense research.

Analyze It Choose a body system. Identify the specialized cells that make up different tissues in that system. Make a poster that describes the types of cells in the system, their specialized jobs, and how their structure helps them carry out their function in supporting your growth and survival.

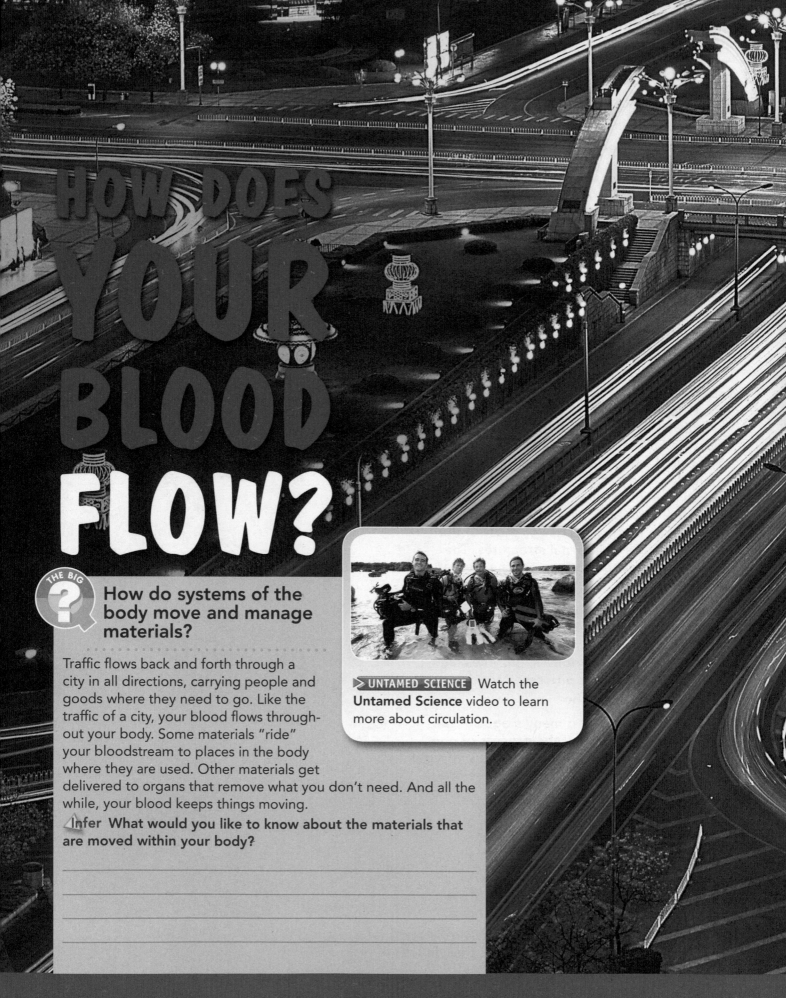

HOW DOES YOUR BLOOD FLOW?

THE BIG ?

How do systems of the body move and manage materials?

Traffic flows back and forth through a city in all directions, carrying people and goods where they need to go. Like the traffic of a city, your blood flows throughout your body. Some materials "ride" your bloodstream to places in the body where they are used. Other materials get delivered to organs that remove what you don't need. And all the while, your blood keeps things moving.

△Infer **What would you like to know about the materials that are moved within your body?**

_____

_____

_____

_____

▶ UNTAMED SCIENCE Watch the **Untamed Science** video to learn more about circulation.

Managing Materials in the Body

12 Getting Started

Check Your Understanding

1. **Background** Read the paragraph below and then answer the question.

Each day, Ken **circulates** from the food pantry to senior centers around the city and then returns to the pantry. He **transports** meals and juice to the seniors and collects their empty bottles. Similarly, your blood circulates in your body. From the heart, your blood carries oxygen and **glucose** to your body cells. It picks up wastes before returning to the heart.

> To **circulate** is to move in a circle and return to the same point.
>
> To **transport** is to carry something from one place to another.
>
> **Glucose** is a sugar that is the major source of energy for the body's cells.

- What materials does your blood transport to your body cells?

_____

_____

> MY READING WEB If you had trouble completing the question above, visit **My Reading Web** and type in *Managing Materials in the Body*.

Vocabulary Skill

Identify Related Word Forms Learn related forms of words to increase your vocabulary. The table below lists forms of words related to key terms.

Verb	Noun	Adjective
respire, *v.* to obtain energy from the breakdown of food molecules	cellular respiration, *n.* the process by which cells obtain energy from the breakdown of food molecules	respiratory, *adj.* concerning respiration
excrete, *v.* to remove or eliminate waste	excretion, *n.* the process by which wastes are removed from the body	excretory, *adj.* concerning excretion

2. **Quick Check** Fill in the blank with the correct form of *respire*.

- Obtaining energy from food is a _____ activity.

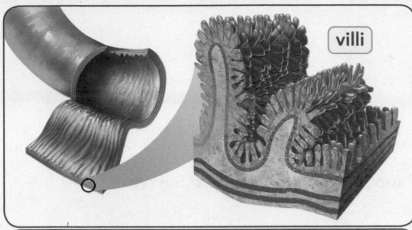

villi

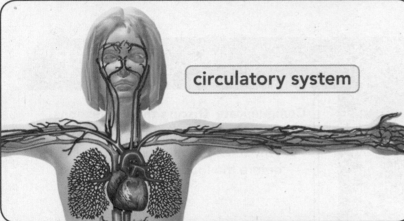

circulatory system

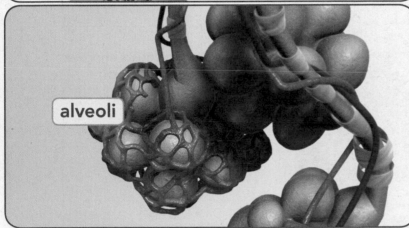

alveoli

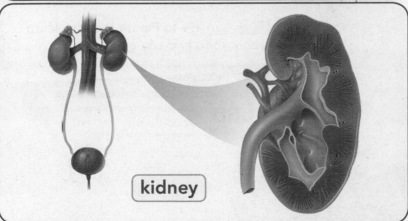

kidney

Chapter Preview

LESSON 1
- calorie • enzyme • esophagus
- peristalsis • villi
- ↻ Reading: Chart
- △ Inquiry: Develop Hypotheses

LESSON 2
- circulatory system • heart
- atrium • ventricle • valve
- artery • aorta • capillary • vein
- hemoglobin
- ↻ Summarize
- △ Observe

LESSON 3
- pharynx
- trachea
- cilia
- bronchi
- lungs
- alveoli
- diaphragm
- larynx
- vocal cords
- ↻ Chart
- △ Communicate

LESSON 4
- excretion
- urea
- urine
- kidney
- ureter
- urinary bladder
- urethra
- nephron
- ↻ Identify the Main Idea
- △ Infer

> VOCAB FLASH CARDS For extra help with vocabulary, visit **Vocab Flash Cards** and type in *Managing Materials in the Body.*

UNLOCK THE BIG ?

🔑 **Why Do You Need Food?**

🔑 **What Happens in Your Digestive System?**

my planet diary

The Science of Food

You know that you need to eat food every day. But did you know that for some people studying food is their job? People called food scientists research and improve the food products you buy at the grocery store. Sometimes, they even think up new foods!

Many food scientists spend a lot of time in a lab. They use what they know about biology and chemistry to test food for nutrition, taste, and shelf life, which is how long the food will last before it spoils. If you like science and food, being a food scientist might be the job for you!

CAREER

Communicate Discuss these questions with a partner. Then write your answers.

1. Why should food scientists test foods before the foods are sold?

_____

_____

_____

2. How might food scientists improve your favorite breakfast food?

_____

_____

_____

_____

_____

▶ PLANET DIARY Go to **Planet Diary** to learn more about food and energy.

Lab zone® Do the Inquiry Warm-Up *Food Claims.*

Vocabulary

- calorie
- peristalsis
- enzyme
- villi
- esophagus

Skills

↻ Reading: Chart

△ Inquiry: Develop Hypotheses

Why Do You Need Food?

All living things need food to stay alive. ⚷ **Food provides your body with materials to grow and to repair tissues. It also provides energy for everything you do.** Exercising, reading, and sleeping require energy. Even maintaining homeostasis takes energy.

Calories When food is used for energy, the amount of energy released is measured in calories. One **calorie** is the amount of energy needed to raise the temperature of one gram of water by one degree Celsius. The unit *Calorie*, with a capital *C*, is used to measure the energy in foods. One Calorie equals 1,000 calories. Everyone needs a certain number of Calories to meet their daily energy needs. However, the more active you are, the more Calories you need.

do the math!

The U.S. Department of Agriculture recommends that people do about 30 to 60 minutes of physical activity most days. The data table shows the Calories a 13-year-old weighing 45 kilograms burned in 30 minutes of each activity.

1 **Graph** Use the data to draw a bar graph.

2 **Name** Write a title for the bar graph.

3 **CHALLENGE** Why does the type of physical activity change a person's dietary needs? Use the graph to explain your answer.

_____

_____

_____

_____

_____

_____

Activity	Calories Burned in 30 minutes
Soccer	275
Dancing	115
Walking	75

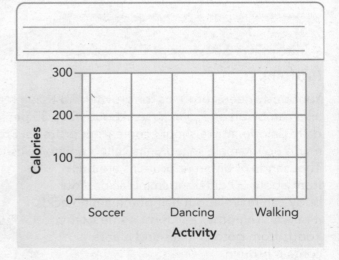

What Nutrients Do You Need?

Your body breaks down the food you eat into nutrients. Nutrients are the substances in food that provide the raw materials and energy the body needs to carry out all its processes. People need six types of nutrients: carbohydrates, fats, proteins, vitamins, minerals, and water.

FIGURE 1 ·······························

> INTERACTIVE ART   **Feeding Your Body**

The nutrients your body needs come from the foods you eat. ✎ **Make Judgments Why do you think it's important to eat a variety of foods every day?**

_____

_____

_____

Carbohydrates

Carbohydrates (kahr boh HY drayts) are a major source of energy. They also provide raw materials to make cell parts. About 45 to 65 percent of your daily Calories should come from carbohydrates. Simple carbohydrates, called sugars, can give you a quick burst of energy. One sugar, glucose, is the major source of energy for your cells. Complex carbohydrates are made of many linked sugar molecules. Starch is a complex carbohydrate. Potatoes, rice, wheat, and corn contain starches. Your body breaks down starches into sugar molecules. In this way, starches provide a steady long-term energy source.

Fats

Like carbohydrates, fats are energy-containing nutrients. However, 1 gram of fat provides 9 Calories of energy, while 1 gram of carbohydrate provides only 4 Calories. Fats form part of the cell membrane. Fatty tissue also protects your organs and insulates your body. No more than 30 percent of your daily Calories should come from fats.

Proteins

Your body needs proteins for growth and tissue repair. Proteins also can be an energy source. About 10 to 35 percent of your daily Calorie intake should come from proteins. Proteins are made up of small, linked units called amino acids (uh MEE noh). Thousands of different proteins are built from about 20 different amino acids. Your body can make about half of the amino acids it needs. The other half must come from food. Foods from both animals and plants contain protein.

Vitamins and Minerals

Unlike some nutrients, vitamins do not provide the body with raw materials and energy. Instead, vitamins act as helper molecules in your body's chemical reactions. The body can make a few vitamins, such as vitamin D, but foods are the source of most vitamins.

Nutrients that are not made by living things are called minerals. Like vitamins, minerals do not provide your body with raw materials and energy. However, your body still needs small amounts of minerals to carry out chemical processes. For example, you need calcium to build bones and teeth, and you need iron to help red blood cells function. Plant roots absorb minerals from the soil. You obtain minerals by eating plants or animals that have eaten plants.

Water

Water is the most important nutrient because all the body's vital processes take place in water. In addition, water helps regulate body temperature and remove wastes. Water accounts for about 65 percent of the average healthy person's body weight because it makes up most of the body's fluids, including blood. Under normal conditions, you need to take in about 2 liters of water every day to stay healthy.

Lab zone® **Do the Quick Lab**
Predicting Starch Content.

🔑 Assess Your Understanding

1a. Define What does a Calorie measure?

_____

_____

b. Draw Conclusions Why do active teenagers have high energy needs?

_____

_____

c. Apply Concepts What do you think is meant by the phrase "a balanced diet"?

_____

_____

_____

_____

_____

_____

got it?..

○ **I get it!** Now I know that food provides the body with _____

_____

○ I need extra help with _____

Go to MY SCIENCE ⓢ COACH *online for help with this subject.*

What Happens in Your Digestive System?

Your digestive system is about 9 meters long from beginning to end. **Figure 2** shows the structures of the digestive system. 🔑 **The digestive system breaks down food, absorbs nutrients, and eliminates waste.** These functions occur one after the other in an efficient, continuous process.

Digestion The process by which your body breaks down food into small nutrient molecules is called digestion. Digestion can be mechanical or chemical. In mechanical digestion, bites of food are torn or ground into smaller pieces. This kind of digestion happens mostly in the mouth and stomach. In chemical digestion, chemicals break foods into their building blocks. Chemical digestion takes place in many parts of the digestive system. Substances made in the liver and pancreas help digestion occur.

Absorption and Elimination

Absorption occurs after digestion. Absorption is the process by which nutrient molecules pass from your digestive system into your blood. Most absorption occurs in the small intestine. The large intestine eliminates materials that are not absorbed.

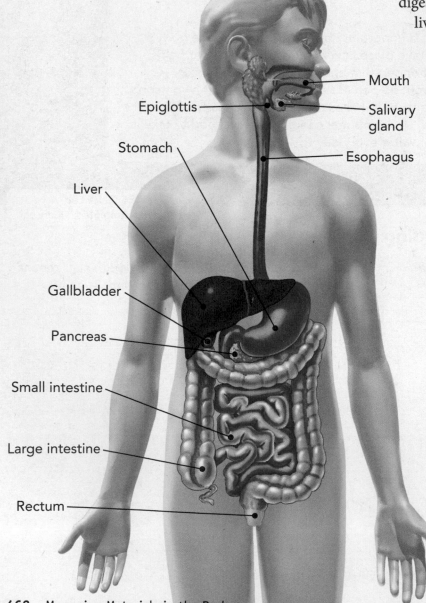

Mouth

Epiglottis

Salivary gland

Stomach

Esophagus

Liver

Gallbladder

Pancreas

Small intestine

Large intestine

Rectum

FIGURE 2 ·······························

The Digestive System
Food passes directly through five organs of your digestive system.

✏️ **Identify** Circle the name(s) of the organ(s) where mechanical digestion mainly occurs. Check the name(s) of the organ(s) where most absorption occurs. Underline the name(s) of the organ(s) where elimination occurs.

The Mouth Have you noticed that smelling food can be enough to start your mouth watering? This response happens because your mouth is where digestion begins. When you bite off a piece of food, both mechanical and chemical digestion begin inside your mouth. Your teeth and tongue carry out mechanical digestion. Your teeth cut, tear, crush, and grind food into small pieces. Your tongue pushes food toward your teeth.

As your teeth work, your saliva (suh LY vuh) moistens food into a slippery mass. Saliva is the fluid released by salivary glands when you eat. Saliva contains a chemical that can break down starches into sugars. This step begins the chemical digestion of your food.

The chemical in saliva that digests starch is an enzyme. An **enzyme** is a protein that speeds up chemical reactions in the body. Your body produces many different enzymes. Each enzyme has a specific chemical shape that enables it to speed up only one kind of reaction. Different enzymes are needed to complete the process of digestion. **Figure 3** shows how enzymes work.

FIGURE 3 ....
How Enzymes Work
Enzymes help break down starches, proteins, and fats.

✎ **Observe** Which molecule does not change?

_____

_____

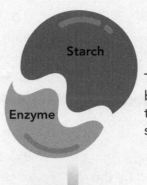

The starch molecule binds to an enzyme that has a matching shape.

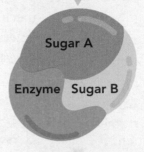

The starch molecule is broken down into two separate sugar molecules.

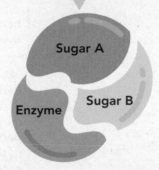

The enzyme and the sugar molecules all separate.

apply it!

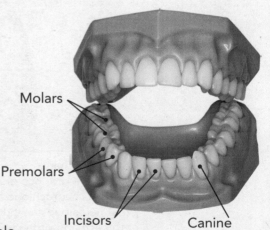

You have four types of teeth. Each type has a specific function.

❶ **Name** Think about eating a carrot. Which type of teeth cuts the carrot into a bite-sized piece? _____

❷ **Identify** Which teeth at the back of your mouth crush and grind the carrot piece? _____ and _____

❸ **Interpret Diagrams** When people tear chicken off a bone, they use their pointed teeth called _____

❹ **Summarize** Write about all the teeth people use to eat an apple.

_____

_____

Molars
Premolars
Incisors
Canine

FIGURE 4 ················

The Stomach

The stomach wall has three muscle layers. The microscopic view shows you the cells that line the inside of the stomach.

✎ **Answer the following questions.**

1. Classify What type of digestion is aided by the action of stomach muscles?

_____

_____

_____

2. Infer How does having different layers of stomach muscles aid digestion?

_____

_____

_____

_____

_____

_____

To the Stomach Food moves from your mouth through your **esophagus** (ih SAHF uh gus) and then into your stomach. The stomach is a J-shaped muscular pouch where most mechanical digestion and some chemical digestion occur. Mechanical digestion occurs as layers of smooth muscle in the stomach wall contract, producing a churning motion. Chemical digestion occurs as the food mixes with digestive juice. Digestive juice is a fluid produced by cells that line the stomach. It contains the enzyme pepsin that chemically digests proteins into short chains of amino acids.

Food usually stays in your stomach for a few hours until mechanical digestion is complete. Now a thick liquid, the food enters the next part of the digestive system. That is where chemical digestion continues and absorption takes place.

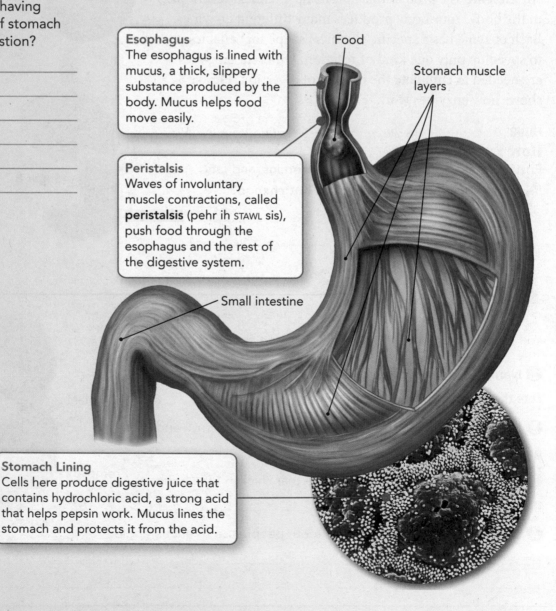

Esophagus
The esophagus is lined with mucus, a thick, slippery substance produced by the body. Mucus helps food move easily.

Food

Stomach muscle layers

Peristalsis
Waves of involuntary muscle contractions, called **peristalsis** (pehr ih STAWL sis), push food through the esophagus and the rest of the digestive system.

Small intestine

Stomach Lining
Cells here produce digestive juice that contains hydrochloric acid, a strong acid that helps pepsin work. Mucus lines the stomach and protects it from the acid.

The Small Intestine
At about 6 meters—longer than some full-sized cars—the small intestine makes up two thirds of the length of the digestive system. The small intestine is the part of the digestive system where most chemical digestion and absorption take place. Its small diameter, from 2 to 3 centimeters wide, gives the small intestine its name.

A great deal happens in the small intestine. When food reaches it, starches and proteins have been partially broken down, but fats have not been digested. 🔑 **Substances produced by the liver, pancreas, and lining of the small intestine help to complete chemical digestion.** The liver and the pancreas send their substances into the small intestine through small tubes.

FIGURE 5 ∙∙∙∙∙∙∙∙∙∙∙∙∙∙∙∙∙∙∙∙∙∙∙∙∙

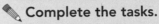

REAL-WORLD INQUIRY **Organs of Digestion**
The liver, pancreas, and gallbladder aid digestion in the small intestine.

✎ **Complete the tasks.**

1. **Identify** Fill in the missing labels.

2. **Develop Hypotheses** How may a blockage in the tube between the gallbladder and the small intestine affect digestion?

_____

_____

_____

_____

_____

Gallbladder
The gallbladder stores bile and releases it into the small intestine.

Liver
The liver has many jobs. One job is making bile for the digestive system. Bile breaks fats into smaller droplets but is not involved in chemical digestion.

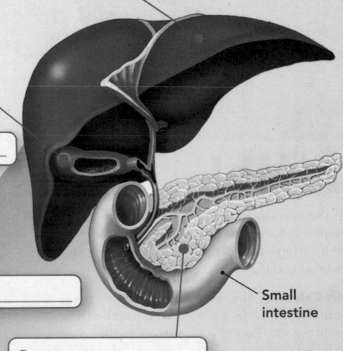

Small intestine

Pancreas
Like the liver, the pancreas has many jobs. One job is to produce enzymes that break down carbohydrates, proteins, and fats.

Absorption in the Small Intestine

After chemical digestion takes place, the small nutrient molecules are ready for the body to absorb. The structure of the small intestine helps absorption occur. The inner surface of the small intestine is folded into millions of tiny finger-shaped structures called **villi** (VIL eye) (singular *villus*). Villi, shown in **Figure 6,** greatly increase the surface area of the small intestine. More surface area means that more nutrients can be absorbed. Nutrient molecules pass from cells on the surface of a villus into blood vessels and are then delivered to body cells.

FIGURE 6 ·····················
Villi
Tiny villi line the folds of the small intestine.

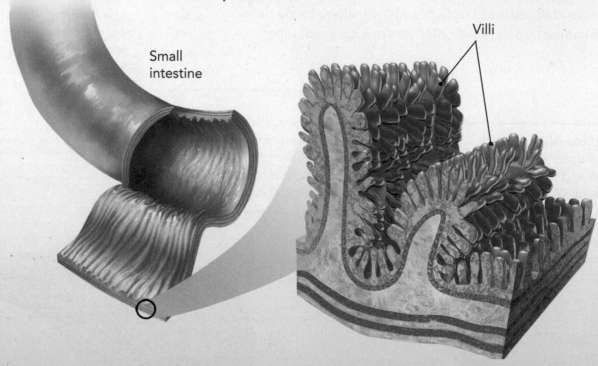

Small intestine

Villi

---

do the math!

If the average person's small intestine had smooth walls, its surface area would be 0.57 m². With villi, the surface area is about 250 m², about the size of a tennis court.

1 Calculate Divide to find how many times greater the surface area is with villi than it is without villi. Round your answer to the nearest whole number.

2 Estimate In Question 1, how did you know which number to divide by to get your answer?

_____

_____

_____

_____

_____

3 CHALLENGE Some people have a wheat allergy that results in villi being destroyed. What problems might these individuals have?

_____

_____

_____

The Large Intestine By the time material reaches the end of the small intestine, most nutrients have been absorbed. The water and undigested food that is left move from the small intestine into the large intestine. The large intestine is the last section of the digestive system. As the material moves through the large intestine, water is absorbed into the bloodstream. The remaining material is readied for elimination from the body.

The large intestine is about 1.5 meters long. It contains bacteria that feed on the material passing through. These bacteria normally do not cause disease. In fact, they are helpful because they make certain vitamins, including vitamin K.

The large intestine ends in a short tube called the rectum. In the rectum waste material is compressed into solid form. This waste material is eliminated from the body through the anus, a muscular opening at the end of the rectum.

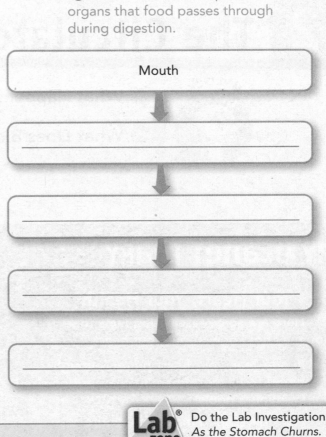

➔ **Chart** Write the sequence of organs that food passes through during digestion.

Mouth

Lab zone ® Do the Lab Investigation *As the Stomach Churns.*

🔑 **Assess Your Understanding**

2a. Define (Chemical/Mechanical) digestion occurs when enzymes break down foods into simpler substances.

b. Apply Concepts How is the stomach similar to a washing machine?

_____

_____

_____

_____

c. Explain How are the liver and pancreas involved in digestion?

_____

_____

_____

_____

d. Relate Cause and Effect How do villi help the small intestine carry out its function?

_____

_____

got it?

○ **I get it!** Now I know that the digestive system works through the actions of organs that include

_____

_____

○ I need extra help with _____

Go to **MY SCIENCE COACH** online for help with this subject.

🔑 **What Happens in Your Circulatory System?**

🔑 **What Does Blood Contain?**

my planet diary

Your Heart, Your Health

Here are some fascinating facts that you may not know about your heart.

- In one year, your heart pumps enough blood to fill more than 30 competition-sized swimming pools!

- A drop of blood makes the entire trip through your body in less than a minute.

- Your heart beats about 100,000 times a day.

- Your heart pushes blood through about 100,000 kilometers of vessels. They would circle Earth more than twice!

- A child's heart is about the size of a fist. An adult's heart is about the size of two fists.

FUN FACTS

Read the following questions. Write your answers below.

1. Why is it important for a person's heart to be healthy?

_____

_____

_____

2. About how many times does your heart beat in a week? In a year?

_____

_____

_____

▷ **PLANET DIARY** Go to **Planet Diary** to learn more about the body's transport system.

 Lab zone Do the Inquiry Warm-Up *Observing a Heart.*

What Happens in Your Circulatory System?

As shown in **Figure 1**, the **circulatory system,** or cardiovascular system, is made up of the heart, blood vessels, and blood. 🔑 **The circulatory system delivers needed substances to cells, carries wastes away from cells, and helps regulate body temperature. In addition, blood contains cells that fight disease.**

Vocabulary

- circulatory system • heart • atrium
- ventricle • valve • artery • aorta
- capillary • vein • hemoglobin

Skills

↻ Reading: Summarize

△ Inquiry: Observe

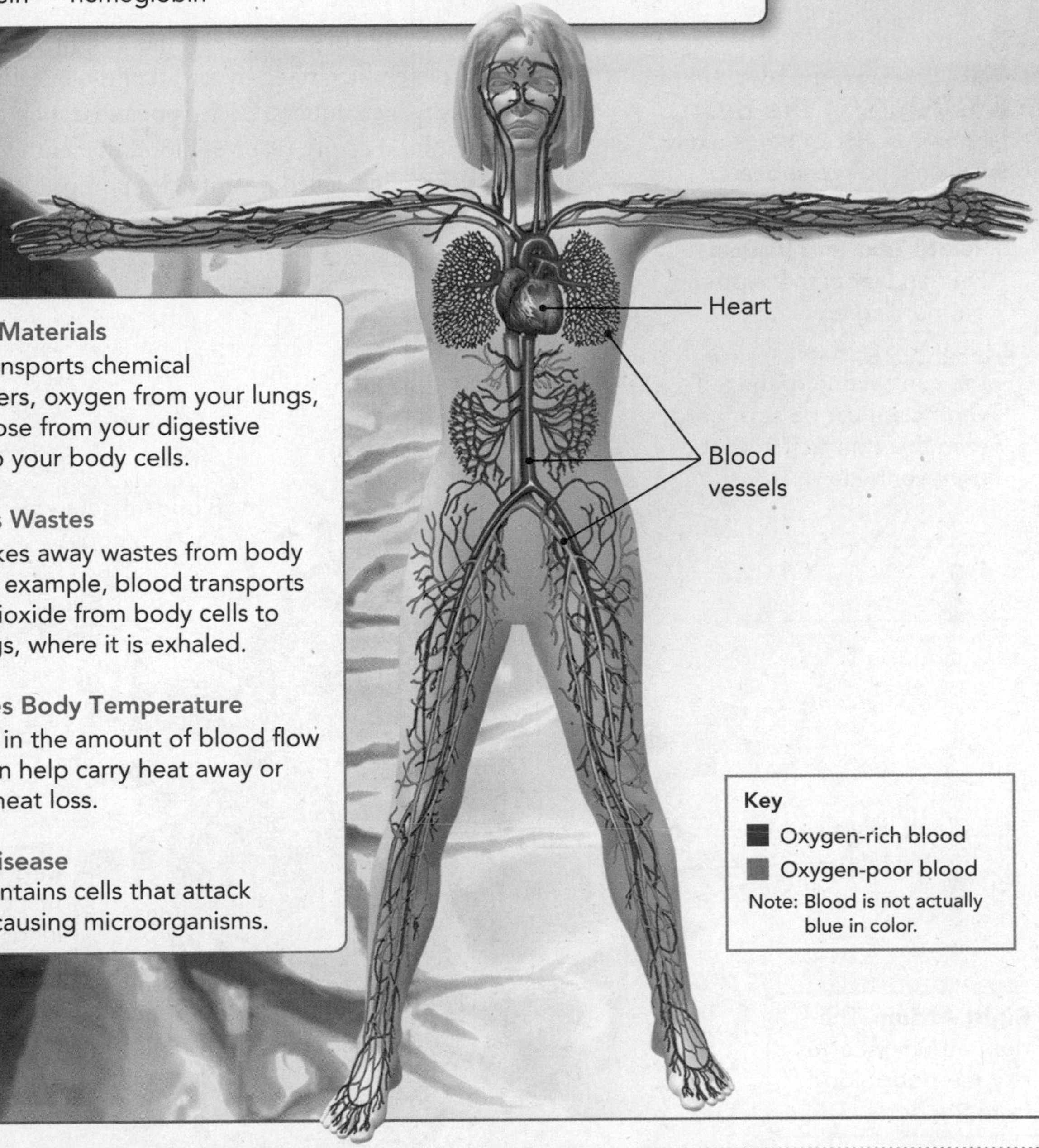

Delivers Materials

Blood transports chemical messengers, oxygen from your lungs, and glucose from your digestive system to your body cells.

Removes Wastes

Blood takes away wastes from body cells. For example, blood transports carbon dioxide from body cells to your lungs, where it is exhaled.

Regulates Body Temperature

Changes in the amount of blood flow in the skin help carry heat away or prevent heat loss.

Fights Disease

Blood contains cells that attack disease-causing microorganisms.

Heart

Blood vessels

Key
■ Oxygen-rich blood
■ Oxygen-poor blood
Note: Blood is not actually blue in color.

FIGURE 1 ···

The Circulatory System

Like roads that link all the parts of a town, your circulatory system links all the parts of your body.

✏ **Use the diagram to answer the questions.**

1. **Infer** What might happen if your circulatory system did not function properly?

_____

_____

_____

2. **Pose Questions** After looking at the diagram, write a question that describes one thing you would like to learn about the circulatory system.

_____

_____

_____

_____

The Heart
Without your heart, your blood would not go anywhere. As **Figure 2** shows, the **heart** is a hollow, muscular organ that pumps blood to the body through blood vessels.

The Heart's Structure The heart has a right side and left side that are completely separated by a wall of tissue called the septum. Each side has two chambers. Each upper chamber, called an **atrium** (AY tree um; plural *atria*), receives blood that comes into the heart. Each lower chamber, called a **ventricle,** pumps blood out of the heart. The pacemaker, a group of cells in the right atrium, sends out signals that regulate heart rate. These signals make the heart muscle contract.

FIGURE 2 ....

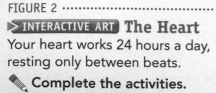

The Heart

Your heart works 24 hours a day, resting only between beats.

✎ **Complete the activities.**

1. **Relate Text and Visuals** Find and label the septum on the diagram.

2. **CHALLENGE** Explain why the contraction of the left ventricle must be stronger than the contraction of the right ventricle.

_____

_____

_____

_____

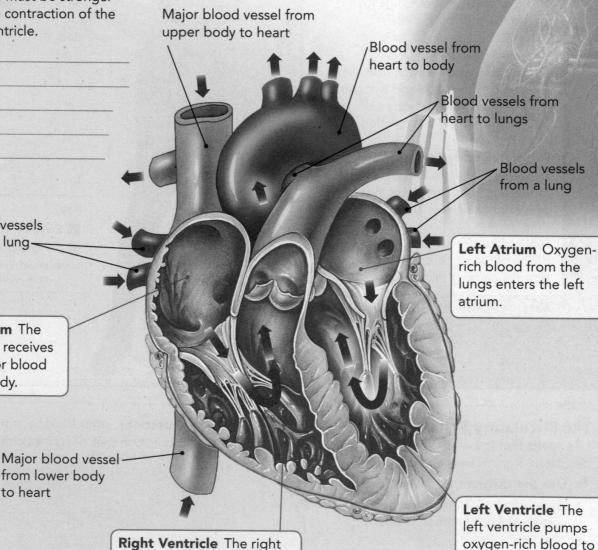

Major blood vessel from upper body to heart

Blood vessel from heart to body

Blood vessels from heart to lungs

Blood vessels from a lung

Blood vessels from a lung

Left Atrium Oxygen-rich blood from the lungs enters the left atrium.

Right Atrium The right atrium receives oxygen-poor blood from the body.

Major blood vessel from lower body to heart

Right Ventricle The right ventricle pumps oxygen-poor blood to the lungs.

Left Ventricle The left ventricle pumps oxygen-rich blood to all parts of the body.

How the Heart Works Valves separate the atria from the ventricles. A **valve** is a flap of tissue that prevents blood from flowing backward. Valves also separate the ventricles and the large blood vessels that carry blood away from the heart.

A heartbeat sounds something like *lub-dup*. First, the heart muscle relaxes and the atria fill with blood. Next, the atria contract, squeezing blood through valves, like those in **Figure 3,** and into the ventricles. Then the ventricles contract. This contraction closes the valves between the atria and ventricles, making the *lub* sound and squeezing blood into large blood vessels. Finally, the valves between the ventricles and blood vessels snap shut, making the *dup* sound. All this happens in less than one second.

The Path of Blood Flow

As you can see in **Figure 4,** the overall pattern of blood flow through the body is similar to a figure eight. The heart is at the center where the two loops cross. In the first loop, blood travels from the heart to the lungs and then back to the heart. In the second loop, blood travels from the heart throughout the body and then back to the heart.

Your body has three kinds of blood vessels: arteries, capillaries, and veins. **Arteries** carry blood away from the heart. For example, blood in the left ventricle is pumped into the **aorta** (ay AWR tuh), the largest artery in the body. From the arteries, blood flows into tiny vessels called **capillaries.** In the capillaries, substances are exchanged between the blood and body cells. From capillaries, blood flows into **veins,** which carry blood back to the heart.

FIGURE 3 ·····································
Heart Valves
Valves control the direction of blood flow through the heart.

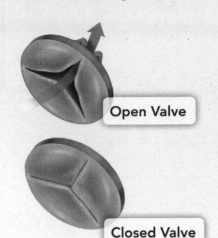

Open Valve

Closed Valve

FIGURE 4 ·····································
Blood Flow
Your heart can pump five liters of blood through the two loops each minute.

✎ **Interpret Diagrams** In each box, write where the blood from the heart travels. Then tell where blood travels after it leaves each part listed below.

Right atrium

_____

Veins from the body

_____

Arteries to the lungs

_____

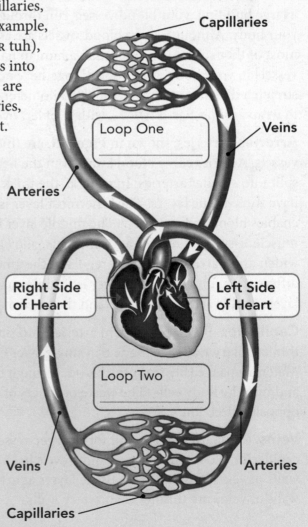

Capillaries

Loop One

Veins

Arteries

Right Side of Heart

Left Side of Heart

Loop Two

Veins

Arteries

Capillaries

471

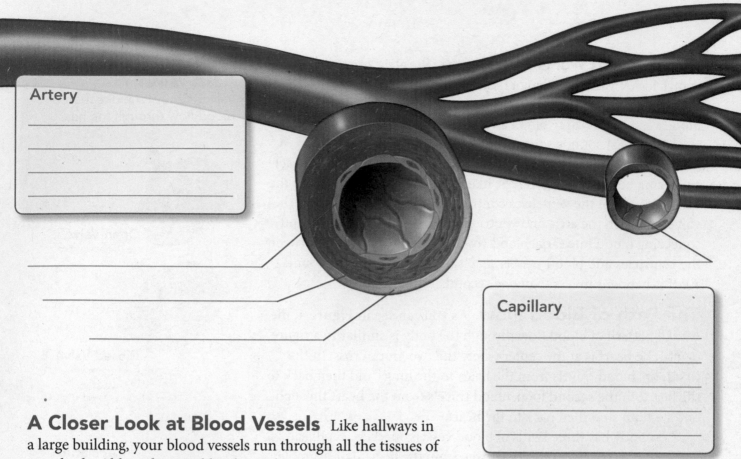

Artery

_____
_____
_____
_____

_____

Capillary

_____
_____
_____
_____
_____

A Closer Look at Blood Vessels

Like hallways in a large building, your blood vessels run through all the tissues of your body. Although some blood vessels are as wide as your thumb, most of them are much finer than a human hair. If all the blood vessels in your body were hooked together end to end, they would stretch a distance of almost 100,000 kilometers. That's long enough to wrap around Earth twice—with a lot left over!

Arteries Arteries, shown in **Figure 5,** are thick-walled, muscular vessels. Arteries carry blood away from the heart. As they do, they split into smaller arteries. In general, the thick, elastic artery walls have three tissue layers. The innermost layer is epithelial tissue that enables blood to flow freely. The middle layer is mostly smooth muscle tissue that relaxes and contracts, allowing the artery to widen and narrow. This layer regulates the amount of blood sent to different organs. The outer layer is flexible connective tissue. These layers enable arteries to withstand the force of pumping blood.

Capillaries Blood flows from arteries into tiny capillaries. The thin capillary walls are made of a single layer of epithelial cells. Materials pass easily from the blood, through the capillary walls, and into the body cells. The waste products of cells pass in the opposite direction.

Veins Capillaries merge and form larger vessels called veins. From capillaries, blood enters veins and travels back to the heart. The walls of veins have the same tissue layers as arteries. However, the walls of veins are thinner than artery walls.

FIGURE 5 ·······················
Blood Vessels
✎ **Read the text before completing the tasks.**

1. **Identify** Underline in the text what happens to blood in each kind of vessel.

2. **Interpret Diagrams** In the diagram above, label the parts of each vessel. Then write in each box how the vessel's structure enables it to function.

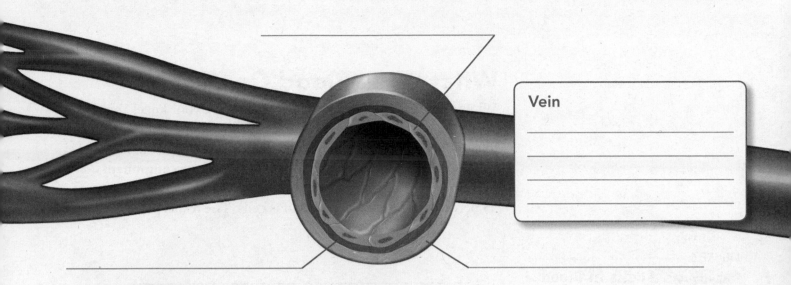

Vein
_____
_____
_____
_____

apply it!

Your pulse results from the alternating relaxation and contraction of arteries as blood is forced through them. Touch the inside of your wrist and find your pulse.

1 ⚠ **Observe** How does your pulse feel through your fingertips?

_____
_____
_____

2 ⚠ **Observe** How many heartbeats do you count in one minute?

_____

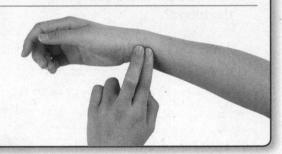

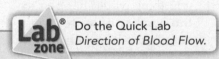 **Lab zone**® Do the Quick Lab
Direction of Blood Flow.

🔑 Assess Your Understanding

1a. Identify Blood returning from the lungs enters the heart at the (right atrium/left atrium/right ventricle/left ventricle).

b. Identify In which direction do arteries carry blood?

_____
_____
_____

c. Draw Conclusions Why is it important for your blood to complete both loops of circulation?

_____
_____
_____
_____
_____

got it? ....

○ **I get it!** Now I know that the circulatory system transports_____

_____

○ **I need extra help with** _____

Go to MY SCIENCE ⓢ COACH online for help with this subject.

What Does Blood Contain?

While riding your bike, you fall off and scrape your knee. Your knee stings, and blood oozes from the open wound. You go inside to clean the scrape. As you do, you wonder about what blood is.

Blood is a complex tissue. **Blood has four components: plasma, red blood cells, white blood cells, and platelets.** About 45 percent of the volume of blood is cells. The rest is plasma.

FIGURE 6 ·······························

▶ VIRTUAL LAB **Cells in Blood**
In addition to red blood cells and white blood cells, blood contains platelets and plasma.
✎ **Use the illustration about blood to complete the tasks.**

1. **Identify** What is the main function of hemoglobin in the blood?

_____

_____

_____

_____

2. **Apply Concepts** What do you think would happen to the number of white blood cells in the body when a person is fighting an infection? Explain your answer.

_____

_____

_____

_____

_____

_____

_____

Red Blood Cells

Red blood cells take up oxygen in the lungs and deliver it to cells throughout the body. Red blood cells, like most blood cells, are produced in bone marrow. Mature red blood cells have no nuclei. Without a nucleus, a red blood cell cannot reproduce or repair itself. Mature red blood cells live only about 120 days.

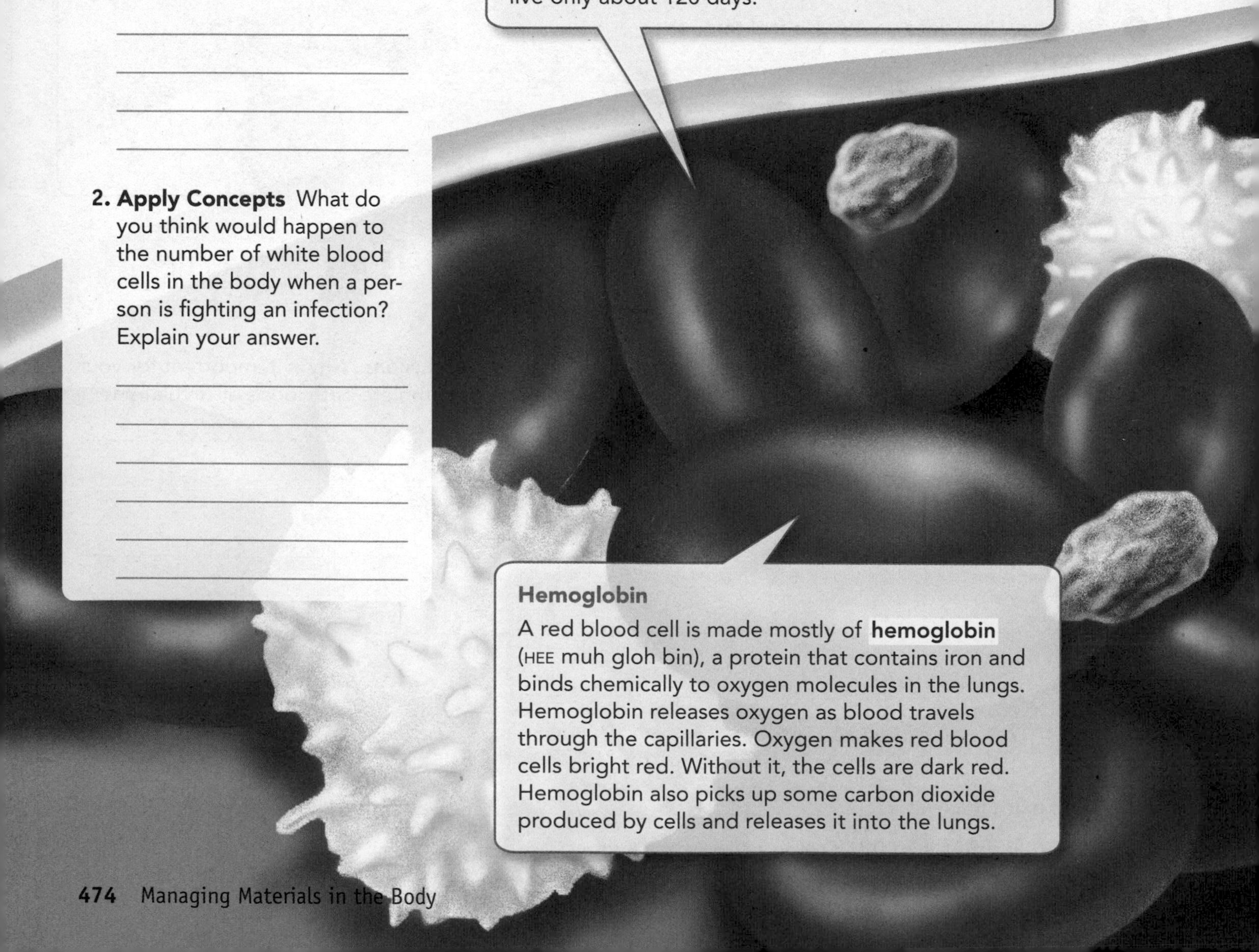

Hemoglobin

A red blood cell is made mostly of **hemoglobin** (HEE muh gloh bin), a protein that contains iron and binds chemically to oxygen molecules in the lungs. Hemoglobin releases oxygen as blood travels through the capillaries. Oxygen makes red blood cells bright red. Without it, the cells are dark red. Hemoglobin also picks up some carbon dioxide produced by cells and releases it into the lungs.

Plasma

Most materials transported in blood travel in the plasma. Plasma carries nutrients, such as glucose, fats, vitamins, and minerals. Plasma also carries chemical messengers that direct body activities, such as how your cells use glucose. In addition, plasma carries away most of the carbon dioxide and many other wastes that cell processes produce. Proteins in the plasma make it look pale yellow. Some of these proteins regulate water in the blood. Some help fight disease. Others help to form blood clots.

Summarize List and describe the materials that plasma carries.

_____
_____
_____
_____
_____
_____
_____
_____
_____

White Blood Cells

Like red blood cells, white blood cells are produced in bone marrow. White blood cells are the body's disease fighters. Some white blood cells recognize disease-causing organisms, such as bacteria, and alert the body to the invasion. Other white blood cells produce chemicals to fight the invaders. Still others surround and kill the organisms. White blood cells are larger than red blood cells and contain nuclei. They may live for days, months, or even years.

Platelets

Platelets (PLAYT lits) are cell fragments that help form blood clots. When a blood vessel is cut, platelets collect and stick to the vessel at the wound. The platelets release chemicals that produce a protein called fibrin (FY brin). Fibrin weaves a net of tiny fibers across the cut. Platelets and blood cells become trapped in the net, and a blood clot forms.

Transfusions for patients in hospitals and other medical facilities create a constant need for blood. In Florida, blood centers across the state collect a total of more than 1,000,000 units of blood each year. (One unit is equal to 450 mL.)

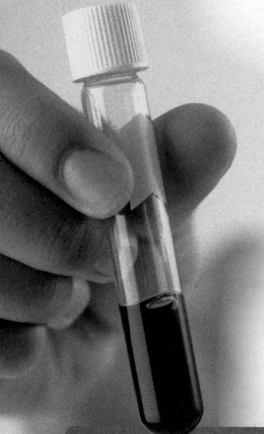

Marker Molecules and Transfusions

A blood transfusion is the transfer of blood from one person to another. Most early attempts at blood transfusion failed, but no one knew why. In the early 1900s, a physician named Karl Landsteiner tried mixing blood samples from two people. Sometimes the two blood samples blended smoothly. At other times, the red blood cells clumped together. In a patient, this clumping would clog the capillaries, causing death.

Blood Types Landsteiner identified the four major types of blood: A, B, AB, and O. Blood types are determined by marker molecules on red blood cells. If your blood type is A, you have the A marker. If your blood type is B, you have the B marker. People with type AB blood have both A and B markers. People with type O blood do not have A or B markers.

Clumping proteins in your plasma recognize red blood cells with "foreign" markers that are not your type. The proteins make cells with foreign markers clump together. For example, blood type A contains anti-B clumping proteins that act against cells with B markers. Blood type O has clumping proteins for both A and B markers. In **Figure 7,** you can see all the blood type marker molecules and clumping proteins.

FIGURE 7

Blood Types and Their Markers

Depending on your blood type, you may have certain marker molecules on your red blood cells and certain clumping proteins in your plasma.

✏️ **Create Data Tables** In the table, label the marker molecules and then identify the clumping proteins.

Blood Types, Marker Molecules, and Clumping Proteins

Blood Type Characteristic	Blood Type A	Blood Type B	Blood Type AB	Blood Type O
Marker Molecules on Red Blood Cells				
Clumping Proteins	anti-B			

apply it!

The marker molecules on your red blood cells determine the type of blood you can safely receive in transfusions. For example, a person with type A blood can receive transfusions of type A or type O blood. But type B blood would cause clumping and would not be safe. Through a process called cross-matching, a patient's blood type is checked so that safe donor types can be determined.

Blood Type	Safe Donor(s)	Unsafe Donor(s)
A	A, O	_____
B	_____	_____
AB	_____	_____
O	_____	_____

1 Infer Use what you know about blood types to complete the table.

2 Predict Which blood type may accept safe transfusions from any other blood type? Why?

_____

_____

_____

3 CHALLENGE Which blood type is a "universal donor," that is, a blood type that can be used in transfusions to anyone? Explain your reasoning.

_____

_____

_____

_____

Rh Factor Landsteiner also discovered a protein on red blood cells that he called *Rh factor*. About 85 percent of the people he tested had this protein. The rest did not. As with blood type, a marker molecule on the red blood cells determines the presence of Rh factor. An Rh-positive blood type has the Rh marker. An Rh-negative blood type does not. Clumping proteins will develop in people with Rh-negative blood if they receive Rh-positive blood. This situation may be potentially dangerous.

Lab zone Do the Quick Lab
Do You Know Your A-B-Os?

Assess Your Understanding

2a. Identify What is plasma?

_____

_____

b. Review What did Karl Landsteiner's observations lead him to discover?

_____

_____

c. Relate Cause and Effect How might a lack of iron in a person's diet affect his or her blood?

_____

_____

_____

_____

got it?

○ **I get it!** Now I know that blood contains _____

_____

○ **I need extra help with** _____

Go to MY SCIENCE COACH *online for help with this subject.*

LESSON

3 The Respiratory System

🔑 **What Is the Role of the Respiratory System?**

🔑 **What Happens When You Breathe?**

MY PLANET DIARY

MISCONCEPTION

The Breath of Life

Misconception: The only gas you exhale is carbon dioxide.

Actually, about 16 percent of the air you exhale is oxygen. The air you inhale is made up of about 21 percent oxygen. Your body only uses a small portion of the oxygen in each breath, so the unused portion is exhaled.

Sometimes, this exhaled oxygen can mean the difference between life and death. If a person stops breathing, he or she needs to get more oxygen quickly. A rescuer can breathe into the person's mouth to give unused oxygen to the person. This process is called rescue breathing.

Read the following question. Then write your answer below.

Why would you want to learn to perform rescue breathing?

_____

_____

_____

_____

_____

_____

▶ PLANET DIARY Go to **Planet Diary** to learn more about the respiratory system.

 Lab **zone**® Do the Inquiry Warm-Up *How Big Can You Blow Up a Balloon?*

What Is the Role of the Respiratory System?

In an average day, you may breathe 20,000 times. You breathe all the time because your body cells need oxygen, which comes from the air. 🔑 **Your respiratory system moves air containing oxygen into your lungs and removes carbon dioxide and water from your body. Your lungs and the structures that lead to them make up your respiratory system.**

Vocabulary

- pharynx • trachea • cilia • bronchi
- lungs • alveoli • diaphragm • larynx • vocal cords

Skills

↻ Reading: Chart
△ Inquiry: Communicate

Breathing and Homeostasis Your body needs oxygen for cellular respiration. During cellular respiration, cells break down glucose, releasing energy. You use energy for activities such as reading this book or playing ball. Your body also uses energy in carrying out processes that maintain homeostasis, such as removing wastes, growing, and regulating body temperature.

Breathing gets oxygen into your body. But cellular respiration depends on body systems working together. The digestive system supplies glucose from food. And the circulatory system carries this glucose and the oxygen from the respiratory system to all the cells in the body.

FIGURE 1 ··

Systems Working Together
Body systems work together, getting the materials needed for cellular respiration to cells.

✏ **Describe System Interactions** Describe how each system provides cells with materials needed for cellular respiration. Then tell how cellular respiration helps the body maintain homeostasis.

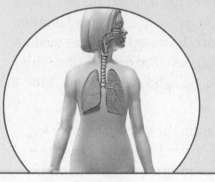

Circulatory System

_____

_____

_____

_____

Respiratory System

_____

_____

_____

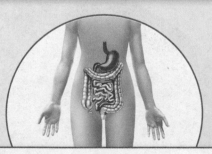

Cellular Respiration and Homeostasis

_____

_____

_____

_____

Digestive System

_____

_____

_____

479

did you
know?................

Substances in the air you breathe can affect your lungs and breathing passages. The Florida Department of Environmental Protection monitors and reports on air quality for the entire state. The reports include data about particles that can cause allergies and other pollutants that can affect human health.

Breathing Structures
When you breathe in, air and particles such as pollen and dust move through a series of structures and then into the lungs. You can see these structures—the nose, pharynx, trachea, and bronchi—on the right. These structures also warm and moisten the air you breathe.

Nose Air enters the body through the nose or the mouth. Hairs in the nose trap large particles. The air passes into spaces called nasal cavities. Some cells lining the nasal cavities produce mucus, a sticky material that moistens the air and traps more particles.

Pharynx and Trachea From the nose, air enters the **pharynx** (FAR ingks), or throat. Both the nose and the mouth connect to the pharynx. So air and food enter the pharynx. From the pharynx, air moves into the **trachea** (TRAY kee uh), or windpipe. When you swallow, a thin flap of tissue called the epiglottis covers the opening of the trachea to keep food out. Cells that line the trachea have **cilia** (SIL ee uh; singular *cilium*), tiny hairlike extensions that can move together in a sweeping motion. The cilia, like those shown in **Figure 2,** sweep the mucus made by cells in the trachea up to the pharynx. If particles irritate the trachea, you cough, sending the particles back into the air. Find the pharynx and trachea in **Figure 3.**

Bronchi and Lungs Air moves from the trachea into the left and right **bronchi** (BRAHNG ky; singular *bronchus*). These two passages take air into the lungs. The **lungs** are the main organs of the respiratory system. Inside the lungs, the bronchi branch into smaller and smaller tubes. At the end of the smallest tubes are **alveoli** (al VEE uh ly; singular *alveolus*), tiny, thin-walled sacs of lung tissue where gases can move between air and blood.

FIGURE 2 ···
Cilia
The photo shows a microscopic view of cilia.

✎ **Answer the questions below.**

1. **Relate Cause and Effect** How does coughing protect the respiratory system?

_____

_____

2. [CHALLENGE] What might happen if you did not have hairs in your nose and cilia in your trachea?

_____

_____

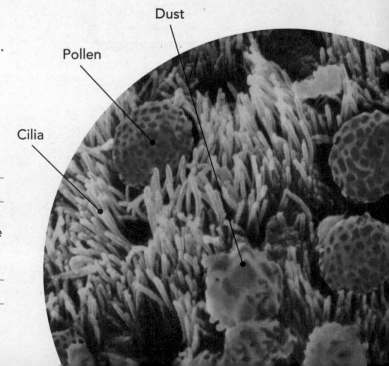

Dust

Pollen

Cilia

FIGURE 3 ··········

Structures of the Respiratory System

Particles in air are filtered out as the air moves through your respiratory system.

⚠️ **Communicate** In your own words, write what each part of the respiratory system does.

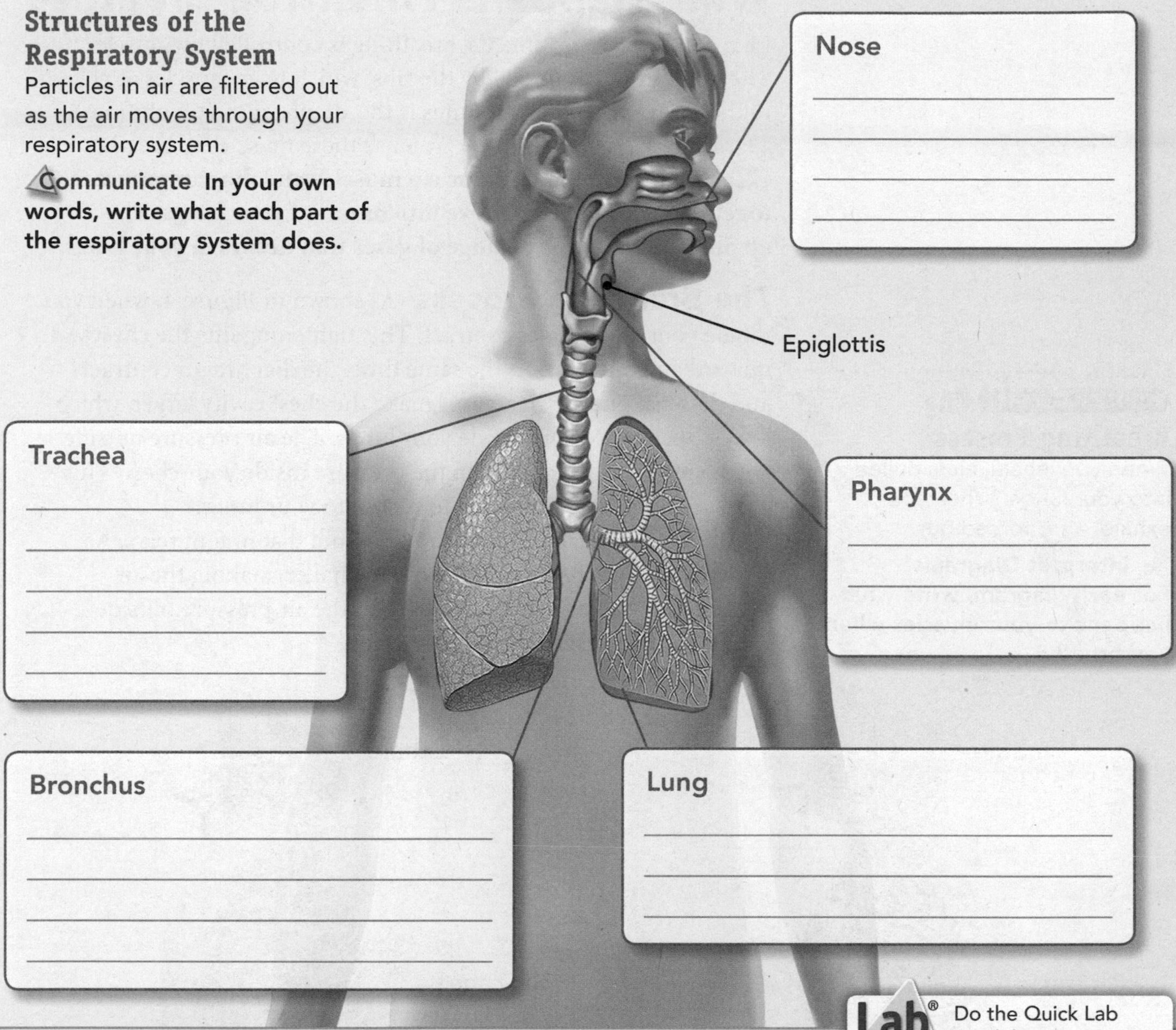

Nose
_____
_____
_____

Epiglottis

Trachea
_____
_____
_____

Pharynx
_____
_____
_____

Bronchus
_____
_____
_____

Lung
_____
_____
_____

Lab zone® Do the Quick Lab *Modeling Respiration.*

🔑 Assess Your Understanding

1a. Review What happens in the lungs?
_____
_____
_____

b. Compare and Contrast How are breathing and cellular respiration different?
_____
_____
_____

got it?

○ **I get it!** Now I know that the respiratory system _____
_____
_____
_____
_____

○ **I need extra help with** _____

Go to **MY SCIENCE COACH** *online for help with this subject.*

What Happens When You Breathe?

Like other body movements, breathing is controlled by muscles. The lungs are surrounded by the ribs, which have muscles attached to them. At the base of the lungs is the **diaphragm** (DY uh fram), a large, dome-shaped muscle. You use these muscles to breathe. **When you breathe, your rib muscles and diaphragm work together, causing air to move into or out of your lungs. This airflow leads to the exchange of gases that occurs in your lungs.**

The Breathing Process   As shown in **Figure 4,** when you inhale your rib muscles contract. This tightening lifts the chest wall upward and outward. At the same time, the diaphragm contracts and flattens. These two actions make the chest cavity larger, which lowers the air pressure inside your lungs. The air pressure outside your body is now higher than the pressure inside your chest. This pressure difference causes air to rush into your lungs.

When you exhale, your rib muscles and diaphragm relax. As they relax, your chest cavity becomes smaller, making the air pressure inside your chest greater than the air pressure outside. As a result, air rushes out of your lungs.

FIGURE 4 ·····························
▶ INTERACTIVE ART **The Breathing Process**
When you inhale, air is pulled into your lungs. When you exhale, air is forced out.

✎ **Interpret Diagrams**
For each diagram, write what happens to your muscles when you breathe.

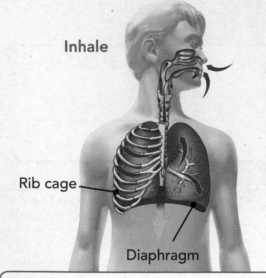

Inhale

Rib cage

Diaphragm

Rib Muscles

_____

_____

_____

Diaphragm

_____

_____

_____

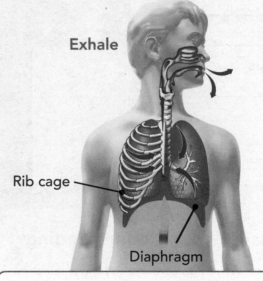

Exhale

Rib cage

Diaphragm

Rib Muscles

_____

_____

_____

Diaphragm

_____

_____

_____

Breathing and Speaking

Did you know that the air that moves out of your lungs when you breathe also helps you to speak? Your **larynx** (LAR ingks), or voice box, is located at the top of your trachea. Two **vocal cords,** which are folds of connective tissue, stretch across the opening of the larynx. When you speak, muscles make the vocal cords contract, narrowing the opening as air rushes through. Then the movement of the vocal cords makes air molecules vibrate, or move rapidly back and forth. This vibration causes a sound—your voice.

✏️ **◑ Chart** In the text, underline and number the steps that help you speak. Then write these steps in the graphic organizer.

Step 1

Step 2

Step 3

apply it!

When you sing, the sounds you make can vary in pitch. That is, you can sing low notes, high notes, and many notes in between. Press your index and middle fingers of one hand gently on the front of your throat.

1 Observe Hum softly, and move your fingers around until you think you have located your voice box. How did humming help you find it?

2 Describe With your fingers still in place, sing softly, switching between low notes and high notes. Describe the differences you felt.

3 Develop Hypotheses How do you think the function of the vocal cords is related to these differences?

Gas Exchange

Gas Exchange Air's final stop in its journey through the respiratory system is an alveolus in the lungs. An alveolus has thin walls and is surrounded by many thin-walled capillaries. **Figure 5** shows some alveoli.

Because the alveoli and the capillaries have very thin walls, certain materials can pass through them easily. After air enters an alveolus, oxygen passes through the wall of the alveolus and then through the capillary wall into the blood. Similarly, carbon dioxide and water pass from the blood into the air within the alveolus. This whole process is called gas exchange.

How Gas Exchange Occurs Imagine that you are a drop of blood. You are traveling through a capillary that wraps around an alveolus. You have a lot of carbon dioxide and a little oxygen. As you move through the capillary, oxygen attaches to the hemoglobin in your red blood cells. Carbon dioxide moves into the alveolus. As you move away from the alveolus, you are rich in oxygen and poor in carbon dioxide.

FIGURE 5 ·······························

▶ **ART IN MOTION** **Gas Exchange**
Gases move across the thin walls of both alveoli and capillaries.

✎ **Relate Text and Visuals** Label each arrow with the gas being exchanged and describe where it is coming from and moving to.

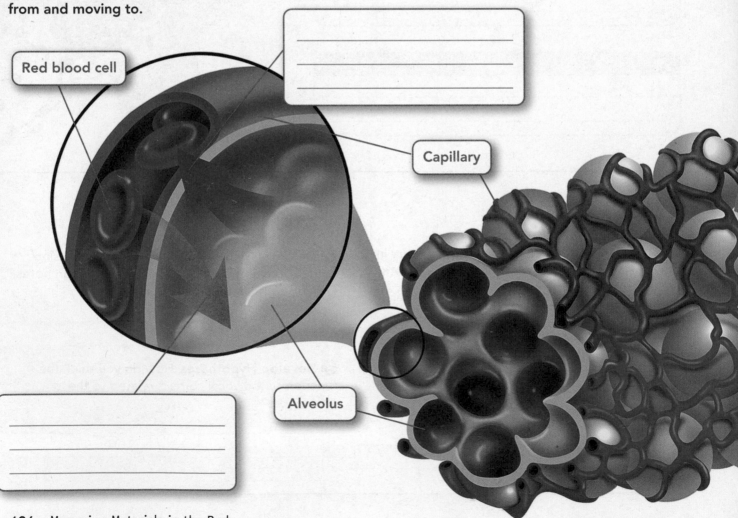

Red blood cell

Capillary

Alveolus

Surface Area for Gas Exchange Your lungs can absorb a large amount of oxygen because of the surface area of the alveoli. An adult's lungs have about 300 million alveoli. Together these alveoli have a surface area of about 100 meters squared (m^2)—the area of the floor in an average classroom! As a result, the alveoli provide a huge amount of surface area for exchanging gases. Therefore, healthy lungs can supply all the oxygen that a person needs—even when the person is very active.

Vocabulary Identify Related Word Forms The verb *absorb* means "to take in." Use this meaning to write a sentence using the noun *absorption*.

Vessel with blood rich in oxygen from lungs

Branch of bronchus

Vessel with blood rich in carbon dioxide from body

Lab zone Do the Lab Investigation *A Breath of Fresh Air*.

🔑 Assess Your Understanding

2a. Identify Where is the larynx located?

_____

_____

b. Explain When you inhale, why does air rush into your lungs?

_____

_____

_____

c. Draw Conclusions How do the alveoli enable people to be very active?

_____

_____

_____

_____

_____

got it?

○ **I get it!** Now I know that when I breathe, air _____

_____

_____

○ **I need extra help with** _____

Go to MY SCIENCE COACH online for help with this subject.

Excretion

🔑 **What Is the Role of the Excretory System?**

🔑 **How Does Excretion Help Your Body Maintain Homeostasis?**

MY PLANET DiARY

Useful Urine

You can recycle plastic, glass, and paper. Did you know that urine can be recycled, too? Some astronauts in space will see their urine turned into drinking water! NASA has developed a machine that will purify the astronauts' urine. The water that is recovered can be used for drinking, among other things.

Why do astronauts need this kind of machine? Large quantities of water are too heavy to carry into space. So the machine runs urine through a filtering system to remove waste. Then iodine is added to the filtered urine to kill any harmful bacteria. What remains is drinkable water.

FUN FACTS

Answer the questions below.

1. How else might the astronauts use the filtered urine?

_____

_____

_____

2. Do you think this system would be useful on Earth? Why or why not?

_____

_____

_____

_____

_____

▶ PLANET DIARY Go to **Planet Diary** to learn more about excretion.

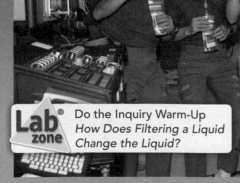

Lab zone Do the Inquiry Warm-Up How Does Filtering a Liquid Change the Liquid?

Vocabulary
- excretion • urea • urine • kidney • ureter
- urinary bladder • urethra • nephron

Skills
- ↻ Reading: Identify the Main Idea
- △ Inquiry: Infer

What Is the Role of the Excretory System?

The human body faces a challenge similar to keeping your room clean. Just as you must clean up papers that pile up in your room, your body must remove wastes from cellular respiration and other processes. The process of removing waste is called **excretion.**

If wastes were not removed from your body, they would pile up and make you sick. 🔑 **The excretory system collects the wastes that cells produce and removes them from the body.** The system includes the kidneys, ureters, urinary bladder, urethra, lungs, skin, and liver. Two wastes that your body must eliminate every day are excess water and urea. **Urea** (yoo REE uh) is a chemical that comes from the breakdown of proteins. As you know, the lungs eliminate some water. Most remaining water is eliminated in a fluid called **urine,** which includes urea and other wastes.

do the math! Analyzing Data

Urine is made up of water, organic solids, and inorganic solids. The organic solids include urea and acids. The inorganic solids include salts and minerals. The solids are dissolved in the water.

❶ **Calculate** Calculate and label on the *Normal Urine Content* graph the percentage of urine that is solids. Calculate and label on the *Solids in Normal Urine* graph the percentage of solids that is urea.

❷ **CHALLENGE** What might a sharp decrease in the percentage of water in a person's urine indicate about the health of that person?

_____

_____

_____

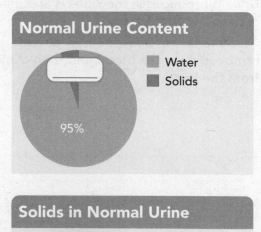

Normal Urine Content

■ Water
■ Solids

95%

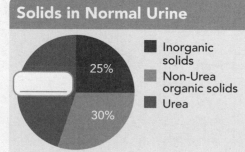

Solids in Normal Urine

■ Inorganic solids
■ Non-Urea organic solids
■ Urea

25%

30%

Structures That Remove Urine

Figure 1 shows the organs that remove urine from the body. Your two kidneys are the major organs of the excretory system. The **kidneys** act like filters. They remove urea and other wastes from the blood but keep materials that the body needs. These wastes are eliminated in the urine. Urine flows from the kidneys through two narrow tubes called **ureters** (yoo REE turz). The ureters carry urine to the **urinary bladder,** a muscular sac that stores urine. Urine leaves the body through a small tube called the **urethra** (yoo REE thruh).

Waste Filtration

Each kidney has about one million nephrons. A **nephron** is a tiny filtering factory that removes wastes from blood and produces urine. The nephrons filter wastes in two stages. First, both wastes and needed materials are filtered out of the blood. Next, much of the needed material is returned to the blood, and the wastes are eliminated from the body. Follow this process in **Figure 2.**

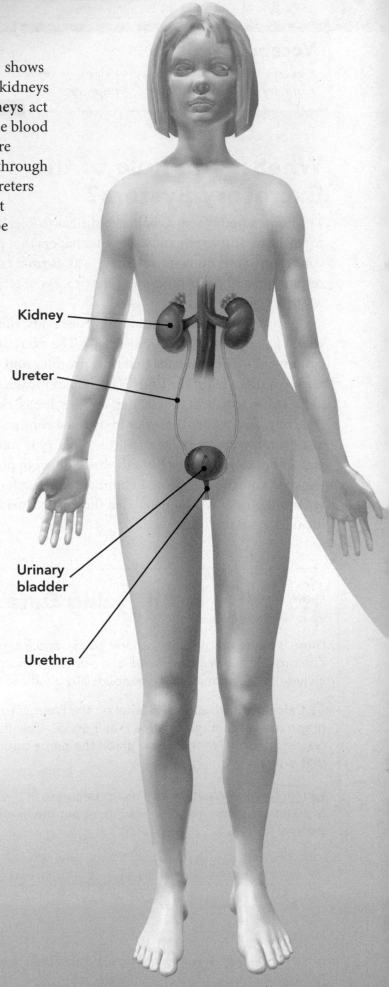

Kidney

Ureter

Urinary bladder

Urethra

FIGURE 1 ·····························

Removing Urine

Urine is produced in the kidneys and then removed from the body.

✎ **Summarize** Describe how urine is removed from the blood and then eliminated from the body.

_____

_____

_____

_____

_____

_____

How the Kidneys Work

Most of the work of the kidneys is done in the nephrons.

✏️ ⚠️ **Infer** In the key, write what each color represents in the diagram. Then explain below why it is important for capillaries to surround the nephron tube.

_____

_____

_____

_____

Key

■ _____

■ _____

■ _____

Stage 1

• Blood flows into the cluster of capillaries in the thin-walled, hollow nephron capsule.

• Urea, glucose, and some water are filtered out of the blood and into the capsule.

• These materials then pass into the nephron tube.

Stage 2

• As the material flows through the nephron tube, most of the needed glucose and water move back into the blood through the capillaries.

• Most of the urea and some of the water stay in the nephron tube and become urine.

Nephron capsule

Nephron tube

Lab zone® Do the Quick Lab _Kidney Function._

🔑 Assess Your Understanding

1a. Name The chemical _____ comes from the breakdown of proteins.

b. Draw Conclusions Why is it important for a kidney to have many nephrons?

_____

_____

_____

got it?

○ **I get it!** Now I know that the function of the excretory system is to _____

_____

○ **I need extra help with** _____

_Go to_ **MY SCIENCE** ⑤ **COACH** _online for help with this subject._

How Does Excretion Help Your Body Maintain Homeostasis?

A buildup of wastes such as urea, excess water, and carbon dioxide can upset your body's balance. 🔑 **Excretion helps to maintain homeostasis by keeping the body's internal environment stable and free of harmful levels of chemicals.** The organs of excretion include the kidneys, lungs, skin, and liver.

Kidneys As the kidneys filter blood, they regulate the amount of water in your body, helping to maintain homeostasis, or internal stability. Remember that as urine is being formed, needed water passes from the nephron tubes into the blood. The amount of water that returns to the blood depends on conditions both outside and inside the body. For example, on a hot day when you have been sweating a lot and have not had much to drink, almost all the water in the nephron tubes will move back into the blood. You will excrete only a small amount of urine. On a cool day when you have drunk a lot of water, less water will move back into the blood. You will excrete a larger volume of urine. Look at **Figure 3**.

Vocabulary Identify Related Word Forms You know the noun *excretion* means "the process of removing wastes." Use this meaning to choose the correct meaning of the verb *excrete*.

○ relating to removing wastes

○ to remove wastes

○ the state of removing wastes

FIGURE 3 ·······································

Fluid Absorption
These three students have been doing different activities all day.

✎ **Relate Text and Visuals** Which student will probably produce the least urine? Explain.

_____

_____

_____

Maria has been in classes all morning. She has had nothing to eat or drink.

Kari has been running sprints. She forgot to bring her water bottle.

Mike has been sitting on the bench and drinking water.

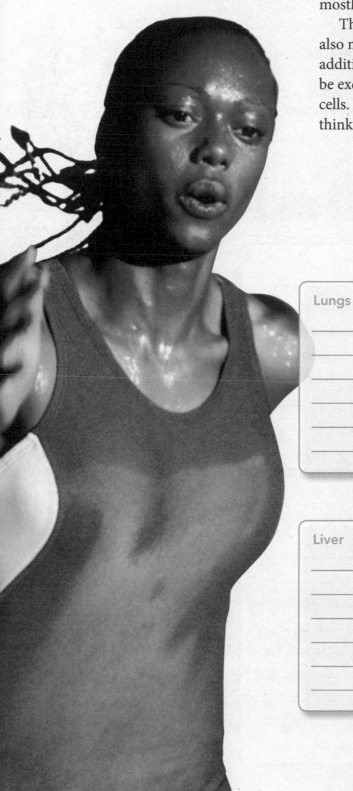

Lungs, Skin, and Liver Organs that function as part of other systems in your body also help keep you healthy by excreting wastes. For example, the lungs of the respiratory system remove carbon dioxide and some water when you exhale. The skin, part of your integumentary system, contains sweat glands that produce perspiration. Perspiration consists mostly of water, salt, and a small amount of urea.

The liver, which functions as part of the digestive system, also makes urea from the breakdown of proteins in the body. In addition, the liver breaks down other wastes into forms that can be excreted. For example, the liver breaks down old red blood cells. It even recycles some of their parts. In this way, you can think of the liver as a recycling factory.

✏️

🔵 **Identify the Main Idea** In your own words, write about each organ's role in excretion.

Lungs
_____
_____
_____
_____

Skin
_____
_____
_____
_____

Liver
_____
_____
_____
_____

Kidneys
_____
_____
_____
_____

EXPLORE THE BIG ?

Moving Things Along

How do systems of the body move and manage materials?

FIGURE 4

The systems of the body work together, helping to maintain homeostasis by changing materials and moving them to where they can be used or excreted.

Complete the following tasks.

1. **Identify** For each system, identify its main function and tell what materials are managed or moved.
2. **Describe System Interactions** Which system is the link for moving materials among the other three systems?

____

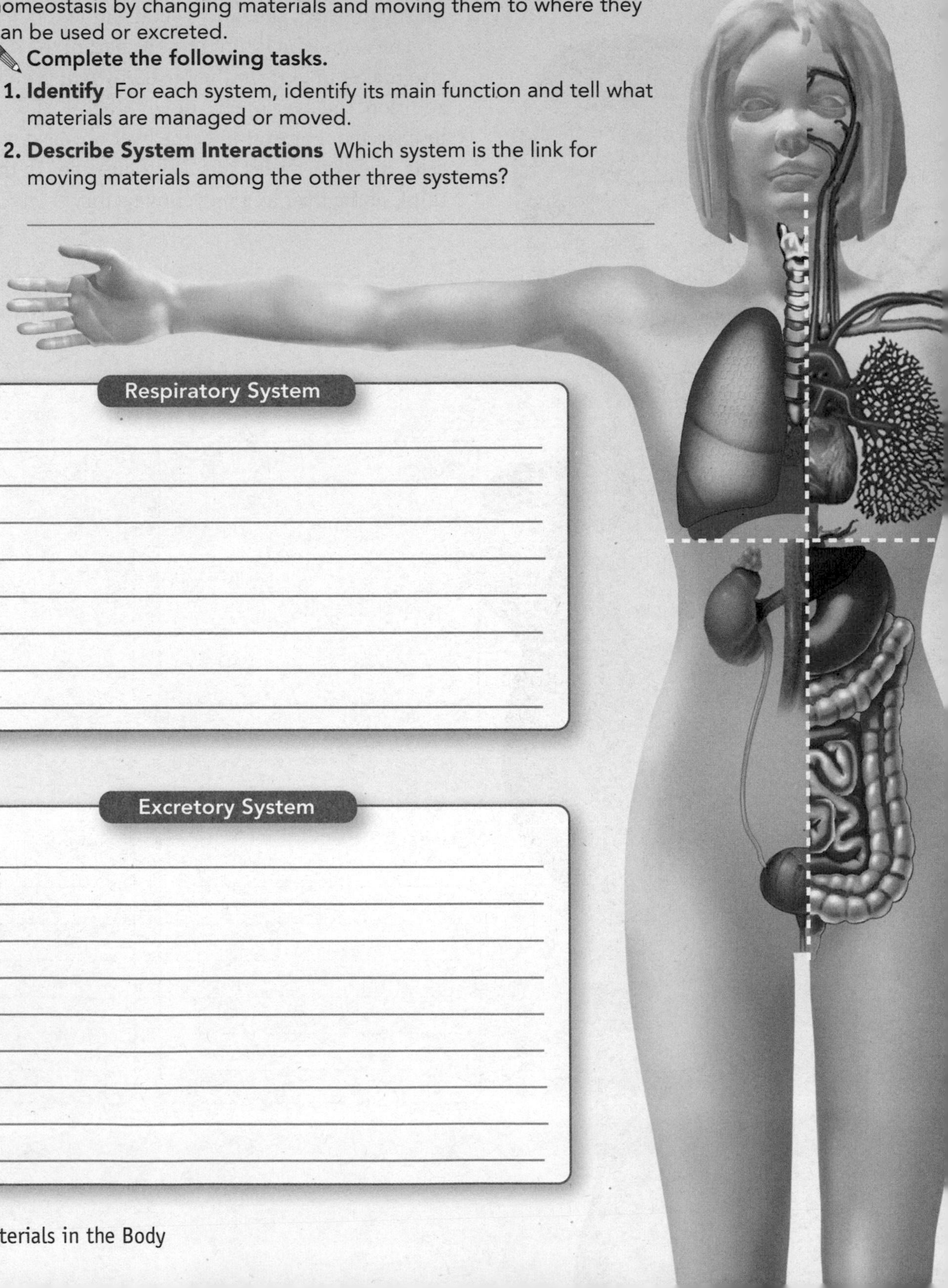

Respiratory System

____

Excretory System

____

Circulatory System

Digestive System

Lab zone® Do the Quick Lab *Perspiration.*

Assess Your Understanding

2a. Review How does removing wastes from the body help maintain homeostasis?

b. Predict On a long bus trip, a traveler does not drink water for several hours. How will the volume of urine she produces that day compare to the volume on a day when she drinks several glasses of water? Explain.

c. ANSWER THE BIG Q How do systems of the body move and manage materials?

got it?

○ **I get it!** Now I know that excretion helps maintain homeostasis in my body by

○ I need extra help with

Go to **MY SCIENCE COACH** *online for help with this subject.*

12 Study Guide

Materials in the body are managed and moved by the _____, _____, _____, and _____ systems.

LESSON 1 Digestion

🔑 Food provides your body with materials for growth and repair. It also provides energy.

🔑 The digestive system breaks down food, absorbs nutrients, and eliminates waste.

🔑 Substances produced by the liver, pancreas, and lining of the small intestine help to complete chemical digestion.

Vocabulary
- calorie • enzyme • esophagus
- peristalsis • villi

LESSON 2 The Circulatory System

🔑 The circulatory system delivers substances to cells, carries wastes away, and regulates body temperature. Blood cells fight disease.

🔑 Blood has four components: plasma, red blood cells, white blood cells, and platelets.

Vocabulary
- circulatory system • heart • atrium • ventricle
- valve • artery • aorta • capillary • vein
- hemoglobin

LESSON 3 The Respiratory System

🔑 Your respiratory system moves air containing oxygen into your lungs and removes carbon dioxide and water from your body. Your lungs and the structures that lead to them make up your respiratory system.

🔑 When you breathe, your rib muscles and diaphragm work together, causing air to move into or out of your lungs. This airflow leads to the exchange of gases that occurs in your lungs.

Vocabulary
- pharynx • trachea • cilia • bronchi • lungs • alveoli
- diaphragm • larynx • vocal cords

LESSON 4 Excretion

🔑 The excretory system collects the wastes that cells produce and removes them from the body.

🔑 Excretion helps maintain homeostasis by keeping the body's internal environment stable and free of harmful levels of chemicals.

Vocabulary
- excretion • urea • urine • kidney • ureter
- urinary bladder • urethra • nephron

Review and Assessment

LESSON 1 Digestion

1. Mechanical digestion begins in the

   a. liver.　　　　**b.** esophagus.

   c. mouth.　　　　**d.** small intestine.

2. _____ is the involuntary contraction of muscles that pushes food forward.

3. Interpret Diagrams How do you think acid reflux, the condition illustrated in the diagram below, affects the esophagus?

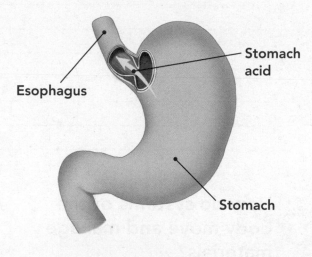

Esophagus

Stomach acid

Stomach

_____

_____

_____

4. Apply Concepts How does the function of the digestive system contribute to homeostasis?

_____

_____

_____

_____

5. 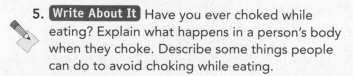 **Write About It** Have you ever choked while eating? Explain what happens in a person's body when they choke. Describe some things people can do to avoid choking while eating.

LESSON 2 The Circulatory System

6. What structure regulates the direction of blood flow through the heart?

   a. ventricle　　　**b.** pacemaker

   c. valve　　　　　**d.** artery

7. The _____ in your body carry blood back to your heart.

8. Classify Which chambers of the heart below are the ventricles? Which chamber receives oxygen-poor blood from the body?

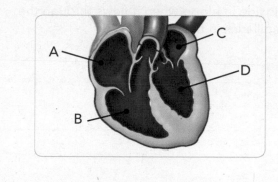

_____

_____

_____

9. Predict Is it safe for a person with blood type O+ to receive a blood transfusion from a person who has blood type A+? Explain.

_____

_____

_____

_____

_____

10. Write About It People who do not have enough iron in their diets sometimes develop anemia, a condition in which their blood cannot carry a normal amount of oxygen. Write a paragraph to explain why this is so.

The Respiratory System

11. Your voice is produced by the

    a. pharynx.   **b.** larynx.

    c. trachea.   **d.** alveoli.

12. Clusters of air sacs in the lungs are _____

13. Classify What part of the respiratory system connects the mouth and nose?

_____

14. Sequence What happens to the carbon dioxide in blood when it flows through the capillaries in the alveoli?

_____

_____

_____

_____

15. Compare and Contrast How do mucus and cilia work together to remove dust that enters your nose? How do they differ?

_____

_____

_____

_____

_____

_____

16. Write About It Suppose you are a doctor with patients who are mountain climbers. Write a letter to these patients that explains how gas exchange is affected at the top of a mountain, where air pressure is lower and there is less oxygen than at lower elevations.

Excretion

17. Urine leaves the body through the

    a. ureters.   **b.** nephrons.

    c. urinary bladder.   **d.** urethra.

18. Urine is stored in the _____

19. Relate Cause and Effect How do the kidneys help maintain homeostasis?

_____

_____

_____

_____

_____

_____

_____

APPLY THE BIG ? **How do systems of the body move and manage materials?**

20. You eat an apple. Describe how the functions of your body systems working together can provide you with energy from the apple.

_____

_____

_____

_____

_____

_____

_____

_____

Standardized Test Prep

Multiple Choice

Circle the letter of the best answer.

1. Which statement below correctly describes the diagram?

   A Blood Vessel A carries blood to the heart.

   B Blood Vessel A is where a pulse can be measured.

   C Blood Vessel B is where diffusion takes place.

   D Blood Vessel B carries blood to the lungs.

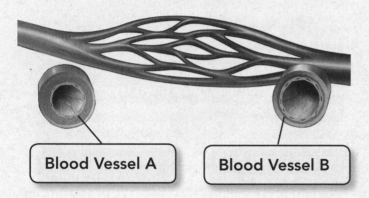

Blood Vessel A **Blood Vessel B**

2. Which of the following nutrients provides the *most* energy for the body?

   A fats

   B proteins

   C carbohydrates

   D vitamins

3. Which of the following parts of the digestive system is paired with its function?

   A esophagus—digests carbohydrates

   B stomach—digests fats

   C large intestine—absorbs water

   D small intestine—begins mechanical digestion

4. Which of the following organs functions as both a respiratory organ and an excretory organ?

   A the liver

   B the skin

   C the kidneys

   D the lungs

5. The correct sequence for the path of blood through the body is

   A heart—lungs—other body parts

   B lungs—other body parts—heart

   C heart—lungs—heart—other body parts

   D heart—other body parts—lungs—heart

Constructed Response

Use the table below and your knowledge of science to help you answer Question 6. Write your answer on a separate sheet of paper.

Blood Types		
Blood Type	Marker Molecules	Clumping Proteins
A	A	anti-B
B	B	anti-A
AB	A and B	none
O	none	anti-A and anti-B

6. A blood bank stores donated blood for transfusions. Which blood type should a blood bank store the most of? People with which blood type will have the greatest chance of finding donated blood that will not cause clumping in a transfusion? Explain your answers.

Artificial Blood

Artist's drawing of an artificial red blood cell ▼

Blood is amazing. It carries oxygen, nutrients, and hormones throughout the body, and carries waste products away from cells. If you have a cut, blood cells called *platelets* quickly patch things up. Blood also carries cells that fight diseases and infections.

If patients lose a lot of blood, doctors must rely on donated blood supplies. This donated blood saves a lot of lives, but it is in short supply. So, scientists have been trying to develop compounds that make it possible to use less blood. One such compound is 50 times more effective at carrying oxygen than red blood cells are. This compound also delivers oxygen through blood vessels that are too damaged to allow red blood cells to pass.

Artificial blood compounds have been used to treat a small number of patients, but they can be expensive to make. Also, no compound can perform all the jobs that blood does. However, researchers hope to produce an artificial blood source that is as good as the real thing!

Write About It Scientists have been trying to find many ways to use less donated blood, including artificial blood. Research problems scientists have come across in developing blood replacements, and write an essay describing these problems.

Understanding Fitness Assessments

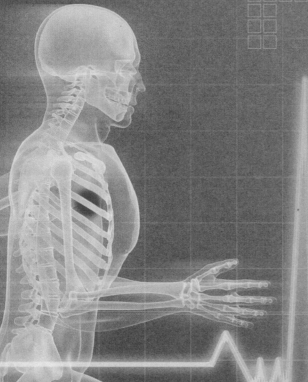

How hard does your heart work to pump blood? One tool for learning about a person's physical fitness is to measure how exercise affects his or her heart rate.

Cardiovascular appraisals measure the difference between a person's heart rate before exercise and during exercise. In simple cardiovascular fitness appraisals, participants check and record their resting heart rates. They then do some form of exercise for a set period of time. The exercises must be aerobic exercises—activities that increase the body's need for oxygen and raise the heart rate. Running, climbing stairs, or riding a bike are common aerobic exercises. After a period of time, participants stop their exercises and immediately check their heart rates again.

The graph below shows how exercise affects the heart rates of two people. Which person is more physically fit? Explain your reasoning.

Analyze It Just how much can you tell about the fitness and activity levels of the two people in the graph? List characteristics of Person A and Person B that might have affected the results of this fitness appraisal. Design a questionnaire that would allow you to find out more about the test subjects.

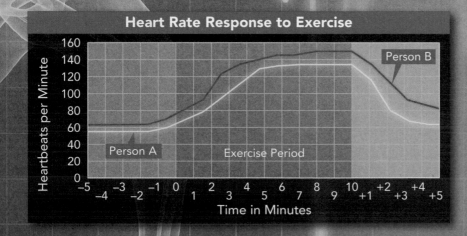

Heart Rate Response to Exercise

Heartbeats per Minute

Person A

Person B

Exercise Period

Time in Minutes

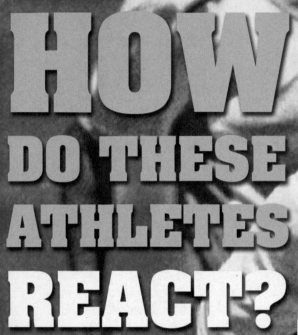

HOW
DO THESE
ATHLETES
REACT?

 THE BIG ?

What systems regulate and control body processes?

Soccer, known as football in most of the world, can be an exciting game. The Brazilian player in yellow is trying to advance the ball past the U.S. players in red and white. As they play the game, all these players rely on their body systems to sense what is happening, think about game strategy, react quickly, and sustain their energy.

⚠️ **Infer** When you are about to collide with someone, how do you react?

_____

_____

_____

_____

▶ UNTAMED SCIENCE Watch the **Untamed Science** video to learn more about the nervous system.

Controlling Body Processes

Check Your Understanding

1. Background Read the paragraph below and then answer the question.

> Rajev wakes up gasping. Smoke enters his nose and stings his eyes. He feels the **involuntary** pounding of his heart. His **sense organs** send signals to his brain—alarms, shouts, smoke, heat, and sirens. Instantly, Rajev interprets the signals and takes **voluntary** action. He crawls to the window as the fire ladder rises below him.

> **Involuntary** action is not under a person's conscious control.
>
> **Sense organs,** such as eyes and ears, are body structures that gather information from your surroundings.
>
> **Voluntary** action is under a person's conscious control.

- Why is Rajev's crawling to the window a voluntary rather than an involuntary action?

_____

_____

> MY READING WEB If you had trouble completing the question above, visit **My Reading Web** and type in *Controlling Body Processes*.

Vocabulary Skill

Prefixes A prefix is a word part that is added to the beginning of a word to change its meaning. The table below lists prefixes that will help you learn terms in this chapter.

Prefix	Meaning	Term
inter-	between, among	interneuron, *n.* a neuron, or nerve cell, that is between other neurons
re-	back, over again	reflex, *n.* an automatic response that occurs rapidly without conscious control

2. Quick Check The prefix *inter-* has more than one meaning. In the table above, circle the meaning of *inter-* that relates to the word *interneuron.*

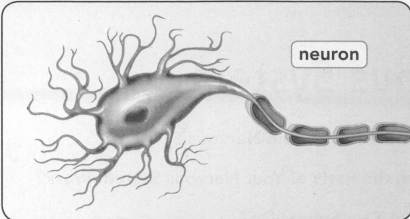

neuron

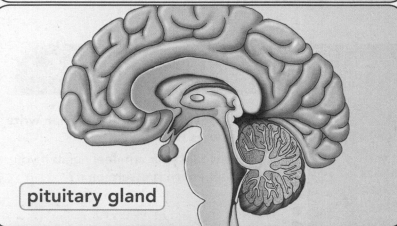

pituitary gland

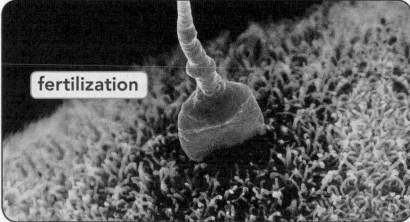

fertilization

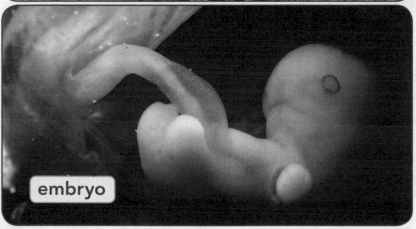

embryo

Chapter Preview

LESSON 1

- neuron • nerve impulse
- nerve • synapse
- central nervous system
- peripheral nervous system
- reflex

🔵 **Identify Supporting Evidence**
🔺 **Infer**

LESSON 2

- gland • duct • hormone
- target cell • hypothalamus
- pituitary gland
- negative feedback

🔵 **Identify the Main Idea**
🔺 **Make Models**

LESSON 3

- fertilization • egg • sperm
- zygote • testes • testosterone
- scrotum • semen • penis
- ovary • estrogen
- Fallopian tube • uterus • vagina
- menstrual cycle • menstruation
- ovulation

🔵 **Sequence**
🔺 **Develop Hypotheses**

LESSON 4

- embryo • fetus • amniotic sac
- placenta • umbilical cord

🔵 **Compare and Contrast**
🔺 **Calculate**

> **VOCAB FLASH CARDS** For extra help with vocabulary, visit **Vocab Flash Cards** and type in *Controlling Body Processes.*

- **What Is the Role of the Nervous System?**

- **How Do the Parts of Your Nervous System Work?**

- **What Do Your Senses Do?**

my PLANET DiARY

FUN FACTS

Wake Up!

Did you ever wake from a nap, only to find that your arm is "asleep"? What causes this "pins-and-needles" sensation? If you lie on your arm for a long period of time, too much pressure is placed on the nerves. The communication between your arm and brain no longer flows smoothly. A decrease in normal signals makes your arm feel odd. The pins-and-needles feeling actually happens when you remove the pressure from the nerves. They begin to send a normal flow of messages from your arm to your brain again. You slowly regain normal feeling in your arm. Remember to change your position often when you sit or lie down. If you don't, you'll end up having to wake up your arms and legs!

Read the following questions. Then write your answers below.

1. Why would your arm feel numb if you put too much pressure on it?

_____

_____

_____

2. Describe a time when one of your limbs fell asleep. How did it feel?

_____

_____

_____

_____

_____

> PLANET DIARY Go to **Planet Diary** to learn more about the nervous system.

 Do the Inquiry Warm-up
How Simple Is a Simple Task?

Vocabulary
- neuron • nerve impulse • nerve
- synapse • central nervous system
- peripheral nervous system • reflex

Skills
↻ Reading: Identify Supporting Evidence
△ Inquiry: Infer

What Is the Role of the Nervous System?

You can use the Internet to chat with a friend hundreds of miles away. You can also use it to gather information from anywhere in the world. Like the Internet, your nervous system is a communications network. It includes the brain, the spinal cord, and the nerves that run throughout the body. It also includes the eyes, ears, and other sense organs. ⌐ **Your nervous system receives information about what is happening both inside and outside your body. It directs how your body responds to this information. In addition, your nervous system helps maintain homeostasis.** Without your nervous system, you could not move, think, or sense the world around you.

Receiving Information Your nervous system makes you aware of what is happening around you. For example, if you were at a cookout like the one shown in **Figure 1,** you would know when the wind was blowing or a fly was buzzing around your head. Your nervous system also checks conditions inside your body, such as the level of glucose in your blood and your internal body temperature.

FIGURE 1 ···

Gathering Information
The nervous system allows people to react to their environment.

✎ **Describe** List four things that your nervous system would help you notice if you were enjoying a meal with this family.

_____

_____

_____

_____

_____

Responding to Information

Any change or signal in the environment that an organism can recognize and react to is called a stimulus (STIM yoo lus; plural *stimuli*). For example, a buzzing fly is a stimulus. After your nervous system analyzes a stimulus, it directs a response. A response is a reaction to a stimulus. Some nervous system responses, such as swatting a fly, are voluntary, or under your control. But heart rate, breathing, sweating, and other necessary processes are involuntary responses to stimuli inside your body.

Maintaining Homeostasis

The nervous system helps maintain homeostasis by directing your body to respond properly to information it receives. For example, when your blood's glucose level drops, your nervous system signals that you are hungry. So, you eat. This action maintains homeostasis by supplying your body with needed nutrients and energy.

apply it!

Soccer goalies rely on their nervous systems.

1 ⚠️ **Infer** Read the headings in each box. Then describe how the goalie is doing each task.

2 **CHALLENGE** Suppose the goalie starts sweating. What may have caused this response?

_____

_____

_____

Receiving Information

_____

_____

_____

Responding to Information

_____

_____

_____

Maintaining Homeostasis

_____

_____

_____

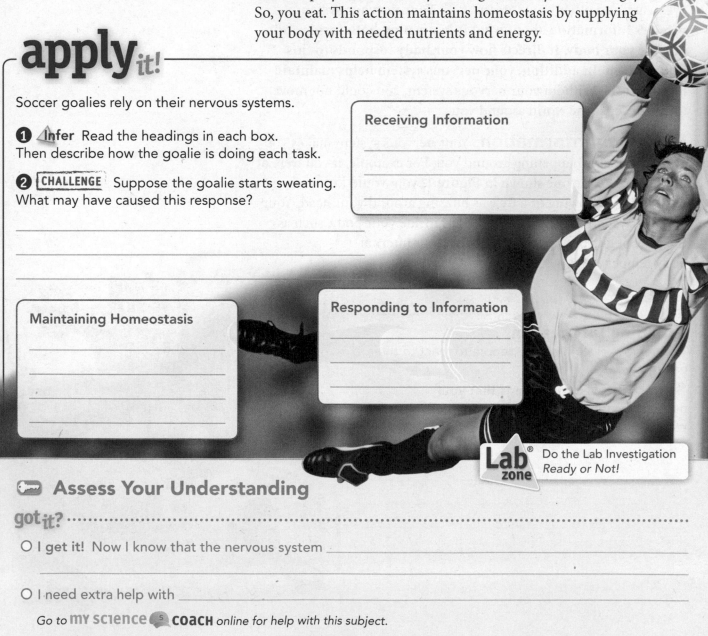

Lab zone® Do the Lab Investigation *Ready or Not!*

🔑 Assess Your Understanding

got it? ....

○ I get it! Now I know that the nervous system _____

_____

○ I need extra help with _____

Go to MY SCIENCE ⓢ COACH online for help with this subject.

How Do the Parts of Your Nervous System Work?

Your nervous system includes your brain, spinal cord, and the nerves that connect these organs to all parts of your body. Individual cells that carry information through your nervous system are called **neurons** (NOO rahnz), or nerve cells. The message that a neuron carries is called a **nerve impulse.** These impulses may occur as either electrical or chemical signals.

Neurons 🔑 **Neurons carry nerve impulses throughout the body.** A neuron has a large cell body that contains a nucleus, threadlike extensions called dendrites, and an axon, as shown in **Figure 2.** Nerve impulses begin in a dendrite and move through the neuron's cell body to the tips of the axon. Axons and their tissue covering make up nerve fibers. Nerve fibers are often arranged in parallel bundles covered with more connective tissue. They look like uncooked spaghetti wrapped in thin plastic. A bundle of nerve fibers is called a **nerve.**

Three Kinds of Neurons Your nervous system includes three kinds of neurons. A sensory neuron picks up a stimulus and converts it into a nerve impulse. The impulse travels along sensory neurons until it reaches an interneuron usually in the brain or spinal cord. An interneuron carries a nerve impulse to another interneuron or to a motor neuron. A motor neuron sends an impulse to a muscle or gland, enabling it to respond.

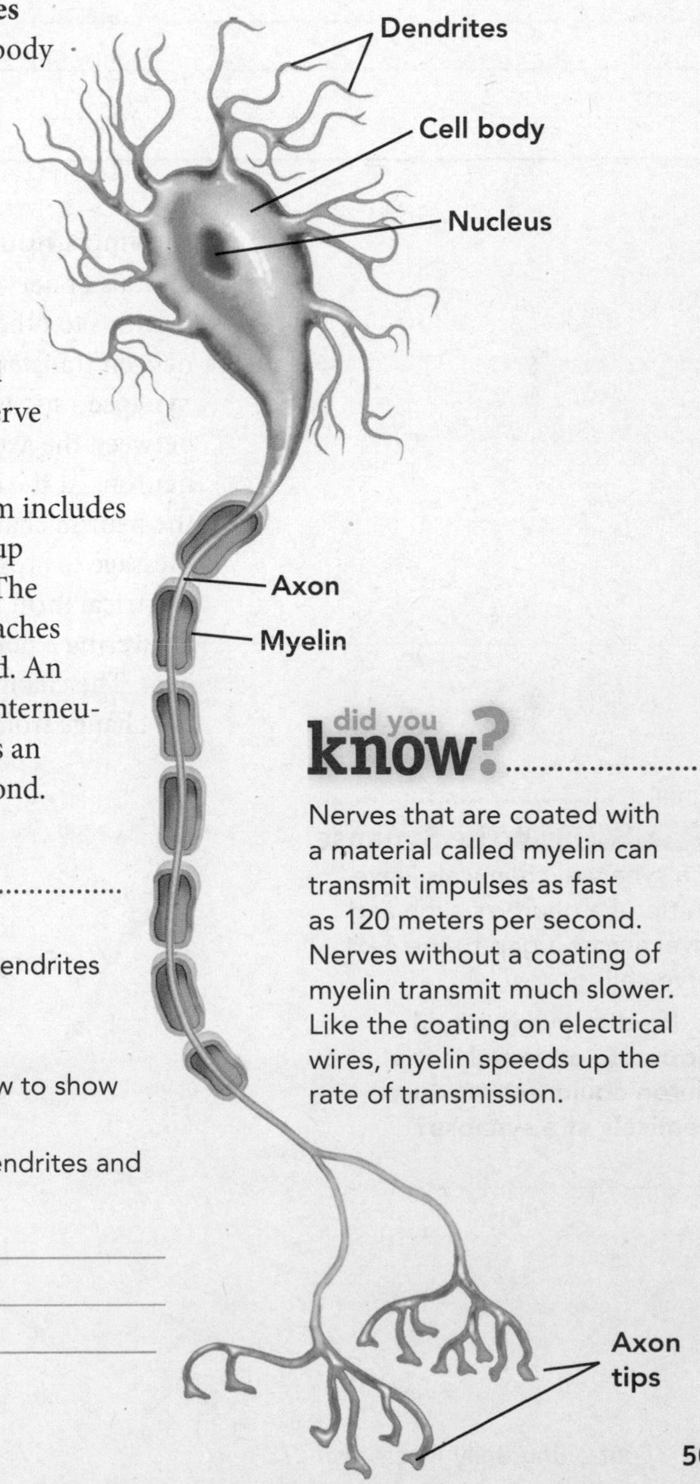

FIGURE 2 ···

Structure of a Neuron

A neuron has only one axon but can have many dendrites that extend from the cell body.

✏ **Use the diagram to complete these tasks.**

1. **Interpret Diagrams** Draw a line with an arrow to show the path of a nerve impulse in the neuron.

2. **Draw Conclusions** How does having both dendrites and an axon help a neuron function?

_____

_____

_____

Dendrites

Cell body

Nucleus

Axon

Myelin

did you know?

Nerves that are coated with a material called myelin can transmit impulses as fast as 120 meters per second. Nerves without a coating of myelin transmit much slower. Like the coating on electrical wires, myelin speeds up the rate of transmission.

Axon tips

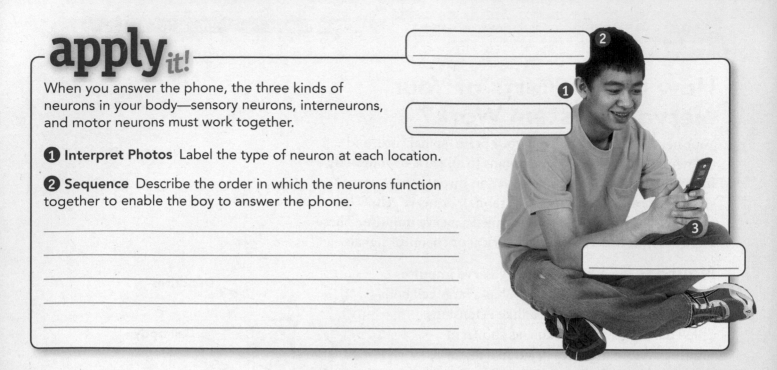

apply it!

When you answer the phone, the three kinds of neurons in your body—sensory neurons, interneurons, and motor neurons must work together.

1 Interpret Photos Label the type of neuron at each location.

2 Sequence Describe the order in which the neurons function together to enable the boy to answer the phone.

_____

_____

_____

_____

Moving Impulses Between Neurons Every day, billions of nerve impulses travel through your nervous system from neurons to other neurons or body structures. The place where a neuron transfers an impulse to another structure is called a **synapse** (SIN aps). **Figure 3** shows the gap within the synapse between the axon tip of one neuron and the dendrite of another neuron. At the axon tips, electrical signals carried through the neuron change into a chemical form. This change allows the message to cross the gap. The message then continues in electrical form through the next neuron. These changes are like answering a phone and then writing down the information you hear. The change from hearing information to writing it is like the change from electrical to chemical form.

FIGURE 3 ····························

▶ ART IN MOTION **The Synapse**

At a synapse, chemicals leave the tip of a neuron's axon and travel across a gap to the next nerve cell.

✎ **Predict** What would happen to an impulse if a neuron could not produce chemicals at a synapse?

_____

_____

_____

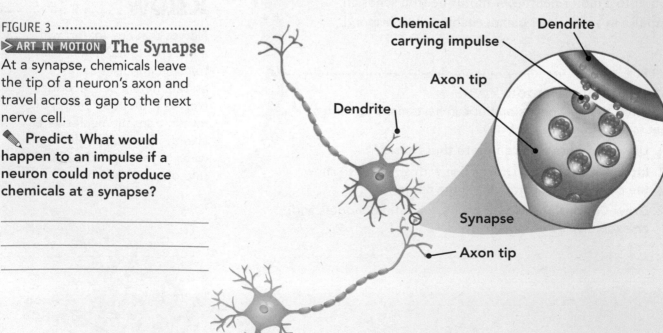

Chemical carrying impulse

Dendrite

Axon tip

Dendrite

Synapse

Axon tip

The Central Nervous System Like a traffic cop directing car drivers through a busy intersection, your nervous system directs your movements. It has two divisions that work together: the central nervous system and the peripheral nervous system. The **central nervous system** includes the brain and spinal cord and acts like the traffic cop. The **peripheral nervous system** includes all the nerves outside of the central nervous system, which are like the car drivers. **Figure 4** shows both systems.

🔑 **The brain is the control center of the central nervous system. The spinal cord is a thick column of nervous tissue that links the brain to the peripheral nervous system.** Most impulses from the peripheral nerves travel through the spinal cord to get to the brain. The brain then directs a response, which usually travels through the spinal cord and back to peripheral nerves.

FIGURE 4 ·······················

The Nervous System
All information about what is happening in the outside world and inside your body travels through your nervous system.

✏ **Use the diagram and the boxes to complete these tasks.**

1. **Identify** Circle the name of each structure that is part of the central nervous system.

2. **Summarize** Explain in your own words the function of the structures in the diagram.

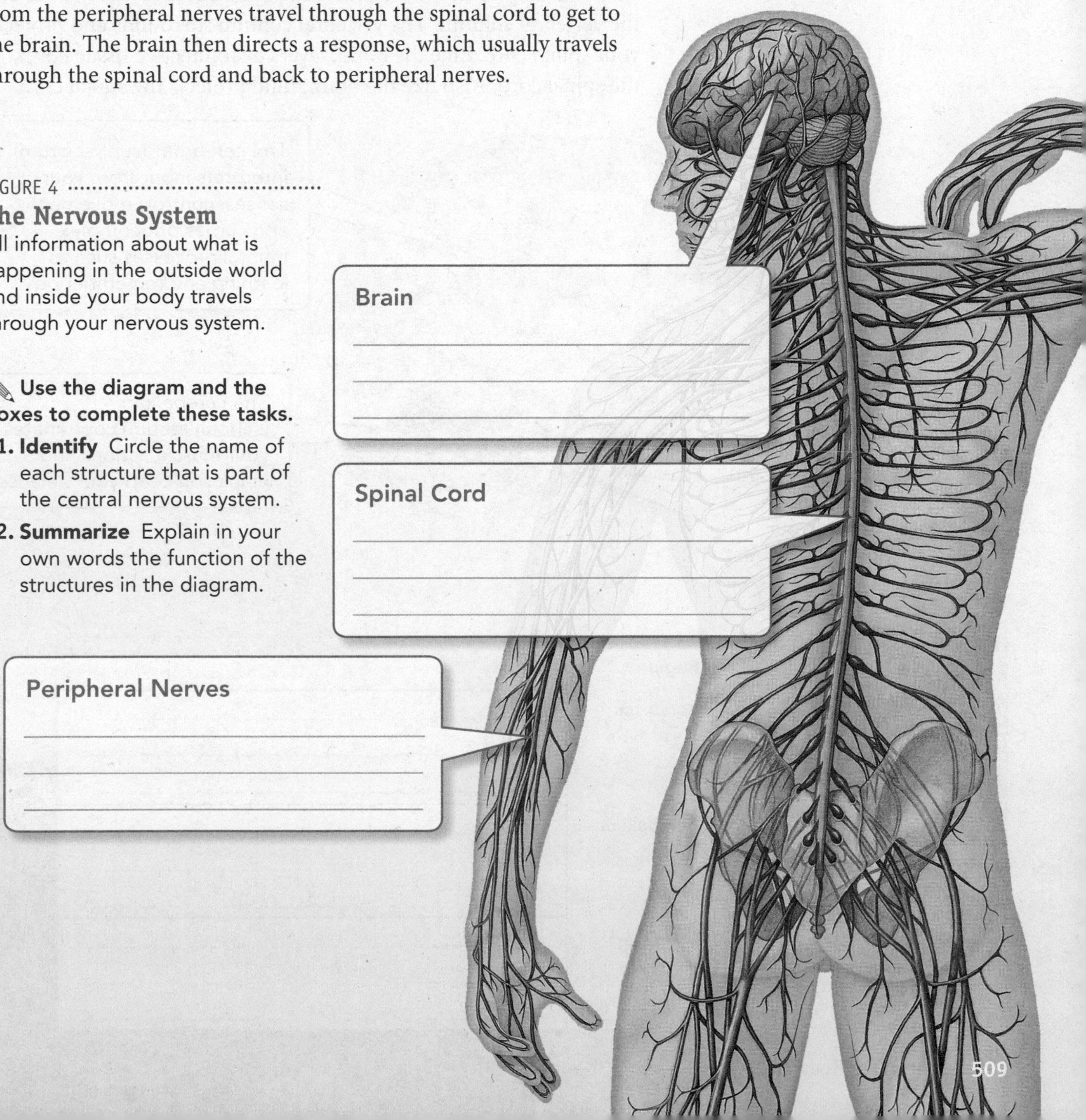

Brain
_____
_____
_____

Spinal Cord
_____
_____
_____

Peripheral Nerves
_____
_____
_____

509

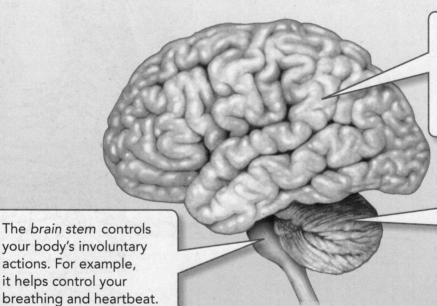

The Brain Your brain has about 100 billion neurons, all of which are interneurons. Each of those neurons may receive up to 10,000 messages from other neurons and may send messages to about 1,000 more! Three layers of connective tissue under the skull cover the brain. Fluid fills the space between the middle layer and the innermost layer of connective tissue. The skull, the connective tissue, and the fluid all help protect the brain from injury. Three main regions of the brain are the brain stem, the cerebellum, and the cerebrum, as shown in **Figure 5.**

The Spinal Cord The brain stem connects to the spinal cord. Run your fingers down the center of your back to feel the bones of the vertebral column. The vertebral column surrounds and protects your spinal cord. Like the brain, layers of connective tissue cover the spinal cord. Also like the brain, fluid protects the spinal cord.

> ✏️ **Identify Supporting Evidence** Which structures protect the brain from injury?
>
> _____
>
> _____
>
> _____

The *cerebrum* (suh REE brum) interprets input from your senses, controls movement, and carries out complex mental processes such as learning and remembering.

The *cerebellum* (sehr uh BEL um) coordinates your muscle actions and helps you keep your balance.

The *brain stem* controls your body's involuntary actions. For example, it helps control your breathing and heartbeat.

FIGURE 5 ·······························

The Brain
Different regions of the brain receive and process different information.

✏️ **Apply Concepts** In the chart, write examples of how you use each region of your brain.

Region	Activity
Cerebrum	
Cerebellum	
Brain stem	

The Peripheral Nervous System

The second division of the nervous system is the peripheral nervous system. The peripheral nervous system is a network of nerves that branches out from the central nervous system and connects it to the rest of the body. The peripheral nervous system is involved in both involuntary and voluntary actions.

The peripheral nervous system has 43 pairs of nerves. Twelve pairs begin in the brain. The other 31 pairs—the spinal nerves—begin in the spinal cord. One nerve in each pair goes to the left side of the body, and the other goes to the right. Look at the spinal nerves shown in **Figure 6.** Each spinal nerve contains axons of both sensory and motor neurons. The sensory neurons carry impulses from the body to the central nervous system. In contrast, the motor neurons carry impulses from the central nervous system to the body.

Somatic and Autonomic Systems

The peripheral nervous system has two groups of nerves. They are the nerves of the somatic (soh MAT ik) nervous system and those of the autonomic (awt uh NAHM ik) nervous system. The somatic nervous system controls voluntary actions, such as using a fork. The autonomic nervous system controls involuntary actions, such as as digesting food.

Vocabulary Prefixes The prefix *auto-* comes from the Greek word for "self." How can this prefix help you to remember the function of the autonomic nervous system?

_____

_____

_____

FIGURE 6 ·····················

The Spinal Nerves

The spinal nerves leave the spinal cord through spaces between the vertebrae.

 **Infer** On the diagram, circle the two spinal nerves that are a pair. Then explain how a spinal nerve is like a two-lane highway.

_____

_____

_____

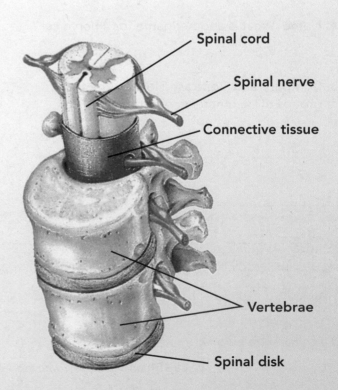

Spinal cord

Spinal nerve

Connective tissue

Vertebrae

Spinal disk

511

FIGURE 7 ······································
▶ INTERACTIVE ART A Reflex Action
Reflexes help protect your body.

✏️ **Relate Text and Visuals** On the diagram, number the steps in a reflex action.

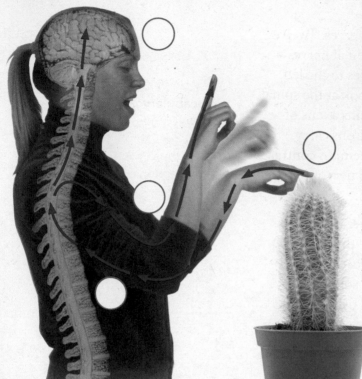

Reflexes The brain usually controls the contraction of skeletal muscles. Sometimes, however, skeletal muscles contract without involving the brain. A **reflex** is an automatic response that occurs rapidly without conscious control. For example, when your finger touches a sharp object, sensory neurons detect a pain stimulus. They send impulses to the spinal cord. Interneurons there pass those impulses directly to motor neurons. The motor neurons cause your arm muscles to contract, pulling your finger away from the sharp object like the cactus in **Figure 7**.

As the reflex action happens, other nerve impulses travel to your brain. As your brain interprets them, you feel a pain in your finger. It takes longer for the pain impulses to reach the brain and be interpreted than it does for the reflex action to occur. By the time you feel the pain, you have already jerked your hand away.

Lab zone® Do the Quick Lab *How Does Your Knee React?*

🔑 Assess Your Understanding

1a. Name What is another name for a nerve cell?

_____

b. Compare and Contrast How do the two groups of peripheral nerves differ?

_____

_____

_____

2a. Identify The part of the brain that helps you keep from falling is the _____.

b. Draw Conclusions Why is it important for the brain to be so well protected?

_____

_____

_____

got it? ··

○ **I get it!** Now I know that messages are carried through the nervous system along structures that

include _____

_____

○ **I need extra help with** _____

Go to **MY SCIENCE ⑤ COACH** *online for help with this subject.*

512 *Controlling Body Processes*

What Do Your Senses Do?

Going to the movie theater can be a treat for your senses. Show times and titles flash on displays. Moviegoers chatter in line. As you walk into the theater, you can smell the popcorn. When you finally sit in your seat, you can feel the texture of the cushions on your body. You take a bite of your snack, and enjoy the show.

🔑 **Your eyes, ears, nose, mouth, and skin are specialized sense organs that enable you to get information from the outside world.** Each of these organs contains sensory neurons that send impulses to your brain. Your brain interprets them, enabling you to understand more about your environment.

How You See You would not be able to enjoy the visual experience of a movie without your sense of sight. Your eyes respond to the stimulus of light. They convert that stimulus into impulses that your brain interprets, enabling you to see.

The eye has many parts, as shown in **Figure 8.** Notice that light rays enter the eye through the pupil. Then they pass through the lens. Muscles attached to the lens adjust its shape and focus light rays on the retina. Because the lens bends light rays, it produces an upside-down image. The retina contains light-sensitive cells that produce nerve impulses. These impulses travel through the optic nerve to the brain. Your brain turns the image right-side up and combines the images from both eyes to produce a single image.

FIGURE 8 ······························

The Eye
Light from an object produces an image on the retina.

✎ **Develop Hypotheses** Hold your hand in front of your face. Look at it with one eye closed, then with the other. Explain why the image of your hand shifts.

_____

_____

_____

_____

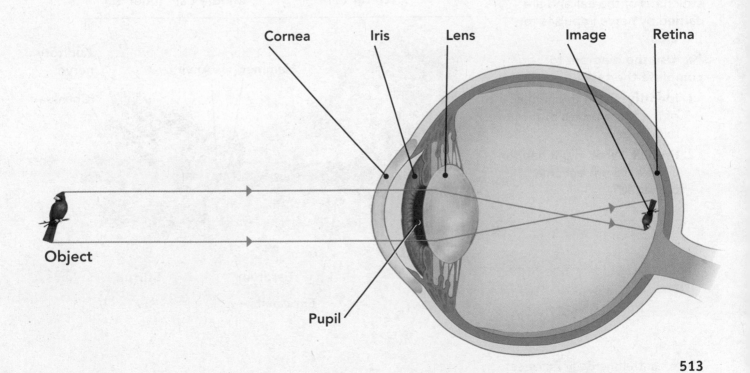

Cornea   Iris   Lens   Image   Retina

Object

Pupil

513

There is a type of berry that can temporarily alter your tastebuds. For about 15 to 30 minutes after eating one of these berries, everything sour tastes sweet. At a Miami, Florida hospital, researchers are studying whether this berry can help cancer patients whose chemotherapy treatments have left them with dulled taste buds.

Taste and Smell The senses of taste and smell work together. Both depend on chemicals in the air or in food. The chemicals trigger responses in receptors in the nose and mouth. Nerve impulses then travel to the brain and are interpreted as smells or tastes.

The nose can distinguish at least 50 basic odors. In contrast, there are only five main taste sensations—sweet, sour, salty, bitter, and a meatlike taste called *umami*. When you eat, however, you experience a wider variety of flavors, since both smell and taste affect the flavor of food.

How You Hear

When you hear your alarm clock ring, your brain tells you that it is time to get up. Most sounds are caused by the vibrations of air particles. The air particle vibrations move outward from the source of the sound, like waves moving out from a stone dropped in the water. In this way, sound is carried as waves. Ears are the sense organs that convert sound waves into nerve impulses that your brain interprets.

The three parts of the ear—outer, middle, and inner—are shown in **Figure 9.** Sound waves enter your outer ear through the ear canal. When the sound waves reach your eardrum, they cause it to vibrate. The vibrations pass to three tiny bones in your middle ear, which transmit the vibrations to your inner ear. There, sensory neurons in the cochlea convert these vibrations into nerve impulses. These impulses travel through the auditory nerve to the brain. Your brain interprets these impulses as sounds.

FIGURE 9

The Ear

Sound waves pass through the structures of the ear and are carried by nerve impulses to the brain.

✎ **Use the diagram to complete the tasks.**

1. **Identify** Circle the names of the three bones of the middle ear.

2. **Predict** What might happen if the eardrum became damaged?

_____

_____

_____

_____

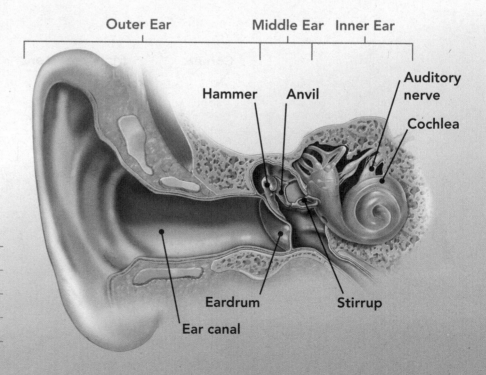

Touch Unlike your other senses, the sense of touch is not found in one place. It is in all areas of your skin. Your skin has different kinds of touch receptors that respond to different stimuli. All of the touch receptors are located in the dermis, or the inner layer of skin.

The receptors that respond to light touch are in the upper part of the dermis. These receptors also let you feel textures, such as smooth glass and rough sandpaper. Receptors deeper in the dermis pick up the feeling of heavy pressure. For example, if you press down hard on your desk, you will feel pressure in your fingertips.

The dermis also contains receptors that respond to temperature and pain. Pain can be one of your most important sensations because it alerts you to danger.

FIGURE 10

Touch

Your skin lets you feel the world around you.

✏ **Classify** In the box next to each photo, describe the kind of touch receptors each person is using.

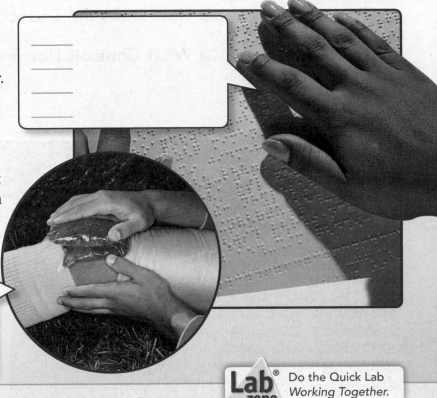

Lab® zone   Do the Quick Lab
Working Together.

🔑 Assess Your Understanding

3a. Name Light-sensitive cells that produce nerve impulses are found in the _____

b. Predict If a head cold interferes with your sense of smell, how do you think your sense of taste would be affected?

_____

_____

c. Describe Describe the eardrum's function.

_____

_____

_____

d. Compare and Contrast How is the sense of touch different from the other senses?

_____

_____

got**it?**

○ **I get it!** Now I know that my sense organs enable me to _____

_____

○ I need extra help with _____

Go to **MY SCIENCE** 💬 **COACH** online for help with this subject.

The Endocrine System

🔑 **How Does the Endocrine System Function?**

🔑 **What Controls Hormone Levels?**

my PLANET DiARY

The Cause of Acne

Misconception: Eating oily foods can cause acne.

Scientists have not found a link between eating certain foods and acne. So, what does cause acne? Much of the blame falls on certain hormones. Your body starts to produce these hormones when you enter adolescence. They stimulate your body to produce an oily substance called sebum. When your body produces too much sebum, some hair follicles in your skin may become blocked. This blockage causes bacteria to get trapped. Because the sebum and bacteria have nowhere to go, your skin becomes inflamed. The result is acne.

MISCONCEPTION

Communicate Discuss the following question with a partner. Write your answer below.

How would you explain to a friend what causes acne?

_____

_____

_____

_____

_____

_____

_____

_____

_____

_____

_____

> PLANET DIARY Go to **Planet Diary** to learn more about the endocrine system.

Lab zone ® Do the Inquiry Warm-Up *What's the Signal?*

Vocabulary
- gland • duct • hormone • target cell • hypothalamus
- pituitary gland • negative feedback

Skills
- Reading: Identify the Main Idea
- Inquiry: Make Models

How Does the Endocrine System Function?

Have you ever been so afraid that you heard your heart thump rapidly in your chest? When something frightens you, your body's endocrine system (EN duh krin) reacts.

Your body has two systems that regulate its activities: the nervous system and the endocrine system. The nervous system regulates most activities by sending nerve impulses throughout the body. **The endocrine system regulates short-term and long-term activities by sending chemicals throughout the body. Long-term changes include growth and development.**

The endocrine system is made up of glands. A **gland** is an organ that produces or releases a chemical. Some glands, such as those producing saliva and sweat, release their chemicals into tiny tubes, or **ducts.** The ducts deliver the chemicals to specific places in the body or to the skin's surface. However, the glands of the endocrine system do not have delivery ducts. The endocrine glands produce and release chemicals directly into the blood. Then the blood carries those chemicals throughout the body.

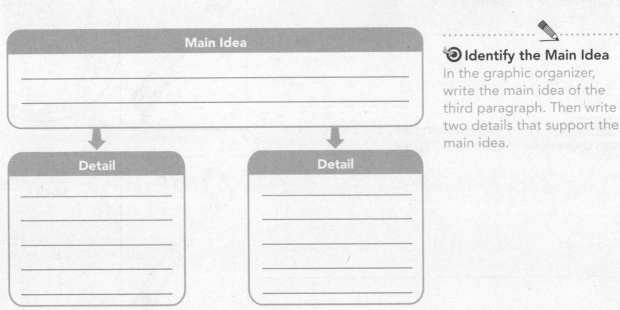

Main Idea

_____

_____

| Detail | Detail |

_____ _____
_____ _____
_____ _____
_____ _____

Identify the Main Idea
In the graphic organizer, write the main idea of the third paragraph. Then write two details that support the main idea.

Hormones

A chemical produced by an endocrine gland is called a **hormone.** Hormones are chemical messengers that travel in the blood. Hormones turn on, turn off, speed up, or slow down the activities of organs and tissues.

Nerve impulses from the brain act quickly. In contrast, hormones usually cause a slower, longer-lasting response. For example, if you see danger, your brain interprets the information and sends an impulse to an endocrine gland. The gland releases the hormone adrenaline into your blood. Adrenaline speeds up your heart rate and breathing rate. Even a quick hormonal response such as releasing adrenaline is much slower than a nerve response.

Each hormone affects specific target cells. **Target cells** are cells that are specialized in a way that enables them to recognize a hormone's chemical structure. Hormones travel in the blood until they find their target cells. Read about the endocrine glands and the hormones they produce in **Figure 1** on the next page.

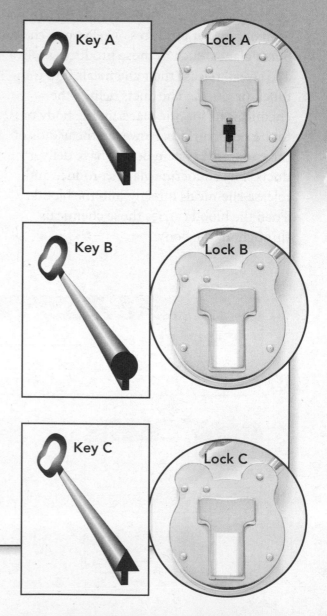

apply it!

Hormones interact with target cells much like keys interact with locks.

1 **Make Models** Look at Key A and Lock A. Then draw the shapes of the keyholes for the locks that Key B and Key C will unlock.

2 **Draw Conclusions** How do a hormone and a target cell function like a key and a lock?

_____

_____

_____

_____

3 [CHALLENGE] What body system does the endocrine system depend on to function? Explain.

_____

_____

_____

_____

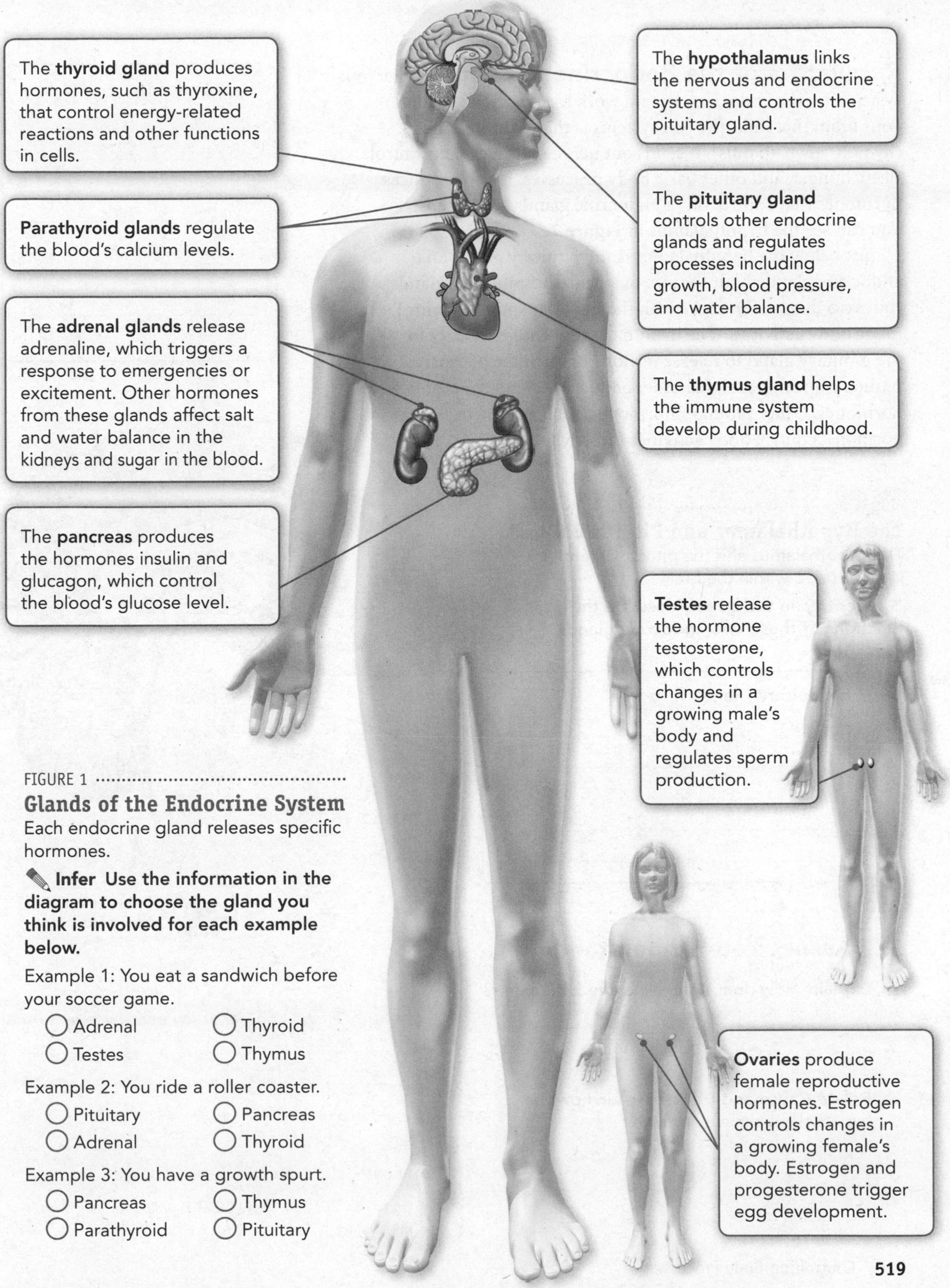

The **thyroid gland** produces hormones, such as thyroxine, that control energy-related reactions and other functions in cells.

Parathyroid glands regulate the blood's calcium levels.

The **adrenal glands** release adrenaline, which triggers a response to emergencies or excitement. Other hormones from these glands affect salt and water balance in the kidneys and sugar in the blood.

The **pancreas** produces the hormones insulin and glucagon, which control the blood's glucose level.

The **hypothalamus** links the nervous and endocrine systems and controls the pituitary gland.

The **pituitary gland** controls other endocrine glands and regulates processes including growth, blood pressure, and water balance.

The **thymus gland** helps the immune system develop during childhood.

Testes release the hormone testosterone, which controls changes in a growing male's body and regulates sperm production.

Ovaries produce female reproductive hormones. Estrogen controls changes in a growing female's body. Estrogen and progesterone trigger egg development.

FIGURE 1 ···

Glands of the Endocrine System

Each endocrine gland releases specific hormones.

✎ **Infer** Use the information in the diagram to choose the gland you think is involved for each example below.

Example 1: You eat a sandwich before your soccer game.

- ○ Adrenal
- ○ Testes
- ○ Thyroid
- ○ Thymus

Example 2: You ride a roller coaster.

- ○ Pituitary
- ○ Adrenal
- ○ Pancreas
- ○ Thyroid

Example 3: You have a growth spurt.

- ○ Pancreas
- ○ Parathyroid
- ○ Thymus
- ○ Pituitary

Regulators of the Endocrine System

The nervous system and the endocrine system work together. The part of your brain that links the two systems is the **hypothalamus** (hy poh THAL uh mus). It sends out nerve messages that control sleep, hunger, and other basic body processes. It also produces hormones that control other endocrine glands and organs. You can see the hypothalamus in **Figure 2**.

Just below the hypothalamus is the pituitary gland, an endocrine gland about the size of a pea. The **pituitary gland** (pih TOO ih tehr ee) works with the hypothalamus to control many body activities. The hypothalamus sends messages to the pituitary gland to release its hormones. Some of those pituitary hormones signal other endocrine glands to produce hormones. Other pituitary hormones, such as growth hormone, control body activities directly.

FIGURE 2 ·······································

The Hypothalamus and Pituitary Gland
The hypothalamus and the pituitary gland are located deep within the brain.

✎ **Identify** In the boxes, describe the functions of these two endocrine glands.

Hypothalamus
_____
_____
_____
_____
_____
_____
_____

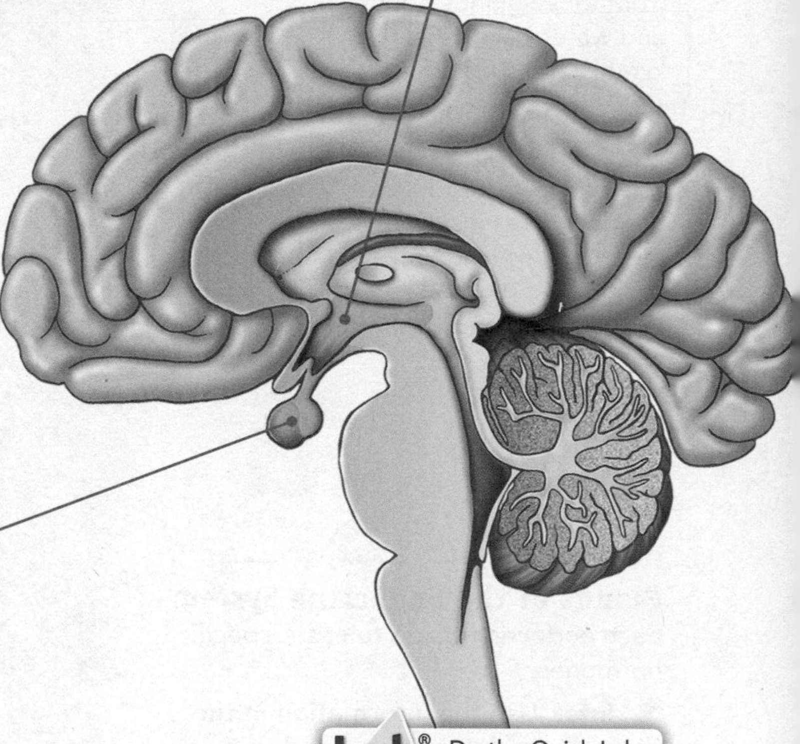

Pituitary Gland
_____
_____
_____
_____

Lab zone® Do the Quick Lab
Making Models.

🔑 **Assess Your Understanding**

1a. Explain How does adrenaline affect the heart?
_____
_____

b. Relate Cause and Effect Explain how the hypothalamus affects growth.
_____
_____
_____

got it?

○ **I get it!** Now I know that my endocrine system
_____
_____
_____

○ I need extra help with _____

Go to **MY SCIENCE** ⓢ **COACH** online for help with this subject.

What Controls Hormone Levels?

Suppose you set a thermostat at 20°C. If the room temperature falls below 20°C, the thermostat signals the furnace to turn on. When heat from the furnace warms the room to 20°C, the thermostat shuts off the furnace. In certain ways, the endocrine system works like a thermostat. It uses a process called **negative feedback** in which a system is turned off by the condition it produces.

🔑 **When the amount of a hormone in the blood reaches a certain level, the endocrine system sends signals that stop the release of that hormone.** In **Figure 3,** you can see how negative feedback regulates the level of the hormone thyroxine in the blood.

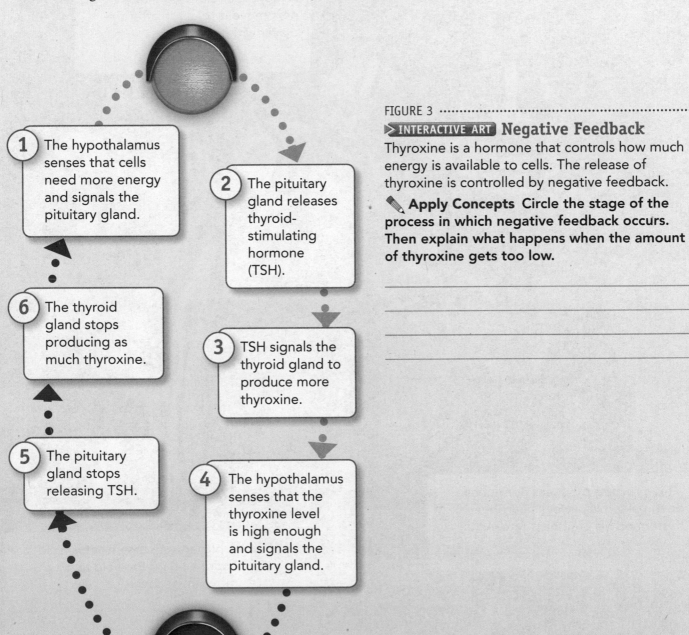

1 The hypothalamus senses that cells need more energy and signals the pituitary gland.

2 The pituitary gland releases thyroid-stimulating hormone (TSH).

6 The thyroid gland stops producing as much thyroxine.

3 TSH signals the thyroid gland to produce more thyroxine.

5 The pituitary gland stops releasing TSH.

4 The hypothalamus senses that the thyroxine level is high enough and signals the pituitary gland.

FIGURE 3 ···

> INTERACTIVE ART **Negative Feedback**

Thyroxine is a hormone that controls how much energy is available to cells. The release of thyroxine is controlled by negative feedback.

✏️ **Apply Concepts** Circle the stage of the process in which negative feedback occurs. Then explain what happens when the amount of thyroxine gets too low.

_____

_____

_____

_____

Sense and Respond

EXPLORE THE BIG Q

What systems regulate and control body processes?

FIGURE 4

REAL-WORLD INQUIRY The fans, players, and referee at this football game react to their surroundings because of their endocrine and nervous systems.

Interpret Photos **Read the descriptions and identify what structures in the nervous system or endocrine system are involved.**

A player understands that his next move is to chase after the player with the ball.

____

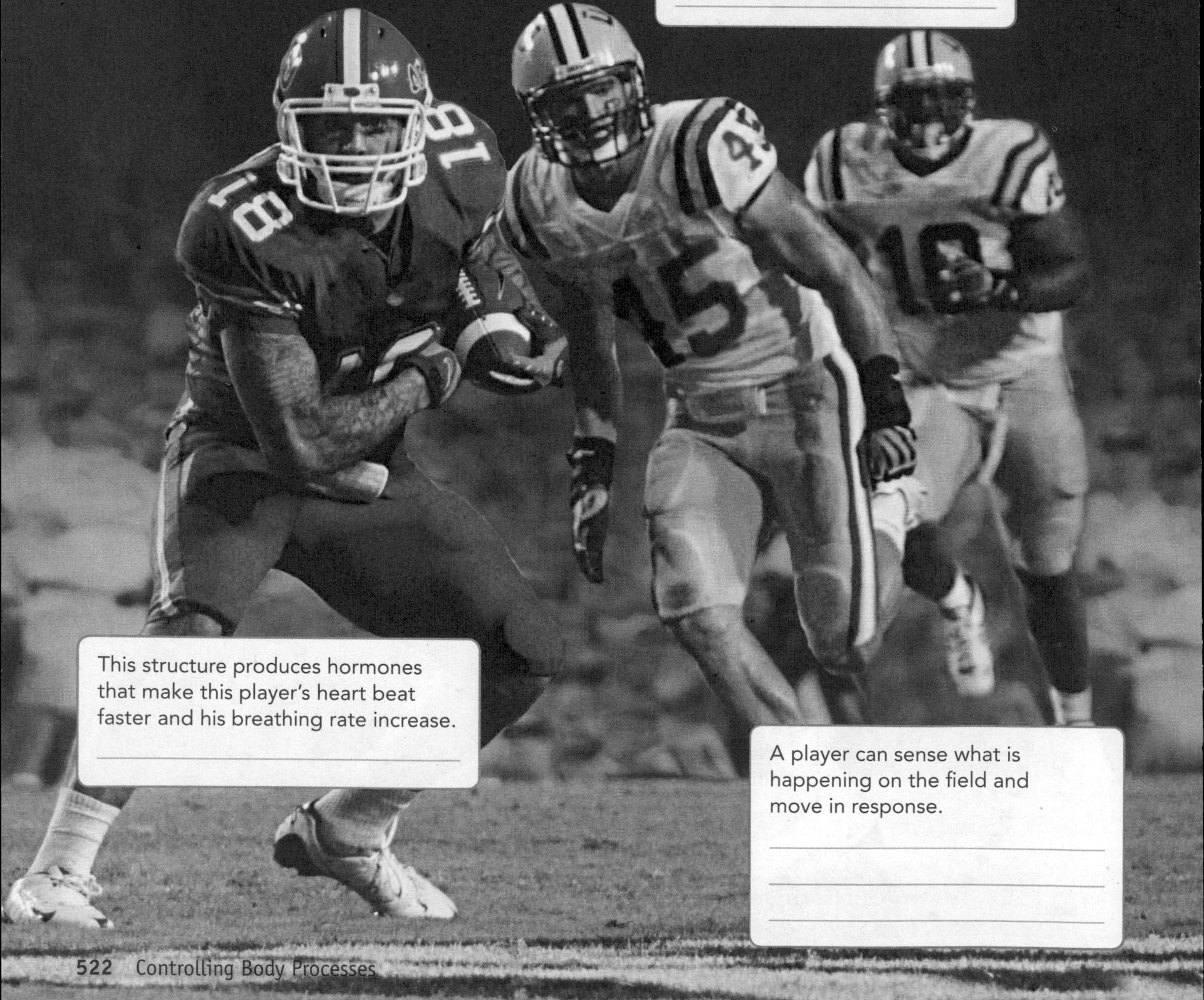

This structure produces hormones that make this player's heart beat faster and his breathing rate increase.

____

A player can sense what is happening on the field and move in response.

____

____

____

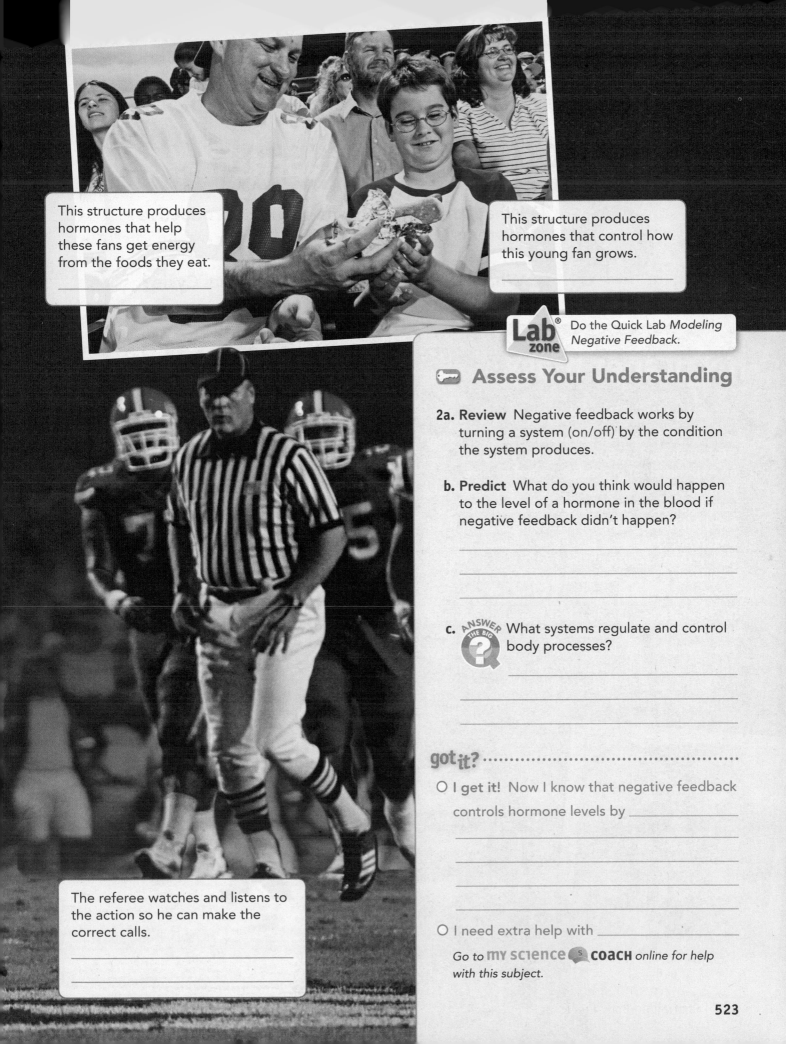

This structure produces hormones that help these fans get energy from the foods they eat.

_____

This structure produces hormones that control how this young fan grows.

_____

The referee watches and listens to the action so he can make the correct calls.

_____

_____

Lab® Do the Quick Lab *Modeling*
zone *Negative Feedback.*

🔑 Assess Your Understanding

2a. Review Negative feedback works by turning a system (on/off) by the condition the system produces.

b. Predict What do you think would happen to the level of a hormone in the blood if negative feedback didn't happen?

_____

_____

_____

c. ANSWER THE BIG ? What systems regulate and control body processes?

_____

_____

_____

got it? ....

○ **I get it!** Now I know that negative feedback controls hormone levels by _____

_____

_____

_____

○ **I need extra help with** _____

Go to **my science** Ⓢ **coach** *online for help with this subject.*

The Male and Female Reproductive Systems

🔑 **What Are the Functions of the Reproductive Systems?**

🔑 **What Happens During the Menstrual Cycle?**

my planet diary

DISCOVERY

In Vitro Fertilization

In 1977, Dr. Patrick Steptoe and Dr. Robert Edwards had been working for years on an experimental procedure called in vitro fertilization. Their goal was to help women who could not become pregnant naturally. In vitro fertilization begins with retrieving an egg from a woman. The egg is placed in a lab dish along with a man's sperm. If the egg is successfully fertilized, it is placed back into the woman's body to grow into a baby.

Dr. Steptoe and Dr. Edwards were unsuccessful time and time again, until they met Lesley and John Brown. The doctors implanted a fertilized egg in Lesley. Nine months later, on July 25, 1978, the world's first in vitro baby was born. Her parents named her Louise Joy Brown.

Communicate Discuss the following questions with a partner. Write your answers below.

1. At what point during the in vitro fertilization process is the egg placed back into the woman's body?

   _____
   _____
   _____

2. What impact do you think in vitro fertilization has had?

   _____
   _____
   _____
   _____

▶ **PLANET DIARY** Go to **Planet Diary** to learn more about the male and female reproductive systems.

 Do the Inquiry Warm-Up
What's the Big Difference?

Louise Joy Brown
at birth

Louise Joy Brown
as an adult

Vocabulary

- fertilization • egg • sperm • zygote • testes
- testosterone • scrotum • semen • penis • ovary
- estrogen • Fallopian tube • uterus • vagina
- menstrual cycle • menstruation • ovulation

Skills

⟳ Reading: Sequence

△ Inquiry: Develop Hypotheses

What Are the Functions of the Reproductive Systems?

Have you noticed how a child's body changes as the child grows? Two different endocrine glands—the ovaries and the testes—release hormones that control many of these changes. They also produce the sex cells that are part of sexual reproduction.

Sexual Reproduction You were once a single cell. That cell resulted from the joining of an egg cell and a sperm cell, which is a process called **fertilization.** An **egg** is the female sex cell. The male sex cell is a **sperm.** Both cells are shown in **Figure 1.** Fertilization is part of sexual reproduction, the process by which males and females produce new individuals. Sexual reproduction involves the production of eggs by the female and sperm by the male. The egg and sperm join together during fertilization. When fertilization occurs, a fertilized egg, or **zygote,** is produced. The zygote contains all the information needed to produce a new human being.

FIGURE 1 ·····································

Egg and Sperm

An egg is one of the largest cells in the body. A sperm cell is much smaller than an egg and can move.

✎ **Describe** In the table, describe each of the cells involved in fertilization.

A sperm penetrating an egg

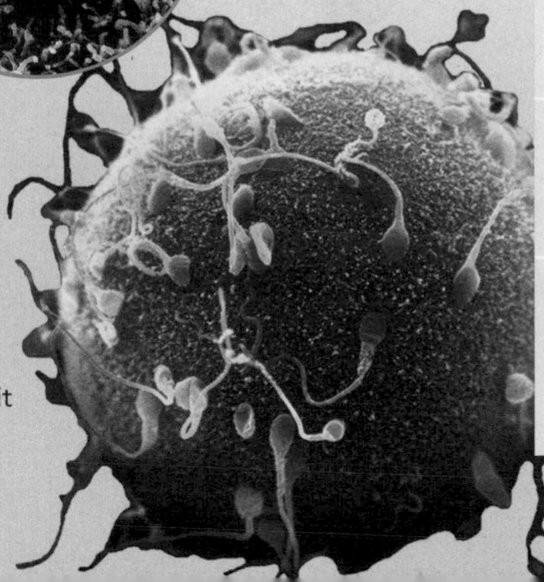

An egg with sperm cells around it

Cell	Description
Sperm	
Egg	
Zygote	

Sperm cells

Male Reproductive System
Look at the organs of the male reproductive system shown in **Figure 2.** 🔑 **The male reproductive system is specialized to produce sperm cells and the hormone testosterone.** The structures of this system include the testes, scrotum, and penis.

The Testes The **testes** (TES teez; singular *testis*) are the organs in which sperm are produced. The testes consist of clusters of tiny, coiled tubes where sperm are formed. In addition to sperm, the testes produce testosterone. The hormone **testosterone** (tes TAHS tuh rohn) controls the development of adult male characteristics. These include facial hair, deepening of the voice, broadening of the shoulders, and the ability to produce sperm.

The testes are located in a pouch of skin called the **scrotum** (SKROH tum). The scrotum holds the testes away from the rest of the body. This distance keeps the testes about 2°C to 3°C below normal body temperature, which is 37°C. The cooler temperature is important because sperm cannot develop properly at 37°C.

FIGURE 2 ·······························

▶ INTERACTIVE ART **Structures of the Male Reproductive System**

✏️ **Complete the tasks.**

1. **Summarize** In the boxes, describe the structure and function of each organ.

2. **Calculate** Find the temperatures at which sperm develop properly.

_____

_____

_____

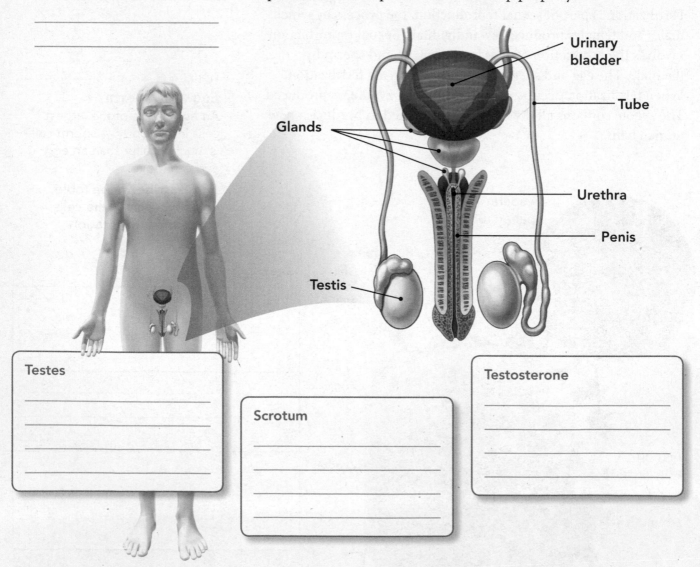

Urinary bladder

Tube

Glands

Urethra

Penis

Testis

Testes

_____

_____

_____

Scrotum

_____

_____

_____

Testosterone

_____

_____

_____

Sperm The production of sperm cells begins during the teenage years. Each sperm cell has a head that contains chromosomes, and a long, whiplike tail. The chromosomes carry the information that controls inherited characteristics, such as blood type. The tail helps the sperm swim in fluid.

After forming in the testes, sperm travel through tubes in the male reproductive system. As they travel, sperm mix with fluids produced by nearby glands, as shown in **Figure 3.** This mixture of sperm cells and fluids is called **semen** (SEE mun). The fluids in semen provide an environment where sperm can swim. Semen also contains nutrients that the sperm use for energy.

Semen leaves the body through an organ called the **penis.** The semen travels through the tube in the penis called the urethra. Urine also leaves the body through the urethra. When semen passes through the urethra, however, muscles near the bladder contract. Those muscles prevent urine and semen from mixing.

⟳ **Sequence** Underline in the paragraphs the path that sperm take to leave the body. Then write the steps on the notepaper below.

FIGURE 3 ···

Sperm Production and Passage From the Body

Sperm are produced in the testes and leave the body through the urethra.

✎ **Use the diagram to complete the tasks.**

1. **Relate Text and Visuals** On the diagram, draw arrows to trace the path that sperm travel through the male reproductive system.

2. **CHALLENGE** Why do sperm need to swim?

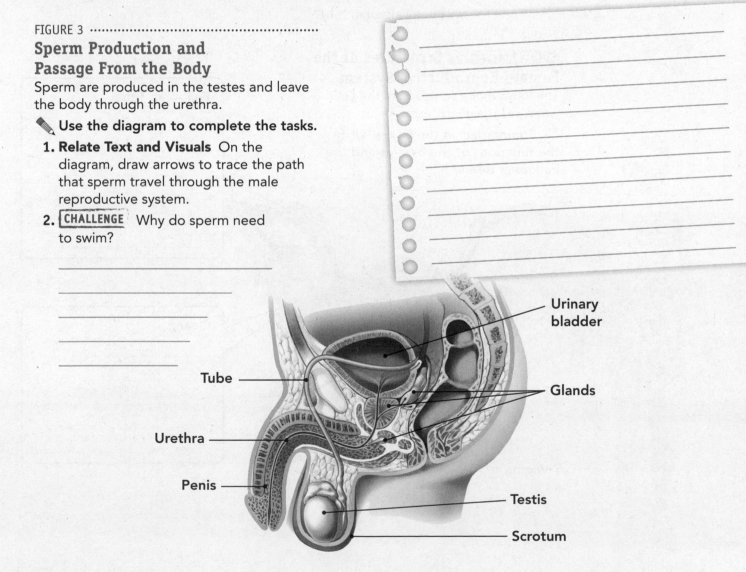

Urinary bladder

Tube

Glands

Urethra

Penis

Testis

Scrotum

did you know? ....

When the female reproductive system becomes mature, the ovaries contain about 400,000 undeveloped eggs. However, only about 450 of those eggs will actually leave the ovaries and reach the uterus during a typical woman's life.

Female Reproductive System ▭ **The female reproductive system is specialized to produce eggs and nourish a developing baby until birth. It also produces estrogen and other hormones.** The organs of this system include the ovaries, Fallopian tubes, uterus, and vagina.

The Ovaries The **ovaries** (OH vuh reez) are the female reproductive structures that produce eggs. They are located slightly below the waist, one on each side of the body, as shown in **Figure 4.** Like the testes in males, the ovaries are also endocrine glands that produce hormones. One hormone, **estrogen** (ES truh jun), triggers the development of some adult female characteristics. For example, estrogen causes the hips to widen and the breasts to develop. Estrogen is also involved in the development of egg cells. Each month, one of the ovaries releases a mature egg into the nearest oviduct, or Fallopian tube. A **Fallopian tube** is the passageway an egg travels from an ovary to the uterus. Fertilization usually occurs within a Fallopian tube.

FIGURE 4 ....

▷ **INTERACTIVE ART** **Structures of the Female Reproductive System**
The word *ovary* comes from the Latin word *ova* meaning "eggs."

✎ **Summarize** In the boxes, write the functions of the ovaries and the Fallopian tubes.

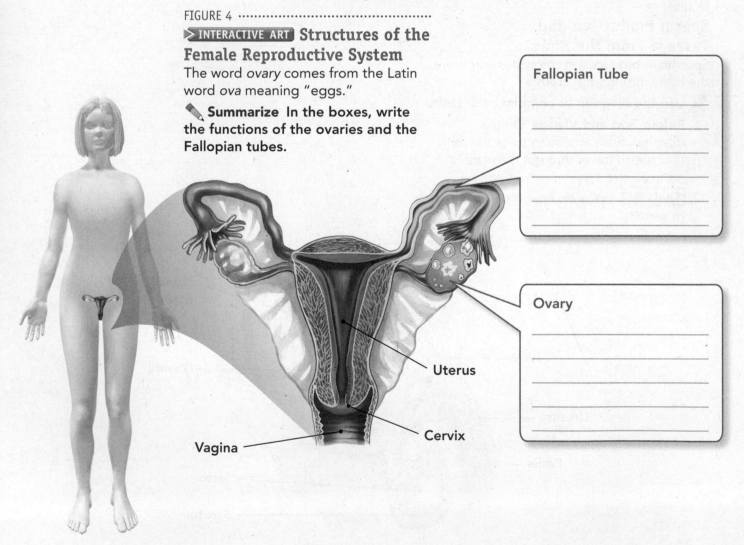

Fallopian Tube

Ovary

Uterus

Cervix

Vagina

Egg Cells From an ovary, an egg travels through the Fallopian tube to the uterus. The **uterus** (YOO tur us) is a hollow, muscular organ. If an egg has been fertilized in the Fallopian tube, it attaches to the wall of the uterus. An unfertilized egg breaks down in the uterus. It leaves through the cervix, an opening at the base of the uterus. The egg then enters the vagina. The **vagina** (vuh JY nuh) is a muscular passageway leading to the outside of the body. The vagina, or birth canal, is the passageway through which a baby leaves its mother's body during childbirth. **Figure 5** shows the female reproductive system.

Vocabulary Identify Related Word Forms When you know the meaning of a word, you can often identify and understand related words. How are the meanings of *fertilized* and *fertilization* related?

_____

_____

_____

FIGURE 5 ·······································

Egg Production and Passage From the Body

Each month, an ovary produces an egg that leaves the body if it is not fertilized.

✎ **Describe** In the boxes, write the functions of the uterus and the vagina.

Fallopian tube

Ovary

Urinary bladder

Cervix

Urethra

Uterus
_____
_____
_____

Vagina
_____
_____
_____

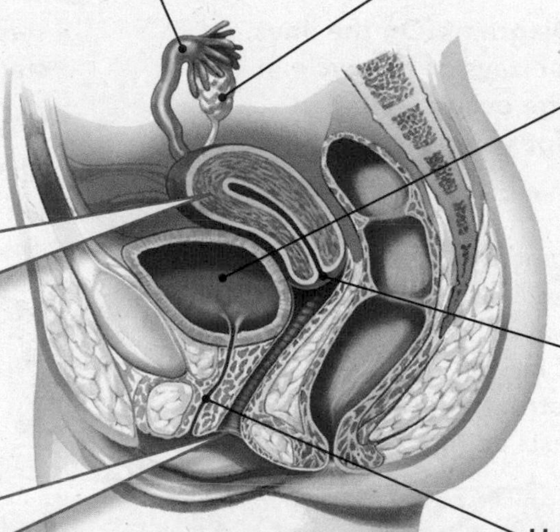

Lab zone® Do the Quick Lab *Reproductive Systems.*

🔑 **Assess Your Understanding**

1a. Review What is fertilization?

_____

_____

b. Relate Cause and Effect What changes does estrogen cause in a female's body?

_____

_____

_____

got it?

○ I get it! Now I know that the male and female reproductive systems _____

_____

_____

○ I need extra help with _____

Go to **MY SCIENCE** ⓢ **COACH** *online for help with this subject.*

What Happens During the Menstrual Cycle?

Usually starting sometime during a girl's teenage years, an egg develops and is released about once a month. This event is part of the **menstrual cycle** (MEN stroo ul), or the monthly cycle of changes that occurs in females. 🔑 **During the menstrual cycle, an egg develops in an ovary. At the same time, the lining of the uterus thickens in a way that prepares the uterus for a fertilized egg.** Follow the stages of the menstrual cycle in **Figure 6**.

FIGURE 6 ·······················

The Menstrual Cycle

The menstrual cycle takes about 28 days.

✎ **Interpret Diagrams** On the lines, write the day or days of the cycle in which each stage occurs. The first stage is done for you.

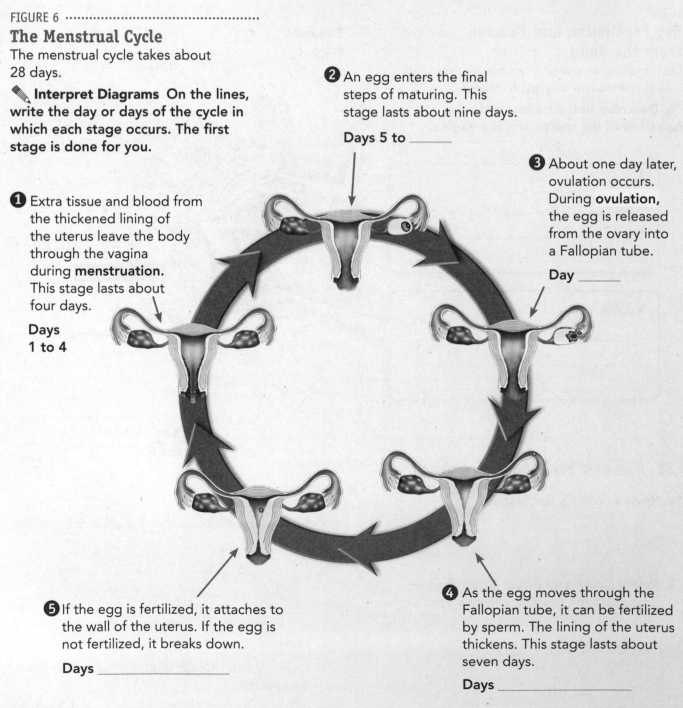

① Extra tissue and blood from the thickened lining of the uterus leave the body through the vagina during **menstruation**. This stage lasts about four days.

Days 1 to 4

② An egg enters the final steps of maturing. This stage lasts about nine days.

Days 5 to _____

③ About one day later, ovulation occurs. During **ovulation**, the egg is released from the ovary into a Fallopian tube.

Day _____

④ As the egg moves through the Fallopian tube, it can be fertilized by sperm. The lining of the uterus thickens. This stage lasts about seven days.

Days _____

⑤ If the egg is fertilized, it attaches to the wall of the uterus. If the egg is not fertilized, it breaks down.

Days _____

do the math!

A woman's hormone levels change throughout her menstrual cycle. One such hormone is called LH.

1 **Graph** Use the data in the table to draw a line graph. Label the axes and write a title for the graph.

Day	1	5	9	13	17	22	25	28
Level of LH	12	13	13	70	12	12	8	10

2 **Read Graphs** On what day was the LH level the lowest? The highest?

_____

_____

3 **Develop Hypotheses** How might LH level and ovulation be related?

_____

_____

_____

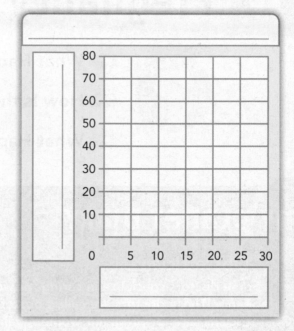

 Do the Quick Lab
Looking at Hormone Levels.

🔑 Assess Your Understanding

2a. Identify In the menstrual cycle, what happens after ovulation occurs?

_____

_____

_____

b. Infer What happens in the menstrual cycle if an egg is fertilized?

_____

_____

_____

got it? ....

○ **I get it!** Now I know that during the menstrual cycle _____

_____

○ **I need extra help with** _____

Go to **my science** **coach** *online for help with this subject.*

UNLOCK THE BIG **Q?**

🔑 **What Happens Before Birth?**

🔑 **How Is the Embryo Protected and Nourished?**

🔑 **What Happens During Childbirth?**

my pLaneT DiaRY

CAREER

Obstetrician

Some doctors specialize in caring for women during pregnancy. These doctors are called obstetricians. Obstetricians care for pregnant women, deliver babies, and make sure the mothers and new babies are healthy in the days that follow childbirth.

If you are interested in becoming an obstetrician, plan on spending at least ten years in school and training after you graduate high school. During this time you will learn how to care for mothers during pregnancy, childbirth, and after delivery. You will also learn about the serious conditions that babies may be born with. This career can be rewarding, even though it takes a lot of time and effort to get there.

Answer the questions below.

1. What are two responsibilities of an obstetrician?

_____

_____

_____

2. Why do you think a woman should see an obstetrician when she is pregnant?

_____

_____

_____

> PLANET DIARY Go to **Planet Diary** to learn more about pregnancy and birth.

Lab zone Do the Inquiry Warm-Up *Prenatal Growth.*

What Happens Before Birth?

When sperm are deposited into the vagina, they swim into and through the uterus and enter the Fallopian tubes. An egg can be fertilized in the Fallopian tubes during the first few days after ovulation. If a sperm fertilizes an egg, pregnancy can occur. The fertilized egg is called a zygote. 🔑 **Before birth, the zygote develops first into an embryo and then into a fetus.**

Vocabulary

- embryo • fetus • amniotic sac
- placenta • umbilical cord

Skills

- Reading: Compare and Contrast
- Inquiry: Calculate

Zygote and Embryo After fertilization, the zygote divides into two cells. These cells continue to divide as they travel toward the uterus. They form a hollow ball of more than one hundred cells by the time they reach the uterus. The ball attaches to the lining of the uterus. From the two-cell stage through the eighth week, a developing human is called an embryo (EM bree oh).

Fetus From the end of the eighth week until birth, a developing human is called a fetus (FEE tus). The internal organs that began to form in the embryo, such as the brain, continue to develop and start to function. The eyes, ears, and nose also develop, as you can see in Figure 1. The heart becomes large enough that a doctor can use a tool to hear it beat. The fetus begins to move and kick.

FIGURE 1 ·····················
> ART IN MOTION **Development of the Fetus**
An embryo develops into a fetus. Note: These photos do not show the actual sizes.

Internet Photos In each box, describe the body parts of the embryo and fetus that you can see.

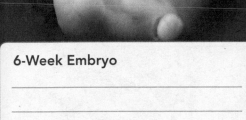

6-Week Embryo

_____
_____
_____
_____

24-Week Fetus

_____
_____
_____
_____

Lab zone® Do the Quick Lab *Way to Grow!*

Assess Your Understanding

got**it?** ···

○ I get it! Now I know that before birth _____
_____

○ I need extra help with _____
   Go to MY SCIENCE ⓢ COACH online for help with this subject.

How Is the Embryo Protected and Nourished?

Soon after the embryo attaches to the uterus, new membranes and structures form. 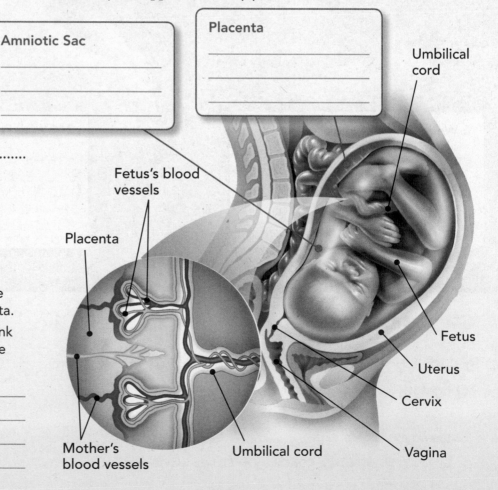 **The membranes and structures that form in the uterus during pregnancy protect and nourish the developing baby.**

Membranes **Figure 2** shows the two membranes that form during development. The **amniotic sac** (am NEE aht ik) surrounds the embryo and is filled with fluid. The fluid cushions and protects the embryo and later the fetus.

Another membrane helps form the **placenta** (pluh SEN tuh), which links the embryo and the mother. In the placenta, the embryo's blood vessels are next to the mother's blood vessels. Their blood does not mix, but substances are exchanged from one bloodstream to the other. The embryo's carbon dioxide and other wastes diffuse to the mother. Nutrients and oxygen diffuse from the mother to the embryo. In addition, drugs, alcohol, and chemicals in tobacco can diffuse from the mother to the embryo and cause it harm. Some effects on the development of the child are immediate. Others may not appear for many years.

⊙ **Compare and Contrast**
In the paragraphs, underline how the amniotic sac and placenta are different. Then write how they are alike below.

_____

_____

_____

FIGURE 2 ·······················

The Amniotic Sac and the Placenta

A fetus needs nourishment and protection to develop properly.

✎ **Complete the tasks.**

1. **Describe** In the boxes, describe the functions of the amniotic sac and the placenta.

2. [CHALLENGE] How do you think it is possible for a baby to be born addicted to drugs?

_____

_____

_____

_____

Amniotic Sac
_____
_____
_____

Placenta
_____
_____

Umbilical cord

Fetus's blood vessels

Placenta

Mother's blood vessels

Umbilical cord

Fetus

Uterus

Cervix

Vagina

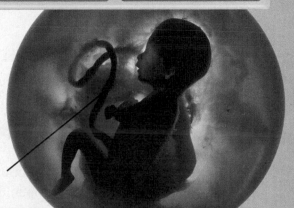

Structures A ropelike structure, called the **umbilical cord,** begins to form between the embryo and the placenta. It contains blood vessels from the embryo that link the embryo to the placenta.

Umbilical cord

do the
math!

A pregnancy is often divided into three stages called trimesters. Each trimester is three months.

1 **Interpret Tables** How much mass does a developing fetus gain during each trimester?

First Trimester _____

Second Trimester _____

Third Trimester _____

2 **Calculate** To find the percentage mass increase in a trimester, divide the mass gained in the trimester by the mass at the start of the trimester. Then multiply by 100. The percentage mass increase for the second trimester is as follows: (614 ÷ 26) x 100 = about 2,361 percent.

Find the percentage mass increase for the third trimester.

_____

_____

Change in Mass of a Developing Baby	
Month of Pregnancy	Mass (grams)
1	0.02
2	2
3	26
4	150
5	460
6	640
7	1,500
8	2,300
9	3,200

Lab zone® Do the Quick Lab *Egg-cellent Protection.*

🗝 Assess Your Understanding

1a. Explain What substances pass from the embryo or fetus to the mother?

_____

_____

_____

b. Relate Cause and Effect Why is it dangerous for a pregnant woman to drink alcohol?

_____

_____

_____

got it? ....

○ **I get it!** Now I know that an embryo or fetus is protected and nourished by _____

_____

○ **I need extra help with** _____

Go to **MY SCIENCE** ⓢ **COACH** online for help with this subject.

What Happens During Childbirth?

After about nine months of development inside a uterus, a baby is ready to be born. 🔑 **The birth of a baby takes place in three stages: labor, delivery, and afterbirth.**

Labor Labor is the first stage of birth. Strong muscle contractions of the uterus cause the cervix to open. Eventually, the opening is large enough for the baby to fit through. Labor may last from about two hours to more than 20 hours.

Delivery and Afterbirth The second stage of birth is called delivery. During a normal delivery the baby is pushed out of the uterus through the vagina. The head usually comes out first. Delivery can last several minutes to an hour or so. Shortly after delivery, the umbilical cord is cut about five centimeters from the baby's abdomen, as you can see in **Figure 3.** Seven to ten days later, the rest of the umbilical cord, which is now dried, falls off. It leaves a scar called the navel, or bellybutton.

Soon after delivery, muscles in the uterus contract, pushing the placenta and empty amniotic sac out through the vagina. This last stage, called afterbirth, usually takes less than an hour.

FIGURE 3 ·····································
Birth
Contractions in the uterus signal the start of labor.

✎ **Sequence** In the boxes below, describe the events in each stage of birth.

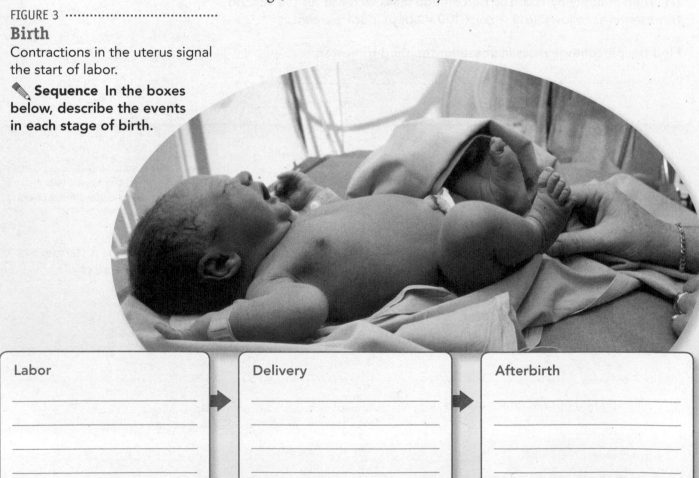

Labor	Delivery	Afterbirth
_____	_____	_____
_____	_____	_____
_____	_____	_____
_____	_____	_____

Birth and the Baby During birth, pressure caused by the muscle contractions briefly decreases the baby's oxygen supply. In response, the baby's endocrine system releases adrenaline, which increases the baby's heart rate. Seconds after delivery, the baby cries and begins breathing. The newborn's heart rate then slows down.

Multiple Births The delivery of more than one baby from a single pregnancy is called a multiple birth. Twin births are the most common multiple births. There are two types of twins: identical and fraternal. **Figure 4** shows how both types develop.

FIGURE 4 ·······························
Multiple Births
Other multiple births, such as triplets, can also be fraternal or identical.

✎ **Interpret Diagrams** Explain on the notebook paper why fraternal twins can be different sexes and identical twins cannot.

Identical Twins
A sperm fertilizes a single egg.

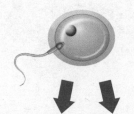

The zygote splits and forms two embryos.

Fraternal Twins
Two sperm fertilize two eggs.

Each zygote forms an embryo.

Lab® zone   Do the Quick Lab *Labor and Delivery.*

🔑 Assess Your Understanding

2a. Name During labor, contractions cause the _____ to open.

b. Apply Concepts Why must a baby start breathing right after birth?

_____

_____

got it?

○ **I get it!** Now I know that childbirth involves

_____

○ **I need extra help with** _____

Go to **my science   coach** online for help with this subject.

13 Study Guide

My _____ and _____ systems help regulate and control my body processes.

LESSON 1 The Nervous System

🔑 Your nervous system receives information about what is happening both inside and outside your body. It directs how your body responds to this information and helps maintain homeostasis.

🔑 Neurons carry nerve impulses throughout the body. The brain is the control center of the central nervous system. The spinal cord links the brain to the peripheral nervous system.

🔑 Your eyes, ears, nose, mouth, and skin are specialized sense organs that enable you to get information from the outside world.

Vocabulary
- neuron • nerve impulse • nerve • synapse • central nervous system
- peripheral nervous system • reflex

LESSON 2 The Endocrine System

🔑 The endocrine system regulates short-term and long-term activities by sending chemicals throughout the body. Long-term changes include growth and development.

🔑 When the amount of a hormone in the blood reaches a certain level, the endocrine system sends signals that stop the release of that hormone.

Vocabulary
- gland • duct • hormone. • target cell • hypothalamus
- pituitary gland • negative feedback

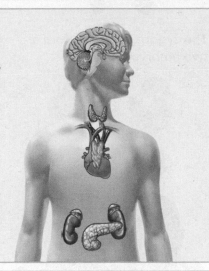

LESSON 3 The Male and Female Reproductive Systems

🔑 The male reproductive system produces sperm and testosterone. The female reproductive system produces eggs and estrogen. It also nourishes a developing baby until birth.

Vocabulary
- fertilization • egg • sperm • zygote
- testes • testosterone • scrotum • semen
- penis • ovary • estrogen • Fallopian tube
- uterus • vagina • menstrual cycle
- menstruation • ovulation

LESSON 4 Pregnancy and Birth

🔑 Before birth, the zygote develops first into an embryo and then into a fetus.

🔑 The membranes and structures that form in the uterus during pregnancy protect and nourish the developing baby.

🔑 The birth of a baby takes place in three stages: labor, delivery, and afterbirth.

Vocabulary
- embryo • fetus • amniotic sac
- placenta • umbilical cord

Review and Assessment

LESSON 1 The Nervous System

1. Which structure links the brain and the peripheral nervous system?

a. the cerebrum   b. the cerebellum

c. the cochlea   d. the spinal cord

2. The senses of _____ and _____ depend on chemicals in the air and food. The sense of _____ depends on the stimulus of light. The sense of _____ depends on the stimulus of sound. The sense of _____ is found in all areas of your skin.

3. Make Generalizations How does the nervous system help maintain homeostasis?

_____

_____

_____

4. Draw Conclusions What is the result if the spinal cord is cut?

_____

_____

_____

5. Apply Concepts As a man walks barefoot along the beach, he steps on a sharp shell. His foot automatically jerks upward, even before he feels pain. What process is this an example of? How does it help protect the man?

_____

_____

_____

_____

6. Write About It The cerebrum, the cerebellum, and the brain stem are regions of the brain that carry out specific functions. Write a brief job description for each of these regions of the brain.

LESSON 2 The Endocrine System

7. The structure that links the nervous system and the endocrine system is the

a. thyroid gland.   b. umbilical cord.

c. target cell.   d. hypothalamus.

8. _____ recognize a hormone's chemical structure.

9. Make Generalizations What is the endocrine system's role?

_____

_____

_____

_____

_____

10. Infer Study the diagram below. Then suggest how the hormones glucagon and insulin might work together to maintain homeostasis in a healthy person.

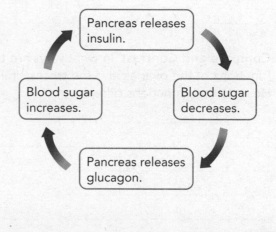

Pancreas releases insulin.

Blood sugar decreases.

Pancreas releases glucagon.

Blood sugar increases.

_____

_____

_____

_____

_____

_____

539

The Male and Female Reproductive Systems

11. The release of an egg from an ovary is called

   a. ovulation.   **b.** menstruation.

   c. fertilization.   **d.** negative feedback.

12. A mixture of sperm and fluids is called

_____

13. Draw Conclusions What is the role of the fluids in semen?

_____

_____

14. Relate Cause and Effect What changes occur in the uterus during the menstrual cycle?

_____

_____

_____

_____

_____

15. Compare and Contrast In what ways are the functions of the ovaries and the testes similar? How do their functions differ?

_____

_____

_____

_____

16. math! The average menstrual cycle is 28 days in length. But it can vary from 21 to 35 days. Ovulation usually occurs 14 days before the end of the cycle. On what day will ovulation occur after the start of a 21-day cycle? A 35-day cycle?

Pregnancy and Birth

17. The membrane that protects and cushions the embryo is called the

   a. umbilical cord.   **b.** scrotum

   c. amniotic sac.   **d.** ovary.

18. The _____ contains blood vessels from the embryo that link the embryo and the placenta.

19. Sequence What three stages of development does a fertilized egg go through before birth?

_____

_____

20. Compare and Contrast Fraternal twins develop from (a single egg/two eggs). Identical twins develop from (a single egg/two eggs).

APPLY THE BIG ? What systems regulate and control body processes?

21. The body goes through many changes during adolescence. Suppose a tumor in the pituitary gland causes the gland to function incorrectly. How might a person's development during adolescence be affected? Explain.

_____

_____

_____

_____

_____

_____

_____

Standardized Test Prep

Multiple Choice

Circle the letter of the best answer.

1. What is the function of the part labeled A on the neuron shown below?

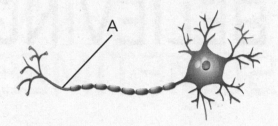

A It carries the nerve impulse toward the cell body.

B It protects the neuron from damage.

C It carries the nerve impulse away from the cell body.

D It picks up stimuli from the environment.

2. You are riding your bike when a small child suddenly darts out in front of you. Which of your endocrine glands is most likely to release a hormone in response to this situation?

A pituitary gland

B adrenal gland

C thyroid gland

D parathyroid gland

3. A change that occurs in girls during puberty is

A their skin wrinkles.

B egg production begins.

C muscle strength decreases.

D ovulation and menstruation begins.

4. A woman gives birth to twins who developed from a single fertilized egg that split early in development. Which of the following is a reasonable prediction that you can make about the twins?

A They will be the same sex.

B They will have similar interests.

C They will not look alike.

D They will have different inherited traits.

5. During pregnancy, which structure permits diffusion of substances from the mother to the fetus?

A zygote

B placenta

C uterus

D fallopian tubes

Constructed Response

Use the diagram below and your knowledge of science to help you answer Question 6. Write your answer on a separate sheet of paper.

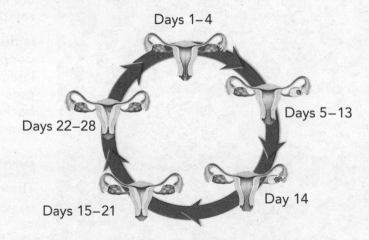

6. Describe what happens during each of the five stages of the menstrual cycle.

SEEING IS BELIEVING ... SOMETIMES

▲ What do you see? What does someone else see? Can you see the faces and the vase at the same time?

Your eyes are constantly checking out the world around you and sending visual information to your brain. Signals from the optic nerves take about one tenth of a second to become a visual image in the brain. Researchers think this lag causes the brain to predict images that will occur one tenth of a second in the future, filling in the gaps. This lag may explain why you see certain types of optical illusions.

Many optical illusions rely on the fact that the brain easily perceives patterns. Scientists think that when there is a gap in a pattern, the brain tries to predict what fills the gap. When these predictions don't match reality, you may end up seeing a false image. You probably experience an optical illusion every day without even noticing it. Television and movies are actually a series of images that are played rapidly, creating the illusion of motion.

Is the figure above an image of a vase or of two people facing each other? You can't see both images at the same time, because your brain gets fooled by thinking there's only one possible background. You can see both images at different times by shifting your attention.

Research It Research more about optical illusions. Then present three of your favorite optical illusions to your class and explain how each one works.

FETAL SURGERY

Michael Skinner had surgery at a very young age. How young? He was the first patient ever to undergo fetal surgery—an operation on a developing fetus.

In 1981, Michael's mother was pregnant with twins. Although one twin was developing normally, doctors noticed that Michael had a serious condition that affected his development. After consulting with medical ethicists who helped them consider the risks, Michael's parents and doctors decided to risk surgery on the fetus. Surgeons used a long needle to reach the fetus inside the mother's uterus and to deliver the treatment Michael needed. The risk paid off, and the surgery was a success!

Hospitals in the United States now perform two types of fetal surgery. In some cases, surgeons use a needle, as they did with Michael Skinner's mother, to deliver treatment. Sometimes, surgeons are able to insert tiny cameras and surgical instruments through a small incision in the uterus. The cameras allow doctors to view the fetus on a computer monitor. These procedures are much less invasive than surgeries in which the uterus is opened. Therefore, they greatly reduce the risks to the mother and the developing fetus.

For other problems, surgeons may need to open the mother's uterus and operate on the fetus directly. At the end of surgery, the surgeon closes the uterus. The fetus is allowed to develop normally inside the mother.

Think About It List three questions you have about fetal surgery. Research to find the answers, and write one or two paragraphs to answer each question.

WHAT CAN YOU DO TO PREVENT DISEASE?

Why do you sometimes get sick?

This three-year-old girl from Somalia is getting a polio vaccine. Polio is spread through contaminated water or food, or by contact with a person infected with the virus. It was a common disease in Somalia. In the United States, polio has been almost eliminated because most babies receive the polio vaccine. Vaccines prevent some viral diseases. Other viral diseases, such as the common cold, have no vaccine.

⚠️ **Infer** What steps can you take to stop a virus such as a cold from spreading?

_____

_____

_____

_____

▶ UNTAMED SCIENCE Watch the **Untamed Science** video to learn more about fighting disease.

Fighting Disease

14 Getting Started

Check Your Understanding

1. **Background** Read the paragraph below and then answer the question.

Camila steps on a nail that punctures her foot. She knows that **bacteria** can cause a disease called tetanus in a wound that is **contaminated**. Fortunately, Camila just received a shot to prevent tetanus. However, to help stop **infection,** she soaks her foot in warm soapy water.

Bacteria are single-celled organisms that lack a nucleus.

An object that is **contaminated** has become unclean and could possibly infect the body.

Infection is the process in which disease-causing microorganisms invade the body and then multiply.

• How can a wound lead to an infection?

_____

_____

_____

> **MY READING WEB** If you had trouble completing the question above, visit **My Reading Web** and type in *Fighting Disease.*

Vocabulary Skill

Latin Word Origins Some terms in this chapter contain word parts with Latin origins. The table below lists some of the Latin words from which these terms come.

Latin Word	Meaning	Key Term
toxicum	poison	toxin, *n.* a poison produced by bacteria that damages cells
tumere	a swelling	tumor, *n.* an abnormal mass of tissue that results from uncontrolled division of cells

2. **Quick Check** In the table above, circle the meaning of the Latin word *toxicum*. The meaning may help you remember the term *toxin.*

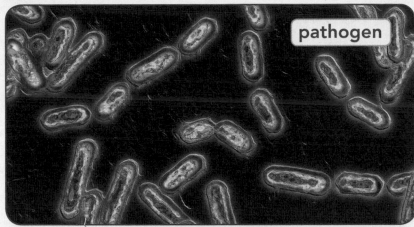

pathogen

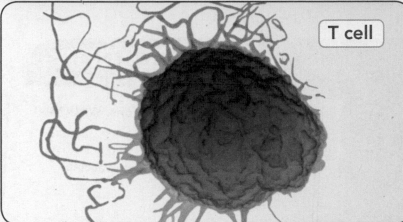

T cell

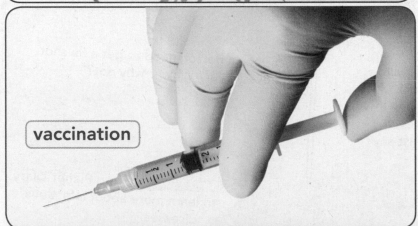

vaccination

allergen

Chapter Preview

LESSON 1
- microorganism • pathogen
- infectious disease • toxin
- 🔁 Identify the Main Idea
- △ Develop Hypotheses

LESSON 2
- inflammatory response
- phagocyte • immune response
- lymphocyte • T cell • antigen
- B cell • antibody
- 🔁 Compare and Contrast
- △ Make Models

LESSON 3
- AIDS • HIV
- 🔁 Sequence
- △ Graph

LESSON 4
- immunity • active immunity
- vaccination • vaccine
- passive immunity • antibiotic
- antibiotic resistance
- 🔁 Relate Cause and Effect
- △ Interpret Data

LESSON 5
- noninfectious disease • allergy
- allergen • histamine • asthma
- insulin • diabetes • tumor
- carcinogen
- 🔁 Summarize
- △ Draw Conclusions

> VOCAB FLASH CARDS For extra help with vocabulary, visit **Vocab Flash Cards** and type in *Fighting Disease.*

Infectious Disease

UNLOCK THE BIG ?

🔑 How Do Pathogens Cause Disease?

🔑 What Pathogens Cause Infectious Disease and How Are They Spread?

my pLaneT DiaRY

Fight the Flu

Misconception: You cannot catch the flu if you have gotten a flu shot.

The flu vaccine decreases your chances of catching the flu, but it does not protect you 100 percent. However, if you get the shot and still end up catching the flu, your symptoms probably will be milder than if you had not gotten vaccinated.

There are many strains of the flu virus. Each year, scientists choose the strains that they think will appear in the United States. Then a vaccine is made that contains those strains. The vaccine is given to people across the country. However, getting a flu shot will not protect you against any strain that is not in the vaccine.

MISCONCEPTION

Read the following questions. Write your answers below.

1. What is one challenge that scientists face when making the flu vaccine?

_____

_____

_____

2. Does a person need to get a flu shot every year? Why or why not?

_____

_____

_____

▷ PLANET DIARY Go to **Planet Diary** to learn more about infectious diseases.

Do the Inquiry Warm-Up
The Agents of Disease.

Vocabulary
- microorganism • pathogen
- infectious disease • toxin

Skills
- ⟳ Reading: Identify the Main Idea
- △ Inquiry: Develop Hypotheses

How Do Pathogens Cause Disease?

In ancient times, people had different ideas about what caused disease. They thought that things such as evil spirits or swamp air caused disease. In fact, they sometimes cut holes in the skulls of sick people to let the evil spirits out. The ancient Greeks thought that disease resulted from an imbalance of four body fluids: blood, phlegm (flem) or mucus, black bile, and yellow bile.

Louis Pasteur and Microorganisms It was not until the 1860s that a French scientist named Louis Pasteur discovered the cause of some diseases. After investigating what causes foods to spoil, Pasteur concluded that **microorganisms,** living things too small to see without a microscope, were the cause. Pasteur thought that microorganisms might be causing disease in animals and people, too. So he investigated a disease attacking silkworms at the time. Pasteur found microorganisms inside silkworms with the disease. He was able to show that these organisms caused the disease. Pasteur's work led to an understanding of what causes most infectious diseases—microorganisms.

⟳ **Identify the Main Idea**
In the graphic organizer, write the main idea of the first paragraph. Then write three details that support the main idea.

Main Idea

NOW

THEN

Then	Now

FIGURE 1 ·······················

Preventing Infection

A clean environment reduces the chance of infection after surgery.

✎ **Communicate** Observe the pictures above. In the table, describe the operating rooms then and now. Then in a small group, discuss how technology affects surgery today. Write your ideas below.

_____

_____

_____

_____

Joseph Lister Pasteur's work influenced a British surgeon named Joseph Lister. Before the twentieth century, surgery was risky because most surgeons operated with dirty instruments and did not wash their hands. The sheets on hospital beds were rarely washed between patients. Even if people lived through an operation, many died later from an infection.

Lister hypothesized that microorganisms cause the infections that often followed surgery. He planned an experiment to test his hypothesis. Before performing operations, he washed his hands and surgical instruments with carbolic acid, a chemical that kills microorganisms. He also sprayed the patients with the acid, as shown in **Figure 1.** After the surgeries, he covered the patients' wounds with bandages dipped in carbolic acid.

Lister's results were dramatic. Before he used his new methods, about 45 percent of his surgical patients died from infection. With Lister's new techniques, only about 15 percent died.

Robert Koch In the 1870s and 1880s, the German physician Robert Koch showed that a specific microorganism causes each disease. For example, the microorganism that causes strep throat cannot cause chickenpox or other diseases. Look at **Figure 2** to see how Koch identified the microorganism for a disease called anthrax.

Organisms that cause disease are called **pathogens.** A disease caused by a pathogen is an **infectious disease.** 🗝 **When you have an infectious disease, pathogens are in your body causing harm.** Pathogens damage large numbers of individual cells, which makes you sick.

FIGURE 2 •••••••••••••••••••••••••••••••••
Koch's Experiment
Koch followed the scientific method in his research of pathogens.

✏ **Draw Conclusions** How would Koch's conclusion have been different if Mouse B's blood had not contained the pathogen found in Mouse A's blood?

_____

_____

_____

_____

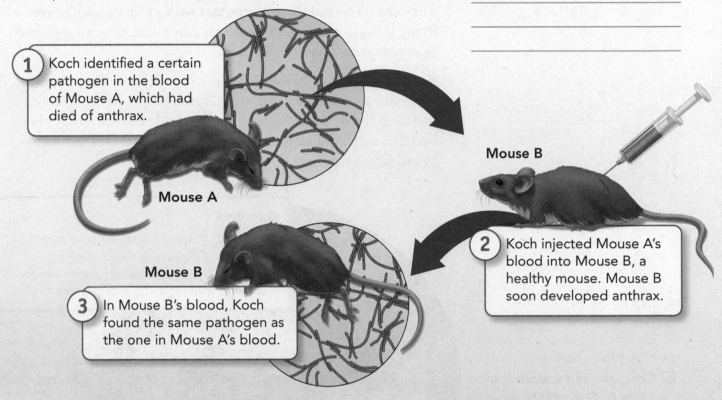

1. Koch identified a certain pathogen in the blood of Mouse A, which had died of anthrax.

Mouse A

Mouse B

2. Koch injected Mouse A's blood into Mouse B, a healthy mouse. Mouse B soon developed anthrax.

Mouse B

3. In Mouse B's blood, Koch found the same pathogen as the one in Mouse A's blood.

Lab zone® Do the Quick Lab *How Do Pathogens Cause Disease?*

🗝 **Assess Your Understanding**

1a. Define What is an infectious disease?

_____

_____

b. Make Generalizations How did Pasteur's work affect Lister's work?

_____

_____

_____

got it?

○ **I get it!** Now I know that pathogens cause

disease by _____

_____

_____

○ **I need extra help with** _____

Go to **MY SCIENCE ⓈCOACH** online for help with this subject.

What Pathogens Cause Infectious Disease and How Are They Spread?

You share Earth with many kinds of organisms. Most of these organisms are harmless, but some can make you sick. Some diseases are caused by multicelled animals, such as worms. However, most pathogens can be seen only with a microscope.

Types of Pathogens 🔑 **The four major types of human pathogens are bacteria, viruses, fungi, and protists. They can be spread through contact with a sick person, other living things, or an object in the environment.** You can see some examples of pathogens in **Figure 3**.

Bacteria Bacteria are one-celled microorganisms. They cause many diseases, including ear infections, food poisoning, tetanus, and strep throat. Some bacteria damage body cells directly. Other bacteria, such as those that cause tetanus, damage cells indirectly by producing a poison, or **toxin**.

FIGURE 3 ·······················
▶ VIRTUAL LAB **Pathogens**
Microscopic organisms cause many common diseases.

✎ **Compare and Contrast** In the table on the next page, use information in the text to write notes about pathogens. Then fill in the circle below to indicate which type of pathogen produces toxins.

- ○ viruses
- ○ bacteria
- ○ protists
- ○ fungi

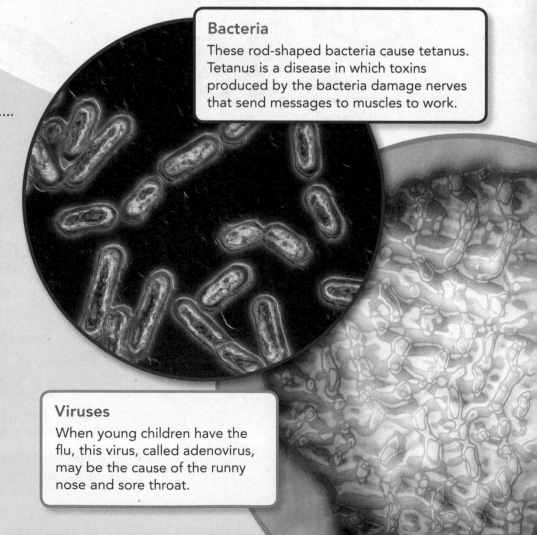

Bacteria
These rod-shaped bacteria cause tetanus. Tetanus is a disease in which toxins produced by the bacteria damage nerves that send messages to muscles to work.

Viruses
When young children have the flu, this virus, called adenovirus, may be the cause of the runny nose and sore throat.

Viruses Viruses are tiny nonliving particles much smaller than bacteria. They can reproduce only inside living cells. The cells are damaged or destroyed when the new virus particles are released. These new virus particles then infect other cells. Viruses cause many diseases including colds and the flu. There are more than 200 kinds of cold viruses alone.

Fungi Some fungi, such as molds and yeasts, also cause infectious diseases. Fungi that cause disease may be one-celled or multicelled living things. Fungi grow best in warm, dark, moist areas of the body. Athlete's foot and ringworm are two fungal diseases.

Protists Most protists are one-celled microorganisms and some can cause disease. They are larger than bacteria but still tiny. One type of protist causes the disease malaria, which is common in tropical areas. African sleeping sickness and hiker's disease are other diseases caused by protists.

Protists
This microorganism is called *Giardia* (jee AHR dee uh). People who drink from streams or lakes with this protist can get an intestinal disease called hiker's disease.

Fungi
This fungus causes a skin infection called athlete's foot.

Pathogen	Size	Characteristics	Type of Disease
Bacteria			
Viruses			
Fungi			
Protists			

Pathogens are spread through contaminated water.

Apply Concepts If you have a cold, what can you do to prevent spreading it?

_____
_____
_____
_____

How Pathogens Are Spread

Pathogens can infect you in several ways. They can spread through contact with an infected person; through soil, food, or water; and through a contaminated object or an infected animal.

Infected People Pathogens often pass from one person to another through direct physical contact, such as kissing and shaking hands. For example, if you kiss someone with an open cold sore, the virus that causes cold sores can get into your body. Pathogens spread indirectly, too. For example, when a person with a cold sneezes, pathogens shoot into the air. People who inhale these pathogens may catch the cold.

Soil, Food, and Water Some pathogens occur naturally in the environment. For example, the bacteria that cause botulism, a severe form of food poisoning, live in soil. These bacteria can produce toxins in foods that have been improperly canned. Other pathogens contaminate food and water and sicken people who eat the food or drink the water. Cholera and dysentery, deadly diseases that cause severe diarrhea, are spread through contaminated food or water.

apply it!

Cholera is a deadly disease caused by bacteria in drinking water. This map shows the locations of cholera cases in the 1854 cholera epidemic in London, England, and the city's water pumps.

❶ Develop Hypotheses Which pump was probably the source of the contaminated water? What evidence do you have?

_____
_____
_____
_____

❷ Pose Questions Suppose a doctor at the time learned that two more people had died of cholera. What two questions would the doctor most likely have asked?

_____
_____

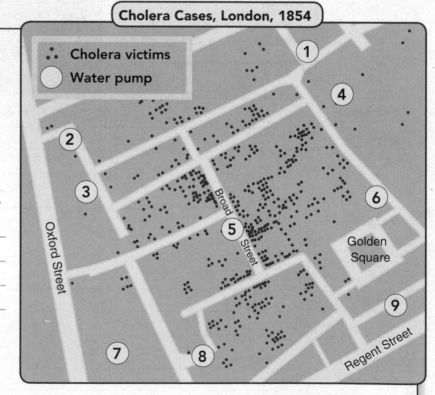

Cholera Cases, London, 1854

- Cholera victims
- Water pump

Oxford Street
Broad Street
Golden Square
Regent Street

Contaminated Objects Some pathogens can survive for a time outside a person's body. People can contact pathogens by using objects, such as towels or keyboards, that an infected person touched. Colds and flu can be spread in this way. Tetanus bacteria can enter the body if a contaminated nail or other object punctures the skin.

Infected Animals If an animal that is infected with certain pathogens bites a person, the pathogens can pass to the person. For example, people get rabies, a serious disease of the nervous system, from the bite of an infected animal, such as a dog or raccoon. In tropical regions, mosquito bites transfer the malaria protist to people. Deer ticks, as shown in **Figure 4,** live mostly in the northeastern and upper mideastern United States. The bites of some deer ticks spread Lyme disease. If left untreated, Lyme disease can damage joints and cause many other health problems.

FIGURE 4 ·············
Deer Ticks and Lyme Disease
To prevent Lyme disease, wear a long-sleeved shirt and tuck your pants into your socks if you plan to walk where ticks may live.

✎ **Infer** Explain how a deer tick could infect you without your realizing it.

_____
_____
_____
_____

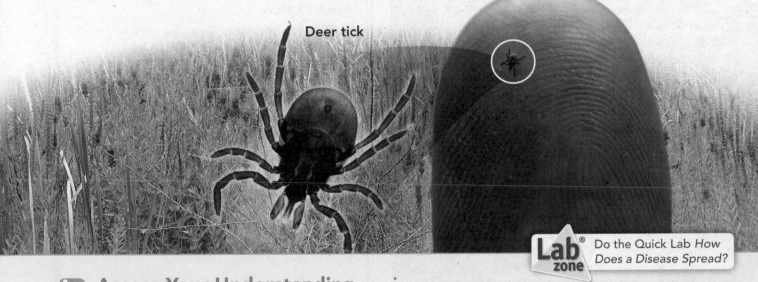

Deer tick

Lab zone® Do the Quick Lab *How Does a Disease Spread?*

🔑 Assess Your Understanding

2a. Identify Name four types of pathogens that cause disease in humans.

_____
_____

b. [CHALLENGE] How could people make bacteria-contaminated water safe to drink in order to prevent illness?

_____
_____
_____

got it?

○ **I get it!** Now I know that disease-causing pathogens include _____

_____ , and they are

spread by _____

_____
_____

○ **I need extra help with** _____

Go to **MY SCIENCE ⬤ᶜ COACH** *online for help with this subject.*

555

The Body's Defenses

UNLOCK THE BIG Q

🔑 **What Is the Body's First Line of Defense?**

🔑 **What Are the Inflammatory and Immune Responses?**

my planet Diary

The Kissing Disease

Have you ever heard of mononucleosis? Also known as mono, or the kissing disease, mononucleosis is most common among older teenagers and people in their twenties. It got its nickname because the disease can be spread through kissing. But, be careful. Because mono is passed through saliva, it can also be spread by sharing cups, forks, straws, and other utensils.

Some common symptoms of mono are fever, sore throat, swollen glands, and fatigue. If you display these symptoms, you might want to pay your doctor a visit, even if you haven't kissed anyone!

FUN FACTS

Read the following questions. Write your answers below.

1. How can mononucleosis be spread?

_____

_____

_____

2. What can you do to lower your chances of catching mono?

_____

_____

_____

> **PLANET DIARY** Go to **Planet Diary** to learn more about the body's defenses.

Lab zone Do the Inquiry Warm-Up *Which Pieces Fit Together?*

Vocabulary
- inflammatory response • phagocyte
- immune response • lymphocyte • T cell
- antigen • B cell • antibody

Skills
↻ Reading: Compare and Contrast
△ Inquiry: Make Models

What Is the Body's First Line of Defense?

You have probably battled invaders in video games. Video games have fantasy battles, but on and in your body, real battles against invading pathogens happen all the time. You are hardly ever aware of these battles because the body's disease-fighting system has lines of defense that effectively eliminate pathogens before they can harm your cells. ⚷ **In the first line of defense, the surface of your skin, breathing passages, mouth, and stomach function as barriers to pathogens. These barriers trap and kill most pathogens with which you come into contact.**

Skin Your skin is an effective barrier to pathogens, as you can see in **Figure 1.** Pathogens on the skin are exposed to destructive chemicals in oil and sweat. Even if these chemicals do not kill them, the pathogens may fall off with dead skin cells. Most pathogens get through the skin only when it is cut. However, blood clots at a cut. Then a scab forms over the cut. So pathogens have little time to enter the body this way.

FIGURE 1 ·······························
Skin as a Barrier
The dots are groups of bacteria. The bacteria were on the skin of a person's hand.

✎ **Use the photo to complete the tasks.**

1. **Identify** In each box, write one of the skin's defenses against pathogens.

2. CHALLENGE Why would you want a cut to bleed some?

_____
_____
_____

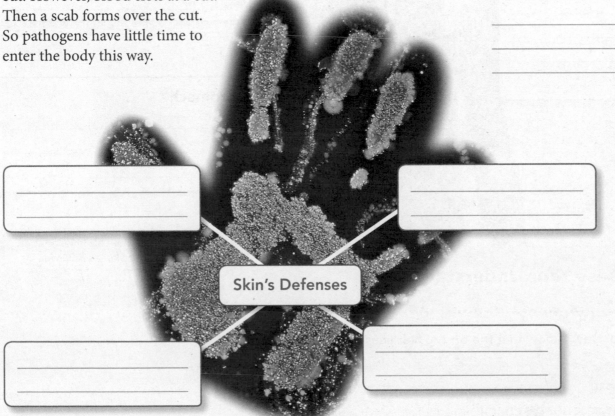

Skin's Defenses

557

Breathing Passages Your breathing passages defend you from many pathogens you inhale. The nose, pharynx, trachea, and bronchi have hairs, mucus, and cilia, all of which trap pathogens from the air. In addition, you sneeze and cough when pathogens irritate your breathing passages. Sneezing and coughing force pathogens out of your body.

Mouth and Stomach Even if foods are handled safely, they still contain potential pathogens. Most of these pathogens are destroyed in your mouth or stomach. Saliva in your mouth contains destructive chemicals, and your stomach produces acid. **Figure 2** shows three of your body's barriers to pathogens.

FIGURE 2 ....

Barriers to Pathogens
Your breathing passages, mouth, and stomach are part of your first line of defense against pathogens.

✏ **Summarize** In each box, write how the barrier protects the body from pathogens.

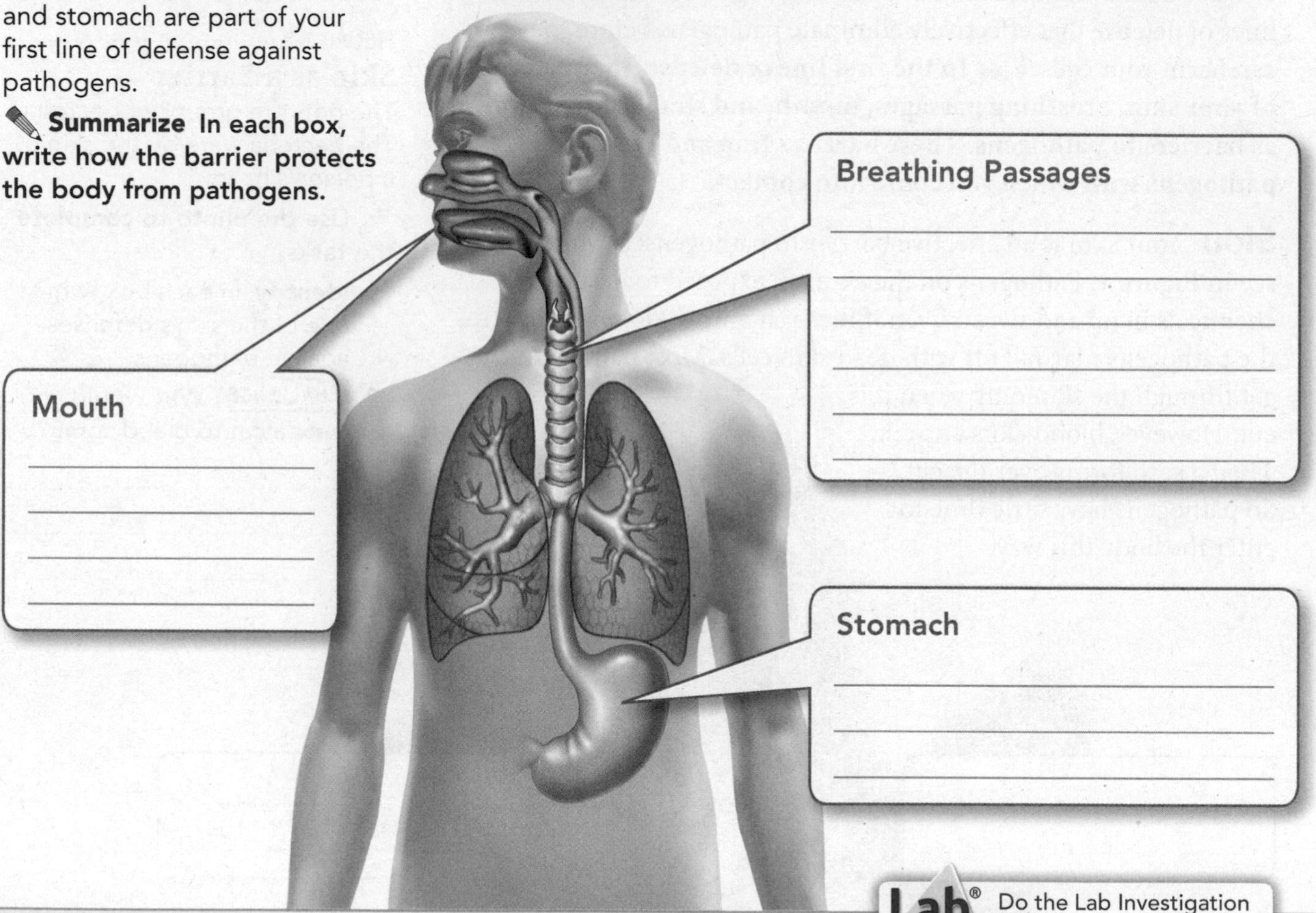

Breathing Passages

Mouth

Stomach

Lab zone Do the Lab Investigation
The Skin as a Barrier.

🔑 Assess Your Understanding

got it? ....

○ **I get it!** Now I know that the body's first lines of defense are _____

_____

○ I need extra help with _____

Go to MY SCIENCE COACH online for help with this subject.

What Are the Inflammatory and Immune Responses?

Sometimes the first line of defense fails, and pathogens get into your body. Fortunately, your body has a second and third line of defense—the inflammatory response and the immune response. **In the inflammatory response, fluid and white blood cells leak from blood vessels and fight pathogens in nearby tissues. In the immune response, certain immune cells in the blood and tissues react to each kind of pathogen with a defense targeted specifically at the pathogen.**

Inflammatory Response Have you ever scraped your knee? When body cells are damaged, they release chemicals that trigger the **inflammatory response,** which is your body's second line of defense. The inflammatory response is the same regardless of the pathogen, so it is a general defense. This response involves white blood cells, inflammation, and sometimes fever.

Vocabulary Latin Word Origins The Latin word *inflammare* means "to set on fire." How does the Latin meaning relate to the word *inflammation*?

_____

_____

_____

Compare and Contrast Use the first paragraph of the text to list how the inflammatory and immune responses are alike and different in the Venn diagram.

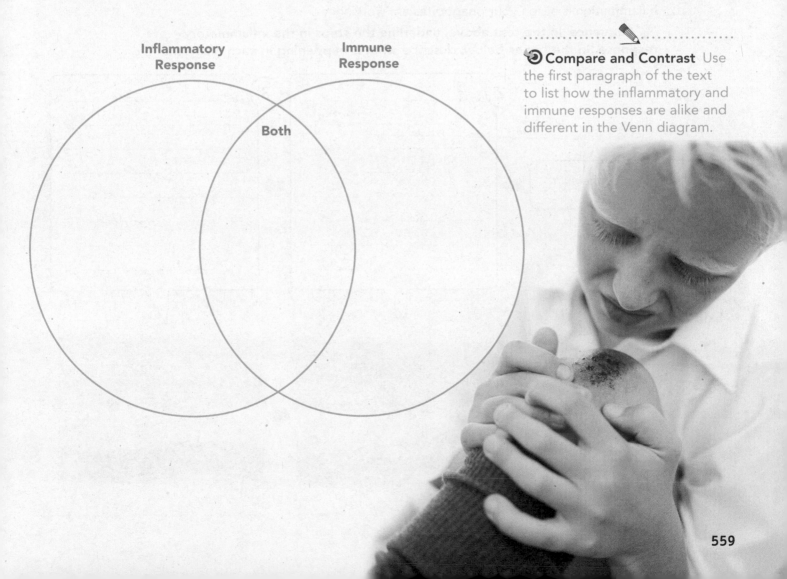

Inflammatory Response | Immune Response | Both

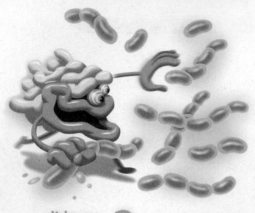

White Blood Cells Most white blood cells are disease fighters. However, each type of white blood cell has a particular function. The type of white blood cell involved in the inflammatory response is the phagocyte. A **phagocyte** (FAG uh syt) is a white blood cell that engulfs pathogens and destroys them by breaking them down.

Inflammation The inflammatory response is shown in **Figure 3.** During this response, capillaries widen in the area with pathogens. This enlargement increases blood flow to the area. Fluid and phagocytes leak out of the enlarged capillaries, and the affected area becomes red and swollen. In fact, if you touch the area, it will feel slightly warmer than usual. The phagocytes engulf the pathogens and destroy them.

Fever Chemicals produced during the inflammatory response sometimes cause a fever. Although a fever makes you feel bad, it helps your body fight the infection. Some pathogens do not grow or reproduce well at higher temperatures.

did you
know?
Your red bone marrow produces about 1 billion new white blood cells every day. Some of them are on patrol in your body right now, looking for pathogens and destroying them.

FIGURE 3

The Inflammatory Response
Inflammation is a sign your phagocytes are working.

✎ **Sequence** In the text above, underline the steps in the inflammatory response. In the boxes below, describe what is happening in each diagram.

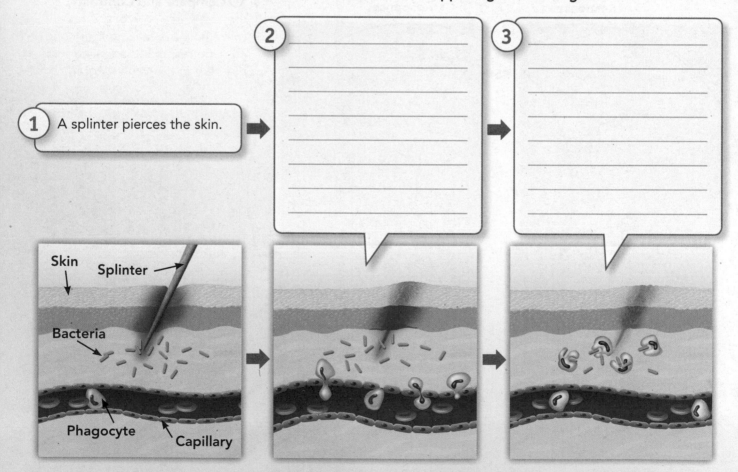

1 A splinter pierces the skin.

2

3

Skin Splinter

Bacteria

Phagocyte Capillary

Immune Response If an infection from a pathogen is severe enough, it triggers the body's third line of defense—the **immune response.** The immune response is controlled by the immune system. The cells of the immune system can distinguish between different kinds of pathogens. They react to invaders with a defense targeted against that pathogen.

The white blood cells that distinguish between different kinds of pathogens are called **lymphocytes** (LIM fuh syts). Your body has two major kinds of lymphocytes: T cells and B cells.

T Cells A **T cell** is a lymphocyte that identifies pathogens and distinguishes one pathogen from another. Each kind of T cell recognizes a different kind of pathogen. What T cells actually recognize are a pathogen's marker molecules, which are called antigens. **Antigens** are molecules that the immune system recognizes either as part of your body or as coming from outside your body. Each different pathogen has its own antigen, with its own chemical structure. Look at **Figure 4** to see how T cells function.

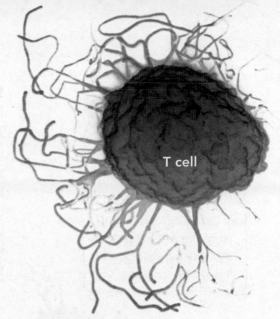

T cell

FIGURE 4 ....
T Cell Function
Healthy people have tens of millions of T cells in their blood.

✎ **Describe** What two roles does a T cell play after it divides?

_____

_____

_____

_____

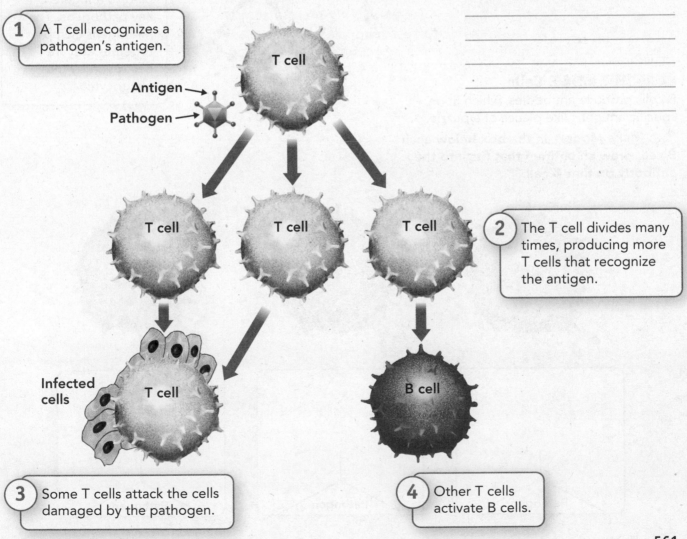

1. A T cell recognizes a pathogen's antigen.

Antigen →

Pathogen →

T cell

T cell

T cell

T cell

2. The T cell divides many times, producing more T cells that recognize the antigen.

Infected cells

T cell

B cell

3. Some T cells attack the cells damaged by the pathogen.

4. Other T cells activate B cells.

B Cells The lymphocytes called **B cells** produce proteins that help destroy pathogens. These proteins are called **antibodies**. Each kind of B cell produces only one kind of antibody, and each kind of antibody has a different structure. Antigen and antibody molecules fit together like pieces of a puzzle. When antibodies bind to the antigens on a pathogen, they mark the pathogen for destruction. Some antibodies make pathogens clump together like those shown in **Figure 5.** Others keep pathogens from attaching to the body cells they might harm. Still other antibodies make it easier for phagocytes to destroy the pathogens.

T cells activate B cells to make antibodies against a pathogen's antigens.

The antibodies then bind to antigens on any pathogens. The pathogens clump together and are destroyed by the phagocytes.

FIGURE 5 ·····································

> **INTERACTIVE ART** **B Cells**

B cells produce antibodies, which fit on specific antigens like pieces of a puzzle.

✎ **Make Models In the box below each B cell, draw an antigen that fits into the antibody on that B cell.**

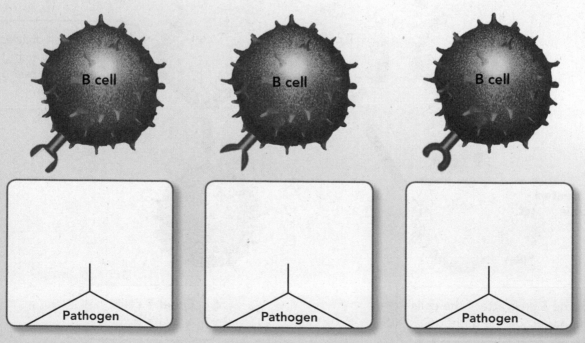

apply it!

Certain bacteria cause strep throat. Your T cells and B cells work together to combat the infection.

❶ Identify Number each step in the immune response.

❷ Sequence Describe each step of the immune response against the bacteria that causes strep throat.

_____
_____
_____
_____
_____
_____
_____
_____
_____
_____
_____
_____
_____
_____

T cell

Antigen →

Pathogen →

T cell   **T cell**   **T cell**

Infected throat cells

T cell

B cell

Antibodies →

Antigen →

Do the Quick Lab
Stuck Together.

🔑 Assess Your Understanding

1a. Name Identify the key cells that are part of the immune response.

_____
_____

b. Explain How does the inflammatory response defend against pathogens?

_____
_____
_____
_____

got it?

○ **I get it!** Now I know the inflammatory and immune responses are the body's _____

_____

_____

○ **I need extra help with** _____

Go to MY SCIENCE ⑤ COACH *online for help with this subject.*

HIV and AIDS

🔑 **How Does HIV Affect the Body?**

🔑 **How Is HIV Spread and Treated?**

my planeT DiaRY

The NAMES Project Foundation— AIDS Memorial Quilt

Headquarters: Atlanta, Georgia

How do you cope with loss? Some who have lost loved ones to AIDS express their feelings by making panels to add to the AIDS Memorial Quilt. Begun in 1987 in San Francisco, the NAMES Project Foundation takes care of the quilt. The quilt is made up of more than 47,000 individual panels from countries all around the world. The panels help people honor those whom they have lost to the tragic disease. The large number of panels sadly illustrates that AIDS has taken so many lives. Yet, the quilt is a symbol of unity that supports continuing research to find a cure for this devastating disease.

PROFILE

Communicate Discuss the following questions with a partner. Write your answers below.

1. The quilt is made up of panels from around the world. What does this tell you about AIDS?

_____

_____

2. Why do you think scientists are important in the fight against AIDS?

_____

_____

_____

▶ PLANET DIARY Go to **Planet Diary** to learn more about HIV and AIDS.

Lab zone Do the Inquiry Warm-Up *How Does HIV Spread?*

Vocabulary
- AIDS
- HIV

Skills
- Reading: Sequence
- Inquiry: Graph

How Does HIV Affect the Body?

Our immune system protects us well. So we usually do not even realize that our body has been attacked by a pathogen. But what happens when our immune system itself is sick?

Acquired immunodeficiency syndrome, or **AIDS,** is a disease caused by a virus that attacks the immune system. The virus that causes AIDS is called the human immunodeficiency virus, or **HIV.** **HIV is the only kind of virus known to attack the human immune system directly and destroy T cells.** Once inside the body, HIV enters T cells and reproduces. People can be infected with HIV—that is, have the virus living in their T cells—for many years before they become sick.

In 1981, the first case of AIDS was reported in the United States. Nearly one million Americans may now be infected with HIV. Many of these people—one in four—do not realize yet that they are infected. However, the disease is not found only in the United States. It is a worldwide epidemic.

do the math!

The table shows the number of men, women, and children under age 15 worldwide living with HIV in 2007.

1 ⚠ **Graph** Use the data in the table to make a bar graph. Then write a title for the graph.

2 Interpret Data What do you notice about the number of men and women living with HIV in 2007?

_____

_____

_____

3 Draw Conclusions What conclusion can you make about the populations the virus affects?

_____

_____

Populations Living With HIV in 2007

Population	Number of People
Men	15.3 million
Women	15.5 million
Children under age 15	2 million

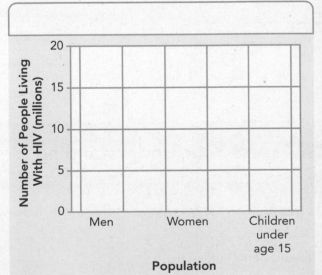

Number of People Living With HIV (millions) — 20, 15, 10, 5, 0

Population: Men, Women, Children under age 15

565

Step 1 A person is infected.

Step 2

_____

_____

_____

_____

Step 3

_____

_____

_____

_____

Step 4

_____

_____

_____

_____

Step 5

_____

_____

_____

HIV and AIDS

When people first become infected with HIV, they often have no symptoms. A month or so later, they may seem to have the flu, but it goes away. Although they may not have symptoms at first, people can still spread the virus.

It may take ten years or more for severe symptoms to appear. However, in time, HIV begins to destroy the T cells it has infected. As the virus destroys T cells like the one shown in **Figure 1,** the body begins to lose its ability to fight disease. This is a symptom of the disease called AIDS.

Infections

People with AIDS start to get diseases that healthy people do not get normally. Development of these infections is one symptom of the disease AIDS. Most people infected with HIV eventually develop the symptoms of AIDS. Many survive attack after attack of infections. Yet, in time, their immune systems fail, and they die.

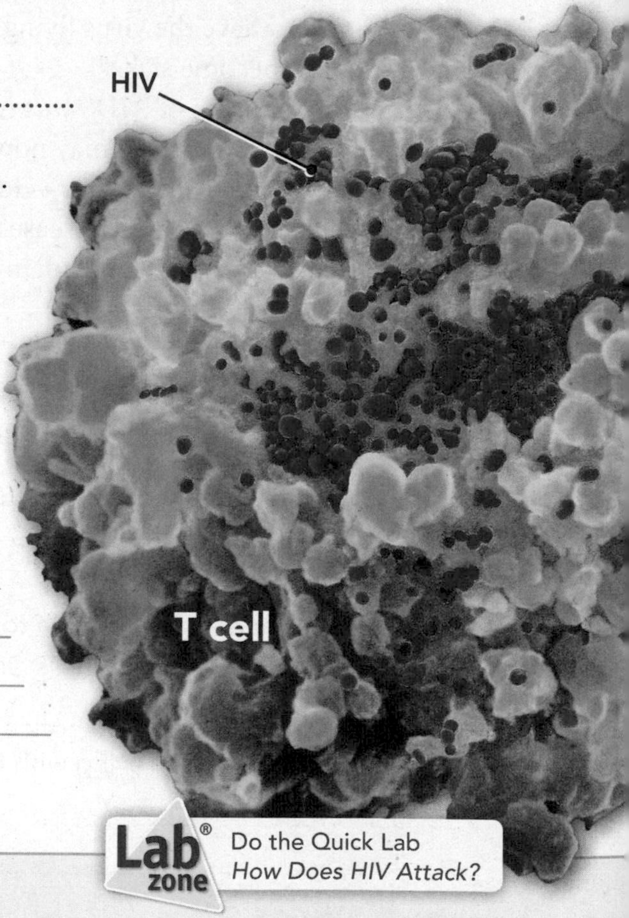

FIGURE 1 ···

HIV

HIV reproduces inside T cells. It then bursts out to attack other T cells.

CHALLENGE **Use what you see in the photo to explain why HIV destroys an immune system.**

_____

_____

_____

_____

_____

_____

HIV

T cell

Lab zone® Do the Quick Lab
How Does HIV Attack?

Assess Your Understanding

got it? ···

O **I get it!** Now I know that HIV affects the body by _____

_____

O **I need extra help with** _____

Go to MY SCIENCE COACH online for help with this subject.

How Is HIV Spread and Treated?

Like all other viruses, HIV can reproduce only inside cells. However, the virus can survive for a short time outside the human body in fluids. These fluids include blood and the fluids that the male and female reproductive systems produce.

🔑 **HIV can spread from one person to another if body fluids from an infected person come in contact with body fluids of an uninfected person.** Sexual contact is one way this transfer happens. HIV may also pass from an infected woman to her baby during pregnancy or childbirth, or through breast milk. Infected blood can also spread HIV. For example, drug users who share needles can pass HIV. Since 1985, all donated blood in the United States has been tested for HIV.

At this time, there is no cure for AIDS. However, combinations of drugs that fight the virus in different ways can delay the development of AIDS and extend life expectancy. See **Figure 2** for information about young people living with AIDS.

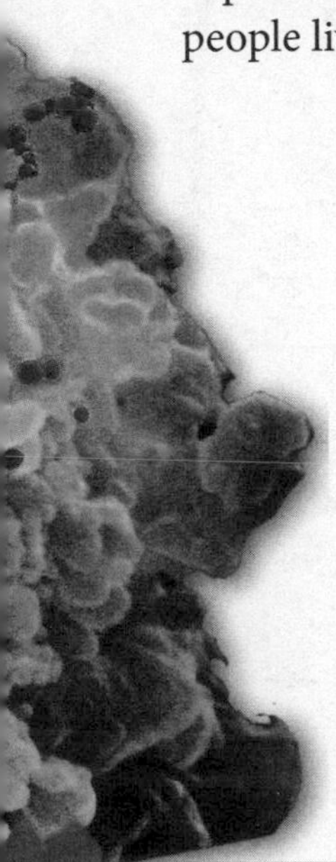

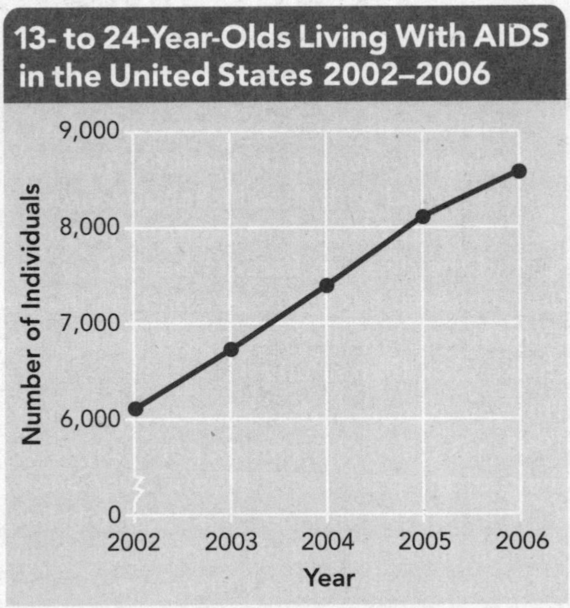

FIGURE 2 ·······················

Young People and AIDS

The graph shows how advances in HIV treatments enabled more people to live with AIDS.

✎ **Read Graphs** Using the graph, estimate how many 13- to 24-year-olds were living with AIDS in 2007.

_____

_____

_____

_____

13- to 24-Year-Olds Living With AIDS in the United States 2002–2006

Number of Individuals (y-axis): 0, 6,000, 7,000, 8,000, 9,000

Year (x-axis): 2002, 2003, 2004, 2005, 2006

Lab zone® Do the Quick Lab
What Will Spread HIV?

🔑 **Assess Your Understanding**

1a. Review Where does HIV reproduce in people?

_____

_____

b. Summarize How is AIDS treated?

_____

_____

got it? ·······························

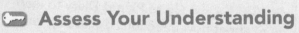

○ **I get it!** Now I know that HIV can spread _____

_____

○ **I need extra help with** _____

Go to **my science** ⓢ **coach** *online for help with this subject.*

Infectious Disease and Your Health

UNLOCK THE BIG Q?

🔑 **How Can You Become Immune?**

🔑 **How Can Infectious Diseases Be Treated and Prevented?**

MY PLANET DiARY

DISCOVERY

Chickenpox Vaccine

Before the chickenpox vaccine was developed, more than 4 million Americans were infected with the chickenpox virus every year. Parents planned chickenpox parties to spread the disease. Parents wanted to expose their children to chickenpox early in life because children are less likely to get seriously ill from chickenpox than adults.

The development of a chickenpox vaccine in 1995 has made chickenpox parties mostly a thing of the past. Now, anyone over one year old can get the vaccine. The vaccine has reduced the likelihood of getting chickenpox to just 10 to 30 percent. Since the vaccine is somewhat new, more research is being done to determine if the vaccine can last through adulthood.

Write your answers to the questions below.

1. What was the purpose of chickenpox parties?

_____

_____

_____

_____

2. Why do you think there is a 10 to 30 percent chance of chickenpox with the vaccine?

_____

_____

_____

▶ **PLANET DIARY** Go to **Planet Diary** to learn more about how infectious diseases affect your health.

Lab zone® Do the Inquiry Warm-Up *Types of Immunity.*

Vocabulary

- immunity • active immunity • vaccination • vaccine
- passive immunity • antibiotic • antibiotic resistance

Skills

↻ **Reading: Relate Cause and Effect**

△ **Inquiry: Interpret Data**

How Can You Become Immune?

People get diseases. However, they get some diseases only once. This is because people develop immunity to some diseases once they recover from them. **Immunity** is the body's ability to destroy pathogens before they can cause disease. Immunity can be active or passive. ⊶ **You acquire active immunity when your own immune system produces antibodies against a pathogen in your body. You acquire passive immunity when the antibodies come from a source outside your body.**

Active Immunity People who have had chickenpox were once invaded by the chickenpox virus. In response, their immune systems produced antibodies. The next time the chickenpox virus invades their bodies, their immune systems will produce antibodies quickly. So they will not become sick with chickenpox again. This reaction is called **active immunity** because the body has produced the antibodies that fight pathogens. Active immunity can result from either getting the disease or being vaccinated. It often lasts for many years. Sometimes it lasts for life.

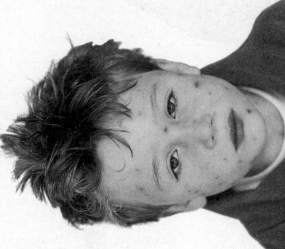

Cause	Effect
Contract chickenpox virus the first time.	_____ _____ _____ _____ _____

↻ **Relate Cause and Effect**
Complete the graphic organizer with the effects of contracting the chickenpox virus.

Cause	Effect
Contract chickenpox virus the second time.	_____ _____ _____ _____ _____

569

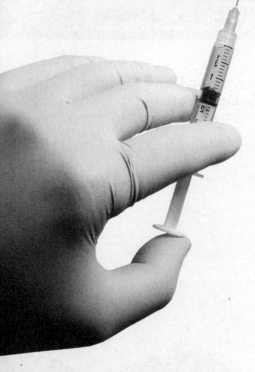

The Immune Response The immune system produces active immunity as part of the immune response. Recall that during the immune response, T cells and B cells help destroy pathogens. After the person recovers, some T cells and B cells keep the "memory" of the pathogen's antigen. If that kind of pathogen invades again, these memory cells recognize the antigen. They start the immune response so quickly that the person often does not get sick.

Vaccination Vaccination is another way of gaining immunity, as shown in **Figure 1. Vaccination** (vac suh NAY shun), or immunization, is the process by which harmless antigens are put into a person's body to produce active immunity. Vaccinations are given by injection, by mouth, or through a nasal spray.

The substance used in a vaccination is a vaccine. A **vaccine** (vak SEEN) usually consists of weakened or killed pathogens that trigger the immune response into action. The T cells and B cells still recognize and respond to the antigens of these weakened or killed pathogens and destroy them. So when you receive a vaccination, you usually do not get sick. However, after destroying these pathogens, your immune system responds by producing memory cells and active immunity to the disease.

FIGURE 1 ·······························
▶ ART IN MOTION **Vaccination**
A vaccine activates the immune response.

✎ **Interpret Diagrams** In the empty boxes, describe what is happening in each diagram.

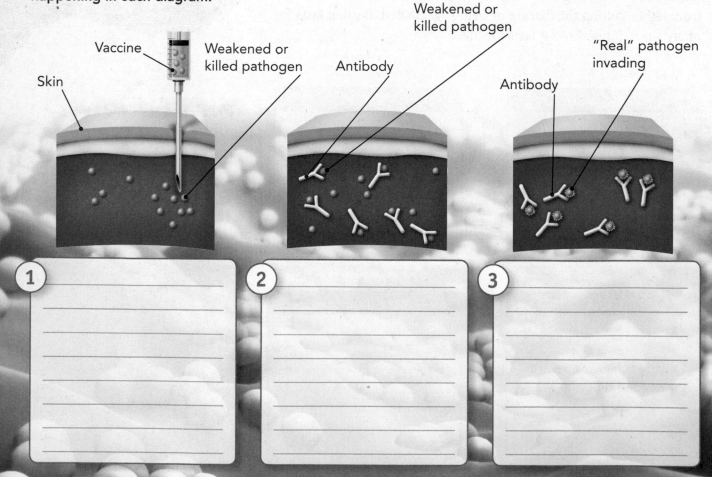

Passive Immunity Some diseases, such as rabies, are uncommon. So people rarely receive vaccinations against them. However, someone who is bitten by an animal with rabies is usually given injections containing antibodies to the rabies antigen. This type of protection is called passive immunity. **Passive immunity** results when antibodies are given to a person. Unlike active immunity, passive immunity usually lasts no more than a few months.

A baby acquires passive immunity to some diseases before birth. This immunity results from antibodies that are passed from the mother's blood into the baby's blood during pregnancy. After birth, these antibodies protect the baby for about six months.

FIGURE 2 ·······························

Immune Responses
Your body can destroy pathogens in two different ways.

✎ **Compare and Contrast** Use the Venn diagram to compare and contrast active immunity and passive immunity.

Active Immunity   **Passive Immunity**

Both

Lab zone ® Do the Quick Lab *Modeling Active and Passive Immunity.*

🔑 Assess Your Understanding

1a. Explain What are two ways that you could acquire active immunity?

_____

_____

_____

b. Develop Hypotheses Why does passive immunity usually not last for long?

_____

_____

_____

got**it?** ···

○ **I get it!** Now I know that I can become immune by _____

_____

○ **I need extra help with** _____

    Go to MY SCIENCE ⓢ COACH online for help with this subject.

How Can Infectious Diseases Be Treated and Prevented?

Bacteria and viruses can cause infectious diseases that require treatment. 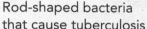 **Bacterial diseases can be treated with specific medications. Viral diseases have no known cure. Both types of diseases can be prevented.**

Bacterial Diseases If you get a bacterial disease, you may be given an antibiotic. An **antibiotic** (an tih by AHT ik) is a chemical that kills bacteria or slows their growth without harming body cells. Antibiotics are made naturally by some bacteria and fungi. They also are made in factories. Some antibiotics, such as amoxicillin, cause the cell walls of certain bacteria to burst.

Over time, many bacteria can become resistant to antibiotics. **Antibiotic resistance** results when some bacteria are able to withstand the effects of an antibiotic. For example, in the 1940s, the use of antibiotics caused the number of tuberculosis cases to drop significantly. Yet, a few tuberculosis bacteria resisted the antibiotics. As resistant bacteria survive and reproduce, the number of resistant bacteria increases. As a result, the number of tuberculosis cases worldwide has increased over the last 20 years.

Rod-shaped bacteria that cause tuberculosis

apply it!

Tuberculosis (TB) is a bacterial disease that affects the lungs. The data table shows the estimated number of new TB cases in 1997, 2002, and 2007.

1 ◢ **Interpret Data** Which country has the greatest problem with TB? Explain how you know.

_____

_____

_____

_____

2 [CHALLENGE] Why are the data presented as the number of new cases per 100,000 people?

_____

_____

_____

Estimated TB Cases per 100,000 Population			
Country	1997	2002	2007
Brazil	67	57	48
China	109	103	98
India	168	168	168
Mexico	39	28	20
Russia	94	108	110
South Africa	360	780	948
United States	7	5	4

Viral Diseases Medicines you take when you have a cold or the flu do not kill the viruses because the viruses are nonliving. But, medicines can reduce your symptoms so you feel better. Always follow the medicine's directions. Medicine can sometimes hide symptoms that should send you to see a doctor.

To recover from a bacterial or viral disease, get plenty of rest and drink fluids. If you do not feel better in a short time, see a doctor.

Prevention There are ways to prevent getting sick from microorganisms. You can avoid contact with infected people and wash your hands often. You can also eat a balanced diet and exercise to stay healthy. To prevent some diseases, such as the flu, you can get a vaccine. However, you cannot get a vaccine for cold viruses.

FIGURE 3 ·····················

Colds and the Flu

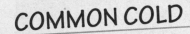 **Describe** Complete the common cold card. Use the flu card as a guide.

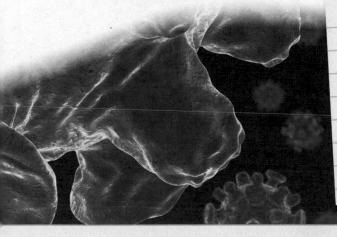

INFLUENZA (Flu)

Symptoms: High fever; sore throat; headache; cough

How It Spreads: Contact with contaminated people or objects; inhaling droplets

Treatment: Bed rest; fluids

Prevention: Vaccine (mainly for the high-risk ill, elderly, and young)

COMMON COLD

Symptoms:

How It Spreads:

Treatment:

Prevention:

Lab zone® Do the Quick Lab *What Substances Can Kill Pathogens?*

 Assess Your Understanding

2a. Review What is the best treatment for viral diseases?

_____

_____

b. Infer Explain why antibiotics are ineffective against viral diseases.

_____

_____

got it? ·····················

○ **I get it!** Now I know that if I get sick, I can treat _____

and prevent _____

○ **I need extra help with** _____

Go to **my science** s **COACH** online for help with this subject.

Noninfectious Disease

How Do Allergies, Asthma, and Diabetes Affect the Body?

What Is Cancer and How Can It Be Treated?

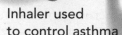

Inhaler used to control asthma

my planet diary

Athletes With Asthma

Asthma is a disease that causes shortness of breath and wheezing or coughing. You may think people who have asthma cannot excel in sports. But asthma does not have to stop anyone from succeeding. Here are some facts about asthma and athletics.

• One out of six athletes in the 1996 Summer Olympics had a history of asthma. Thirty percent of them won a medal.

• 22 percent of the athletes in the 1998 Winter Olympics suffered from asthma.

• Jerome Bettis (NFL football player), Jackie Joyner-Kersee (Olympic track and field medalist), Hakeem Olajuwon (NBA basketball player), and Amy VanDyken (Olympic swimmer) all live with asthma.

SCIENCE STATS

Answer the following questions.

1. Why might people think that someone with asthma cannot play sports?

_____

_____

_____

_____

2. What would you tell a friend who has asthma and wants to join the swim team?

_____

_____

_____

▶ PLANET DIARY Go to **Planet Diary** to learn more about noninfectious disease.

 Do the Inquiry Warm-Up *Causes of Death, Then and Now*

Vocabulary

- noninfectious disease • allergy • allergen
- histamine • asthma • insulin • diabetes
- tumor • carcinogen

Skills

- ↻ Reading: Summarize
- △ Inquiry: Draw Conclusions

How Do Allergies, Asthma, and Diabetes Affect the Body?

Americans are living longer than ever before. A person who was born in 2000 can expect to live about 77 years. In contrast, a person who was born in 1950 could expect to live only about 68 years, and a person born in 1900 only about 50 years.

Progress against infectious disease is one reason why life spans have increased. However, as most infectious diseases have become less common, noninfectious diseases have grown more common. **Noninfectious diseases** are diseases that are not caused by pathogens. Unlike infectious diseases, noninfectious diseases cannot be transmitted from person to person. Two noninfectious diseases, cardiovascular disease and cancer, are the first and second leading causes of death from disease in the United States. Allergies, asthma, and diabetes are other noninfectious diseases. While not often fatal, these diseases are chronic. That is, they reappear frequently over time. **Allergies cause an inflammatory response by the body. Asthma affects breathing, while diabetes affects how body cells take up glucose.**

✎ **Summarize** Use your own words to summarize the information about diseases on this page.

Allergies People who sneeze a lot in the spring may not have a cold. Instead, they may be showing a symptom of an allergy. An **allergy** is a reaction caused when the immune system is overly sensitive to a foreign substance—something not normally found in the body.

Any substance that causes an allergy is an **allergen.** Allergens include pollen, dust, molds, some foods, pet dander (dandruff), and even some medicines. Unfortunately, the bodies of many people react to one or more allergens.

Allergens may get into your body when you inhale them, eat them in food, or touch them. Allergens signal cells in the body to release a substance called histamine. **Histamine** (HIS tuh meen) is a chemical that is responsible for the symptoms of an allergy, such as a rash, sneezing, and watery eyes. Drugs that interfere with the action of histamine, called antihistamines, may lessen this reaction. However, if you have an allergy, the best way to prevent allergy symptoms is to try to avoid the substance to which you are allergic.

apply it!

Suzy ate some strawberries. A short time later, she broke out in a rash.

❶ Identify What might have caused Suzy's rash?

_____

❷ Sequence Explain how eating strawberries can cause a rash.

_____
_____
_____

❸ Predict What might a doctor prescribe to relieve Suzy's rash?

_____
_____

Asthma Some allergic reactions can cause a condition called asthma. **Asthma** (AZ muh) is a disease in which the airways in the lungs narrow significantly. This narrowing causes wheezing, coughing, and shortness of breath. Other factors that may trigger asthma attacks include stress and heavy exercise. Tobacco smoke, air pollution, strong odors, and respiratory infections can also trigger an attack. More than 20 million Americans have asthma.

Figure 1 shows a normal airway and an airway affected by asthma. During an asthma attack, the muscles around the airways tighten, narrowing the airways. At the same time, the inner walls of the airways become irritated, red, swollen, and warm. They produce mucus. The mucus clogs the airways and makes breathing even more difficult.

Someone who is having an asthma attack needs medicines, such as an inhaler, to open the airways and reduce swelling. A severe attack may require emergency care. An asthma attack can be fatal.

FIGURE 1 ···

Airways With and Without Asthma

Asthma is a common condition among young people.

✎ **Relate Text and Visuals** Look at the diagram of a normal airway. Then in each box of the second diagram, describe what happens in an airway affected by asthma.

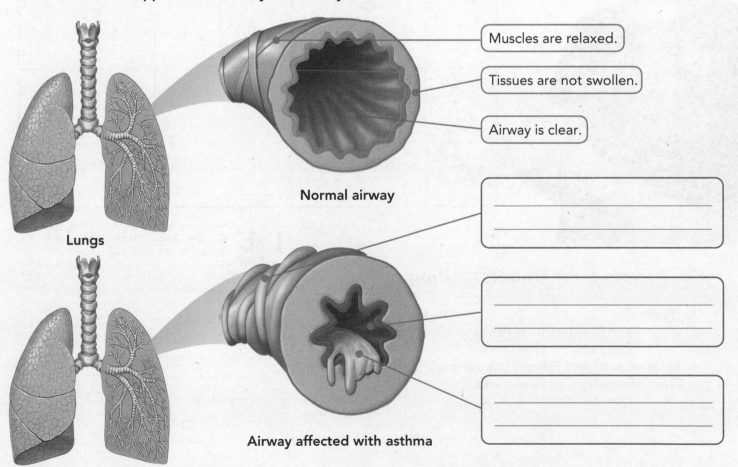

Muscles are relaxed.

Tissues are not swollen.

Airway is clear.

Normal airway

Lungs

Airway affected with asthma

FIGURE 2 ·······························

Glucose Testing
The student is using a device called a glucometer to measure the amount of glucose in his blood.

✏️ 🔄 **Summarize** Write notes in the table about Type I and Type II diabetes.

Diabetes One function of the pancreas is to produce insulin. **Insulin** (IN suh lin) is a substance that enables body cells to take glucose from the blood and use it for energy. In the condition called **diabetes** (dy uh BEE teez), either the pancreas produces too little insulin or body cells do not use insulin properly. People with diabetes, or diabetics, have high levels of glucose in their blood but not enough of it in their body cells. If untreated, diabetics may lose weight and feel weak and hungry. They also may urinate often and feel thirsty.

Diabetes has two main forms. Type I diabetes often begins in childhood. The pancreas produces little or no insulin. People with this condition need insulin injections. Type II diabetes usually develops in adults. Either body cells stop responding normally to insulin or the pancreas stops making enough insulin. Some Type II diabetics can control their symptoms through diet, weight control, and exercise instead of insulin injections. All diabetics must check their blood frequently, as shown in **Figure 2**.

Type of Diabetes	Cause	Symptoms	Treatment
Type I			
Type II			

Lab zone® Do the Quick Lab *What Happens When Air Flow Is Restricted?*

🔓 Assess Your Understanding

1a. Name _____ is a disorder in which airways of the lungs narrow significantly.

b. Relate Cause and Effect How are insulin levels affected in Type I diabetes?

_____

_____

got**it?**

○ **I get it!** Now I know that allergies, asthma, and diabetes affect _____

_____

○ **I need extra help with** _____

Go to MY SCIENCE Ⓢ COACH online for help with this subject.

What Is Cancer and How Can It Be Treated?

Usually, the body produces new cells at about the same rate that other cells die. 🔑 **However, cancer is a disease in which cells multiply uncontrollably, over and over, destroying healthy tissue. Treatments include surgery, radiation, and drugs.**

How Cancer Develops As cells divide over and over, they often form abnormal masses of cells called **tumors.** Not all tumors are cancerous. Cancerous tumors invade and destroy the healthy tissue around them. Eventually, cells from a tumor may break away from the tumor and enter the blood or lymph vessels. The blood or lymph carries the cancer cells to other parts of the body, where they may form new tumors. Unless stopped by treatment, cancer progresses through the body.

Causes of Cancer Different factors may work together to cause cancer. Inherited characteristics make some people more likely to develop certain cancers. For example, daughters of mothers who had breast cancer have an increased chance of developing breast cancer themselves. Factors in the environment, called **carcinogens** (kahr SIN uh junz), can also cause cancer. The tar in cigarette smoke is a carcinogen.

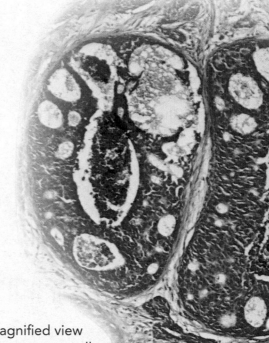

Magnified view of cancerous cells

do the math!

This data table shows the estimated number of new cases of different cancers in the United States in 1981 and 2007.

❶ **Interpret Tables** Which type of cancer has increased the most from 1981 to 2007 in men? In women?

Men _____

Women _____

❷ ⚠ **Draw Conclusions** Explain why the number of new cancer cases might increase as tests to detect cancer improve.

_____

_____

_____

_____

_____

Estimated New Cancer Cases

Type of Cancer	New Cases (1981)	New Cases (2007)
Men		
Prostate	70,000	218,890
Lung	88,000	114,760
Colon and Rectum	58,000	79,130
Oral Cavity and Pharynx	18,400	24,180
Women		
Breast	110,000	178,480
Lung	34,000	98,620
Colon and Rectum	62,000	74,630
Uterus	54,000	50,230

Cancer Treatment

Surgery, radiation, and drugs are used to treat cancer. If cancer is detected before it has spread, doctors may remove tumors with surgery. After surgery, radiation or drugs may be used to kill remaining cancer cells.

Radiation treatment uses high-energy waves to kill cancer cells. When these waves are aimed at tumors, the intense energy damages and kills cancer cells. Drug therapy is the use of chemicals to destroy cancer cells. It is often called chemotherapy. However, many of these chemicals can destroy some normal cells, too. Both radiation and chemotherapy can have side effects, such as nausea and hair loss.

Cancer Prevention

People can reduce their risk of cancer by avoiding carcinogens, such as those in tobacco and sunlight. A low-fat diet that includes plenty of fruits and vegetables can help prevent cancers of the digestive system.

Also, people can get regular checkups to increase their chance of surviving cancer. The earlier cancer is detected, the more likely it can be treated successfully. In **Figure 3,** you can see a blackened spot on skin. This spot is a skin cancer called melanoma. Exposing unprotected skin to sunlight too often contributes to the development of skin cancer. It is especially important to avoid sunburns, which damage skin cells.

FIGURE 3 ·······································

Melanoma

Melanoma is the most serious skin cancer. It can affect many other organs in your body if not treated quickly.

✎ **On the notebook paper, write answers to the questions below.**

1. **Explain** What can you do to prevent skin cancer?
2. **CHALLENGE** What steps might a doctor take to treat melanoma?

Melanoma

INVISIBLE INVADERS

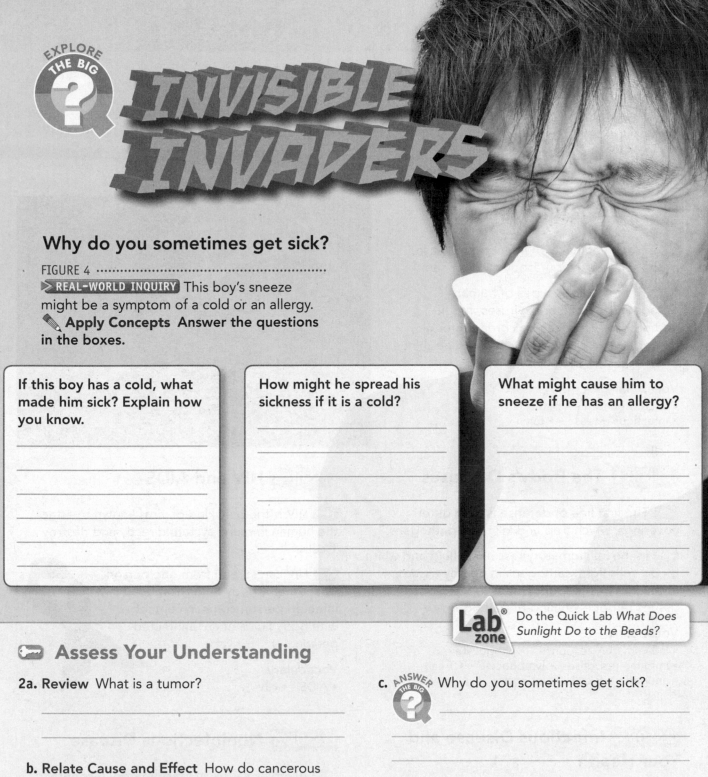

Why do you sometimes get sick?

FIGURE 4 ···

> **REAL-WORLD INQUIRY** This boy's sneeze might be a symptom of a cold or an allergy.

✎ **Apply Concepts** Answer the questions in the boxes.

If this boy has a cold, what made him sick? Explain how you know.
_____
_____
_____
_____
_____

How might he spread his sickness if it is a cold?
_____
_____
_____
_____
_____

What might cause him to sneeze if he has an allergy?
_____
_____
_____
_____
_____

Lab zone ® Do the Quick Lab *What Does Sunlight Do to the Beads?*

🔑 Assess Your Understanding

2a. Review What is a tumor?

_____

_____

b. Relate Cause and Effect How do cancerous tumors harm the body?

_____

_____

c. ANSWER THE BIG ? Why do you sometimes get sick?

_____

_____

_____

_____

_____

got it? ···

○ **I get it!** Now I know that cancer is _____

_____

○ **I need extra help with** _____

Go to **MY SCIENCE COACH** online for help with this subject.

A _____ in my body may cause an _____ disease.
I can also get sick from a _____ disease.

LESSON 1 Infectious Disease

🔑 When you have an infectious disease, pathogens are in your body causing harm.

🔑 The four major types of human pathogens are bacteria, viruses, fungi, and protists. They can be spread through contact with a sick person, other living things, or an object in the environment.

Vocabulary
- microorganism
- pathogen
- infectious disease
- toxin

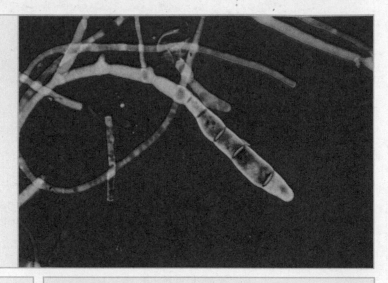

LESSON 2 The Body's Defenses

🔑 The first line of defense is your outer coverings, which trap and kill most pathogens.

🔑 In the inflammatory response, fluid and white blood cells fight pathogens in nearby tissues. In the immune response, cells in the blood and tissues target each kind of pathogen.

Vocabulary
- inflammatory response
- phagocyte
- immune response
- lymphocyte
- T cell
- antigen
- B cell
- antibody

LESSON 3 HIV and AIDS

🔑 HIV is the only kind of virus known to attack the human immune system directly and destroy T cells.

🔑 HIV can spread from one person to another if body fluids from an infected person come in contact with body fluids of an uninfected person.

Vocabulary
- AIDS
- HIV

LESSON 4 Infectious Disease and Your Health

🔑 You acquire active immunity when your own immune system produces antibodies. You acquire passive immunity when the antibodies come from a source outside your body.

🔑 Bacterial diseases can be treated with medications. Viral diseases have no known cure.

Vocabulary
- immunity
- active immunity
- vaccination
- vaccine
- passive immunity
- antibiotic
- antibiotic resistance

LESSON 5 Noninfectious Disease

🔑 Allergies cause an inflammatory response by the body. Asthma affects breathing, while diabetes affects how body cells take up glucose.

🔑 Cancer is a disease in which cells multiply uncontrollably, destroying healthy tissue. Treatments include surgery, radiation, and drugs.

Vocabulary
- noninfectious disease
- allergy
- allergen
- histamine
- asthma
- insulin
- diabetes
- tumor
- carcinogen

Review and Assessment

LESSON 1 **Infectious Disease**

1. Organisms that cause disease are called

   a. histamines.   **b.** pathogens.

   c. phagocytes.   **d.** toxins.

2. _____ are living things too small to see with a microscope that cause most infectious diseases.

3. Classify What are the four ways in which a person can become infected with a pathogen?

_____

_____

_____

_____

_____

_____

4. Compare and Contrast Describe how bacteria and viruses are alike and different in terms of how they cause disease.

_____

_____

_____

_____

_____

5. Apply Concepts Can you catch a cold by sitting in a chilly draft? Explain.

_____

_____

_____

6. **Write About It** Write a short speech that Joseph Lister might have delivered to other surgeons to convince them to use his surgical techniques. In the speech, Lister should explain why his techniques were so successful.

LESSON 2 **The Body's Defenses**

7. Proteins produced by B cells are called

   a. phagocytes.   **b.** T cells.

   c. antibodies.   **d.** pathogens.

8. _____ engulf pathogens and destroy them.

9. Communicate How does the body make it difficult for a pathogen to reach a part of the body where it can cause disease?

_____

_____

_____

_____

_____

_____

10. Interpret Diagrams In the diagram below, identify each labeled structure and its role in the immune response.

_____

_____

_____

_____

_____

_____

_____

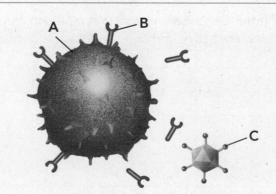

14 Review and Assessment

LESSON 3 HIV and AIDS

11. HIV attacks the human immune system and destroys

    a. B cells.   **b.** antigens.

    c. antibodies.   **d.** T cells.

12. HIV spreads from an infected person to an uninfected person through the contact of

_____

13. Relate Cause and Effect How does the destruction of T cells interfere with the body's ability to fight disease?

_____

_____

_____

_____

LESSON 4 Infectious Disease and Your Health

14. Which of the following produce active immunity without causing illness?

    a. vaccines   **b.** antibody injections

    c. antibiotics   **d.** phagocytes

15. _____ are chemicals that can kill bacteria without harming body cells.

16. Infer Describe one way that a person can acquire active immunity and passive immunity.

_____

_____

_____

_____

_____

LESSON 5 Noninfectious Disease

17. Abnormal tissue masses are called

    a. allergies.   **b.** cancer.

    c. diabetes.   **d.** tumors.

18. An _____ is any substance that causes an allergy.

19. **Write About It** For some people, dander of a cat causes an allergic reaction. On a separate paper, describe how a person's body responds when exposed to this allergen. How can they lessen the reaction?

APPLY THE BIG ? Why do you sometimes get sick?

20. Strep throat is an example of an infectious disease, while asthma is an example of a noninfectious disease. Compare and contrast what causes these diseases and how your body protects you from them.

_____

_____

_____

_____

_____

_____

_____

_____

_____

_____

Standardized Test Prep

Multiple Choice

Circle the letter of the best answer.

1. SARS is a respiratory disease caused by a virus. Use the data table to decide which statement below is true.

SARS Cases (Nov. 2002–July 2003)

Country	No. of Cases	No. of Deaths
Canada	251	43
China, mainland	5,327	349
China, Taiwan	346	37
Singapore	238	33
United States	29	0

  A Most of the people who got SARS died.
  B Most SARS cases were in mainland China.
  C Most SARS cases were in North America.
  D Most SARS cases were in Singapore.

2. All of the following are the body's defenses against pathogens *except*

  A a physical barrier such as the skin.
  B the inflammatory response.
  C the immune response.
  D attacks by red blood cells.

3. Abnormal masses of cells that can lead to cancer are called

  A vaccines
  B phagocytes
  C tumors
  D antibodies

4. Which of these diseases occurs when the airways in the lungs narrow significantly during an allergic reaction?

  A asthma
  B diabetes
  C AIDS
  D melanoma

5. Which of the following is paired correctly?

  A rabies: infectious disease
  B diabetes: infectious disease
  C AIDS: noninfectious disease
  D allergy: infectious disease

Constructed Response

Use the graph below and your knowledge of science to help you answer Question 6. Write your answer on a separate sheet of paper.

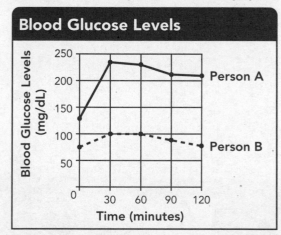

6. In a glucose tolerance test, a doctor gives a patient a sugar drink and measures the blood glucose level over time. The graph above shows two people's test results. Which person may have diabetes? Explain your answer.

585

Making H2O A-OK

What runs, but never walks? *Water!* Even though water is all around us, over 1 billion people across the world can only dream of having clean drinking water. Every day, about 4,000 children die from water-related diseases because they drink unsafe water. But now, a packet of powder the size of a ketchup packet at a cafeteria can stop this from happening.

Scientists have created a powder that can purify dirty, polluted water in 30 minutes. Just one small packet of the stuff can clean 2.5 gallons of water! The powder is made up of bleach and iron sulfate. The bleach kills bacteria and viruses. The iron sulfate causes solids in the water, such as metals like lead, to bind together in clumps. These clumps can be filtered out using a cotton cloth.

With helpful technology like this, more kids will be able to have safe and clean drinking water.

Write About It Natural disaster victims, such as those who survive a hurricane or a flood, often have a hard time getting clean drinking water. Write a letter to a rescue agency, such as the Red Cross, explaining the importance of having clean drinking water and what they can do to purify the water.

Museum of Science.

Colwell's Gift

Cholera is an infection of the intestines that is spread by drinking water or eating food contaminated with cholera bacteria. It causes diarrhea, vomiting, and cramps. When cholera strikes, approximately one victim in 20 can become seriously ill, and may die within hours. Because most places in the United States have safe drinking water, we don't see a lot of cholera here. But in many developing countries, cholera is still common.

For a long time, scientists could not predict cholera epidemics. Outbreaks happened suddenly, with no warning. And after the epidemic, scientists could not detect the cholera bacteria in the water. So, where did the bacteria go, and how did they reappear so suddenly?

Rita Colwell suspected that the cholera bacteria were present in the water in an inactive state between outbreaks. She thought that the bacteria became active when the water temperature rose.

After many years, Colwell proved her hypothesis. Using new methods, scientists were able to detect the inactive cholera bacteria in water where they had not previously been able to detect cholera. Satellite data also confirmed that cholera outbreaks occur when ocean temperatures rise. Warmer water causes cholera bacteria to multiply. Now, scientists use this information to help prevent future cholera outbreaks.

Illustrate It Rita Colwell developed a simple cloth filter to help prevent the spread of cholera. Research the life cycle of cholera bacteria. Prepare an information card that uses diagrams to explain how Colwell's filter helps to stop the spread of bacteria.

Why Do Clownfish Play With Poison?

How do living things affect one another?

Clownfish live among the poisonous and stinging tentacles of sea anemones to avoid being eaten by larger fish. Amazingly, the clownfish do not get stung! This is because a fluid called mucus protects the skin of the fish. ⚠️ **Develop Hypotheses How might a sea anemone benefit from having clownfish around?**

_____

_____

_____

_____

_____

_____

▶ **UNTAMED SCIENCE** Watch the **Untamed Science** video to learn more about interactions between organisms.

Populations and Communities

15 Getting Started

Check Your Understanding

1. **Background** Read the paragraph below and then answer the question.

Raquel planted a garden in a sunny area near her home. First, she loosened the **soil,** so the plant roots could easily grow. If days passed with no **precipitation,** she watered the plants. That was all she had to do—the rest of what the plants needed came from the **atmosphere!**

> **Soil** is made up of rock fragments, water, air, and decaying plant and animal matter.
>
> Rain, hail, sleet, and snow are all types of **precipitation.**
>
> Earth's **atmosphere** contains oxygen, carbon dioxide, nitrogen, and other gases.

• How do soil, precipitation, and the atmosphere help a plant grow?

_____

_____

_____

> **MY READING WEB** If you had trouble completing the question above, visit **My Reading Web** and type in *Populations and Communities.*

Vocabulary Skill

Latin Word Origins Some key terms in this chapter contain word parts with Latin origins. The table below lists two of the Latin words that key terms come from.

Latin Word	Meaning of Latin Word	Example
aptare	to fit	adaptation, *n.* a characteristic that allows an organism to live successfully in its environment
migrare	to move	immigration, *n.* movement into a population

2. **Quick Check** The terms *immigration* and *emigration* both come from the Latin word *migrare.* Circle the meaning of *migrare* in the table above.

organism

immigration

adaptation

predation

Chapter Preview

LESSON 1
- organism • habitat
- biotic factor • abiotic factor
- species • population
- community • ecosystem
- ecology

↺ **Compare and Contrast**
△ **Draw Conclusions**

LESSON 2
- birth rate • death rate
- immigration • emigration
- population density
- limiting factor
- carrying capacity

↺ **Relate Cause and Effect**
△ **Infer**

LESSON 3
- natural selection • adaptation
- niche • competition • predation
- predator • prey • symbiosis
- mutualism • commensalism
- parasitism • parasite • host

↺ **Relate Text and Visuals**
△ **Classify**

LESSON 4
- succession • primary succession
- pioneer species
- secondary succession

↺ **Compare and Contrast**
△ **Observe**

> **VOCAB FLASH CARDS** For extra help
with vocabulary, visit **Vocab Flash
Cards** and type in *Populations and
Communities.*

Living Things and the Environment

🔑 **What Does an Organism Get From Its Environment?**

🔑 **What Are the Two Parts of an Organism's Habitat?**

🔑 **How Is an Ecosystem Organized?**

MY PLANET DiARY

DISCOVERY

Love Song

The gray, golden brown, and Goodman's mouse lemurs are some of the world's smallest primates. These three lemurs look similar. Looking so similar makes it difficult for the lemurs to find members of their own kind or species during mating season. However, it seems that the lemurs can identify their own species by song. Scientists recorded the mating calls of the three species of lemurs. They discovered that the lemurs reacted more to the calls from their own species. This allows the lemurs to pick the right mate, even at night.

Goodman's mouse lemur

Communicate Answer these questions. Discuss your answers with a partner.

1. If you were looking for your sneakers among several pairs that looked just like yours, what characteristics would make it easier for you to find them?

_____

_____

2. What do you think would happen if a lemur mated with a different kind of lemur?

_____

_____

▶ PLANET DIARY Go to **Planet Diary** to learn more about habitats.

Golden brown mouse lemur

Gray mouse lemur

Lab®**zone** Do the Inquiry Warm-Up *What's in the Scene?*

Vocabulary

- organism • habitat • biotic factor • abiotic factor
- species • population • community • ecosystem
- ecology

Skills

- Reading: Compare and Contrast
- Inquiry: Draw Conclusions

What Does an Organism Get From Its Environment?

If you were to visit Alaska, you might see a bald eagle fly by. A bald eagle is one type of **organism,** or living thing. Different types of organisms live in different types of surroundings, or environments. **An organism gets food, water, shelter, and other things it needs to live, grow, and reproduce from its environment.** An environment that provides the things a specific organism needs to live, grow, and reproduce is called its **habitat.**

In a forest habitat, mushrooms grow in the damp soil and wood-peckers build nests in tree trunks. Organisms live in different habitats because they have different requirements for survival and reproduction. Some organisms live on a prairie, with its flat terrain, tall grasses, and low rainfall amounts. A prairie dog, like the one shown in **Figure 1,** obtains the food and shelter it needs from a prairie habitat. It could not survive on this rocky ocean shore. Likewise, the prairie would not meet the needs of a sea star.

FIGURE 1 ···

What's Wrong With This Picture?
Most people would never expect to see a prairie dog at the beach.
✎ **List** Give three reasons why this prairie dog would not survive in this habitat.

_____

_____

_____

_____

Lab zone® Do the Quick Lab
Organisms and Their Habitats.

Assess Your Understanding

got it? ···

○ I get it! Now I know that an organism's environment provides _____

_____

○ I need extra help with_____

Go to MY SCIENCE COACH online for help with this subject.

What Are the Two Parts of an Organism's Habitat?

To meet its needs, a prairie dog must interact with more than just the other prairie dogs around it. 🗝 **An organism interacts with both the living and nonliving parts of its habitat.**

Biotic Factors What living things can you see in the prairie dog's habitat shown in **Figure 2**? The parts of a habitat that are living, or once living, and interact with an organism are called **biotic factors** (by AHT ik). The plants that provide seeds and berries are biotic factors. The ferrets and eagles that hunt the prairie dog are also biotic factors. Worms and bacteria are biotic factors that live in the soil underneath the prairie grass. Prairie dog scat, owl pellets, and decomposing plant matter are also biotic factors.

Abiotic Factors Not all of the factors that organisms interact with are living. **Abiotic factors** (ay by AHT ik) are the nonliving parts of an organism's habitat. These factors, as shown in **Figure 2,** include sunlight, soil, temperature, oxygen, and water.

✏ **Compare and Contrast** In the paragraphs at the right, circle how biotic and abiotic factors are similar and underline how they are different.

FIGURE 2 ·············
Factors in a Prairie Habitat
A prairie dog interacts with many biotic and abiotic factors in the prairie habitat.

✎ **Relate Text and Visuals** Add another biotic factor to the picture. For each abiotic factor, draw a line from the text box to an example in the picture.

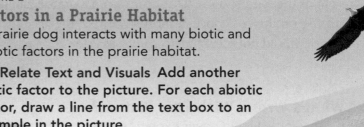

Sunlight Because sunlight is needed for plants to make their own food, it is an important abiotic factor for most living things.

Soil Soil consists of varying amounts of rock fragments, nutrients, air, water, and the decaying remains of living things. The soil in an area influences the kinds of plants and animals that can live and grow there.

Temperature The temperatures that are typical in an area determine the types of organisms that can live there.

Oxygen Most living things require oxygen to carry out their life processes. Organisms on land obtain oxygen from air. Aquatic organisms obtain oxygen that is dissolved in the water around them.

Water All living things require water to carry out their life processes. Plants and algae need water along with sunlight and carbon dioxide to make their own food. Other living things depend on plants and algae for food.

apply it!

Salt is an abiotic factor found in some environments. To see how the amount of salt affects the hatching of brine shrimp eggs, varying amounts of salt were added to four different 500-mL beakers.

❶ **Observe** In which beaker(s) did the eggs, shown as purple circles, hatch? _____

❷ **Infer** The manipulated variable was
_____

❸ **Infer** The responding variable was _____
_____

❹ [CHALLENGE] Beaker _____ was the control.

❺ ⚠ **Draw Conclusions** What can you conclude about the amount of salt in the shrimps' natural habitat?
_____
_____
_____

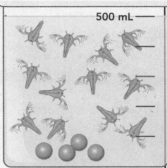
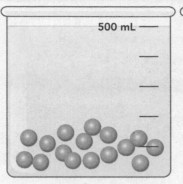

Beaker A
500 mL spring water

Beaker B
500 mL spring water
+ 2.5 g salt

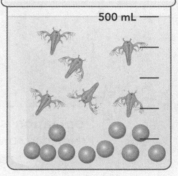
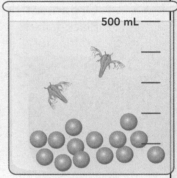

Beaker C
500 mL spring water
+ 7.5 g salt

Beaker D
500 mL spring water
+ 15 g salt

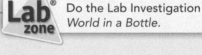
Do the Lab Investigation
World in a Bottle.

🔑 **Assess Your Understanding**

1a. Interpret Diagrams List two biotic and two abiotic factors in **Figure 2.**
_____
_____
_____
_____

b. ⚠ **Draw Conclusions** Name two abiotic factors in your habitat and explain how your life would be different without them.
_____
_____
_____
_____

got it? ....

○ **I get it!** Now I know that the two parts of an organism's habitat are _____
_____

○ **I need extra help with** _____

Go to **my science** ⊙ **COACH** online for help with this subject.

Ecological Organization

How do living things affect one another?

FIGURE 3 ···

▷ REAL-WORLD INQUIRY In this figure, the smallest level of organization is the organism. The largest is the entire ecosystem.

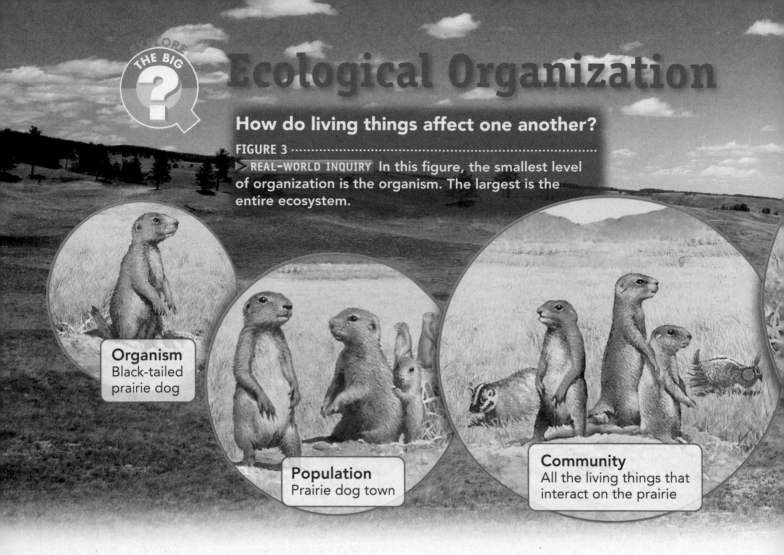

Organism
Black-tailed prairie dog

Population
Prairie dog town

Community
All the living things that interact on the prairie

How Is an Ecosystem Organized?

Most organisms do not live all alone in their habitat. Instead, organisms live together in populations and communities that interact with abiotic factors in their ecosystems.

Organisms Black-tailed prairie dogs that live in prairie dog towns on the Nebraska plains are all members of one species. A **species** (SPEE sheez) is a group of organisms that can mate with each other and produce offspring that can also mate and reproduce.

Populations All the members of one species living in a particular area are referred to as a **population.** The prairie dogs in the Nebraska town are one example of a population.

Communities A particular area contains more than one species of organism. The prairie, for instance, includes prairie dogs, hawks, snakes, and grasses. All the different populations that live together in an area make up a **community.**

✎ **Apply Concepts** Draw or write how an ecosystem of your choice is organized. Identify each level. Include biotic and abiotic examples.

Ecosystem
All the living and nonliving things that interact on the prairie

Ecosystems The community of organisms that live in a particular area, along with their non-living environment, make up an **ecosystem.** A prairie is just one of the many different ecosystems found on Earth. Other ecosystems are deserts, oceans, ponds, and forests.

Figure 3 shows the levels of organization in a prairie ecosystem. 🔑 **The smallest level of organization is a single organism, which belongs to a population that includes other members of its species. The population belongs to a community of different species. The community and abiotic factors together form an ecosystem.**

Because the populations in an ecosystem interact with one another, any change affects all the different populations that live there. The study of how organisms interact with each other and with their environment is called **ecology.**

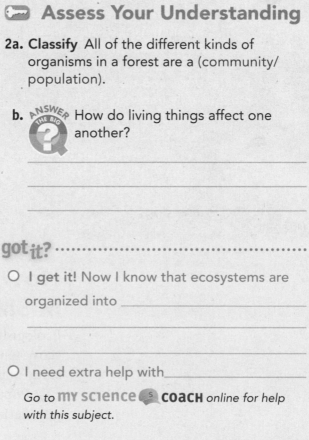

Lab® zone Do the Quick-Lab *Organizing an Ecosystem.*

🔑 **Assess Your Understanding**

2a. Classify All of the different kinds of organisms in a forest are a (community/population).

b. 🅰️ How do living things affect one another?

_____

_____

_____

got it? •

○ **I get it!** Now I know that ecosystems are

organized into _____

_____

○ **I need extra help with**_____

Go to **MY SCIENCE COACH** online for help with this subject.

597

Populations

🔑 How Do Populations Change in Size?

🔑 What Factors Limit Population Growth?

MY PLANET DiARY

Prairie Dog Picker-Upper

Did you know that vacuum cleaners do more than just clean carpets? Across the Great Plains, farmers are using specially designed vacuum cleaners to help them remove black-tailed prairie dogs from the farm land. Prairie dogs can eat crops, cause soil erosion, and endanger cattle and farm machinery. The prairie dog vacuum uses a 4-in. plastic hose to suck prairie dogs out of the ground at 483 km/h! The prairie dogs end up in a padded tank, usually unharmed. They are then relocated or donated to the U.S. Fish and Wildlife Service to be fed to endangered eagles, hawks, and black-footed ferrets.

Prairie dogs

TECHNOLOGY

Communicate Discuss these questions with a group of classmates. Write your answers below.

1. If all of the prairie dogs were removed, how do you think the prairie ecosystem would be affected?

_____

_____

_____

2. Should prairie dogs be used as food for endangered species? Explain.

_____

_____

_____

▶ PLANET DIARY Go to **Planet Diary** to learn more about populations.

 Lab zone ® Do the Inquiry Warm-Up Populations.

How Do Populations Change in Size?

Ecologists are scientists who study biotic and abiotic factors of an ecosystem and the interactions between them. Some ecologists study populations and monitor the sizes of populations over time. 🔑 **Populations can change in size when new members join the population or when members leave the population.**

Vocabulary

- birth rate • death rate • immigration
- emigration • population density
- limiting factor • carrying capacity

Skills

↻ **Reading: Relate Cause and Effect**
△ **Inquiry: Infer**

Births and Deaths The most common way in which new individuals join a population is by being born into it. If more individuals are born into a population than die in any period of time, a population can grow. So when the **birth rate,** the number of births per 1,000 individuals for a given time period, is greater than its **death rate,** the number of deaths per 1,000 individuals for a given time period, the population may increase. The main way that individuals leave a population is by dying. If the birth rate is the same as the death rate, then the population may stay the same. In situations where the death rate is higher than the birth rate, then the population may decrease.

do the math!

Depending on the size and age of the female, an American Alligator can lay between 10 and 50 eggs per year.

❶ **Graph** Using the data table and colored pencils, create a double bar graph showing alligator births and deaths for four years.

❷ Label the *x*-axis and *y*-axis.

❸ Write a title for the graph.

❹ Fill in the graph using the colors shown.

❺ **Develop Hypotheses** What factors might explain the number of births and deaths in Year 3?

_____
_____
_____
_____
_____
_____
_____

Data Table

Year	Births	Deaths
1	32	8
2	28	13
3	47	21
4	33	16

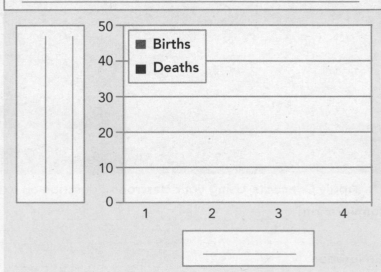

■ Births
■ Deaths

The Population Statement

When the birth rate in a population is greater than the death rate, the population will generally increase. This can be written as a mathematical statement using the "is greater than" sign:

If birth rate > death rate, population size increases.

However, if the death rate in a population is greater than the birth rate, the population size will generally decrease. This can also be written as a mathematical statement:

If death rate > birth rate, population size decreases.

Immigration and Emigration

The size of a population also can change when individuals move into or out of the population. **Immigration** (im ih GRAY shun) means moving into a population. **Emigration** (em ih GRAY shun) means leaving a population. For instance, if food is scarce, some members of an antelope herd may wander off in search of better grassland. If they become permanently separated from the original herd, they will no longer be part of that population.

Vocabulary Latin Word Origins
Both the terms *immigration* ("moving into a population") and *emigration* ("moving out of a population") come from the Latin word *migrare* ("to move"). What do you think the prefixes *im–* and *e–* mean?

_____

_____

_____

_____

FIGURE 1

Immigration

In 1898, white-tailed deer were almost extinct in Iowa due to over-hunting. The deer population was reestablished as animals from Minnesota, Wisconsin, and Missouri immigrated into Iowa.

✎ **Apply Concepts** Using your classroom, describe an example of each of the following.

Immigration: _____

_____

Emigration: _____

_____

populations size can be displayed on a line graph. Figure 2 shows a graph of the changes in a rabbit population. The vertical axis identifies the number of rabbits in the population, while the horizontal axis shows time. The graph represents the size of the rabbit population over a ten-year period.

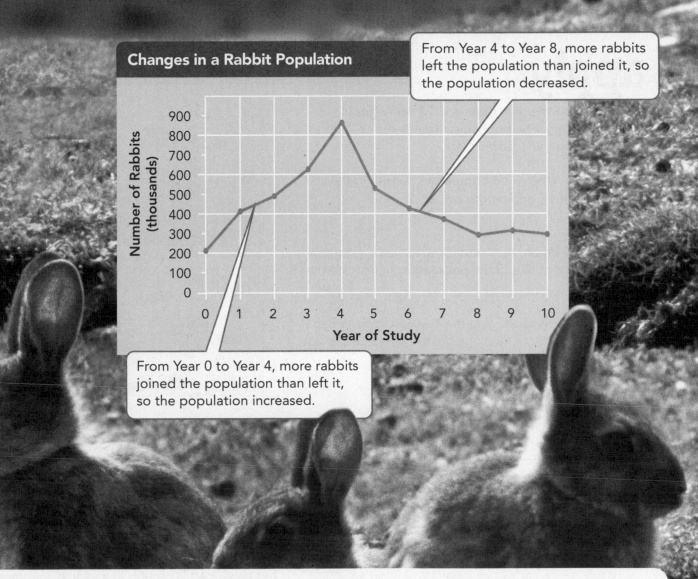

Changes in a Rabbit Population

From Year 4 to Year 8, more rabbits left the population than joined it, so the population decreased.

From Year 0 to Year 4, more rabbits joined the population than left it, so the population increased.

FIGURE 2 ·······································

> INTERACTIVE ART **Changes in a Rabbit Population**

✎ This graph shows how the size of a rabbit population changed over ten years.

1. **Interpret Data** In Year _____, the rabbit population reached its highest point.

2. **Read Graphs** What was the size of the rabbit population in that year? _____

3. CHALLENGE How do you think the rabbit population affected the fox population over the same ten-year period? Explain your reasoning.

_____
_____
_____
_____
_____
_____
_____

Population Density Sometimes an ecologist needs to know more than just the total size of a population. In many situations, it is helpful to know the **population density**—the number of individuals in an area of a specific size. Population density can be written as an equation:

$$\text{Population density} = \frac{\text{Number of individuals}}{\text{Unit area}}$$

For example, suppose you counted 20 butterflies in a garden measuring 10 square meters. The population density would be 20 butterflies per 10 square meters, or 2 butterflies per square meter.

apply it!

In the pond on the top, there are 10 flamingos in 8 square meters. The population density is 1.25 flamingos per square meter.

❶ Calculate What is the population density of the flamingos in the pond on the bottom?

_____

❷ Infer If 14 more flamingos landed in the pond on the bottom, what would the population density be then?

_____

❸ CHALLENGE What do you think would happen if the population density of flamingos in the pond on the bottom became too great?

_____

_____

_____

◄—— 4 meters ——►

2 meters

2 meters

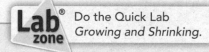
Do the Quick Lab
Growing and Shrinking.

🔑 **Assess Your Understanding**

1a. Review Two ways to join a population are _____ and _____.

Two ways to leave a population are _____ and _____.

b. Calculate Suppose a population of 8 wolves has produced 20 young in a year. If 7 wolves have died, how many wolves are in the population now? (Assume no wolves have moved into or out of the population for other reasons.)

_____

got it? ....

○ **I get it!** Now I know that population size changes due to _____

_____

○ **I need extra help with** _____

Go to MY SCIENCE Ⓢ COACH *online for help with this subject.*

What Factors Limit Population Growth?

When the living conditions in an area are good, a population will generally grow. But eventually some environmental factor will cause the population to stop growing. A **limiting factor** is an environmental factor that causes a population to stop growing or decrease in size. **Some limiting factors for populations are weather conditions, space, food, and water.**

Climate Changes in climate conditions, such as temperature and the amount of rainfall, can limit population growth. A cold spring season can kill the young of many species of organisms, including birds and mammals. Unusual events like floods, hurricanes, and the tornado shown in **Figure 3**, can also have long-lasting effects on population size.

FIGURE 3 ·······························

Weather as a Limiting Factor

A tornado or flood can destroy nests and burrows.

✎ **Identify** Name two types of natural disasters that you think can also limit population growth.

_____

_____

Tornado funnel touching ground

↻ **Relate Cause and Effect** As you read about the four factors that can limit populations, fill in the graphic organizer below.

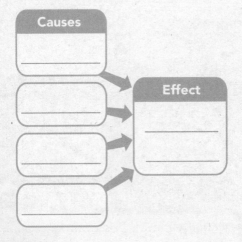

Causes

Effect

did you

know? ....

Some plants, like the black walnut tree, release chemicals into the environment that discourage other plants from growing too close. This process is called allelopathy (uh luh LOP uh thee).

Space Space is another limiting factor for populations. Gannets are seabirds that are usually seen flying over the ocean. They come to land only to nest on rocky shores. But the nesting shores get very crowded. If a pair does not find room to nest, they will not be able to add any offspring to the gannet population. So nesting space on the shore is a limiting factor for gannets. If there were more nesting space, more gannets would be able to nest. The population could increase.

Figure 4 shows how space is also a limiting factor for plants. The amount of space in which a plant grows determines whether the plant can obtain the sunlight, water, and soil nutrients it needs. For example, many pine seedlings sprout each year in forests. But as the seedlings grow, the roots of those that are too close together run out of space. Branches from other trees may block the sunlight the seedlings need. Some of the seedlings then die, limiting the size of the pine population.

Food and Water Organisms require food and water to survive. When food and water are in limited supply, they can be limiting factors. Suppose a giraffe must eat 10 kilograms of leaves each day to survive. The trees in an area can provide 100 kilograms of leaves a day while remaining healthy. Five giraffes could live easily in this area, because they would need just 50 kilograms of food a day. But 15 giraffes could not all survive—there would not be enough food. No matter how much shelter, water, and other resources there were, the population would not grow much larger than 10 giraffes. The largest population that an area can support is called its **carrying capacity.** The carrying capacity of this giraffe habitat would be 10 giraffes. The size of a population can vary, but usually stays near its carrying capacity because of the limiting factors in its habitat.

FIGURE 4 ···

Space as a Limiting Factor

If no more tulip plants can grow in this field, the field has reached its carrying capacity for tulips.

✎ **List Name three things a plant needs to survive.**

_____

apply it!

Giant pandas live in the mountains of south central China. Most (99 percent) of the pandas' diet is made up of the bamboo plant. Bamboo is not nutrient rich. Pandas spend 55 percent of their day eating between 9 and 38 kilograms of bamboo. Getting enough bamboo to eat can be a challenge. Farming and the timber industry have destroyed the pandas' habitat and bamboo forests. In addition, when a bamboo plant flowers, the plant dies and does not regrow for several years. It is difficult for scientists to know exactly how many giant pandas exist in the wild. The best estimate is that there are about 1,600 of them. Due to the small population size, this species is classified as endangered.

✎ **Communicate** Write a letter to the editor that describes how food and space may be limiting factors for the giant panda species. Add a headline to your letter.

_____
_____
_____
_____
_____
_____
_____
_____

Lab zone Do the Quick Lab Elbow Room.

🔑 Assess Your Understanding

2a. Summarize When the climate changes or there is not enough _____ or _____ or _____, a population can (begin/stop) growing in size.

b. Relate Cause and Effect Choose a limiting factor and describe the factor's effect on population growth.

_____
_____
_____

got it? ....

○ I get it! Now I know that populations can be limited when _____
_____

○ I need extra help with _____

Go to MY SCIENCE ⑤ COACH *online for help with this subject.*

Interactions Among Living Things

🔑 **How Do Adaptations Help an Organism Survive?**

🔑 **What Are Competition and Predation?**

🔑 **What Are the Three Types of Symbiosis?**

MY PLANET DIARY

FUN FACT

Predator Power

What predator can close its jaws the fastest? You might think it is a lion or a shark, but you would be wrong. It is the trap-jaw ant that has the fastest strike in the animal kingdom. The trap-jaw ant closes its mouth around its prey in 0.13 milliseconds at speeds of 35 to 64 meters per second! The force created when its jaw snaps shut also helps the ant escape danger by either jumping up to 8.3 centimeters high or 39.6 centimeters sideways.

A trap-jaw ant stalks its prey.

Communicate Answer the questions below. Discuss your answers with a partner.

1. How does the trap-jaw ant's adaptation help it avoid becoming the prey of another organism?

_____

_____

_____

2. What are some adaptations that other predators have to capture prey?

_____

_____

_____

▶ PLANET DIARY Go to **Planet Diary** to learn more about predators.

 Do the Inquiry Warm-Up *Can You Hide a Butterfly?*

How Do Adaptations Help an Organism Survive?

As day breaks, a sound comes from a nest tucked in the branch of a saguaro cactus. Two young red-tailed hawks are preparing to fly. Farther down the stem, a tiny elf owl peeks out of its nest in a small hole. A rattlesnake slithers around the base of the saguaro, looking for breakfast. Spying a shrew, the snake strikes it with needle-like fangs. The shrew dies instantly.

Vocabulary

- natural selection • adaptation • niche • competition
- predation • predator • prey • symbiosis • mutualism
- commensalism • parasitism • parasite • host

Skills

⊙ **Reading:** Relate Text and Visuals

△ **Inquiry:** Classify

Figure 1 shows some organisms that live in, on, and around the saguaro cactus. Each organism has unique characteristics. These characteristics affect the individual's ability to survive and reproduce in its environment.

Natural Selection A characteristic that makes an individual better suited to a specific environment may eventually become common in that species through a process called **natural selection.** Natural selection works like this: Individuals whose unique characteristics are well-suited for an environment tend to survive and produce more offspring. Offspring that inherit these characteristics also live to reproduce. In this way, natural selection results in **adaptations,** the behaviors and physical characteristics that allow organisms to live successfully in their environments. For example, the arctic hare has fur that turns from gray to white in the winter which helps camouflage the hare against the snow.

Individuals with characteristics poorly suited to a particular environment are less likely to survive and reproduce. Over time, poorly suited characteristics may disappear from the species. If a species cannot adapt to changes in its environment, the entire species can disappear from Earth and become extinct.

FIGURE 1 ·······································

Saguaro Community

✏️ **Describe** Circle two examples of how organisms interact in this scene. Describe each one.

_____

_____

_____

_____

Red-tailed hawk
Purple martin
Flycatcher
Woodpecker
Elf owl
Saguaro cactus
Wasps
Gila monster
Rattlesnake
Scorpion
Roadrunner

Niche The organisms in the saguaro community have adaptations that result in specific roles. The role of an organism in its habitat is called its **niche.** A niche includes what type of food the organism eats, how it obtains this food, and what other organisms eat it. A niche also includes when and how the organism reproduces and the physical conditions it requires to survive. Some organisms, like the birds in **Figure 2,** share the same habitat but have very specific niches that allow them to live together. 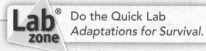 **Every organism has a variety of adaptations that are suited to its specific living conditions and help it survive.**

apply it!

Organisms occupy many niches in an environment like the one in this picture.

1 **Identify** List two abiotic factors in the picture.

_____

2 **Interpret Diagrams** Describe the niche of the squirrel in the picture.

_____

_____

3 **Make Generalizations** What adaptations might the squirrel have that make it able to live in this environment?

_____

_____

Lab zone® Do the Quick Lab *Adaptations for Survival.*

Assess Your Understanding

1a. Define Adaptations are the _____ and _____ characteristics that allow organisms to live successfully in their environments.

b. Explain How are a snake's sharp fangs an adaptation that help it survive in the saguaro community?

_____

_____

got it? •••

○ **I get it!** Now I know that adaptations are_____

_____

○ **I need extra help with** _____

Go to **MY SCIENCE** **COACH** *online for help with this subject.*

What Are Competition and Predation?

During a typical day in the saguaro community, a range of interactions takes place among organisms. 🔑 **Two major types of interactions among organisms are competition and predation.**

Competition Different species can share the same habitat and food requirements. For example, the flycatcher and the elf owl both live on the saguaro and eat insects. However, these two species do not occupy exactly the same niche. The flycatcher is active during the day, while the owl is active mostly at night. If two species occupy the same niche, one of the species might eventually die off. The reason for this is **competition.** The struggle between organisms to survive as they attempt to use the same limited resources is called competition. For example, weeds in a garden compete with vegetable crops for soil nutrients, water, and sunlight.

In any ecosystem, there are limited amounts of food, water, and shelter. Organisms that share the same habitat often have adaptations that enable them to reduce competition. For example, the three species of warblers in **Figure 2** specialize in feeding only in a certain part of the spruce tree.

Cape May Warbler
This species feeds at the tips of branches near the top of the tree.

Bay-Breasted Warbler
This species feeds in the middle part of the tree.

Yellow-Rumped Warbler
This species feeds in the lower part of the tree and at the bases of the middle branches.

FIGURE 2 ·······························
Niche and Competition

✏️ Each of these warbler species occupies a very specific location in its habitat. By feeding on insects in different areas of the tree, the birds avoid competing for food and are able to live together.

1. **Predict** What could happen if these warbler species fed in the same location on the tree?

_____

_____

_____

_____

2. **List** For what resources do the tree and the grass compete?

_____

_____

_____

_____

_____

609

FIGURE 3 ·······················

Predation

This tiger shark and this albatross are involved in a predator-prey interaction.

✎ **Interpret Photos**
Label the predator and the prey in the photo.

Predation In **Figure 3**, a tiger shark bursts through the water to seize an albatross in its powerful jaws. An interaction in which one organism kills another for food or nutrients is called **predation.** The organism that does the killing is the **predator.** The organism that is killed is the **prey.** Even though they do not kill their prey, organisms like cows and giraffes are also considered predators because they eat plants.

Predation can have a major effect on a prey population size. Recall that when the death rate exceeds the birth rate in a population, the population size can decrease. So, if there are too many predators in an area, the result is often a decrease in the size of the prey population. But a decrease in the number of prey results in less food for their predators. Without adequate food, the predator population can decline. Generally, populations of predators and their prey rise and fall in related cycles.

FIGURE 4 ·····························

Predator Adaptations

A jellyfish's tentacles contain a poisonous substance that paralyzes tiny water animals. The sundew is a plant that is covered with sticky bulbs on stalks. When a fly lands on a bulb, it remains snared in the sticky goo while the plant digests it.

✎ **Make Models** Imagine an ideal predator to prey upon a porcupine. Draw or describe your predator below and label its adaptations.

Predator Adaptations Predators, such as those in **Figure 4**, have adaptations that help them catch and kill their prey. A cheetah can run very fast for a short time, enabling it to catch its prey. Some predators, such as owls and bats, have adaptations that enable them to hunt at night when their prey, small mammals and insects, are active.

Prey Adaptations How do organisms avoid being killed by effective predators? The smelly spray of a skunk and the sharp quills of a porcupine help keep predators at a distance. As you can see in **Figure 5**, organisms have many kinds of adaptations that help them avoid becoming prey.

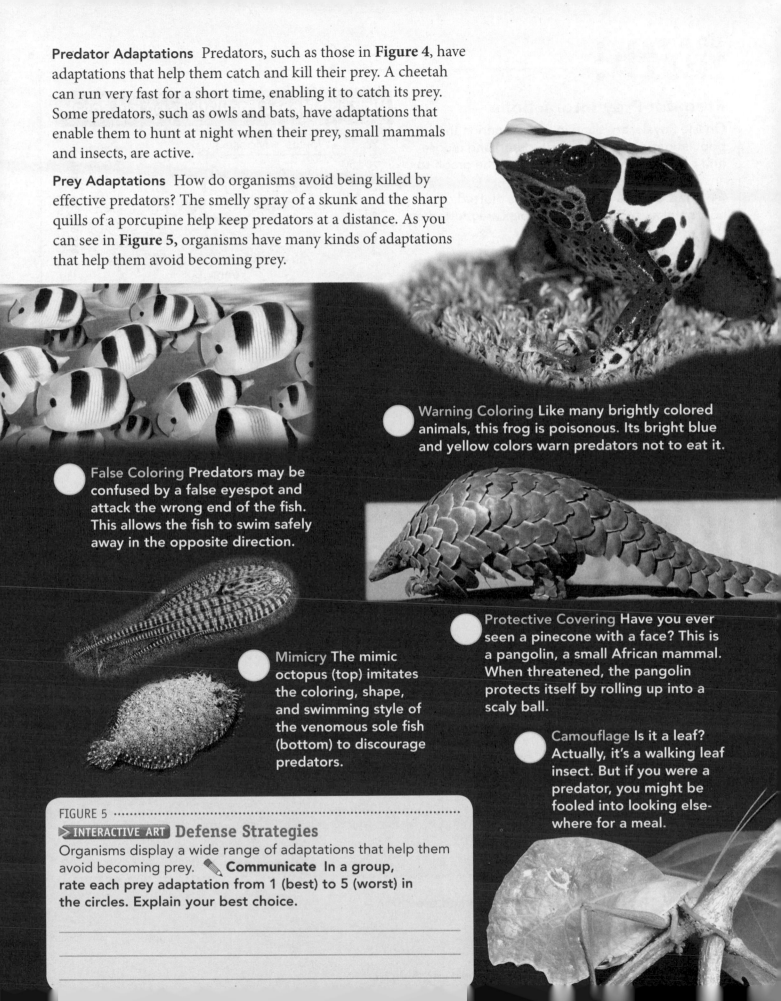

Warning Coloring Like many brightly colored animals, this frog is poisonous. Its bright blue and yellow colors warn predators not to eat it.

False Coloring Predators may be confused by a false eyespot and attack the wrong end of the fish. This allows the fish to swim safely away in the opposite direction.

Mimicry The mimic octopus (top) imitates the coloring, shape, and swimming style of the venomous sole fish (bottom) to discourage predators.

Protective Covering Have you ever seen a pinecone with a face? This is a pangolin, a small African mammal. When threatened, the pangolin protects itself by rolling up into a scaly ball.

Camouflage Is it a leaf? Actually, it's a walking leaf insect. But if you were a predator, you might be fooled into looking elsewhere for a meal.

FIGURE 5 ···

> INTERACTIVE ART Defense Strategies

Organisms display a wide range of adaptations that help them avoid becoming prey. ✏ **Communicate** In a group, rate each prey adaptation from 1 (best) to 5 (worst) in the circles. Explain your best choice.

_____

_____

_____

do the math!

Predator-Prey Interactions

On Isle Royale, an island in Lake Superior, the populations of wolves (the predator) and moose (the prey) rise and fall in cycles. Use the graph to answer the questions.

1 **Read Graphs** What variable is plotted on the horizontal axis? What two variables are plotted on the vertical axis?

_____

2 **Interpret Data** How did the moose population change between 2002 and 2007? What happened to the wolf population from 2003 through 2006?

_____
_____
_____

3 **Draw Conclusions** How might the change in moose population have led to the change in the wolf population?

_____
_____
_____
_____

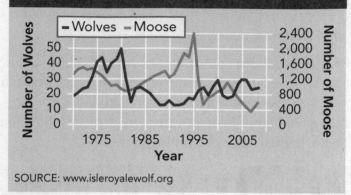

Wolf and Moose Populations on Isle Royale

— Wolves — Moose

SOURCE: www.isleroyalewolf.org

4 **Explain** What adaptations does a wolf have that make it a successful predator?

_____
_____

5 **Predict** How might disease in the wolf population one year affect the moose population the next year?

_____
_____
_____
_____

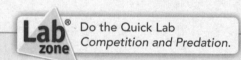
Do the Quick Lab
Competition and Predation.

Assess Your Understanding

2a. Review Two main ways in which organisms

interact are_____

and _____ .

b. Describe Give an example of competition. Explain your answer.

_____
_____

c. Apply Concepts Owls often prey on mice. What adaptations do you think the mice have that help them avoid becoming prey?

_____
_____
_____
_____

got it? ....

O **I get it!** Now I know that competition and predation_____

O **I need extra help with** _____

Go to MY SCIENCE ⓢ COACH online for help with this subject.

What Are the Three Types of Symbiosis?

In addition to competition and predation, symbiosis is a third type of interaction among organisms. **Symbiosis** (sim bee OH sis) is any relationship in which two species live closely together and at least one of the species benefits. ⟨🔑⟩ **The three main types of symbiotic relationships are mutualism, commensalism, and parasitism.**

Mutualism In some relationships, two species may depend on one another. This is true for some species of acacia trees and stinging ants in South America. The stinging ants nest only in the acacia tree, whose thorns discourage the ants' predators. The tree also provides the ants' only food. The ants, in turn, attack other animals that approach the tree and clear competing plants away from the base of the tree. This relationship is an example of **mutualism** (MYOO choo uh liz um). A relationship in which both species benefit is called mutualism. Other examples of mutualism can be seen in **Figure 6.**

FIGURE 6 ·····················

Mutualism
✏️ An oxpecker rides and snacks aboard an impala. The oxpecker eat ticks living on the impala's ears. This interaction is an example of mutualism because both organisms benefit.

1. Infer How does the oxpecker benefit?

_____

2. Infer How does the impala benefit?

_____

3. [CHALLENGE] Explain how the relationship between the hummingbird and the flower is an example of mutualism.

_____

_____

613

Commensalism Have you ever seen a bird build a nest in a tree? The bird gets a place to live while the tree is unharmed. This relationship is an example of commensalism. **Commensalism** (kuh MEN suh liz um) is a relationship in which one species benefits and the other species is neither helped nor harmed. In nature, commensalism is not very common because two species are usually either helped or harmed a little by any interaction.

Parasitism Many family pets get treated with medication to prevent tick and flea bites. Without treatment, pets can suffer from severe health problems as a result of these bites. A relationship that involves one organism living with, on, or inside another organism and harming it is called **parasitism** (PA ruh sit iz um). The organism that benefits is called a **parasite.** The organism it lives on or in is called a **host.** The parasite is usually smaller than the host. In a parasitic relationship, the parasite benefits while the host is harmed. Unlike a predator, a parasite does not usually kill the organism it feeds on. If the host dies, the parasite could lose its source of food or shelter.

Some parasites, like fleas and ticks, have adaptations that enable them to attach to their host and feed on its blood. Other examples of parasitism are shown in **Figure 7.**

✎ **Relate Text and Visuals** List the names of the parasites and the hosts in **Figure 7.**

Parasites	Hosts
_____	_____
_____	_____
_____	_____
_____	_____
_____	_____

A parasitic cowbird laid its eggs in a yellow warbler's nest. The cowbird chick is outcompeting the warbler chicks for space and food.

Fish lice feed on the blood and other internal fluids of fish.

Dwarf mistletoe is a small parasitic flowering plant that grows into the bark of trees to obtain water and nutrients.

FIGURE 7 ·····································
Parasitism
There are many examples of parasitic relationships. Besides fleas, ticks, and tapeworms, some plants and birds are parasites. ✎ **Explain** Why doesn't a parasite usually kill its host?

_____

_____

_____

apply it!

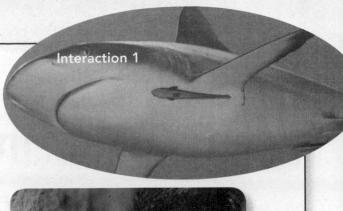
Interaction 1

Classify Each photograph on the right represents a different type of symbiosis. Classify each interaction as mutualism, commensalism, or parasitism. Explain your answers.

Interaction 1: A remora fish attaches itself to the underside of a shark without harming the shark, and eats leftover bits of food from the shark's meals.

Interaction 2: A vampire bat drinks the blood of horses.

Interaction 3: A bee pollinates a flower.

❶ Interaction 1

_____

_____

❷ Interaction 2

_____

_____

❸ Interaction 3

_____

_____

Interaction 2

Interaction 3

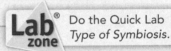
Do the Quick Lab
Type of Symbiosis.

🗝 Assess Your Understanding

3a. Identify The three types of symbiosis are

_____, _____,

and _____.

b. Classify Microscopic mites live at the base of human eyelashes, where they feed on tiny bits of dead skin. What type of symbiosis could this be? Explain your answer.

_____

_____

_____

c. Compare and Contrast Name each type of symbiosis and explain how the two species are affected.

_____

_____

_____

_____

_____

_____

_____

got it? ....

○ **I get it!** Now I know that the three types of symbiosis differ in _____

_____

○ **I need extra help with** _____

Go to **MY SCIENCE COACH** online for help with this subject.

Changes in Communities

How Do Primary and Secondary Succession Differ?

my planet Diary

Fighting Fire With Fire

Wildfires are often reported in the national news. The images associated with these reports show how damaging these fires can be to property and to some ecosystems. What you may not know is that fire can actually help fight wildfires! Controlled burns, or prescribed burns, are fires that are purposely and care-fully set by professional foresters. Prescribed burns are used to remove materials such as dead, dry branches and leaves that can fuel wildfires. A wildfire that occurs in an area that has previously been burned would cause less damage and be easier for firefighters to control.

This forester is carefully igniting a controlled burn.

MISCONCEPTION

Communicate Discuss these questions with a classmate. Write your answers below.

1. Why should only professional foresters set prescribed fires?

_____

_____

2. What do you think could be some other benefits to using prescribed burns in an ecosystem?

_____

_____

_____

> PLANET DIARY Go to **Planet Diary** to learn more about succession.

 Do the Inquiry Warm-Up *How Communities Change.*

How Do Primary and Secondary Succession Differ?

Fires, floods, volcanoes, hurricanes, and other natural disasters can change communities very quickly. But even without disasters, communities change. The series of predictable changes that occur in a community over time is called **succession**.

Vocabulary

- succession
- primary succession
- pioneer species
- secondary succession

Skills

- Reading: Compare and Contrast
- Inquiry: Observe

Primary Succession

When a new island is formed by the eruption of an undersea volcano or an area of rock is uncovered by a melting sheet of ice, no living things are present. Over time, living things will inhabit these areas. **Primary succession** is the series of changes that occurs in an area where no soil or organisms exist.

Figure 1 shows how an area might change following a volcanic eruption. Just like the pioneers that first settled new frontiers, the first species to populate an area are called **pioneer species.** They are often carried to the area by wind or water. Typical pioneer species are mosses and lichens. Lichens are fungi and algae growing in a symbiotic relationship. As pioneer species grow, they help break up the rocks. When the organisms die, they provide nutrients that enrich the thin layer of soil that is forming on the rocks.

As plant seeds land in the new soil, they begin to grow. The specific plants that grow depend on the climate of the area. For example, in a cool, northern area, early seedlings might include alder and cottonwood trees. Eventually, succession may lead to a community of organisms that does not change unless the ecosystem is disturbed. Reaching this mature community can take centuries.

FIGURE 1 ·····························

> ART IN MOTION **Primary Succession**

Primary succession occurs in an area where no soil and no organisms exist.

✎ **Sequence** In the circles, number the stage of primary succession to show the correct order of events.

Soil Creation
As pioneer species grow and die, soil forms. Some plants grow in this new soil.

Pioneer Species
The first species to grow are pioneer species such as mosses and lichens.

Volcanic Eruption
Shortly after a volcanic eruption, there is no soil, only ash and rock.

Fertile Soil and Maturing Plants
As more plants die, they decompose and make the soil more fertile. New plants grow and existing plants mature in the fertile soil.

617

FIGURE 2 ···

> ART IN MOTION   **Secondary Succession**

Secondary succession occurs following a disturbance to an ecosystem, such as clearing a forest for farmland.

✏ **Describe** Write a brief title that describes what happens at each of the four stages of secondary succession.

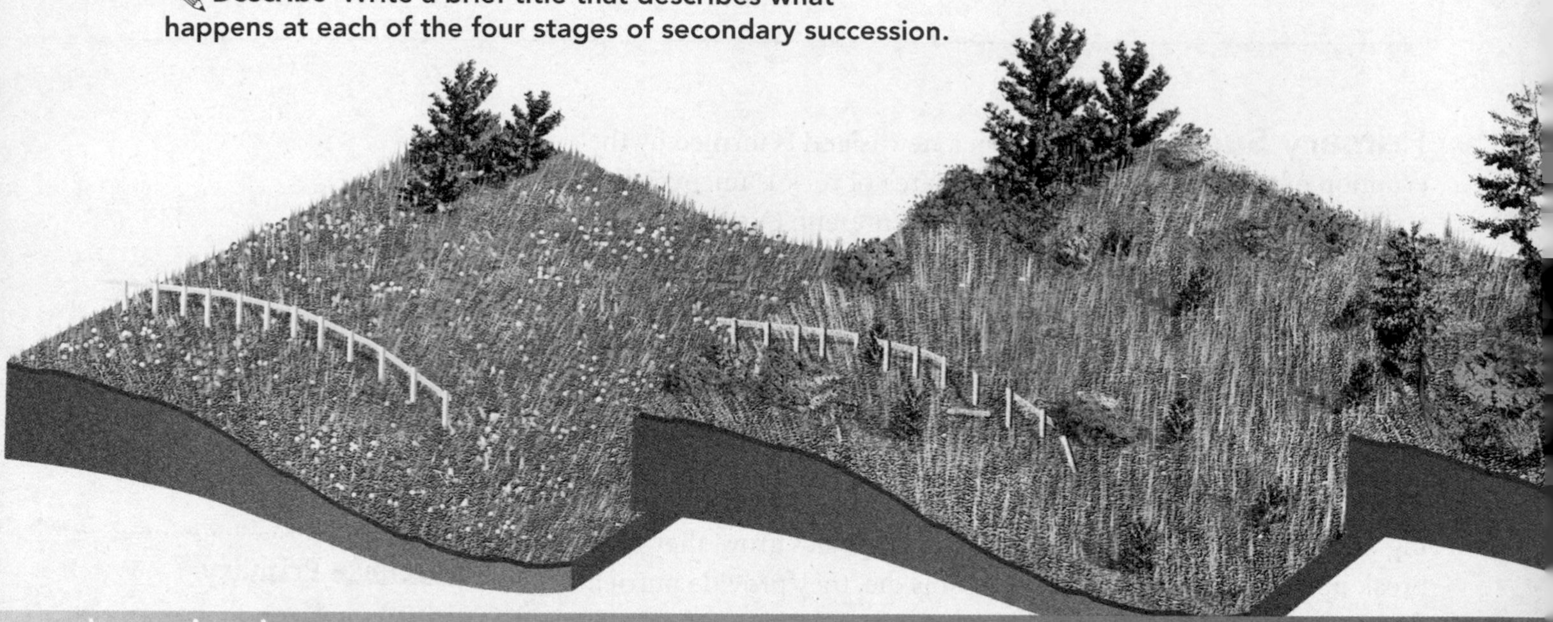

Increasing time

Title: _____

Grasses and wildflowers have taken over this abandoned field.

Title: _____

After a few years, pine seedlings and other trees replace some of the grasses and wildflowers.

apply it!

⊙ **Compare and Contrast** Based on your reading, complete the table below.

Factors in Succession	Primary Succession	Secondary Succession
Possible Cause	Volcanic eruption	_____
Type of Area		
Existing Ecosystem?		

Secondary Succession   In October 2007, huge wildfires raged across Southern California. The changes following the California fires are an example of secondary succession. **Secondary succession** is the series of changes that occurs in an area where the ecosystem has been disturbed, but where soil and organisms still exist. Natural disturbances that have this effect include fires, hurricanes, and tornadoes. Human activities, such as farming, logging, or mining, may also disturb an ecosystem and cause secondary succession to begin.

🔑 **Unlike primary succession, secondary succession occurs in a place where an ecosystem currently exists.** Secondary succession usually occurs more rapidly than primary succession because soil already exists and seeds from some plants remain in the soil. You can follow the process of succession in an abandoned field in **Figure 2.** After a century, a forest develops. This forest community may remain for a long time.

Title: _____

As tree growth continues, the trees begin to crowd out the grasses and wildflowers.

Title: _____

Eventually, a forest of mostly oak, hickory, and some pine dominates the landscape.

Lab zone® Do the Quick Lab _Primary or Secondary._

🔑 Assess Your Understanding

1a. Define Pioneer species are the _____ species to populate an area.

b. 🔺Observe Is grass poking through a sidewalk crack primary or secondary succession? Why?

_____

_____

_____

c. CHALLENGE Why are the changes during succession predictable?

_____

_____

_____

_____

got it? ....

○ I get it! Now I know that primary and secondary succession differ in _____

_____

○ I need extra help with _____

Go to MY SCIENCE ⓢ COACH online for help with this subject.

15 Study Guide

Living things interact in many ways, including competition and _____, as well as through symbiotic relationships such as mutualism, commensalism, and _____.

LESSON 1 Living Things and the Environment

🔑 An organism gets the things it needs to live, grow, and reproduce from its environment.

🔑 Biotic and abiotic factors make up a habitat.

🔑 The levels of organization in an ecosystem are organism, population, and community.

Vocabulary
- organism • habitat • biotic factor
- abiotic factor • species • population
- community • ecosystem • ecology

LESSON 2 Populations

🔑 Populations can change in size when new members join the population or when members leave the population.

🔑 Some limiting factors for populations are weather conditions, space, food, and water.

Vocabulary
- birth rate • death rate • immigration
- emigration • population density
- limiting factor • carrying capacity

LESSON 3 Interactions Among Living Things

🔑 Every organism has a variety of adaptations that are suited to its specific living conditions to help it survive.

🔑 Two major types of interactions among organisms are competition and predation.

🔑 The three main types of symbiotic relationships are mutualism, commensalism, and parasitism.

Vocabulary
- natural selection • adaptation • niche • competition
- predation • predator • prey • symbiosis • mutualism
- commensalism • parasitism • parasite • host

LESSON 4 Changes in Communities

🔑 Unlike primary succession, secondary succession occurs in a place where an ecosystem currently exists.

Vocabulary
- succession
- primary succession
- pioneer species
- secondary succession

Review and Assessment

LESSON 1 Living Things and the Environment

1. A prairie dog, a hawk, and a snake are all members of the same

   a. niche.   **b.** community.

   c. species.   **d.** population.

2. Grass is an example of a(n) _____ in a habitat.

3. Sequence Put these levels in order from the smallest to the largest: population, organism, ecosystem, community.

_____

_____

4. Apply Concepts Name two biotic and two abiotic factors you might find in a forest ecosystem.

_____

_____

5. Draw Conclusions In 1815, Mount Tambora, a volcano in Indonesia, erupted. So much volcanic ash and dust filled the atmosphere that 1816 is referred to as the "Year Without a Summer." How might a volcanic eruption affect the abiotic factors in an organism's habitat?

_____

_____

_____

_____

_____

6. Write About It Write at least one paragraph describing your habitat. Describe how you get the food, water, and shelter you need from your habitat. How does this habitat meet your needs in ways that another would not?

LESSON 2 Populations

7. All of the following are limiting factors for populations except

   a. space.   **b.** food.

   c. time.   **d.** weather.

8. _____ occurs when individuals leave a population.

Use the data table to answer the questions below. Ecologists monitoring a deer population collect data during a 30-year study.

Year	0	5	10	15	20	25	30
Population (thousands)	15	30	65	100	40	25	10

9. Graph Use the data to make a line graph.

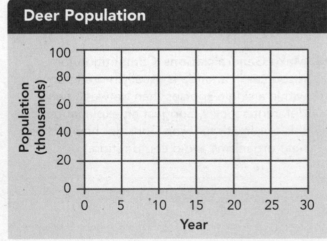

Deer Population

10. Interpret Data In which year was the deer population the highest? The lowest?

_____

11. Develop Hypotheses In Year 16 of the study, this region experienced a severe winter. How might this have affected the deer population?

_____

_____

_____

_____

621

15 Review and Assessment

12. In which type of interaction do both species benefit?

a. predation   b. mutualism

c. commensalism   d. parasitism

13. A parasite lives on or inside its _____.

14. Relate Cause and Effect Name two prey adaptations. How does each adaptation protect the organism?

_____

_____

_____

_____

_____

_____

15. Make Generalizations Competition for resources in an area is usually more intense within a single species than between two different species. Suggest an explanation for this observation. (*Hint:* Consider how niches help organisms avoid competition.)

_____

_____

_____

_____

_____

16. Write About It Some scientists think that the relationship between clownfish and sea anemones is an example of commensalism. Other scientists think that the relationship is mutualism. If this relationship is actually mutualism, how might both the clownfish and sea anemone benefit?

LESSON 4 Changes in Communities

17. The series of predictable changes that occur in a community over time is called

a. natural selection   b. ecology

c. commensalism   d. succession

18. _____ are the first species to populate an area.

19. Classify Lichens and mosses have just begun to grow on the rocky area shown below. What type of succession is occurring? Explain.

_____

_____

_____

APPLY THE BIG Q

How do living things affect one another?

20. Humans interact with their environment on a daily basis. These interactions can have both positive and negative effects. Using at least four vocabulary terms from this chapter, describe a human interaction and the effect it has on the environment.

_____

_____

_____

_____

_____

_____

_____

_____

_____

Standardized Test Prep

Multiple Choice

Circle the letter of the best answer.

1. Symbiotic relationships include mutualism, commensalism, and parasitism. Which of the images below shows mutualism?

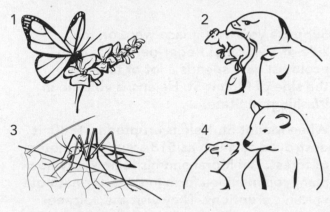

   A Image 1   **B** Image 2
   C Image 3   **D** Image 4

2. In general, which of the following is a true statement about population size?

   A If birth rate < death rate, population size increases.

   B If death rate < birth rate, population size decreases.

   C If birth rate > death rate, population size increases.

   D If death rate > birth rate, population size increases.

3. Ecosystems have different levels of organization. A group of similar organisms makes up a _____, which, along with other types of organisms, makes up a(n) _____.

   A species, population

   B habitat, ecosystem

   C population, community

   D population, habitat

4. Three different bird species all live in the same trees in an area, but competition between the birds rarely occurs. Which of the following is a likely explanation for this lack of competition?

   A The three species occupy different niches.

   B The three species eat the same food.

   C The three species have a limited supply of food.

   D The three species live in the same part of the trees.

5. Which of the following is a typical pioneer species?

   A grass

   B lichen

   C pine trees

   D soil

Constructed Response

Use the diagram below and your knowledge of science to help you answer Question 6. Write your answer on a separate piece of paper.

6. An organism interacts with both the biotic and abiotic factors in its habitat. List three biotic factors and three abiotic factors shown in the drawing above.

SUCCESSION ECOLOGIST

These lupine plants are growing out of the volcanic ash on Mount St. Helens, 20 years after its last eruption.

Suppose your workplace were on the side of a volcano! Roger del Moral is an ecologist who spends a lot of time on the side of Mount St. Helens, a volcano in Washington State.

When Mount St. Helens erupted in 1980, it destroyed as much as 518 square kilometers of forest. Del Moral and his team study how plant communities form in the aftermath of volcanic eruptions. They visit the volcano regularly to identify plants and estimate the remaining populations of plants to describe how the plant communities are recovering. This work enables researchers to develop more effective ways to help areas recover from human-caused environmental changes.

Del Moral loves his work and says, "My work on Mount St. Helens allows me to follow my passion, train students, and contribute to a better understanding of how the world works."

If you are interested in ecology, try volunteering or interning at a local park or field museum. National parks also have Junior Naturalist programs designed to give you experience in the field.

Compare It Find a park in your neighborhood or town and describe the kinds of plants you find. Make a table in which you list each kind of plant, describe it, describe where it grew, and draw conclusions about the reasons why it might have grown there.

BINOCULAR BOOT CAMP

▼ Populations of common and rare birds can be estimated based on input from students like you!

Scientists need all the help they can get estimating large populations! Binocular Boot Camp, a program for kids in Sonoma Valley, California, trains kids to identify the songs, calls, and flight patterns of birds. Participants form teams and identify and count as many birds as they can in one afternoon. The information they gather gets entered into a huge database of bird observations.

You don't have to go to Binocular Boot Camp to help, though. For four days in February, schools, clubs, and individuals in the United States and Canada take part in the Great Backyard Bird Count (GBBC). All you need to do is count birds for 15 minutes, then fill out a form to help scientists learn how climate change, habitat change, and other factors affect bird populations.

Research It Find out more about the GBBC. Design a poster or use presentation software to create a presentation to convince your school to participate.

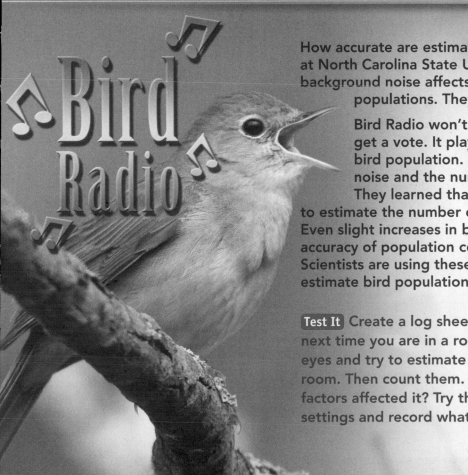

Bird Radio

How accurate are estimates of bird populations? Scientists at North Carolina State University wondered whether background noise affects scientists' ability to count bird populations. They used Bird Radio to find out.

Bird Radio won't be on the top 40—unless birds get a vote. It plays bird songs to simulate a wild bird population. Researchers adjusted background noise and the number of different bird songs. They learned that this affected people's ability to estimate the number of "birds" singing on Bird Radio. Even slight increases in background noise reduced the accuracy of population counts by up to 40 percent! Scientists are using these data to develop better ways to estimate bird populations.

Test It Create a log sheet for population estimates. The next time you are in a room with other people, close your eyes and try to estimate the number of people in the room. Then count them. Was your estimate close? What factors affected it? Try this experiment in five different settings and record what happens each time.

WHERE DOES FOOD COME FROM?

How do energy and matter move through ecosystems?

Flying around hunting for food, this barn owl spots a mouse for dinner. But what did the mouse eat? Perhaps it nibbled on seeds or a caterpillar. Then you might ask, where did the seeds and caterpillar get their food?

Develop Hypotheses Where do living things get their food?

_____

_____

_____

_____

_____

_____

> **UNTAMED SCIENCE** Watch the **Untamed Science** video to learn more about ecosystems and biomes.

Ecosystems and Biomes

Check Your Understanding

1. Background Read the paragraph below and then answer the question.

One morning, Han walks to the park and sits by the pond. He has just studied **ecosystems** in class, and now, looking at the pond, he realizes he sees things in a new way. He notices a turtle sunning itself on a rock, and knows that the sun and rock are **abiotic factors,** while the turtle, and other living things, are **biotic factors.**

The community of organisms that live in a particular area, along with their nonliving environment, make up an **ecosystem.**

Abiotic factors are the nonliving parts of an organism's habitat.

Biotic factors are the living parts of an organism's habitat.

• Name one more biotic factor and one more abiotic factor that Han might see at the pond.

_____

_____

> MY READING WEB If you had trouble answering the question above, visit **My Reading Web** and type in *Ecosystems and Biomes.*

Vocabulary Skill

Prefixes Some words can be divided into parts. A root is the part of the word that carries the basic meaning. A prefix is a word part that is placed in front of the root to change the word's meaning. The prefixes below will help you understand some vocabulary in this chapter.

Prefix	Meaning	Example
bio-	life	biodiversity, *n.* the number of different species in an area
inter-	between	intertidal, *adj.* ocean zone between the highest high-tide line and the lowest low-tide line

2. Quick Check Circle the prefix in each boldface word below.

• There was an **intermission** between the acts of the play.

• The **biosphere** is the area where life exists.

consumer

precipitation

desert

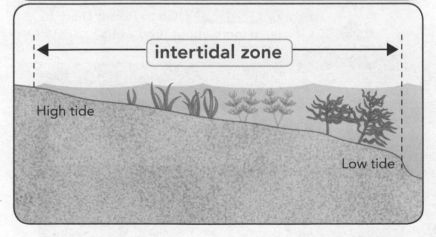

intertidal zone

High tide

Low tide

Chapter Preview

LESSON 1
- producer • consumer
- herbivore • carnivore • omnivore
- scavenger • decomposer
- food chain • food web
- energy pyramid

↻ **Relate Text and Visuals**
△ **Classify**

LESSON 2
- evaporation • condensation
- precipitation • nitrogen fixation

↻ **Sequence**
△ **Infer**

LESSON 3
- biome • climate • desert
- rain forest • emergent layer
- canopy • understory • grassland
- savanna • deciduous tree
- boreal forest • coniferous tree
- tundra • permafrost

↻ **Compare and Contrast**
△ **Draw Conclusions**

LESSON 4
- estuary
- intertidal zone
- neritic zone

↻ **Outline**
△ **Communicate**

LESSON 5
- biodiversity • keystone species
- gene • extinction
- endangered species
- threatened species
- habitat destruction
- habitat fragmentation • poaching
- captive breeding

↻ **Compare and Contrast**
△ **Infer**

> **VOCAB FLASH CARDS** For extra help with vocabulary, visit **Vocab Flash Cards** and type in *Ecosystems and Biomes.*

Energy Flow in Ecosystems

UNLOCK THE BIG Q?

🔑 What Are the Energy Roles in an Ecosystem?

🔑 How Does Energy Move Through an Ecosystem?

my planet Diary

I'll Have the Fish

Scientists have noticed something fishy going on with the wolves in British Columbia, Canada. During autumn, the wolves ignore their typical food of deer and moose and feast on salmon instead. Salmon are very nutritious and lack the big horns and hoofs that can injure or kill wolves. Plus, there are plenty of fish in a small area, making them easier to find and catch.

Many animals, including the wolves, depend upon the salmon's annual mating trip upstream. Losing this important food source to overfishing would hurt the populations of bears, wolves, birds, and many other animals.

DISCOVERY

Communicate Discuss these questions with a classmate. Write your answers below.

1. What are two reasons the wolves may eat fish in autumn instead of deer or moose?

_____

_____

2. What effect could overfishing salmon have on an ecosystem?

_____

_____

_____

_____

▶ PLANET DIARY Go to **Planet Diary** to learn more about food webs.

Lab zone Do the Inquiry Warm-Up *Where Did Your Dinner Come From?*

Vocabulary

- producer   • consumer   • herbivore   • carnivore
- omnivore   • scavenger   • decomposer   • food chain
- food web   • energy pyramid

Skills

↻ Reading: Relate Text and Visuals
△ Inquiry: Classify

What Are the Energy Roles in an Ecosystem?

Do you play an instrument in your school band? If so, you know that each instrument has a role in a piece of music. Similar to instruments in a band, each organism has a role in the movement of energy through its ecosystem.

An organism's energy role is determined by how it obtains food and how it interacts with other organisms. **Each of the organisms in an ecosystem fills the energy role of producer, consumer, or decomposer.**

Producers Energy enters most ecosystems as sunlight. Some organisms, like the plants and algae shown in **Figure 1,** and some types of bacteria, capture the energy of sunlight and store it as food energy. These organisms use the sun's energy to turn water and carbon dioxide into food molecules in a process called photosynthesis.

An organism that can make its own food is a **producer.** Producers are the source of all the food in an ecosystem. In a few ecosystems, producers obtain energy from a source other than sunlight. One such ecosystem is found in rocks deep beneath the ground. Certain bacteria in this ecosystem produce their own food using the energy in hydrogen sulfide, a gas that is present in their environment.

Tape grass and water milfoil

FIGURE 1 ·····················
Producers
Producers are organisms that can make their own food.

✎ **Identify** Complete the shopping list below to identify the producers that are part of your diet.

○ wheat _____
○ corn _____
○ banana _____
○ _____
○ _____
○ _____
○ _____
○ _____
○ _____

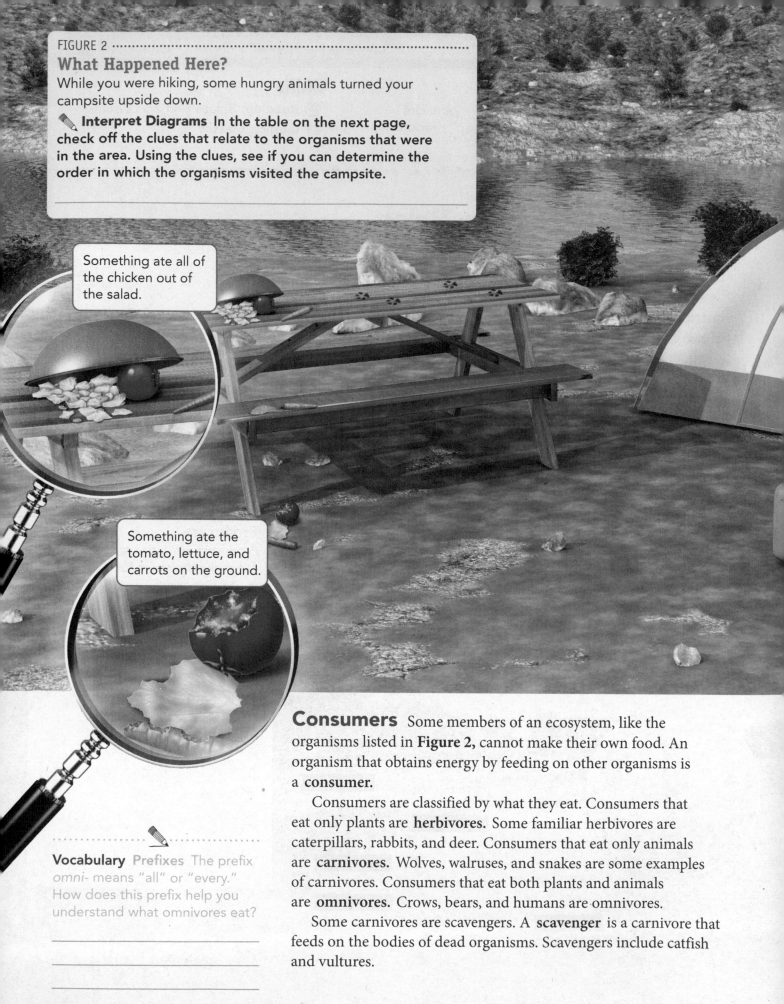

FIGURE 2 ·······································

What Happened Here?

While you were hiking, some hungry animals turned your campsite upside down.

✎ **Interpret Diagrams** In the table on the next page, check off the clues that relate to the organisms that were in the area. Using the clues, see if you can determine the order in which the organisms visited the campsite.

Something ate all of the chicken out of the salad.

Something ate the tomato, lettuce, and carrots on the ground.

Vocabulary Prefixes The prefix *omni-* means "all" or "every." How does this prefix help you understand what omnivores eat?

_____

_____

_____

Consumers Some members of an ecosystem, like the organisms listed in **Figure 2,** cannot make their own food. An organism that obtains energy by feeding on other organisms is a **consumer.**

Consumers are classified by what they eat. Consumers that eat only plants are **herbivores.** Some familiar herbivores are caterpillars, rabbits, and deer. Consumers that eat only animals are **carnivores.** Wolves, walruses, and snakes are some examples of carnivores. Consumers that eat both plants and animals are **omnivores.** Crows, bears, and humans are omnivores.

Some carnivores are scavengers. A **scavenger** is a carnivore that feeds on the bodies of dead organisms. Scavengers include catfish and vultures.

Clues	Bear	Mold	Rabbit	Wolf
Can easily reach the table top				
Grows on food and breaks it down				
Small enough to enter and exit tent				
Gets energy from meat				
Strong enough to open cooler				
Not a picky eater				
Gets energy from plants				

Something ate the apples and beef jerky from inside the tent.

Something ate strawberries, even some of the moldy ones.

Decomposers If an ecosystem had only producers and consumers, the raw materials of life, such as carbon and nitrogen, would stay locked up in wastes and the bodies of dead organisms. However, there are organisms in ecosystems that prevent this from happening. **Decomposers** break down biotic wastes and dead organisms and return the raw materials to the ecosystem.

You can think of decomposers as nature's recyclers. While obtaining energy for their own needs, decomposers return simple molecules to the environment. These molecules can be used again by other organisms. Mushrooms, bacteria, and mold are common decomposers.

Lab zone® Do the Quick Lab
Observing Decomposition.

🔑 Assess Your Understanding

1a. Describe An organism's energy role is determined by how it obtains _____ and how it _____ with other organisms.

b. Apply Concepts What is the main source of energy for all three energy roles? Why?

_____
_____
_____
_____
_____
_____
_____

got it? ·

O **I get it!** Now I know that the energy roles in an ecosystem are _____
_____
_____

O **I need extra help with** _____
_____

Go to MY SCIENCE ⓢ COACH *online for help with this subject.*

633

How Does Energy Move Through an Ecosystem?

As you have read, energy enters most ecosystems as sunlight and is converted into food by producers. This energy is transferred to the organisms that eat the producers, and then to other organisms that feed on the consumers. **Energy moves through an ecosystem when one organism eats another.** This movement of energy can be shown as food chains, food webs, and energy pyramids.

Food Chains One way to show how energy moves in an ecosystem is with a food chain. A **food chain** is a series of events in which one organism eats another and obtains energy. You can follow one example of a food chain in **Figure 3.**

Food Webs A food chain shows only one possible path along which energy can move through an ecosystem. Most producers and consumers are part of many food chains. A more realistic way to show the flow of energy through an ecosystem is with a food web. As shown in **Figure 4,** a **food web** consists of many overlapping food chains in an ecosystem.

Organisms may play more than one role in an ecosystem. Look at the crayfish in **Figure 4.** A crayfish is an omnivore that is a first-level consumer when it eats plants. But when a crayfish eats a snail, it is a second-level consumer.

Just as food chains overlap and connect, food webs interconnect as well. A gull might eat a fish at the ocean, but it might also eat a mouse at a landfill. The gull, then, is part of two food webs—an ocean food web and a land food web. All the world's food webs interconnect in what can be thought of as a global food web.

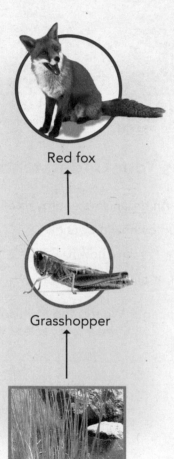

Red fox

Grasshopper

Plants

FIGURE 3 ·····························
Food Chain
In this food chain, you can see how energy moves from plants, to a grasshopper, to the fox. The arrows show how energy moves up the food chain, from one organism to the next.

Classify Using what you have learned about food chains, draw or describe a food chain from your local ecosystem. Show at least three organisms in your food chain. Name each organism and label it as a producer, consumer, or decomposer.

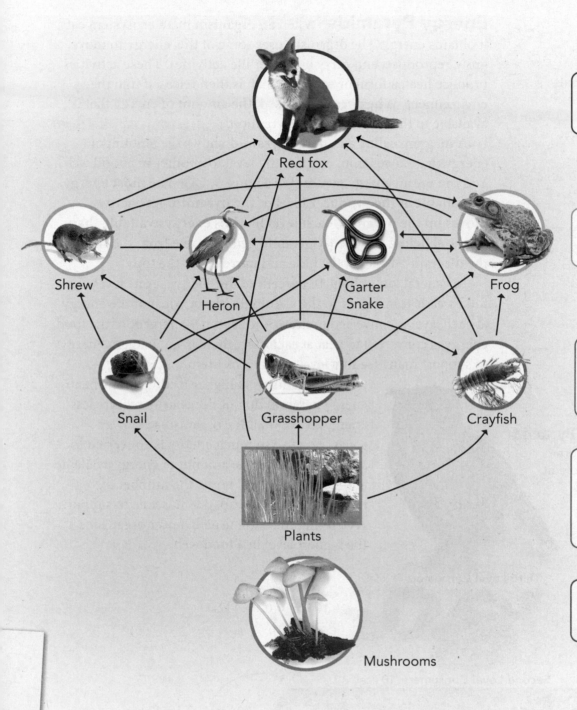

Third-level consumers eat the second-level consumers.

Second-level consumers eat the first-level consumers.

First-level consumers are organisms that feed directly on the producers.

Producers form the base of the food web. The first organism in a food chain is always a producer.

Decomposers consume the wastes and remains of other organisms.

Red fox

Shrew

Heron

Garter Snake

Frog

Snail

Grasshopper

Crayfish

Plants

Mushrooms

FIGURE 4 ·······························

> INTERACTIVE ART **Food Web**

A food web consists of many interconnected food chains.

✎ **Complete the tasks.**

1. **Interpret Diagrams** Pick two organisms from the food web. Draw arrows connecting them to the decomposers.

2. ↻ **Relate Text and Visuals** How can the fox be both a second-level and third-level consumer?

_____
_____
_____
_____
_____
_____

Energy Pyramids

Energy Pyramids When an organism in an ecosystem eats, it obtains energy. The organism uses some of this energy to move, grow, reproduce, and carry out other life activities. These activities produce heat, a form of energy, which is then released into the environment. When heat is released, the amount of energy that is available to the next consumer is reduced.

A diagram called an **energy pyramid** shows the amount of energy that moves from one feeding level to another in a food web. You can see an energy pyramid in **Figure 5**. 🔑 **The most energy is available at the producer level of the pyramid. As energy moves up the pyramid, each level has less energy available than the level below.** An energy pyramid gets its name from the shape of the diagram—wider at the base and narrower at the top.

In general, only about 10 percent of the energy at one level of a food web is transferred to the next higher level. Most of the energy at each level is converted to heat. Since about 90 percent of the food energy is converted to heat at each step, there is not enough energy to support many feeding levels in an ecosystem.

The organisms at higher feeding levels of an energy pyramid do not necessarily require less energy to live than the organisms at lower levels. Because so much energy is converted to heat at each level, the amount of energy available at the producer level limits the number of consumers that the ecosystem is able to support. As a result, there are usually fewer organisms at the highest level in a food web.

✏️ **Relate Text and Visuals**
Look at the energy pyramid. Why is a pyramid the best shape to show how energy moves through an ecosystem?

_____

_____

_____

_____

_____

_____

FIGURE 5 ·······················

▶ **VIRTUAL LAB** **Energy Pyramid**
This energy pyramid diagram shows the energy available at each level of a food web and how it is calculated. Energy is measured in kilocalories, or kcal.

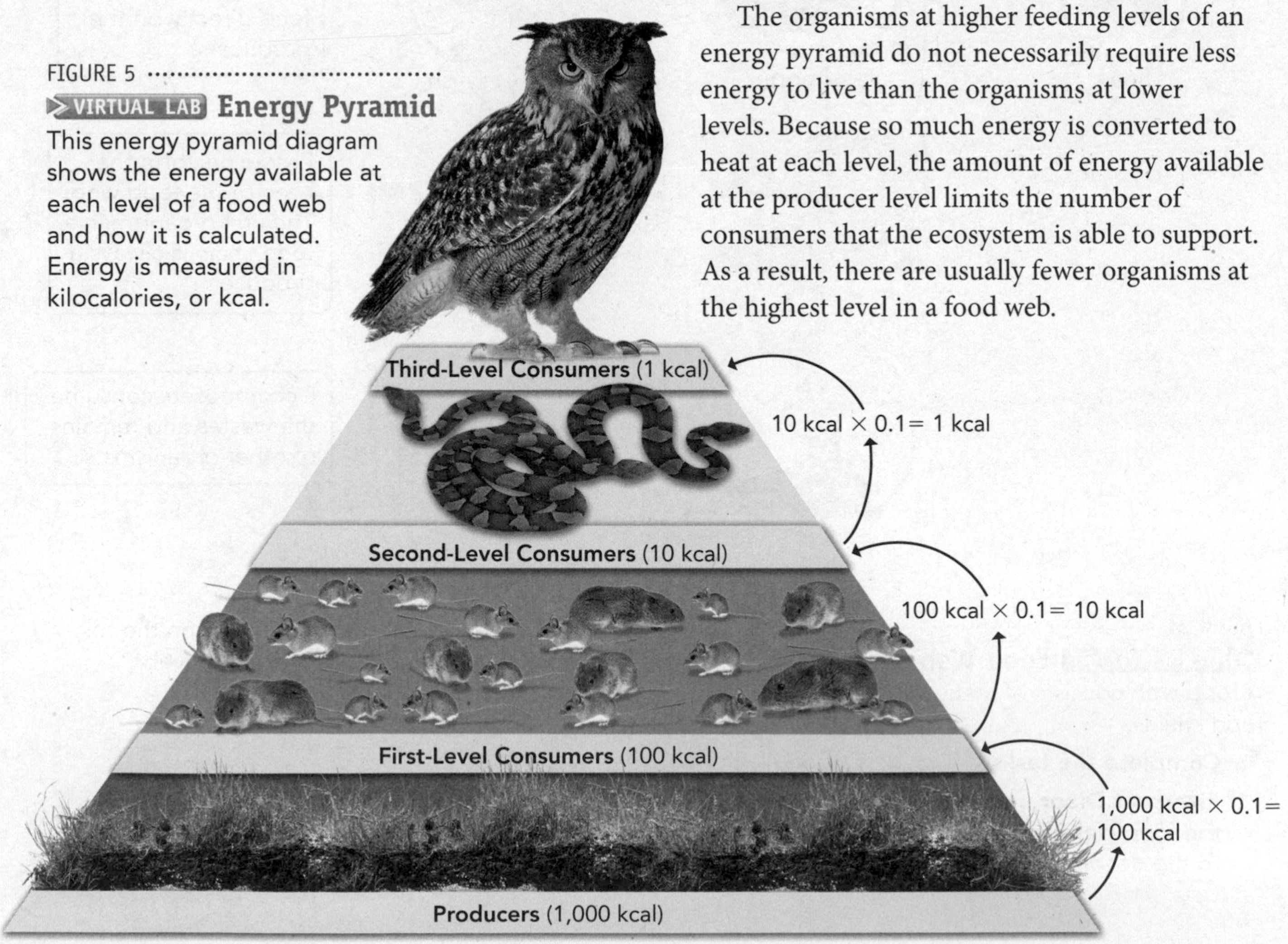

Third-Level Consumers (1 kcal)

10 kcal × 0.1 = 1 kcal

Second-Level Consumers (10 kcal)

100 kcal × 0.1 = 10 kcal

First-Level Consumers (100 kcal)

1,000 kcal × 0.1 = 100 kcal

Producers (1,000 kcal)

do the math!

Energy Pyramids

Suppose that the producers at the base of an energy pyramid contain 330,000 kilocalories.
Calculate Using **Figure 5** as a guide, label how much energy would be available at each level of the pyramid based on the questions below.

1 If mice ate all of the plants, how much energy would be available to them as first-level consumers?

2 If all of the mice were eaten by snakes, how much energy would the snakes receive?

3 If all of the snakes were eaten by the owl, how much energy would the owl receive?

4 [CHALLENGE] About how much energy would the owl use for its life processes or lose as heat? _____

5 [CHALLENGE] How much energy would be stored in the owl's body? _____

Third-Level Consumers

Second-Level Consumers

First-Level Consumers

330,000 kcal
Producers

Lab zone® Do the Lab Investigation *Ecosystem Food Chains.*

🔑 Assess Your Understanding

2a. Define A food (web/chain) is a series of events in which one organism eats another and obtains energy. A food (web/chain) consists of many overlapping food (webs/chains).

b. Compare and Contrast Why is a food web a more realistic way of portraying an ecosystem than a food chain?

_____

_____

_____

c. Relate Cause and Effect Why are there usually fewer organisms at the top of an energy pyramid?

_____

_____

_____

_____

_____

_____

got it? ··

○ **I get it!** Now I know that energy moves through an ecosystem when_____

_____

○ **I need extra help with** _____

   Go to my science ⑤ **coach** *online for help with this subject.*

Cycles of Matter

UNLOCK THE BIG ?

🔑 **What Processes Are Involved in the Water Cycle?**

🔑 **How Are the Carbon and Oxygen Cycles Related?**

🔑 **How Does Nitrogen Cycle Through Ecosystems?**

MY PLANET DIARY

DISASTER

Canaries and Coal

Have you ever stopped to listen to a bird sing? If you were a coal miner in the early 1900s, your life may have depended on it! Sometimes miners stumbled upon pockets of carbon monoxide, a toxic, odorless gas that makes it difficult for the body to get enough oxygen. Without fresh air circulating in the mineshafts, the miners would fall asleep and eventually die. To prevent this disaster from happening, canaries were used to monitor the air quality. A singing canary indicated that all was well. If the canary stopped singing and died, the miners knew that they needed to quickly leave the mine.

Answer the question below.
Do you think it was ethical, or fair, to use canaries this way? Explain.

_____
_____
_____
_____

▶ PLANET DIARY Go to **Planet Diary** to learn more about cycles of matter.

 Do the Inquiry Warm-Up *Are You Part of a Cycle?*

What Processes Are Involved in the Water Cycle?

Recycling is important for ecosystems because matter is limited. To understand how matter cycles through an ecosystem, you need to know a few terms that describe the structure of matter. Matter is made up of tiny particles called atoms. Two or more atoms that are joined and act as a unit make up a molecule. For example, a water molecule consists of two hydrogen atoms and one oxygen atom.

Water is essential for life. The water cycle is the continuous process by which water moves from Earth's surface to the atmosphere and back. 🔑 **The processes of evaporation, condensation, and precipitation make up the water cycle.**

Vocabulary
- evaporation
- condensation
- precipitation
- nitrogen fixation

Skills
- ↻ Reading: Sequence
- △ Inquiry: Infer

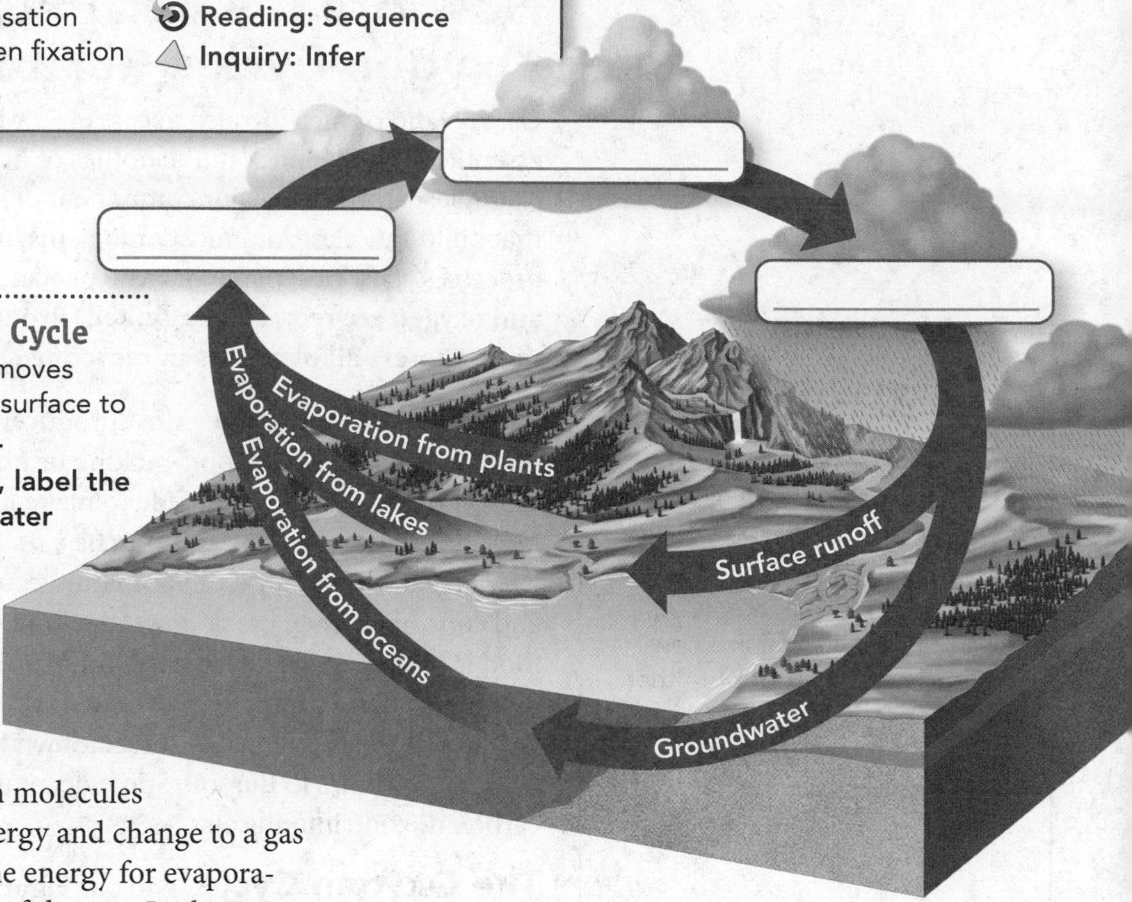

FIGURE 1 ·······················

▶ INTERACTIVE ART **Water Cycle**
In the water cycle, water moves continuously from Earth's surface to the atmosphere and back.

✎ **Identify** As you read, label the three processes of the water cycle in the diagram.

Evaporation from plants

Evaporation from lakes

Evaporation from oceans

Surface runoff

Groundwater

Evaporation
How does water from the ground get into the air? The process by which molecules of liquid water absorb energy and change to a gas is called **evaporation.** The energy for evaporation comes from the heat of the sun. In the water cycle, liquid water evaporates from oceans, lakes, and other sources and forms water vapor, a gas, in the atmosphere. Smaller amounts of water also evaporate from living things. Plants release water vapor from their leaves. You release liquid water in your wastes and water vapor when you exhale.

Condensation
As water vapor rises higher in the atmosphere, it cools down. The cooled vapor then turns back into tiny drops of liquid water. The process by which a gas changes to a liquid is called **condensation.** The water droplets collect around dust particles and form clouds.

Precipitation
As more water vapor condenses, the drops of water in the clouds grow larger. Eventually the heavy drops fall to Earth as **precipitation**—rain, snow, sleet, or hail. Precipitation may fall into oceans, lakes, or rivers. The precipitation that falls on land may soak into the soil and become groundwater, or run off the land, flowing back into a river or ocean.

Lab® zone Do the Quick Lab Following Water.

🔑 Assess Your Understanding

got it? ···························

○ I get it! Now I know that the processes of the water cycle are _____

_____

_____

○ I need extra help with _____

_____

_____

Go to MY SCIENCE Ⓢ COACH online for help with this subject.

How Are the Carbon and Oxygen Cycles Related?

Carbon and oxygen are also necessary for life. Carbon is an essential building block in the bodies of living things. For example, carbon is a major component of bones and the proteins that build muscles. And most organisms use oxygen for their life processes. 🔑 **In ecosystems, the processes by which carbon and oxygen are recycled are linked. Producers, consumers, and decomposers all play roles in recycling carbon and oxygen.**

The Carbon Cycle Most producers take in carbon dioxide gas from the air during food-making or photosynthesis. They use carbon from the carbon dioxide to make food—carbon-containing molecules such as sugars and starches. As consumers eat producers, they take in the carbon-containing molecules. Both producers and consumers then break down the food to obtain energy. As the food is broken down, producers and consumers release carbon dioxide and water into the environment. When producers and consumers die, decomposers break down their remains and return carbon molecules to the soil. Some decomposers also release carbon dioxide into the air.

The Oxygen Cycle Look at **Figure 2**. Like carbon, oxygen cycles through ecosystems. Producers release oxygen as a result of photosynthesis. In fact, photosynthesis is responsible for most of the oxygen in Earth's atmosphere. Most organisms take in oxygen from the air or water and use it to carry out their life processes.

Human Impact Human activities also affect the levels of carbon and oxygen in the atmosphere. When humans burn oil and other plant-based fuels, carbon dioxide is released into the atmosphere. Carbon dioxide levels can also rise when humans clear forests for lumber, fuel, and farmland. Increasing levels of carbon dioxide are a major factor in global warming.

As you know, producers take in carbon dioxide during photosynthesis. When trees are removed from the ecosystem, there are fewer producers to absorb carbon dioxide. There is an even greater effect if trees are burned down to clear a forest. When trees are burned down, additional carbon dioxide is released during the burning process.

apply it!

Producers, consumers, and decomposers all play a role in recycling carbon and oxygen.

⚠️ **Infer** On the lines below, describe how you think a cow eating grass is part of both the carbon and oxygen cycles.

_____

_____

_____

_____

_____

_____

_____

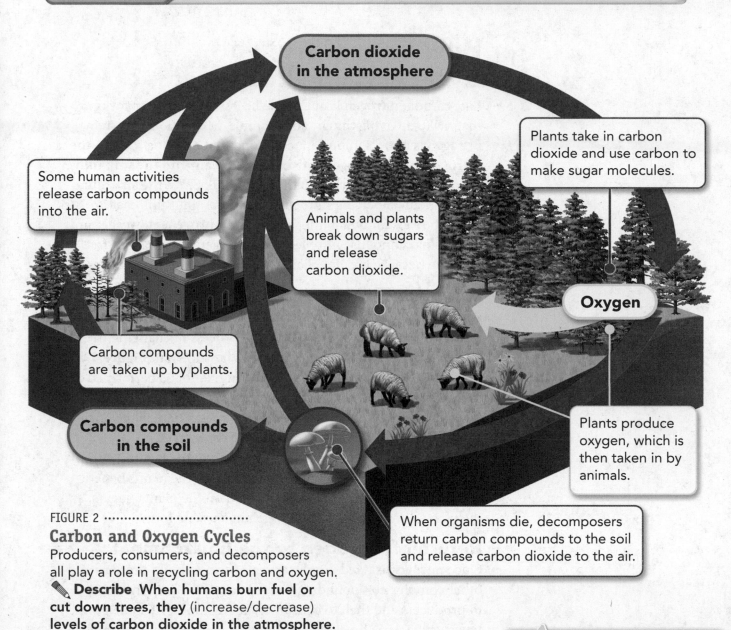

Carbon dioxide in the atmosphere

Some human activities release carbon compounds into the air.

Plants take in carbon dioxide and use carbon to make sugar molecules.

Animals and plants break down sugars and release carbon dioxide.

Oxygen

Carbon compounds are taken up by plants.

Carbon compounds in the soil

Plants produce oxygen, which is then taken in by animals.

When organisms die, decomposers return carbon compounds to the soil and release carbon dioxide to the air.

FIGURE 2 ....
Carbon and Oxygen Cycles
Producers, consumers, and decomposers all play a role in recycling carbon and oxygen.
✏️ **Describe** When humans burn fuel or cut down trees, they (increase/decrease) levels of carbon dioxide in the atmosphere.

 Lab zone Do the Quick Lab *Carbon and Oxygen Blues.*

🔑 Assess Your Understanding

1a. Identify Carbon and oxygen are both
_____ in an ecosystem.

b. Develop Hypotheses How might the death of all the producers in a community affect the carbon and oxygen cycles?

_____
_____
_____
_____

got it?

○ **I get it!** Now I know that the carbon and oxygen cycles are related by _____

_____
_____
_____

○ **I need extra help with** _____

_____

Go to **MY SCIENCE** ⬢ **COACH** *online for help with this subject.*

How Does Nitrogen Cycle Through Ecosystems?

Like carbon, nitrogen is one of the necessary building blocks that make up living things. For example, in addition to carbon, nitrogen is also an important component of proteins. 🗝 **In the nitrogen cycle, nitrogen moves from the air into the soil, into living things, and back into the air or soil.** Since the air around you is about 78 percent nitrogen gas, you might think that it would be easy for living things to obtain nitrogen. However, most organisms cannot use nitrogen gas. Nitrogen gas is called "free" nitrogen because it is not combined with other kinds of atoms.

Nitrogen Fixation Most organisms can use nitrogen only after it has been "fixed," or combined with other elements to form nitrogen-containing compounds. The process of changing free nitrogen into a usable form of nitrogen, as shown in **Figure 4,** is called **nitrogen fixation.** Most nitrogen fixation is performed by certain kinds of bacteria. These bacteria live in bumps called nodules (NAHJ oolz) on the roots of legumes. These plants include clover, beans, peas, alfalfa, peanuts, and some trees.

The relationship between the bacteria and the legumes is an example of mutualism. Both the bacteria and the plants benefit from this relationship: The bacteria feed on the plants' sugars, and the plants are supplied with nitrogen in a usable form.

Return of Nitrogen to the Environment

Once nitrogen is fixed, producers can use it to build proteins and other complex compounds. Nitrogen can cycle from the soil to producers and then to consumers many times. At some point, however, bacteria break down the nitrogen compounds completely. These bacteria then release free nitrogen back into the air, causing the cycle to continue.

FIGURE 3 ·····································

Growth in Nitrogen-Poor Soil

Pitcher plants can grow in nitrogen-poor soil because they obtain nitrogen by trapping insects in their tube-shaped leaves. The plants then digest the insects and use their nitrogen compounds.

✏ **Circle the correct word in each sentence.**

1. **Identify** If nitrogen in the soil isn't (fixed/free), then most organisms cannot use it.

2. CHALLENGE The relationship between the pitcher plant and the insects is an example of (competition/predation/symbiosis).

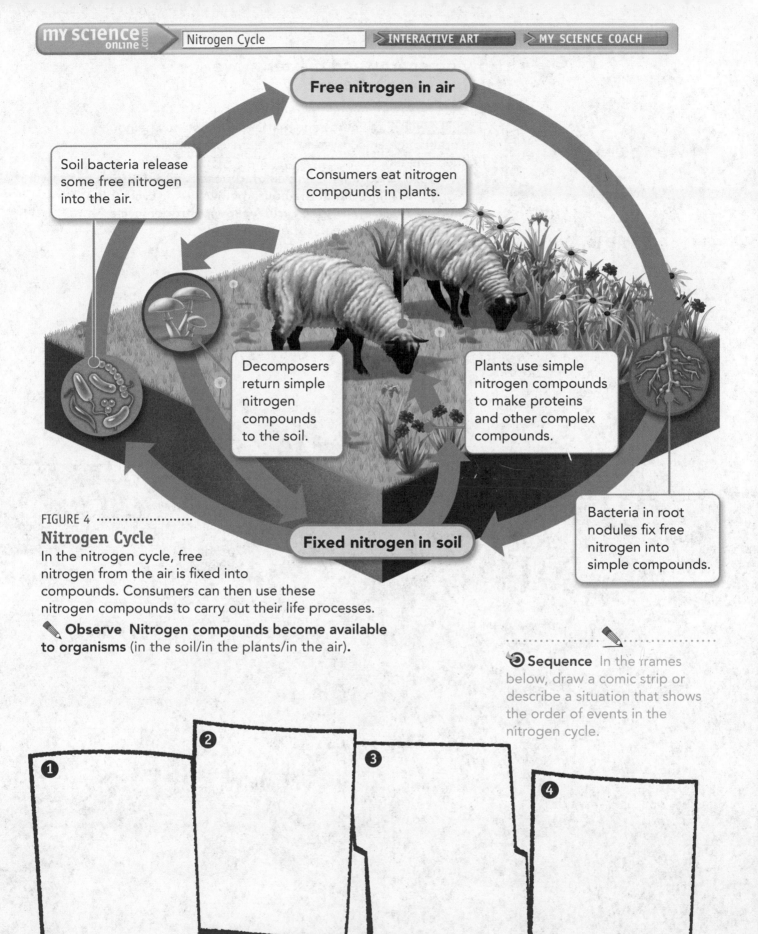

Free nitrogen in air

Soil bacteria release some free nitrogen into the air.

Consumers eat nitrogen compounds in plants.

Decomposers return simple nitrogen compounds to the soil.

Plants use simple nitrogen compounds to make proteins and other complex compounds.

Bacteria in root nodules fix free nitrogen into simple compounds.

Fixed nitrogen in soil

FIGURE 4 ....

Nitrogen Cycle

In the nitrogen cycle, free nitrogen from the air is fixed into compounds. Consumers can then use these nitrogen compounds to carry out their life processes.

✏️ **Observe** Nitrogen compounds become available **to organisms** (in the soil/in the plants/in the air).

⟳ **Sequence** In the frames below, draw a comic strip or describe a situation that shows the order of events in the nitrogen cycle.

❶

❷

❸

❹

Cycles of Matter

EXPLORE THE BIG **?**

How do energy and matter move through ecosystems?

FIGURE 5 ···

> **INTERACTIVE ART** Energy and matter are constantly being cycled through an ecosystem. These cycles can occur at the same time.

✎ **Interpret Diagrams** Using colored pencils, draw arrows to represent the following in the figure below: water cycle (blue), carbon cycle (purple), oxygen cycle (yellow), nitrogen cycle (orange), food chain (green). Label each cycle.

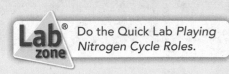
Do the Quick Lab *Playing Nitrogen Cycle Roles.*

🔑 Assess Your Understanding

2a. Describe (Fixed/Free) nitrogen is not combined with other kinds of atoms.

b. Predict What might happen in a community if farmers did not plant legume crops?

_____

_____

_____

_____

_____

_____

_____

_____

_____

c. ANSWER THE BIG **?** How do energy and matter move through ecosystems?

_____

_____

_____

_____

_____

_____

_____

_____

_____

got**it?** ....

○ I get it! Now I know that the nitrogen cycle

_____

_____

_____

○ I need extra help with _____

_____

Go to MY SCIENCE S COACH *online for help with this subject.*

UNLOCK
THE BIG
?

🔑 **What Are the Six Major Biomes?**

---

my planeT DiaRY

That's Super Cool!

Misconception: It is always fatal when body temperatures drop below freezing.

Fact: In the tundra, arctic ground squirrels hibernate up to eight months a year. During this time, a squirrel's body temperature drops below freezing! This is called supercooling and gives the squirrel the lowest body temperature of any mammal. Without waking, a squirrel will shiver for several hours every couple of weeks to increase its body temperature.

MISCONCEPTION

Answer the question below.

What do you think are the advantages of supercooling?

_____

_____

_____

_____

_____

_____

▶ **PLANET DIARY** Go to **Planet Diary** to learn more about biomes.

Lab ® Do the Inquiry Warm-Up
zone *How Much Rain Is That?*

What Are the Six Major Biomes?

Imagine that you are taking part in an around-the-world scientific expedition. On this expedition you will collect data on the typical climate and organisms of each of Earth's biomes. A **biome** is a group of ecosystems with similar climates and organisms.

🔑 **The six major biomes are desert, rain forest, grassland, deciduous forest, boreal forest, and tundra.** It is mostly the **climate**—the average annual temperature and amount of precipitation—in an area that determines its biome. Climate limits the species of plants that can grow in an area. In turn, the species of plants determine the kinds of animals that live there.

Vocabulary

- biome • climate • desert • rain forest
- emergent layer • canopy • understory • grassland
- savanna • deciduous tree • boreal forest
- coniferous tree • tundra • permafrost

Skills

🔁 Reading: Compare and Contrast
△ Inquiry: Draw Conclusions

Desert Biomes The first stop on your expedition is a desert. You step off the bus into the searing heat. A **desert** is an area that receives less than 25 centimeters of rain per year. Some of the driest deserts may not receive any precipitation in a year! Deserts often undergo large shifts in temperature during the course of a day. A scorching hot desert like the Namib Desert in Africa cools rapidly each night when the sun goes down. Other deserts, such as the Gobi in central Asia, have a yearly average temperature that is below freezing.

Organisms that live in the desert, like the fennec in **Figure 1**, must be adapted to little or no rain and to extreme temperatures. For example, the stem of a saguaro cactus has folds that are similar to the pleats in an accordion. The stem expands to store water when it is raining. Gila monsters can spend weeks at a time in their cool underground burrows. Many other desert animals are most active at night when the temperatures are cooler.

FIGURE 1 ·······························

Desert

Organisms must be adapted to live in the desert.

✏ **Complete these tasks.**

1. [CHALLENGE] How do you think the fennec's ears and fur are adaptations to the desert's extreme temperatures?

   _____

   _____

   _____

2. **List** Write five things you'll need to be well adapted to desert conditions. Pack carefully!

Supply List

○ wide-brimmed hat
○ _____
○ _____
○ _____
○ _____
○ _____

Equator

Desert Biomes

Desert

647

Compare and Contrast As
you read about temperate and
tropical rain forests, fill in the
Venn diagram.

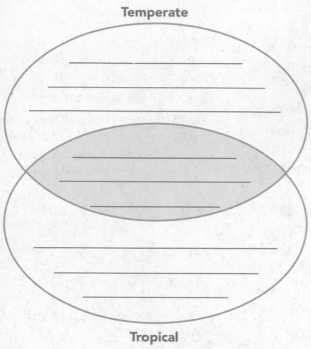

Temperate

Tropical

Rain-Forest Biomes The second stop on
your expedition is a rain forest. **Rain forests** are
forests in which large amounts of rain fall year-
round. This biome is living up to its name—it's
pouring! After a short shower, the sun reappears.
However, very little sunlight reaches the ground.

Plants are everywhere in the rain forest. Some
plants, like the vines hanging from tree limbs,
even grow on other plants! And animals are
flying, creeping, and slithering all around you.

Temperate Rain Forests You may think that
a rain forest is a warm, humid "jungle" in the
tropics. But there is another type of rain forest.
The Pacific Northwest of the United States
receives more than 300 centimeters of rain a
year. Huge trees grow there, including redwoods,
cedars, and firs. Many ecologists refer to this
ecosystem as a temperate rain forest. The term
temperate means "having moderate temperatures."

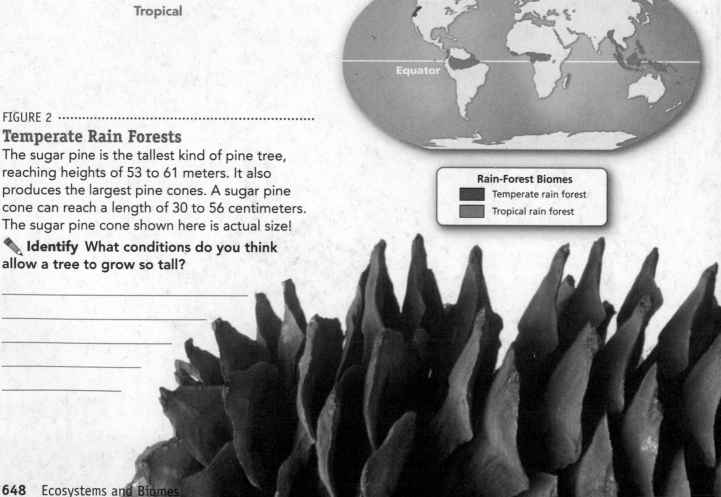

Equator

Rain-Forest Biomes
▬ Temperate rain forest
▬ Tropical rain forest

FIGURE 2

Temperate Rain Forests
The sugar pine is the tallest kind of pine tree,
reaching heights of 53 to 61 meters. It also
produces the largest pine cones. A sugar pine
cone can reach a length of 30 to 56 centimeters.
The sugar pine cone shown here is actual size!

✎ **Identify** What conditions do you think
allow a tree to grow so tall?

Tropical Rain Forests As you can see on the map, tropical rain forests are found in regions close to the equator. The climate is warm and humid all year long, and there is a lot of rain. Because of these climate conditions, an amazing variety of plants grow in tropical rain forests.

Trees in the rain forest form several distinct layers. The tallest layer of the rain forest which receives the most sunlight and can reach up to 70 meters, is the **emergent layer.** Underneath, trees up to 50 meters tall form a leafy roof called the **canopy.** Below the canopy, a layer of shorter trees and vines, around 15 meters high, form an **understory.** Understory plants grow well in the shade formed by the canopy. The forest floor is nearly dark, so only a few plants live there. Look at the tree layers in **Figure 3.**

The abundant plant life in tropical rain forests provides habitats for many species of animals. Ecologists estimate that millions of species of insects live in tropical rain forests. These insects serve as a source of food for many reptiles, birds, and mammals. Many of these animals, in turn, are food sources for other animals. Although tropical rain forests cover only a small part of the planet, they probably contain more species of plants and animals than all the other biomes combined.

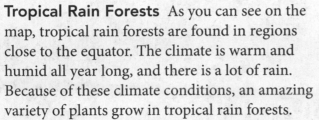

FIGURE 3 ···

Tropical Rain Forests
On the edge of this tropical rain forest, an amazing variety of organisms can be found in the different layers.

✏ **Relate Text and Visuals** Based on your reading, label the four distinct layers of the tropical rain forest in the boxes above.

FIGURE 4 ·····························

Grasslands

The rhea, cassowary, and ostrich are grassland birds that live on different continents.

✎ **Interpret Maps** On the world map, identify the continents in which these three birds are located. List three characteristics that these grassland birds all share.

_____

_____

_____

_____

Grassland Biomes The third stop on the expedition is a grassy plain called a prairie. Temperatures are more comfortable here than they were in the desert. The breeze carries the scent of soil warmed by the sun. This rich soil supports grasses as tall as you. Startled by your approach, sparrows dart into hiding places among the waving grass stems.

Although the prairie receives more rain than a desert, you may notice only a few scattered areas of trees and shrubs. Ecologists classify prairies, which are generally found in the middle latitudes, as grasslands. A **grassland** is an area that is populated mostly by grasses and other nonwoody plants. Most grasslands receive 25 to 75 centimeters of rain each year. Fires and droughts are common in this biome. Grasslands that are located closer to the equator than prairies are known as savannas. A **savanna** receives as much as 120 centimeters of rain each year. Scattered shrubs and small trees grow on savannas, along with grass.

Grasslands are home to many of the largest animals on Earth— herbivores such as elephants, bison, antelopes, zebras, giraffes, kangaroos, and rhinoceroses. Grazing by these large herbivores maintains the grasslands. Their grazing keeps young trees and bushes from sprouting and competing with the grass for water and sunlight. You can see some grassland birds in **Figure 4**.

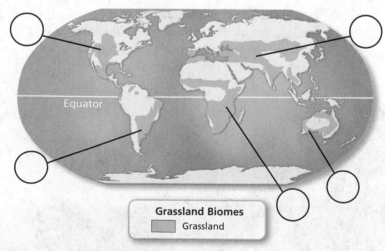

Equator

Grassland Biomes
Grassland

Deciduous Forest Biomes Your trip to the fourth biome takes you to another forest. It is now late summer. Cool mornings here give way to warm days. Several members of the expedition are busy recording the numerous plant species. Others are looking through binoculars, trying to identify the songbirds.

You are now visiting a deciduous forest biome. Many of the trees in this forest are **deciduous trees** (dee SIJ oo us), trees that shed their leaves and grow new ones each year. Oaks and maples are examples of deciduous trees. Deciduous forests receive enough rain to support the growth of trees and other plants, at least 50 centimeters of rain per year. Temperatures can vary greatly during the year. The growing season usually lasts five to six months.

The variety of plants in a deciduous forest creates many different habitats. Many species of birds live in different parts of the forest, eating the insects and fruits in their specific areas. Mammals such as chipmunks and skunks live in deciduous forests. In a North American deciduous forest you might also see wood thrushes and white-tailed deer.

If you were to return to this biome in the winter, you would not see much wildlife. Many of the bird species migrate, or fly great distances, to warmer areas. Some of the mammals hibernate, or enter a state of greatly reduced body activity similar to sleep. Look at **Figure 5.** During the winter months, animals that hibernate get energy from fat stored in their bodies.

did you know?

How far would you be willing to migrate? The bobolink has one of the longest songbird migration routes. The birds travel south from southern Canada and the northern United States to northern Argentina. This migration route is approximately 20,000 kilometers round trip!

Equator

Deciduous Forest Biomes
Deciduous forest

FIGURE 5 ·······················

Deciduous Forest

Most of the trees in a deciduous forest have leaves that change color and drop to the forest floor each autumn. In the leaves, this dormouse hibernates through the winter.

✎ **Infer** Is hibernation an adaptation to life in a deciduous forest? Explain your answer.

_____

_____

_____

_____

_____

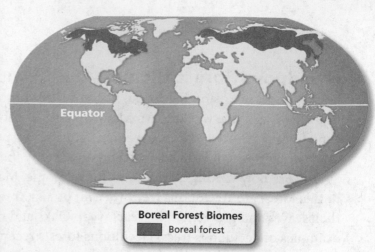

Boreal Forest Biomes

Boreal forest

FIGURE 6 ....

Boreal Forest

✎ This lynx and snowshoe hare are adapted to life in the boreal forest.

1. Infer Choose the best answer. The feet of each animal are an adaptation to its

○ food.   ○ climate.

○ predators.   ○ all of the above

2. Explain Defend your answer.

_____

_____

_____

_____

_____

Boreal Forest Biomes Now the expedition heads north to a colder biome, the boreal forest. The term *boreal* means "northern," and **boreal forests** are dense forests found in upper regions of the Northern Hemisphere. The expedition leaders claim they can identify a boreal forest by its smell. When you arrive, you catch a whiff of the spruce and fir trees that blanket the hillsides. Feeling the chilly early fall air, you pull a jacket and hat out of your bag.

Boreal Forest Plants Most of the trees in the boreal forest are **coniferous trees** (koh NIF ur us), trees that produce their seeds in cones and have leaves shaped like needles. The boreal forest is sometimes referred to by its Russian name, the *taiga* (TY guh). Winters in these forests are very cold. The snow can reach heights well over your head! Even so, the summers are rainy and warm enough to melt all the snow.

Tree species in the boreal forest are well adapted to the cold climate. Since water is frozen for much of the year, trees must have adaptations that prevent water loss. Coniferous trees, such as firs and hemlocks, all have thick, waxy needles that prevent water from evaporating.

Boreal Forest Animals Many of the animals of the boreal forest eat the seeds produced by the coniferous trees. These animals include red squirrels, insects, and birds such as finches. Some herbivores, such as moose and beavers, eat tree bark and new shoots. The variety of herbivores in the boreal forest supports many predators, including lynx, otters, and great horned owls. **Figure 6** shows an herbivore and its predator.

Tundra Biomes As you arrive at your last stop, the driving wind gives you an immediate feel for this biome. The **tundra** is extremely cold and dry. Expecting deep snow, many are surprised to learn that the tundra may receive no more precipitation than a desert.

Most of the soil in the tundra is frozen all year. This frozen soil is called **permafrost.** During the short summer, the top layer of soil thaws, but the underlying soil remains frozen. Because rainwater cannot soak into the permafrost, shallow ponds and marshy areas appear in the summer.

Tundra Plants Mosses, grasses, and dwarf forms of a few trees can be found in the tundra. Most of the plant growth takes place during the long days of the short summer season. North of the Arctic Circle, the sun does not set during midsummer.

Tundra Animals In summer, the insects are abundant. Insect-eating birds take advantage of the plentiful food by eating as much as they can. But when winter approaches, these birds migrate south. Mammals of the tundra include caribou, foxes, and wolves. The mammals that remain on the tundra during the winter grow thick fur coats. What can these animals find to eat on the tundra in winter? The caribou scrape snow away to find lichens. Wolves follow the caribou and look for weak members of the herd to prey upon.

FIGURE 7

Tundra
Although the ground is frozen for most of the year, mosses, grasses, and dwarf willow trees grow here.

✎ **Communicate** Discuss with a partner why there are no tall trees on the tundra. Describe two factors that you think may influence tree growth.

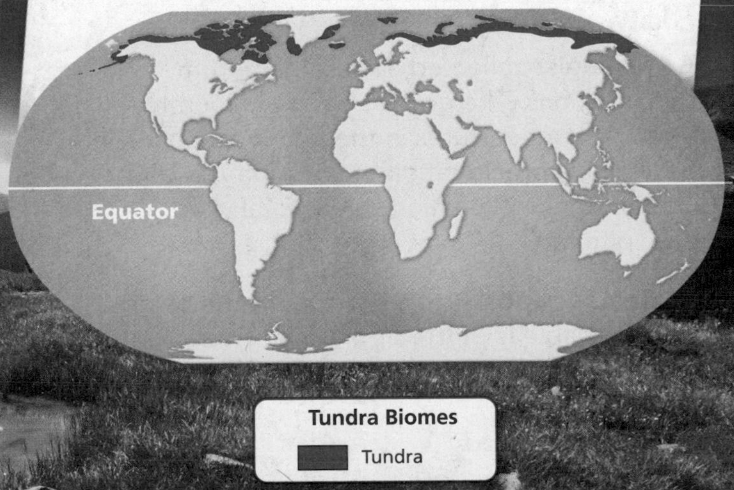

_____

_____

_____

_____

_____

_____

_____

_____

Equator

Tundra Biomes

Tundra

Mountains and Ice Legend
- Mountains
- Ice

Equator

FIGURE 8 ·······························

> **INTERACTIVE ART** **Mountains**
Mountains are not part of any major biome.

Mountains and Ice Some land areas are not classified as biomes. Recall that biomes are defined by abiotic factors such as climate and soil, and by biotic factors such as plant and animal life. Because the organisms that live in these areas vary, mountain ranges and land covered with thick ice sheets are not considered biomes.

The climate of a mountain changes from its base to its summit. If you were to hike all the way up a tall mountain, you would pass through a series of biomes. At the base, you might find grasslands. As you climbed, you might pass through deciduous forest and then boreal forest. As you neared the top, your surroundings would resemble the cold, dry tundra.

Other places are covered year-round with thick ice sheets. Most of Greenland and Antarctica fall into this category. Organisms that are adapted to life on ice include leopard seals and polar bears.

do the math!

Biome Climates

An ecologist collected climate data from two locations. The graph shows the monthly average temperatures in the two locations. The total yearly precipitation in Location A is 250 centimeters. In Location B, the total yearly precipitation is 14 centimeters.

① **Read Graphs** Provide a title for the graph. What variable is plotted on the horizontal axis? On the vertical axis?

_____

② **Interpret Data** Study the graph. How would you describe the temperature over the course of a year in Location A? In Location B?

_____

_____

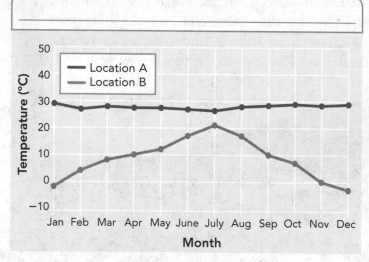

③ **Draw Conclusions** Given the precipitation and temperature data for these locations, in which biome would you expect each to be located?

_____

_____

_____

apply it!

Key of Earth Biomes
- ☐ Desert
- ☐ Temperate rain forest
- ☐ Tropical rain forest
- ☐ Grassland
- ☐ Deciduous rain forest
- ☐ Boreal forest
- ☐ Tundra

❶ Interpret Maps Using the colors shown in the biome maps throughout this lesson, color in the key above. Use the key to color in the areas on the map of North America.

❷ Draw Conclusions Where are most of the boreal forests located? Why are there no boreal forests in the Southern Hemisphere?

_____

_____

_____

_____

_____

❸ Describe Mark the area in which you live with an X on the map. What is the climate like where you live? How do you think your climate affects which organisms live there?

_____

_____

_____

_____

_____

_____

_____

Lab zone® Do the Quick Lab
Inferring Forest Climates.

⚷ Assess Your Understanding

1a. Review _____ and

_____ are the two

main factors that determine an area's biome.

b. Infer What biome might you be in if you were standing on a bitterly cold, dry plain with only a few, short trees scattered around?

_____

got it? ....

○ **I get it!** Now I know that the six major biomes are _____

_____

○ **I need extra help with** _____

    Go to MY SCIENCE ⓢ COACH *online for help with this subject.*

Aquatic Ecosystems

🔑 **What Are the Two Major Aquatic Ecosystems?**

my planeT DiaRY

TECHNOLOGY

Underwater *Alvin*

Meet *Alvin*, an HOV (Human-Occupied Vehicle). Equipped with propulsion jets, cameras, and robotic arms, *Alvin* helps scientists gather data and discover ecosystems that exist deep in the ocean. Built in 1964, *Alvin* was one of the world's first deep-ocean submersibles and has made more than 4,500 dives. *Alvin* is credited with finding a lost hydrogen bomb, exploring the first known hydrothermal vents, and surveying the wreck of the *Titanic*.

Calculate Suppose that on each of the 4,500 dives *Alvin* has made, a new pilot and two new scientists were on board. How many scientists have seen the deep ocean through *Alvin's* windows? How many people, in total, traveled in *Alvin*?

_____

_____

▶ **PLANET DIARY** Go to **Planet Diary** to learn more about aquatic ecosystems.

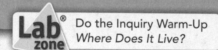

Lab zone® Do the Inquiry Warm-Up *Where Does It Live?*

What Are the Two Major Aquatic Ecosystems?

Since almost three quarters of Earth's surface is covered with water, many living things make their homes in and near water. 🔑 **There are two types of aquatic, or water-based, ecosystems: freshwater ecosystems and marine (or saltwater) ecosystems.** All aquatic ecosystems are affected by the same abiotic, or nonliving, factors: sunlight, temperature, oxygen, and salt content. Sunlight is an important factor in aquatic ecosystems because it is necessary for photosynthesis in the water just as it is on land. Half of all oxygen produced on Earth comes from floating algae called phytoplankton. Because water absorbs sunlight, there is only enough light for photosynthesis to occur near the surface or in shallow water.

Vocabulary
- estuary • intertidal zone
- neritic zone

Skills
- Reading: Outline
- Inquiry: Communicate

Freshwater Ecosystems No worldwide expedition would be complete without exploring Earth's waters. Even though most of Earth's surface is covered with water, only 3 percent of the volume is fresh water. Freshwater ecosystems include streams, rivers, ponds, and lakes. On this part of your expedition, you'll find that freshwater biomes provide habitats for a variety of organisms.

Streams and Rivers At the source of a mountain stream, the water flows slowly. Plants take root on the bottom, providing food for insects and homes for frogs. These consumers then provide food for larger consumers. Stream currents increase as streams come together to make larger streams, often called rivers. Animals here are adapted to strong currents. For example, trout have streamlined bodies to swim in the rushing water. As the current speeds up, it can become cloudy with sediment. Few plants or algae grow in this fast-moving water. Consumers such as snails feed on leaves and seeds that fall into the stream. At lower elevations, streams are warmer and often contain less oxygen, affecting the organisms that can live in them.

Ponds and Lakes Ponds and lakes are bodies of still, or standing, fresh water. Lakes are generally larger and deeper than ponds. Ponds are often shallow enough that sunlight can reach the bottom, allowing plants to grow there. In large ponds and most lakes, however, algae floating at the surface are the major producers. Many animals are adapted for life in still water. Dragonflies, snails, and frogs live along the shores of ponds. In the open water, sunfish feed on insects and algae close to the surface. Scavengers such as catfish live near the bottoms of ponds. Bacteria and other decomposers also feed on the remains of other organisms.

Outline As you read, make an outline on a separate sheet of paper that includes the different types of aquatic ecosystems. Use the red headings for the main ideas and the black headings for the supporting details.

FIGURE 1
Freshwater Ecosystems
Water lilies live in ponds and lakes.
Answer the questions.

1. **Identify** What are two abiotic factors that can affect water lilies?

_____

_____

_____

2. **CHALLENGE** What adaptations do fish have that allow them to live in water?

_____

_____

_____

_____

657

High tide

Low tide

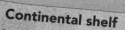

Continental shelf

Marine Ecosystems

The expedition now heads to the coast to explore some marine biomes. On your way, you'll pass through an estuary. An **estuary** (ES choo ehr ee), is found where the fresh water of a river meets the salt water of an ocean. Algae and plants provide food and shelter for animals, including crabs and fish. Many animals use the calm waters of estuaries for breeding grounds. Last, you explore the different ocean zones as described in **Figure 2**.

Ocean Zones		
Zone	**Location**	**Inhabitants**
Intertidal zone	Located on the shore between the highest high-tide line and the lowest low-tide line	Organisms must be able to survive pounding waves and the sudden changes in water levels and temperature that occur with high and low tides. For example, barnacles and sea stars cling to the rocks while clams and crabs burrow in the sand.
Neritic zone	Region of shallow water found below the low-tide line and extending over the continental shelf	Sunlight passes through shallow water, allowing photosynthesis to occur. Many living things, such as algae and schools of fish, live here. Coral reefs can also be found here in warmer waters.
Surface zone, open ocean	Located beyond the neritic zone and extending from the water's surface to about 200 meters deep	Sunlight penetrates this zone, allowing photosynthesis to occur in floating phytoplankton and other algae. Tuna, swordfish, and some whales depend on the algae for food.
Deep zone, open ocean	Located beneath the surface zone to the ocean floor	Little, if any, sunlight passes through. Animals feed on the remains of organisms that sink down. Organisms, like the giant squid and anglerfish, are adapted to life in the dark.

FIGURE 2 ·······················

Marine Ecosystems

The ocean is home to a number of different ecosystems.

✎ **Classify** Using the clues, determine at which depth each organism belongs. In the circles in the ocean, write the letter for each organism in the correct zone.

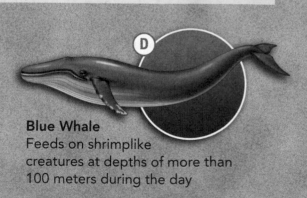

C

D

Yellowfin Tuna
Found in open waters and has been known to eat squid

Blue Whale
Feeds on shrimplike creatures at depths of more than 100 meters during the day

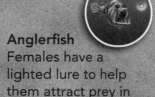

A

Anglerfish
Females have a lighted lure to help them attract prey in the dark.

B

Tripod Fish
This fish has three elongated fins to help it stand.

E

Swordfish
Often seen jumping out of the water to stun smaller fish

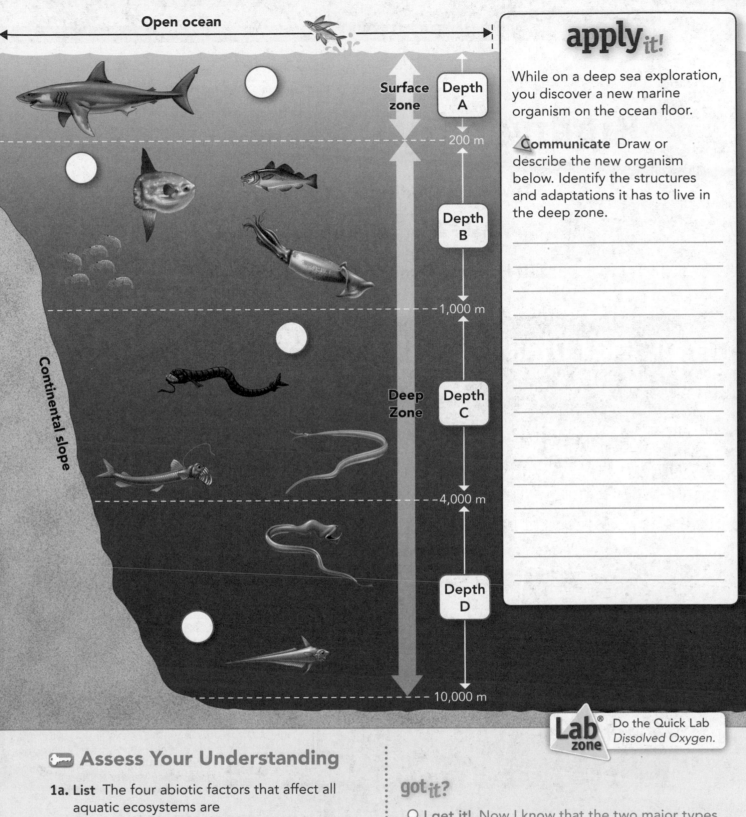

Open ocean

Surface zone

Depth A

200 m

Depth B

1,000 m

Deep Zone

Depth C

4,000 m

Depth D

10,000 m

Continental slope

apply it!

While on a deep sea exploration, you discover a new marine organism on the ocean floor.

Communicate Draw or describe the new organism below. Identify the structures and adaptations it has to live in the deep zone.

_____

_____

_____

_____

_____

_____

_____

_____

_____

_____

_____

_____

_____

_____

Lab zone Do the Quick Lab *Dissolved Oxygen.*

🔑 Assess Your Understanding

1a. List The four abiotic factors that affect all aquatic ecosystems are

_____

_____

b. Make Generalizations Why is sunlight important to all aquatic ecosystems?

_____

_____

got it?

○ **I get it!** Now I know that the two major types of aquatic ecosystems are _____

_____

○ **I need extra help with** _____

_____

Go to **MY SCIENCE COACH** *online for help with this subject.*

Biodiversity

UNLOCK THE BIG Q?

🔑 **What Is Biodiversity's Value?**

🔑 **What Factors Affect Biodiversity?**

🔑 **How Do Humans Affect Biodiversity?**

MY PLANET DIARY

BLOG

Posted by: Max

Location: Hagerstown, Maryland

I went to summer camp to learn about wildlife and how to protect it. One of the activities that I liked the most was making "bat boxes." These are wooden homes for brown bats, which often need places to nest. Making these houses is important, because without brown bats, there would be too many mosquitoes. I hope the bats like their new homes as much as I loved making them.

Communicate Discuss the question with a group of classmates. Then write your answers below.

How do you think helping the bats in an area helps other species nearby?

_____

_____

_____

_____

_____

_____

_____

▶ PLANET DIARY Go to **Planet Diary** to learn more about biodiversity.

Lab zone Do the Inquiry Warm-Up *How Much Variety Is There?*

What Is Biodiversity's Value?

No one knows exactly how many species live on Earth. As you can see in **Figure 1,** scientists have identified more than 1.6 million species so far. The number of different species in an area is called the area's **biodiversity.** It is difficult to estimate the total biodiversity on Earth because many areas have not been thoroughly studied.

Vocabulary

- biodiversity
- keystone species
- gene
- extinction
- endangered species
- threatened species
- habitat destruction
- habitat fragmentation
- poaching
- captive breeding

Skills

↻ Reading: Compare and Contrast

△ Inquiry: Infer

There are many reasons why preserving biodiversity is important. One reason to preserve biodiversity is that wild organisms and ecosystems are a source of beauty and recreation. ⚷ **In addition, biodiversity has both economic value and ecological value within an ecosystem.**

Economic Value Many plants, animals, and other organisms are economically valuable for humans. These organisms provide people with food and supply raw materials for clothing, medicine, and other products. No one knows how many other useful species have not yet been identified. Ecosystems are economically valuable, too. Many companies now run wildlife tours to rain forests, savannas, mountains, and other places. This ecosystem tourism, or ecotourism, is an important source of jobs and money for such nations as Brazil, Costa Rica, and Kenya.

Ecological Value All the species in an ecosystem are connected to one another. Species may depend on each other for food and shelter. A change that affects one species can affect all the others.

Some species play a particularly important role in their ecosystems. A **keystone species** is a species that influences the survival of many other species in an ecosystem. Sea otters, as shown in **Figure 2,** are one example of a keystone species.

FIGURE 1 ·····························

Species Diversity

There are many more species of insects than plant or other animal species on Earth!

✎ **Calculate** What percentage of species shown on the pie graph do insects represent? Round your answer to the nearest tenth.

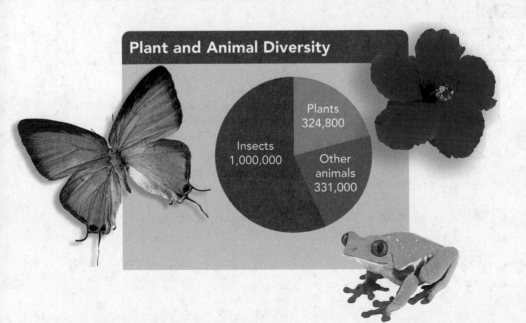

Plant and Animal Diversity

Plants 324,800

Insects 1,000,000

Other animals 331,000

FIGURE 2 ·············

Keystone Otters

Sea otters are a keystone species in the kelp forest ecosystem.

✏️ **Describe** Read the comic. In the empty panel, draw or explain what happened to the kelp forest when the otters returned. Write a caption for your panel.

The sea otter is a keystone species in a kelp forest ecosystem.

In the 1800s, many otters were killed for their fur.

Without otters preying on them, the population of kelp-eating sea urchins exploded, destroying kelp forests.

Under new laws that banned the hunting of sea otters, the sea otter population grew again.

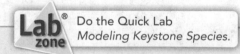

Do the Quick Lab
Modeling Keystone Species.

🔑 Assess Your Understanding

got it? ···

○ **I get it!** Now I know that biodiversity has _____

○ **I need extra help with** _____

　Go to **MY SCIENCE** 🟤 **COACH** online for help with this subject.

What Factors Affect Biodiversity?

Biodiversity varies from place to place on Earth. **Factors that affect biodiversity in an ecosystem include climate, area, niche diversity, genetic diversity, and extinction.**

Climate The tropical rain forests of Latin America, southeast Asia, and central Africa are the most diverse ecosystems in the world. The reason for the great biodiversity in the tropics is not fully understood. Many scientists hypothesize that it has to do with climate. For example, tropical rain forests have fairly constant temperatures and large amounts of rainfall throughout the year. Many plants grow year-round. This continuous growing season means that food is always available for other organisms.

Area See **Figure 3**. Within an ecosystem, a large area will usually contain more species than a small area. For example, you would usually find more species in a 100-square-meter area than in a 10-square-meter area.

did you know? ....

Rain forests cover only about seven percent of the Earth's land surface. But they contain more than half of the world's species, including the chimpanzee!

FIGURE 3 ·······················
Park Size
A park manager has received three park plans. The dark green area represents the park.

10 m
10 m

✎ **Complete each task.**

1. **Identify** Circle the plan the manager should choose to support the most biodiversity.

2. **Calculate** Suppose that 15 square meters of the park could support seven species of large mammals. About how many species could the park you circled support?

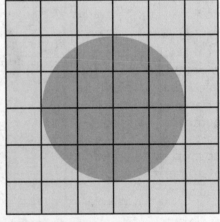

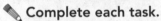

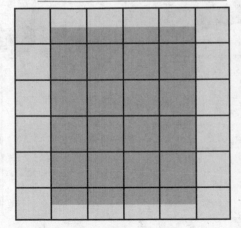

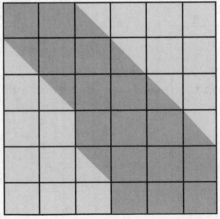

Niche Diversity Coral reefs are the second most diverse ecosystems in the world. Found only in shallow, warm waters, coral reefs are often called the rain forests of the sea. A coral reef supports many different niches. Recall that a niche is the role of an organism in its habitat, or how it makes its living. A coral reef enables a greater number of species to live in it than a more uniform habitat, such as a flat sandbar, does.

Genetic Diversity Diversity is very important within a species. The greatest genetic diversity exists among species of unicellular organisms. Organisms in a healthy population have diverse traits such as color and size. **Genes** are located within cells and carry the hereditary information that determines an organism's traits. Organisms inherit genes from their parents.

The organisms in one species share many genes. But each organism also has some genes that differ from those of other individuals. Both the shared genes and the genes that differ among individuals make up the total gene pool of that species. Species that lack a diverse gene pool are less able to adapt to and survive changes in the environment.

apply it!

New potato plants are created from pieces of the parent plant. So a potato crop has the same genetic makeup as the parent plant. In 1845, Ireland was struck by a potato famine. A rot-causing fungus destroyed potato crops, which were an important part of the Irish diet. Many people died of starvation, and many more left the country to find food.

❶ **Apply Concepts** How did a potato crop without a variety of different genes lead to the Irish potato famine of 1845?

_____

_____

_____

_____

❷ [CHALLENGE] What could farmers do to prevent another potato famine?

_____

_____

_____

_____

Extinction of Species The disappearance of all members of a species from Earth is called **extinction.** Extinction is a natural process that occurs when organisms do not adapt to changes in their environment. In the last few centuries, the number of species becoming extinct has increased dramatically. Once a population drops below a certain level, the species may not recover. People have directly caused the extinction of many species through habitat destruction, hunting, or other actions.

Species in danger of becoming extinct in the near future are called **endangered species.** Species that could become endangered in the near future are called **threatened species.** Endangered and threatened species are found on every continent and in every ocean.

Green sea turtle ▲

FIGURE 4 ·····································

Endangered Species

Large animals, like the green sea turtle, are the most publicized endangered species. Did you know insects and plants can also be endangered? ✏️ ◢**Infer** **Why do you think some endangered species get more attention than others?**

_____

_____

_____

_____

_____

Blackburn's ▲
sphinx moth

Hawaiian alula ▲

Lab zone® Do the Quick Lab
Grocery Gene Pool.

🔑 **Assess Your Understanding**

1a. Review A (smaller/larger) area will contain more species than a (smaller/larger) area.

b. Explain How is biodiversity related to niches?

_____

_____

_____

c. 🔄 **Compare and Contrast** What is the difference between an endangered species and a threatened species?

_____

_____

_____

got it? ···

○ **I get it!** Now I know that the factors that affect biodiversity include _____

_____

○ I need extra help with _____

Go to **MY SCIENCE** ⓢ **COACH** online for help with this subject.

How Do Humans Affect Biodiversity?

Humans interact with their surroundings every day. The many choices people make impact the environment and affect species. 🔑 **Biodiversity can be negatively or positively affected by the actions of humans.**

Damaging Biodiversity A natural event, such as a hurricane, can damage an ecosystem, wiping out populations or even entire species. Human activities can also threaten biodiversity and cause extinction. These activities include habitat destruction, poaching, pollution, and the introduction of exotic species.

Habitat Destruction The major cause of extinction is **habitat destruction,** the loss of a natural habitat. Clearing forests or filling in wetlands changes those ecosystems. Breaking larger habitats into smaller, isolated pieces, or fragments, is called **habitat fragmentation.** See **Figure 5.** Some species may not survive such changes to their habitats.

Poaching The illegal killing or removal of wildlife from their habitats is called **poaching.** Some endangered species are valuable to poachers. Animals can be sold as pets or used to make jewelry, coats, belts, or shoes. Plants can be sold as houseplants or used to make medicines.

Pollution Some species are endangered because of pollution. Pollution may reach animals through the water they drink, the air they breathe, or the food they eat. Pollutants may kill or weaken organisms or cause birth defects.

Exotic Species Introducing exotic species into an ecosystem can threaten biodiversity. Exotic species can outcompete and damage native species. The gypsy moth was introduced into the United States in 1869 to increase silk production. Gypsy moth larvae have eaten the leaves off of millions of acres of trees in the northeastern United States.

FIGURE 5 ··

Habitat Fragmentation

Breaking habitats into pieces can have negative effects on the species that live there.

✏️ **Interpret Diagrams** In the first diagram below, a road divides a habitat in two. On the second diagram, redraw the road so it divides the habitat's resources equally.

Protecting Biodiversity

Some people who preserve biodiversity focus on protecting individual endangered species. Others try to protect entire ecosystems. Three methods of protecting biodiversity are captive breeding, laws and treaties, and habitat preservation.

Captive Breeding **Captive breeding** is the mating of animals in zoos or on wildlife preserves. Scientists care for the young, and then release them into the wild. Much of the sandhill crane habitat in the United States has been destroyed. To help the population, some cranes have been taken into captivity. The young are raised and trained by volunteers to learn the correct behaviors, such as knowing how and where to migrate. They are then released into the wild.

✎ Compare and Contrast
The photos on top show young sandhill cranes being raised by their parents. The photos on the bottom show humans copying this process to increase the crane population. What is a possible disadvantage of the human approach?

_____

_____

_____

_____

Life in a Coral Reef

How do natural and human activities change ecosystems?

FIGURE 6 ···

▷ VIRTUAL LAB This photo shows the diversity of the organisms in a coral reef ecosystem. The coral and sponges provide living space for algae and shelter for crabs, fishes, and other animals. Some fishes eat the algae.

✎ Predict Answer the questions in the boxes.

Suppose many more orange fish immigrate to this ecosystem, doubling the species' population. How might the increased numbers of orange fish impact other populations in the ecosystem? Explain.

_____

_____

_____

Laws and Treaties In the United States, the Endangered Species Act prohibits trade of products made from threatened or endangered species. This law also requires the development of plans to save endangered species. The Convention on International Trade in Endangered Species is an international treaty that lists more than 800 threatened and endangered species that cannot be traded for profit or other reasons anywhere in the world.

Habitat Preservation The most effective way to preserve biodiversity is to protect whole ecosystems. Protecting whole ecosystems saves endangered species, the species they depend upon, and those that depend upon them. Many countries have set aside wildlife habitats as parks and refuges. Today, there are about 7,000 nature parks, preserves, and refuges in the world.

Suppose people start to overfish this area. How might this change the ecosystem? Explain.

_____
_____
_____
_____
_____

Suppose a tsunami, a huge ocean wave, were to hit this ecosystem, destroying much of the reef. Do you think the ecosystem would come back after the tsunami? Explain.

_____
_____
_____
_____
_____
_____
_____

Lab® Do the Quick Lab
zone Humans and Biodiversity.

Assess Your Understanding

2a. Define What is poaching?

_____
_____
_____
_____

b. How do natural and human activities change ecosystems?

_____
_____
_____
_____

got it? ....

○ I get it! Now I know that humans affect biodiversity_____
_____

○ I need extra help with _____

Go to MY SCIENCE ⓢ COACH online for help with this subject.

16 Study Guide

Producers, _____, and _____ help to cycle energy through ecosystems.

LESSON 1 **Energy Flow in Ecosystems**

🔑 Each of the organisms in an ecosystem fills the energy role of producer, consumer, or decomposer.

🔑 Energy moves through an ecosystem when one organism eats another.

🔑 The most energy is available at the producer level of the pyramid. As energy moves up the pyramid, each level has less energy available than the level below.

Vocabulary
• producer • consumer • herbivore • carnivore
• omnivore • scavenger • decomposer • food chain • food web • energy pyramid

LESSON 2 **Cycles of Matter**

🔑 The processes of evaporation, condensation, and precipitation make up the water cycle.

🔑 The processes by which carbon and oxygen are recycled are linked. Producers, consumers, and decomposers play roles in recycling both.

🔑 Nitrogen moves from the air into the soil, into living things, and back into the air or soil.

Vocabulary
• evaporation • condensation
• precipitation • nitrogen fixation

LESSON 3 **Biomes**

🔑 The six major biomes are desert, rain forest, grassland, deciduous forest, boreal forest, and tundra.

Vocabulary
• biome • climate • desert • rain forest
• emergent layer • canopy • understory
• grassland • savanna • deciduous tree
• boreal forest • coniferous tree • tundra
• permafrost

LESSON 4 **Aquatic Ecosystems**

🔑 There are two types of aquatic, or water-based, ecosystems: freshwater ecosystems and marine (or saltwater) ecosystems.

Vocabulary
• estuary
• intertidal zone
• neritic zone

LESSON 5 **Biodiversity**

🔑 Biodiversity has both economic value and ecological value within an ecosystem.

🔑 Factors that affect biodiversity in an ecosystem include climate, area, niche diversity, genetic diversity, and extinction.

🔑 Biodiversity can be negatively or positively affected by the actions of humans.

Vocabulary
• biodiversity • keystone species • gene
• extinction • endangered species
• threatened species • habitat destruction • habitat fragmentation • poaching • captive breeding

Review and Assessment

LESSON 1 **Energy Flow in Ecosystems**

1. A diagram that shows how much energy is available at each feeding level in an ecosystem is a(n)

  a. food web.   **b.** food chain.

  c. water cycle.   **d.** energy pyramid.

2. A(n) _____ is a consumer that eats only plants.

3. Interpret Diagrams Which organisms in the illustration are producers? Consumers?

_____

_____

_____

_____

_____

_____

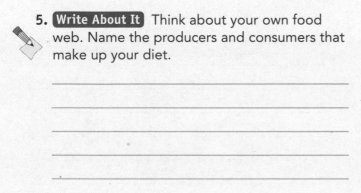

4. Compare and Contrast How are food chains and food webs different?

_____

_____

_____

5. **Write About It** Think about your own food web. Name the producers and consumers that make up your diet.

_____

_____

_____

_____

_____

_____

LESSON 2 **Cycles of Matter**

6. When drops of water in a cloud become heavy enough, they fall to Earth as

  a. permafrost.   **b.** evaporation.

  c. precipitation.   **d.** condensation.

7. Evaporation, condensation, and precipitation are the three main processes in the

_____

_____

8. Infer Which process is responsible for the droplets visible on the glass below? Explain.

_____

_____

_____

_____

9. Classify Which group of organisms is the source of oxygen in the oxygen cycle? Explain.

_____

_____

10. Make Generalizations Describe the roles of producers and consumers in the carbon cycle.

_____

_____

_____

_____

_____

_____

11. Draw Conclusions What would happen if all the nitrogen-fixing bacteria disappeared?

_____

_____

_____

_____

671

16 Review and Assessment

Biomes

12. Little precipitation and extreme temperatures are main characteristics of which biome?

   a. desert   **b.** grassland

   c. boreal forest   **d.** deciduous forest

13. A _____ is a group of ecosystems with similar climates and organisms.

14. Compare and Contrast How are the tundra and desert similar? How are they different?

_____

_____

_____

_____

_____

_____

Aquatic Ecosystems

15. In which ocean zone would you find barnacles, sea stars, and other organisms tightly attached to rocks?

   a. neritic zone   **b.** intertidal zone

   c. estuary ecosystem **d.** freshwater ecosystem

16. Coral reefs are found in the shallow, sunny waters of the _____.

17. Compare and Contrast How are a pond and lake similar? How do they differ?

_____

_____

_____

_____

_____

_____

Biodiversity

18. The most effective way to preserve biodiversity is through

   a. captive breeding

   b. habitat destruction

   c. habitat preservation

   d. habitat fragmentation

19. _____ occurs when all members of a species disappear from Earth.

20. Predict How could the extinction of a species today affect your life in 20 years?

_____

_____

_____

_____

APPLY THE BIG ?

How do energy and matter cycle through ecosystems?

21. Many acres of the Amazon rain forest have been destroyed to create farmland. Describe how the amount of energy in the food web for this area might be affected. How might the carbon and oxygen cycle also be affected?

_____

_____

_____

_____

_____

_____

_____

_____

_____

_____

_____

Standardized Test Prep

Multiple Choice

Circle the letter of the best answer.

1. At which level of this energy pyramid is the *least* energy available?

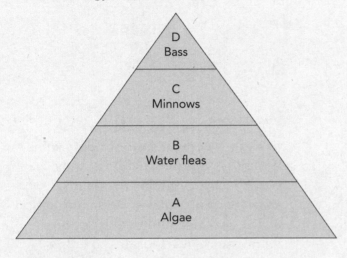

A Level A		**B** Level B	
C Level C		**D** Level D	

2. You are in an area in Maryland where the fresh water of the Chesapeake Bay meets the Atlantic Ocean. Which of the following terms describes where you are?

A tundra	**B** estuary
C neritic zone	**D** intertidal zone

3. Which pair of terms could apply to the same organism?

A carnivore and producer

B consumer and carnivore

C scavenger and herbivore

D producer and omnivore

4. Which of the following terms describes a species that is in danger of becoming extinct in the near future?

A captive species

B keystone species

C endangered species

D threatened species

5. Which of the following human activities has a positive impact on Earth's ecosystems?

A habitat fragmentation

B urban growth

C soil monitoring

D landfill development

Constructed Response

Use the diagram below and your knowledge of science to help you answer Question 6. Write your answer on a separate piece of paper.

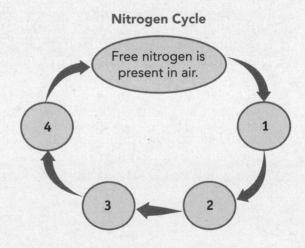

Nitrogen Cycle

6. Describe each numbered part of the cycle shown in the diagram above.

A Lake Can't last forever

Much like living things, lakes change over time and even have life spans. Scientists call this change "lake succession". One way this occurs is through eutrophication.

Eutrophication refers to the addition of nutrients to bodies of water. It occurs naturally, but human activity can speed up the process. Nutrients—especially phosphorus and nitrogen—are necessary for algae and plants to grow in lakes. However, too many nutrients, such as those from fertilizers and sewage, can lead to excessive algae growth or "blooms."

These blooms often kill plant and animal life by upsetting the oxygen and carbon dioxide cycles. Decomposers, such as bacteria, feed off the algae, using up dissolved oxygen in the water in the process. This limits the amount and kinds of aquatic life that can live there.

Over many years, a lake becomes shallower when it fills with dying plant and animal matter. Material also builds up from outside the lake. The lake becomes a marsh that, over time, turns into dry land.

Research It With your classmates, analyze a body of water to determine its ability to support life. To study biotic factors, obtain and identify samples of organisms. Find information about how to count the kinds and numbers of invertebrates to judge pollution levels. Then look at abiotic factors. Use thermometers, probeware, and water chemistry kits to determine temperature, dissolved oxygen, and pH levels. Research information about how these factors affect the survival of organisms. Compile findings in a table and graph data. Pass records on to future classes to interpret and predict changes over time.

Trees: Environmental Factories

Some of the most important members of your community don't volunteer. They consume huge amounts of water and they make a mess. Despite these drawbacks, these long-standing community members do their share. Who are these individuals? They're trees!

Keeping it clean: Trees remove pollutants from the air. Some researchers have calculated the value of the environmental cleaning services that trees provide. One study valued the air-cleaning service that trees in the Chicago area provide at more than $9 million every year.

Keeping it cool: Trees provide shade and lower air temperature by the process of transpiration. Pollutants, like ozone and smog, form more easily when air temperatures are high, so by keeping the air cool, trees also keep it clean.

Acting locally and globally: Trees help fight global environmental problems such as climate change. Trees remove carbon dioxide from the air and store the carbon as they grow. Experts estimate that urban trees in the United States remove more than 700 million tons of carbon from the air every year.

Helping the local economy: Trees are also good for business. One study found that shoppers spend more money in urban areas where trees are planted than they do in similar areas that don't have trees!

Schools, clubs, and civic groups all over the United States volunteer to plant trees in their communities. ▶

Research It Examine a topographical map of the area where you live. Compare it to an aerial photograph from a library or local archive. Identify areas with a lot of trees, and areas that you think could benefit from more trees. Create a proposal to plant trees in one of the areas you identified. What kinds of trees will you plant? What do those trees need in order to grow well?

GLOSSARY

A

abiotic factor A nonliving part of an organism's habitat. (594)
factor abiótico La parte sin vida del hábitat de un organismo.

absorption **1.** The process by which nutrient molecules pass through the wall of the digestive system into the blood. (419) **2.** The process by which an object takes in, or absorbs, light.
absorción **1.** Proceso en el cual las moléculas de nutrientes pasan a la sangre a través de las paredes del sistema digestivo. **2.** Proceso en el cual un objeto recibe, o absorbe, luz.

active immunity Immunity that occurs when a person's own immune system produces antibodies in response to the presence of a pathogen. (569)
inmunidad activa Inmunidad que ocurre cuando el sistema inmunológico de una persona produce anticuerpos en respuesta a la presencia de un patógeno.

active transport The movement of materials across a cell membrane using cellular energy. (68)
transporte activo Proceso que usa la energía celular para mover materiales a través de la membrana celular.

adaptation An inherited behavior or physical characteristic that helps an organism survive and reproduce in its environment. (185, 309, 607)
adaptación Comportamiento o característica física hereditaria que le permite a un organismo sobrevivir y reproducirse en su ambiente.

AIDS (acquired immunodeficiency syndrome) A disease caused by a virus that attacks the immune system. (565)
SIDA (síndrome de inmunodeficiencia adquirida) Enfermedad causada por un virus que ataca el sistema inmunológico.

algae Plantlike protists. (231)
algas Protistas con características vegetales.

alleles The different forms of a gene. (113)
alelos Diferentes formas de un gen.

allergen A substance that causes an allergy. (576)
alérgeno Sustancia que causa la alergia.

allergy A disorder in which the immune system is overly sensitive to a foreign substance. (576)
alergia Trastorno fisiológico en el cual el sistema inmunológico es extremadamente sensible a sustancias externas.

alveoli Tiny sacs of lung tissue specialized for the movement of gases between air and blood. (480)

alvéolos Sacos diminutos de tejido pulmonar que se especializan en el intercambio de gases entre el aire y la sangre.

amniotic egg An egg with a shell and internal membranes that keep the embryo moist; a major adaptation to life on land characteristic of reptiles, birds, and egg-laying mammals. (389, 534)
huevo amniótico Huevo con cáscara y membranas internas que mantiene al embrión húmedo; adaptación principal a la vida en la tierra, característica de los reptiles, las aves y los mamíferos que ponen huevos.

amphibian A vertebrate whose body temperature is determined by the temperature of its environment, and that lives its early life in water and its adult life on land. (330)
anfibio Animal vertebrado cuya temperatura corporal depende de la temperatura de su entorno, y que vive la primera etapa de su vida en el agua y su vida adulta en la tierra.

angiosperm A flowering plant that produces seeds enclosed in a protective fruit. (268)
angiosperma Planta con flores que produce semillas encerradas en una fruta protectora.

annual A flowering plant that completes its life cycle in one growing season. (281)
anual Planta con flores que completa su ciclo de vida en una sola temporada de crecimiento.

antibiotic A chemical that kills bacteria or slows their growth without harming body cells. (572)
antibiótico Sustancia química que mata las bacterias o disminuye la velocidad de su crecimiento sin dañar las células del cuerpo humano.

antibiotic resistance The ability of bacteria to withstand the effects of an antibiotic. (572)
resistencia a los antibióticos Capacidad de la bacteria de resistir los efectos de los antibióticos.

antibody A protein produced by a B cell of the immune system that destroys pathogens. (562)
anticuerpo Proteína producida por una célula B del sistema inmunológico que destruye patógenos.

antigen A molecule that the immune system recognizes either as part of the body or as coming from outside the body. (561)
antígeno Molécula que el sistema inmunológico puede reconocer como parte del cuerpo o como un agente extraño.

aorta The largest artery in the body; receives blood from the left ventricle. (471)
aorta La arteria más grande del cuerpo; recibe sangre del ventrículo izquierdo.

artery A blood vessel that carries blood away from the heart. (471)
arteria Vaso sanguíneo que transporta la sangre que sale del corazón.

arthropod An invertebrate that has an external skeleton, a segmented body, and jointed appendages. (322)
artrópodo Invertebrado que tiene un esqueleto externo, un cuerpo segmentado y apéndices articulados.

asexual reproduction A reproductive process that involves only one parent and produces offspring that are genetically identical to the parent. (7)
reproducción asexual Proceso reproductivo que consiste de un solo reproductor y que produce individuos que son genéticamente idénticos al reproductor.

asthma A disease in which the airways in the lungs narrow significantly. (577)
asma Enfermedad en la que las vías respiratorias de los pulmones se estrechan considerablemente.

atrium An upper chamber of the heart that receives blood. (470)
aurícula Cavidad superior del corazón que recibe la sangre.

autotroph An organism that is able to capture energy from sunlight or chemicals and use it to produce its own food. (11, 82)
autótrofo Organismo capaz de capturar y usar la energía del Sol o de las sustancias químicas para producir su propio alimento.

auxin A plant hormone that speeds up the rate at which a plant's cells grow and controls a plant's response to light. (290)
auxina Hormona vegetal que acelera la velocidad del crecimiento de las células de una planta y que controla la respuesta de la planta a la luz.

B

B cell A lymphocyte that produces proteins that help destroy pathogens. (562)
célula B Linfocito que produce proteínas que ayudan a destruir patógenos.

bacteria Single-celled organisms that lack a nucleus; prokaryotes. (217)
bacteria Organismos unicelulares que no tienen un núcleo; procariotas.

biennial A flowering plant that completes its life cycle in two years. (281)
bienal Planta con flores que completa su ciclo de vida en dos años.

bilateral symmetry A body plan in which a single imaginary line divides the body into left and right sides that are mirror images of each other. (314)
simetría bilateral Esquema del cuerpo en el que una línea imaginaria divide el cuerpo en dos partes, izquierda y derecha, que son el reflejo la una de la otra.

binary fission A form of asexual reproduction in which one cell divides, forming two identical cells. (221)
fisión binaria Forma de reproducción asexual en la que una célula se divide y forma dos células idénticas.

binary star A star system with two stars. (149)
estrella binaria Sistema estelar de dos estrellas.

binomial nomenclature The classification system in which each organism is given a unique, two-part scientific name indicating its genus and species. (16)
nomenclatura binaria Sistema de clasificación en el que cada organismo tiene un nombre científico específico de dos partes que indica el género y la especie.

biodiversity The total number of different species on Earth, including those on land, in the water, and in the air. (660)
biodiversidad Número total de especies diferentes que habitan la Tierra, incluyendo especies terrestres, marinas y del aire.

biome A group of ecosystems with similar climates and organisms. (646)
bioma Grupo de ecosistemas con organismos y climas parecidos.

biotic factor A living or once living part of an organism's habitat. (594)
factor biótico Parte viva, o que alguna vez tuvo vida, del hábitat de un organismo.

bird A vertebrate whose body temperature is regulated by its internal heat, lays eggs, and has feathers and a four-chambered heart. (332)
ave Vertebrado cuya temperatura corporal es regulada por su calor interno, que produce huevos y que tiene plumas y un corazón de cuatro cavidades.

birth rate The number of births per 1,000 individuals for a certain time period. (599)
tasa de natalidad Número de nacimientos por 1,000 individuos durante un período de tiempo determinado.

boreal forest Dense forest of evergreens located in the upper regions of the Northern Hemisphere. (652)
bosque boreal Bosque denso donde abundan las plantas coníferas y que se encuentra en las regiones más al norte del Hemisferio Norte.

GLOSSARY

brain **1.** An organized grouping of neurons in the head of an animal with bilateral symmetry. (353) **2.** The part of the central nervous system that is located in the skull and controls most functions in the body.
encéfalo **1.** Conjunto organizado de neuronas ubicado en la cabeza de animales con simetría bilateral. **2.** Parte del sistema nervioso ubicada en el cráneo y que controla la mayoría de las funciones del cuerpo.

branching tree diagram A diagram that shows probable evolutionary relationships among organisms and the order in which specific characteristics may have evolved. (27)
árbol ramificado Diagrama que muestra las relaciones evolucionarias probables entre los organismos y el orden en que ciertas características específicas podrían haber evolucionado.

bronchi The passages that direct air into the lungs. (480)
bronquios Conductos que dirigen el aire hacia los pulmones.

budding A form of asexual reproduction in which a new organism grows out of the body of a parent. (238)
gemación Forma de reproducción asexual en la que una porción del cuerpo de un reproductor se separa y forma un nuevo organismo.

C

---

calorie The amount of energy needed to raise the temperature of one gram of water by 1°C. (459)
caloría Cantidad de energía que se necesita para elevar en 1°C la temperatura de un gramo de agua.

cambium A layer of cells in a plant that produces new phloem and xylem cells. (272)
cámbium Una capa de células de una planta que produce nuevas células de floema y xilema.

cancer A disease in which some body cells grow and divide uncontrollably, damaging the parts of the body around them. (157)
cáncer Enfermedad en la que algunas células del cuerpo crecen y se dividen sin control, y causan daño a las partes del cuerpo que las rodean.

canopy A leafy roof formed by tall trees in a rain forest. (649)
dosel Techo de hojas que forman los árboles en la selva tropical.

capillary A tiny blood vessel where substances are exchanged between the blood and the body cells. (471)

capilar Vaso sanguíneo diminuto donde se intercambian sustancias entre la sangre y las células del cuerpo.

captive breeding The mating of animals in zoos or wildlife preserves. (667)
reproducción en cautiverio Apareamiento de animales en zoológicos y reservas naturales.

carbohydrate An energy-rich organic compound, such as a sugar or a starch, that is made of the elements carbon, hydrogen, and oxygen. (60)
carbohidrato Compuesto orgánico rico en energía, como un azúcar o almidón, formado por los elementos carbono, hidrógeno y oxígeno.

carcinogen A substance or a factor in the environment that can cause cancer. (579)
carcinógeno Sustancia o factor ambiental que puede causar cáncer.

cardiac muscle Involuntary muscle tissue found only in the heart. (440)
músculo cardiaco Tejido de músculo involuntario, que sólo se encuentra en el corazón.

carnivore A consumer that obtains energy by eating only animals. (367, 632)
carnívoro Consumidor que adquiere su energía al alimentarse de animales solamente.

carrier A person who has one recessive allele and one dominant allele for a trait. (165)
portador Persona que tiene un alelo recesivo y un alelo dominante para un rasgo.

carrying capacity The largest population that a particular environment can support. (604)
capacidad de carga Población mayor que un ambiente en particular puede mantener.

cartilage A connective tissue that is more flexible than bone and that protects the ends of bones and keeps them from rubbing together. (329, 347, 436)
cartílago Tejido conector más flexible que el hueso, que protege los extremos de los huesos y evita que se rocen.

cell The basic unit of structure and function in living things. (6, 40, 409)
célula Unidad básica de la estructura y función de todos los seres vivos.

cell cycle The series of events in which a cell grows, prepares for division, and divides to form two daughter cells. (94)
ciclo celular Serie de sucesos en los que una célula crece, se prepara para dividirse y se divide para formar dos células hijas.

cell membrane A thin, flexible barrier that surrounds a cell and controls which substances pass into and out of a cell. (49, 409)
membrana celular Barrera delgada y flexible alrededor de la célula que controla lo que entra y sale de la célula.

cell theory A widely accepted explanation of the relationship between cells and living things. (42)
teoría celular Explicación ampliamente aceptada sobre la relación entre las células y los seres vivos.

cell wall A rigid supporting layer that surrounds the cells of plants and some other organisms. (49)
pared celular Capa fuerte de apoyo alrededor de las células de las plantas y algunos otros organismos.

cellular respiration The process in which oxygen and glucose undergo a complex series of chemical reactions inside cells, releasing energy. (87, 220, 372)
respiración celular Proceso en el cual el oxígeno y la glucosa pasan por una serie compleja de reacciones químicas dentro de las células y así liberan energía.

central nervous system The division of the nervous system consisting of the brain and spinal cord. (509)
sistema nervioso central División del sistema nervioso formada por el cerebro y la médula espinal.

chemotherapy The use of drugs to treat diseases such as cancer. (159)
quimioterapia Uso de medicamentos para tratar enfermedades como el cáncer.

chlorophyll A green photosynthetic pigment found in the chloroplasts of plants, algae, and some bacteria. (83, 255)
clorofila Pigmento verde fotosintético de los cloroplastos de las plantas, algas y algunas bacterias.

chloroplast An organelle in the cells of plants and some other organisms that captures energy from sunlight and changes it to an energy form that cells can use in making food. (55, 256)
cloroplasto Orgánulo de las células vegetales y otros organismos que absorbe energía de la luz solar y la convierte en una forma de energía que las células pueden usar para producir alimentos.

chordate An animal that has a notochord, a nerve cord, and throat pouches at some point in its life. (325)
cordado Animal que tiene un notocordio, un cordón nervioso y bolsas en la garganta en determinada etapa de su vida.

chromosome A threadlike structure within a cell's nucleus that contains DNA that is passed from one generation to the next. (94)
cromosoma Estructura filamentosa en el núcleo celular que contiene el ADN que se transmite de una generación a la siguiente.

cilia Tiny, hairlike projections on the outside of cells that move in a wavelike manner. (229, 480)
cilio Estructuras diminutas parecidas a pelos, ubicadas en el exterior de las células y que ondulan.

circulatory system An organ system that transports needed materials to cells and removes wastes. (377, 468)
sistema circulatorio Sistema de órganos que transporta los materiales que la célula necesita y elimina los desechos.

classification The process of grouping things based on their similarities. (15)
clasificación Proceso de agrupar cosas según sus semejanzas.

climate The average annual conditions of temperature, precipitation, winds, and clouds in an area. (646)
clima Condiciones promedio anuales de temperatura, precipitación, viento y nubosidad de un área.

clone An organism that is genetically identical to the organism from which it was produced. (169)
clon Organismo genéticamente idéntico al organismo del que proviene.

cnidarian A radially symmetrical invertebrate that uses stinging cells to capture food and defend itself. (319)
cnidario Invertebrado de simetría radiada que usa células urticantes para obtener alimentos y defenderse.

codominance A situation in which both alleles for a gene are expressed equally. (123)
codominancia Situación en la que ambos alelos de un gen se manifiestan de igual manera.

commensalism A type of symbiosis between two species in which one species benefits and the other species is neither helped nor harmed. (614)
comensalismo Tipo de relación simbiótica entre dos especies en la cual una especie se beneficia y la otra especie ni se beneficia ni sufre daño.

community All the different populations that live together in a particular area. (596)
comunidad Todas las poblaciones distintas que habitan en un área específica.

compact bone Hard and dense, but not solid, bone tissue that is beneath the outer membrane of a bone. (435)
hueso compacto Tejido de hueso denso y duro, pero no sólido, que se encuentra debajo de la membrana externa de un hueso.

GLOSSARY

competition The struggle between organisms to survive as they attempt to use the same limited resources in the same place at the same time. (609)
competencia Lucha por la supervivencia entre organismos que se alimentan de los mismos recursos limitados en el mismo lugar y al mismo tiempo.

complete metamorphosis A type of metamorphosis with four distinct stages: egg, larva, pupa, and adult. (392)
metamorfosis completa Tipo de metamorfosis de cuatro etapas: huevo, larva, pupa y adulto.

compound A substance made of two or more elements chemically combined in a specific ratio, or proportion. (59)
compuesto Sustancia formada por dos o más elementos combinados químicamente en una razón o proporción específica.

condensation The change in state from a gas to a liquid. (639)
condensación Cambio del estado gaseoso al estado líquido.

cone The reproductive structure of a gymnosperm. (284)
cono Estructura reproductora de una gimnosperma.

coniferous tree A tree that produces its seeds in cones and that has needle-shaped leaves coated in a waxy substance to reduce water loss. (652)
árbol conífero Árbol que produce sus semillas en piñones y que tiene hojas en forma de aguja y cubiertas por una sustancia cerosa que reduce la pérdida de agua.

conjugation A form of sexual reproduction in which a unicellular organism transfers some of its genetic material to another unicellular organism. (221)
conjugación Forma de reproducción sexual en la que un organismo unicelular transfiere su material genético a otro organismo unicelular.

connective tissue A body tissue that provides support for the body and connects all its parts. (410)
tejido conector Tejido del cuerpo que mantiene la estructura del cuerpo y une todas sus partes.

consumer An organism that obtains energy by feeding on other organisms. (632)
consumidor Organismo que obtiene energía al alimentarse de otros organismos.

contractile vacuole The cell structure that collects extra water from the cytoplasm and then expels it from the cell. (228)
vacuola contráctil Estructura celular que recoge el agua sobrante del citoplasma y luego la expulsa de la célula.

controlled experiment An experiment in which only one variable is manipulated at a time. (9)

experimento controlado Experimento en el cual sólo se manipula una variable a la vez.

convergent evolution The process by which unrelated organisms evolve similar characteristics. (29)
evolución convergente Proceso por el cual organismos no relacionados exhiben una evolución de características similares.

cotyledon A leaf produced by an embryo of a seed plant; sometimes stores food. (268)
cotiledón Hoja producida por el embrión de una planta fanerógama; a veces almacena alimentos.

critical night length The number of hours of darkness that determines whether or not a plant will flower. (291)
duración crítica de la noche El número de horas de oscuridad que determina si florecerá una planta o no.

cuticle The waxy, waterproof layer that covers the leaves and stems of most plants. (258)
cutícula Capa cerosa e impermeable que cubre las hojas y los tallos de la mayoría de las plantas.

cytokinesis The final stage of the cell cycle, in which the cell's cytoplasm divides, distributing the organelles into each of the two new daughter cells. (98)
citocinesis Última etapa del ciclo celular en la que se divide el citoplasma y se reparten los orgánulos entre las dos células hijas nuevas.

cytoplasm The thick fluid region of a cell located inside the cell membrane (in prokaryotes) or between the cell membrane and nucleus (in eukaryotes). (51, 217, 409)
citoplasma Región celular de líquido espeso ubicada dentro de la membrana celular (en las procariotas) o entre la membrana celular y el núcleo (en las eucariotas).

D

day-neutral plant A plant with a flowering cycle that is not sensitive to periods of light and dark. (291)
planta de día neutro Planta con un ciclo de floración que no es sensible a la luz o la oscuridad.

death rate The number of deaths per 1,000 individuals for a certain time period. (599)
tasa de mortalidad Número de muertes por 1,000 individuos durante un período de tiempo determinado.

deciduous tree A tree that sheds its leaves during a particular season and grows new ones each year. (651)
árbol caducifolio Árbol que pierde las hojas durante una estación específica y al que le salen hojas nuevas cada año.

decomposer An organism that gets energy by breaking down biotic wastes and dead organisms, and returns raw materials to the soil and water. (225, 633)
descomponedor Organismo que obtiene energía al descomponer desechos bióticos y organismos muertos, y que devuelve materia prima al suelo y al agua.

dermis The inner layer of the skin. (447)
dermis Capa más interna de la piel.

desert A dry region that on average receives less than 25 centimeters of precipitation per year. (647)
desierto Región seca en la que se registra un promedio menor de 25 centímetros de precipitación anual.

development The process of change that occurs during an organism's life to produce a more complex organism. (7)
desarrollo Proceso de cambio que ocurre durante la vida de un organismo, mediante el cual se crea un organismo más complejo.

diabetes A condition in which the pancreas fails to produce enough insulin or the body's cells cannot use it properly. (578)
diabetes Condición en la que el páncreas no puede producir suficiente insulina o las células del cuerpo no la pueden usar correctamente.

diaphragm A large, dome-shaped muscle located at the base of the lungs that helps with breathing. (482)
diafragma Músculo grande y redondo situado en la base de los pulmones que ayuda a la respiración.

dicot An angiosperm that has two seed leaves. (268)
dicotiledónea Angiosperma cuyas semillas tienen dos cotiledones.

diffusion The process by which molecules move from an area of higher concentration to an area of lower concentration. (66, 373)
difusión Proceso por el cual las moléculas se mueven de un área de mayor concentración a otra de menor concentración.

digestion The process that breaks down complex molecules of food into smaller nutrient molecules. (370)
digestión Proceso que descompone las moléculas complejas de los alimentos en moléculas de nutrientes más pequeñas.

digestive system An organ system that has specialized structures for obtaining and digesting food. (370)
sistema digestivo Sistema de órganos que tiene estructuras especializadas para ingerir y digerir alimentos.

DNA Deoxyribonucleic acid; the genetic material that carries information about an organism and is passed from parent to offspring. (62)
ADN Ácido desoxirribonucleico; material genético que lleva información sobre un organismo y que se transmite de padres a hijos.

DNA replication Before a cell divides, the process in which DNA copies itself. (148)
replicación del ADN Proceso en el que el ADN se duplica, antes de que la célula se divida.

dominant allele An allele whose trait always shows up in the organism when the allele is present. (113)
alelo dominante Alelo cuyo rasgo siempre se manifiesta en el organismo, cuando el alelo está presente.

dormancy A period of time when an organism's growth or activity stops. (292)
latencia Período de tiempo durante el cual se detiene el crecimiento o la actividad de un organismo.

double helix The shape of a DNA molecule. (62)
doble hélice Forma de una molécula de ADN.

duct A tiny tube through which chemicals are released from a gland. (517)
ducto Conducto diminuto por el cual se liberan sustancias químicas de una glándula.

E

echinoderm A radially symmetrical marine invertebrate that has an internal skeleton and a system of fluid-filled tubes. (323)
equinodermo Invertebrado marino de simetría radiada que tiene un esqueleto interno y un sistema de apéndices en forma de tubos llenos de líquido.

ecology The study of how organisms interact with each other and their environment. (597)
ecología Estudio de la forma en que los organismos interactúan entre sí y con su medio ambiente.

ecosystem The community of organisms that live in a particular area, along with their nonliving environment. (597)
ecosistema Comunidad de organismos que viven en un área específica, y el medio ambiente que los rodea.

ectotherm An animal whose body temperature is determined by the temperature of its environment. (327)
ectotermo Animal cuya temperatura corporal es determinada por la temperatura de su medio ambiente.

GLOSSARY

egg A female sex cell. (525)
óvulo Célula sexual femenina.

element A pure substance that cannot be broken down into other substances by chemical or physical means. (58)
elemento Sustancia que no se puede descomponer en otras sustancias por medios químicos o físicos.

embryo 1. The young organism that develops from a zygote. (276) **2.** A developing human during the first eight weeks after fertilization has occurred. (533)
embrión 1. Organismo joven que se desarrolla a partir del cigoto. **2.** Un ser humano en desarrollo durante las primeras ocho semanas después de llevarse a cabo la fertilización.

emergent layer The tallest layer of the rain forest that receives the most sunlight. (649)
capa emergente Capa superior de la selva tropical, que recibe la mayor cantidad de luz solar.

emigration Movement of individuals out of a population's area. (600)
emigración Traslado de individuos fuera del área de una población.

endangered species A species in danger of becoming extinct in the near future. (665)
especie en peligro de extinción Especie que corre el riesgo de desaparecer en el futuro próximo.

endocytosis The process by which the cell membrane takes particles into the cell by changing shape and engulfing the particles. (69)
endocitosis Proceso en el que la membrana celular absorbe partículas al cambiar de forma y envolver las partículas.

endoplasmic reticulum An organelle that forms a maze of passageways in which proteins and other materials are carried from one part of the cell to another. (51)
retículo endoplasmático Orgánulo que forma un laberinto de conductos que llevan proteínas y otros materiales de una parte de la célula a otra.

endoskeleton An internal skeleton; structural support system within the body of an animal. (323)
endoesqueleto Esqueleto interno; sistema estructural de soporte dentro del cuerpo de un animal.

endospore A structure produced by prokaryotes, such as bacteria, in unfavorable conditions; a thick wall encloses the DNA and some of the cytoplasm. (222)
endospora Estructura que las procariotas, como las bacterias, producen en condiciones desfavorables; capa gruesa que encierra al ADN y parte del citoplasma.

endotherm An animal whose body temperature is regulated by the internal heat the animal produces. (327)
endotermo Animal cuya temperatura corporal es regulada por el calor interno que produce.

energy pyramid A diagram that shows the amount of energy that moves from one feeding level to another in a food web. (636)
pirámide de energía Diagrama que muestra la cantidad de energía que fluye de un nivel de alimentación a otro en una red alimentaria.

enzyme 1. A type of protein that speeds up a chemical reaction in a living thing. (61, 463) **2.** A biological catalyst that lowers the activation energy of reactions in cells.
enzima 1. Tipo de proteína que acelera una reacción química de un ser vivo. **2.** Catalizador biológico que disminuye la energía de activación de las reacciones celulares.

epidermis The outer layer of the skin. (447)
epidermis Capa externa de la piel.

epiglottis A flap of tissue that seals off the windpipe and prevents food from entering the lungs. (84)
epiglotis Lámina de tejido que sella la tráquea y evita que los alimentos entren en los pulmones.

epithelial tissue A body tissue that covers the interior and exterior surfaces of the body. (410)
tejido epitelial Tejido del cuerpo que cubre las superficies interiores y exteriores.

esophagus A muscular tube that connects the mouth to the stomach. (464)
esófago Tubo muscular que conecta la boca con el estómago.

estrogen A hormone produced by the ovaries that controls the development of eggs and adult female characteristics. (528)
estrógeno Hormona producida por los ovarios que controla el desarrollo de los óvulos y de las características femeninas adultas.

estuary A kind of wetland formed where fresh water from rivers mixes with salty ocean water. (658)
estuario Tipo de pantanal que se forma donde el agua dulce de los ríos se junta con el agua salada del océano.

eukaryote An organism whose cells contain a nucleus. (24)
eucariota Organismo cuyas células contienen un núcleo.

evaporation The process by which molecules at the surface of a liquid absorb enough energy to change to a gas. (639)

evaporación Proceso mediante el cual las moléculas en la superficie de un líquido absorben suficiente energía para pasar al estado gaseoso.

evolution Change over time; the process by which modern organisms have descended from ancient organisms. (186)
evolución Cambios a través del tiempo; proceso por el cual los organismos modernos se originaron a partir de organismos antiguos.

excretion The process by which wastes are removed from the body. (487)
excreción Proceso por el cual se eliminan los desechos del cuerpo.

exocytosis The process by which the vacuole surrounding particles fuses with the cell membrane, forcing the contents out of the cell. (69)
exocitosis Proceso en el que la vacuola que envuelve partículas se funde con la membrana celular, expulsando así el contenido al exterior de la célula.

exoskeleton External skeleton; a tough, waterproof outer covering that protects, supports, and helps prevent evaporation of water from the body of many invertebrates. (322)
exoesqueleto Esqueleto exterior; una cobertura fuerte e impermeable que protege, soporta y ayuda a prevenir la evaporación del agua del cuerpo de muchos invertebrados.

external fertilization When eggs are fertilized outside of a female's body. (386)
fertilización externa Cuando los óvulos se fertilizan fuera del cuerpo de la hembra.

extinction The disappearance of all members of a species from Earth. (665)
extinción Desaparición de la Tierra de todos los miembros de una especie.

F

Fallopian tube A passageway for eggs from an ovary to the uterus. (528)
trompa de falopio Pasaje por el que pasan los óvulos de un ovario al útero.

fermentation The process by which cells release energy by breaking down food molecules without using oxygen. (90)
fermentación Proceso en el que las células liberan energía al descomponer las moléculas de alimento sin usar oxígeno.

fertilization The process in sexual reproduction in which an egg cell and a sperm cell join to form a new cell. (111, 282, 525)
fertilización Proceso de la reproducción sexual en el que un óvulo y un espermatozoide se unen para formar una nueva célula.

fetus A developing human from the ninth week of development until birth. (533)
feto Humano en desarrollo desde la novena semana de desarrollo hasta el nacimiento.

filter feeder An animal that strains its food from water. (368)
comedores por suspensión Animal que filtra sus alimentos del agua.

fish A vertebrate whose body temperature is determined by the temperature of its environment, and that lives in the water and has fins. (329)
pez Vertebrado cuya temperatura corporal es determinada por la temperatura de su medio ambiente, que vive en el agua y que tiene aletas.

flagellum A long, whiplike structure that helps a cell to move. (217)
flagelo Estructura larga con forma de látigo, que ayuda a la célula a moverse.

flower The reproductive structure of an angiosperm. (278)
flor Estructura reproductora de una angiosperma.

follicle Structure in the dermis of the skin from which a strand of hair grows. (447)
folículo Estructura en la dermis de la piel de donde crece un pelo.

food chain A series of events in an ecosystem in which organisms transfer energy by eating and by being eaten. (634)
cadena alimentaria Serie de sucesos en un ecosistema por medio de los cuales los organismos transmiten energía al comer o al ser comidos por otros.

food web The pattern of overlapping feeding relationships or food chains among the various organisms in an ecosystem. (634)
red alimentaria Patrón de las relaciones de alimentación superpuestas o de cadenas alimentarias entre los diferentes organismos de un ecosistema.

fossil The preserved remains or traces of an organism that lived in the past. (183)
fósil Restos o vestigios conservados de un organismo que vivió en el pasado.

frond The leaf of a fern plant. (264)
fronda Hoja de un helecho.

GLOSSARY

fruit The ripened ovary and other structures of an angiosperm that enclose one or more seeds. (287)
fruto Ovario maduro y otras estructuras de una angiosperma que encierran una o más semillas.

fruiting body The reproductive structure of a fungus that contains many hyphae and produces spores. (238)
órgano fructífero Estructura reproductora de un hongo, que contiene muchas hifas y produce esporas.

fungus A eukaryotic organism that has cell walls, uses spores to reproduce, and is a heterotroph that feeds by absorbing its food. (237)
hongo Organismo eucariótico que posee paredes celulares, usa esporas para reproducirse y es un heterótrofo que se alimenta absorbiendo sus alimentos.

G

gametophyte The stage in the life cycle of a plant in which the plant produces gametes, or sex cells. (280)
gametofito Etapa del ciclo vital de una planta en la que produce gametos, es decir, células sexuales.

gene A sequence of DNA that determines a trait and is passed from parent to offspring. (113, 664)
gen Secuencia de ADN que determina un rasgo y que se pasa de los progenitores a los hijos.

gene therapy The process of changing a gene to treat a medical disease or disorder. An absent or faulty gene is replaced by a normal working gene. (171)
terapia genética Proceso que consiste en cambiar un gen para tratar una enfermedad o un trastorno médico. El gen ausente o defectuoso se cambia por un gen con función normal.

genetic engineering The transfer of a gene from the DNA of one organism into another organism, in order to produce an organism with desired traits. (169)
ingeniería genética Transferencia de un gen desde el ADN de un organismo a otro, para producir un organismo con los rasgos deseados.

genetics The scientific study of heredity. (111)
genética Ciencia que estudia la herencia.

genotype An organism's genetic makeup, or allele combinations. (120)
genotipo Composición genética de un organismo, es decir, las combinaciones de los alelos.

genus A classification grouping that consists of a number of similar, closely related species. (16)

género Clase de agrupación que consiste de un número de especies similares y estrechamente relacionadas.

germination The sprouting of the embryo out of a seed; occurs when the embryo resumes its growth following dormancy. (277)
germinación Brotamiento del embrión a partir de la semilla; ocurre cuando el embrión reanuda su crecimiento tras el estado latente.

gestation period The length of time between fertilization and birth of a mammal. (387)
período de gestación Tiempo entre la fertilización y el nacimiento de un mamífero.

gland An organ that produces and releases chemicals either through ducts or into the bloodstream. (420, 517)
glándula Órgano que produce y libera sustancias químicas por los ductos o al torrente sanguíneo.

Golgi apparatus An organelle in a cell that receives proteins and other newly formed materials from the endoplasmic reticulum, packages them, and distributes them to other parts of the cell. (54)
aparato de Golgi Orgánulo de la célula que recibe, empaqueta y distribuye a otras partes de la célula las proteínas y otros materiales que se forman en el retículo endoplasmático.

gradualism Pattern of evolution characterized by the slow and steady accumulation of small genetic changes over long periods of time. (198)
gradualismo Evolución de una especie por medio de la acumulación lenta pero continua de cambios genéticos a través de largos períodos de tiempo.

grassland An area populated mostly by grasses and other nonwoody plants that gets 25 to 75 centimeters of rain each year. (650)
pradera Área poblada principalmente por hierbas y otras plantas no leñosas, y donde caen entre 25 y 75 centímetros de lluvia cada año.

gymnosperm A plant that produces seeds directly on the scales of cones—not enclosed by a protective fruit. (266)
gimnosperma Planta que produce semillas directamente sobre las escamas de los conos—sin estar encerradas en un fruto protector.

H

habitat An environment that provides the things a specific organism needs to live, grow, and reproduce. (593)
hábitat Medio que provee lo que un organismo específico necesita para vivir, crecer y reproducirse.

habitat destruction The loss of a natural habitat. (666)
destrucción del hábitat Pérdida de un hábitat natural.

habitat fragmentation The breaking of a habitat into smaller, isolated pieces. (666)
fragmentación del hábitat Desintegración de un hábitat en porciones aisladas más pequeñas.

heart A hollow, muscular organ that pumps blood throughout an organism's body. (470)
corazón Órgano hueco y muscular que bombea la sangre por todas partes del cuerpo de un organismo.

hemoglobin An iron-containing protein that binds chemically to oxygen molecules; makes up most of red blood cells. (474)
hemoglobina Proteína que contiene hierro, y que se enlaza químicamente las moléculas de oxígeno; forma la mayoría de los glóbulos rojos.

herbivore A consumer that obtains energy by eating only plants. (367, 632)
herbívoro Consumidor que come sólo plantas para obtener energía.

heredity The passing of traits from parents to offspring. (110)
herencia Transmisión de rasgos de padres a hijos.

heterotroph An organism that cannot make its own food and gets food by consuming other living things. (11, 82)
heterótrofo Organismo que no puede producir sus propios alimentos y que se alimenta al consumir otros seres vivos.

heterozygous Having two different alleles for a particular gene. (120)
heterocigoto Que tiene dos alelos distintos para un gen particular.

histamine A chemical that is responsible for the symptoms of an allergy. (576)
histamina Sustancia química responsable de los síntomas de una alergia.

HIV (human immunodeficiency virus) The virus that causes AIDS. (565)
VIH (virus de la inmunodeficiencia humana) Virus que causa el SIDA.

homeostasis The condition in which an organism's internal environment is kept stable in spite of changes in the external environment. (13, 309, 423)
homeostasis Condición en la que el medio ambiente interno de un organismo se mantiene estable a pesar de cambios en el medio ambiente externo.

homologous structures Structures that are similar in different species and that have been inherited from a common ancestor. (194)
estructuras homólogas Estructuras parecidas de especies distintas y que se han heredado de un antepasado común.

homozygous Having two identical alleles for a particular gene. (120)
homocigoto Que tiene dos alelos idénticos para un gen particular.

hormone 1. A chemical that affects growth and development. 2. The chemical produced by an endocrine gland. (290, 421, 518)
hormona 1. Sustancia química que afecta el crecimiento y el desarrollo. 2. Sustancia química producida por una glándula endocrina.

host An organism that a parasite lives with, in, or on, and provides a source of energy or a suitable environment for the parasite to live. (211, 614)
huésped Organismo dentro del o sobre el cual vive un parásito y que provee una fuente de energía o un medio apropiado para la existencia del parásito.

hybrid An offspring of crosses that has two different alleles for a trait. (114)
híbrido Descendiente de cruces que tiene dos alelos distintos para un rasgo.

hybridization A selective breeding method that involves crossing different individuals to bring together the best traits from both parents. (168)
hibridación Técnica reproductiva en la que se cruzan individuos distintos para reunir los mejores rasgos de ambos progenitores.

hyphae The branching, threadlike tubes that make up the bodies of multicellular fungi. (237)
hifas Delgados tubos ramificados que forman el cuerpo de los hongos multicelulares.

hypothalamus A part of the brain that links the nervous system and the endocrine system. (520)
hipotálamo Parte del encéfalo que une el sistema nervioso con el sistema endocrino.

I

immigration Movement of individuals into a population's area. (600)
inmigración Movimiento de individuos al área de una población.

immune response Part of the body's defense against pathogens in which cells of the immune system react to each kind of pathogen with a defense targeted specifically at that pathogen. (561)

GLOSSARY

reacción inmunológica Parte de la defensa del cuerpo contra los patógenos, en la que las células del sistema inmunológico reaccionan a cada tipo de patógeno con una defensa específica.

immunity The body's ability to destroy pathogens before they can cause disease. (569)
inmunidad Capacidad del cuerpo para destruir los patógenos antes de que causen enfermedades.

impulse An electrical message that carries information in the nervous system. (352)
impulso Mensaje eléctrico que transporta información por el sistema nervioso.

inbreeding A selective breeding method in which two individuals with similar sets of alleles are crossed. (168)
endogamia Técnica reproductiva en la que se cruzan dos individuos con conjuntos de alelos parecidos.

incomplete dominance A situation in which one allele is not completely dominant over another allele. (123)
dominancia incompleta Situación en la que un alelo no es completamente dominante sobre el otro.

incomplete metamorphosis A type of metamorphosis with three stages: egg, nymph, and adult. (393)
metamorfosis incompleta Tipo de metamorfosis de tres etapas: huevo, ninfa y adulto.

infectious disease A disease caused by the presence of a living thing in the body that can pass from one organism to another. (551)
enfermedad infecciosa Enfermedad causada por la presencia de un ser vivo en el cuerpo y que puede pasar de un organismo a otro.

inflammatory response Part of the body's defense against pathogens, in which fluid and white blood cells leak from blood vessels into tissues and destroy pathogens by breaking them down. (559)
reacción inflamatoria Parte de la defensa del cuerpo contra los patógenos en la cual los fluidos y los glóbulos blancos salen de los vasos sanguíneos hacia los tejidos y destruyen los patógenos descomponiéndolos.

insulin A hormone produced in the pancreas that enables the body's cells to take in glucose from the blood and use it for energy. (578)
insulina Hormona producida por el páncreas, que permite que las células del cuerpo absorban glucosa de la sangre y la usen como energía.

internal fertilization When eggs are fertilized inside a female's body. (386)
fertilización interna Cuando los óvulos se fertilizan dentro del cuerpo de la hembra.

interneuron A neuron that carries nerve impulses from one neuron to another. (352)
interneurona Neurona que transporta los impulsos nerviosos de una neurona a otra.

interphase The first stage of the cell cycle that takes place before cell division occurs, during which a cell grows and makes a copy of its DNA. (94)
interfase Primera etapa del ciclo celular que ocurre antes de la división celular y durante la cual la célula crece y duplica su ADN.

intertidal zone An area between the highest high-tide line on land and the point on the continental shelf exposed by the lowest low-tide line. (658)
zona intermareal Área entre el punto más alto de la marea alta y el punto más bajo de la marea baja.

invertebrate An animal without a backbone. (310)
invertebrado Animal sin columna vertebral.

involuntary muscle A muscle that is not under conscious control. (439)
músculo involuntario Músculo que no se puede controlar conscientemente.

J

joint A place in the body where two bones come together. (348, 416, 433)
articulación Lugar en el cuerpo en donde se unen dos huesos.

K

keystone species A species that influences the survival of many other species in an ecosystem. (661)
especie clave Especie que tiene un impacto en la supervivencia de muchas otras especies de un ecosistema.

kidney A major organ of the excretory system; removes urea and other wastes from the blood. (488)
riñón Órgano importante del sistema excretorio; elimina la urea y otros desechos de la sangre.

L

larva The immature form of an animal that looks very different from the adult. (384)
larva Forma inmadura de un animal que luce muy distinta al adulto.

larynx The voice box; located in the top part of the trachea, underneath the epiglottis. (483)
laringe Caja de la voz; está ubicada en la parte superior de la tráquea debajo de la epiglotis.

lichen The combination of a fungus and either an alga or an autotrophic bacterium that live together in a relationship that benefits both organisms. (243)
liquen Combinación de un hongo y una alga o bacteria autotrópica que viven juntos en una relación mutuamente beneficiosa.

ligament Strong connective tissue that holds bones together in movable joints. (433)
ligamentos Tejido conector resistente que une dos huesos en las articulaciones móviles.

limiting factor An environmental factor that causes a population to decrease in size. (603)
factor limitante Factor ambiental que causa la disminución del tamaño de una población.

lipid An energy-rich organic compound, such as a fat, oil, or wax, that is made of carbon, hydrogen, and oxygen. (61)
lípido Compuesto orgánico rico en energía, como una grasa, aceite o cera, formado por los elementos carbono, hidrógeno y oxígeno.

long-day plant A plant that flowers when the nights are shorter than the plant's critical night length. (291)
planta de día largo Planta que florece cuando la duración de la noche es más corta que la duración crítica.

lung 1. An organ found in air-breathing vertebrates that exchanges oxygen and carbon dioxide with the blood. 2. In humans, one of two main organs of the respiratory system. (480)
pulmón 1. Órgano que tienen los vertebrados que respiran aire, que intercambia oxígeno y dióxido de carbono en la sangre. 2. En los humanos, uno de los dos órganos principales del sistema respiratorio.

lymphocyte A white blood cell that distinguishes between each kind of pathogen. (561)
linfocito Glóbulo blanco que distingue cada tipo de patógeno.

lysosome A cell organelle which contains chemicals that break down large food particles into smaller ones and that can be used by the rest of the cell. (55)
lisosoma Orgánulo de una célula, que tiene sustancias químicas que convierten partículas grandes de alimentos en partículas más pequeñas que el resto de la célula puede utilizar.

M

mammal A vertebrate whose body temperature is regulated by its internal heat, and that has skin covered with hair or fur and glands that produce milk to feed its young. (333)
mamífero Vertebrado cuya temperatura corporal es regulada por su calor interno, cuya piel está cubierta de pelo o pelaje y que tiene glándulas que producen leche para alimentar a sus crías.

mammary gland An organ in female mammals that produces milk for the mammal's young. (333)
glándula mamaria Órgano de los mamíferos hembra que produce leche para alimentar a sus crías.

marrow The soft connective tissue that fills the internal spaces in bone. (435)
médula ósea Tejido conector suave que llena los espacios internos de un hueso.

marsupial A mammal whose young are born at an early stage of development, and which usually continue to develop in a pouch on their mother's body. (333)
marsupial Mamífero cuyas crías nacen en una etapa muy temprana del desarrollo, y que normalmente continúan el desarrollo en una bolsa del cuerpo de la madre.

medusa A cnidarian body form characterized by an open umbrella shape and adapted for a free-swimming life. (384)
medusa Cnidario con cuerpo que tiene la forma de una sombrilla abierta y que está adaptado para nadar libremente.

meiosis The process that occurs in the formation of sex cells (sperm and egg) by which the number of chromosomes is reduced by half. (132)
meiosis Proceso durante la formación de las células sexuales (espermatozoide y óvulo) por el cual el número de cromosomas se reduce a la mitad.

melanin A pigment that gives the skin its color. (447)
melanina Pigmento que da color a la piel.

menstrual cycle The monthly cycle of changes that occurs in the female reproductive system, during which an egg develops and the uterus prepares for the arrival of a fertilized egg. (530)
ciclo menstrual Ciclo mensual de cambios del sistema reproductor femenino, durante el cual se desarrolla un óvulo y el útero se prepara para la llegada del óvulo fecundado.

menstruation The process in which the thickened lining of the uterus breaks down and blood and tissue then pass out of the female body through the vagina. (530)
menstruación Proceso en el cual el recubrimiento grueso del útero se rompe, y sangre y tejido salen del cuerpo femenino a través de la vagina.

GLOSSARY

messenger RNA Type of RNA that carries copies of instructions for the assembly of amino acids into proteins from DNA to ribosomes in the cytoplasm. (151)
ARN mensajero Tipo de ARN que lleva, del ADN a los ribosomas del citoplasma, copias de instrucciones para sintetizar a los aminoácidos en proteínas.

metabolism The combination of chemical reactions through which an organism builds up or breaks down materials. (6)
metabolismo Combinación de reacciones químicas mediante las cuales un organismo compone o descompone la materia.

metamorphosis A process in which an animal's body undergoes major changes in shape and form during its life cycle. (391)
metamorfosis Proceso por el cual el cuerpo de un animal cambia de forma radicalmente durante su ciclo vital.

microorganism A living thing too small to see without a microscope. (549)
microorganismo Ser vivo que es tan pequeño que sólo es visible a través de un microscopio.

microscope An instrument that makes small objects look larger. (42)
microscopio Instrumento que permite que los objetos pequeños se vean más grandes.

mitochondria Rod-shaped organelles that convert energy in food molecules to energy the cell can use to carry out its functions. (51)
mitocondria Estructura celular con forma de bastón que transforma la energía de las moléculas de alimentos en energía que la célula puede usar para llevar a cabo sus funciones.

mitosis The second stage of the cell cycle during which the cell's nucleus divides into two new nuclei and one set of DNA is distributed into each daughter cell. (95)
mitosis Segunda etapa del ciclo celular, durante la cual se divide el núcleo de la célula en dos núcleos nuevos y el conjunto del ADN se reparte entre cada célula hija.

mollusk An invertebrate with a soft, unsegmented body; most are protected by a hard outer shell. (321)
molusco Invertebrado con cuerpo blando y sin segmentos; la mayoría tienen una concha exterior dura que les sirve de protección.

molting The process of shedding an outgrown exoskeleton. (346)
muda de cubierta Proceso de cambiar un exoesqueleto viejo por uno nuevo.

monocot An angiosperm that has only one seed leaf. (268)

monocotiledónea Angiosperma cuyas semillas tienen un solo cotiledón.

monotreme A mammal that lays eggs. (333)
monotrema Mamífero que pone huevos.

motor neuron A neuron that sends an impulse to a muscle or gland, causing the muscle or gland to react. (352)
neurona motora Neurona que envía un impulso a un músculo o glándula y hace que el músculo o la glándula reaccione.

multicellular Consisting of many cells. (6, 56)
multicelular Que se compone de muchas células.

multiple alleles Three or more possible alleles of a gene that determine a trait. (124)
alelo múltiple Tres o más alelos posibles del gen que determina un rasgo.

muscle A tissue that contracts or relaxes to create movement. (349)
músculo Tejido que se contrae o relaja para crear movimiento.

muscle tissue A body tissue that contracts, or shortens, making body parts move. (410)
tejido muscular Tejido del cuerpo que se contrae o encoge, y permite que se muevan las partes del cuerpo.

mutation Any change in the DNA of a gene or a chromosome. (155)
mutación Cualquier cambio del ADN de un gen o cromosoma.

mutualism A type of symbiosis in which both species benefit from living together. (613)
mutualismo Tipo de relación simbiótica entre dos especies en la cual ambas especies se benefician de su convivencia.

N
---

natural selection The process by which organisms that are best adapted to their environment are most likely to survive and reproduce. (188, 607)
selección natural Proceso por el cual los organismos que se adaptan mejor a su ambiente tienen mayor probabilidad de sobrevivir y reproducirse.

negative feedback A process in which a system is turned off by the condition it produces. (521)
reacción negativa Proceso en el cual un sistema cesa de funcionar debido a la condición que produce.

nephron Small filtering structure found in the kidneys that removes wastes from blood and produces urine. (488)
nefrona Estructura diminuta de filtración ubicada en los riñones, que elimina los desechos de la sangre y produce la orina.

neritic zone The area of the ocean that extends from the low-tide line out to the edge of the continental shelf. (658)
zona nerítica Área del océano que se extiende desde la línea de bajamar hasta el borde de la plataforma continental.

nerve A bundle of nerve fibers. (507)
nervio Conjunto de fibras nerviosas.

nerve impulse The message carried by a neuron. (507)
impulso nervioso Mensaje que una neurona transporta.

nervous system An organ system that receives information from the environment and coordinates a response. (351)
sistema nervioso Sistema de órganos que recibe información del medio ambiente y coordina una respuesta.

nervous tissue A body tissue that carries electrical messages back and forth between the brain and other parts of the body. (410)
tejido nervioso Tejido del cuerpo que transporta impulsos eléctricos entre el cerebro y otras partes del cuerpo.

neuron A cell that carries information through the nervous system. (352, 507)
neurona Célula que transporta información a través del sistema nervioso.

niche How an organism makes its living and interacts with the biotic and abiotic factors in its habitat. (608)
nicho Forma en que un organismo vive e interactúa con los factores bióticos y abióticos de su hábitat.

nitrogen bases Molecules that contain nitrogen and other elements. (145)
bases nitrogenadas Moléculas que contienen nitrógeno y otros elementos.

nitrogen fixation The process of changing free nitrogen gas into nitrogen compounds that plants can absorb and use. (642)
fijación del nitrógeno Proceso que consiste en transformar el gas de nitrógeno libre en compuestos de nitrógeno que las plantas pueden absorber y usar.

noninfectious disease A disease that is not caused by a pathogen. (575)
enfermedad no infecciosa Enfermedad que no es causada por un patógeno.

nonvascular plant A low-growing plant that lacks true vascular tissue for transporting materials. (260)
planta no vascular Planta de crecimiento lento que carece de tejido vascular verdadero para el transporte de materiales.

notochord A flexible rod that supports a chordate's back just below the nerve cord. (325)
notocordio Cilindro flexible que sostiene la columna de un cordado, debajo del cordón nervioso.

nucleic acid A very large organic molecule made of carbon, oxygen, hydrogen, nitrogen, and phosphorus, that contains the instructions cells need to carry out all the functions of life. (62)
ácido nucleico Molécula muy grande formada por carbono, oxígeno, hidrógeno y fósforo, que porta las instrucciones necesarias para que las células realicen todas las funciones vitales.

nucleus 1. In cells, a large oval organelle that contains the cell's genetic material in the form of DNA and controls many of the cell's activities. (23, 50, 409) **2.** The central core of an atom which contains protons and neutrons. **3.** The solid core of a comet.
núcleo 1. En las células, orgánulo grande y ovalado que contiene el material genético de la célula en forma de ADN y que controla muchas de las funciones celulares. **2.** Parte central del átomo que contiene los protones y los neutrones. **3.** Centro sólido de un cometa.

nutrient 1. A substance such as nitrogen or phosphorus that enables plants and algae to grow. **2.** Substances in food that provide the raw materials and energy needed for an organism to carry out its essential processes. (419)
nutriente 1. Sustancia como el nitrógeno o el fósforo que hace posible que las plantas y algas crezcan. **2.** Sustancias de los alimentos que dan el material y la energía que un organismo necesita para sus funciones vitales.

nymph A stage of incomplete metamorphosis that usually resembles the adult insect. (393)
ninfa Estado de la metamorfosis incompleta que generalmente se asemeja al insecto adulto.

O

omnivore A consumer that obtains energy by eating both plants and animals. (367, 632)
omnívoro Consumidor que come plantas y animales para obtener energía.

organ A body structure that is composed of different kinds of tissues that work together. (57, 313, 411)
órgano Estructura del cuerpo compuesta de distintos tipos de tejidos que trabajan conjuntamente.

GLOSSARY

organ system A group of organs that work together to perform a major function. (57, 412)
sistema de órganos Grupo de órganos que trabajan juntos para realizar una función importante.

organelle A tiny cell structure that carries out a specific function within the cell. (50)
orgánulo Estructura celular diminuta que realiza una función específica dentro de la célula.

organism A living thing. (5, 593)
organismo Un ser vivo.

osmosis The diffusion of water molecules across a selectively permeable membrane. (67)
ósmosis Difusión de moléculas de agua a través de una membrana permeable selectiva.

osteoporosis A condition resulting from a loss of minerals in which the body's bones become weak and break easily. (437)
osteoporosis Condición producida por la pérdida de minerales en la que los huesos del cuerpo se vuelven frágiles y se quiebran fácilmente.

ovary 1. A flower structure that encloses and protects ovules and seeds as they develop. (279) **2.** Organ of the female reproductive system in which eggs and estrogen are produced. (528)
ovario 1. Estructura de una flor que encierra y protege a los óvulos y las semillas durante su desarrollo. **2.** Órgano del sistema reproductivo femenino en el que se producen los óvulos y el estrógeno.

ovulation The process in which a mature egg is released from the ovary into a Fallopian tube. (530)
ovulación Proceso en el cual el óvulo maduro sale del ovario y pasa a las trompas de falopio.

ovule A plant structure in seed plants that produces the female gametophyte; contains an egg cell. (284)
óvulo Estructura vegetal de las plantas de semilla que produce el gametofito femenino; contiene una célula reproductora femenina.

P

parasite An organism that benefits by living with, on, or in a host in a parasitism interaction. (211, 614)
parásito Organismo que se beneficia al vivir dentro de o sobre un huésped en una relación parasítica.

parasitism A type of symbiosis in which one organism lives with, on, or in a host and harms it. (614)
parasitismo Tipo de relación simbiótica en la cual un organismo vive con o en un huésped y le hace daño.

passive immunity Immunity in which antibodies are given to a person rather than produced within the person's own body. (571)
inmunidad pasiva Inmunidad en la que una persona recibe anticuerpos en vez de producirlos en su propio cuerpo.

passive transport The movement of dissolved materials across a cell membrane without using cellular energy. (66)
transporte pasivo Movimiento de materiales a través de una membrana celular sin usar energía celular.

pasteurization A process of heating food to a temperature that is high enough to kill most harmful bacteria without changing the taste of the food. (224)
pasteurización Proceso de calentamiento de los alimentos a una temperatura suficientemente alta como para matar la mayoría de las bacterias dañinas sin que cambie el sabor.

pathogen An organism that causes disease. (551)
patógeno Organismo que causa enfermedades.

peat Compressed layers of dead sphagnum mosses that accumulate in bogs. (296)
turba Capas comprimidas de musgos esfagnáceos muertos que se acumulan en las marismas.

penis The organ through which both semen and urine leave the male body. (527)
pene Órgano por el cual salen del cuerpo masculino tanto el semen como la orina.

perennial A flowering plant that lives for more than two years. (281)
perenne Planta con flores que vive más de dos años.

peripheral nervous system The division of the nervous system consisting of all of the nerves located outside the central nervous system. (509)
sistema nervioso periférico División del sistema nervioso formada por todos los nervios ubicados fuera del sistema central nervioso.

peristalsis Waves of smooth muscle contractions that move food through the esophagus toward the stomach. (464)
peristalsis Contracciones progresivas de músculo liso que mueven el alimento por el esófago hacia el estómago.

permafrost Permanently frozen soil found in the tundra biome climate region. (653)
permagélido Suelo que está permanentemente congelado y que se encuentra en el bioma climático de la tundra.

petal A colorful, leaflike structure of some flowers. (278)
pétalo Estructura de color brillante, similar a una hoja, que algunas flores poseen.

phagocyte A white blood cell that destroys pathogens by engulfing them and breaking them down. (560)
fagocito Glóbulo blanco que destruye los patógenos envolviéndolos y descomponiéndolos.

pharynx The throat; part of both the respiratory and digestive systems. (480)
faringe Garganta; parte de los sistemas respiratorio y digestivo.

phase One of the different apparent shapes of the moon as seen from Earth. (22)
fase Una de las distintas formas aparentes de la Luna vistas desde la Tierra.

phenotype An organism's physical appearance, or visible traits. (120)
fenotipo Apariencia física, o rasgos visibles, de un organismo.

phloem The vascular tissue through which food moves in some plants. (263)
floema Tejido vascular de algunas plantas por el que circulan los alimentos.

photoperiodism A plant's response to seasonal changes in the length of night and day. (291)
fotoperiodicidad Respuesta de una planta a los cambios estacionales del día y de la noche.

photosynthesis The process by which plants and other autotrophs capture and use light energy to make food from carbon dioxide and water. (82, 255)
fotosíntesis Proceso por el cual las plantas y otros autótrofos absorben la energía de la luz para producir alimentos a partir del dióxido de carbono y el agua.

pigment 1. A colored chemical compound that absorbs light. 2. A colored substance used to color other materials. (231)
pigmento 1. Compuesto químico que absorbe luz. 2. Sustancia de color que se usa para teñir otros materiales.

pioneer species The first species to populate an area during succession. (617)
especies pioneras La primera especie que puebla un área durante la sucesión.

pistil The female reproductive part of a flower. (279)
pistilo Parte reproductora femenina de una flor.

pituitary gland An endocrine gland that regulates many body activities and controls the actions of several other endocrine glands. (520)

glándula pituitaria Glándula endocrina que regula muchas actividades corporales y controla las acciones de varias otras glándulas endocrinas.

placenta An organ in most pregnant mammals, including humans, that links the mother and the developing embryo and allows for the passage of materials between them. (333, 390, 534)
placenta Órgano de la mayoría de los mamíferos preñados, incluyendo a los seres humanos, que conecta a la madre con el embrión en desarrollo y que permite el intercambio de materiales entre ellos.

placental mammal A mammal that develops inside its mother's body until its body systems can function independently. (333)
mamífero placentario Mamífero que se desarrolla dentro del cuerpo de la madre hasta que sus sistemas puedan funcionar por sí solos.

poaching Illegal killing or removal of wildlife from their habitats. (666)
caza ilegal Matanza o eliminación de la fauna silvestre de su hábitat.

pollen Tiny structure (male gametophyte) produced by seed plants that contain the cell that later becomes a sperm cell. (266)
polen Diminuta estructura (gametofito masculino) producida por las plantas de semilla que contiene la célula que más adelante se convertirá en un espermatozoide.

pollination The transfer of pollen from male reproductive structures to female reproductive structures in plants. (278)
polinización Transferencia del polen de las estructuras reproductoras masculinas de una planta a las estructuras reproductoras femeninas.

polygenic inheritance The inheritance of traits that are controlled by two or more genes, such as height in humans. (124)
herencia poligénica Herencia de los rasgos controlados por dos o más genes, como la altura en los seres humanos.

polyp A cnidarian body form characterized by an upright vase shape and usually adapted for a life attached to an underwater surface. (384)
pólipo Cnidario con cuerpo de forma tubular y que está adaptado para vivir fijo en un fondo acuático.

population All the members of one species living in the same area. (596)
población Todos los miembros de una especie que viven en el mismo lugar.

population density The number of individuals in an area of a specific size. (602)

GLOSSARY

densidad de población Número de individuos en un área de un tamaño específico.

pore An opening through which sweat reaches the surface of the skin. (447)
poros Aberturas a través de las cuales sale el sudor a la superficie de la piel.

precipitation Any form of water that falls from clouds and reaches Earth's surface as rain, snow, sleet, or hail. (639)
precipitación Cualquier forma del agua que cae de las nubes y llega a la superficie de la tierra como lluvia, nieve, aguanieve o granizo.

predation An interaction in which one organism kills another for food or nutrients. (610)
depredación Interacción en la cual un organismo mata a otro para alimentarse u obtener nutrientes de él.

predator The organism that does the killing in a predation interaction. (610)
depredador Organismo que mata durante la depredación.

prey An organism that is killed and eaten by another organism in a predation interaction. (610)
presa Organismo que es consumido por otro organismo en el proceso de depredación.

primary succession The series of changes that occur in an area where no soil or organisms exist. (617)
sucesión primaria Serie de cambios que ocurren en un área donde no existe suelo ni organismos.

probability A number that describes how likely it is that a particular event will occur. (117)
probabilidad Número que describe cuán probable es que ocurra un suceso.

producer An organism that can make its own food. (631)
productor Organismo que puede generar su propio alimento.

prokaryote A unicellular organism that lacks a nucleus and some other cell structures. (23)
procariota Organismo unicelular que carece de un núcleo y otras estructuras celulares.

protein Large organic molecule made of carbon, hydrogen, oxygen, nitrogen, and sometimes sulfur. (61)
proteína Molécula orgánica grande compuesta de carbono, hidrógeno, oxígeno, nitrógeno y, a veces, azufre.

protist A eukaryotic organism that cannot be classified as an animal, plant, or fungus. (227)
protista Organismo eucariótico que no se puede clasificar como animal, planta ni hongo.

protozoan A unicellular, animal-like protist. (227)
protozoario Protista unicelular con características animales.

pseudopod A "false foot" or temporary bulge of cytoplasm used for feeding and movement in some protozoans. (228)
seudópodo "Pie falso" o abultamiento temporal del citoplasma que algunos protozoarios usan para alimentarse o desplazarse.

punctuated equilibrium Pattern of evolution in which long stable periods are interrupted by brief periods of more rapid change. (199)
equilibrio puntual Patrón de la evolución en el que los períodos largos estables son interrumpidos por breves períodos de cambio rápido.

Punnett square A chart that shows all the possible combinations of alleles that can result from a genetic cross. (118)
cuadrado de Punnett Tabla que muestra todas las combinaciones posibles de los alelos que se pueden derivar de un cruce genético.

pupa The third stage of complete metamorphosis, in which a larva develops into an adult insect. (392)
pupa Tercera etapa de la metamorfosis completa, en la que la larva se convierte en insecto adulto.

purebred An offspring of crosses that has the same form of traits. (111)
raza pura Descendiente de cruces, que tiene los mismos rasgos.

R

radial symmetry A body plan in which any number of imaginary lines that all pass through a central point divide the animal into two mirror images. (314)
simetría radiada Esquema del cuerpo en el que cualquier número de líneas imaginarias que atraviesan un punto central dividen a un animal en dos partes que son el reflejo la una de la otra.

rain forest A forest that receives at least 2 meters of rain per year, mostly occurring in the tropical wet climate zone. (648)
selva tropical Bosque donde caen al menos 2 metros de lluvia al año, principalmente en la zona climática tropical húmeda.

recessive allele An allele that is hidden whenever the dominant allele is present. (113)
alelo recesivo Alelo que no se manifiesta cuando el alelo dominante está presente.

reflex An automatic response that occurs rapidly and without conscious control. (512)

reflejo Respuesta automática que ocurre rápida e involuntariamente.

replication The process by which a cell makes a copy of the DNA in its nucleus before cell division. (94)
replicación Proceso en el que la célula copia el ADN de su núcleo antes de la división celular.

reptile A vertebrate whose temperature is determined by the temperature of its environment, that has lungs and scaly skin, and that lays eggs on land. (331)
reptil Vertebrado cuya temperatura corporal es determinada por la temperatura de su medio ambiente, que tiene pulmones y piel escamosa y que pone huevos en la tierra.

respiratory system An organ system that enables organisms to exchange gases with their surroundings. (373)
sistema respiratorio Sistema de órganos que permite al organismo intercambiar gases con su entorno.

response An action or change in behavior that occurs as a result of a stimulus. (7, 351, 420)
respuesta Acción o cambio del comportamiento que ocurre como resultado de un estímulo.

rhizoid A thin, rootlike structure that anchors a moss and absorbs water and nutrients for the plant. (261)
rizoide Estructura fina parecida a una raíz que sujeta un musgo al suelo, y que absorbe el agua y los nutrientes para la planta.

ribosome A small grain-shaped organelle in the cytoplasm of a cell that produces proteins. (50, 217)
ribosoma Orgánulo pequeño con forma de grano en el citoplasma de una célula que produce proteínas.

root cap A structure that covers the tip of a root, protecting the root from injury as the root grows through soil. (271)
cofia Estructura que cubre la punta de una raíz y la protege de cualquier daño mientras crece en la tierra.

S

savanna A grassland located close to the equator that may include shrubs and small trees and receives as much as 120 centimeters of rain per year. (650)
sabana Pradera que puede tener arbustos y árboles pequeños, ubicada cerca del ecuador y donde pueden caer hasta 120 centímetros de lluvia al año.

scavenger A carnivore that feeds on the bodies of dead or decaying organisms. (632)
carroñero Carnívoro que se alimenta de los restos de organismos muertos o en descomposición.

scientific theory A well-tested explanation for a wide range of observations or experimental results. (186)
teoría científica Explicación comprobada de una gran variedad de observaciones o resultados de experimentos.

scrotum An external pouch of skin in which the testes are located. (526)
escroto Bolsa de piel externa en donde se encuentran los testículos.

secondary succession The series of changes that occur in an area where the ecosystem has been disturbed, but where soil and organisms still exist. (618)
sucesión secundaria Serie de cambios que ocurren en un área después de la perturbación de un ecosistema, pero donde todavía hay suelo y organismos.

seed The plant structure that contains a young plant and a food supply inside a protective covering. (266)
semilla Estructura vegetal que contiene una planta joven y una fuente alimenticia encerradas en una cubierta protectora.

selectively permeable A property of cell membranes that allows some substances to pass across it, while others cannot. (65)
permeabilidad selectiva Propiedad de las membranas celulares que permite el paso de algunas sustancias y no de otras.

semen A mixture of sperm and fluids. (527)
semen Mezcla de esperma y fluidos.

sensory neuron A neuron that picks up stimuli from the internal or external environment and converts each stimulus into a nerve impulse. (352)
neurona sensorial Neurona que recoge los estímulos del medio ambiente interno o externo y convierte a cada estímulo en un impulso nervioso.

sepal A leaflike structure that encloses and protects the bud of a flower. (278)
sépalo Estructura similar a una hoja que encierra y protege el capullo de una flor.

sex chromosomes A pair of chromosomes carrying genes that determine whether a person is male or female. (163)
cromosomas sexuales Par de cromosomas portadores de genes que determinan el sexo (masculino o femenino) de una persona.

sex-linked gene A gene that is carried on a sex (X or Y) chromosome. (164)
gen ligado al sexo Gen de un cromosoma sexual (X o Y).

GLOSSARY

sexual reproduction A reproductive process that involves two parents that combine their genetic material to produce a new organism which differs from both parents. (7)
reproducción sexual Proceso de reproducción que involucra a dos reproductores que combinan su material genético para producir un nuevo organismo que es distinto a los dos reproductores.

shared derived characteristic A characteristic or trait, such as fur, that the common ancestor of a group had and passed on to its descendants. (27)
característica derivada compartida Característica o rasgo, como el pelaje, del ancestro común de un grupo que éste pasa a sus descendientes.

short-day plant A plant that flowers when the nights are longer than the plant's critical night length. (291)
planta de día corto Planta que florece cuando la duración de la noche es más larga que la duración crítica.

skeletal muscle A muscle that is attached to the bones of the skeleton and provides the force that moves the bones; also called striated muscle. (415, 440)
músculo esquelético Músculo que está conectado a los huesos del esqueleto y que proporciona la fuerza que mueve los huesos; llamado también músculo estriado.

skeleton 1. The inner framework made up of all the bones of the body. (415, 431) **2.** A framework that shapes and supports an animal, protects its internal organs, and allows it to move in its environment.
esqueleto 1. Estructura interna compuesta de todos los huesos del cuerpo. **2.** Estructura que da forma y soporte a un animal, protege sus órganos internos y le permite moverse en su medio ambiente.

smooth muscle Involuntary muscle found inside many internal organs of the body. (440)
músculo liso Músculo involuntario que se halla dentro de muchos órganos internos del cuerpo.

species A group of similar organisms that can mate with each other and produce offspring that can also mate and reproduce. (16, 183, 596)
especie Grupo de organismos semejantes que pueden cruzarse y producir descendencia fértil.

sperm A male sex cell. (525)
esperma Célula sexual masculina.

spongy bone Layer of bone tissue that has many small spaces and is found just inside the layer of compact bone. (435)
hueso esponjoso Capa de tejido óseo que tiene muchos orificios pequeños y que se encuentra próxima a la capa de hueso compacto.

spontaneous generation The mistaken idea that living things arise from nonliving sources. (8)
generación espontánea Idea equivocada de que los seres vivos surgen de fuentes inertes.

spore In bacteria, protists, and fungi, a thick-walled, tiny cell capable of surviving unfavorable conditions and then growing into a new organism. (234)
espora En las bacterias, los protistas y los hongos, una minúscula célula de paredes gruesas capaz de sobrevivir condiciones desfavorables y crecer hasta convertirse en un organismo.

sporophyte The stage in the life cycle of a plant in which the plant produces spores. (280)
esporofito Etapa del ciclo vital de una planta en la que produce esporas.

stamen The male reproductive part of a flower. (278)
estambre Parte reproductora masculina de una flor.

stimulus Any change or signal in the environment that can make an organism react in some way. (7, 351, 420)
estímulo Cualquier cambio o señal del medio ambiente que puede causar una reacción en un organismo.

stoma A small opening on the underside of a leaf through which oxygen, water, and carbon dioxide can move. (274)
estomas Pequeños orificios en la superficie inferior de la hoja a través de los cuales ocurre el intercambio de oxígeno y dióxido de carbono.

stress 1. A force that acts on rock to change its shape or volume. **2.** The reaction of a person's body to potentially threatening, challenging, or disturbing events. (426)
presión 1. Fuerza que actúa sobre las rocas y que cambia su forma o volumen. **2. estrés** Reacción del cuerpo de un individuo a sucesos como posibles amenazas, desafíos o trastornos.

striated muscle A muscle that appears banded; also called skeletal muscle. (440)
músculo estriado Músculo con forma de franjas; también se llama músculo esquelético.

succession The series of predictable changes that occur in a community over time. (616)
sucesión Serie de cambios predecibles que ocurren en una comunidad a través del tiempo.

swim bladder An internal gas-filled organ that helps a bony fish stabilize its body at different water depths. (358)
vejiga natatoria Órgano interno lleno de gas que ayuda a un pez con esqueleto a estabilizar su cuerpo a distintas profundidades.

symbiosis Any relationship in which two species live closely together and that benefits at least one of the species. (613)
simbiosis Cualquier relación en la cual dos especies viven muy cerca y al menos una de ellas se beneficia.

synapse The junction where one neuron can transfer an impulse to the next structure. (508)
sinapsis Confluencia donde una neurona puede transferir un impulso a la siguiente estructura.

T

T cell A lymphocyte that identifies pathogens and distinguishes one pathogen from another. (561)
célula T Linfocito que identifica a los patógenos y distingue un patógeno de otro.

tadpole The larval form of a frog or toad. (394)
renacuajo Estado de larva de una rana o un sapo.

target cell A cell in the body that recognizes a hormone's chemical structure. (518)
célula destinataria Célula del cuerpo que reconoce la estructura química de una hormona.

taxonomy The scientific study of how living things are classified. (15)
taxonomía Estudio científico de cómo se clasifican los seres vivos.

tendon Strong connective tissue that attaches muscle to bone. (440)
tendón Tejido conectivo resistente que une un músculo a un hueso.

testis Organ of the male reproductive system in which sperm and testosterone are produced. (526)
testículo Órgano del sistema reproductor masculino en el que se producen el esperma y la testosterona.

testosterone A hormone produced by the testes that controls the development of sperm and adult male characteristics. (526)
testosterona Hormona producida por los testículos que controla el desarrollo del esperma y las características del hombre adulto.

threatened species A species that could become endangered in the near future. (665)
especie amenazada Especie que puede llegar a estar en peligro de extinción en el futuro próximo.

tissue A group of similar cells that perform a specific function. (57, 256, 313, 410)
tejido Grupo de células semejantes que realizan una función específica.

toxin A poison that can harm an organism. (552)
toxina Veneno que puede dañar un organismo.

trachea The windpipe; a passage through which air moves in the respiratory system. (480)
tráquea Conducto por el cual circula el aire en el sistema respiratorio.

trait A specific characteristic that an organism can pass to its offspring through its genes. (110)
rasgo Característica específica que un organismo puede transmitir a sus descendientes a través de los genes.

transfer RNA Type of RNA in the cytoplasm that carries an amino acid to the ribosome during protein synthesis. (151)
ARN de transferencia Tipo de ARN del citoplasma que lleva un aminoácido al ribosoma durante la síntesis de proteínas.

transpiration The process by which water is lost through a plant's leaves. (275)
transpiración Proceso por el cual las hojas de una planta pierden agua.

tropism The response of a plant toward or away from a stimulus. (289)
tropismo Respuesta de una planta acercándose o apartándose del estímulo.

tumor A mass of rapidly dividing cells that can damage surrounding tissue. (158, 579)
tumor Masa de células que se dividen rápidamente y que puede dañar los tejidos que la rodean.

tundra An extremely cold, dry biome climate region characterized by short, cool summers and bitterly cold winters. (653)
tundra Bioma de la región climática extremadamente fría y seca, que se caracteriza por veranos cortos y frescos e inviernos sumamente fríos.

U

umbilical cord A ropelike structure that forms between the embryo or fetus and the placenta. (535)
cordón umbilical Estructura con forma de cuerda que se forma en el útero entre el embrión o feto y la placenta.

understory A layer of shorter trees and vines that grows in the shade of a forest canopy. (649)
sotobosque Capa de árboles de poca altura y plantas trepadoras que crecen bajo la sombra del dosel de un bosque.

GLOSSARY

unicellular Made of a single cell. (6, 56)
unicelular Compuesto por una sola célula.

urea A chemical that comes from the breakdown of proteins. (487)
urea Sustancia química que resulta de la descomposición de proteínas.

ureter A narrow tube that carries urine from one of the kidneys to the urinary bladder. (488)
uretra Conducto estrecho que lleva la orina desde uno de los riñones a la vejiga urinaria.

urethra A small tube through which urine leaves the body. (488)
uretra Conducto pequeño a través del cual la orina sale del cuerpo.

urinary bladder A sacklike muscular organ that stores urine until it is eliminated from the body. (488)
vejiga urinaria Órgano muscular con forma de saco que almacena la orina hasta que se elimine del cuerpo.

urine A watery fluid produced by the kidneys that contains urea and other wastes. (487)
orina Fluido acuoso producido por los riñones que contiene urea y otros materiales de desecho.

uterus The hollow muscular organ of the female reproductive system in which a fertilized egg develops. (529)
útero Órgano muscular hueco del sistema reproductor femenino en el que se desarrolla un óvulo fertilizado.

V

vaccination The process by which harmless antigens are deliberately introduced into a person's body to produce active immunity; also called immunization. (570)
vacunación Proceso por el cual antígenos inocuos se introducen deliberadamente en el cuerpo de una persona para producir una inmunidad activa; también se le llama inmunización.

vaccine A substance used in a vaccination that consists of pathogens that have been weakened or killed but can still trigger the body to produce chemicals that destroy the pathogens. (214, 570)
vacuna Sustancia que se inyecta en la vacunación; consiste de patógenos débiles o muertos que pueden estimular al cuerpo a producir sustancias químicas que destruyan esos patógenos.

vacuole A sac-like organelle that stores water, food, and other materials. (54, 256)

vacuola Orgánulo en forma de bolsa que almacena agua, alimentos y otros materiales.

vagina A muscular passageway leading to the outside of a female's body; also called the birth canal. (529)
vagina Pasaje muscular que se extiende hasta una abertura del cuerpo de una mujer; también llamada canal de nacimiento.

valve A flap of tissue in the heart or a vein that prevents blood from flowing backward. (471)
válvula Lámina de tejido del corazón o de una vena que impide que la sangre fluya hacia atrás.

variation Any difference between individuals of the same species. (189)
variación Cualquier diferencia entre individuos de la misma especie.

vascular plant A plant that has true vascular tissue for transporting materials. (263)
planta vascular Planta que tiene tejido vascular verdadero para el transporte de materiales.

vascular tissue The internal transporting tissue in some plants that is made up of tubelike structures that carry water, food, and minerals. (258)
tejido vascular Tejido interno de algunas plantas compuesto de estructuras tubulares que transportan agua, alimentos y minerales.

vein 1. A narrow deposit of a mineral that is sharply different from the surrounding rock. **2.** A blood vessel that carries blood back to the heart. (471)
vena 1. Placa delgada de un mineral que es marcadamente distinto a la roca que lo rodea. **2.** Vaso sanguíneo que transporta la sangre al corazón.

ventricle A lower chamber of the heart that pumps blood out to the lungs or body. (470)
ventrículo Cavidad inferior del corazón que bombea sangre a los pulmones o el cuerpo.

vertebrae The bones that make up the backbone of an organism. In humans, the 26 bones that make up the backbone. (326, 431)
vértebras Huesos que componen la columna vertebral de un organismo. En los humanos, los 26 huesos que componen la columna vertebral.

vertebrate An animal with a backbone. (310)
vertebrado Animal con columna vertebral.

villi Tiny finger-shaped structures that cover the inner surface of the small intestine and provide a large surface area through which digested food is absorbed. (466)
vellosidades Pequeñas estructuras con forma de dedo que cubren la superficie interna del intestino delgado y proporcionan una superficie amplia a través de la cual se absorbe el alimento digerido.

virus A tiny, nonliving particle that enters and then reproduces inside a living cell. (210)
virus Partícula diminuta inerte que entra en una célula viva y luego se reproduce dentro de ella.

vocal cords Folds of connective tissue that stretch across the opening of the larynx and produce a person's voice. (483)
cuerdas vocales Pliegues de tejido conector que se extienden a lo largo de la abertura de la laringe y que producen la voz de una persona.

voluntary muscle A muscle that is under conscious control. (439)
músculo voluntario Músculo que se puede controlar conscientemente.

W

water vascular system A system of fluid-filled tubes in an echinoderm's body. (358)
sistema vascular de agua Sistema de vasos llenos de líquido en el cuerpo de un equinodermo.

X

xylem The vascular tissue through which water and minerals move in some plants. (263)
xilema Tejido vascular de algunas plantas por el que circulan agua y nutrientes.

Z

zygote A fertilized egg, produced by the joining of a sperm and an egg. (282, 525)
cigoto Óvulo fertilizado, producido por la unión de un espermatozoide y un óvulo.

INDEX
Page numbers for key terms are printed in **boldface** type.

INDEX

INDEX

Page numbers for key terms are printed in **boldface** type.

INDEX

Page numbers for key terms are printed in **boldface** type.

INDEX

Page numbers for key terms are printed in **boldface** type.

S

INDEX

ACKNOWLEDGMENTS

Staff Credits

The people who made up the *Interactive Science* team—representing composition services, core design digital and multimedia production services, digital product development, editorial, editorial services, manufacturing, and production—are listed below:

Jan Van Aarsen, Samah Abadir, Ernie Albanese, Chris Anton, Zareh Artinian, Bridget Binstock, Suzanne Biron, Niki Birbilis, MJ Black, Nancy Bolsover, Stacy Boyd, Jim Brady, Laura Brancky, Katherine Bryant, Michael Burstein, Pradeep Byram, Jessica Chase, Jonathan Cheney, Sitha Chhor, Arthur Ciccone, Allison Cook-Bellistri, Brandon Cole, Karen Corliss, Rebecca Cottingham, AnnMarie Coyne, Bob Craton, Chris Deliee, Paul Delsignore, Michael Di Maria, Diane Dougherty, Nancy Duffner, Kristen Ellis, Kelly Engel, Theresa Eugenio, Amanda Ferguson, Jorgensen Fernandez, Kathryn Fobert, Alicia Franke, Louise Gachet, Julia Gecha, Mark Geyer, Steve Gobbell, Paula Gogan-Porter, Jeffrey Gong, Sandra Graff, Robert M. Graham, Maureen Griffin, Adam Groffman, Lynette Haggard, Christian Henry, Karen Holtzman, Guy Huff, Susan Hutchinson, Sharon Inglis, Marian Jones, Sumy Joy, Chris Kammer, Sheila Kanitsch, Courtenay Kelley, Chris Kennedy, Toby Klang, Alyse Kondrat, Greg Lam, Russ Lappa, Margaret LaRaia, David Leistensnider, Ben Leveille, Thea Limpus, Charles Luey, Dotti Marshall, Kathy Martin, Robyn Matzke, John McClure, Mary Beth McDaniel, Krista McDonald, Tim McDonald, Rich McMahon, Cara McNally, Bernadette McQuilkin, Melinda Medina, Angelina Mendez, Maria Milczarek, Claudi Mimo, Mike Napieralski, Deborah Nicholls, Dave Nichols, Anthony Nuccio, William Oppenheimer, Jodi O'Rourke, Julie Orr, Ameer Padshah, Lorie Park, Celio Pedrosa, Jonathan Penyack, Linda Zust Reddy, Jennifer Reichlin, Stephen Rider, Charlene Rimsa, Walter Rodriguez, Stephanie Rogers, Marcy Rose, Rashid Ross, Anne Rowsey, Manuel Sanchez, Logan Schmidt, Amanda Seldera, Laurel Smith, Nancy Smith, Ted Smykal, Sandy Schneider, Emily Soltanoff, Cindy Strowman, Dee Sunday, Barry Tomack, Elizabeth Tustian, Patricia Valencia, Ana Sofia Villaveces, Stephanie Wallace, Amanda Watters, Christine Whitney, Brad Wiatr, Heidi Wilson, Heather Wright, James Yagelski, Tim Yetzina, Rachel Youdelman.

Photographs

Every effort has been made to secure permission and provide appropriate credit for photographic material. The publisher deeply regrets any omission and pledges to correct errors called to its attention in subsequent editions.

Unless otherwise acknowledged, all photographs are the property of Pearson Education, Inc.

Photo locators denoted as follows: Top (T), Center (C), Bottom (B), Left (L), Right (R), Background (Bkgd)

Cover

agefotostock/Superstock

Front Matter

vi (TR) Kevin Schafer/Alamy; vii (TR) Nature Picture Library; viii (TR) Ocean/Corbis; ix (TR) Blickwinkel/Schmidbauer/Alamy Images; xi (TR) Mark Conlin/Alamy; xii (TR) AGE Fotostock/PhotoLibrary Group, Inc.; xiii (TR) Tristan Lafranchis/Peter Arnold/PhotoLibrary Group, Inc.; xiv (TR) National Geographic Image Collection; xv (TR) Stephen Dalton/Science Source; xvi (TR) Peter Rowlands/PR Productions; xvii (TR) Photo Researchers, Inc.; xviii (TR) ©Kevin Fleming/Corbis; xix (TR) Sayyid Azim/©Associated Press; xx (TR) Gary Bell/Corbis; xxi (TR) Marko König/Corbis; xxx (C) iStockphoto; (R) Thomas Deerinck, NCMIR/Science Source; xxxii (CR) AURORA, (B) Nature Picture Library; xxxiii (B) Nature Picture Library; xxxiv (Bkgrd) Michael Meisl/Oxford Scientific/Photolibrary Group, Inc.; xxxvi (Bkgrd) Kevin Schafer/Alamy

1 (BR) Jane Allan/Fotolia; 3 (TCL) Joshua Haviv/Fotolia, (BCL) Eye of Science/Photo Researchers, Inc., (TL) Shutterstock; 4 (CR) Sam Ogden/Science Source; 5 (BL) Kjell Sandved/Oxford Scientific/PhotoLibrary Group, Inc., (TR) Matt Meadows/Peter Arnold/PhotoLibrary Group, Inc., (TL) Paroli Galperti/PhotoLibrary Group, Inc., (TC) Shutterstock; 6 (TR) Kerstin Hinze/Nature Picture Library, (TL) Photo Researchers, Inc., (BL) Science Photo Library RF/Photolibrary Group, Inc.; 7 (TR) ©John Kaprielian/Photo Researchers, Inc., (BL) Gentoo Multimedia/Fotolia, (CL) Ingo Arndt/Nature Picture Library; 8 (BL) Dan Duchars/PhotoLibrary Group, Inc., (TCL) Jürgen and Christine Sohns/Picture Press/PhotoLibrary Group, Inc.; 9 Ian Thraves/Alamy; 11 (Bkgrd) Arco Images GmbH/ Alamy; 12 (B) Jose Fuste Raga/Age Fotostock/PhotoLibrary Group, Inc., (TL) Pichugin Dmitry/Shutterstock; 13 (TLC) Steve Byland/Shutterstock, (TL) Tony Campbell/Fotolia; 14 (BL)/©Chip Clark/Smithsonian Institution; 15 (BR) Ilian Animal/Alamy Images; 16 (T) Joshua Haviv/Fotolia, (BL) Eric Isselée/Shutterstock, (BR) Rod Williams/Nature Picture Library; 17 (TR) Alan Gleichman/Shutterstock; 18 (CL) FloridaStock/Shutterstock; 20 (CR) Stuart Wilson/Science Source; 21 (TL) Armando Frazao/iStockphoto, (TR) Eric Isselée/Shutterstock, (TCL) Hemera Technologies/Jupiter Images, (TC) JinYoung Lee/Shutterstock, (TCR) Joseph Calev/Shutterstock, (TC) Kim Taylor/Nature Picture Library; 22 (TR) alle/Fotolia; 23 (TCR) SciMAT/Photo Researchers, Inc., (BR) Eye of Science/Science Source; 24 (L) Eric V. Grave/Science Source, (BCR) Eye of Science/Photo Researchers, Inc., (Bkgrd) Ron Erwin/All Canada Photos/Corbis; 25 (CL) Nicolas Larento/Fotolia; 26 (TR) Nature Picture Library; 28 (Bkgrd) Elenathewise/Fotolia, (CL) Photo courtesy of Research in Review, Florida State University: U. Treesucon, David Redfield Expedition. Used by permission, (BL) Tim Laman/Nature Picture Library; 29 (BL) Jasmina007/Shutterstock, (BL) Nick Garbutt/Nature Picture Library; 30 (BL) Eric V. Grave/Science Source, (BCR) Alan Gleichman/Shutterstock, (TR) Photo Researchers, Inc.; 32 (TCR)/Virgin Galactic; 34 (Bkgrd) Alfred Wolf/Explorer/Photo Researchers, Inc.; 35 (BR) Rebecca Ellis/iStockphoto; 36 (B) Nature Picture Library; 39 (BCL) iStockphoto, (BL) Michael Abbey/Photo Researchers, Inc., (TL) Perennou Nuridsany/Photo Researchers, Inc.; 40 (CR) Biophoto Associates/Photo Researchers, Inc.; 41 (Bkgrd) Nils-Johan Norenlind/AGE Fotostock; 42 (CL) Dr. Cecil H. Fox/Photo Researchers, Inc., (CL) Dr. Jeremy Burgess/Photo Researchers, Inc., (BCR) Science Museum, London/DK Images, (Inset) Steve Gschmeissner/Photo Researchers, Inc.; 43 (Inset) John Walsh/Photo Researchers, Inc., (Inset) M. I. Walker/Photo Researchers, Inc., (BCR) Perennou Nuridsany/Photo Researchers, Inc.; 44 (BR)/©DK Images, (CR) TheRocky41/Shutterstock, (BCR) Millard H. Sharp/Photo Researchers, Inc., (CL) Paul Taylor/Riser/Getty Images, (BCL) Wes Thompson/Corbis Yellow/Corbis;

46 (C) ©A. Syred/Photo Researchers, Inc.; 48 (Bkgrd) Dr. Torsten Wittmann/Photo Researchers, Inc.; 50 (CL) Alfred Paskieka/Photo Researchers, Inc., (BR) Bill Longcore/Photo Researchers, Inc.; 51 (CL) CNRI/Photo Researchers, Inc.; 54 (TL) Professors Pietro M. Motta & Tomonori Naguro/Photo Researchers, Inc.; 55 (TR) Biophoto Associates/Photo Researchers, Inc.; 56 (BL) Biophoto Associates/Photo Researchers, Inc., (BR) Thomas Deerinck, NCMIR/Science Source, (TR) Ed Reschke/Getty Images, (TL) Profs. P. Motta and S. Correr/Science Photo Library/Photo Researchers, Inc.; 58 (Bkgrd) Tierbild Okapia/Photo Researchers, Inc.; 59 (Bkgrd) Digital Vision/Getty Images; 60 (BL) David Murray/©DK Images, (BR) iStockphoto; 61 (TR) Tstarr/Shutterstock; 64 (BC) Michael Lamotte/Cole Group/Photodisc/Getty Images; 67 (TR, TCR) Perennou Nuridsany/Photo Researchers, Inc.; 69 (CR, CL, C) Michael Abbey/Photo Researchers, Inc.; 70 (TR) Science Museum, London/DK Images; 72 (BCR)/©DK Images; 74 (BL) David M. Phillips/Photo Researchers, Inc., (Inset, Bkgrd) Kim Taylor and Jane Burton/Dorling/©DK Images; 75 (Inset) Martin Shields/Photo Researchers, Inc.; 76 (Bkgrd) Ocean/Corbis; 79 (B) Kent Wood/Getty Images, (BCL) Ed Reschke/Peter Arnold/PhotoLibrary Group, Inc., (TL) SuperStock, (TCL) Vincenzo Lombardo/Photodisc/Getty Images; 80 (CR) David Cook/blueshiftstudios/Alamy; 81 (BCL) AURORA, (Bkgrd) Robbert Koene/Getty Images, (BCR) SuperStock; 83 (Bkgrd) Rich Iwasaki/Getty Images; 85 (Bkgrd) Yuji Sakai/Digital Vision/Getty Images; 86 (Bkgrd) Pete Saloutos/Flirt/Corbis; 90 (Bkgrd) Vincenzo Lombardo/Photodisc/Getty Images; 91 (Bkgrd) Noah Clayton/Riser/Getty Images; 92 (C, Bkgrd) George Grall/National Geographic Image Collection; 93 (CR) Eric Bean/The Image Bank/Getty Images, (L) Helmut Gritscher/Peter Arnold/PhotoLibrary Group, Inc., (Inset) Michael Poliza/Getty Images; 96 (TR, TCL, B) Ed Reschke/Peter Arnold/PhotoLibrary Group, Inc.; 97 (TC, CR, B) Ed Reschke/Peter Arnold/PhotoLibrary Group, Inc.; 98 (C) Kent Wood/Getty Images, (TCR) Dr. Gopal Murti/Photo Researchers, Inc.; 100 (TR, BR) Ed Reschke/Peter Arnold/PhotoLibrary Group, Inc.; 104 (CL) Andres Rodriguez/Alamy; 105 (Bkgrd) Thomas Deerinck, NCMIR/Photo Researchers, Inc.; 106 (C) SuperStock; 109 (BCL) Brand X Pictures/Jupiter Images, (BCL) Frank Krahmer/Getty Images, (TCL) iStockphoto; 110 (TC) Bettman/Corbis, (C) Maximilian Stock/Getty Images; 112 (CL) Andrea Jones/Alamy Images; 115 (TC) Herman Eisenbeiss/Photo Researchers, Inc., (Bkgrd) Monika Gniot/Shutterstock, (TCR) WildPictures/Alamy Images; 116 (Inset) J. Pat Carter/AP Images/©Associated Press, (Bkgrd) NOAA; 117 (CR) Brand X Pictures/Jupiter Images; 118 (Bkgrd) Monika Gniot/Shutterstock; 120 (R) Alexandra Grablewski/Jupiter Images; 121 (Bkgrd) Agg/Dreamstime LLC, (C) iStockphoto, (CR) Jomann/Dreamstime LLC; 122 (Bkgrd) Erik Rumbaugh/iStockphoto, (C) Joel Sartore/National Geographic/Getty Images; 123 (BR) ©DK Images, (BCL) Brand X Pictures/Jupiter Images, (BCR) CreativeAct-Animals Series/Alamy, (BCL) Frank Krahmer/Getty Images; 124 (TC) Geoff Dann/©DK Images, (TCR) Jay Brousseau/Stone/Getty Images, (TC) John Daniels/Ardea; 125 (BCR) Blickwinkel/Schmidbauer/Alamy Images, (C) Luis Carlos Torres/iStockphoto, (BC) Michael Melford/National Geographic/Getty Images, (BR) Naile Goelbasi/Taxi/Getty Images, (BCL) Radius Images/Photolibrary Group, Inc., (B) Randy Faris/Spirit/Corbis, (BC) Stuart McClymont/Stone/Getty Images; 126 (BL, BCL) ©DK Images, (BC) Brand X Pictures/Jupiter Images, (BCL) CreativeAct-Animals Series/Alamy, (BC) Frank Krahmer/Getty Images, (BCL) Joel Sartore/National Geographic/Getty Images, (BCL) Radius Images/Photolibrary Group, Inc., (Bkgrd) Serg64/Shutterstock, (TCL) Stuart McClymont/Stone/Getty Images, (Bkgrd) Tomas Bercic/iStockphoto; 128 (BR) Patrick Landmann/Science Source, (BL) James King-Holmes/Science Source; 129 (BC) Cathlee/iStockphoto, (BL) Eric Isselée/iStockphoto, (C) Frank Greenaway/©DK Images, (Inset) Jamie Marshall/©DK Images, (BR) Jane Burton/©DK Images, (BR) proxyminder/iStockphoto; 134 (BL) Blickwinkel/Schmidbauer/Alamy Images; 138 (Bkgrd) We Shoot/Alamy Images; 139 (BR) Dorling Kindersley/©DK Images; 140 (Bkgrd) David Doubilet/National Geographic/Getty Images; 143 (BCL) Christian Charisius/Reuters Media, (BL) Scott Camazine/Science Source; 144 (T) Gerald C. Kelley/Photo Researchers, Inc., (BCR) Omikron/Photo Researchers, Inc., (CL) Science Source/Photo Researchers, Inc.; 146 (CL) Andrew Syred/Photo Researchers, Inc., (BR) Mark Evans/iStockphoto; 149 (TR) Dr. Gopal Murti/Science Photo Library/Photo Researchers, Inc.; 150 (CL)/©DK Images, (TR) Bedrock Studios/©DK Images; 154 (B) Peter Cade/Getty Images, (Inset) Russell Glenister/image100/Corbis; 156 (TL) ©Jim Stamates/Getty Images, (Inset) Christian Charisius/Reuters Media; 157 (BR) Andy Crawford/©DK Images, (CR) Scott Camazine/Science Source; 161 (BR) Timothey Kosachev/iStockphoto; 162 (TL) China Daily China Daily Information Corp-CDIC/Reuters Media; 163 (CR) ©Department of Clinical Cytogenetics Addenbrookes Hospital/Science Photo Library/Photo Researchers, Inc., (BC) Addenbrookes Hospital/Photo Researchers, Inc.; 164 (TR, BR) Jupiterimages/Brand X/Alamy/Alamy, (BC) Prisma/Superstock; 166 (BL) AFP/Stringer/Getty Images, (Bkgrd) Anke van Wyk/Shutterstock; 169 (Inset) Ed Reschke/Peter Arnold/PhotoLibrary Group, Inc., (BR) Splashnews/NewsCom; 171 (Bkgrd) Yonhap, Choi Byung-kil/©Associated Press; 176 (Bkgrd) D. Robert Franz/ImageState/Alamy Images, (BL) Denis Poroy/©Associated Press; 177 (C) Anthony Tueni/Alamy Images, (TL) Dave King/©DK Images; 178 Mark Conlin/Alamy; 182 (Inset)/©DK Images, (Bkgrd) Andreas Gross/Westend 61/Alamy Images, (TC) PoodlesRock/Corbis; 183 (BCR) Enzo & Paolo Ragazzini/Corbis, (T) Oyvind Martinsen/Alamy, (BCL) N. Reed of QED Images/Alamy, (BC) Wardene Weisser/Bruce Coleman Inc./Alamy Images; 184 (CR) Joe McDonald/Corbis, (BCL) Rosemary Calvert/Getty Images, (TL) Steve Bloom Images/Alamy; 186 (CL) GK Hart/Vikki Hart/Getty Images, (Bkgrd) Photo-Max/iStockphoto, (C) Steve Shott/©DK Images, (CR) Tracy Morgan/©DK Images; 187 (TR) Derrell Fowler, (TL) Georgette Douwma/Nature Picture Library, (TC) The Art of Animals.co.uk/PetStock Boys/Alamy Images; 190 (BL) Mark Conlin/Getty Images; 191 (Bkgrd) Copyright ©2007 Maury Hatfield. All Rights Reserved; 192 (BL) Gordon Wiltsie/National Geographic Image Collection, (CR, BR) Model by Tyler Keillor/University of Chicago; 194 (BCR)/SuperStock, (BC) Ed Robinson/Design Pics/Corbis, (BCL) Winfried Wisniewski/Cusp/Corbis; 196 (TCR)/Cook Islands Biodiversity/(C)/John T. Rotenberry; 197 (Bkgrd) Momatiuk--Eastcott/Corbis, (TCR) T. Leeson/Photo Researchers, Inc., (TCL) Thomas & Pat Leeson/Photo Researchers, Inc.; 200 (TR, TCR) Joe McDonald/Corbis, (TCR) T. Leeson/Photo Researchers, Inc., (BCR) Thomas & Pat Leeson/Photo Researchers, Inc.; 202 (TCR) S.Borisov/Shutterstock; 204 (TCL) Joshua Roper/

ACKNOWLEDGMENTS

Alamy; **206** (Bkgrd) Topic Photo Agency IN/AGE Fotostock; **208** (Bkgrd) Mark Newman/Stock Connection; **209** (BL) Getty Images; **210** (Inset) Biosphoto/Peter Arnold/PhotoLibrary Group, Inc.; **214** (Bkgrd) evok20/Fotolia; **216** (C) Rick Souders/Index Stock Imagery/PhotoLibrary Group, Inc.; **217** (Bkgrd) Brian J. Ford/Brian J Ford; **218** (C) Chris Bjornberg/Photo Researchers, Inc., (C) VEM/Photo Researchers, Inc., (CR) CMSP/Getty Images; **219** (BCL), RGB Ventures LLC dba SuperStock / Alamy, (BR) Rob Whitrow/Garden Picture Library/PhotoLibrary Group, Inc., (BR, BL) Shutterstock; **220** (TL) SciMAT / Science Source, (Bkgrd) Comstock Images/AGE Fotostock, (TR) Science Photo Library/Photo Researchers, Inc.; **221** (BL) Dr. Linda M. Stannard, University of Cape Town / Science Source, (BCR) George Grall/National Geographic Image Collection, (BL) Luká Hejtman/iStockphoto; **223** (Bkgrd) Stuart Westmorland/Photographer's Choice/Getty Images; **224** (TL) Scimat / Science Source, (Bkgrd) RGB Ventures LLC dba SuperStock/Alamy; **226** (Bkgrd), (Inset)/Gioia Photography; **227** (BR) Andrew Syred / Science Source, (BL) Eye of Science/Photo Researchers, Inc., (BC) Steve Gschmeissner/Science Source; **229** (Inset) Larry West/Photo Researchers, Inc.; **231** (BCR) Getty Images, (BR) Steve Gschmeissner/Photo Researchers, Inc.; **232** (TL) David McCarthy/Photo Researchers, Inc., (BR) marinethemes/Kelvin Aitken/Image Quest 3-D, (TR) Steve Gschmeissner/Photo Researchers, Inc.; **233** (TR) David McCarthy/Photo Researchers, Inc., (TCR) Getty Images, (TC) Lawrence Naylor/Photo Researchers, Inc., (TCL) Steve Gschmeissner/Photo Researchers, Inc.; **234** (B) Biophoto Associates/Science Source; **235** (Bkgrd) Chad Bridwell/Fotolia; **236** (Bkgrd) Scott Camazine/Photo Researchers, Inc.; **238** (CR) Ed Reschke/Peter Arnold/PhotoLibrary Group, Inc., (CL) Getty Images; **239** (TCL) Michael Lander/Nordic/Getty Images, (Inset) ScienceFoto/Oxford Scientific/PhotoLibrary Group, Inc.; **240** (Bkgrd) Gary Meszaros/Photo Researchers, Inc.; **242** (BCL) Beppe Arvidsson/Scanpix/PhotoLibrary Group, Inc., (TL) Emilio Ereza/AGE Fotostock, (TCR) Jeff Barnard/AP Photos; **243** (CL) Jeffrey L. Rotman/Corbis, (BL) TED MEAD/PhotoLibrary Group, Inc.; **244** (TCR) evok20/Fotolia; **245** (C) Chris Bjornberg/Photo Researchers, Inc., (CR) VEM/Photo Researchers, Inc.; **248** (Bkgrd) Dean Murray/iStockphoto; **249** (BC) Michel Viard/Jacana/Photo Researchers, Inc., (TR) PASIEKA/SPL/Science Photo Library/Alamy; **250** (Bkgrd) Laurent Bouvet/Easy-Pix/AGE Fotostock; **253** (TCL) Howard Rice/©DK Images, (BL) Nature Picture Library; **255** (B) Theodore Clutter / Science Source, (BR) Paul Paladin/iStockphoto; **256** (TL) Lusoimages/Shutterstock, (TCL) Perennou Nuridsany/Photo Researchers, Inc.; **258** (TCL) Kjell Sandved/Photo Researchers, Inc.; **260** (Inset) Garden Picture Library/Francesca Yorke/PhotoLibrary Group, Inc.; **261** (Inset) John Serrao/Photo Researchers, Inc., (Bkgrd) czamfir/Fotolia; **262** (Inset)/Dr. David T. Webb, (TL) Adrian Davies/Nature Picture Library, (CL) Daniel Vega/Age fotostock/PhotoLibrary Group, Inc.; **263** (Bkgrd) Howard Rice/Garden Picture Library/PhotoLibrary Group, Inc.; **265** (C) Albert Aanensen/Nature Picture Library, (TCL) Philippe Clement/Nature Picture Library; **267** (TL) Christine M. Douglas/©DK Images, (BCL) Joanna Pecha/iStockphoto, (BL) M. Philip Kahl/Photo Researchers, Inc., (TC) Peter Anderson/©DK Images; **268** (BCR) Anna Subbotina/Shutterstock, (CL) Howard Rice/©DK Images, (TL) K. Kaplin/Shutterstock; **270** (CL) Fletcher & Baylis/Photo Researchers, Inc.; **271** (CR) Derek Croucher/Alamy Images, (C) Lynwood M. Chace/Photo Researchers, Inc.; **272** (C) Manfred Kage/Peter Arnold/PhotoLibrary Group, Inc., (TL) Peter Hestbaek/Shutterstock; **274** (Bkgrd) Pakhnyushcha/Shutterstock; **278** (BCL) Kim Taylor/Nature Picture Library, (BR, BL) Nature Picture Library, (BC) Niall Benvie/Nature Picture Library, (BR) Simon Williams/Nature Picture Library, (BCL) All Canada Photos/Alamy; **280** (Bkgrd) Ocean/Corbis; **282** (B) Ed Reschke/Peter Arnold/PhotoLibrary Group, Inc.; **283** (Bkgrd) Christine M. Douglas/©DK Images, (TR) Tristan Lafranchis/Peter Arnold/PhotoLibrary Group, Inc.; **284** (Bkgrd) Andrew Browne/Ecoscene/Corbis; **285** (TCL) Trent Dietsche/Alamy, (C) Breck P. Kent/Breck P. Kent Natural History Photography, (C) Patti Murray/Animals Animals/Earth Scenes/Animals Animals/Earth Scenes; **286** (B)/Dwight R. Kuhn, (BL) Medio Images/Photodisc/PhotoLibrary Group, Inc.; **287** (Bkgrd) Nature Picture Library, (TC) Peter Chadwick/©DK Images, (CR, C) Peter Chapwick/©DK Images, (CR) Peter Chapwick/©DK Images; **288** (Bkgrd)/Dr Kerry-Ann Nakrieko; **290** (TL) Maryann Frazier/Photo Researchers, Inc.; **291** (Bkgrd) Mark Turner/Garden Picture Library/PhotoLibrary Group, Inc.; **292** (TL) Carole Drake/Garden Picture Library/PhotoLibrary Group, Inc.; **294** (Bkgrd) Gary K. Smith/Nature Picture Library; **295** (Bkgrd) Albinger/AGE Fotostock; **296** (Bkgrd) Nature Picture Library; **297** (TR) Tom Mayes/Cal Sport Media/Zuma Press, Inc.; **298** (TC) Kjell Sandved/Photo Researchers, Inc., (BR) Nature Picture Library; **302** (BR) Susumu Nishinaga/Photo Researchers, Inc.; **303** (Bkgrd) Ames/NASA; **304** (Bkgrd) age Fotostock 3/SuperStock; **307** (BCL) Andrew J. Martinez/Photo Researchers, Inc., (BL) Fritz Polking/Peter Arnold/PhotoLibrary Group, Inc., (TCL) National Geographic Image Collection, (TL) Nature Picture Library; **308** (Bkgrd) DLILLC/Corbis, (C) Nature Picture Library; **309** (BCL) Jason Edwards/National Geographic Image Collection, (CL) Pixtal/SuperStock, (C) Stock Connection, (BCR) Anthony Mercieca / Science Source; **311** (TR) Connie Coleman/Photographer's Choice/Getty Images, (TC) Don Hammond/Design Pics/Corbis, (TCR) Volodymyr Krasyuk/Fotolia, (TC) Keith Leighton/Alamy; **312** (Bkgrd) Comstock Images/Jupiter Images; **313** (BCR) Neil Fletcher/Oxford University/Museum of Natural History/©DK Images; **314** (BR) Bill Curtsinger/National Geographic Image Collection, (BCR) G. Mermet/Peter Arnold/PhotoLibrary Group, Inc., (BC) Getty Images, (TR) National Geographic Image Collection, (B) Photo Researchers, Inc.; **315** (TCR) B.A.E., Inc./Alamy, (Bkgrd, BCR) D. Hurst/Alamy, (BC) Image Source/SuperStock, (BCR) Photodisc/Alamy, (BCR) Tatiana Popova/iStockphoto; **316** (Bkgrd) ©Gray Hardel/Corbis, (Inset) Kaz Chiba/Stockbyte/Getty Images, (BCR) WaterFrame/Alamy; **317** (Bkgrd) Purestock/Getty Images; **318** (C) Daniel Aneshansley/Cornell University/Thomas Eisner; **319** (BCR) Michael DeFreitas Underwater/Alamy Images, (Bkgrd) WaterFrame / Alamy, (Bkgrd) Malcolm Ross/Alamy; **320** (CR) Dr. Richard Kessel & Dr. Gene Shih/Visuals Unlimited/Getty Images, (BL) Photo Fun/Shutterstock, (BC) M.I. (Spike) Walker/Alamy Images, (Bkgrd) Tim Gainey/Alamy; **321** (BC) Andrew J. Martinez/Photo Researchers, Inc., (BR) David Fleetham/Mira, (BCL) Sebastian Duda/Shutterstock; **322** (Bkgrd) ©Grant Faint/Getty Images, (TCR) Dave King/©DK Images, (BCR) Dave King/DK Images, (TCR) Jupiterimages/Creatas/Alamy, (C) National Geographic Image Collection; **323** (TCL) ©Grant Faint/Getty Images, (TC) Brandon D. Cole/Corbis, (CR) NatureDiver/Shutterstock, (TR) Andrew J. Martinez/Science

714

Source, (TCL) Kaz Chiba/Stockbyte/Getty Images; **324** (TR) Silver/Fotolia; (Bkgrd) Tsuneo Nakamura/Volvox Inc./Alamy; **325** (BC) Heather Angel/Natural Visions; **326** (T) Dave King/©DK Images, (Bkgrd) David Peart/©DK Images; **327** (CR) Alan & Sandy Carey/Photo Researchers, Inc., (BCR) Christian Bauer/TIPS North America, (CR) Fritz Polking/Peter Arnold/PhotoLibrary Group, Inc., (BCR) John Cancalosi/AGE Fotostock; **328** (Bkgrd) Richard Cummins/Corbis; **329** (Inset) Heather Angel/Natural Visions/Alamy Images, (BL) Pavlo Vakhrushev/Fotolia, (Bkgrd) Stephen Frink/Stone/Getty Images, (CL) Marevision/Getty Images; **330** (TL) Arterra Picture Library/Alamy, (Bkgrd) Alex L. Fradkin/Stockbyte/Getty Images, (TCR) Nick Garbutt/Nature Picture Library; **331** (Inset) blickwinkel/Alamy, (TR) Karl Shone/©DK Images, (Bkgrd) Sarah Leen/National Geographic Image Collection; **332** (CL) Marvin Dembinsky Photo Associates/Alamy, (CR) Franco/Bonnard/Peter Arnold/PhotoLibrary Group, Inc., (TL) Hermann Brehm/Nature Picture Library, (Bkgrd) Shunsuke Yamamoto Photography/Getty Images; **333** (TR) Joe McDonald/Corbis, (CL) Nature Picture Library, (BC) Tom McHugh/Photo Researchers, Inc.; **334** (BC) Christian Bauer/TIPS North America, (BR) David Fleetham/Mira, (BR) Nature Picture Library, (CL) Photo Researchers, Inc., (C) Stock Connection; **336** (BCR) Jupiter Images; **337** (BCR) Geoff Brightling/Peter Minister, modelmaker/©DK Images, (BCR) Getty Images, (BCR) Jerry Young/©DK Images; **338** (CL) Bart Nedobre/Alamy Images; **339** (Bkgrd) Cornel Stefan Achirei/Alamy Images, (Bkgrd) Doug Steley/Alamy, (TR) Tom McHugh/Photo Researchers, Inc.; **340** (Bkgrd) Stephen Dalton/Science Source; **343** (CL) Stephen Dalton/Science Source, (TCL) HorusVisual/Fotolia; **344** (B) Alan Carey/Corbis, (TR) David A. Northcot/Corbis; **345** (Inset) Getty Images; **346** (BC) Frank Greenaway/©DK Images, (BCR) Keith Leighton/Alamy, (Bkgrd) Vibrant Image Studio/Shutterstock, (CR) Wayne Mckown/Dreamstime LLC; **348** (TL) HorusVisual/Fotolia, (CR) Steve Bloom Images/Alamy Images; **350** (B) ©Corbis; **351** (BCR) Stephen Dalton/Science Source; **354** (Inset) Geoff Brightling/©DK Images, (Bkgrd) Nature Picture Library; **356** Platinum Gpics/Alamy, (TC) Shutterstock; **357** (CR) ©Royalty-Free/Corbis, (CL) M. Delpho/Peter Arnold/PhotoLibrary Group, Inc., (C) Steve Goodwin/iStockphoto; **359** (Bkgrd) blickwinkel/Schmidbauer/Alamy Images, (CR) Mark Conlin/Alamy Images, (TL) Will & Deni McIntyre/Corbis, (CL) Natural Visions/Alamy; **360** (TL) Charles Stirling (Diving)/Alamy Images, (Inset) Blaine Harrington III/Alamy, (Inset) Smaointe/Alamy Images; **361** (BR) Daryl Balfour/Gallo Images/Alamy, (TL) Juergen Hasenkopf/Alamy Images, (Bkgrd) Remi Benali/Corbis, (TR) Perytskyy/Fotolia; **362** (C) Bernd Zoller/Imagebroker/Alamy Images, (TL) Gijs Bekenkamp/Alamy Images, (Bkgrd) Photodisc/PhotoLink/Getty Images; **363** (TL) Bob Jensen/Alamy Images, (B) D. Hurst/Alamy, (BL) Ellen McKnight/Alamy Images, (C) Idamini/Alamy, (TR, BR) Rolf Richardson/Alamy Images; **366** (TCR) Eric Isselée/iStockphoto, (BCL) Joel Sartore/National Geographic Image Collection; **367** (BR) Darren Greenwood/Design Pics/Jupiter Images, (BC) Keith Levit/Shutterstock, (TCR) Nancy Nehring/iStock Exclusive/Getty Images, (BL) Tom Brakefield/Digital Vision/Getty Images; **368** (Bkgrd) Gregory G. Dimijian/Photo Researchers, Inc., (BL) Duncan Noakes/Fotolia; **369** (TR)/Jeff Rotman Photography, (Inset) Gary Lewis/PhotoLibrary Group, Inc., (Bkgrd) Kim Taylor & Jane Burton/ ©DK Images, (C)

National Geographic Image Collection, (TL) Rich Reid/National Geographic Image Collection, (CL) Steve Kaufman/age fotostock/PhotoLibrary Group, Inc.; **372** (CR) Mike Kemp/Rubberball Productions/Getty Images; **373** (Bkgrd) Mark J. Barrett/Alamy Images; **374** (BR) Peter Leahy/Shutterstock, (CR) Georgette Douwma/Nature Picture Library, (BL) Rico/Shutterstock; **375** (TR) Dreamstime/Dreamstime LLC; **376** (TL) Karen Givens/Shutterstock, (TCL) Karen H. Johnson/iStockphoto, (TR) Linn Currie/Shutterstock; **377** (CR) Sapsiwai/Shutterstock; **378** (Bkgrd) Dwight Nadig/iStockphoto, (TL) Jeff Lepore/Photographer's Choice/Getty Images; **380** (TCR, Bkgrd) Kathy Keatley Garvey; **381** (Bkgrd) Colin Milkins/Oxford Scientific (OSF)/PhotoLibrary Group, Inc.; **382** (TC, BCR) ©DK Images, (T) DLILLC/Corbis; **383** (TR) K.L. Kohn/Shutterstock, (B) David Chapman/Alamy; **386** (Bkgrd) Oxford Scientific/Getty Images; **388** (BL) David G. Knowles/David Knowles; **389** (BR) Juniors Bildarchiv/PhotoLibrary Group, Inc.; **391** (Inset) Alistair Dove/Alamy Images, (Bkgrd) Andrew J. Martinez/Photo Researchers, Inc., (Inset) George D. Lepp/Corbis; **392** (BL) Rick & Nora Bowers/Alamy, (BR) Rick & Nora Bowers/Alamy, (BC) SF Photo/Shutterstock; **393** (BL) Design Pics Inc./Alamy, (CR) Design Pics Inc./Alamy; **395** (B) Patricia Fogden/Corbis; **396** (TR) JinYoung Lee/Shutterstock, (B) Keren Su/China Span/Alamy; **399** (CR) Shutterstock; **400** (TR) Daryl Balfour/Gallo Images/Alamy; **402** (L) Mark Conlin/Alamy Images; **403** (Bkgrd) Niels Poulsen/Alamy; **407** (TL) Dr. Gopal Murti/Photo Researchers, Inc., (BCL) Ed Reschke/PhotoLibrary Group, Inc., (TCL) Innerspace Imaging/Photo Researchers, Inc., (BL) Ocean/Corbis; **408** (BCL) Mads Abildgaard/iStockphoto; **409** (Bkgrd) Dr. Gopal Murti/Photo Researchers, Inc.; **410** (B) ©DK Images, (TCL) Biophoto Associates/Photo Researchers, Inc., (TL) Innerspace Imaging/Photo Researchers, Inc., (TL) Michael Abbey/Science Source; **414** (BL) Lebedinski Vladislav/Shutterstock; **415** (B) Claro Cortes IV/Reuters/Corbis Wire/Corbis, (BR) Jeff Rotman/Nature Picture Library; **416** (CL) Juice Images/Photolibrary Group, Inc.; **418** (Bkgrd) Photodisc/White/Photolibrary Group, Inc.; **420** (CL)/©DK Images; **421** (TC) tedestudio/iStockphoto; **422** (TCR) O. Burriel/Photo Researchers, Inc.; **423** (Bkgrd) Mike Chew/keepsake RM/Corbis; **424** (Bkgrd) Duomo TIPS RF/Photolibrary Group, Inc.; **426** (Bkgrd) Michael Meisl/Oxford Scientific/Photolibrary Group, Inc., (TR) Mike Kemp/Rubberball/AGE Fotostock; **427** (TR)/SuperStock, (TL) John Henley/Flirt/Corbis; **428** (Bkgrd) Michael Wong/Flirt/PhotoLibrary Group, Inc.; **430** (TR)/Bone Clones, (BR) Nick Caloyanis/National Geographic Image Collection; **431** (BL) Comstock/Punchstock, (BR) Steve Gorton/©DK Images; **433** (B) Corbis/AGE Fotostock; **436** (TL) JGI/Blend Images/Getty Images, (BR) moodboard/Corbis; **437** (CR) Professor Pietro M. Motta/Science Source, (CL) Steve Gschmeissner/Photo Researchers, Inc.; **438** (Bkgrd) Dan Galic/Alamy; **440** (BCL) Eric V. Grave/Photo Researchers, Inc., (C) Science Photo Library/Photo Researchers, Inc.; **441** (BCR) Ed Reschke/PhotoLibrary Group, Inc., (TR) Image Source/AGE Fotostock; **443** (TC) Nasa/Corbis; **444** (B)/Custom Medical Stock Photo, (TR) Mauritius/SuperStock; **445** (BR) Tom Carter/Alamy Images; **446** (CL) Alloy Photography/Corbis, (C) David Vintiner/zefa/Corbis, (CR) Ocean/Corbis; **448** (CL) John Henley/Flirt/Corbis; **450** (TCR) Martin Lee/Mediablitz Images Limited (UK)/Alamy Images; **453** ©Jaren Jai Wicklund/Shutterstock, ©Petit Format/Photo Researchers, Inc. **454** (Bkgrd) Raga Jose Fuste/AGE Fotostock; **458** (BL)

ACKNOWLEDGMENTS

Jonathan Gelber/BlueMoon Stock/Alamy; **459** (TCR) Jupiterimages/Polka Dot/Alamy; **460** (TL) Angelo Cavalli/zefa/Corbis; **463** (BR) ©Royalty-Free/Corbis; **468** (TCR) Sheila Terry/Photo Researchers, Inc.; **469** (Bkgrd) Zephyr/Photo Researchers, Inc.; **470–471** 3D Clinic/Getty; **473** (BL) Tim Ridley/©DK Images; **476** (CL) Photodisc/Alamy; **478** (BR) UpperCut Images/Masterfile Corporation; **480** (CL) BananaStock/Jupiter Images, (BR) Eddy Gray/Photo Researchers, Inc.; **483** (CL) Anne Ackermann/Digital Vision/Getty Images; **486** (TL, B) Science Source; **487** (TCR) JGI/Jamie Grill/Corbis; **490** (BL), (BR) Anderson Ross/Digital Vision/Getty Images, (BC) Steve Skjold/Alamy Images; **491** (Bkgrd) Pete Saloutos/Corbis; **494** (BCR) Pete Saloutos/Corbis; **498** (Bkgrd) Laguna Designs/Photo Researchers, Inc.; **499** (Bkgrd) Sebastian Kaulitzki/iStockphoto; **500** (Bkgrd) AFP/Getty Images; **503** (B) Dopamine/Photo Researchers, Inc., (BC) Gary Cornhouse/Digital Vision/Alamy; **504** (R) Science Photo Library/Alamy Images; **505** (BR) Larry Dale Gordon/The Image Bank/Getty Images; **506** (TL) Creative Studios/Alamy, (BR) Mile Powell/Allsport Concepts/Getty Images; **510** (Bkgrd) Gregor Schuster/Ionica/Getty Images; **512** (BC) Image Source/Corbis; **515** (Inset) Michael Nemeth/The Image Bank/Getty Images, (Bkgrd) Ocean/Corbis; **516** (Bkgrd) Fuse/Jupiter Images, (BR) Keith Leighton/Alamy; **517** (CR) Sandy Huffaker/Stringer/Getty Images; **518** (CR) Adrian Brockwell/Alamy, (TL) Tom Sanders/Aurora/Getty Images; **524** (C) Adrian Arbib/Encyclopedia/Corbis, (BL) Keystone/Stringer/Hulton Archive/Getty Images; **525** (BL) David M. Phillips/Photo Researchers, Inc.; **526** (Inset) Gary Cornhouse/Digital Vision/Alamy; **531** (Bkgrd) Tig Photo/Alamy; **532** (Bkgrd) Michelle Del Guercio/The Medical File/PhotoLibrary Group, Inc.; **533** (CL) Dopamine/Photo Researchers, Inc., (CR) Tim Vernon, LTH NHS Trust/Photo Researchers, Inc.; **535** (TR) Getty Images; **536** (BC) BSIP/PhotoLibrary Group, Inc.; **537** (BL) Big Cheese Special/Big Cheese Photo LLC/Alamy, (BL) Tony Freeman/PhotoEdit, Inc.; **543** (L) Jonathan Davies/iStockphoto; **544** (Bkgrd) Sayyid Azim/©Associated Press; **547** (TL) Custom Medical Stock Photo, (BCL) D. Hurst/Alamy, (BL) Frank Krahmer/Terra/Corbis, (TCL) Stem Jems/Photo Researchers, Inc.; **548** (B) David Grossman/Alamy Images; **549** (Bkgrd) Andrew Brookes/Corbis; **550** (TL) Bettmann/Corbis, (TR) Jochen Sands/Digital Vision/Getty Images; **552** (BC) Custom Medical Stock Photo, (BR) BSIP/Corbis; **553** (BCR) Joaquin Carrillo-Farga/Science Source, (TR) SPL/Photo Researchers, Inc.; **554** (TL) Jose Pedro Fernandes/Alamy; **555** (Bkgrd) Bruce Heinemann/Stockbyte/Getty Images, (C) Ed Reschke/PhotoLibrary Group Inc., Inc/Alamy Images, (CR) Karen Kasmauski/Corbis; **556** (TR) Viktor Fischer/Alamy; **557** (B) Science Pictures Ltd./Photo Researchers, Inc.; **559** (BR) Stockbyte/Getty Images; **561** (TR) Stem Jems/Photo Researchers, Inc.; **564** (TR) Digital Vision/Alamy, (Bkgrd) Hisham Ibrahim/PhotoV/Alamy; **565** (R) Alex Segre/Alamy Images; **566** (C) NIBSC/Photo Researchers, Inc.; **568** (B) Justin Leighton/Alamy Images, (Bkgrd) VEM/Photo Researchers, Inc.; **569** (CR) Digital Vision/Getty Images; **570** (TL) D. Hurst/Alamy, (B) MedicalRF/Alamy; **571** (TR) Stockbyte/Getty Images; **572** (TCR) MedicalRF/Getty Images; **573** (C) Stephen Sweet/Alamy; **574** (TR) Judith Collins/Alamy; **575** (Inset) Altrendo Images/Getty Images, (Bkgrd) Frank Krahmer/Terra/Corbis, (BL) Santokh Kochar/Photodisc/Getty Images; **576** (Inset) Chris Rout/Alamy Images, (Bkgrd) Crystal Cartier Photography/Brand X Pictures/Jupiter Images;

578 (CL) David Kelly Crow/PhotoEdit, Inc.; **579** (R) Eye of Science/Photo Researchers, Inc.; **580** (B) Michael Keller/Corbis, (Inset) Scott Camazine/Alamy Images; **581** (Bkgd) leungchopan/Fotolia; **582** Joaquin Carrillo-Farga/Science Source; **586** (L) Tom Merton/OJO Images/Getty Images; **587** (Bkgrd) Adrian Arbib/Alamy Images; **588** (Bkgrd) Gary Bell/Corbis; **591** (BL) Christian Kosanetzky/Alamy, (BCL) Photoshot/AGE Fotostock, (CL) Tom Brakefield/Getty Images; **592** (BL) Dr. Jörn Köhler, (TCR) David Haring/DUPC/Getty Images, (Bkgrd) Nick Garbutt/Nature Picture Library, (BR) Peter Arnold/PhotoLibrary Group, Inc.; **593** (BCR) Bruno Morandi/Corbis, (Inset) Tom Brakefield/Getty Images; **596** (B) Jason O. Watson/Alamy; **599** (CR) Chris Johns/National Geographic Image Collection; **600** (BC) Tom Brakefield/Getty Images; **601** (Bkgrd) Kim Taylor/Nature Picture Library; **603** (Bkgrd) Weatherstock/Peter Arnold/PhotoLibrary Group, Inc.; **604** (Bkgrd) ©Matt Brown/Corbis, (Bkgrd) Tim Mannakee/Corbis; **605** (TR) Taylor S. Kennedy/National Geographic Image Collection; **606** Alex Wild; **609** (BCL) Jim Zipp/Photo Researchers, Inc., (BL) Michael P. Gadomski/Photo Researchers, Inc., (CL) Glenn Bartley/Corbis; **610** (BC) Christian Kosanetzky/Alamy, (BL) Klaas Lingbeek- van Kranen/Getty Images, (BCR) sndr/iStockphoto; **611** (CR) age Fotostock/SuperStock, (BCL) Ethan Daniels/Alamy Images, (BCL) Fabrice Bettex/Alamy Images, (TL) Jeff Hunter/Getty Images, (TR) Michael D. Kern/Nature Picture Library, (BR) Nature's Images/Photo Researchers, Inc.; **612** (TR) Bill Curtsinger/National Geographic Image Collection; **613** (BCL) Mogens Trolle/Shutterstock, (BCR) Steve Byland/Fotolia; **614** (BR)/Courtesy of USDA, Agricultural Research Service, (BCR) WaterFrame/Alamy, (CL) Jeff Foott/Getty Images; **615** (CR) Dietmar Nill/Nature Picture Library, (TCR) Bruce Dale/Getty Images, (TR) Steve Jones/Corbis; **616** (Bkgrd) Ilene MacDonald/Alamy; **620** (CR) WaterFrame/Alamy; **624** (Bkgrd)/Roger del Moral; **625** (BL) Chris Gomersall/Alamy Images, (TR) Dave & Les Jacobs/Blend Images/Getty Images; **626–627** (Bkgrd) Marko König/Corbis; **629** (TL)/©DK Images, (BCL) Karen Huntt/Photographer's Choice/Getty Images; **630** (BC) Ian McAllister/All Canada Photos/PhotoLibrary Group, Inc.; **631** (B) Jerome Wexler/Photo Researchers, Inc., (Inset) Ted Kinsman/Photo Researchers, Inc.; **634** (T)/©DK Images, (Inset) ©DK Images, (Inset) iStockphoto; **635** (Inset)/©DK Images, (Inset) ©DK Images, (Inset) DK Images, (Inset) Frank Greenaway/©DK Images, (Inset) Geoff Brightling/©DK Images, (Inset) iStockphoto, (Inset) Jerry Young/©DK Images, (Inset) Judy Ledbetter/iStockphoto, (Inset) Nicholas Homrich/iStockphoto; **636** (Inset, BL, BC) ©DK Images, (BC) DK Images, (CC) GlobalP/iStockphoto; **638** (CL) Juniors Bildarchiv/Alamy; **640** (BL) Emma Firth/©DK Images; **642** (BL) Dr. Paul A. Zahl/Photo Researchers, Inc.; **647** (Inset) Floridapfe from S.Korea Kim in cherl/Getty Images, (Bkgrd) Karen Huntt/Photographer's Choice/Getty Images; **648** (BC) Peter Chadwick/©DK Images; **649** (C) Theo Allofs/Corbis; **650** (TC) Arco Images GmbH/Alamy Images, (TL) Juan-Carlos Munoz/Peter Arnold/PhotoLibrary Group, Inc., (TR) Peter Lillie/PhotoLibrary Group, Inc.; **651** (BR) Tim Shepard, Oxford Scientific Films/©DK Images; **652** (BL) ©Tom Brakefield/Corbis, (TL) Randy Green/Taxi/Getty Images; **653** (B) deberarr/Fotolia; **654** (Bkgrd) blickwinkel/Alamy; **656** (TC) Sandy Felsenthal/Corbis; **657** (CL) PIER/Stone/Getty Images; **660** (BCL) Jerome Whittingham/iStockphoto;

661 (BCR) arlindo 71/iStockphoto, (TCR) arlindo71/iStockphoto, (BL) Ocean/Corbis, (BC) kikkerdirk/Fotolia, (BC) PhotographerOlympus/iStockphoto; 663 (CR) kiamsoon/iStockphoto; 664 (BCR) mbongo/Fotolia; 665 (CR), (CL) Betsy Gange/Hawaii Dept. of Land and Natural Resources/©Associated Press, (TR) Image Quest 3-D; 667 (BR), (BC)/©Operation Migration, Inc., (TR) Kevin Schafer/Alamy, (CL) Markus Botzek/Bridge/Corbis, (BL) Kim Mitchell/Whooping Crane Eastern Partnership, (TC) James Caldwell/Alamy; 670 (TCR) iStockphoto; 671 (CR) Cheerz/Dreamstime LLC; 674 (B) ©Masterfile Royalty-Free, (Bkgrd) Westend 61 GmbH/Alamy Images; 675 (Bkgrd) Brent Waltermire/Alamy Images, (Inset) Jupiter Images/Creatas/Alamy

this is your book

you can write in it

718